THE COLLECTED LETTERS OF
JOSEPH CONRAD

GENERAL EDITOR:
FREDERICK R. KARL

VOLUME 2

THE COLLECTED LETTERS
OF JOSEPH CONRAD

VOLUME 2   1898–1902

EDITED BY

FREDERICK R. KARL

AND

LAURENCE DAVIES

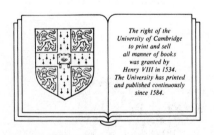

The right of the
University of Cambridge
to print and sell
all manner of books
was granted by
Henry VIII in 1534.
The University has printed
and published continuously
since 1584.

CAMBRIDGE UNIVERSITY PRESS

CAMBRIDGE

LONDON   NEW YORK   NEW ROCHELLE

MELBOURNE   SYDNEY

Published by the Press Syndicate of the University of Cambridge
The Pitt Building, Trumpington Street, Cambridge CB2 1RP
32 East 57th Street, New York, NY 10022, USA
10 Stamford Road, Oakleigh, Melbourne 3166, Australia

©Cambridge University Press 1986

First published 1986

Printed in Great Britain at the University Press, Cambridge

British Library cataloguing in publication data
Conrad, Joseph
The collected letters of Joseph Conrad.
Vol. 2, 1898–1902
1. Conrad, Joseph – Biography   2. Novelists, English – 20th century – Biography
I. Title   II. Karl, Frederick R.   III. Davies, Laurence
823'.912   PR6005.04Z/

Library of Congress cataloguing in publication data
(Revised for vol. 2)

Conrad, Joseph, 1857–1924.
The collected letters of Joseph Conrad.
English and French.
Includes bibliographical references and indexes.
Contents: v. 1. 1861–1897 – v. 2. 1898–1902.
1. Conrad, Joseph, 1857–1924 – Correspondence.
2. Novelists, English – 20th century – Correspondence.
I. Karl, Frederick Robert, 1927–   .
II. Davies, Laurence, 1943–   .   III. Title.
PR6005.04Z48   1983   823'.912   82-14643

ISBN 0 521 24216 9 (vol. 1)
ISBN 0 521 25748 4 (vol. 2)

CE

This volume is dedicated to the curators:

Bruce Brown, Colgate University Library
Stanley Brown, Baker Library, Dartmouth College
Clive Driver, formerly of the Rosenbach Foundation
David Farmer, formerly of the Humanities Research Center,
University of Texas at Austin
Kenneth Lohf, Columbia University Special Collections
Lola Szladits, The Berg Collection, New York Public Library
Marjorie Wynne, Beinecke Library, Yale University

CONTENTS

List of plates   *page* ix

Map   x

Acknowledgments   xi

List of holders of letters   xiii

Published sources of letters   xv

Chronology   xix

Introduction to Volume Two   xxi

Conrad's correspondents, 1898–1902   xxix

Editorial procedures   xxxv

Letters   1

Silent corrections to the text   471

Corrigenda for Volume One   473

Index of recipients   475

Index of names   477

PLATES

between pages 186 and 187

1 X-ray photograph of Conrad's hand: Conrad was intrigued by contemporary physics
2 and 3 How to secure a funnel: Conrad to Graham, 7 January 1898
4 Joseph Conrad, *c.* 1900, taken by Wells
5 Jessie and Borys Conrad, 1899
6 Stephen Crane shows a smugglers' den at Brede Place
7 Cora Crane, war correspondent
8 Helen and Katherine Sanderson, 1899
9 Ted Sanderson with oboe, *c.* 1896
10 Gabriela Cunninghame Graham at Gartmore, 1900
11 W. E. Henley, by William Rothenstein
12 Ivy Walls Farm
13 John Galsworthy, by R. H. Sauter
14 G. F. W. Hope
15 George Gissing, taken by Wells
16 Wells pedals off: presentation inscription in *Tales of Space and Time*

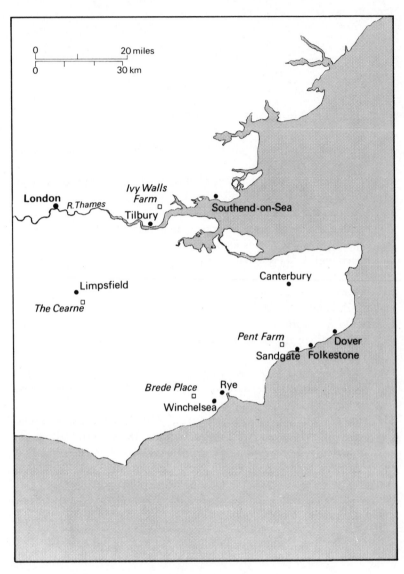

South-east England

ACKNOWLEDGMENTS

Holders of manuscripts are listed separately, but we thank them here, wholeheartedly, for their co-operation.

Many of the people acknowledged in the first volume gave us help that affects the entire edition, and we offer them all our redoubled thanks. For aid and good counsel in preparing Volume Two, however, we express our particular gratitude to Dr Nigel Cross, Dr Krystyna Dietrich, Ms Nancy Essery, Mr Malcolm Forbes, Jr, Professor Eloise Knapp Hay, Mr P. G. Hunter, Dr Owen Knowles, Professor Thomas Moser, Professor Barry Scherr, Mr Raymond B. Sutton, Jr, Mrs C. E. Taylor, Mr Hans van Marle, and Professor Cedric Watts.

For giving us access to his important discoveries about the correspondence with Clifford, we owe a special debt of gratitude to Dr Allan Hunter.

Some of Frederick R. Karl's work on this volume was funded by the National Endowment for the Humanities, a federal agency to which both editors have cause to be grateful.

The late Anne Royal was characteristically generous with her knowledge and enthusiasm: 'los muertos abren los ojos a los que viven'.

HOLDERS OF LETTERS

Berg	The Berg Collection: Astor, Lenox and Tilden Foundations, New York Public Library
BL	The British Library
Castle	Mrs Alfred L. Castle
Chichester	Cobden MSS, West Sussex County Record Office, Chichester
Clifford	Mr Hugh Clifford-Holmes
Colgate	Colgate University Library, Hamilton, New York
Columbia	Special Collections Division, Columbia University, New York
Dartmouth	Baker Library, Dartmouth College, Hanover, New Hampshire
Duke	Duke University Library, Durham, North Carolina
Forbes	Mr Malcolm Forbes, Jr
Free	The Free Library of Philadelphia
Heinemann	William Heinemann, Ltd, London
Illinois	University of Illinois Library, Champaign–Urbana
Indiana	Lilly Library, University of Indiana, Bloomington
Lamb	The late Katharine Hueffer Lamb
Leeds	Brotherton Library, University of Leeds
Morgan	The Pierpont Morgan Library, New York
Murray	John Murray, Ltd, London
Mursia	The late Ugo Mursia
Neville	Mr Maurice F. Neville
NLS	The National Library of Scotland, Edinburgh
Northwestern	Northwestern University Library, Evanston, Illinois
NYPL	Miscellaneous Manuscripts Division, New York Public Library
NYU	The Fales Collection, New York University Libraries
POSK	The Polish Library, London
Quiller-Couch	Miss F. Quiller-Couch
RLF	The Royal Literary Fund, London
Rosenbach	The Philip M. and A. S. W. Rosenbach Foundation, Philadelphia
SO	Mr Jamie Sutton

Spiridion	Dr Jan Spiridion
Sutton	Mr Raymond B. Sutton, Jr
Syracuse	Syracuse University Library, Syracuse, New York
Taylor	Mrs C. E. Taylor
Texas	Humanities Research Center, University of Texas at Austin
UCL	The Library of University College, London
Virginia	Tracy W. McGregor Collection, University of Virginia Library, Charlottesville
Warsaw	The National Library of Poland, Warsaw
Wellington	The Honourable Company of Master Mariners, H.Q.S. *Wellington*, London
Williams	Chapin Library, Williams College, Williamstown, Massachusetts
Yale	The Beinecke Rare Book and Manuscript Library, Yale University, New Haven, Connecticut

We offer renewed thanks to the individuals and institutions listed above.

PUBLISHED SOURCES OF LETTERS

Baines   Jocelyn Baines, *Joseph Conrad: A Critical Biography*. Weidenfeld and Nicolson, 1960

Blackburn   William Blackburn, ed., *Joseph Conrad: Letters to William Blackwood and David S. Meldrum*. Durham, N.C.: Duke University Press, 1958

Coustillas   Pierre Coustillas, 'Conrad and Gissing', *Cahiers d'Etudes et de Recherches Victoriennes et Edouardiennes*, 2 (1975), 43–4

Curreli   Mario Curreli, ed., 'Four Unpublished Conrad Letters', *Conradiana*, 7 (1976), 209–17

Danilewicz   Maria Danilewicz, ed., *Joseph Conrad: Listy do Johna Galsworthy 'ego*. B. Swiderski, 1957

G.   Edward Garnett, ed., *Letters from Joseph Conrad, 1895–1924*. Nonesuch Press, 1928

G. & S.   John A. Gee and Paul J. Sturm, trans. and ed., *Letters of Joseph Conrad to Marguerite Poradowska*. New Haven: Yale University Press, 1940

Hunter   Allan Hunter, ed., 'Letters from Joseph Conrad', *Notes and Queries*, forthcoming

J-A   G. Jean-Aubry, ed., *Joseph Conrad: Life and Letters*. 2 volumes. Heinemann, 1927

Keating   George T. Keating, *A Conrad Memorial Library: The Collection of George T. Keating*. Garden City, N.Y: Doubleday, Doran, 1929

Krishnamurti   G. Krishnamurti, ed., *Joseph Conrad: A Letter to William Nicholson*. The Eighteen Nineties Society, 1985

Knowles   Owen Knowles and G. W. S. Miskin, ed., 'Unpublished Conrad Letters: The H.Q.S. *Wellington* Collection', *Notes and Queries*, forthcoming

Letters   Frederick R. Karl and Laurence Davies, ed., *The Collected Letters of Joseph Conrad*. Cambridge University Press, Vol. 1, 1983

L.fr.   G. Jean-Aubry, ed., *Lettres françaises*. Paris: Gallimard, 1929

Listy	Zdzisław Najder, ed., Halina Carroll, trans., *Joseph Conrad: Listy*. Warsaw: Państwowy Instytut Wydawniczy, 1968
Marrot	H. V. Marrot, ed., *The Life and Letters of John Galsworthy*. New York: Scribner's, 1936
Najder	Zdzisław Najder, ed., Halina Carroll, trans., *Conrad's Polish Background: Letters to and from Polish Friends*. Oxford University Press, 1964
Najder (1970)	'Joseph Conrad: A Selection of Unpublished Letters', *Polish Perspectives* (Warsaw), 13 (1970), no. 2, 31–45
Rapin	René Rapin, ed., *Lettres de Joseph Conrad à Marguerite Poradowska*. Geneva: Droz, 1966
Ray	Martin Ray, ed., 'Conrad and Wells: Yet Another Undated Letter', *Notes and Queries*, 228 (30 August 1983), 323–5
Stallman	R. W. Stallman and Lillian Gilkes, ed., *Stephen Crane: Letters*. New York University Press, 1960
Stape	J. H. Stape, ed., 'Conrad and Mr. "Colesworthy": Two Unpublished Letters and a Reply', *Conradiana*, 14 (1983), 230–2
Watts	C. T. Watts, ed., *Joseph Conrad's Letters to R. B. Cunninghame Graham*. Cambridge University Press, 1969

Certain unreliable magazine publications are not listed here but cited in the provenance notes accompanying the text.

OTHER FREQUENTLY CITED WORKS

Conrad, Jessie	*Joseph Conrad and His Circle*. Jarrold's, 1935
Conrad, Jessie	*Joseph Conrad as I Knew Him*. Garden City, N.Y: Doubleday, Page, 1926
Ford, Ford Madox	*Joseph Conrad: A Personal Remembrance*. Duckworth, 1924
Gilkes, Lillian	*Cora Crane*. Bloomington: Indiana University Press, 1960
Heilbrun, Carolyn G.	*The Garnett Family*. George Allen & Unwin, 1961

Jean-Aubry G., ed.	*Twenty Letters to Joseph Conrad*. First Edition Club, 1926
Karl, Frederick R.	*Joseph Conrad: The Three Lives*. New York: Farrar, Straus, Giroux, 1979
Mackenzie, Norman and Jeanne	*H. G. Wells: A Biography*. New York: Simon & Schuster, 1973
Najder, Zdzisław ed., and Halina Carroll, trans.	*Conrad under Familial Eyes*. Cambridge University Press, 1983
Najder, Zdzisław	*Joseph Conrad: A Chronicle*. New Brunswick, N.J.: Rutgers University Press, 1983
Sherry, Norman	*Conrad: The Critical Heritage*. Routledge & Kegan Paul, 1973
Sherry, Norman	*Conrad's Eastern World*. Cambridge University Press, 1966
Stallman, R. W.	*Stephen Crane: A Biography*. New York: George Braziller, 1968
Watts, Cedric and Laurence Davies	*Cunninghame Graham: A Critical Biography*. Cambridge University Press, 1979

Unless otherwise noted, references to Conrad's work come from the Kent Edition, published by Doubleday, Page in twenty-four volumes (Garden City, N.Y., 1925).

CHRONOLOGY, 1898–1902

15 January 1898	Borys Conrad born at Ivy Walls Farm, Essex.
4 April 1898	*Tales of Unrest* published (26 March in U.S.).
9 April 1898	Essay on Daudet in *Outlook*.
23 April 1898	Review of Clifford's *Studies in Brown Humanity* for *Academy*.
May? 1898	Began 'Youth'.
May? 1898	Began 'Jim: A Sketch', precursor of *Lord Jim*.
3 June 1898	Finished 'Youth' (*Blackwood's Magazine*, September).
4 June 1898	Essay on Marryat and Cooper in *Outlook*.
23 June 1898	Meldrum asked for a volume of sea-stories (*Youth*).
June 1898	Sold serial rights for *The Rescue* – completed 1919.
September 1898	Visit to Scotland in search of employment.
26 October 1898	Moved to Pent Farm, Kent.
October 1898	Collaboration on 'Seraphina' (*Romance*) discussed with Ford.
Mid? December 1898	Began 'Heart of Darkness'.
14 January 1899	*Tales of Unrest* 'crowned' by *Academy*.
6 February 1899	Finished 'Heart of Darkness' (*Blackwood's*, February–April).
October 1899	Began revising Ford's draft of *The Inheritors*.
February 1900	MS of *The Inheritors* submitted to Heinemann.
14 July 1900	Finished *Lord Jim* (*Blackwood's*, October 1899–November 1900).
20 July–18 August 1900	The Conrads and the Hueffers on a working holiday in Belgium, where Borys fell dangerously ill.
September 1900	Became a client of J. B. Pinker (who had offered his services in August 1899).

September–October 1900	Began 'Typhoon'.
15 October 1900	*Lord Jim* appeared as a book.
10–11 January 1901	Finished 'Typhoon' (*Pall Mall Magazine*, January–March).
Mid January	Began 'Falk'.
May 1901	Finished 'Falk', began 'Amy Foster'.
16 June 1901	Finished 'Amy Foster' (*Illustrated London News*, December).
26 June 1901	*The Inheritors* published.
Mid January 1902	Finished 'To-morrow' (first mentioned November 1901; published *Pall Mall Magazine*, August 1902).
Early March 1902	Finished *Romance* (published October 1903, after heavy cutting).
17 March 1902	Began 'The End of the Tether'.
23 June 1902	A large batch of 'The End of the Tether', MS and TS, destroyed in a fire.
Early July 1902	Grant of £300 from the Royal Literary Fund.
4 September 1902	*Typhoon* published in the U.S. (without accompanying stories).
16 October 1902	Finished 'The End of the Tether' (*Blackwood's*, July–December).
13 November 1902	*Youth* appeared as a book.

INTRODUCTION TO VOLUME TWO

From a distance and in briefest summary, the story of Conrad's life between 1898 and 1902 looks cheerful. He acquires a son, a collaborator, and a literary agent. He moves to a charming (albeit badly plumbed) farmhouse in Kent within calling distance of half the day's most gifted authors. Among other works, he writes 'Youth', 'Heart of Darkness', 'Typhoon', 'Amy Foster' and *Lord Jim*. The period ends with the first stirrings of *Nostromo*. It begins with reviews of *The Nigger of the 'Narcissus'*, sometimes obtuse or uncomprehending, but always respectful and often enthusiastic – a spectrum of response to be repeated over and over. Meanwhile, serious critics and serious fellow novelists come to recognize him as, in Gissing's words: 'The strongest writer – in every sense of the word – at present publishing in English' (*Critical Heritage*, p. 140).

Yet this pattern of artistic achievement, critical success, and domestic consolidation bears scant resemblance to the texture of the correspondence day by day and month by month. The letters abound in unhappiness:

So I turn in this vicious circle and the work itself becomes like the work in a treadmill – a thing without joy – a punishing task.

(To Sanderson, 12 October 1899)

I can't rope in a complete thought; I am exhausted mentally and very depressed.

(To Graham, 28 July 1900)

Time lost. Spirits low. Weather too horrible . . . Irritability, weakness, pain, with their natural train of consequences. That's the budget.

(To Galsworthy, 24 March 1901)

Writers suffer strange distortions in their sense of time and space. By the nature of the work, they feel lonely in a crowd and unproductive when two meagre weeks follow four prolific ones. Their sense, moreover, of distance from what they have done or are doing is subject to drastic fluctuations: now the urge to run away, now the urge to linger, perhaps too long. These psychic shifts are hard for the most equable of people to bear – and equability was not among Conrad's virtues.

His distress, however, cannot simply be put down to the curse of a manic-depressive temperament or the usual horrors of creation. He faced a series of accidents and crises: the almost fatal illness of his son; the burning of 'The End of the Tether' as it lay in manuscript; and, constantly, the calling-in of old debts. 'What a drama', Henry James wrote to Edmund Gosse; 'altogether the circumjacent crash of things' (Blackburn, p. xxvii). Meanwhile, his agent and his publishers wanted a steady flow of material; his reviewers, even the enthusiastic ones, often misunderstood his work and, in any case, their enthusiasm did little to satisfy his doctor, his butcher, or his landlord. 'He is poor and a gentleman and proud', Crane observed of him (Stallman, pp. 283–4), accurately locating the point where character and circumstances met with the greatest possible discomfort. However loftily he might remind Pinker that 'there are other virtues than punctuality' (8 January 1902), Conrad knew the connection between an empty page and an empty larder.

In other words, the present-day reader approaches Conrad's correspondence with a certitude that Conrad could not share. We read any dead person's letters with a hindsight denied their author, and hindsight, like the prospect of the noose for Johnson's forger, concentrates the mind wonderfully. Conrad, however, lived with and in more than the usual degree of uncertainty. He was strongly aware of his distinctiveness as a writer. 'I am *modern* ... My work shall not be an utter failure because it has the solid basis of a definite intention' (to William Blackwood, 31 May 1902), but he had a counter-awareness almost as strong of his inability to follow that intention through: 'The more I write the less substance do I see in my work. The scales are falling off my eyes' (to Garnett [31 March 1899]). Further, the more serious the writing, the more powerful the autonomy it demanded. In spite of his devotion to the idea of form, Conrad rarely had an accurate notion of how his work would turn out. Referring to what, in the scientific rather than economic sense, might be called the inflation of *Lord Jim* from 'A Sketch' to a *nouvelle*, and from a *nouvelle* to a full-blown novel, Conrad assured George Blackwood (20 May 1902) 'That sort of thing does not happen twice.' But, as *Nostromo*, 'The End of the Tether', and *Under Western Eyes* attest, it did. As he told Ford (28 April 1901), 'I am finishing the Falk story but with me such a statement may mean anything.'

It is not surprising, therefore, that Conrad acquired an expert knowledge of last posts and early trains. Yet letters to Pinker and Blackwood make spirited ripostes to the charge of laziness – and rightly so. Attacks of physical or spiritual illness apart, Conrad wrote hard. His was a busy procrastination, the product not of a reluctance to begin but of a reluctance to conclude. Whether he gambled on deadlines in order to squeeze the last possible droplet of significance from his material, or whether he did it out of philosophical and personal distaste for closure, the fervour of Conrad's artistic convictions actually made the atmosphere of doubt that enveloped him all the more suffocating.

At least he had the assurance of many friends. In the second volume of his letters, correspondents familiar from the first such as Edward Garnett, Ted and Helen Sanderson, R. B. Cunninghame Graham, Stephen Crane, Aniela Zagórska, Marguerite Poradowska and H. G. Wells are joined by Neil Munro, Arnold Bennett, Hugh Clifford, H.-D. Davray and, most notably, by John Galsworthy (a longstanding friend) and Ford Madox Ford. Many Sanderson, Wells, and Galsworthy letters and virtually all those to Ford appear here for the first time in English.

In matters of literary business – matters that often touched him to the heart – he dealt with S. S. Pawling, the McClure brothers, C. K. Shorter, and Lewis Hind, but for Conrad the most important figures were William Blackwood, David Meldrum, and J. B. Pinker. Encouraged by Meldrum, a writer himself and a sympathetic go-between, Blackwood brought out *Youth* and *Lord Jim*, displaying a tolerance of the latter work's unexpected growth that might astonish a modern editor. With Pinker relations were less ceremonious and often less cordial. Nevertheless, Conrad came to rely on him as financial manager as well as agent; the surviving letters, a good twelve hundred of them and almost all unpublished, demonstrate the intensity and complexity of the relationship. Indeed the shift in allegiance from the stately Edinburgh publisher who had been friends with Trollope to the ever-alert transatlantic commuter and maker of deals epitomizes the course of modern publishing. Yet Conrad had to negotiate with them both, a task he brought off with a good deal of persistence, occasional cunning, some indignation, and a quantity of wishful thinking that led him to promise what he could not always deliver. When he faced the inevitable reproaches of these two very different Scotsmen (to Pinker, 8 January, to Blackwood, 31 May 1902), he detailed his artistic mission as eloquently as he ever did, providing what amounted to two chapters of an apologia.

In the reply to Pinker, Conrad asked:

Am I a confounded boy? I have had to look death in the eye once or twice. It was nothing. I had not then a wife and child. It was nothing to what I have to go through now pen in hand before what to *me* spells failure. I am no sort of airy R. L. Stevenson ... I dare say he was punctual – but I don't envy him.

At issue was the delay in finishing *Romance*, the second collaboration with Ford Madox Ford. Conrad and Ford had much in common, in spite of the sixteen-year disparity in age and Conrad's greater experience of literature and the world. Garnett was appalled by the prospect of their collaboration, yet it had its logic. They were committed to a lofty concept of fiction and short of cash. (Ford was another proud but poor gentleman.) They encouraged each other's dreams of a work that might be popular though not contemptible. Even Ford's youthfulness was an asset; it suited Conrad in his exuberant moods, and it turned their projects into a deliciously absurd as well as a desperate gamble:

For indeed unless beguiled by a malicious fiend what man would undertake it? ... Therefore I am anxious. And I am quite excited for there is an excitement in braving heaven itself as it were, in giving form to an idea, in clothing the breath of our life with day. How fine and how insane!   [23 April 1902]

When it was time to publish *The Inheritors*, their satire of sentiment and heartlessness in public life, Conrad wrote, with the linguistic zaniness that certain close friends brought out:

The time of our conjunction approaches and from shock heavenly fire struck would base metals into gold transmute! (in other words: from Bsh Public's pocket extract shekels.)   [28 June? 1901]

They were intimates, conspirators, and tempters of providence.

Although the earliest surviving Galsworthy letters appear in Volume Two, the friendship went back to 1893 and a voyage on the *Torrens*. The correspondence with Conrad (and with Garnett) shows how much help and encouragement he needed in his early days as an author. In person – Galsworthy was one of the Pent's most faithful visitors – and in writing, Conrad was ever ready to oblige. Here, for example, he assesses the shaping of characters in *A Man of Devon*:

Your attitude to them should be purely intellectual, more independant*, freer, less rigorous than it is. You seem for their sake to hug your conceptions of right or wrong too closely. There is exquisite atmosphere in your tales. What they want now is more air.   (11 November 1901)

Galsworthy lent Conrad money, guaranteed his financial exploits and, as the letter of 1 June 1902 suggests, even laundered his funds.

I trust Your letter'll act like magic – but are you not tired of assissting* (in the French and English sense) at my sordid man[o]euvrings?   [4 June 1902?]

From the tone of the letters, however, it is clear that the friendship meant far more than a complicity between rich amateur (for, at the turn of the century, amateur he still was) and debt-ridden professional. Their relationship was a warmer and more constant affair than that.

Other writers not addressed in Volume One included W. E. Henley, Neil Munro, Arnold Bennett, Hugh Clifford, and H.-D. Davray. For their expression of literary attitudes and their sympathetic engagement with the recipients, the letters to the first three deserve more than passing attention, but those to Clifford and to Davray are particularly significant. Clifford had a double claim to Conrad's notice: he had praised his work while politely challenging his knowledge of Malay life; soon after, Conrad had reviewed *Studies in Brown Humanity* as a collection of truthful but artistically slight sketches – 'One cannot expect to be, at the same time, a ruler of men and an irreproachable player on the flute' (*Notes on Life and Letters*, p. 60). But the piquancy of their conjunction is less important than its timing; the acquaintance began in spring 1899, just when *Lord Jim*, that study of values and loyalties in a colonial and near-colonial setting, was starting to grow out of 'Tuan Jim: A Sketch'. As its implications ramified the story would have grown in any case, but the amiable sparring with Clifford must at the least have prepared Conrad for the main event.

If Clifford revived Conrad's involvement with the East, Davray helped maintain his allegiance to the Continent. Davray's life was devoted to the marrying of French and English literature. His monthly review of new British and Irish writing for the *Mercure de France* and his many personal contacts (he was as at home with Wells as he was with Mallarmé) made him an admirable advocate. Conrad spelled out his literary intentions to him with unusual exactness.

This volume continues the correspondence with relations such as Marguerite Poradowska and Aniela Zagórska and with well-established friends. In many cases, their circumstances were changing. Cunninghame Graham was imprisoned in the Atlas Mountains and later had to sell his family home. Garnett escaped from Fisher Unwin's clutches. Helen Watson and Ted Sanderson married and had their first child; not long after, Ted went off to soldier in South Africa. Crane covered the war in Cuba, hid in low company for a while, and returned to England where, with Cora Crane, he presided over the feudal hospitality and worse than feudal sanitation of Brede Place. When, to everyone's distress, he died in 1900, his role as master of ceremonies to the extraordinary group of writers settled in Kent and East Sussex was taken up by H. G. Wells.

All these people received memorable letters. For instance there are the accounts of British literary life sent to Aniela Zagórska, the arguments over socialism with Cunninghame Graham, the bantering exchanges with Wells, and the terrible reports of depression to Garnett and to Sanderson. Through all this richness and variety, however, certain obsessions recur.

Here one must be careful: the span of this volume is determined by the needs of publishing. Nevertheless, the years from 1898 to 1902 do have a distinctive quality. During this period, Conrad tried exceptionally hard to understand his place in the scheme of things. He faced the problem in terms of family, profession, the sense of his own being, national and historical identity, and the physical universe itself.

We hear the two ends of the gamut in the notorious, resonantly ironic skirmish with Graham of 14 January 1898, which follows the second law of thermodynamics to an emotional if not necessarily logical conclusion. Conrad takes the discoveries of contemporary physics to heart: 'The fate of a humanity condemned ultimately to perish from cold is not worth troubling about.' He adds a postscript:

This letter missed this morning's post because an infant of male persuasion arrived and made such a row that I could not hear the Postman's whistle. It's a fine commentary upon this letter!

The birth of his first child came just when Conrad was preoccupied with endings, not least the prospect of his own. Borys diverted and delighted (see, for instance, the postscript to Sanderson, 12 October 1899) but compounded his worries. What if Conrad died soon, leaving a baby, a sheaf of debts and obligations, and a widow who was already responsible for two orphaned sisters? Knowing how much he had staked on his literary future, imagining oblivion, Conrad dwelled on life-insurance schemes.

In between the cosmic and the personal lie all the worlds of culture and of history. The diversity of his mind shows in Conrad's language. Not only all Europe contributed to its making but a good bit of Asia and Africa too. Sentences in French and music-hall Cockney jostle Italian oaths and Arabic pieties in a style that, writing to Mrs Bontine (4 December 1898), he himself called 'macaronic'. Yet, day by day, he was confronted with the problem of national allegiance. He sent Garnett a particularly full inventory of his origins on 20 January 1900. In his homeland, he was denounced by a merciless section of the intelligentsia as a writer who had sold his gifts for alien rewards. In his adopted land, he lived frugally in country places where a foreign voice and foreign manners were noticed. During the South African war he tried to stay on reasonable terms with his cousin Aniela, who looked on the Boers as gallant victims, with Ted Sanderson, ever-loyal to the Union Jack, and with Cunninghame Graham, who saw the whole bloody affair as a fight between two burglars.

Above all, Conrad sought to locate himself as a writer – as if he had fallen into a Steinian dream and was lost:

And oh! dear Ted — it *is* a fool's business to write fiction for a living. It is indeed.

It is strange. The unreality of it seems to enter one's real life, penetrate into the bones, make the very heart beats pulsate illusions through the arteries.

(To Sanderson, 12 October 1899)

The anxiety was metaphysical – in his worst moods, witness the letter to Garnett of 16 September 1899, he writes like a spectre on parole from limbo – and it was artistic. Explicitly a modern writer, Conrad shared the company of Garnett, Crane and Ford, but he swam in a sea dominated by imposing fossils like Hall Caine, S. R. Crockett, and Marie Corelli.

Writing, however, was the cure as well as the cause. The fiction of those years engages the same problems as the letters. The terrifying vastness of the cosmos makes the outermost backdrop for 'Typhoon', cultural bonds and cultural isolation figure largely in 'Amy Foster', *Lord Jim*, and even *Romance*; imperial and Darwinian histories give 'Heart of Darkness' its ironic frame, and the summing-up of a single life at the point of death its laconic centre.

In the Preface to *The Nigger*, Conrad cites the need to do 'the highest kind of justice to the visible universe'. This in turn means the need to do justice to himself, to his own sense of things. The problems of location and identity, political, moral, metaphysical, psychological, may be beyond solution, but the problem of dealing with them artistically is not. Few readers would dispute the claim that 'Heart of Darkness' and *Lord Jim* express more, represent more, do more than *Almayer's Folly* or *An Outcast of the Islands*. The former are 'classic Conrad' in a way that the latter, however fine, are not. About the turn of the century, he undertook experiments so successful that we usually forget they are experiments at all. That is as true of the 'lesser' works (a strictly relative description) as of the masterpieces; 'Typhoon' is not a repetition of *The Nigger*, nor does 'Amy Foster' repeat 'The Idiots'. Yet there were also false starts and false continuations: this volume records glimpses of *Chance* (1913) and *The Shadow Line* (1917), and further blindman's-bluff with *The Rescue*

(1919). In those works he did not yet have what he once called '*the belief*' (*Letters*, 1, p. 297). What was worse, circumstances drove him to seek artistic perfection in monthly instalments – a pursuit indeed '*ewig—usque ad finem* ...'.

Again and again he reached that end. The years from 1898 to 1902 were a time not of promise but of fulfilment, when Conrad became completely Conrad. One novelist to another, he advised Galsworthy to remove himself from his work (11 November 1901). Conrad followed this counsel of Flaubertian detachment himself, refining his ironic sense, inventing Marlow. Nevertheless, the farther back he stood, the stronger was his presence. Of the fiction as much as of the letters, we might ask 'Who but Conrad?'

And this was a time of reflection on his own history, his own memories. Graham described 'Heart of Darkness' as written 'in the fervent contemplation of his tracks' (to Garnett, MS Texas). Less intensely, that is also true of 'Youth'. If we recall Conrad's anxiety about his eyesight, even 'The End of the Tether' looks like deflected autobiography, a coming-to-terms with having left the sea. This time of reinterpretation ended late in 1902, when he turned to *Nostromo*, the most imagined book so far. He tells the reader of *The Nigger* that his 'task ... is, before all, to make you *see*'. In the fiction and the letters of the period before us, he was trying to see for himself.

Laurence Davies

Dartmouth College

CONRAD'S CORRESPONDENTS
1898–1902

Enoch Arnold BENNETT (1867–1931), the prolific chronicler of Staffordshire, London, and cosmopolitan life; his Naturalist approach to fiction and his financial success made him the butt of Modernist writers such as Woolf and Pound.

George BLACKWOOD (1876–1942) was more 'business-like' than his uncle William and next in line as head of the Edinburgh publishing house.

William BLACKWOOD (1836–1912), editor of *Blackwood's Edinburgh Magazine*, published some of Conrad's early work, including *Youth* and *Lord Jim*, in book and serial forms.

The Hon. Ann Elizabeth BONTINE (née Elphinstone Fleeming, 1828–1925), was Cunninghame Graham's widowed mother. Of Scottish Whig and Spanish ancestry, she lived in London and took a well-informed interest in politics and the arts.

Minnie BROOKE, a friend of Jane Cobden Unwin, visited the Conrads on their honeymoon. Her husband, the Reverend Arthur Brooke, was the rector of Slingsby in the North Riding of Yorkshire.

Jeanne or Janina, Baronne de BRUNNOW (née Taube, 1864–1943), a friend from Conrad's boyhood in Cracow and a ward of his uncle Tadeusz Bobrowski. She married a general in the Russian army.

Harriet Mary CAPES (1849–1936), who lived in Winchester, wrote inspirational stories for children. She was a great admirer of Conrad's works; he dedicated *A Set of Six* to her.

Wilfrid Hugh CHESSON (1870–1952) could claim, as a reader at Fisher Unwin when Conrad submitted *Almayer's Folly*, to be among the first to recognize his talent.

Sir Hugh CLIFFORD (1866–1941), a colonial administrator, was serving as British Resident in Pahang, Malaya, when he wrote one of the earliest general appreciations of Conrad's work. Later, he was appointed to the Governorships of Labuan and North Borneo, the Gold Coast, Nigeria, Ceylon, and the Straits Settlements. He published many volumes of stories and sketches, collaborated on a Malay dictionary, and produced a Malay translation of the colonial penal code.

Edward CLODD (1840–1930), a prosperous banker, wrote on folklore and science.

Cora CRANE (née Howorth, 1865–1910) travelled as Stephen's wife. A once and future brothel-keeper, she wrote short stories and was the first woman war-correspondent.

Stephen CRANE (1871–1900), poet, novelist, and journalist, had already written *Maggie: A Girl of the Streets* (1893) and *The Red Badge of Courage* (1895) when he met Conrad in October 1897. Between that date and his death from tuberculosis, Crane reported the Spanish–American war, and presided over the generous hospitality of Brede Place.

Henry-Durand DAVRAY (1873–1944) encouraged French and British writers to know each other better. He appeared regularly in the *Mercure de France* and edited its Collection of Foreign Authors. Among those he translated were Kipling, Meredith, Wells, and Conrad.

Ernest DAWSON (1884–1960), brother of A. J., was introduced to Conrad by Henley and Wells. Major Dawson contributed reminiscences of life in Burma to *Blackwood's*.

Ford Madox FORD (1873–1939) provided in his memoirs and novels some of the best English fiction of the twentieth century. He was also a poet and a brilliant editor. At the time of his collaboration on *Romance* and *The Inheritors*, however, his list of publications was short. He changed his name from Hueffer to Ford in 1919; characteristically, he had retained the German name all through his service in the Great War.

John GALSWORTHY (1867–1933) met Conrad on the *Torrens* in 1893. The early work was tentative, but he went on to win a Nobel prize (an honour denied his friend) for his fiction and his plays. Like the Forsytes, his family had plenty of money, and he helped Conrad with many loans and outright gifts.

David GARNETT (1892–1981), 'Bunny', was the son of Constance and Edward. A novelist deeply involved with Bloomsbury, his autobiographies have much to say about the intelligentsia of early-twentieth-century England.

Edward GARNETT (1868–1937), a publisher's reader and critic, was the husband of Constance, the translator. They lived at The Cearne, a meeting-place for writers, artists, anarchists, socialists, and Russian refugees. Edward's encouragement of Conrad was typical of his generous attention to new writers.

Richard GARNETT (1835–1906), Edward's father, wrote *The Twilight of the Gods and Other Tales* (1888) and many literary biographies. Keeper of Printed Books from 1890 to 1899 and before that Superintendent of the Reading-Room, his extraordinary knowledge of the British Museum Library made him the ideal person to consult about any bibliographical problem.

George GISSING (1857–1903) led a sad but productive life. His novels include *New Grub Street* (1891), *The Odd Women* (1893), and *In the Year of Jubilee* (1894).

Edmund GOSSE (1849–1928), poet, literary historian and biographer, had great influence in the literary world. His autobiographical *Father and Son* appeared in 1907; his critical enthusiasms included Ibsen and Donne. In 1894 he read the MS of *Almayer's Folly*, and in 1902 he procured Conrad's grant from the Royal Literary Fund.

Gabriela Cunninghame GRAHAM (née de la Balmondière, 1860?–1906), Robert's Chilean-born wife, wrote stories, essays and poems, studied mysticism, and was active in the Spanish women's movement. Her biography of Saint Teresa of Avila appeared in 1894.

Robert Bontine Cunninghame GRAHAM (1852–1936), socialist and (according to some scholars) rightful King of Scotland, had worked and travelled widely in the Americas. He drew on his experiences in many volumes of tales, sketches, and essays and also in his histories of the Spanish conquest. From 1886 to 1892 he represented North-West Lanarkshire in Parliament; he spent four and a half weeks in gaol for his part in the Bloody Sunday demonstration of 1887. His enduring friendship with Conrad began in 1897.

William Ernest HENLEY (1849–1903), poet, critic, and editor, published the serial version of *The Nigger* in his *New Review*. He is said to have been the model for Long John Silver.

Charles Lewis HIND (1862–1927) edited the *Academy* from 1896 to 1903.

Elsie HUEFFER (née Martindale, 1876–1924), married Ford in 1894, against her parents' wishes. She wrote several novels and published her translations from de Maupassant in 1903.

Ford Hermann Madox HUEFFER: see FORD.

Spiridion KLISZCZEWSKI (Joseph Spiridion) was the son of Józef, who had taken refuge in Britain after the failure of the Polish insurrection of 1830–1. In 1885, Conrad sent Spiridion his first known letters in English.

Józef KORZENIOWSKI (1863–1921), a historian and librarian, lived in Cracow. He was not related to Conrad.

David S. MELDRUM (1864–1940) was the literary adviser in Black-wood's London office; he became a partner in 1903 and retired in 1910. Among the first to recognize Conrad's talent, he published his own novel, *The Conquest of Charlotte*, in 1902.

Sir Algernon METHUEN (originally Stedman, 1856–1924) founded his company in 1889. Besides text-books, which were the source of the firm's prosperity, he published works by Kipling, Stevenson, Maeterlinck and, later, six titles by Conrad.

Neil MUNRO (1864–1930), the Scottish poet, novelist, and critic, was a fellow contributor to *Blackwood's*.

Alexander Henry Hallam MURRAY (1854–1934) was a partner in the family firm of John Murray, and a writer and illustrator of travel books.

William NICHOLSON (1872–1949), the painter, graphic artist, and set-designer, collaborated with his brother-in-law; they were the 'Beggarstaff Brothers'.

Sydney S. PAWLING (1862–1923), partner of William Heinemann, admired Conrad's early work and introduced him to Crane. Pawling published *The Nigger* and advanced money on *The Rescue*, incomplete for many years.

James Brand PINKER (1863–1922), a Scotsman, was one of the first literary agents in London. At various times he represented Ford, James, Crane, Wells, Bennett, and D. H. Lawrence. From 1900 on, he also acted for Conrad and helped him through many financial crises.

Marguerite PORADOWSKA (née Gachet, 1848–1937), the widow of Conrad's cousin Aleksander, and thus his 'Aunt'. Her novels of French, Belgian, and Polish life such as *Yaga* (1887) and *Le Mariage du fils Grandsire* (1894) were well-known in their day. Between 1895 and 1900 there is an enigmatic gap in the correspondence.

Sir Arthur Thomas QUILLER-COUCH (pseudonym 'Q', 1863–1944) had been a lecturer in classics and associate editor of the *Speaker*. After settling in Fowey ('Troy Town'), he wrote many volumes of fiction and other prose. He edited the original *Oxford Book of English Verse* and, in 1912, became King Edward VII Professor of English Literature at Cambridge.

Mabel REYNOLDS, Galsworthy's younger sister, was born in 1871. She took an interest in literature; her husband, Tom, was a musician.

Arthur Llewelyn ROBERTS (1855–1919) was Secretary of the Royal Literary Fund, a charity that helps needy writers.

Edward Lancelot ('Ted') SANDERSON (1867–1939) took passage on the *Torrens* in 1893; on that voyage, Conrad read him a draft of *Almayer's Folly*. Sanderson taught at Elstree, his family's preparatory school in Hertfordshire. After service in the Boer War he remained in Africa, first in Johannesburg then in Nairobi; he returned in 1910 to be Headmaster of Elstree.

Helen Mary SANDERSON (née Watson) married Ted in 1898. She was a Scotswoman full of moral and intellectual vigour.

Clement King SHORTER (1859–1926) edited the *Illustrated London News* and the *Sketch*; later he founded *Tatler* and *Sphere*. His literary works included books on the Brontës.

Jane Cobden UNWIN (1851–1949) carried on the radical traditions of her father, Richard. She was active in feminist and other political causes.

T. Fisher UNWIN (1848–1935), Jane's husband, published *Almayer's Folly, An Outcast of the Islands*, and *Tales of Unrest*. Neither his business practices nor his adherence to the Liberal party endeared him to Conrad.

Helen Mary WATSON: see SANDERSON.

John WATSON managed the Northern Newspaper Syndicate from Kendal, in the Lake District.

Herbert George WELLS (1866–1946) began his friendship with Conrad with anonymous reviews of *Almayer's Folly* and *An Outcast*. They were good friends for over ten years, and Conrad liked the scientific romances such as *The Invisible Man* and *The Time Machine*, but their differing social, literary, and political ideas led to an estrangement.

Jane WELLS (née Amy Catherine Robbins, 1872–1927) had been Wells's student and became his second wife. A collection of her writings appeared in 1928.

Aniela ZAGÓRSKA (née Unrug, 1881–1943) was the wife of Conrad's cousin Karol. She followed contemporary literature closely and her daughter, also Aniela, translated some of Conrad's works.

EDITORIAL PROCEDURES

Hoping to balance the comfort of the reader against the requirements of the scholar, we have adopted the following conventions:

1. The texts stay faithful to Conrad's spelling, accentuation, and punctuation, but letters missing from within words are supplied in square brackets. Rather than use *sic*, we mark words that might be taken as misprints with an asterisk. Missing apostrophes are not restored.

2. Where absolutely necessary to the sense, missing pronouns and auxiliary verbs are also supplied in brackets. Gaps in the text, such as those caused by damage to the MS, appear thus: [...].

3. Again when sense dictates, full-stops are tacitly provided and quotation marks completed; words apparently repeated by accident have been deleted. A list of silent emendations will be found at the end of the volume.

4. Especially in pronouns, Conrad used capitals more profusely than a native speaker would. We preserve his usage, but distinguishing between upper and lower case must often be a matter of judgment rather than certainty. The same is true of locating paragraph breaks.

5. For the letters in French we observe the same conventions, but use square brackets and asterisks more sparingly; Conrad's erratic accentuation we leave as it is.

6. For the convenience of those who do not read the letters in sequence, information in footnotes may appear more than once.

7. Although he kept the surname Hueffer until 1919, Conrad's collaborator is called Ford Madox Ford throughout the edition. His first wife (divorced before the change of name) appears as Elsie Hueffer, and the couple as the Hueffers.

8. American readers should note that Conrad used the British system of abbreviating dates; thus 3.6 would mean 3 June, not 6 March.

9. In this and subsequent volumes the Nonesuch rather than the less reliable Bobbs-Merrill edition of the letters to Garnett provides the copy-text when no manuscript is available.

10. This edition collects all available letters, but only the more interesting telegrams; references to some others appear in the notes.

Thanks to variations in wording and lay-out, headings on Pent Farm stationery often help to place undated letters. The following letterheads appear in this volume (several later forms will appear in Volume Three):

Type one (black: all others are red), 17 November 1898 to 2 February 1899:

STATION:
SANDLING JUNCTION,
S.E.R.

**PENT FARM,
STANFORD, Near HYTHE.**

Type two, 7 February 1899 to 25 March 1899:

STATION:-
SANDLING JUNCTION. S.E.R.

**PENT FARM,
STANFORD,
Near HYTHE.**

Type three, 17 April 1899 to 25 November 1899 (after first use of type four): **STATION** now begins to the right of **SANDLING** but is still at an angle of 60°.
Type four, 24 October 1899 to 20 February 1900: **STATION** is now 50° to the horizontal.
Type five, 3 April 1900 to 20 July 1900: **STATION** is 30° to the horizontal.

Type six, mid September 1900 to 14 February 1901:

STATION:
SANDLING JUNCTION
S.E.R.

**PENT FARM,
STANFORD, Near HYTHE,
KENT.**

Type seven, 23 February 1901 to 12 March 1902: **STATION** at 60°; comma above **N** of **KENT**.

Type eight, 17 March 1902 to 4 November 1902: **STATION** at 50°; **JUNCTION** begins above stop between **E** and **R**.

Type nine, 5 November 1902 to June 1903: **JUNCTION** begins above **R**.

The headings are associated with these papers:

Type one: 175×110 mm, watermark STRAKER

Types two to five: 179×112 mm, watermark BURYCOURT VELLUM WOVE

Types six to nine: 175×113mm, watermark ROCKLEIGH MILL ORIGINAL

The dimensions give the size of sheets as folded, ready for writing.

1898

To Minnie Brooke

Text MS Texas; Unpublished

3^d. Jan 1898
Stanford le Hope
Essex.

Dear Mrs Brooke.[1]

A letter—in a very contrite tone—left here early on Xmas Eve for Slingsby Rectory. Has it reached you? Meantime your good and forgiving missive reached my unworthy hands. But I trust that by this time you have read my wishes and my news.

I am very much touched by the kindness that prompted you to write. Jess was delighted. And so life goes on: we are ever greedy of kindness and most so when we least deserve it. But perhaps this year at last I shall succeed in turning over a new leaf. Good resolutions are written there; but the page is heavier than lead—alas! And I have learned to mistrust my strenght.*

I shall not repeat here my wishes. The feeling is lasting and the written words will come into your hands at some time or other; and I shall think and feel then as I have felt and thought before, as I shall think and feel in the future.

My books!—Well if You must know, one has appeared in Dec^{er} published by Heinemann;[2] another shall appear in the spring from Mr Unwin's house.[3] They appear, are praised and drop into the past like a stone into water. A small ripple—gone for ever. It is bread—hardly that even; probably as much as I deserve.

I am always your very faithful and
obedient servant

Jph Conrad.

P.S. Jessie sends her love. As I wrote, we are in daily expectation of an *event*. She is getting on very well but I am very anxious all the same. I shall let you know—before long. May it be good![4]

---

[1] A friend of the Fisher Unwins, Mrs Brooke had met the Conrads on their honeymoon. Her husband was rector of Slingsby in the North Riding of Yorkshire.
[2] *The Nigger of the 'Narcissus'.*   [3] *Tales of Unrest*, 4 April.
[4] Borys Conrad was born on 15 January.

To R. B. Cunninghame Graham
Text MS Dartmouth; J-A, I, 220; Watts 58

Stanford le Hope.
7th Jan 98.

Cher ami.[1]

Business first.[2] If a damned stack fetched away in a gale it would have to stay down I fancy. But if it got only loose then chains, wire rope, any blamed thing you could lay hands on would serve to secure it. Never saw a stack quit its post, tho' I saw a cold green sea go right down into one. *Yes.* A *fore*-stay-sail and a main stay-sail (if carried) could be set to steady the roll of a steamship, providing the gale was not too heavy. Fore stay-sail alone—hardly; tho' it's quite conceivable. In a serious affair they would be useless and in any one case would speedily vanish; the necessity of steaming head to sea causing a tremendous strain on the canvass.

And in exchange will You tell me whether that life-boat that capsized (of which you wrote) was a steam-lifeboat? And what does your brother think of steam-lifeboats?[3] I hate machinery but candidly must own that it seems to me that in most cases steam's the thing for that work.

A year of happy life for every good word spoken of the *Nigger*–to You! Had you the pluck to read it again? Eh! Man! Ye are perfectly fearless! What mad thing will you do next?

Read the *Badge*. It won't hurt you—or only very little. Crane-ibn-Crane el Yankee is all right. The man sees the outside of many things and the inside of some.[4]

I am making preparations to receive the Impenitent Thief which* all the honours due to his distinguished position. I always thought a lot of

---

[1] Robert Bontine Cunninghame Graham (1852–1936) was a Scottish laird, a Nationalist, a Socialist, and a traveller in distant places. His friendship with Conrad, which started in 1897, developed very rapidly: the letter before this one (20 December) began 'My dear Sir'.

[2] Graham also wrote. He was experimenting with short pieces that combined in various proportions fiction, autobiography, and speculative essay. The information given here was used in 'S.S. *Atlas*': *Saturday Review*, 14 and 21 May.

[3] A former naval officer, Graham's brother Charles had been appointed deputy chief inspector for the Royal National Lifeboat Institution. Conrad held that lifeboats should be mechanically powered (Watts, p. 61).

[4] Stephen Crane's *The Red Badge of Courage* appeared in 1895; he first met Conrad in October 1897. Although immediately fond of him, Conrad had reservations about his work (letters to Garnett, 5 December 1897, to Graham, 19 January 1900). The language of the previous paragraph acknowledges Graham's passion for Scotland; this one, his passion for North Africa.

that man.[1] He was no philistine anyhow—and no Jew, since he had no eye for the shent-per-shent business the other fellow spotted at once.[2] I hope your essay is sympathetic.

Do send everything you write—it does a fellow good. Or at any rate let us know where the things are so that I may scuffle around to get them.

As to the Saga it confirms me in my conviction that you have a fiendish gift of showing the futility—the ghastly, jocular futility of life.[3] Et c'est très fin—très fin. C'est finement vu et c'est exprimé avec finesse—presque a mots couverts, avec de l'esprit dans chaque phrase.[4] Excuse this polyglot epistle to the faithful.

Ever Yours

J. Conrad

P.S. Re-reading your letter—

That's how a stack would go perhaps.[5] And this would give you an idea how to secure it again. Here both lanyards to S have been carried away—say, by a roll. the thing is then to catch the ends of chains hook quick a spare tackle into the big link and the ring on deck and set taut. Should chains go same principle of action must be followed or should only one of each pair of chains go then could secure in a hurry thus with a rope (5 inch line) the steam-pipe would check the fall of a funnel and it would go over slowly and land on one of the ship's boats—probably— and smash it no doubt. Or if pitched forward it would damage the bridge—and the man on it too very likely. But the most dramatic circumstance would be the hellish mess of soot blowing about or washing over the deck. Does the plot hinge on the funnel? You must have a *plot*! If you haven't, every fool reviewer will kick you because

---

[1] Luke 23.39–43. In a letter to Garnett, Conrad calls the malefactor 'one of my early heroes' (11 June 1897). Graham's essay 'The Impenitent Thief' appeared in the January 1898 issue of H.M. Hyndman's *Social-Democrat*. See also the letters to Graham of 23 and 31 January.

[2] In the 1890s, 'shent-per-shent' was an anti-Semitic catch-phrase. Watts (p. 62) cites an example of its use in the *Labour Leader* (27 March 1897), a paper to which Graham contributed.

[3] Graham's short story 'Snaekoll's Saga' was published in the *Saturday Review*, 18 and 25 December 1897. It tells of an Icelandic farmer whose great ambition is to cross his country's deserts of ice. He sets off with his horse, Snaekoll, but only the horse reaches the other side. Presumably Snaekoll has survived by eating his master. Both the 'Saga' and 'S.S. *Atlas*' were reprinted in *The Ipané* (T. Fisher Unwin, 1899).

[4] 'And it's very subtle – very subtle. It's subtly observed and it's artfully expressed – virtually by innuendoes, with intelligence in every phrase.'

[5] For Conrad's drawings, see plates 2 and 3.

there can't be literature without plot.[1] I am in a state of wild excitement
about the stack. Let's know quick what happened in the tramp. A
Scotch tramp is a very good tramp. The Engineers tell anecdotes, the
mates are grim and over all floats the flavour of an accent that gives a
special value to every word pronounced on her deck. You must know
I've a soft spot for Scotchmen.[2] Be easy on the tramp.

Ah! Amigo! I've thought of Rajah Laut in London and if not in the
W-H[3] then next thing to it. But I haven't the heart. I Haven't! Not yet.
I am now busy about his youth—a gorgeous romance—gorgeous as to
feeling I mean. Battles and loves and so on.[4]

To Edward Garnett
Text MS Sutton; G. 115 (in part)

7th Jan 98.
[Stanford-le-Hope]

My dear Garnett.[5]

I've been putting off writing so as to send you the MS. at the same
time. But I want to have a little more still, for you to see, so that you may
judge of the way I take hold of the actual story.[6]

I had a most kind appreciative, good letter from your wife—and more
shame to me not to have acknowledged it. Present my excuses. I was
delighted. I've pasted it in my copy of the N[igger]: the most prized
words of praise and specially interesting as disclosing the woman's point
of view to look at such a rough performance.[7]

---

[1] See the letter to Garnett, 7 January, p. 9 note 1. The present letter, as Watts points out,
anticipates 'Typhoon' – and 'Typhoon' was collected in a volume dedicated to Graham.
[2] Conrad served on the Scottish clipper *Duke of Sutherland* in 1878/9, and the barque
Highland Forest in 1887.
[3] Western Hemisphere?
[4] In *Almayer's Folly* and *An Outcast of the Islands*, Tom Lingard is called Rajah Laut—King
of the Sea. *The Rescue*, the 'gorgeous romance', presents an earlier period of his fictional
career. Norman Sherry discusses the origins of this character in *Conrad's Eastern World*,
pp. 89–118.
[5] Edward Garnett (1868–1937) was working for T. Fisher Unwin. In his career as a
publisher's reader, Garnett had a remarkable influence on the course of twentieth-
century literature. *The Nigger of the 'Narcissus'* is dedicated to him.
[6] *The Rescue.*
[7] Constance Garnett (1862–1946), the celebrated translator of Russian literature, wrote
to Conrad on 30 December. Having thanked Conrad for praising her work on Turgenev
and having noted an affinity of thought and style between the two novelists, she
continues: 'I feel so grateful for the insight you have given me into the sailors. It is such
as they are the everlasting fascinating masculine enigma for us women. The artist is
more than half feminine, and him we can make shift by glimpses to understand, at least

The P[atron] writes he can't anyhow place the *Return* and I give it up. What upset me is that he means to fire off the book *at once!*[1] At the same time Pawling writes me he is going to start the Nigger upon the book-sellers.[2] He is going to "bang it" he says. If the books clash it will be fatal to both of them.

I wrote a temperate letter to the P. telling him that I sold him the book for spring publication—end March at earliest—and that it was so agreed plainly in our conversation. That I object to publication at once—thinking it bad for the *stories*—from a business point of view. He must let the Reviewers have their say about one thing before throwing at them another.[3] Firm and polite. Reminded him of our talk. Said I hold him to it. But really I am helpless. The man is unsafe—and I am a fool.

I think I am going to have the 2^d part of the *Rescue* written by first week in Febr^y. Meantime things are pretty serious with me. Casting about for ways to obtain bread and *peace* the following commercial transaction suggested itself to me.[4] To be faithful to Pawling I have practically thrown away a safe £300. Blackwood would have given that. His man here told me so.[5] Now Pawling himself wrote that he had almost positive hopes to get for me £400 in serial rights alone. (Here & in Am[erica]). But serial rights must be waited for and the book is not finished. What I think of proposing to Pawling is this: I shall *sell* him outright the <u>serial</u> rights of the *Rescue* for *£240* and as the book is not finished (and even if it was) I don't want cash down. I want him to pay me say *£20* p. month. Perhaps before he had made 3 such payments he may find a place for the Rescue (having then a half finished book to show). It's no concern of mine. I don't even want to know for how much *he* sold it. I want him to go on with the monthly payments (£20) for a year (£240)—even if the book is finished in another six months.[6] And if he *thought* he could get 400 for me then he *ought* to get *300* for himself. I

as well as any way he is understood by his common fellow men.' The whole letter is reproduced in G., p. 111.

1 T. Fisher Unwin, whom Garnett and Conrad mockingly dubbed The Enlightened Patron of Letters, published *Tales of Unrest* on 4 April. It was his last Conrad title.
2 Sydney S. Pawling, a partner of William Heinemann, who had published *The Nigger* in December (but bearing an 1898 publication date).
3 All the stories but 'The Return' had appeared in periodicals; the most recent were 'An Outpost of Progress' (*Cosmopolis*, June/July) and 'Karain' (*Blackwood's*, November 1897).
4 Garnett leaves out the rest of the paragraph. He also omits the *Notes* that constitute the bulk of the following paragraph and part of the one after that.
5 David Meldrum, literary adviser in the London office of William Blackwood, the Edinburgh publisher.
6 *The Rescue*, in six parts, did not appear until 1920. Conrad first mentioned it in 1896.

think that the extra £60 (or perhaps more) will make the business not so bad for him and even cover the extra risk of such a transaction. This is the risk of my illness or death before finishing the story. However my health is not particularly bad (and without worry would be better) and I have no reason to expect death this year. Remain accidents. (Rwy. boating and snow) For that I have a £1000 policy out of which (should I break my neck in some way) any advance he would have made till then can be repaid by my wife.

As You have done so much for me—in fact everything—with Pawling I submit this plan to you and should you dislike it I shall forbear mentioning it to our friend. I don't want to do anything that would look as if I were trying to get *at* Pawling. To my mind it appears a simple commercial transaction in which risk and profit are on one side and a great convenience on the other. *Note* that by this arrangement he never stands to lose anything like even 200 pounds. He would stop the monthly payments in case of my decease and the book shall be finished in six months and by this time the amount will be paid at £20 p. and would be *only £120*. And I think that the risk is so small that to propose the affair is not quite like begging on my part. What do you think? Would you add to the many acts of brotherly regard and give your thought to this—and then tell me frankly what You think. That I must borrow money somewhere is very evident; and no man can so well understand the only security I offer than Pawling. I don't think he would be *annoyed* by such a proposal. Do you? After all I've given him in Nov^er a very fair chance to choke me off, which he would *not* take.[1] He believes in me? Or is it only the stress of competition?

At any rate I do not wish to say anything till nearly ½ the book is written. (2 parts complete). He writes to me in a most friendly manner and seems pleased with the reviews. He says that he is going to work the *N* off on the booksellers after the 15th inst when they have finished stock-taking. I have confidence in him but don't expect much. Still perhaps the Nigger may exist for a few years and so not be a bad spec for him. *Note* (Should I make the proposal above and be accepted I would let the royalties of the *Nigger* (I've only had the value of 1.500 copies) remain with him as further security to diminish the amount of any loss—should I peg out naturally).

I had 23 reviews. One indifferent (The Standard) and *one bad (the*

---

[1] Pawling had accepted *The Rescue* on the strength of the first part.

Academy).[1] Two or three of a hesitating kind in prov[incial] papers. The rest unexpectedly appreciative. Did I tell you I had a warm letter from Quiller Couch? He is going to say something about the Book in Pall Mall Magazine for Febry.[2]—I'll be sending You the R[escue] next week. A damned pot boiler. But I am quite interested myself tho' I write without pleasure.

Ever Yours

Jph Conrad

Jessie sends her love and thanks to Your wife. She wants to know whether Bunny[3] remembers her. We are standing by here.

To T. Fisher Unwin
Text MS Berg; Unpublished

7th Jan 1898.
[Stanford-le-Hope]

Dear Mr Unwin.[4]

I am sorry to hear You have given up the placing of the *Return*. The story is none the worse for it, however—and it may do the Vol good to have *one* at least that has not appeared before.[5] I did not for a moment suppose that the magazine you mention would care to publish that tale. It is not much their style—but it is a serious loss to me.

As to the publication of the book I can hardly suppose You mean to do it before the spring. You mentionned* next autumn—and I stipulated for next spring (which I understood to mean *end* March at the *very* earliest) to which you agreed. But as your letter *may* mean that you

---

[1] Although regretting the absence of an elaborate plot, the *Standard* found 'all this nothingness . . . admirably told' (24 December 1897). The *Academy* also regretted the absence of intrigue ('no plot and no petticoats') and claimed that the book's material was better suited to a short story. While conceding Conrad's 'originality and energy', the reviewer complains about 'the tense, exaggerated, highly poetic diction', which he considers out of place in a sailor's narrative: 'it is a cause of unfeigned regret that the presentation lacks tact and discrimination, so that merits which should have been open and attractive are to be discovered only by conquering a sense of repulsion' (1 January 1898). The latter, unsigned review is reprinted in Norman Sherry, *Conrad: The Critical Heritage*, pp. 94–6.

[2] A. T. Quiller-Couch ('Q') contributed a regular article on old and new books, 'From a Cornish Window'. His enthusiastic remarks are on pp. 428–9 of the February number.

[3] The Garnetts' son, David, who was nearly seven.

[4] T. Fisher Unwin (1848–1935) had already published *Almayer's Folly* (1895) and *An Outcast of the Islands* (1896). *Tales of Unrest* would be his last book by Conrad.

[5] See the preceding letter to Garnett.

intend publishing next month—or even next week I wish to submit to you my reasons against that course.

—Imprimis my last book the *Nigger* had not as yet its chance. It looks as tho' it would be discussed; and many important reviews have not yet appeared.[1] I had letters about it from various people. I know that even as late as middle Febr^y a *causerie* about it shall appear by Quiller Couch in a popular magazine. The book is worth notice as much perhaps by its faults as by its qualities—and I think that *notice* it will get. Now it strikes me that another work of mine launched on its heels, so to speak, won't get its fair value of attention, besides interfering with the sale of the previous work while doing no good, commercially, for itself. I want—and of course you do also—to have the *vol* of short stories noticed, noticed *properly*. They also deserve it. The longer the discussion of the last published book the better it shall be for its successor. Let the critics have their say out about one thing before they begin on another or else they will neglect one of them. Now you may take my word that they won't neglect the *unique* sea tale. They will slate or praise it—it's all one to me but there will be no conspiracy of silence. It seems to me, then, that it would be better business as well as carrying out the spirit (*and even the words*) of our understanding, to publish the *Tales of Unrest* about the 25th March or the first week in April.[2] I was so firmly convinced that such was your intention that I furnished a note to that effect to the Editor of *Literature*[3]—and I see other papers are copying it already.

After all you can well afford to follow my desire in that matter. The book can hardly be a loss to you, since for my last (I don't mind telling you) I get *17½ and 20%* on *pub. price* in England[4] and *15 cents* per copy in the States: terms considerably higher than those I asked you for the Tales. Let us then say: *The Return* shall appear for the first time in the vol. The vol: shall appear after the 25th of March—as I understood from the first.

With kind regards faithfully yours

Jph. Conrad.

PS I'm sorry I can't come to town but I shall be wanted at home the next week or two. It would have been more satisfactory to talk the matter

[1] *Literature*, for example, did not discuss *The Nigger* until March 26.

[2] It appeared on 4 April.

[3] The note, which appeared on 1 January (p. 348), announced *Tales of Unrest* for spring publication. It also announced that Conrad was at work on *The Rescue*, a romance that 'will relate events which the author has known or heard of, and sketch portraits of remembered people'.

[4] According to a letter to Garnett (27 September 1897), Conrad actually received 15% and 20%.

over. I trust You are well. *The Return* is not a tale for puppy dogs nor for maids of thirteen. I am not in the least ashamed of it. Quite the reverse. All the others had attracted notice when they appeared. I am very anxious about these tales. Give them a fair chance. Congratulate you about Hugh Wynne a fine book.[1] Was it appreciated?

To John Galsworthy

Text MS Forbes; Unpublished

[early January 1898][2]

[Stanford-le-Hope]

My dear Galsworthy.[3]

I send back the MS to-night. The chapters are all they should be. The last line *excellent*. Good luck to the book.[4]

Don't you feel like an orphan since You finished?

F[isher] U[nwin] is trying to play me a dirty trick. He got possession of the whole manuscript under pretence of placing the *Return* (serially) and now suddenly writes that he is tired of trying for it—so concludes to publish the book at once! Neither in previous letters nor in conversation did he ever give the slightest hint of such an intention. In fact the scoundrel pretended a desire to delay pub^{on} till autumn. He got the book for a song and now wants to make money by the stir of the *N of the N.* not caring how he may injure me. I wrote temperately that I object absolutely. But what can I do? The man is unsafe and I am a fool when dealing with such a type for I can't understand it.

Try for higher terms than You are disposed to accept. He will never give you what the book is *worth*—nobody would of course; but *he* won't even give you what the book should *fetch*. Generosity on Your part would be misplaced.

Yes! I am immensely pleased with the work. Not everybody's writing and not everybody's reading either. There is something in your sen-

---

[1] S. Weir Mitchell's *Hugh Wynne, Free Quaker* (T. Fisher Unwin, 1897), a historical novel about the American war of independence.

[2] Evidently the letter to Unwin of 7 January, deploring over-eager publication of *Tales of Unrest*, had already been written. This letter must date from the same day or soon after; Conrad wrote again on the sixteenth.

[3] John Galsworthy (1867–1933), novelist: his friendship with Conrad went back to a voyage on the *Torrens* in 1893.

[4] *Jocelyn*, a novel submitted to Unwin at the end of January. Unwin rejected it, but Duckworth took it on.

tences that touches me time and again in a tender spot. I like it. And
I believe it will be appreciated. I do. I don't despair of mankind. The
best of luck to you and the story.

Ever Yours

J.C.

To Edward Garnett
Text MS Williams; G.117

Monday.[1]
9.1.98
[Stanford-le-Hope]

Dearest G.

Your letter is most helpful. I shall write to C[unninghame]
Graham to night. I am in *intimate* correspondence with him. He
writes to me every week once or even twice. He is struck. Pawling is
(lately) also in correspondence with him. What about I don't know
but P did mention this to me incidentally in his last letter.

I can speak plainly to C.G. about the *Sat R* idea. I don't know
whether he is on very good terms with F.H. tho'.[2] Fact to note: *all* the
fiction (it may be called) the *S.R* publishes is furnished by C.G.
alone.

I don't see why P[awling] should fail to fix serial of *Rescue* since
Blackwood was positively ready to accept it. The only question is
time. The *Rescue* would have perhaps to wait a year or so for a place.
Scribners would have made offer if they had not been full for 98 &
99. And even then if the book had been *finished* they would have made
an offer. So their letter to P (I've seen it) says. Still this may be a too
sanguine view. I send You by this post my copy of "*N*" with *notices*.

Thanks millions of times. You are a whole mountain of bricks—to
think and scheme for me so. I'm indeed blessed in *this* friendship.

Ever Yours

Jph Conrad.

---

[1] Monday was actually the tenth.
[2] According to Garnett, he had advised Conrad to try placing short stories and serialized
novels with the *Saturday Review* (London). Its editor, Frank Harris, despite his
insufferable conceit, had managed to attract a brilliant array of contributors, among
them Shaw, Wells, and Graham.

Look in the *"N"* copy *back* and front. The Lond. Dailies are all in front. Are these good *selling* notices?[1] I don't think so.

After I hear from C.G. I may try Q^2 but this I am more reluctant to do. Do write what you think of *"N"* and Why. I study it and there seems now like a flavour of failure about it.

To Stephen Crane
Text MS Columbia; Stallman 167

Wednesday [12? January 1898][3]
[Stanford-le-Hope]

My dear Crane[4]

I hope You haven't been angry with me. Fact is my dear fellow I've been having a hell of a time—what with one thing and another.[5] Had I come that day I would have been no good at all. I am hardly yet in a decent frame of mind.

I am curious to know Your idea; but I feel somehow that collaborating with you would be either cheating or deceiving You.[6] In any case disappointing you. I have no dramatic gift. *You* have the terseness, the clear eye the easy imagination. You have all—and I have only the accursed faculty of dreaming. My ideas fade—Yours come out sharp cut as cameos—they come all living out of Your brain and bring images—

---

[1] Such comments on *The Nigger* as this from the *Daily Chronicle* (22 December 1897) must have been a mixed blessing: 'the value of the book lies in the telling, and not in the events of the tale'.

[2] A. T. Quiller-Couch at the *Pall Mall Magazine*.

[3] The references at the end of the letter to Jessie Conrad's imminent delivery suggest the twelfth, but the fifth would also be possible.

[4] Stephen Crane (1871–1900), poet, novelist, and journalist, lived at the time in Oxted, Surrey.

[5] Awaiting the birth of a child, arguing with Unwin, fretting about reviews of *The Nigger*, squeezing out *The Rescue*, going deeper and deeper into debt.

[6] Crane proposed that they collaborate on a play set in the American west. His innocence about the theatre was only rivalled by Conrad's distaste for it. Nevertheless they did toy with the idea, or so Conrad claimed in 1923 (Preface to Thomas Beer's *Stephen Crane*, reprinted in *Last Essays*, Doubleday, 1926; this Preface attributed the proposal to 1899, but the letter to Sanderson of 3 February 1898 confirms the earlier date). 'The general subject consisted in a man personating his "predecessor" (who had died) in the hope of winning a girl's heart ... the action, I fear, would have been frankly melodramatic. Crane insisted that one of the situations should present the man and the girl on a boundless plain standing by their dead ponies after a furious ride (a truly Crane touch). I made some objections. A boundless plain in the light of a sunset could be got into a back-cloth, I admitted; but I doubted whether we could induce the management of any London theatre to deposit two stuffed horses on its stage' (*Last Essays*, pp. 115–16). The idea of a 'predecessor' surfaced again in 'The Planter of Malata' (1914).

and bring light. Mine bring only mist in which they are born, and die. I would be only a hindrance to you—I am afraid. And it seems presumptuous of me to think of helping You. You want no help. I have a perfect confidence in your power—and why should you share with me what then may be of profit and fame in the accomplished task?

But I want to know! Your idea is good—I am certain. Perhaps you, yourself, don't know how good it is. I ask you as a friend's favour to let me have a sketch of it when you have the time and in a moment of inclination. I shall—if you allow me write You *all* I think of it, about it, around it. Then you shall see how worthless I would be to you. But if by any chance such was not your deliberate opinion—if you should really, honestly, artistically think I could be of some use—then my dear Crane I would be only too glad to work by Your side and with your lead. And Quien sabe? Something perhaps would get itself shaped to be mangled by the scorn or the praise of the Philistines.

Take your time and answer me. My wife sends kind regards. We are standing by for a regular bust-up. It may come any day. I can't write. The Dly Mail has given a bad notice to the *Nigger*.[1] There's no other news here.

Yours ever

Jph. Conrad.

This letter has been held back and now since I can't come I send it. My Sister in law must go away to morrow,[2] and I can't leave my wife all alone here. Do write your idea. I am anxious

Yours

J.C.

To T. Fisher Unwin
Text MS Syracuse; Unpublished

14 Jan. 98.

[Stanford-le-Hope]

Dear Mr Unwin.

Thanks very much for Smith's letter. Of course I would be very glad to have the story accepted in the States if its publication there would not

---

[1] 7 December 1898: 'we must admit that in many respects this present work is a disappointment'. This was one of the reviews that bewailed the absence of a blatant plot.
[2] Jessie Conrad had four sisters. One of them, Dolly, helped out for six months after the baby was born.

interfere with your plans for the book.[1] I may mention that nothing of mine shall appear (at any rate in book form) this year—except these Tales. I trust they will be liked—(or at least read) enough to make their publication profitable to us both.

With kind regards
Very faithfully Yours
Jph. Conrad

To R. B. Cunninghame Graham

Text MS Dartmouth; J-A, I, 221; Watts 63

10 pm. 14 Jan. 98.
Stanford le Hope
Essex

Cher ami.

A really friendly letter and my conscience smote me at every word read when I thought of your work upon which I intrude with my miserable affairs.

Semm! Pronounce the Name—and write to F. Harris.[2] This *is* a service and a most important one. I would rather owe it to you than to any one else—in fact don't *see* myself owing it to any one else. Frankly (you may have guessed) I was pretty nearly in my last ditch before I thought of attacking Harris. I talked to you in my letter as if I were ready to face fire and water and an Editor, but my heart was in my boots. Yours is a helping hand. And if You don't think you are thus sacrificing an old friend to a new one—well then Say the Name—and write.

And since you offer to do me this good turn I had better tell you that it would be rather important for me to have the publication begin as soon as possible—say in two–three months. By that time there would be a good lot of copy to go on with while I twisted the remainder out of my bowels. (It's wonderful how this fool-business of writing is serious to one.) The book is by no means near its termination. About 30000 out of 90000 words are ready.[3] Won't it be too cheeky approaching H. with such a small beginning?

---

[1] Smith must have been an American editor or publisher (rather than Reginald Smith, Unwin's rival at Smith, Elder). 'The Return' made its first appearance in the United States when Scribner's published *Tales of Unrest* on 26 March.

[2] For Conrad's hopes of publishing in the *Saturday Review* (a periodical that normally took only short fiction) see letters to Garnett, 9/10 and 15 January. 'Semm': the Judaic concept of the power of naming.

[3] The final version of *The Rescue* runs to about 140,000 words.

I would be very glad, very, to see him—in any case. But You know I am shy of my bad English. At any rate prepare him for a "b—y furriner" who will talk gibberish to him at the rate of 10 knots an hour. If not forewarned the phenomenon might discourage him to the point of kicking me downstairs. This is submitted to your wisdom which embraces the world and the men in it from Patagonia to Iceland.[1] Our ears are open.

Was the fire serious? And has Your wife got over the emotion? You know when I sprung that affair of mine on you I had no idea of the accumulation of troubles in Gartmore.[2] But all the same it was dam' unkind of you to lead me on gently to make an ass of myself about smoke stacks and stay-sails and then fire off at me a lot of sailor talk about going down the leach of a top-sail.[3] What don't you know! From the outside of a sail to the inside of a prison![4] When I think of you I feel as tho' I had lived all my life in a dark hole without ever seeing or knowing anything.

Nothing would be more delightful to me than to read a review of the *N* by you.[5] I never dreamed you would care to do this thing. I do not know who, when and how it is to be reviewed. But is the *N* worthy of your pen and especially of your thought! Is it too late. Do you really mean it?—There will be a *vol* of short stories app^g in March. One of them *The Outpost*. Now if you are really anxious to give me a good slating . . . .

"Put the tongue out" why not?[6] One ought to really. And the machine will run on all the same. The question is, whether the fatigue of the muscular exertion is worth the transient pleasure of indulged scorn. On the other hand one may ask whether scorn, love, or hate are justified in the face of such shadowy illusions. The machine is thinner than air and as evanescent as a flash of lightning. The attitude of cold unconcern is the only reasonable one. Of course reason is hateful—but why? Because it demonstrates (to those who have the courage) that we, living, are out of life—utterly out of it. The mysteries of a universe made of drops of fire

---

[1] Two locales of Graham's travels and his fiction: others included North and West Africa, Texas, and Paraguay.

[2] Graham was in the last stages of an unsuccessful struggle to keep the debt-ridden family estate in Perthshire.

[3] Leech: 'The perpendicular or sloping side of a sail' *OED*.

[4] For his part in the 'Bloody Sunday' demonstration (Trafalgar Square, 1887), Graham spent four-and-a-half weeks in Pentonville prison. He described his experiences in 'Sursum Corda' (*Saturday Review*, 19 June 1897).

[5] There is no evidence of Graham's having written a review. For his reactions to *The Nigger*, see Conrad's letter of 14 December 1897.

[6] 'An Outpost of Progress' ends with the discovery of Kayerts, who has hanged himself: 'And, irreverently, he was putting out a swollen tongue at his Managing Director.'

and clods of mud do not concern us in the least. The fate of a humanity condemned ultimately to perish from cold is not worth troubling about. If you take it to heart it becomes an unendurable tragedy. If you believe in improvement you must weep, for the attained perfection must end in cold, darkness and silence.[1] In a dispassionate view the ardour for reform, improvement for virtue, for knowledge, and even for beauty is only a vain sticking up for appearances as though one were anxious about the cut of one's clothes in a community of blind men. Life knows us not and we do not know life—we don't know even our own thoughts. Half the words we use have no meaning whatever and of the other half each man understands each word after the fashion of his own folly and conceit. Faith is a myth and beliefs shift like mists on the shore; thoughts vanish; words, once pronounced, die; and the memory of yesterday is as shadowy as the hope of to-morrow[2]—only the string of my platitudes seems to have no end. As our peasants say: "Pray, brother, forgive me for the love of God". And we don't know what forgiveness is, nor what is love, nor where God is. Assez.

Yesterday I've finished the Life.[3] Ça m'a laissé une profonde impression de tristesse comme si j'avais vécu toutes les pages du livre. I can say no more just now.

Ever Yours

Jph Conrad.

15th/1/98
PS. This letter missed this morning's post because an infant of male persuasion[4] arrived and made such a row that I could not hear the Postman's whistle. It's a fine commentary upon this letter! But salvation lies in being illogical. Still I feel remorse.

---

[1] The conviction that entropy would triumph on a cosmic scale was widespread as the century neared its close. In the farthest epoch he reaches, Wells's Time-traveller sees an ailing sun and a freezing world. For verbal parallels between this letter and an essay by Anatole France, consult Yves Hervouet, *Ariel* (Calgary), 1 (1970), 84–99.

[2] This sense of mutability anticipates the ending of 'Youth', written in early June.

[3] The biography of Saint Teresa of Avila by Graham's wife, Gabriela Cunninghame Graham.

[4] Alfred Borys.

To Edward Garnett
Text MS NYU; G. 119

15th 1.98
[Stanford-le-Hope]

My dear Garnett

Infant of male persuasion arrived to-day and made a great row. Everything is going on well here.

I had a warm letter from Graham. He offers to write Harris—thinks the idea splendid—and so on. I have in him a friend at court indeed. I replied telling him to go ahead.

Chesson wrote me a splendid letter about the *Nigger*.[1] It quite cheered me. I haven't written anything of the story since I saw you, but I think of it every day.

Crane wrote me, also, a penitent letter for not replying to mine at Xmas. He says he finds it easier to write *about* me than to me. Says he has written about me, but *where* he says not.[2]

Graham said incidentally he would have liked to review the *Nigger*. I told him he may be in time yet.

Upon the whole the Harris business might come off if Graham's letter reached him when he is in good temper. I shall let you know without delay how it turns out.

My kindest regards to your wife.

Ever yours

Jph. Conrad

Sinjohn[3] writes me that the *N[igger]* is in great request at his club—Junior Carlton. Great guns! I wish they would buy it

---

[1] See the next letter.

[2] Crane's only published remarks on Conrad appeared in March: 'Concerning the English "Academy"', *Bookman* (New York), 7, 22–4. They concern *The Nigger*, in which Conrad 'comes nearer to an ownership of the mysterious life on the ocean than anybody who has written in this century'.

[3] Galsworthy, who published his first four books under the pseudonym 'John Sinjohn'. He was about to submit *Jocelyn* to T. Fisher Unwin, Garnett's employer.

To W. H. Chesson
Text MS Yale; Keating 34

Sunday 16. Jan 98.
Stanford-le-Hope
Essex

Dear Mr Chesson[1]

Your unexpected and delightful letter reached me yesterday morning. I would have answered it at once had it not been that the house was in a state of disorganization on account of the arrival of an infant of the male persuasion. However this fuss is over thank God.

Your letter shows such a comprehension of the state of mind which produced the story, that had you given blame instead of generous praise it would still have been a rare pleasure to be thus understood—seized in the act of thinking, so to speak. Of all that has been said about the book this what you say gives the most intimate satisfaction, because you not only see what the book is but what it might have been. When you say, "One almost regrets Donkin being one of the crew," I take it as the very highest praise I have received—inconceivably different in its insight within those dark and inarticulate recesses of mind where so many thoughts die at the moment of birth, for want of personal strenght*—or of moral rectitude—or of inspired expression.

One would like to write a book for your reading.

This is what touched me most. The other words of commendation I take as Your recognition of a tendency of mind repulsive to many, understood by few, clearly seen by You—and which I cannot help thinking of as not wholly without merit. But a tendency of mind is nothing without expression and that the expression should please you is in my opinion my very great fortune.

It is to your letter (now incorporated with my copy of the *Nigger*)[2] that in moments of doubt and weariness I shall turn with the greatest confidence as to an infaillible* remedy for the black disease of writers. I've read it several times since yesterday.

---

[1] Like Garnett, W. H. Chesson (1870–1952) worked for Unwin. Chesson edited the manuscript of *Almayer's Folly* and had probably seen it before Garnett did. See Ugo Mursia, *The True 'Discoverer' of Joseph Conrad's Literary Talent* (Varese, Italy, 1971).

[2] The letter – and the book – are now at Yale. It is easy to see why Conrad was delighted. Chesson rebuts the standard reviewers' objections: 'words will not contain my contempt for those who deprecate the lack of story or plot ... I dismiss too, cheerfully, the argument that a seaman ... is not to write with fervid orchestral style against which the colloquial speech of his comrades sounds with double futility and increased clearness'.

I have also corrected all the *like* into *as* in my copy. One is so strangely blind to one's own prose; and the more I write the less sure I am of my English. Thanks for going to the trouble of pointing out to me the passages. I don't think the *N* will have a 2ᵈ Ed: but if—in years to come—it ever has, the corrections shall be made.[1] Believe me very gratefully and faithfully Yours,

Jph. Conrad.

PS. I trust you haven't bought the book. I haven't forgotten I have the privilege to owe you a copy. But I am coming to Town soon and the precious debt shall be discharged.

To Minnie Brooke
Text MS Texas; Unpublished

Sunday. [16 January 1898][2]
[Stanford-le-Hope]

Dear Mrs Brooke.

Excuse this post card. Can't lay hands on anything else and want this to go to day.

The event came off happily yesterday about noon. The mother and the child (a very noisy boy) are doing well—unexpectedly so.

Jessie sends her love. She is in the seventh heaven. I would tell You how I feel if I didn't suspect You know it without my telling. I was very glad to get your letter and to see you take interest in the notices of my *Nigger*. It is just like you to be so forgiving. We would like to have news of You and your little boy. Poor little chap. I've been a sick child too and feel for him. I am your very faithful and obedient servant.

Jph Conrad.

The letter as a whole, available in Keating, pp. 35–6, insists on the novel's shapeliness, its psychological acuity, and its ironic power.

[1] Eventually Conrad made corrections for the Heinemann collected edition of 1921.

[2] Date from postmark.

To Stephen Crane

Text MS Columbia; Stallman 169

16th Jan 98.

Stanford le Hope

Essex

My dear Crane

Dont you bother about writing unless You feel like it. I quite understand how you feel about it—and am not likely to forget you because you don't write. Still mind that when You do write You give me a very great pleasure.

A male infant arrived yesterday and made a devil of a row. He yelled like an Apache and ever since this morning has been on the war path again. It's a ghastly nuisance.

Look here—when you are coming to town next time just fling a sixpence away on a wire (the day before) to me and I shall try to run up too.[1] If detained shall wire care Heinemann. Ever Yours

Jph Conrad.

Say—what about the *Monster*. The damned story has been haunting me ever since.[2] I think it *must* be fine. It's a subject for you.

To John Galsworthy

Text MS Forbes; J-A, I, 223[3]

Sunday [16 January 1898][4]

[Stanford-le-Hope]

Dear Galsworthy.

Writing to F[*isher*] U[*nwin*] I would say: "as to terms of publication I would suggest the following arrangement — — — — — — — — — " I wouldn't take up an unyielding position.[5]

The good lady in the North judges from a remote standpoint. It never probably occurred to her to ask herself what you intended doing—how near you've come to that intention. Now I contend that (if I understood our attitude of mind) You have absolutely done what you set out to do.

---

[1] Crane was living twenty miles south of London, and Conrad roughly the same distance east.

[2] Since discussing it with Crane, perhaps on the visit to Stanford-le-Hope, 29 November. The story of the hideously burned and heroic Black was published in August 1898.

[3] Jean-Aubry omits the third paragraph.

[4] The reference to the new baby gives the date.

[5] Galsworthy was about to submit *Jocelyn*, his first novel. Unwin had published a collection of short stories, *From the Four Winds*, at Galsworthy's expense.

I contend that the people You take being what they are, the book is *their* psychology; if it had gone deeper it would have found nothing. This is my opinion. And the merit of the book (apart from distinguished literary expression) is just in this: You have given the exact measure of your characters in a language of great felicity, with measure, with poetical appropriateness to characters tragic indeed but within the bounds of their nature. That's what makes the book valuable apart from its many qualities as a piece of literary work.

In fact the force of the book is in its fidelity to the surface of life—to the surface of events—to the surface of things and ideas. Now this is not being shallow. If the episode of life you describe strikes your critic as without profundity it is not because the *treatment* is not deep. To me you have absolutely touched the bottom and the achievement is as praiseworthy as though you had plumbed the very ocean. It is not your business to invent depths—to invent depths is not art either. Most things and most natures have nothing but a surface. A fairly prosperous man in the state of modern society is without depth—but he is complicated—just in the way you show him. I don't suppose you admire such beings any more than I do. Your book is a dispassionate analysis of highminded and contemptible types—and you awaken sympathy, interest, feeling in an impartial, artistic way.[1] It is an achievement. I am rather angry with your critic for so wholly missing the value and the *fundamental* art of the book. As to the essential beauty of the work she could not very well have said less. The book is *desperately* convincing. She quarrels with you for not making it inspiring! Just like a clever woman. You and I know there is very little inspiration in such a phase of life—but women won't have it so. Prepare yourself to be misunderstood right and left. The work is good. And *as work* it *is* inspiring. Even so!

I am anxious to see the added chapter. If you have a duplicate copy please send the three chapters without delay. Interpolating like this is a dangerous experiment.

F.U. climbed down with a very bad grace but only after I had written a letter containing several hard truths as to his methods of conduct.[2] To give you the measure of the man—he tries to turn off the thing into an innocent joke. I wrote him I didn't see any reason why he should joke with me.

---

[1] *Jocelyn* is a novel of unhappy marriage and adultery. Conrad cannot yet have known about Galsworthy's involvement with Ada, his cousin's wife.
[2] Over the publication of *Tales of Unrest*.

An infant of male persuasion arrived yesterday. All is going on well here. I feel greatly relieved and hope to do some work now.

I should like to know what agreement you make with Unwin. I've told Garnett to look out for your MS. He is simply overwhelmed with work.

> Affectionately
> Ever Yours
>
> Jph. Conrad.

I am glad to hear your club reads the "*N*"
The Nigger lenght.* 50.000 words. You are well within limits of a 6/- book.

To Aniela Zagórska

Text Wiadomości Literackie (Warsaw) 1929, no. 51; J-A, 1,
224; Najder 223[1]

> Stanford-le-Hope,
> Essex.
> 21st January, 1898

Chère Cousine,[2]

I have received the wafer[3]—accompanied by a bitter complaint that was not quite deserved. Les apparences mentent quelquefois.[4] But that does not altogether excuse me.

The baby was born on the 17th of this month[5] and I particularly waited these three days in order to be able to inform you definitely that tout va bien. The doctor reports that it is a magnificent boy. He has dark hair, enormous eyes—and looks like a monkey. What upsets me is that my wife maintains that he is also very much like me. Enfin! Please do not draw hasty conclusions from this surprising coincidence. My wife must be wrong.

He will be christened in the Chapel of the Cloister of the Carmelites in Southwark (London).[6] The principle on which his name was chosen is

---

[1] Translation from Najder (but ending from Jean-Aubry).

[2] Aniela Zagórska (1881–1943), wife of Karol Zagórski, Conrad's second cousin once removed. They lived in Lublin.

[3] In Poland, pieces of the wafer served on Christmas Eve are saved for absent relations (Najder, p. 223).

[4] 'Appearances sometimes lie.'

[5] On the fifteenth: procrastinator's licence.

[6] In the middle of February, or so he told Mrs Brooke (25 January). However, Zdzisław Najder has established that Borys was not baptized until 29 January 1899– in a church near the Pent (*Joseph Conrad: A Chronicle*, p. 250). The Carmelites lived in North Kensington, not in Southwark; in any case, the house of a closed order would be an odd

the following: that the rights of the two nations must be respected. Thus, my wife representing the Anglo-Saxons chose the Saxon name Alfred. I found myself in an embarrassing situation. I wanted to have a purely Slavonic name, but one which could not be distorted either in speech or in writing—and at the same time one which was not too difficult for foreigners (non-Slavonic). I had, therefore, to reject names such as Władysław, Bogusław, Wienczysław etc., I do not like Bohdan: so I decided on Borys, remembering that my friend Stanisław Zaleski gave this name to his eldest son, so that apparently a Pole may use it.[1] Unless, Aniela dear, you care to suggest a nicer name (and there is still time) please remember that there is a certain Alfred Borys Konrad Korzeniowski, whom I commend to your heart in the name of God and of those who, after a life full of trouble and suffering, remain in your and my memory.

I kiss your hands. A warm embrace for Karol. My wife sends her dear love to all of you.

Your loving,
Konrad Korzeniowski.

She says that it is now only that she feels she belongs to the family. She is extremely pleased with herself and with the whole world. C'est naif mais touchant.

Both our love to the dear girls.

To R. B. Cunninghame Graham

Text MS Dartmouth; J-A, I, 229; Watts 68

Sunday. [23 January 1898][2]
[Stanford-le-Hope]

Cher ami

I've got a bad wrist; that's why I did not write sooner. I gave it complete rest. Much better now.

The Impenitent Thief has been read more than once.[3] I've read it several times alone and I've read it aloud to my wife. Every word has

---

venue for a christening. Had Conrad required its aid, there was a Polish church in the East End.

[1] The name is characteristically Russian – as Conrad seems to realize. About four years younger than Conrad, Zaleski was a long-standing family friend and had helped execute the will of Tadeusz Bobrowski, Conrad's uncle.

[2] Citing the letters of 14 and 31 January, Watts gives cogent arguments for this date.

[3] In the January issue of the *Social-Democrat*. Edited by an avowed Marxist, this monthly stood farther to the left than the modern associations of its title might suggest. 'The Impenitent Thief' was reprinted in *Success* (Duckworth, 1902). This essay praises the

found a home. You with your ideals of sincerity, courage and truth are strangely out of place in this epoch of material preoccupations. What does it bring? What's the profit? What do we get by it? These questions are at the root of every moral, intellectual or political movement. Into the noblest cause men manage to put something of their baseness; and sometimes when I think of You here, quietly You seem to me tragic with your courage, with your beliefs and your hopes. Every cause is tainted: and you reject this one, espouse that other one as if one were evil and the other good while the same evil you hate is in both, but disguised in different words. I am more in sympathy with you than words can express yet if I had a grain of belief left in me I would believe you misguided. You are misguided by the desire of the impossible—and I envy you. Alas! What you want to reform are not institutions—it is human nature. Your faith will never move that mountain. Not that I think mankind intrinsically bad. It is only silly and cowardly. Now *You* know that in cowardice is every evil—especially that cruelty so characteristic of our civilisation. But without it mankind would vanish. No great matter truly. But will You persuade humanity to throw away sword and shield? Can you persuade even me—Who write these words in the fulness of an irresistible conviction? No. I belong to the wretched gang. We all belong to it. We are born initiated, and succeeding generations clutch the inheritance of fear and brutality without a thought, without a doubt without compunction—in the name of God.

These are the thoughts suggested by the man who wrote an essay on the Impenitent Thief.[1] Forgive their disconnected impertinence. You'll have to forgive me many things if you continue to know me on the basis of sincerity and friendship.

I wanted to say a word or so about the technique of the essay but I can't.[2] A la prochaine—donc

Ever Yours

Jph Conrad

consistency of the thief who, in St Luke's account of the crucifixion, rails at Christ. In effect, the thief has refused to take the Pascalian gamble: 'Repentance is a sort of fire insurance, hedging on what you will – an endeavour to be all things to all men and to all gods.'

[1] With its emphasis on the ubiquity and inevitability of human suffering, the essay itself is far from utopian. Its appearances in such militant company, however, gave Conrad the chance to tilt at his friend's genuine commitment to Socialism. In *Cunninghame Graham*, Watts and Davies contend that this commitment was accompanied by much more pragmatism and even scepticism than Conrad (who perhaps saw reflections of his revolutionary father) was willing to recognize.

[2] Throughout, Conrad's hand had been trembling.

To John Galsworthy
Text MS Forbes; Unpublished

Monday [24 January 1898][1]
[Stanford-le-Hope]

My dear Galsworthy

Thanks for your good wishes. We on our side wish that You should never know unhappiness and in the work, the new work of your brain and heart find always the intimate satisfaction of your own approval and the justice of public recognition. I've been very unwell myself this morning. A kind of nervous disturbance which has left me tired out. I return F.U.'s letter. I think you ought to stick to him. He has *means* to push a book—the connection and the best agent in the trade. Terms—I should say: 5d per copy first 500. Then 10d up to 2000. Afterwards 12d. Ask more than you would take. F.U. shall haggle or I am much mistaken.

My wife's kind regards. I am ever yours

Jph Conrad

To Edward Garnett
Text MS Yale; G. 120

Monday evening [24 January 1898][2]
[Stanford-le-Hope]

Dear Garnett

I have your letter and the proofs.[3] You are the best of fellows to go through all that disgusting kind of toil for me. And my ingratitude is so complete, is so black that I can by no means be ashamed of it. This morning for half an hour or perhaps a little less I disliked you with the utmost cordiality and sat brooding about some way to do You a serious mischief. But now—at 5 pm—I feel I could bear the sight of You without showing any unholy emotion.

Yes. Seriously. You are right in everything—even in the suggestion to let the story go as it is. It shall go—and be hanged to it. It is bad—and in

---

[1] The contents place this letter between that of 16 January, which suggests a general formula for submitting *Jocelyn*, and Galsworthy's letter to Unwin, 29 January (Marrot, *Life and Letters*, p. 111), which borrows Conrad's advice in both letters almost verbatim.
[2] Garnett's dating.
[3] Of *Tales of Unrest*.

sober truth I can't bear the sight of it any more.[1] Let it go. No one will notice it particularly, and even if someone arose to solemnly curse it, the story and the curse would be forgotten before the end of the week.

My very sincere thanks to Mrs. Garnett for saying a good word—the only good word—for the woman. Tell Her please that as to the story I think it is as false as a sermon by an Archbishop. Exactly. This is to you.[2] Another man goes out than the man who came in. T'other fellow is dead. You have missed the symbolism of the new gospel (that's what the Return is) altogether—and You call yourself a critic! The only weak point in the story is the slamming of the street door at the end. I ought to have stopped on the "... not even a footstep on the thick carpet ... as though no sooner outside he had died and his body had vanished together with his soul" and then in leaded type "He never returned". That would have made the newspaper boys sit up. They would have wanted to know where he went to, how he got downstairs; they would have made guesses at it—they would have called it realism, naturalism, or new humour. I've missed fame by a hair's breadth. And then we could have hired some chinaman of letters to explain that the whole story is transcendental symbolico-positivist with traces of illuminism. I've missed my best chance. Enough fooling. It strikes me I am "taking up your valuable time".

Ever Yours

J Conrad.

Jess sends her love to Mrs Garnett and desires me to state that the baby is a very fine baby. I disclaim all responsibility for that statement. *Do* you really think the volume *will do*?

To Minnie Brooke

Text MS Texas; Unpublished

25 Jan 1898
Stanford-le-Hope
Essex.

Dear Mrs Brooke.

My wife shall write as soon as she may sit up; meantime let me thank you in both our names for the coverlet—and still more, for the friendly thought.

---

[1] Conrad's revulsion from 'The Return' was strong and long-lasting. When, many years later, he looked at it again, 'the reading rendered me dumb for the remainder of the day, not exactly with astonishment but with a sort of dismal wonder' (*Tales of Unrest*, Author's Note, p. x).

[2] Sentence added in margin.

Everything is going on all right here and on the 14th of next month I think Jess will be strong enough to travel to London where the boy shall be christened. His names are to be: Alfred Borys Conrad, which last he may use for a surname as his father does.

We are very much concerned about your little boy. Have You had a very trying time? Am I right in my surmise that You are staying in Wales on his account? We would dearly like to hear good news of You and the children.

Excuse the hurry of this letter but I ought to have written yesterday and must not miss the post to-day. I am afraid You will not like my last book; it is too salty and tarry.[1] I shall send you my vol: of short stories in March, as soon as it comes out. I am dear Mrs Brooke your most obedient and faithful servant.

Jph. Conrad Korzeniowski.

To Cora Crane

Text MS Columbia; Stallman 169 (in part)

25 Jan 1898
Stanford-le-Hope
Essex

Dear Mrs Crane.[2]

My wife shall write as soon as she is allowed to sit up. Meantime let me send You our warmest thanks for the beautiful flowers and for your very kind invitation.

I would hesitate to inflict myself upon you with the tribe—but since You call your fate upon your own head the temptation to please ourselves is too irresistible. So, all being well, we shall descend upon your peaceful homestead on the 19th.[3] I have grounds for hope that by that date my wife shall be able to travel. We shall meantime devote all our energies to the taming of the baby lest he should break out and devastate your countryside, which, I feel, would put you and Crane in a false position vis-a-vis your neighbours. Perhaps a strong iron cage

---

[1] Conrad worried that bad language and exclusive maleness would offend women readers of *The Nigger*.

[2] Stephen and Cora Crane (née Howorth, 1865–1910) travelled as husband and wife; her legal husband, who had refused a divorce years before, lived in what is now Ghana. The Cranes had met while Cora was proprietor of the Hotel de Dream in Jacksonville, Florida, a combination of brothel and salon. In 1897, reporting the conflict between Greece and Turkey, Cora Crane became the first woman war-correspondent; later, she wrote short stories.

[3] Of February. The Cranes lived in Oxted, Surrey.

would be the most effective expedient; however we shall judge at the time the exact degree of his ferocity and act accordingly. My most earnest consideration had been also given to the matter of a good reliable keeper—which you with such kind forethought mention yourself. My wife will want some help, not being even at the best of times very athletic. Could we—instead of a nurse—whom we have not—bring Dolly, whom we have. Dolly is a young person with her hair down her back, and of extreme docility. I have the distinction of being her brother-in-law. She is now (and for the next six months) staying with us for the sake of her health and to help my wife. Will you frankly tell me whether there is the slightest objection to this plan. As Crane perhaps told you I am cheeky but easily repressed. You must really forgive me the coolness of my impudence.

The child is, I am sorry to say, absolutely callous to the hono[u]r awaiting him of his very first visit being to your house. I talked myself hoarse trying to explain to him the greatness of the occurrence—all in vain. I want Crane to give it his artistic benediction and call upon its head the spirit—the magnificent spirit that is his familiar—the genius of his work. And then when our writing days are over he who is a child to day may write good prose—may toss a few pearls before the Philistines. I am dear Mrs. Crane Your most obedient and faithful servant

Jph Conrad.

To R. B. Cunninghame Graham
Text MS Dartmouth; J-A, 1, 225; Watts 70

31 Jan 98.
[Stanford-le-Hope]

Cher et excellent ami.

In the wrist there was gout or some other devil which rendered it quite powerless, besides it being horribly painful. It's all over now.

It is good of you to push my fortunes. You are the only man—in this or any other country—who took any effective interest in them. Still I think that F. Harris should not be pressed.[1] You have given him two broadsides and if the man will not surrender, well then let him run.

Now the first sensation of oppression has worn off a little what remains with one after reading the Life of Sta Theresa[2] is the impression

---

[1] To publish Conrad's work in the *Saturday Review*.
[2] Gabriela Cunninghame Graham's *Santa Teresa* (1894, 2 vols.), a work that attends to the active at least as much as to the contemplative aspect of the saint's life.

of a wonderful richness; a world peopled thickly—with the breath of
mysticism over all—the landscapes, the walls, the men, the woman. Of
course I am quite incompetent to criticise such a work; but I can
appreciate it. It is vast and suggestive; it is a distinct acquisition to the
reader—or at least to me; it makes one *see* and reflect. It is absorbing like
a dream and as difficult to keep hold of. And it is—to me—profoundly
saddening. It is indeed old life re-vived.[1] And old life is like new life after
all—an uninterrupted agony of effort. Yes. Egoism is good, and altruism
is good, and fidelity to nature would be the best of all, and systems could
be built, and rules could be made—if we could only get rid of
consciousness. What makes mankind tragic is not that they are the
victims of nature, it is that they are conscious of it. To be part of the
animal kingdom under the conditions of this earth is very well—but as
soon as you know of your slavery the pain, the anger, the strife—the
tragedy begins. We can't return to nature, since we can't change our
place in it. Our refuge is in stupidity, in drunken[n]ess of all kinds, in
lies, in beliefs, in murder, thieving, reforming—in negation, in
contempt—each man according to the promptings of his particular
devil. There is no morality, no knowledge and no hope; there is only the
consciousness of ourselves which drives us about a world that whether
seen in a convex or a concave mirror is always but a vain and floating
appearance. "Ôte-toi de là que je m'y mette"[2] is no more of a sound rule
than would be the reverse doctrine. It is however much easier to
practice.

What made you suspect that I wanted vous faire une querelle
d'Allemand[3] about the technique of the Impenitent Thief? I leave that
to Wells, who is in the secret of the universe—or at least of the planet
Mars.[4] It struck me when reading your essay that the style was not the
Cunninghame Graham I've known hitherto. As to the matter, however,
there was not the slightest doubt—and, as I have said, every word has
found a home. As to the form: *c'est plus d'un seul jet*[5] if I may say so. It
grips in a different way. The pictures and the figures are drawn without
lifting pencil from paper. I like it very well. It's just the thing for that

---

[1] During her travels, Graham found many traces of the Castille Teresa had known in the
   sixteenth century, yet these traces made the gap between past and present seem all the
   wider; time and place were physically accessible but spiritually remote. 'There will be
   no more saints', wrote Graham in her Epilogue.
[2] 'Make room for me.'
[3] 'To pick a groundless quarrel with you.'
[4] Home of the invaders in *The War of the Worlds*, just published.
[5] 'It's more than a single stroke', i.e. 'there's more than one effect'.

essay whether You did it of set purpose or by caprice or, perhaps, unconsciously?

I am glad your brother likes the *Nigger*.[1] Symons reviewing *Trionfo della Morte* (trans:) in the last *Sat. Rev.* went out of his way to damn Kipling and me with the same generous praise. He says that *Captains Courageous* and the *Nigger* have no idea behind them.[2] I don't know. Do you think the remark is just? Now straight!

I haven't written to your brother. I am not going to inflict myself upon the whole family. I shall devote all my spare time and what's left of my energy to worrying you alone of the whole of your House. And why not? Haven't you rushed upon your fate? I am like the old man of the sea.[3] You can't get rid of me by the apparently innocent suggestion of writing to your brother. Seriously speaking I was afraid of trespassing—and then each man is so busy with his own futility that the handwriting of a stranger cannot be very welcome to him. Is he a naval officer? I _am_ glad he likes the nigger. Please tell him so—if you ever do write to him.

"The Rescue: A Romance of Shallow Waters", spreads itself, more and more shallow, over innumerable pages. Symons (who lives on ideas) shall have an indigestion if he reads it. It would be for him like swallowing a stone; for there *I know* there are no ideas. Only a few types and some obscure incidents upon a dismal coast where Symons's humanity ends and raw mankind begins.

And so the end! The lamp is dim and the night is dark. Last night a heavy gale was blowing and I lay awake thinking that I would give ever so much (the most flattering criticism) for being at sea, the soul of some patient faithful ship standing up to it under lower topsails and no land anywhere within a thousand miles. Wouldn't I jump at a command if some literary shipowner suddenly offered it to me![4]

Thanks for your inquiries. My wife and the boy are very well. I was very sorry to hear of your wife's indisposition. Nothing serious I hope. If your horse has not eaten you up entirely[5] I trust you will write before the end of the week.

Ever Yours

Jph Conrad.

---

[1] Graham's brother Charles, younger by a year, an inspector of lifeboats and retired naval officer.
[2] In the 29 January *Saturday Review* (85, 145–6) Arthur Symons praised a translation of d'Annunzio's *Trionfo della Morte* at the expense of Conrad and Kipling, whose latest books he thought finely told but conceptually weak.
[3] A demonic character in *The Thousand and One Nights* who will not let go.
[4] For Graham's efforts on Conrad's behalf, see pp. 75–6.
[5] The fate of the daring farmer in Graham's 'Snaekoll's Saga'.

To W. H. Chesson
Text MS Yale; Unpublished

[late January 1898][1]
[Stanford-le-Hope]

Dear Mr Chesson

I obtained this copy for you wishing to present the book to you in this shape, unlovely indeed, but which in this sordid age has the merit of not having its price—for, it can't be bought.[2] It seems to me that thus I can show better how much I have been comforted by the generous warmth of your appreciation.

Believe me always faithfully
Jph. Conrad.

To Edward Garnett
Text G. 121

Wednesday [2 February 1898][3]
[Stanford-le-Hope]

Dearest Garnett.

This is a free evening before I go into harness again to pull out of the mire, out of the slough of despond that damned and muddy romance.[4] I am getting on—and it is very very bad. Bad enough I sometimes think to make my fortune.

The news I want you to know are

1st. The Cranes have invited the lot of us man woman and child to stay with them ten days—from 19th February—and I've accepted for I feel that if there is no break I will go crazy or go out altogether.

2nd. Harris keeps quiet like a man in hiding. Graham blasphemes and curses.

3rd. I've gone and done it. I write for the press!!!!!! I've sent to the *Outlook* an unconceivably silly thing about A. Daudet. "Words! words! words!" Apparently that's what they want. They asked for more. Today I've sent another silly thing about Kipling.[5] It took me one and a half days to write 1500 words. I can do this kind of thing quicker than the muddy romance. Damn! I've lost the last shred of belief in myself. I

---

[1] Chesson received his presentation copy of *The Nigger* on 1 February.
[2] Bound in paper, the book was one of eight printed in July 1897. One went to Garnett's mother, the rest to the copyright libraries.
[3] Garnett's dating, confirmed by resemblances to the following day's letter to Sanderson.
[4] *The Rescue.*
[5] The Daudet piece was reprinted in *Notes on Life and Letters*; the Kipling was never published.

simply *dare not* send you the MS. But ultimately I shall. It is unredeemed trash. Are you near enough to Crane to be invaded?[1] My wife shall want to show the blessed baby to your wife. I hate babies. Will you manage to see me while I am there? Do you object to read 100 pages of my handwriting? It feels like a lot of wheels in my head.

I am sending you here a bit of the *Sat. Rev.* Symons criticising trans: of Annunzio mentions Kipling and myself as you can see.

Frankly—is the remark true?

That the Voynich book sells does not surprise me. Some people will take it as an attack on the Popish religion.[2] La bêtise humaine est capable de tout.

It is bad with me when the thought does not unfold itself easily when talking to a friend. I feel I am boring you with this letter—and yet don't wish to stop. I can't say half the things I want to say.

I want to hear you speak—I do. I want to come in contact with your thought.

I am again thinking of attacking Pawling.[3] Something must be done and that soon. With a book half written I can talk better to the man. He is a good fellow. I should not like him to curse the day he set eyes on me. If he feels so sure of *Scribners* why not accept my proposal on a business basis: Acquire from me my serial rights. The risk will be great enough to prove his goodwill and friendship anyhow. As to asking him to, plainly speaking, pension me I don't think I can. Moreover do you think he would care to keep a private author on the staff? I won't do anything without giving you information in time for a last word of advice. For after all you are the serpent and I am a bedraggled silly dove.

Jess sends her love—she intends to write tomorrow to your wife. Everybody here is in rude health at which I am sorry because of the enormous appetites which is so expensive—and the stores running low at that.

Ever yours

Jph. Conrad

---

[1] About three miles away.

[2] E. L. Voynich's *The Gadfly*, set in Latin America and Risorgimento Italy, is strongly anti-clerical.

[3] Asking Heinemann's partner to do something with *The Rescue*.

To E. L. Sanderson

Text MS Yale; J-A, 1, 227

3ᵈ Febr. 98.
[Stanford-le-Hope]

My dear Ted.[1]

I haven't yet thanked you for Your congratulations and the classical greeting to the boy. I liked it immensely. May your wishes expressed in the words of old Ajax come true.[2] But the child is born to a dismal heritage. I like sometimes to forget the past.

There isn't much to say. All goes well here—and for that I am inexpressibly thankful. I work. I reproach myself with my incapacity to work more. Yet the work itself is only like throwing words into a bottomless hole. It seems easy, but it is very very fatiguing.

And so I've taken to writing for the press. More words—another hole. Still the degradation of daily journalism has been spared to me so far. There is a new weekly coming. Its name The Outlook; its price three pence sterling, its attitude—literary; its policy—Imperialism, tempered by expediency; its mission—to make money for a Jew; its editor Percy Hurd (never heard of him); one of its contributors Joseph Conrad—under the heading of "Views and Reviews."

The first number comes out on Saturday next. There will be in it something of mine about a Frenchman who is dead and therefore harmless.[3] I've just sent off a second contribution. It is a chatter about Kipling provoked by a silly criticism. It's called—Concerning a certain criticism;[4] I'll send you the number in which it appears, probably N° 2.

Stephen Crane is worrying me to write a play with him.[5] He won't believe me when I swear by all the gods and all the muses that I have no dramatic gift. Probably something will be attempted but I would bet nothing shall be done. This is all my news. And now Your turn—when You *really* can spare the time. Do not think hardly of me because I don't

---

[1] Edward Lancelot Sanderson (1867–1939) taught at Elstree, the family-owned preparatory school. When he sailed on the *Torrens* in 1893, he became friendly with Conrad, the first mate; between Cape Town and London, Conrad read him a draft of *Almayer's Folly* (memorandum by Helen Sanderson, MS Taylor).

[2] Sanderson had read classics at King's College, Cambridge.

[3] The Daudet article appeared 9 April.

[4] This lost contribution was probably an answer to Symons (see letter to Graham, 31 January).

[5] Discussed in a letter to Crane, 12(?) January. Conrad's first attempt at playwriting came with the dramatization of 'To-morrow' in 1904. (He also took a modest part in writing 'The Ghost', Christmas 1899, an entertainment that numbered among its authors Henry James, Wells, Gissing, and Rider Haggard.)

write often. I think of you more perhaps than I would if I saw you every day; and when the good time comes we shall foregather—and find no change.

Ever Yours

Jph. Conrad

To R. B. Cunninghame Graham
Text MS Dartmouth; Watts 74

4th Febr 98

[Stanford-le-Hope]

Cher ami.

I was glad to get your good letter. From his point of view Runciman is right. It would stereotype the paper.[1] And after all they did take a line which at any rate is not philistinish.

Pawling is a good friend to me and I think that my acceptance by "Scribner's"—thanks to his efforts—is assured *if* I can wait till they have space. Barrie blocks the way.[2] I shall scout around energetically to find a shop where they take in pawn the *future* of *writers*.

I haven't said half what I wanted to say about S*ta* Theresa—and what I have said has been stupidly expressed. I am glad Mrs Cunninghame Graham is not angry. This is the sweetness of women, for there is nothing more exasperating than an ignorant appreciation.

—How did you come to know such a delightful man as your friend of the barquentine?[3] A coaster eh? I've served in a coaster. Also a barque*ne*. "Skimmer of the Seas" what a pretty name![4] But she is gone and took a whole lot of good fellows away with her into the other world. Comme c'est vieux tout ça! In that craft I began to learn English from East Coast chaps each built as though to last for ever, and coloured like a Christmas card. Tan and pink—gold hair and blue eyes with that Northern straight-away-there look! Twenty two years ago! From Lowestoft to Newcastle and back again. Good school for a seaman. As soon as I can

---

[1] By committing many issues to the serial publication of a novel. Runciman was assistant editor (and music critic) of the *Saturday Review*.

[2] *Scribner's Magazine* had accepted J. M. Barrie's novel *Tommy and Grizel*, which was to run in monthly parts.

[3] Perhaps Honest Tom Bilson, skipper of the barque *Wilberforce*. He figures in Graham's 'Bristol Fashion', a story of double-dealing on the West African coast (*Saturday Review*, 5 and 12 February).

[4] Actually, *Skimmer of the Sea*, the three-masted collier on which Conrad served from July to September 1878. It went down with all hands in October 1881.

sell my damaged soul for two and six I shall transport my damaged body
there and look at the green sea, over the yellow sands. Eheu! Fugaces![1]
Excuse these tears.

And to think you were dining my wretched carcass at the Devonshire[2]
while you might have been on board the "Tourmaline" giving invaluable tips to her owner about Sidi Haschem.[3] Sir—you have sinned. But
as your sinning was my profit you are forgiven. But why the devil have
they been arrested. One should never be arrested. And where exactly?
Tho' I can read you with ease (honor bright) the proper names stump
me.[4] Is it West Coast of Morocco? or about cape Blanco? I am lost in
conjectures.

On the 19th all our tribe man, woman and child shift camp to Oxted to
dwell for ten days in the tents of the Beni-Crane. A risky experiment.

Ever Yours

Jph. Conrad.

To Aniela Zagórska
Text J-A, i, 228; Najder 224[5]

6.2.98.
Stanford-le-Hope

My dearest Aniela,

It is still more painful and hard to think of you than to realize my
loss;[6] if it was not so, I would pass in silence and darkness these first
moments of suffering. Neither you, nor he, know—can know—what
place you occupy in my life—how my feelings, my thoughts and my

---

[1] 'Eheu fugaces ... Labuntur anni.' 'Alas, the fleeting years are slipping by': Horace,
   Odes, ii, xiv.
[2] Graham's club: he had entertained Conrad there on 26 November.
[3] Major A. G. Spilsbury, acting for the Globe Venture Syndicate, had been running guns
   aboard the *Tourmaline*; he intended trading them to separatists in the Sus of southwes-
   tern Morocco. On his second expedition, he was caught by the Royal Moroccan Navy.
   The suspicion of foreigners caused by the first expedition was partly responsible for
   Graham's capture as he tried to cross the Atlas. Although attracted to Spilsbury
   personally, Graham detested his methods. Watts (pp. 76–7) gives more details and
   suggests that Conrad turned *Tourmaline* into *Tremolino* when retelling his own activities
   as a gun-runner. Sidi Haschem was a chieftain in the Sus.
[4] 'I am one of the few men living', boasted Shaw in the Notes to *Captain Brassbound's
   Conversion*, a play that owes much to Graham's Moroccan exploits, 'who can decipher
   the curious alphabet in which he writes his private letters.'
[5] Polish original lost: Najder's text, given here, comes from a collation of Jean-Aubry's
   text with Aniela Zagórska's fuller MS translation into French, now at Yale.
[6] The death, 19 January, of Conrad's cousin, Karol Zagórski.

remembrances have been centred round you both and your children.[1] And perhaps I myself did not know until now how much I depended on his memory, his heart, and his personality—who, even when seen only once, could arouse such feelings of devotion and confidence. He had the gift of drawing all hearts to him and from the moment when I saw him for the first time, fourteen years ago,[2] I was overcome with affection for him, as the man most akin to me in thought and by blood—after my Uncle, who took the place of my parents. Not a single day passed but I found myself thinking of you both—et dans les moments pénibles l'idée qu'il y aurait un jour où je pourrais lui confesser ma vie toute entière et être compris de lui: cette pensée était ma plus grande consolation. Et voilà que cet espoir—le plus précieux de tous—s'est éteint pour toujours.[3]

The sound of human words does not bring consolation—there is no consolation on this earth. Time can soften but not efface sorrow. I have never felt so near to you and your little girls until this moment when we feel together the injustice of Fate which has loaded you with the burden of life without any support. In the presence of your grief I dare not speak of mine. I only ask you to believe in my attachment to you and in my memory of the mourned husband and father who, with you, was my whole family.

My wife said to me with tears in her eyes: 'I felt as if I knew him'—and seeing her tears, it seemed to me that never had I cared for him so much as now. Unfortunately she never knew him—although she 'had often heard me speak of him—for I was not capable of appreciating the worth of such a man. I did not know him thoroughly; but I believe that I understood him. I had a profound affection for him, I always went to him in my thoughts. And now I feel quite alone—even as you.

I kiss your hands, my poor Aniela, I also kiss your little daughters, for whose sake you must be courageous. Be sure of my affection and devotion to you.

K. Korzeniowski.

---

[1] Aniela and Karola. The younger Aniela was to translate many of Conrad's works into Polish.

[2] In the summer of 1883 in what is now Czechoslovakia. Conrad saw his cousin again in 1890, this time in Poland.

[3] 'And in moments of pain, the idea that there would be a day when I should be able to confess my whole life to him and be understood by him: this idea was my greatest consolation. And there is that hope, the most precious of all, gone for good.'

To Edward Garnett
Text MS Yale; G. 124

Thursday. [10 February 1898][1]
[Stanford-le-Hope]

Dearest G.

Just a word to thank you for your invitation. We shall certainly call on you[2] but as to inflicting the baby and all for more than a day—well it would be taking a mean advantage of your hospitality.

—I saw Pawling the other day. He is very nice. Thinks prospect of Scribners distinctly good. What he wants me to do is to get ready as much of the story as I can and send it off to Am: by the mail of the 23^{d} inst. so as to reach N.Y. while Heinemann is still there.[3] (He left yesterday). I shall therefore write all I can up to the last moment—and Pawling says he shall get the *typing* done in one day. I must write another chapter and correct shorten and arrange part 1st. Then about 45000 words shall go to the Yanks—and we shall see.

Jess sends her thanks and love. She is very keen on that visit. You may live yet to regret bitterly your indiscretion in suggesting its possibility.

In haste   Ever Yours
Jph. Conrad.

To Stephen Crane
Text MS Columbia; Stallman 175

Tuesday [15 February 1898][4]
[Stanford-le-Hope]

My dear Crane.

I've been rather seedy lately—all worry I think. But I am going to put my worries aside and have a real good time with you. I shall wire You on Sat: by what train we are coming; some time in the afternoon but not late. I shall bring a lot of paper and You shall find a pen. I am anxious to know what You have done with Your idea for a play.[5] A play to write is no play. I believe You can do anything.

Ever Yours
J. Conrad.

Our kindest regards to Mrs. Crane. Baby sends a friendly howl.

---

[1] Garnett's dating. This letter must come after a reply to the letter of 2 February. 17 February might also be possible.
[2] While staying nearby, with the Cranes.
[3] Heinemann and Pawling were partners; the story was *The Rescue*.
[4] Date from postmark.   [5] The collaboration mooted on 12(?) January.

To R. B. Cunninghame Graham

Text MS Dartmouth; Watts 77

16 Febr 98
[Stanford-le-Hope]

Cher ami.

I did not write because I was beastly seedy—nerve trouble—a taste of hell. All right now.

Thanks for sending me the paper and the letter about it which reached me in an incomplete state—4 pages missing. Yes it did me good to read about the good fellows. That was a good ship because of the men in her. Yes you do appreciate that kind of thing and that's why I seem to understand you in whatever You say.

The *Bristol Fashion* business is excellently well put.[1] You seem to know a lot about every part of the world and, what's more, you *can* say what you know in a most individual way. The skipper of the barque is "pris sur le vif".[2] I've known the type. And the tongue is put out all along in a fine, effective way.[3] More power to your pen!

You have *not* sent any kind of guide book!!![4]

An extreme weariness oppresses me. It seems as though I had seen and felt everything since the beginning of the world. I *suspect* my brain to be yeast and my backbone to be cotton. And I *know* that the quality of my work is of the kind to confirm my suspicions. I would yell for help to anybody—man or devil if I could persuade myself that anybody would care—and, caring, could help. Well. No more. Ever Yours.

Conrad.

To T. Fisher Unwin

Text MS Leeds; Unpublished

17 Febr. 98.
[Stanford-le-Hope]

Dear Mr Unwin.

Have you heard about the *Return*? I would be very disappointed if the thing should fail in the States because I have had comm[unicati]on with the Bacheller Syndicate[5] who wish to have there the first refusal of my

[1] The second part of 'Bristol Fashion' had appeared in the 12 February *Saturday Review*.
[2] 'Taken from life.'   [3] An echo from the letter of 14 January.
[4] Graham must have mentioned his *Notes on the District of Menteith* (1895).
[5] Irving Bacheller's syndicate had sent Crane on a reporting tour of Mexico and western USA in 1895 and published a shortened version of *The Red Badge of Courage* in various newspapers.

work and offer to act as my agents without commission, for serial publication.

With kind regards
faithfully Yours

Jph. Conrad

To Spiridion Kliszczewski
Text MS Spiridion; Unpublished

[21 February 1898][1]
C/o Stephen Crane Esq.
Ravensbrook
Oxted
Surrey.

My dear friend.[2]

Could you lend me a five pound note for a couple of weeks? I find myself a little short while on a visit here; but since last week my prospects have improved wonderfully.[3]

This visit does lots of good to my prospects. You see I come to you in a little difficulty of that kind because if I went to other people I could certainly get it but it would lay open to them the nakedness of the land. I hope you won't think me a nuisance. If you do send please send a *note* to the address above.

Excuse this blackmailing letter. In
great haste.
Affectionately Yours

Jph. Conrad.

To Jane Cobden Unwin
Text MS Chichester; Curreli

22ᵈ Febry 98.
[letterhead: Ravensbrook,
Oxted, Surrey]

Dear Mrs Unwin.[4]

I am so sorry we cannot accept Your kind invitation. My good host has arranged something for every day and on Saturday I am engaged to stay here and meet some people who are coming on purpose to have the

---

[1] Date from postmark.
[2] Kliszczewski (also known as Joseph Spiridion) was the son of a watchmaker who, having escaped after the Polish insurrection of 1830–1, eventually took refuge in Wales.
[3] Thanks to Crane's North American contacts?
[4] Jane Cobden Unwin (1851–1949), active in feminist and Radical causes, was the daughter of Richard Cobden and married to T. Fisher Unwin.

felicity of beholding me[1] in "my habit, as I live".[2] And on Monday a very important business calls me to London. It is indeed very probable that we shall have to curtail our stay here considerably.[3]

Perhaps You will kindly express to Mr Zangwill my regret at missing this opportunity of making his acquaintance.[4] His mention of the *Nigger* in the "Academy" has given me a great pleasure.[5] It was an unexpected reward for a disinterested admiration for his work—dating far back, to the days of *Premier and the Painter* which I read by chance on the Indian Ocean—a copy with covers torn off and two pages missing. Tempi passati![6] But the admiration of his talent, of his art so individual and so sincere has grown with the passing years.

With friendly regards to Mr Unwin. I am dear Mrs Unwin Your most obedient and faithful servant.

Jph Conrad

To Spiridion Kliszczewski
Text MS Rosenbach; Unpublished

23 Febr 98
[letterhead: Ravensbrook]

My dear Friend

I've received a five-pound (£5) note for which let this letter be a receipt. Thanks for your friendly readiness.

Yes. I understand Your feeling—every bit of it. Give our most hearty greeting to dear Clement and may happiness attend him,[7] all yours and Yourself

in haste

Ever Yours affectionately
Jph Conrad

Jess sends her love

---

[1] Among them, Harold Frederic, the American novelist, and perhaps Ford Madox Ford (Hueffer): Jessie Conrad, *Joseph Conrad and His Circle*, p. 58. The first extant letter to Ford (29 September) suggests acquaintance but not intimacy; they may not have met until early in that month.

[2] A refraction of *Hamlet* III. iv. 136.

[3] The Conrads went on to visit the Garnetts and did not return home until 4 March.

[4] Israel Zangwill (1864–1926), writer and Zionist, already famous for *The Children of the Ghetto* (1892) and *The King of Schnorrers* (1894). He published with Heinemann, not with Unwin.

[5] 8 January: Zangwill was one of the writers asked to nominate books for the *Academy* 'crown'.

[6] 'Times gone by!' This novel, a collaboration, came out in 1888.

[7] Kliszczewski's son.

To S. S. Pawling
Text MS Heinemann; Unpublished

27th Febr. 98
[letterhead: Ravensbrook]

My dear Pawling.[1]

I am perfectly satisfied with the terms you have obtained from Maclure.[2] I shall go right ahead with the story and hope to finish it in five months—at the outside, probably in four.

One thing is absolutely necessary if I am to write and keep good time. I must have £20 per month for these five months—to commence in March each month paid in advance. On my side I promise not to write during that time anything but the story. In July I would have had £100 and you would have the story complete and then some further arrangement as to payment could be made.

The only risk is of me going off the hooks in a natural way. I have a £1000 accident insurance policy so that you would lose nothing if I fall out of the boat. But even should I kick the bucket unexpectedly there are 500 pounds of mine knocking about loose in the world, on which I can't lay hands now, but which are sure to turn up all right before long.

Please tell me at once whether you accept this proposal. Write to me c/o E. Garnett. The Cearne—Kent Hatch. N^r Edenbridge where I shall be till the 4th of March. On the 6th I shall be home and at work.

                                              Ever yours

                                                        Jph Conrad.

To Stephen Crane
Text MS Columbia; Stallman 170

5th Febr [March] 98.[3]
Stanford-le-Hope

Dear Stephen.

We got home last night. Ever since I've left You I am wondering how you have passed through Your crisis.[4] I would like to hear all is well; it hurts me to think You are worried. It is bad for You and it is bad for your

---

[1] Sydney S. Pawling (1862–1923) had gone into partnership with Heinemann about five years previously. *The Nigger* was published at Pawling's instigation.
[2] The S. S. McClure Company had offered to buy North American serial rights to *The Rescue*.
[3] As Najder observes (*Chronicle*, p. 540, n. 135), Conrad mistook the date. Clearly he has just returned from the visits to Garnett and Crane—and this is his thank-you letter.
[4] Debts.

art. All the time I was at the Garnetts we have been talking of You. We conclude you must be kept quiet; but who is going to work that miracle?

We trust in Mrs. Crane and in the sagacity of publishers. That last is not much to trust to—I admit. Still! . . .

I've had letters of thanks from Pearson[1] and Blackwood for inducing You to call on them. The Pearson man writes he hopes they shall be able very soon to do something quite satisfactory to Mr Crane "if he gives us an opportunity". The Blackwood man sends an invite to lunch for the week after next to you and me if you will condescend to accept that invitation through me. It appears old Blackwood is coming to London himself to make your and my acquaintance. He is a good old Scotchman and if you like the idea drop me a line to name the day. It is left to you.[2]

Your whisky old man has effected a cure and I feel quite fit for work. How long that disposition will last only the devil in charge of my affairs knows. I miss You horribly. In fact Ravensbrook and its inhabitants have left an indelible memory. Some day—perhaps next year—we must take a house together—say in Brittany for 3 months or so. It would work smoothly—I am sure.

Present my respectful and most friendly regards to Your wife and assure Her of our gratitude for Her more than charming hospitality. My wife sends her love to the whole household. She is going to write in a day or two—as soon as we are a little settled.

Give me some news—good, if You can.

Ever Yours

Jph Conrad.

To R. B. Cunninghame Graham

Text MS Dartmouth; J-A, 1, 230; Watts 79

5th March 98.
Stanford-le-Hope.

Cher ami.

I see you don't bear malice for my delays in correspondence so I don't apologise.

The Guide book simply *magnificent* Everlastingly good![3] I've read it

---

[1] Of *Pearson's Magazine*.

[2] Blackwood gave the luncheon at the Garrick Club, 25 March.

[3] Graham's distinctive guide to ancestral terrain, *Notes on the District of Menteith* (1895), dedicated to the local poacher, with 'All rights reserved, except in the Republic of Paraguay'. Graham's evocation of life on the Caledonian frontier anticipates 'Heart of Darkness': 'What an abode of horror it must have been to the unfortunate centurion, say

last night having only then returned home. During my visit to the
Cranes we talked of you and your work every day. Stephen is a great
admirer of Yours. The man after all knows something. Harold Frederic[1]
also enthused with perfect sincerity. My opinion of them has gone up a
hundred points.

Your engineer is immense! Wish I had seen him. It is good of You to
think of me when such a subject comes in your way.[2] I never seem to
meet any one of that kind—now. I am on the shelf—I am dusty.

Yes. We Poles are poor specimens. The strain of national worry has
weakened the moral fibre—and no wonder when You think of it. It is
not a fault; it is a misfortune. Forgive my jeremiads. I don't repine at the
nature of my inheritance but now and then it is too heavy not to let out a
groan.

I've sold my american *serial* rights of the *Rescue* for £250 to Maclure (of
New York). I get another *£50* on acc/t of book rights in the states (15%
royalty) I think—upon the whole—this is not bad. Pawling arranged it
all for me—free of charge. The worst is the book is not finished yet and
must be delivered end July at the latest. Pawling told me they
(Heinemann) are going to publish your book—the Morocco book I
understand.[3] I wait for it *anxiously*. My short tales—"Tales of Unrest"—
shall appear (from Unwin's shop) on the 25th of this month.[4]

Well! Till next time . . . .

Ever Yours

Jph. Conrad

PS It was Harold Frederic who wrote the criticism of the *Nigger* in the
Satur: R. He affirmed to me that Runciman had cut out the best
passages.[5] I tried to persuade him I did not care a hang—which is true.

from Naples, stranded in a marsh far from the world, in a climate of the roughest, and
blocked on every side by painted savages!'
[1] Crane's friend, foreign correspondent for the *New York Times*, best known for his novel
The Damnation of Theron Ware (1896).
[2] Here Watts sees a possible origin for 'An Anarchist' (1906).
[3] *Mogreb-el-Acksa*: Conrad's enthusiastic response to the book came in letters of 1, 4, and 9
December 1898.
[4] In the United States, 26 March; in Great Britain, 4 April.
[5] Runciman was assistant editor of the *Saturday Review*. The unsigned review (12
February; *Critical Heritage*, p. 98) treats *Almayer*, *An Outcast*, and 'An Outpost' as
competent variations on a Stevensonian theme. While *The Nigger*, especially in the storm
scene, shows Conrad developing a new and praiseworthy mode, his characterization is
thin – and James Wait is a downright bore. 'In a word, Mr. Conrad has not realised, as
yet, the importance of what is called "human interest."' Concerning *The Nigger*,

To Edward Garnett

Text G. 124

Sunday evening [13 March 1898][1]
[Stanford-le-Hope]

Dearest G.

Thanks ever so much for your letter, and more still for your promise to come on Friday next. Do come early. Could you get here for lunch. There is a train from Fenchurch Street at 11.35 a.m.

You have already cheered me up. I did miss you dreadfully. I had really a hard time of it and not a soul to turn to.

Jess sends her kind regards and is anxious for you to see the baby. The poor girl is a perfect slave to it—but thinks she likes it.

Of course we can put you up—and you shall sleep as long as you like or the baby likes.

Could you find out any facts about the sales of the *Tales*. Unwin wrote me the book went off well!!? What could have been his object?

Ever yours

Conrad

My friendly regards to Mrs. Garnett. Jess sends her love to her and to Bunny. Remember me to that promising youth!

To Cora Crane

Text MS Columbia; Stallman 176

Tuesday. [15 March 1898]
[Stanford-le-Hope]

Dear Mrs. Crane.

I am sorry to say I am not well enough to keep Stephen's engagement for Saturday evening.[2] It is nervous trouble and the doctor advises me to keep very quiet. I think I ought to follow his advice. A dinner in town means sleeping in town and I simply don't feel equal to it. I hope Stephen won't be angry; but really I do not feel at all well. I am writing to day to Meldrum[3] saying that Stephen would like to meet M^r

Frederic had already had a plate-smashing, pistol-waving disagreement with Crane (Stallman, *Stephen Crane*, p. 332).

[1] Presumably because of the postmark, Garnett assigns this letter to 14 March. Given this date, the reference to the success of *Tales of Unrest* is puzzling – unless Conrad means the advance sales by Unwin's travellers.

[2] To dine at the Savage Club. Crane wrote to Conrad on the seventeenth, urging him to come, and Conrad did (*Last Essays*, pp. 114–15). This train of events dates the letter.

[3] Blackwood's man in London.

Blackwood if it can be managed on Saturday next. If the thing is arranged I shall try to come up on that day for the lunch, but must get home in the afternoon.

I am so glad Stephen is writing; it consoles me from* my own inability to work. I haven't written three pages since I left You. I simply *can't.*

I am like a man under a fiendish spell cast over the power of thinking.

My wife and Dolly[1] send their love to You all. Believe me dear Mrs Crane Your faithful and affectionate servant

Joseph Conrad.

To Cora Crane
Text MS Columbia; Stallman 177

17.3.98
[Stanford-le-Hope]

My dear Mrs Crane

You are both awfully good to me. The only reason why I would hesitate to accept Your kind proposal[2] is that I am afraid the company of a wretched creature like me *won't* do any good to Stephen, who is an artist and therefore responsive to outside moods. Now my mood is unhealthy; and I would rather forbear seeing Stephen all my life—(notwithstanding my affection for the man and admiration for the artist)—than bring a deteriorating element into his existence. You, knowing him better than any one, may tell best whether my fear is justified.

However for this time I am inclined to be selfish and say yes. I haven't yet heard from the Blackwood man. I instructed him to write direct to Stephen about the Saturday lunch business. We shall no doubt both get a letter tomorrow (Friday). If *yes* we shall meet where he appoints. If *not*, then perhaps Stephen would wire to me on Saturday—as early as possible.

Wife and Dolly send their love to all, and I am dear Mrs Crane always most faithfully your

Jph Conrad.

To Edward Garnett
Text MS Sutton; G. 125

Monday. [21 March 1898][3]
[Stanford-le-Hope]

My dear Garnett

Well. It isn't so bad as I expected if in every two pages only one and a half are too bad for anything.

---

[1] Dolly George, who was helping her sister with the baby.
[2] To spend the night in Oxted after the dinner at the Savage.
[3] Garnett's dating.

To tell you the truth I hate the thing with such great hatred that I don't want to look at it again.[1] I've read your remarks. Gospel truth—except where you try to cheer me on. I shall certainly go on—that is if I can. The best about the work is that it is *sold*. They've got to take it. But the thought that such rubbish is produced at the cost of positive agony fills me with despair. I have not an atom of courage left.

It was awful good of You to read and annotate. I don't know how to thank you. I shall try to do something before it appears as a book. Now I haven't the strenght* nor the pluck.

My kindest regards to Mrs. Garnett. Love to Bunny.[2] Is his cold better? I *haven't* been well.

Ever Yours

J. Conrad

My wife sends her love to you all.

To E. L. Sanderson

Text MS Yale; Unpublished

23^d March 1898
[Stanford-le-Hope]

My dear Ted,

It is good of You to remember me in the midst of Your occupations, preparations, exaltations and botherations. Well, dear old chap all this will be soon over. Peace and content are before you, and not everyone can say as much.[3]

I am glad to hear You are pretty fit. I am somewhat less limp but the work does not progress much for there is a curious inability to think clearly. A bad sign I should say; only I won't say. Not yet. I haven't given up hope but I don't feel very happy or very certain about the future.

If you've thought of me I have thought of you both. What is the date of the great event? In spirit I shall be by Your side on the most fateful day of a man's life—and that it is going to be the beginning of a serene happiness is my absolute conviction.

No more now or I will miss the post. Jess sends kind regards.

Ever Yours

Jph Conrad.

The baby is very well.

[1] *The Rescue.*   [2] David Garnett.
[3] Ted Sanderson and Helen Watson were to marry in April.

To Cora Crane

Text MS Columbia; Stallman 178

24ᵗʰ March 98
[Stanford-le-Hope]

Dear Mrs Crane

Thanks for Your letter. I am glad to hear Stephen is at work. I am not.

I shall be at Heinemann's a little before one. I think it's the best place for us to meet on Friday before going to feed at old Blackwood's expense. The time of feeding is 1.30 and the locality Garrick Club.[1]

Jessie and Dolly send their best love to you and Mrs Rudie.[2] The baby has set up a carriage and is so puffed up with pride that there is no bearing him. He behaved like an accomplished ruffian when Stephen was here and has hurt my feelings so much that we haven't been on speaking terms since.

I am, dear Mrs Crane,

Most sincerely yours

Jph. Conrad

To T. Fisher Unwin

Text MS Berg; Unpublished

26ᵗʰ March [1898]
[Stanford-le-Hope]

Dear Mr Unwin.

Thanks for your note informing me of the publication of the Tales.[3] I, of course have no suggestions to offer feeling certain that you will do everything needful to give the book a good send off.

The only thing I would ask is, that, as you correspond with Baron Tauchnitz,[4] you would mention the Volume to him, should the reviews be favourable, as I anticipate they shall be. As a matter of fact in that book I come nearer to the popular notion of tale-telling than in any previous work of mine. All the stories had attracted notice when they

---

[1] The day after the luncheon, Meldrum wrote to Blackwood: 'I was so glad you could meet Crane and Conrad – the two foremost of the youngest writers just now, and types of the men we want to get round the firm' (Blackburn, pp. 20–1). Two advances from Blackwood (9 and 16 April) enabled Crane to set off as a correspondent for the Spanish–American war.

[2] Described by Cora Crane's biographer as 'the ever devoted and enigmatic Mrs Ruedy' (Lillian Gilkes, *Cora Crane*, p. 75).

[3] 4 April 1898.

[4] The German publisher, whose paperback series, *The Collection of British Authors*, enjoyed large sales on the Continent.

appeared in serial form. The only thing against the book is the general *slump* in short stories; an illogical phenomenon, since the intrinsic value of a work can have nothing to do with its lenght.*

Would you send an early copy to Mr Cunninghame Graham? He is now in London. *39 Chester Square.*[1] I think it possible he may write a review[2]—and he is very friendly to me and my work.

> I am, dear Mr Unwin very
> faithfully Yours,
>
> Jph Conrad

To Edward Garnett

Text MS Sutton; J-A, 1, 231; G. 126

29th March. [1898]
[Stanford-le-Hope]

My dear Garnett.

I am ashamed of myself. I ought to have written to you before but the fact is I have not written anything at all. When I received your letter together with part II^d of R[*escue*] I was in bed—this beastly nervous trouble. Since then I've been better but have been unable to write. I sit down religiously every morning, I sit down for eight hours every day—and the sitting down is all. In the course of that working day of 8 hours I write 3 sentences which I erase before leaving the table in despair. There's not a single word to send you. Not one! And time passes—and McClure waits[3]—not to speak of Eternity for which I don't care a damn. Of McClure however I am afraid.

I ask myself sometimes whether I am bewitched, whether I am the victim of an evil eye? But there is no "jettatura" in England[4]—is there? I assure you—speaking soberly and on my word of honour—that some-times it takes all my resolution and power of self control to refrain from butting my head against the wall. I want to howl and foam at the mouth but I daren't do it for fear of waking that baby and alarming my wife. It's no joking matter. After such crises of despair I doze for hours till half conscious that there is that story I am unable to write. Then I wake up, try again—and at last go to bed completely done-up. So the days pass and nothing is done. At night I sleep. In the morning I get up with the horror of that powerlessness I must face through a day of vain efforts.

In these circumstances as you imagine I feel not much inclination to

---

[1] His mother's address. [2] No such review is known. [3] For a serial version.
[4] As opposed to Italy, Garnett's holiday destination.

write letters. As a matter of fact I had a great difficulty in writing the most commonplace note. I seem to have lost all *sense* of style and yet I am haunted, mercilessly haunted by the *necessity* of style. And that story I can't write weaves itself into all I see, into all I speak, into all I think, into the lines of every book I try to read. I haven't read for days. You know how bad it is when one *feels* one's liver, or lungs. Well I feel my brain. I am distinc[t]ly conscious of the contents of my head. My story is there in a fluid—in an evading shape. I can't get hold of it. It is all there—to bursting, yet I Can't get hold of it no more than you can grasp a handful of water.

There! I've told You all and feel better. While I write this I am amazed to see that I can write. It looks as though the spell were broken but I hasten, I hasten lest it should in five minutes or in half an hour be laid again.

I tried to correct Part II^d according to Your remarks. I did what I could—that is I knocked out a good many paragraphs. It's so much gained. As to alteration, rewriting and so on I haven't attempted it—except here and there a trifle—for the reason I could not think out anything different to what is written. Perhaps when I come to my senses I shall be able to do something before the *book* comes out. As to the serial it must go anyhow. I would be thankful to be able to write anything, anything, any trash, any rotten thing—something to earn dishonestly and by false pretences the payment promised by a fool.

That's how things stand to-day; and to-morrow would be more mysterious if it were not so black! I write You a nice cheery letter for a good-bye: don't I, dear old fellow. That's how we use our friends. If I hadn't written I would have burst.

Good luck to you and buon' viaggio signore. Think of me sometimes. Are you going to Milan? It's 24 years since I saw the Cathedral in moonlight.[1] Tempi passati—I had young eyes then. Don't give all your time to the worship of Bot[t]icelli. Somebody should explode that superstition. But there, *You* know better. It is good of you to think of the boy. He is bigger every day. I would like to make a bargeman of him: strong, knowing his business and thinking of nothing. That is *the* life my dear fellow. Thinking of nothing! O! bliss. I had a lunch with Blackwood good old smoothbore. Also Cunning: Graham came down to see me the day before dining with your father.[2] Has been in bed since but writes every second day. Recommend my short stories to your friend. Have you

---

[1] In 1873, on a tour of Germany, Switzerland, and Italy with his tutor, Adam Pulman.
[2] Richard Garnett, man of letters, Keeper of Printed Books at the British Museum.

seen the Nigger notice in *Literature* of last week. Amazing.[1] Jess sends her best love.

Vale frater[2]

Yours ever

J.C.

To E. L. Sanderson

Text MS Yale; Unpublished

30th March 1898.

[Stanford-le-Hope]

Dearest Ted.

I have waited for the arrival of the brass clock—promised to you in the fulness of heart over the bachelor tobacco at the "Fortune"[3]—for the 15th century dial that was (if You had gone to the expense of having it repaired) to me[a]sure the moment of Your happiness in the 19th. Apparently it is as unattainable as though it had remained in the 15th century. It shall be conquered tho' but I will have to go to Poland for it—I guess. My letters abusive, plaintive, remonstrative all had one answer: "Not to be found". And yet it is not an object that could fall through a crack in the floor.

You are the sufferer, let us hope only for a time. Meanwhile I wanted you to have something from me[4] which you could use often—as a reminder of my affection, of my friendship and my fidelity. And here I send a trifle that represents so much of my best feelings

Ever Yours

Conrad.

To Helen Watson

Text MS Yale; J-A, 1, 233

2^d April 1898

Stanford-le-Hope

Essex

Dear Miss Watson.[5]

Permit me to answer informally and through You the invitation we have had to Your wedding, since it is to Your friendly feeling and Your memory that we owe it.

---

[1] The reviewer is excited by the very features that distressed some other critics – 'there are no adventures, beyond the supreme and continuous adventure of the sea'. The book is 'an epical fragment' distinguished by narrative power and the authenticity of one 'who speaks at first hand from intimate knowledge' (*Literature*, 26 March, 354).

[2] 'Farewell, brother': a variation on the ending of Catullus, CI.

[3] A mediaeval pilgrims' hostel in the grounds of Elstree School. Carved over the door was the wheel of fortune.

[4] A wedding present. [5] Ted Sanderson's fiancée, a Scot of great moral intensity.

That we cannot give way to our very strong desire to be present at the ceremony is, believe me, the fault of the unbending circumstances. The despotism of the baby, my wretched health and the necessities of my work prevent me from leaving home.[1] And, indeed, were there no inexorable obstacles I would perhaps, perhaps hesitate out of my sincere affection for you both to show my sour face and (let us charitably say) my constitutional melancholy on the day of all days when all the omens should speak of unalterable serenity, and peace, and joy.

But if the face is sour and the mind (more or less) diseased the heart, I trust, has not been touched by a subtle evil; and though you who found your wor[l]dly welfare upon the uncorruptible promises of Eternity have no need of men's wishes to be the forerunners of your happiness, yet You will allow me to send mine the most true—the most sincere— straight from a heart, let us hope, untouched by evil.

Jess joins me in this imperfect expression of feelings. She is happy with Your happiness and begs You to believe that her thoughts, like mine, will be with You both on the momentous day. Believe me, dear Miss Watson with true affection and profound respect Your most faithful obedient servant

J. Conrad Korzeniowski.

To R. B. Cunninghame Graham
Text MS Dartmouth; Watts 81

Thursday. [7 April? 1898][2]
[Stanford-le-Hope]

Cher ami.

Only a word. I had your letter last night and am overjoyed to learn you like the stories. I wonder if they will bring me the needed success. I don't think so—and with mixed feelings don't know whether I am pleased or sorry.

I send back the letter. *If* what the sheik said is true then it is hard to find an excuse for the Major.[3] The whole business seems to have been managed in a mysteriously silly manner. I've done better in my time but

---

1 The marriage was to be solemnized in Scotland.
2 This letter seems to predate that of 14 April – which can be dated firmly. Graham has read *Tales of Unrest*, published 4 April. Unless he saw an advance copy (in which case 31 or even 24 March might be considered), only 7 April fits.
3 More references to Major A. G. Spilsbury and his weapon-peddling (letter of 4 February). Graham gives an extended account of the affair in *Mogreb-el-Acksa* (1898), Appendix C.

then I didn't act for a syndicate.[1] And by the bye the sheik in saying the word "*Yahudi*" was only half wrong. Isn't the Globe Syd^cte managed by one Sassoon?[2]

However my criticism is impertinent since I do not know *all* the circumstances. But it looks like a wretched fizzle.

Let me know how you get on. I am still lame. Ever Yours

Conrad.

My wife sends her kind regards

To E. L. Sanderson
Text MS Yale; Unpublished

9th April 1898
[Stanford-le-Hope]

My dear Ted.

Forgive me if I don't come to see the last of You in your bachelor character. I have twinges in all my joints and a beastly cold ambitious to become influenza. I must check its aspiration.

I think of You daily with unmingled feeling of satisfaction since you are approaching the end of trouble and worries and the beginning of happiness; and I am fortunate enough to gain (as is so seldom the case) another and a precious friendship by your marriage. Last week I wrote my last letter to Miss Watson in reply to an invitation to the wedding, which we had through her kind and friendly thought. Obviously we couldn't come. I wrote to say so and also to say a part, a very small part (because words are so inadequate) of what I feel. When next I address her on paper it will be as Mrs E. L Sanderson and you two will be facing the world side by side. May your hearts never falter and may your courage be ever sustained by that Higher Power to which You both commit your hearts and your fate.

I send three cheers and one more after you as You turn out of the darkness of bachelor ways into the broad path of married life, and in this

---

[1] In *The Mirror of the Sea*, Conrad claims that, during his time in Marseilles (1874–8), he smuggled arms to the Carlist rebels in Spain; he may have done the same for insurgents in Colombia: Karl, *Three Lives*, pp. 143, 157–61, 171–2.

[2] C. E. Sassoon, member of a prominent Jewish family, was a director. Graham ends his story of confederacy between disaffected Muslims and Christian gun-runners with a letter from a Moroccan friend who translates the complaint of a captured sheik: 'Oh, le Nazrani m'a trompé, ce sont des trompeurs les chrétiens, il m'avait promis que des frégates et des soldats anglais débarqueront ... par Dieu, ce chrétien doit être un Juif! mais c'était écrit, Allah Ackbar.'

primitive demonstration Jessie joins me with all her heart. Our thoughts
are with you both.

Ever Yours

Jph. Conrad

To Spiridion Kliszczewski
Text MS Williams; J-A, 1, 273

12th April [1898]¹
Stanford-le-Hope

My Dear Old Friend

Here's the latest volume of my works which I beg you to accept for
yourself and dear Mrs. Spiridion.

I haven't written for a very long time as it seems to me: but both you
and I are busy men, each in our way. I daresay you will forgive me. After
six hours pen in hand one does not seem to have anything more to
write—even to one's best friend.

The book I've been writing since last December and am writing still is
sold already for serial appearance both in America and also here. The
price is not so bad, considering I get £250 for *serial* rights in both
countries. Then, for *book form* I shall probably get £100 in all. Well one
can live on that. But meantime I am living on these prospects the book
not being finished as yet. I am trying to complete it by end July and if the
health holds out, I shall not doubt do it. I must ask you to forgive my
delay in repaying the amount I owe you, though I do not for a moment
suppose you are impatient.

When you have a moment of spare time give me the news of your
wife's and your own health and tell us all about your boys. We often talk
of them and especially of Clem for whom my wife has a soft spot. May
your prosperity always increase and your shadow never grow less.

What do you think of foreign affairs? I am simply sick to see the blind
and timid bungling of the men at the head of affairs. This is this
country's very last chance to assert itself in the face of Russia and indeed
of the whole* Europe. I am convinced that at this moment all the
chances would be in favour of England and after a first success there
would be no lack of friends and allies. But there! What's the use talking;

---

¹ Jean-Aubry assigns this letter to 1899, but its content (the copy of *Tales of Unrest*, the
prospects for *The Rescue*) clearly places it a year earlier.

I am not foreign minister.[1] Jessie sends her love to all. She is pretty well. The baby flourishes exceedingly. He is very big and seems very strong. I am afraid he is tasking my wife's strenght* to the utmost.

> Well! Good-bye for the present.
> My affectionate greetings to you
> all. I am always yours
> Jph Conrad.

To Aniela Zagórska
Text J-A, 1, 234; Najder 225[2]

12.4.98
Stanford-le-Hope

My dear Aniela,

Forgive my long silence. The bad state of my health is the reason why the news of our terrible bereavement has put me in such a state of nervous excitement that I am quite unable to follow my thoughts or to write a couple of lines.

I am filled with admiration for your courage and the strength of mind with which you bear this awful blow inflicted by Fate.[3] I have not written, but I can tell you that every day I have been with you in my thoughts.

The exigencies of life do not bring relief—they only drive back the outward show of grief. The day before yesterday I returned to my work; it could not be otherwise. And it is thus, with poignant grief in my heart, that I write novels to amuse the English!

I thank you for your letter which I read with much sadness and which brings me nearer to your grief; in sharing your feelings and your sorrow, I do not feel so much alone! I feel as if in sorrow, at least, I were near you. Alas! it is impossible to remove the consciousness of the distance which separates us. There is a wish to take the hand and to hear the sound of the voice, but it cannot be. My wife and child are well, thanks be to God. As for me, I am not ill, but I am not well either. And then the

---

[1] The Marquess of Salisbury was both Prime Minister and Foreign Secretary. Early in 1898, he tried to improve relations with Russia just when that country was consolidating its hold over Port Arthur in Manchuria.
[2] For textual source, see n. 5 to letter of 6 February. The ending has not survived.
[3] The death of her husband, 19 January.

uncertainty of our destiny oppresses me. We live with difficulty, from day to day—et c'est tout! My reputation grows, but popularity remains behind. The work is not easy and every day seems more difficult to me. Que la vie est cruelle et bête! But enough for today.

To R. B. Cunninghame Graham
Text MS Dartmouth; J-A, 1, 233; Watts 82

Thursday. [14 April 1898][1]
[Stanford-le-Hope]

Cher et excellent ami.

Yesterday I hobbled out and away to London. Not hearing from you imagined all kinds of serious things. So I called at Chester Square.[2] The bird was flown! I thought "very good!" but had a suspicion you went away too early. Your letter confirms my surmise. I thought it wasn't a common cold you had. If I was You (or rather if You were me) I would take it easy for a couple of weeks. It would pay better in the long run.

The cutting is valuable. Do you possess Lavery's portrait of yourself? Of Lavery I know only the _Girl in White_, but I knew he had done some oriental things.[3]

Don't you take it into your head you are getting old.[4] You are simply run down and strong men feel it so much more than weaklings like me—who have felt overtasked ever since the age of 28.[5] True! And yet I had another ten years of sea—and did my work too. It isn't your body—it's your brain that is tired. The battery wants recharging. Time, with common caution, will do that. My wife was very much concerned about you. Women have a curious insight sometimes. She said to me after you left. "I am sorry Mr Cunninghame Graham came. He ought to have been at home. I am sure he will be ill."—I said "Oh bosh! You don't know anything; that kind of man is never ill." I consider you played a mean trick on me with your affectation of influenza. My position as an infallible man is badly shaken at home. I never had it elsewhere.

---

1 This letter follows Graham's visit to Ivy Walls farm on Good Friday (8 April), as described by Jessie Conrad, _Joseph Conrad and His Circle_, p. 58.
2 Home of Graham's mother, Mrs Bontine.
3 'A Girl in White' was shown at the Goupil Gallery, London, in June 1891 (Watts, p. 83). John Lavery (1856–1941) painted Graham, whom he had met in North Africa, several times. The two Scotsmen were close. 'I think I did something to help Graham in the creation of his masterpiece – himself': Lavery, _The Life of a Painter_ (1940), p. 92.
4 Graham was almost 46.
5 The time of Conrad's struggles to qualify as a first mate and master.

I am glad you like *Karain*. I was afraid you would despise it. There's something magazine'ish about it. Eh? It was written for Blackwood.[1]

There is twilight and soft clouds and daffodils—and a great weariness. Spring! Excellentissime—Spring? We are annually lured by false hopes. Spring! Che coglioneria![2] Another illusion for the undoing of mankind.

Enough!

—Do spare yourself if not for your own sake then for the sake of the horse.

Ever Yours

Jph. Conrad

To C. L. Hind
Text MS Yale; Unpublished

16th April 1898
Stanford-le-Hope
Essex

Dear Sir.[3]

Mr Clifford's book[4] reached me only yesterday—the 15th—tho' his letter within is dated on the 5th. I mention this to show that I have at once (tho' busy with another work) answered to Your kind proposal—this being the best manner of showing my appreciation of it.

The book is interesting, has insight, sympathy and, of course, unrival[l]ed knowledge of the subject. But it is not literature. This being so I have, in the enclosed review, followed an unliterary train of thought, which however, I trust has a grain of truth in it.[5]

I have signed my review. I am of course aware that it is the high standing and the intellectual authority of the publication which gives its final value to the criticism appearing in its pages. And it is this conviction which induced me to avail myself of your offer. Yet it seems to me that fundamentally, in the matter of criticism it is always the individual voice that speaks and, if so, then the individual should not be hidden. The responsibility for truth or error is on his shoulders also.

---

[1] Published November 1897. Graham would have read the story in *Tales of Unrest*.
[2] 'Balls!'
[3] Charles Lewis Hind (1862–1927) edited the *Academy*, an important literary weekly, from 1896 to 1903.
[4] Hugh Clifford's volume of Malay sketches, *Studies in Brown Humanity*.
[5] The review appeared in the *Academy*, 23 April, and is collected in *Notes on Life and Letters*, pp. 58–60. For Clifford's reaction, see the letter to him of 17 May 1899.

I say this not knowing whether the rule of unsigned articles is imperative in the *Academy*.[1] In any case I hope you will find the enclosed suitable for your columns.

I am, dear Sir, very faithfully
yours

Jph. Conrad

The Editor of the *Academy*

To Cora Crane
Text MS Columbia; Stallman 179

19th April 1898
[Stanford-le-Hope]

My dear Mrs Crane

We imagine how lonely you must have felt after Stephen's departure. The dear fellow wired me from Queenstown,[2] just before going aboard I suppose. Jess is very concerned about you and wishes me to ask you to drop her a line on your arrival in Ireland. I think your going there would be a good thing as solitude after separation is sometimes very hard to bear.

We thought of asking You to come here at once but on receiving Stephen's wire I imagined you were all in Ireland already. However you will be more entertained at the Frederic's[3] for a time, and on your return to England I hope you will have the will and the courage to undertake the risky experiment of coming to us with Mrs Ruedy. Moreover I fancy Stephen's absence won't be very prolonged[4] and we may have the felicity of seeing you all here together. I trust you will let me know how he fares whenever you hear from him. He is not very likely to write to anyone else—if I know the man.

Jess and Dolly send their very best love to you and Mrs Ruedy. The baby flourishes exceedingly and its mother is more of a slave than ever. I am as usual ineffective and lazy.

Believe me dear Mrs Crane your
very faithful friend and servant

Jph. Conrad.

---

[1] The review was signed.
[2] Cobh, County Cork, often the last port of call for westbound liners.
[3] Harold Frederic was convalescing in Ireland.
[4] He returned from his Cuban adventures the following January.

To C. L. Hind [?][1]
Text J-A, 1, 235

23rd April, 1898
[Stanford-le-Hope]
My Dear Sir,

It is a sore temptation, but I don't think I ought to review Crane's last book.[2] The excellent fellow in the goodness of his heart has been praising me beyond my merits on his own side of the water[3] and his generous utterances have been quoted here. I've not enough standing and reputation to put me above the suspicion of swinging back the censer. Consequently my review would do no good to Crane's work, which deserves a warm appreciation. I've seen many of these stories in MS. and others in proofs and have discussed them all ends up with him; yet what can be said and explained during an all-night talk may wear a different complexion in the cold austerity of print. Upon the whole then I think I had better not. Pardon all this long letter, for the simple purpose of saying no. But I wished you to understand why I can't avail myself of your flattering offer.

To R. B. Cunninghame Graham
Text MS Dartmouth; J-A, 1, 235; Watts 84

1st May 1898.
[Stanford-le-Hope]
Cher et excellent ami.

I take it for granted you are not angry with me for my silence. Wrist bad again, baby ill, wife frightened, damned worry about my work[4] and about other things, a fit of such stupidity that I could not think out a single sentence—excuses enough in all conscience, since I am not the master but the slave of the peripeties and accidents (generally beastly) of existence.

And yet I wanted badly to write, principally to say: "Je ne comprends pas du tout!" I had two letters from you. The first announced an inclosure which was not there. The next (a week ago by the gods!) alluded no doubt to the absent enclosure and said you corrected proof (of a sea-phrase) by wire. It being Saturday I jumped at my N° of the S.R. making sure to see there the story of the Scotch tramp on a

---

[1] A speculation: Hind had just commissioned another review from Conrad.
[2] *The Open Boat and Other Stories.*
[3] In the *Bookman* (March 1898).
[4] *The Rescue*, as ever – and perhaps the start of 'Youth'.

Christmas Eve.[1] Nix! Exasperation followed by resignation on reflecting that unless the world came to a sudden end I would worm out of you the secret of these letters. I want to know! Istaghfir Allah![2] O! Sheik Mohammed![3] I take refuge with the One the Invincible.

By all means Viva l'España!!!![4]

I would be the first to throw up my old hat at the news of the slightest success. It is a miserable affair whichever way you look at it. The ruffianism on one side, an unavoidable fate on the other, the impotence on both sides, though from various causes, all this makes a melancholy and ridiculous spectacle. Will the certain issue of that struggle awaken the Latin race to the sense of its dangerous position?[5] Will it be any good if they did awaken? Napoleon the Third had that sense and it was the redeeming trait of his rule.[6] But, perhaps, the race is doomed? It would be a pity. It would narrow life, it would destroy a whole side of it which had its morality and was always picturesque and at times inspiring. The others may well shout Fiat Lux![7] It will be only the reflected light of a silver dollar and no sanctimonious pretence will make it resemble the real sunshine. I am sorry, horribly sorry. Au diable! Après tout cela doit m'être absolument égal.[8] But it isn't for some obscure reason or other. Which shows my folly. Because men are "fourbes lâches, menteurs, voleurs, cruels"[9] and why one should show a preference for one manner of displaying these qualities rather than for another passes my comprehension in my meditative moments.

However I need not worry about the Latin race. My own life is difficult enough. It arises from the fact that there is nothing handy to steal and I never could invent an effective lie—a lie that would sell, and last, and be admirable. This state of forced virtue spreads a tinge of fearsome melancholy over my wasted days.—But I am ever Yours

Conrad.

[1] 'S. S. *Atlas*', with its sketch of a whisky-reeking Hogmanay at sea, did not come out in the *Saturday Review* until 14 and 21 May.

[2] 'Astaghfir Allah!': 'I ask God's forgiveness!' – a formula often used in polite self-deprecation: Hans Wehr, *A Dictionary of Modern Written Arabic* (Ithaca, 1976), p. 678.

[3] On his way to the forbidden city of Tarudant, Graham had attempted to pass himself off as Sheik Mohammed el Fasi, descendant of the Prophet.

[4] Over the war of '98, Graham took the Spanish part; his own ancestry aside, he felt that unabashed imperialism, however deplorable, was preferable to the covert kind (Watts and Davies, pp. 173–4, 215–18).

[5] Threatened by the ambitions of the 'northern' powers.

[6] In 'Autocracy and War' (1905), Conrad sees the Franco-Prussian war as marked by an unprecedented degree of nationalistic hatred (*Notes on Life and Letters*, pp. 105–6).

[7] Genesis 1.3. The ironic joining of light, greed and civilisation foreshadows 'Heart of Darkness'.

[8] 'After all, that should not matter to me in the least.'

[9] 'Mean-spirited cheats, liars, thieves, cruel people.'

To R. B. Cunninghame Graham
Text MS Dartmouth; Watts 85

17 May 98
[Stanford-le-Hope]

Excellentissime,

Heer's* Garnett's letter.[1] I've looked in of course because he told me I may. I've heard all this said with greater warmth of appreciation, since You have been (in Your work) a subject of long discussions between us. By the Gods! *Atlas* is magnificently good.[2] Vous taillez dans le vif là dedans![3] My envy of your power grows with every new thing I see. I am glad—very glad the sketches are going to be collected. One will be able to live with them then. Now one hunts for them in a waste of paper and printer's ink.

I wonder how things are with you. I trust Your Wife is better by now. I would like to know.

I am still miserably unwell, working against the grain while all the time I think it's no good no good. Quelle misére!

Ever Yours

Conrad

To Edward Garnett
Text MS Sutton; G. 129

18 May 98
[Stanford-le-Hope]

My dear Garnett.

I've sent off Your letter to Cunningh[a]me Graham. I've looked into it. What you say is just. Your idea of the "colonial" series is excellent.[4]

What shall I say? Things aren't well with me dear friend. I grow a little hopeless now. Writing is as difficult as ever.

Forgive me if I do not come to see you in town. And yet I want to see You very much. When you are again abreast of Your work and can find

---

[1] Garnett had long admired Graham's work but not yet met him. On 16 May, Garnett wrote to propose that a collection of Graham's sketches, essays, and stories should be the first volume in Unwin's Over-Seas Library – an avowedly experimental series illustrating the life of English-speakers overseas (Watts and Davies, pp. 169–71).

[2] 'S. S. *Atlas*' was reprinted in *The Ipané* (1899), the volume conceived by Garnett.

[3] 'Therein, you're cutting to the quick.'

[4] Garnett's manifesto, printed on the end-papers of each volume, reads in part: 'The Over-Seas Library makes no pretence at Imperial drum-beating, or putting English before Colonial opinion. It aims, instead, at getting the atmosphere and outlook of the new peoples recorded, if such is possible.'

time run down to see me here. A word the day before will do. I am not
likely to move from here.

My wife sends her kindest regards and hopes we shall see you soon. A
ridiculously small quantity of the *Rescue* has been done. I am horribly
sick of life.

Ever Yours

Jph. Conrad

To Edward Garnett
Text MS Colgate; G. 130

Saturday [28 May or 4 June?
1898][1]
[Stanford-le-Hope]

Dearest G.

I've sent you today a copy of the *Children etc*, 3 or 4 of your own books
and that amazing masterpiece *Bel-Ami*.[2] The technique of that work
gives to one acute pleasure. It is simply enchanting to see how it's done.

I've sold (I think) the sea thing[3] to B[lackwood] for £35 (13000
words). Meldrum thinks there's no doubt—but still B must see it
himself. McClure[4] has been the pink of perfection. "We will be glad to
get as much as we can for you in America"—and so on. He is anxious to
have a book of short tales. I think *Jim* (20.000) Youth (13.000) A
seaman (5.000) Dynamite (5.000)[5] and another story of say 15.000
would make a volume for B here and for McC. there. That is after serial
pub*on*. I broached the subject and they seem eager. Have made no
conditions but said I would like to know what B. would offer. As to
McC. I leave it vague for the present.

The Rescue shall not begin till *October* next. That means bookform
for winter season of 1899. A long time to wait—and to find it after all a
dead frost—perhaps.

I don't feel a bit more hopeful about the writing of Rescue than

---

[1] Garnett has simply '[May 1898]'. This letter clearly falls between the one to Garnett
dated 18 May and one also dated '[May 1898]' which really belongs to 7 June. Although
21 May is possible, the later dates better fit the negotiations over 'Youth'.

[2] Guy de Maupassant's novel (1885) and *The Children of the Sea*, the American edition of
The Nigger (1897).

[3] 'Youth': Blackwood accepted the story on 9 June (Blackburn, p. 23).

[4] Either S. S. McClure or Robert, his London representative.

[5] 'Jim' grew into *Lord Jim* and 'Dynamite' into *Chance* (written 1911–12); the fate of 'A
Seaman' is unknown, but it may be 'the sketch of old Captain Loutit' (letter to
Meldrum, 22 August 1899).

before. It's like a curse. I can't *imagine* anything. How do you like C. Graham?

Jess sends her love to you all

Ever Yours

Jph. Conrad

I told C. Graham to get Mrs Garnett's translation of Turgeniev.[1] He admires T. but only read the French rendering. My most friendly regards to your wife.

To Helen Sanderson
Text MS Yale; J-A, 1, 238

3 June 1898
[Stanford-le-Hope]

Dear Mrs. Sanderson.[2]

Your letter is all that's good and kind and charming to read and I thank you very much for it. I can't imagine any letter from you that could be anything else to me. So Your remarks at the end—since you know my feelings toward the House of Sanderson, in all its ramifications—seem not so much the outcome of modesty as of mistrust of my own peevish disposition. You are here humbly (but firmly) requested not to do it again. To hint that reading Your letter could be for me a loss of time is at least unkind—if not bitterly ironic. My dear Mrs Sanderson, the friendships contracted at Elstree,[3] Ted's solid affection, Your friendly feeling—are the clearest gains of my life; and such letters as yours assure me that I've not lost that without which I would be forlorn indeed, and ruined beyond retrieving.

When your letter arrived I was finishing a short story[4] and I put off my answer till the end was reached. Half an hour ago I've written the last word and without loss of time, after a short stroll up the meadow, sat down to expostulate with you—a little—but mostly to thank you for all You say and for the kindness that shines between the lines of Your letter.

---

[1] Starting in 1894, Constance Garnett produced seventeen volumes of translations from Turgenev. All in all she translated about seventy volumes from the Russian (Heilbrun, *The Garnett Family*, p. 183). Edward Garnett sent Graham a copy of *Smoke* (Graham/Garnett correspondence, Texas).

[2] Helen Sanderson (née Watson) came from Galloway, in Scotland. She had been married in April (see letter to Sanderson, 9 April).

[3] With many of Ted Sanderson's thirteen brothers and sisters and, especially, with Sanderson's mother; almost all Conrad's letters to her were destroyed.

[4] 'Youth'.

I am anxious to see You and Ted in your new home. The servant trouble, the financial shortcomings are of the kind one gets used to. Just as well one should—since they are unavoidable. And in time the household machine will run smooth—but You must not let it grind you small.

And you mustn't let other things grind you at all. In these matters the great thing is to be faithfully yourself. I am quite alive to the circumstances, to the difficulties that surround you. They must be faced "in propria persona" so to speak. You and Ted—Ted and You—the two, the one must meet them by being faithful to yourselves—and by that alone. This seems vague—yet it is my clear thought for which I cannot find another form. Nothing more difficult than expression. And if—at times—you feel defeated, believe me it will be a delusion, because no circumstances of man's contriving can be stronger than a personality upheld by faith and conscience. There! I wish I could say something really helpful—something practical to you—and here I am unable to present anything but a belief. I believe it is truth. For the rest I so completely trust your tact and Ted's *instinct* of the world (his knowledge of it of course being granted) that I contemplate your future with interest with sympathy—but without uneasiness.

There's hardly room left to thank you for the invitation. Of course I am eager to come—and I shall very soon—my visit being to St Mary's.[1]

> Believe me dear Mrs Sanderson
> Your most faithful friend &
> servant
>
> > Joseph Conrad.

Hand-shake to Ted. I am inexpressibly glad to hear good news of his health. I feel criminal in not answering his letter. Will he receive me if I come?

To David Meldrum

Text MS Duke; Blackburn 21

> Friday. [3 June 1898][2]
> [Stanford-le-Hope]

Dear Mr Meldrum.[3]

I send you the end of *Youth* Sorry for the delay but had lots of interruptions.

I beg you will read it and if it should not commend itself to you send it

[1] A house in the grounds of Elstree School.
[2] The reference in the preceding letter to finishing 'Youth' gives the date.
[3] David S. Meldrum (1864–1940) was a literary adviser to William Blackwood and represented the Edinburgh publisher's interests in London.

back at once. If *you* do *not* think Mr Blackwood would like it I can't wait for his return.[1]

I'll send *Jim* along on Monday—as much as there is of him.[2]

I would be awfully pleased to see you here—soon. Drop me a line a day before.

Faithfully yours

Jph Conrad.

To William Nicholson
Text Krishnamurti

3 June 1898
Stanford le Hope
Essex

My dear Nicholson,[3]

Ever so many thanks for the Don Quixote[4] received this morning and for the words written thereon. It was good of you to remember me. I like the Knight very much. You have given him a lovely face and the individuality of the horse is as engaging as that of the rider. May you flourish exceedingly. You and your art and all that belongs to you in a greater or lesser degree.

Your faithful admirer

Joseph Conrad

To David Meldrum
Text MS Duke; Blackburn 21

Saturday. [4 June 1898][5]
[Stanford-le-Hope]

Dear Mr Meldrum.

Last night I posted You the last pages of *Youth*. Here I send the first 18 pages of *Jim: A Sketch* just to let you see what it is like. It will give You an idea of the spirit the thing is conceived in. I rather think it ought to be worked out in no less than 20-25 thousand words. Say *two* numbers of "Maga".

Suppose You let Mr Blackwood have a sight of it? I leave it however to your judgment. The MS is sent to *you*, just to form an opinion; I would want it back but at Your convenience.

---

[1] From taking the cure at Aix-les-Bains, 6 June.

[2] Work on 'Youth' and the beginnings of *Lord Jim* may have gone on simultaneously, but the chronology is not clear.

[3] Painter, graphic artist, and set-designer (1872–1949). He and his brother-in-law, James Pryde, collaborated as the 'Beggarstaff Brothers'.

[4] Nicholson's design for a poster of Sir Henry Irving in that role.

[5] Conrad finished 'Youth' the day before.

As to book-form publication You understand I do not wish to—so to speak—intrude the matter upon Mr Blackwood. I am averse to concluding anything as to a work not yet in existence. Nevertheless I would be glad to know what Mr Blackwood would offer for it. All being well we could perhaps be ready for the next spring season.[1] The SS McClure C^o would have the book in the States.

What do You think of a day in the country? Say the week after next. Fix Your own day and drop me a word. There is a train from Fenchurch Street at *11.35* which would bring You here in time for lunch. Last train at night at 8. But we could put you up and you would be in London at 9.30 next day.

Very faithfully Yours
Jph Conrad.

To Edward Garnett
Text MS Colgate; J-A, 1, 236; G. 131

Tuesday. [7 June 1898][2]
[Stanford-le-Hope]

Dearest G.

Thanks for your letter. I am glad you like C.–Graham who certainly is unique.

As to *Rescue* you are under a 'misapyrehension' as Shaw[3] would have said. I intend to write nothing else. I am not even going to finish Jim now. Not before Sept^{ber}. The talk about short stories has been commenced by those men B[lackwood] and McC[lure] and seeing them willing to discuss the future I gave them an idea of what I would do. The fact however remains that this *Rescue* makes me miserable—frightens me—and I shall not abandon it—even temporarily—I must get on with it, and it will destroy my reputation. Sure!

B has returned yesterday and Meldrum wrote me saying I shall hear from him very soon.

Thanks for your care for your thought. Alas no one can help me. In the matter of R. I have lost all sense of form and I can't see *images*. But what to write I *know*. I have the action only the hand is paralysed when it comes to giving expression to that action.

If I am too miserable I shall groan to you, O! best of men.

Ever Yours
J. Conrad

---

[1] *Lord Jim* was completed in July 1900.
[2] Garnett places this letter in May, but Blackburn (p. 22) has established Blackwood's return on 6 June – 'yesterday'. An envelope postmarked 7 June is in the Sutton collection.   [3] In *The Rescue*, the mate of Lingard's brig.

To William Blackwood
Text MS NLS: Blackburn 23

11th June 1898
Stanford-le-Hope
Essex.

Dear Mr Blackwood[1]

Thank you very much for Your good letter[2] and for the cheque for £*40* of which £35 in payment for the story entitled *Youth* and £5 on account of the story (yet unfinished) entitled *Jim: A sketch.*

My thanks however are due both for the matter and for the manner, and if the first superficially viewed appears a business transaction where the word thanks may be taken as a conventional expression, I beg you to believe I have a very clear sense of the inestimable value of the second. Inestimable is deliberately written. Man does not live by bread alone, and very little bread will go a long way towards sustaining life— without making it more supportable. For that last one must turn to men and be often disappointed. A word of appreciation, a f[r]iendly act performed in a friendly manner these are as rare as nuggets in gold-bearing sand and suddenly enrich the most obscure the most solitary existence.

This being the trend of my thought you may imagine I was gratified by the terms of Your letter apart from the "bis dat qui . . ." You know the proverb.[3] And for that also my thanks are due.

I trust You will like *Youth.* Its only merit is its being a bit of life. Of course I feel it could have been made better if it had fallen into better hands; but at any rate the sentiment which guided me was genuine.

I hope You have, in Aix-les-Bains, stored up health for a good long time. If the British Public, who is a kind of inferior Providence for the use of Authors, wills it I shall go there myself next year. I am, dear Mr Blackwood very faithfully Yours

Joseph Conrad.

---

[1] Editor of *Blackwood's Edinburgh Magazine* ('Maga') and head of the family company. Conrad's association with the house ran from 1897 to 1903.
[2] Accepting 'Youth' for *Blackwood's* (Blackburn, p. 23).
[3] 'Bis dat qui cito dat': 'he who gives promptly gives twice' (attributed to Publius Syrus).

To R. B. Cunninghame Graham

Text MS Dartmouth; J-A, 1, 239; Watts 87

11 June 1898.
[Stanford-le-Hope]

Cher et excellent ami

Thanks ever so much for the book.[1]

I have read it once so far.

The more I read you the more I admire. This is a strong word but not a bit too strong for the sensation it is supposed to describe. In your Wife's sketches I came again with delight upon the hand that had called to life the incomparable saint[2] and the mankind of that place and time.

I and Garnett have used up most of the adjectives we know in talking you over yesterday. He has sent me the *Bloody Niggers* and the Labour Leader.[3] Très bien!!

You are the perfection of scorn—not vulgar scorn mind, not scorn that would fit any utterance. No! Scorn that is clear in the thought and lurks in the phrase. The philosophy of unutterable scorn.

Ah! Amigo de mi corazon[4] (is that right?) you may fling contempt and bitterness, and wit and hard wisdom, hard unpractical wisdom, at this world and the next—l'ignoble boule roulera toujours portant des êtres infimes et méchants dans un univers qui ne se comprends pas lui-même.[5]

I put first (of yours) *Horses* then *Father Arch*[6]—or bracket them. But I like every line of the others. Of your Wife's *The Will*[7] is a perfect little thing and Yuste-Batuecas and Plasencia are pictures of a rare charm. They breathe like things of life seen in a dream. Ever Yours

Jph Conrad.

P.S. You are the most *undemocratic* of men. By what perversion of

[1] *Father Archangel of Scotland, and Other Essays* (1896), a collection by Gabriela and R. B. Cunninghame Graham.

[2] Teresa of Avila.

[3] 'Bloody Niggers', a diatribe against racial arrogance in general and imperialism in particular, appeared in the *Social-Democrat* (April 1897), 1, 104–9 and, as 'Niggers', in *The Ipané*. Cedric Watts gives the original in *Selected Writings of Cunninghame Graham* (1981). Graham often contributed to the *Labour Leader*, an offshoot of Keir Hardie's *Miner*; Garnett had passed on 'Castles in the Air' from the 30 April issue (Graham to Garnett, 3 June, MS Texas).

[4] 'Amigo de mi corazón': 'friend of my heart'. Graham had a Spanish grandmother.

[5] 'The vile ball will keep on rolling, carrying mean and wicked creatures into a universe that doesn't understand itself.'

[6] 'The Horses of the Pampas' and 'Father Archangel of Scotland'.

[7] 'A Will', 'Yuste', 'The Batuecas', and 'La Vera de Plasencia' – all by Graham's wife.

sentiment vous vous êtes fourré dans une galère qui n'arrivera nulle part? Du reste ça importe peu.[1] The truth of your personality is visible, would be visible anywhere.

P.P.S. No. The *Vanishing Race* decidedly is first in my affection.

P.P.P.S. I have also received *Badminton* with the most interesting Bolas.[2] You are good to let me have all you publish. Continuez. Yahudi[3] seems greatly impressed by you. Just like his cheek.

To R. B. Cunninghame Graham

Text MS Dartmouth; Watts 88

15 June 1898
[Stanford-le-Hope]

Cher et excellent ami.

I need not tell you how delighted I am with your declaration of friendly purposes. Please tell the kind Author of Sta Theresa that we both are waiting impatiently for the day when we shall have the honour and pleasure of seeing her in our camping place in the wilds of Essex.

This is the kindest and the most friendly thing that has been done to me for many years and I hope you will persevere in your charitable and rash intention.

Yes. B[loody] N[iggers] is or are good—very good, very telling; in fact they tell one all about you.[4] And the more one is told the more one wants to hear more. Mais—cher ami—ne Vous eparpillez pas trop. Vos pensées courent de par le monde comme des chevaliers errants, tandis qu'il faudrait les tenir en main, les assembler, en faire une phalange penetrante et solide[5]—peut être victorieuse—qui sait?— Peut-être————

Et puis—pourquoi prêchez Vous au convertis?[6] Mais je deviens stupide. Il n y a pas des convertis aux idées de l'honneur, de la justice, de la pitié, de la liberté. Il n y a que des gens qui sans savoir, sans

---

[1] 'Have you ended up in a galley that won't get anywhere? Besides, that doesn't much matter.'

[2] An essay on the *boleadoras* used by South American ranchers, collected in *The Ipané*.

[3] T. Fisher Unwin.

[4] 'I take it Africa was brought about in sheer ill-humour. No one can think it possible that an all-wise God (had he been in his sober senses) would create a land and fill it full of people destined to be replaced by other races from across the seas. Better, by far, to have made the "niggers" white and let themselves by degrees all become Englishmen, than put us to the trouble of exterminating whole tribes of them to carry out his plan!' (*Selected Writings*, p. 66).

[5] Uncharacteristically, Graham did make extensive changes before republishing his polemic in *The Ipané*.

[6] In a left-wing weekly.

comprendre, sans sentir s'extasient sur les mots, les repètent, les crient, s'imaginent y croire—sans croire a autre chose qu'au gain, a l'avantage personel, a la vanité satisfaite. Et les mots s'envolent; et il ne reste rien, entendez vous? Absolument rien, oh homme de foi! Rien. Un moment, un clin d'oeil et il ne reste rien—qu'une goutte de boue, de boue froide, de boue morte lancée dans l'espace noir, tournoyant autour d'un soleil éteint. Rien. Ni pensée, ni son, ni âme. Rien.[1]

Jess sends her best regards. I am ever Yours

Jph Conrad.

P.S. Mes devoirs a Madame Votre Femme et mes remerciments.

To E. L. Sanderson
Text MS Yale; J-A, 1, 240

15th June 98
[Stanford-le-Hope]

Dearest old Ted

I do not deserve the display of your patience and endurance towards me. It was good and next to angelic to write to me when I had not answered your letter after the end of the honeymoon. I did not answer; I do nothing; I have no time; I shall take arrears of correspondence with me into my grave—I fear. I am incorrigible. And by the by: what a good title for a play—a serious comedy in five acts: The Incorrigible. Almost any phase of life could be treated under that title.

Excuse me: I have play on the brain; nothing definite; just *play* in the abstract.

I am coming to see You in your own nest. Every day counts. When I'll get there is another matter. I am in a state of deadly, indecent funk. I've obtained a ton of cash from a Yank under, what strikes me, are false

---

[1] 'But—dear friend—don't spread yourself too thin. Your thoughts gad about the world like knights-errant, whereas they should be held back, gathered together to form a solid and penetrating phalanx—perhaps victorious—who knows?—perhaps—.

'And then—why do you preach to the converted? But I'm becoming stupid. There are no converts to ideas of honour, justice, pity, freedom. There are only people who, without knowledge, understanding, or feeling, drive themselves into a frenzy with words, repeat them, shout them out, imagine they believe in them—without believing in anything but profit, personal advantage, satisfied vanity. And words fly away; and nothing remains, do you understand? Absolutely nothing, oh man of faith! Nothing. A moment, a twinkling of an eye and nothing remains—but a clot of mud, of cold mud, of dead mud cast into black space, rolling around an extinguished sun. Nothing. Neither thought, nor sound, nor soul. Nothing.'

pretences.[1] The Child of the Screaming Eagle is as innocent as a dove. He *thinks* the book he bought will be finished in July while I *know* that it is a physical and intellectual impossibility to even approach the end by that date. He sends on regular cheques which is—according to his lights—right, but I pocket them serenely which—according to my lights—looks uncommonly like a swindle on my part. And would you believe it? Sometimes I feel a kind of guilty exultation, a kind of corrupt joy in living thus on the proceeds of dishonesty. As we get older we get worse. At least some of us do. Others again remain young for ever. Thus the supply of tolerably decent people is kept up.

But as I don't wish to see Your door closed against me I hasten to inform You, that, partly from fear and partly from remorse, I have invited the Yank to lunch here to-morrow. In that way I return some part of my ill-gotten gains and may have an opportunity to break the fatal news gently to him. If I survive the interview you shall certainly see me very soon.

I am glad you liked my thing in the *Outlook*. Was it the Views & Reviews article about Marryat & Cooper?[2] It seems to have pleased various people—and the Editor (a decent little chap)[3] most of all.

However that kind of thing does not pay.

I have written a species of short story for Blackwood.[4] That pays pretty well. It is a sort of sea narrative without head or tail. When it will appear I don't know, and care not since the cash I've had—and have spent—alas!—already.

I am so-so. My wife is pretty well and the boy thrives alarmingly well. To day is his fifth (monthly) birthday and he has two teeth. Jess sends her kindest regards to you both and I am, speaking to both of You

Ever Yours

Jph Conrad

To David Meldrum

Text MS Duke; Blackburn 24

15th June 98
[Stanford-le-Hope]

My dear Meldrum.

I had Your letter and a wire from McClure. Next week will suit me, any day it suits You; but I rather think McClure is coming anyhow—tomorrow probably. I've wired to know for certain.

[1] From Robert McClure, for the serialization of *The Rescue* by S. S. McClure.
[2] 'Tales of the Sea', *Outlook*, 4 June, reprinted in *Notes on Life and Letters*.
[3] Percy Hurd.   [4] 'Youth'.

I had no intention to come to town for the next month. Could I not give my mind and advice (both pretty worthless but very much at your service if you have occasion for such rubbish) in writing? But if the thing is really so that I can be of any use I could run down on Friday or Sat. Just drop me a line.

I received *Jim* all right. Thanks. In any case we shall meet next week and till then Au revoir

Yours faithfully

Jph. Conrad.

To David Meldrum

Text MS Duke; Blackburn 25

20th June 1898[1]
Stanford le Hope

Dear Mr Meldrum.

We shall expect You on Thursday for lunch.[2] Let me know what train You are coming by so that I can meet you. There's a good train at *9.45* AM. arriving here at *10.46*. Should this be too early then the *11.45* brings You here at *one*.

McClure has been here last Friday; came late and spent the night. I think he is busy all this week. We talked of war and politics mostly. I hope he wasn't too bored.

Expecting a word from you I am
dear Mr Meldrum
Yours very faithfully

Jph. Conrad.

To Cora Crane

Text MS Columbia; Stallman 182

Stanford-le-Hope
27 June 1898

Dear Mrs Crane.

I am, we are, horribly ashamed of ourselves for leaving Your good and welcome letter so long without a reply. But we reckon upon your generous forgiveness.

I was delighted to hear good news of dear Stephen. The life on board

---

[1] A Monday.
[2] They discussed publishing a volume of sea-stories, the origin of *Youth* (Blackburn, p. 25).

that tug of his will set him up in strenght* and appetite for years.[1] Have
You heard from him since you wrote? I suppose he landed with the army
and is in the thick of everything that's going. I've only heard lately he is
going to write for Blackwood.[2] They think a lot of him and expect—as
well they may—first rate work. Meldrum was here (I suppose You've
heard of him? Blackwoods man in London) the other day and spoke of
Stephen with real enthusiasm. They are anxious but not impatient.—

We had a hard time of it. Jess is overworked and we positively *can't* get
a decent girl. The pea-pickers are not come yet but are expected in a day
or two and my wife is afraid lest they should bring some disease and
harm the baby.[3] It is most unlikely tho'.

Garnett told me You had secured a house after Your own heart.[4] My
congratulation on that and still more on the success of American arms
especially on the exploit of Hobson! That was worth all the Manila
battle![5] Magnificent.

It looks as though the war would drag after all. I think you had better
not wait for Stephen's return and come to us with Mrs Ruedy[6] (to whom
my respectful duty) *at* *least* for the promised day and for longer if You
can stand it. I am afraid You would get bored. We lead a wretched,
shut-up, existence in the most primitive surroundings.[7]

Jessie will write to suggest the time but in reality you must consult
your own convenience. The poor girl is doing all the house-work,
nursing and cooking, herself. She is very cheerful about it but it makes
me miserable to see her toiling like this from morning to night. Oh! for a
success, a beastly popular success! I long for it on that account. My work
goes on desperately slow. I think with difficulty and write without
enthusiasm but still the book crawls on towards its lame and impotent
end. But the end is not yet. Enough lamentations!

A word as to Your health, Your doings and Your plans would be very

---

[1] He was in the Caribbean, covering the Spanish–American war from a base on the
tugboat *Three Friends*.
[2] Crane, who was also retained by the New York *World*, owed Blackwood two articles.
Conrad later told the story of obtaining that commission (*Last Essays*, pp. 117–18).
[3] She recalled her fears in *Joseph Conrad and His Circle*, pp. 60–2.
[4] Brede Place, a massive fourteenth-century manor house in East Sussex, complete with
dungeon, chapel, secret passages, and a ghost. The Cranes did not go there until
January.
[5] The Spanish East Indian Fleet was destroyed by Admiral Dewey in Manila bay;
Lieutenant Hobson sank the *Merrimac*, thereby bottling up the West Indian fleet in
Santiago harbour.
[6] Cora Crane's companion since the Jacksonville days.
[7] For the splendours and miseries of Ivy Walls Farm, see *Joseph Conrad and His Circle*,
pp. 50–1.

welcome. We send you here an amateur photograph of Jess and baby
(doesn't he look like a little pig?) and another of our house—a side view.

My wife and Dolly send their very best love to you and Mrs Ruedy
and I am, dear Mrs Crane, your most obedient and faithful friend and
servant

Jph. Conrad.

PS I was so pleased to hear my tales are a success amongst the socialists
of Ten[n]essee. I feel quite proud of it.

To Edward Garnett

Text MS Colgate; G. 132

[late June? 1898][1]
[Stanford-le-Hope]

Dearest Garnett.

Thanks. Do come when you can.

I send you a few pages of P III.[2] The rest is not typed yet.

I am awfully behind and though I can work my regular gait I cannot
make up for the lost 3 months. I am full of anxiety. Here, I have already
had a 100 pounds on acct! And the end is not in sight. Horrid mess I am
in.

I'll tell you everything when you do come. I am living in a hell of my
own. Thanks for the books.

Ever Yours

Conrad

Jess sends her love to you all. The boy is teething and is in a devil of a
temper night and day.

---

[1] Garnett gives 'June': a date towards the end of the month would match the visit
proposed here and paid by 12 July.
[2] *The Rescue.*

To R. B. Cunninghame Graham
Text MS Dartmouth; J-A, 1, 242; Watts 90

Saturday. [2 or 9 July 1898][1]
[Stanford-le-Hope]

Très illustre Seigneur.

I write at once because to-morrow is Sunday et dans le village arriéré where you sojourn now there is no postal delivery to-morrow.[2]

Pourquoi-pas? It is a jolly good idea for the play.[3] Of that particular bit of history (and of every other) I have but the slightest, the haziest idea. In the way of writing I *do not* see Your limitations. Revez la dessus, and something very good may come out of it. You are as romantic as the rest of us. Nous sommes tous dans cette galère.[4] The thing is—the expression. Now as to that I have no doubt. You'll find it for the simple reason it is in you. Il s'agit de fouiller au plus profond[5] and you will reach the vein. I am only afraid You would make it too good—much too good for scenic success. The gods are stupid. You'll not be conventional enough, for them to understand you.

These are brave oaths! Ils me mettent du coeur au ventre.[6] I shall write to you re Sir F.E. when I hear.[7] It occurs to me however that it may not happen for a long time—may never happen! Quien sabe? La plus belle fille du monde ne peut donner que ce qu'elle a.[8] You know this proverb? Therefore if before you return to your native wilds you come across the Donald creature just whisper softly into his ear.[9] I've served in so many Scotch ships (from the Duke of Sutherland to the Highland Forest[10]—the list is too long) that I imagine myself to possess some sort

---

[1] Internal evidence shows that Graham was in London but had not been able to visit Ivy Walls. He arrived from Scotland 27 or 28 June (Graham/Garnett correspondence, Texas); on 15 July he met Conrad in London. 2 and 9 July are, therefore, the only feasible dates.

[2] London, a city not favoured with Sunday mails. A letter posted on a Saturday morning in the Essex countryside, however, would be delivered in the West End that afternoon. ~~Translations apart, no play of Graham's has survived.

[4] 'We are all in the same boat.'

[5] 'It's a question of digging right to the bottom.'   [6] 'They make me bold.'

[7] Conrad hoped to see Sir Francis Evans about a job with the Union Line, which ran steamers to South Africa.

[8] 'The most beautiful girl in the world can only give what she's got.'

[9] Sir Donald Currie, head of Donald Currie & Co., Shipowners, proprietors of the Castle Line: Graham was helping Conrad find a command; the story that, for literature's sake, Graham secretly dissuaded shipowners from hiring his friend is touching but unlikely (Watts and Davies, pp. 149–50).

[10] In 1878/9 and 1887, respectively.

of claim. A word from Sir Donald would go a long way with any firm north of the Tweed. Let the big-wigs compete for the honour of employing the immortal author of—of—I forgot now.

I conclude from your letter I shan't see you here this time. Tans pis. Let me know when you are passing through London on your way to Morrocco.* Veuillez presenter mes très respectueux devoirs a Madame Votre Femme. Ever Yours

Jph. Conrad.

Boris is better. I find it difficult yet to forgive him for preventing your visit here. On ne rattrappe l'occasion qui passe, qui est passée![1]

To Edward Garnett
Text MS Sutton; G. 133

Tuesday [12 July 1898][2]
[Stanford-le-Hope]

My dear Garnett

This day with You has done me good. I feel much calmer and more hopeful about my work. I still think it very bad and do not feel that eagerness to show it to You which in the past impelled me to forward successive chapters hot from the oven—for Your inspection. However I send two parts by this morning's post. You shall read and see; I am afraid to think of what you will say. I am afraid that even as an infamous pot-boiler this book[3] is too unskillfully made. I think I went wrong from the beginning but now I am waist deep and there is no going back.

My kindest regards to Mrs Garnett. My wife sends her love. We are well here.

Ever Yours

Jph Conrad

---

[1] 'One doesn't recapture the chance that passes, that has passed.'
[2] Date from Garnett.
[3] *The Rescue.*

To Spiridion Kliszczewski
Text MS Spiridion; Unpublished

> 12th July 1898.
> Stanford-le-Hope.
> Essex.

Dear old Friend.

I would have written sooner but what with the press of work on one hand and laziness to take a pen on the other I've been sadly delayed.

Thanks for Hubert's letters. Apart from the interest attaching to his experiences and views (not to mention the feelings of friendship for him as your son) I've been struck by his descriptive ability and by the clear easy style—not without a distinct charm. I had a real pleasure in reading these letters and I repeat my thanks to your wife and yourself for having given me the opportunity.

Is Clem[1] then coming to London? I suppose you will come with him to see him settled. If so you must take a run down here and see us. You needn't be told that during Clem's residence in London we shall be glad, we shall be very happy to see him as often as he can spare time to run down to Stanford. Sundays or week days, early and late our door shall fly open for him. And if weary with London atmosphere he wants a breath of fresh air he can find it here. If he cycles—two hours over easy roads will bring him to our door.

I am happy to see *the dispute* is about to be settled. I can quite imagine how everyone must suffer. Is your loss really very serious? You say you are dropping money every week; I am grieved to hear it; you've worked too hard for it not to deserve better luck.

My wife's best love to Mrs. Spiridion and all the family. My kind remembrances and regards to your wife and boys. I am always your affectionate friend.

> Jph. Conrad.

P.S. I've fallen behind with my work. Since May however I get on better. My health was very indifferent all the first part of the year. I shall write you again end this month.

---

[1] His son Clement.

To A. T. Quiller-Couch
Text MS Quiller-Couch; Unpublished

Stanford-le-Hope
Essex
13th July 1898

My dear Sir.[1]

Many thanks for your letter. It has given me a great, a very great pleasure. Nothing would please me more than to act upon your suggestion. Unfortunately there is always some nigger in the fence. I am now struggling with a book—a mass of verbiage with some dim idea so well lost in it that I, even I have a long time ago lost sight of it. This thing sits on my shoulder like the old Man of the sea, and embitters my life. I write, I write and the wretched thing doesn't move an inch.

On the other hand Mr. Blackwood is waiting for some short stories. These however would have been too long for your magazine.

But I am exceedingly loth to let this opportunity you offer pass away from me. Will you allow me to answer in this way:

As soon as there is a break in the clouds I shall think out something 4-5000 words in length, and send it to Fowey[2] for you to look at. If tolerable you shall give me the usual rate of your magazine, and allow McClure to copyright it for the States. This will cause no delay.

But I can give you no idea of when I may be ready with it. It may be months.

I saw the notice of the new Magazine under your Editorship[3] and I need not say that, on the strength of your name, I wished it all possible luck. You have laid hold of the big end of a very heavy job. There is in mankind a bias, a tendency, that drives it towards the cheap, towards the worthless, in letters, in art, in politics, in sentiment, in—by all the gods that sit grinning above—in the very love itself. A trace of the original ape I suppose. To drive it on an upward path you must pat the ape on the back lest it turn and rend you.

This is an immoral theory but I've left my morality on the sea. Still I

---

[1] Arthur Thomas Quiller-Couch (pseudonym 'Q', 1863–1944), man of letters, compiler of the original *Oxford Book of English Verse* (1900), later a professor of English at Cambridge.

[2] The Cornish seaside village ('Troy Town' in his fiction) where 'Q' had gone to live, seeking native soil and a better climate than London could offer.

[3] A puzzling reference: 'Q' had been an assistant editor of the *Speaker* since 1890 and also wrote a literary column for the *Pall Mall Magazine* (in whose February number he had praised *The Nigger*); with these exceptions, ill-health had forced him to cut back his work for periodicals.

am very pleased that you, when about to fight for the good cause, have
thought of me. I am afraid, afraid—I don't quite deserve it.

My best wishes for your attempt and for the magazine. Believe me,
dear Sir,

Very faithfully yours

Jph. Conrad

To R. B. Cunninghame Graham

Text MS Dartmouth; J-A, 1, 241; Watts 92

19 July 1898
[Stanford-le-Hope]

Cher ami.

Thanks for Cyrano.[1] I haven't yet read it but shall do so before the
sun rises again.

I've seen Sir Francis Evans this morning. He was full of business with
twenty people waiting for an interview, but he received me at once and
was kindness itself. The upshot of it is this: It is of course impossible to
place me in the Union Line[2]—I said I did not even dream of such a
thing but explained that I thought he might have some tramp or good
collier. The Company he said owns no tramps or colliers but he might
hear of something of the kind and in such a case "would let me know."
— He has my card but my address is not on it. Perhaps you would drop
him a line pour l'entretenir dans la bonne voie[3] and mention where I
live. — He said he would be "extremely pleased to do anything for a
friend of Mr Cunninghame Graham". Thereupon I salaamed myself
out and another man rushed in.

Something may come of it. In any case many thanks. Since you have
begun that trouble yourself I feel less compunction in asking you to keep
it up when an opportunity offers. Now some shadow of possibility to go
to sea has been thus presented to me I am almost frantic with the
longing to get away. Absurd!

I return Don Jaime's[4] letters. It *is* amusing. The glimpse into the

---

[1] Edmond Rostand's play: French original, 1897: English version, July 1898. Resemblances between Graham and its hero would not be hard to find.
[2] On a passenger ship, that is.   [3] 'To keep him in the right direction.'
[4] James Fitzmaurice Kelly (1857–1923), an authority on Spanish literature whose literary and scholarly virtues Graham often praised.

"cuisine" of criticism is very entertaining. I would expect anything from a man like Traill. C'est une vieille ganache.[1] He wrote once a book about Flaubert for which he deserves to be disembowelled and flung to die on a garbage-heap.[2] Who's Watt? And why is he inimical to the Ingenious Hidalgo, as presented by Don Jaime?[3] Moi je suis naif et je ne comprends pas. Enough of this twaddle. Ever Yours.

Conrad.

Mes devoirs a Madame Votre Femme. Jess who sends her kind regards is as anxious for the sea as I am.[4] She is very touched by Your references to Borys, in your letters, and full of gratitude for your efforts on my behalf.

To R. B. Cunninghame Graham
Text MS Dartmouth; J-A, 1, 243; Watts 94

Saturday
30th July
98
[Stanford-le-Hope]

Très cher ami.

This morning I had the Aurora from Smithers N° 2 of the 500 copies.[5]

C'est, tout simplement, magnifique yet I do not exactly perceive what on earth they have been making a fuss about.[6]

I am afraid Henley is a horrible bourgeois.[7] Who drew the frontispiece? I can't imagine anybody whose name I know. Is it an English drawing? It does not look like it.[8] I notice variations in the text as I've read it in the typewritten copy. This seems the most finished piece of work you've ever done. Il y a une note, une resonnance là dedans, vibrant de ligne en ligne. C'est très fort.[9] No one will see it.

---

[1] 'He's an old fogey.' H. D. Traill (1842–1900), author of *The New Fiction, and Other Essays on Literary Subjects* (1897) and editor of *Literature*.

[2] Conrad must have meant J. E. Tarver's *Gustave Flaubert As Seen in His Works and Correspondence* (1895), the only work on Flaubert in English at that time.

[3] Traill had published a letter from Henry E. Watts, who asserted that Kelly was unfit to edit Cervantes. According to Kelly: 'His game is to play to the Protestant gallery, to make out *Don Quixote* a covert attack on the Inquisition' (letter to Graham, 7 March, MS Texas).

[4] She explains her position in *Joseph Conrad and His Circle*, pp. 59–60.

[5] Graham's *Aurora la Cujiñí: A Realistic Sketch in Seville*, a booklet about a legendary gypsy dancer, published by Leonard Smithers.

[6] Graham's references to lesbianism, sweaty arm-pits and the aphrodisiac effects of blood had made it hard to find a publisher.

[7] As editor of the *New Review*, W. E. Henley had refused *Aurora*.

[8] An old lithograph, found in Madrid by Graham and Will Rothenstein.

[9] 'There's a note, a resonance in there, ringing from line to line. It's very powerful.'

I had a note from Fisher Unwin written evidently for the purpose to inform me that he had met "Our Mutual Friend (!) Mr Cunninghame Graham at Wilfrid's* Blunt."[1]

Quel toupet![2] As long as such a man exists I *will not* admit equality, fraternity—as to liberty vous et moi nous savons bien a quoi nous en tenir.[3] I've read the little book three times this morning—and behold! I am disgusted with what I write. No matter.

Blackwoods Magazine for this month has an appreciation of F. M. Kelly's edition of Don Quixote.[4] Very fair. Nothing striking but distinct recognition.

I do like the attitude of the *Maga* on the Spanish business.[5]

If one could set the States & Germany by the ears! That would be *real fine*. I am afraid however that the thieves shall agree in the Philip[p]ines. The pity of it!

Viva l'España! Anyhow.

Do you believe in a speedy peace. Write me all you know. I would like to see the thing over and done with tho' mind I think that Spain is perfectly invulnerable now and may keep the Yanks capering around for an indefinite time.[6]

When do you start for Morocco?

I've been seedy—in my head—in my idiotic cabeza. I feel lazy (always did) and sleepy. When I've written a page I feel it ought to be sold to the ten-cent paper man in New York.[7] It's all it's good for.

C'est Zolaesque ce que je viens d'écrire Hein?[8] But look at the circumlocutions. If you want to know how I exactly feel to my work put the above into plain Zola language and it will give you a faint idea then.

Assez. Toujours le votre

J Conrad.

Mes devoirs a Madame Votre Femme.

[1] Like Graham, Wilfrid Scawen Blunt (1840–1922) campaigned against imperialism and went to gaol on political charges. He was also a poet, a traveller, and a breeder of Arabian horses.

[2] 'What cheek!'   [3] 'We well know, you and I, what to believe.'

[4] Conrad refers to the August issue of *Blackwood's*. For Kelly, see letter of 19 July.

[5] Presented by the United States as a crusade for freedom, the Spanish–American war was really a struggle between an old imperial power and a new one, a conflict in which Britain's sympathies should go to Spain: *Blackwood's*, Vol. 164, pp. 283–9.

[6] Spain accepted American terms on 12 August. By the Treaty of Paris, 10 December, the United States acquired Guam and Puerto Rico, and bought the Philippines.

[7] Such popular magazines as *McClure's* and *Munsey's* cost a dime.

[8] Comparisons with Zola's novels began in a review of *Almayer's Folly* (*Critical Heritage*, p. 52); Watts points to a more recent example: *Illustrated London News*, 5 February 1898.

To R. B. Cunninghame Graham
Text MS Dartmouth; Watts 98

Stanford-le-Hope
Essex
2^d August 1898

Très cher ami.

Indeed I do understand, and though I do not want to say much I wish you to know that I feel the pain of your defeat with an intimate comprehension.[1] I know you well enough to be certain that the fight was a good fight. It is a satisfaction but not a consolation—not to me at least tho' it may be to you. When one responds with such depth as one has to a friend's trouble it is difficult to delude oneself as to the brutality of facts. The end is seen—nothing else. He who strove has the memories of blows struck—of hopes—of sensations. I have only the knowledge of the catastrophe—as unexpected as a stab in the dark.

It is good of you to think of my miserable affairs.—When one hears news of that kind the natural selfishness leaps out and the first pain is the pain of perceiving how useless one is. And there is humiliation in this finding out that all one's friendship goodwill, affection that seemed so strong, so far reaching are powerless to ward off the slightest pain or the greatest misfortune, are as though they had not been!

I did not intend to disregard your wishes but indeed I understand too well to be altogether silent. Ever yours.

Jph Conrad

Mes hommages très respectueux a Madame Votre Femme. Jess sends her kind regards.

---

[1] Conrad, another member of a land-owning family, sympathized deeply with Graham's efforts to keep Gartmore, in Perthshire. When Graham inherited the estate in 1883, he also inherited debts of £61,000 incurred by his demented father. The prolonged agricultural depression made recovery impossible; in 1900, Graham sold house and land to a Glasgow tycoon.

To Edward Garnett
Text MS Virginia; G. 133

3^d Aug. 98
[Stanford-le-Hope]

My dear Garnett.

I am not dead tho' only half alive. Very soon I shall send you some MS. I am writing hopelessly—but still I am writing.[1] How I feel I cannot express. Pages accumulate and the story stands still.

I feel suicidal.

Drop me a line and tell me where and how you are. If you could come down it would be an act of real friendship and also of charity.

My kind regards and Jessie's love to your wife. Jess is knocked up with the boy's teething performances. He has (and she has also) a rough time of it.

I am afraid there's something wrong with my thinking apparatus. I am utterly out of touch with my work—and I can't get in touch. All is darkness.

Ever Yours

Jph. Conrad

To R. B. Cunninghame Graham
Text MS Dartmouth; J-A, 1, 224; Watts 100

3^d Aug 98
[Stanford-le-Hope]

Excellent Ami.

Thanks for letter with communication from Sir Donald.[2]

It is sound advice but does not meet the case. If I wanted to do what he advises I would hunt up some of my old skippers. That however I can't do. It would be giving up everything to begin life for the third time and I am not young enough for that. Do not worry about that affair. If I thought that in the midst of your troubles my silly desire to get out to sea added to your occupations my conscience wouldn't let me sleep.

Je suis triste a crever.[3] I think of you preparing your capitulation with fate et j'ai le coeur gros. Fourteen years! How much that means in the

---

[1] *The Rescue.*   [2] Sir Donald Currie, of the Castle Line.
[3] 'I'm sad enough to die' – sad about his literary and Graham's financial misfortunes.

past—and for the future too—since this fight must have grown and taken root in your life.

Toujours a vous de coeur

Jph Conrad

Jess sends her best regards. She understands enough to be very sorry. Write only when you have time. Could I do anything in the way of reading the proofs for you?[1]

To T. Fisher Unwin
Text MS Leeds; Unpublished

8th Aug 98

[Stanford-le-Hope]

Dear Mr Unwin.

I forward you a post card which reached me to-day. I am writing to M[r] Bussow to say that personally I would be very pleased to have the *Outcast* translated into German.[2] The business question I leave to you since you have a half share in the rights.

Would You communicate with this Mr Bussow? I know nothing about him. And I think it would be expedient to find out something, before giving him the authorisation he asks for. He may publish in a hole-and-corner manner in some obscure provincial town—which would be undesirable. On the other hand he may be a satisfactory person. I am not in a position to make inquiries and so perhaps you may be inclined to take this matter in hand.

With kind regards

very faithfully Your

Jph. Conrad.

---

1 The proofs of *Mogreb-el-Acksa*: in the end, Conrad did not read them but did help Graham at other times.
2 The German translation, by Elsie McCalman, appeared in 1934. *The Nigger* (1912) was the first Conrad novel published in German.

To Edward Garnett
Text MS Indiana; G. 134

Saturday. [13 August 1898][1]
[Stanford-le-Hope]

Dearest G.

I trust you completely and if in your judgment you lean towards mercy—as it seems to me—well this mercy is very welcome and perhaps not altogether undeserved. In any case it is human for it brings alleviation to a very real (though ridiculous) suffering. So, the thing is vivid—and seen? It is good news to me, because, unable to try for something better, higher, I did try for the visual effect. And I must trust to that for the effect of the whole story from which I cannot evolve any meaning—and have given up trying. The book will be of 15000 words.[2] That's certain. I am able to write now. I shall be better able after I've seen you.[3] I must be getting well since, looking back, I see how ill, mentally, I have been these last four months. The fear of this horror coming back to me makes me shiver. As it is it has destroyed already the little belief in myself I used to have. I am appalled at the absurdity of my situation—at the folly of my hopes, at the blindness that had kept me up in my gropings. Most appalled to feel that all the doors behind me are shut and that I must remain where I have come blundering in the dark.

I am looking forward to your coming. I have some plans for my manner of life and for work which I shall talk over with you. I hope this uncautious frankness won't scare you away. Cunng^{me} Graham is very unhappy. Shall tell you when we meet. He got into his head to get me the command of a steamer or ship and swears he will do it. Meantime he is again in Paris about his eyesight. I saw his wife (for twenty minutes) the author of the St^a Theresa book—you know. Details when we meet. Ever yours

Conrad.

My kindest regards and Jessie's love to your wife.

---

[1] Garnett has 3 August – which was not a Saturday. Graham's visit to Paris (between 7 and 16 August) fixes the real date.

[2] Conrad meant 150,000 – an accurate prediction of *The Rescue's* ultimate length.

[3] Garnett seems to have paid more than one visit in August: letter to Graham, 27 August; letter from Garnett to Graham, 26 August (Watts, p. 104), referring to a visit 'the other day'.

To C. K. Shorter

Text MS Wellington; Knowles

Tuesday. 23^d Aug 98.

[Stanford-le-Hope]

Dear Mr Shorter.[1]

I return proofs of chap*rs* I. II III.[2]

The beginning of chap III falls about the middle of slip 8.

In a day or two Mr R McClure shall be in possession of nearly the whole of part III. in all 60.000 words. Another 40-50 will complete the story.

Allow me at this opportunity to tell you how much I appreciate Your generous recognition of my work. The attitude of Your publications towards my books has been a source of the greatest pleasure to me—especially the reference to the Nigger in one of the last papers contributed to the News by the late Mr James Payn.[3]

Believe me, dear Mr Shorter

Very faithfully Yours

Jph. Conrad.

To C. K. Shorter

Text MS Berg; Unpublished

Stanford-le-Hope. Essex.

Wednesday 24th Aug. 1898

Dear Mr. Shorter.

I could not catch this morning's post to answer your letter of yesterday's date.

Had I obtained the slightest hint of what you now propose doing, say two months ago I would have disregarded the urgent representations of my medical man and gone on driving at the *Rescue*. What the book would have been like in that case I do not like to say—or even think of. At any rate it would have been all there for you to judge and decide.

As it is I must ask You whether *six weeks* is enough to prepare for the press an instalment of the story. If so then I can promise to deliver the last pages six weeks before the last date fixed for their appearance. It is very probable that by the middle of October all the story will be in your

---

[1] Clement King Shorter (1859–1926), editor of the *Illustrated London News* and the *Sketch*. Later, he founded *Sphere* and *Tatler*, and wrote books on the Brontës.

[2] Of *The Rescue*, unfinished but accepted for publication in the weekly *Illustrated London News*; Shorter had acquired the necessary rights from the McClures.

[3] He compared *The Nigger* to books by Zola and Hugo (5 February 1898).

hands but to feel quite safe I must take the very outside limit. Say 15th
Nov. You will kindly remember I was told the book was to begin *in a
monthly* in October, so that your extremely flattering offer to use the tale
for the *News* finds me altogether unprepared.

I cannot adequately express my regret; the more so that I have to a
certain extent misled Mr R. McClure (not in bad faith tho') but through
being too sanguine as to my rate of work.

Should you still (after this confession) intend my work for the *News*
may I be permitted to suggest that it would perhaps be safer to effect a
few cuttings in Part II. There are a few bits of description and analysis
which could come out or could be shortened without injury to the *tale*
proper. As it is the story must be a close fit; and part III & IV could not
be touched without interfering with the action.

If you think my idea opportune perhaps you will send me the MS of
Part II?

Believe me, dear Mr Shorter,
very faithfully yours
Jph. Conrad

To R. B. Cunninghame Graham
Text MS Dartmouth; J-A, 1, 244; Watts 100

26th Aug 98
[Stanford-le-Hope]

Cher et bon.

I return the pages *To Wayfaring Men.*[1] I read them before I read your
letter and I have been deeply touched. I think I can understand the
mood from which the thing flowed. And if I can't understand your
mood—which is probable—I can understand my own emotion at the
reading of these pages—a silly thing for which you should disclaim
respo[n]sibility because your words are meant for better men.

Ah! The lone tree on the horizon and then bear a little—(a very little)
to the right. Haven't we all ridden with such directions to find no house
but many curs barking at our heels. Can't miss it? Well perhaps we
can't. And we don't ride with a stouter heart for that. Indeed my friend
there is a joy in being lost, but a sorrow in being weary.

I don't know whether it is because I know too much—but there seems

[1] The Preface to *Mogreb-el-Acksa*, to be published in December. This letter echoes and
comments on the Preface, which ends with a picture of travellers on the pampas
straining their eyes for a sight of shelter as night comes down.

to me to be a deeper note in this preface than in any of your writings I've seen. But what business have you O! Man! coming with your uncomprehended truth—a thing less than mist but black—to make me sniff at—the stink of the lamp.

Ride on to the tree and to the right—for verily there is a devil at the end of every road. Let us pray to the potbellied gods, to gods with more legs than a centipede and more arms than a dozen windmills, let us pray to them to guard us from the mischance of arriving somewhere. As long as we don't pray to the gods made in man's image we are sure of a most glorious perdition.

Don't know tho! I wouldn't give two pence for all its glory—and I would pray to a god made like a man in the City—and do you know for what? For a little forgetfulness. Say half an hour. Oh bliss. I would give him my soul for it and he would be cheated. To be cheated is godlike. It is your devil who makes good bargains, legends notwithstanding.

Meantime let us look at Soheil[1] and reflect that it is a speck in the eternal night even as we are. Only we don't shine. At least some of us don't. We are as celestial as the other bodies—only we are obscure. At least some of us are. But we all have our illusion of being wayfarers. No more than Soheil, amigo! The appointed course must be run. Round to the left or round to the right what matters if it is a circle. Ask Soheil. And if you get an answer I shall with my own hands give you a piece of the moon. Ever Yours

J. Conrad.

I've got your short note. Thanks for sending on my papers. Look here! Shorter of the Ill. Lon. News who bought *Rescue* from McClure suddenly decided to put it into the last quarter of the News. Begins in Oct[er]! I thought I had months before me and am caught. The worst is I had advances from McClure. So I must write or burst. It is too awful. Half the book is not written and I have only to 1st Nov[er] to finish it! I could not take a command till December because I am in honour bound to furnish the story to time. Yet to get to sea would be salvation. I am really in a deplorable state, mentally. I feel utterly wretched. I haven't the courage to tackle my work.

---

[1] The Arabic name for Canopus. Graham took as epigraph for *Mogreb* the Arab proverb 'Show me Sohail and I will show you the moon'; he had also written an essay called 'Sohail'.

To R. B. Cunninghame Graham

Text MS Dartmouth; J-A, 1, 246; Watts 103

27 Aug 1898
[Stanford-le-Hope]

Cher et excellentissime.

I have been thinking of You every day and more than once a day.

Garnett just left. He showed me your preface to the Fisher Unwin's volume of Your sketches.[1] We howled with satisfaction over it. Vous êtes tout a fait unique et inimitable.

He read *Aurora* here. He thinks it is simply great. On the other hand he abused you bitterly for spoiling the effects of *Victory*.[2] As he said he had written to you about it I shan't repeat his criticism. Moreover I dissent.

Sometimes I feel deeply distressed. At times a little angry. But I think and think—et la terre tourne. How long O Lord! How Long?[3]

If this miserable planet had perception a soul, a heart, it would burst with indignation or fly to pieces from sheer pity.

I am making desperate efforts to write something. Why the devil did I ever begin. Que tonteria!

I am writing coglionerie[4] while I don't know how the Teufel I am going to live next month. The very sea breeze has an execrable taste. Assez.

Ever Yours

Jph. Conrad.

Mes devoirs très respectueux a Madame Votre Femme. Jess sends her kind regards.

Can't understand Rimbaud at all.[5] You overrate my intelligence. Je ne suis bon qu'a lire Cyrano and such like coglionerie.[6] That's what I am fit for only since I am no longer fit to carry sacks of wheat in a hold. I wish you would come to shoot me.

---

[1] *The Ipané* (1899).

[2] A fulmination touched off by American successes in Cuba: *Westminster Gazette*, 13 July, reprinted in *Thirteen Stories* (1900).

[3] This familiar abbreviation of Psalms 13. 1 originated in Macaulay's *Marriage of Tirzah*.

[4] 'Que tonteria' (Spanish): 'What madness'; 'coglionerie' (Italian, from 'coglioni': 'balls'): 'nonsense'.

[5] Conrad usually disclaimed any ability to read poetry, but in a letter to Blackwood, 8 February 1899, he writes: 'I happen to know Rimbaud's verses.'

[6] Graham had sent him a copy of *Cyrano de Bergerac* (letter of 19 July).

To Helen Sanderson
Text MS Yale; J-A, 1, 246

31 Aug^st 1898
[Stanford-le-Hope]

Dear Mrs Sanderson.

Thanks for your kind and friendly letter. I have been passing through a period of ill health and worries and had no heart to write. It is good of you to remember me.

I am glad of the good news. Of course I will come if you still want me. Don't I want to come! If there is a place I wish to see it is Elstree.

I am in the midst of various difficulties—but the baby is well. He is very large and noisy and (they say) intelligent. He has broken ever so many things—a proof of intelligence indubitably. He has not put anything together yet and it is that I am anxious to see. He is very precious and very objectionable. I want Ted to let me know what is the *very* earliest age a boy may be sent to school—say to Elstree?

The *Rescue* is to appear as a serial in the Illustrated London News—to begin on Oct^er the first and end with the year.[1] This is sprung on me suddenly; I am not ready; the "artist" is in despair; various Jews are in a rage; McClure weeps; threats of cancelling contracts are in the air—it is an inextricable mess. Dates are knocked over like ninepins; proofs torn to rags; copy rights trampled under foot. The last shred of honour is gone—also the last penny. The baby however is well. He is singing a song now. I don't feel like singing—I assure You.

My head feels as if full of sawdust. Of course many people's heads are full of sawdust—the tragic part of the business is in my being aware of it. The man who finds out that apparently innocent truth about himself is henceforth of no use to mankind. Which proves the saving power of illusions.

I am like a tight-rope dancer who in the midst of his performance should suddenly discover that he knows nothing about tight-rope dancing. He may appear ridiculous to the spectators but a broken neck is the result of such untimely wisdom. I am trying to be as serious as I know how—for indeed the matter is serious enough to me.

Still I have till Nov^er the 15th to find out whether I can dance on a tight-rope. That honourable occupation shall engross all my energies—up to that date. Afterwards—the deluge,[2] probably. Should I break my neck I hope You will sometimes remember the acrobat. If his head was

---

[1] Of course, it did not.   [2] 'Après nous le déluge': Mme de Pompadour.

full of sawdust his heart—well we will not talk of his heart since that also must die and turn to dust.

If You catch sight of the brown covers of Blackwood's Magazine (for Sept^er) there is a thing of mine there called Youth: A Narrative[1] and if You have time perhaps You will look at it. I would like You to see it very much. A bit of life—nothing more—not well done—"a small thing—but mine own."[2]

After all—chi lo sa?[3]—perhaps I may yet save neck.* And then won't I inflict myself on all my friends! It shall be a pilgrimage, beginning at Elstree. Received with kindness I shall make myself insupportable out of pure lightness of heart, and shall depart in the midst of rejoicings. It is too good to come to pass I fear!.

Jessie sends her love. She is pretty well and under proper subjection to the baby.

> Believe me dear Mrs Sanderson
> your most affectionate and
> obedient friend and servant.
>> Jph. Conrad.

My immense love to dear old Ted. I shall write to him soon—or at least as soon as I can. I am going to stay with my friend Garnett for a fortnight to do a monstrous heap of work; if a silly novel may be so called.

To H. G. Wells
Text MS Illinois; J-A, 1, 248

> 6th Sept 1898.
> The Cearne.
> Kent Hatch
> N^r Edenbridge[4]

My dear Sir.[5]

I am profoundly touched by your letter—and Lucas[6] whom I expect to see this evening shall have my warmest thanks for his share in procuring me this unexpected piece of real good fortune.

[1] On 30 August, William Blackwood wrote to Conrad: '"Youth" will be a favourite item for Maga's readers this month I expect, and for myself I now look forward to "Jim: A Sketch", which I hope makes good progress' (Blackburn, p. 28).

[2] 'An ill-favoured thing, Sir, but mine own', says Touchstone, *As You Like It*, V.iv.

[3] 'Who knows?' [4] Garnett's address.

[5] Wells (1866–1946) wrote anonymous reviews of *Almayer's Folly* and *An Outcast* for the *Saturday Review*; without knowing his identity, Conrad sent a letter to the author of the second review, thus initiating their friendship.

[6] E. V. Lucas (1868–1936), journalist, essayist, critic, and Garnett's friend.

A few days ago I learned with great concern the news of your illness.[1] It saddened me the more because for the last two years (since your review of the *Outcast* in *S.R* compelled me to think seriously of many things till then unseen)[2] I have lived on terms of close intimacy with you, referring to you many a page of my work, scrutinising many sentences by the light of your criticism. You are responsible for many sheets torn up and also for those that remained untorn and presently meeting your eye have given me the reward of your generous appreciation.

It has been treasured, and if two letters I wrote to you in that time were never sent it is only a further proof of our intimacy. I had obtained so much from you that it was unnecessary to presume further. And, indeed, there was perhaps a deficiency of courage. I am no more valorous than the rest of us. We all like, in our audacities, to feel something solid at our back. Such a feeling is unknown to me. This confession is induced by honesty which You will take for what it is worth. To be dishonest is a dangerous luxury for most of us, I fancy, and I am sure it is so for me.

As to the flaws of "Youth"[3] their existence is indisputable. I felt what you say myself—in a way. The feeling however which induced me to write that story was genuine (for once) and so strong that it poked its way through the narrative (which it certainly defaces) in good many places. I tell you this in the way of explanation simply. Otherwise the thing is unjustifiable.

Looking at your letter so dim in the sunlight, I cannot help thinking what a lucky day it was for me when in 1880 I shipped in the "Palestine".[4] And it was a gloomy rainy day too. Well. Peace to its ashes. Only four years ago poor old Beard[5] ran after me outside the South West India Dock gates. He was a little grayer, a little more twisted and gnarled. He was very grimy and had a chocolate coloured muffler round his throat. He told me he had piloted a foreigner down the North sea. His eyes were perfectly angelic. This is not a sentimental exaggeration but an honest attempt to convey the effect. He was so bent that he was always looking upwards so to speak. In the poky bar of a

---

[1] A kidney abscess: Norman and Jeanne Mackenzie, *H. G. Wells*, pp. 137–8.
[2] Wells (16 May 1896; *Critical Heritage*, pp. 73–6) hailed the 'greatness' in Conrad, but rebuked him for his wordiness: 'his story is not so much told as seen intermittently through a haze of sentences.'
[3] In the September issue of *Blackwood's*.   [4] He sailed on 21 September 1881.
[5] In 'Youth', the narrative of his ill-fated voyage, the *Palestine* became the *Judea*, and the captain became John rather than Elijah Beard.

little pub he told me "Since my wife died I can't rest". He had not been able to snatch her in his arms that time.[1] He said he was glad I "got on" and did not allude to our voyage towards Bankok. I should think he *can* rest where he is now.

Yes. The story should have been ended when you say or perhaps at the next paragraph describing the man sleeping in the boats. I am afraid I am wearying you not a little but it has been such a pleasure to talk to you a bit that I gave rein to my ferocious selfishness—for once. I would like to hear how your recovery progresses and when you are *going back to work*. May it be soon! I—for one— can not have enough of Your work. *You* have done me good. You have been doing me good every day for many months past. Some day You will perhaps deny me—cast me out—but it will be too late. I shall be always yours.

Joseph Conrad.

To Ford Madox Ford
Text MS Yale; Unpublished

29 Sept 1898
Ivy Walls
Stanford-le-Hope
Essex.

Dear Mr. Hueffer.[2]

I've just got back from Glasgow and write without loss of time asking you to conclude the affair with the landlord.[3] I would prefer to be a quarterly tenant; should he wish however to let for a year do not let that small matter stand in the way. This opportunity is a perfect godsend to me. It preserves what's left of my piety and belief in a benevolent

---

[1] When a steamer is about to collide with the *Judea*, Captain Beard scoops up his wife and puts her in the ship's boat.

[2] When he met Conrad, Ford Hermann Madox Hueffer (1873–1939) had published a novel, a biography, a volume of poetry, and several fairy tales. According to Jessie Conrad (*Joseph Conrad and His Circle*, p. 58), whose evidence can be unreliable, the first meeting happened during the visit to the Cranes in February. Otherwise, it happened in early September, when Conrad was staying with the Garnetts; the Hueffers had leased a cottage close by, among the Russian exiles and simple-lifers of 'Dostoevsky Corner'.

On 4 June 1919, Hueffer became Ford Madox Ford, the name by which he is known for his distinguished career as a novelist, memoirist, and editor. No solution to the problem of what to call him can avoid inconsistency. The present editors follow the example of modern scholars such as Mizener and Moser in using the name Ford throughout; his wife (who never carried that name) will be called Elsie Hueffer; and the couple will be called the Hueffers.

[3] Ford was going to sub-let Pent Farm to the Conrads.

Providence and probably also my sanity.[1] I shall run down as soon as I can, after first consulting your convenience by a wire. Say early next week? We would move in directly You leave[2] so as not to have the house standing empty more than a day or two.

If you were to kindly drop me a line just to say it's all right I would recover that serenity becoming a self made philosopher and a pilgrim on the stony path of Art.

Very Faithfully Yours,
Jph. Conrad.

Kind regards from us both to Mrs. Hueffer[3] and compliments to the Lady Christina.

To Edward Garnett
Text MS Sutton; G. 135

29th Sep[t] 1898
[Stanford-le-Hope]

Dearest G.

I got back to-day. Nothing decisive happened in Glasgow; my impression however is that a command will come out of it sooner or later[4]—most likely later, when the pressing need is past and I had found my way on shore. I do not regret having gone. McIntyre is a scientific swell who talks art, knows artists of all kinds—looks after their throats, you know.[5] He has given himself a lot of trouble in my interest and means to hammer away at it till I do get something.

All day with the shipowners and in the evening dinner, phonograph, X rays, talk about *the* secret of the universe and the nonexistence of, so called, matter. The secret of the universe is in the existence of horizontal waves whose varied vibrations are at the bottom of all states of

---

[1] Jessie hated Ivy Walls, and Joseph had gone through a miserable period of depression there. Quite apart from the prospect of congenial literary company in the neighbourhood, the Pent, an eighteenth-century Kentish house at the foot of the South Downs about five miles from Hythe, offered a welcome change of scenery from the forlorn marshes of Essex.

[2] The Hueffers had made a temporary return to the Pent; in their absence, it had been sub-let to Walter Crane, the artist and socialist.

[3] Elsie Martindale had married Ford in May 1894 in spite of vigorous opposition from her father. She was seventeen, and Ford twenty. Their daughter Christina was born 3 July 1897.

[4] Aided and abetted by Graham, Conrad's search for a ship had begun earlier in the year.

[5] Dr John McIntyre (1857–1928), Graham's friend and Conrad's host, one of the first radiologists.

consciousness. If the waves were vertical the universe would be different. This is a truism. But, don't you see, there is nothing in the world to prevent the simultaneous existence of vertical waves, of waves at any angles; in fact there are mathematical reasons for believing that such waves do exist. Therefore it follows that two universes may exist in the same place and in the same time[1]—and not only two universes but an infinity of different universes—if by universe we mean a set of states of consciousness; and note, *all* (the universes) composed of the same matter, *all matter* being only that thing of inconceivable tenuity through which the various vibrations of waves (electricity, heat, sound, light etc.) are propagated, thus giving birth to our sensations—then emotions —then thought. Is that so?

These things I said to the D^r while Neil Munro[2] stood in front of a Röntgen machine[3] and on the screen behind we contemplated his backbone and his ribs. The rest of that promising youth was too diaphanous to be visible. It was so—said the Doctor—and there is no space, time, matter, mind as vulgarly understood, there is only the eternal something that waves and an eternal force that causes the waves—it's not much—and by the virtue of these two eternities exists that Corot and that Whistler in the dining room upstairs (we were in a kind of cellar) and Munro's here writings and your Nigger and Graham's politics and Paderewski's playing (in the phonograph)[4] and what more do you want?

What we wanted (apparently) was more whisky. We got it. Mrs McIntyre went to bed. At one o'clock Munro and I went out into the street. We talked. I had read up the Lost Pibroch[5] which I do think wonderful in a way. We foregathered very much indeed and I believe Munro didn't get home till five in the morning. He turned up next day and burned incense before me, and saw me into the train after a dinner at the Art club (not to speak of the whisky).

This is the true and faithful report of our gestes in Glesga.[6] I returned to the bosom of my family at 1 pm today and wrote to Hueffer at once to clinch the matter (there's no matter) of Pent Farm (which is only a vain

[1] In this encounter with more-or-less modern physics, Watts (pp. 107–8) sees the genesis of *The Inheritors* with its invaders from the Fourth Dimension.
[2] Scottish novelist, story-teller, and Conradian.
[3] An X-ray machine: Röntgen discovered the principle in 1895.
[4] Conrad listened to his compatriot's piano-playing on another recent invention: gramophone discs were first used in 1887.
[5] *The Lost Pibroch* (1896): a collection of stories.
[6] 'Glesga': phonetic rendering; 'gestes': 'deeds'.

and delusive appearance). I hope I may get it. If I don't I shall vanish into space (there's no space) and the vibrations that make up me, shall go to the making of some other fool.

I feel less hopeless about things and particularly about the damned thing called *the Rescue*. Tomorrow I write but this evening I feel merry. When I feel sure of Pent Farm I shall be comparatively happy.

If we get fixed there you must come and stay with us a good long time when your wife is in France. This is what I am looking forward to now. Look ever forward, ever forward. What a sell! For me to look forward is folly—but then it's good. Don't you throw cold water on my vision. There's no reason why you should. We shall work. By heavens and earth we shall work!

We three send our love to you three.

Ever yours

Jph. Conrad

To T. Fisher Unwin

Text MS Texas; Unpublished

2^d Oct 1898
[Stanford-le-Hope]

Dear Mr Unwin.

Very many thanks for the copies of agreement, which are to day to hand. Sorry for the trouble I gave You.

Faithfully Yours

Jph. Conrad.

To Ford Madox Ford

Text MS Yale; *Listy* 143; Original unpublished

Stanford-le-Hope
Essex.
2^d Oct 1898.

My dear Mr Hueffer.

I am very much concerned to hear your body is making itself so objectionable to you.[1] It is very good of you to write at lenght* and I am immensely pleased at the arrangement. Pray do not think of shortening Your stay on my account.[2] My nerves are simply ridiculous, and not

---

[1] Ford had an eye infection.
[2] The Hueffers had moved back to the Pent for a few weeks; afterwards, they were to go back to Gracie's Cottage, near Limpsfield, where their lease ran until March.

deserving of deference. I am, of course, cowed, but I *think* of them with contempt.

As you mention 3 weeks we shall take it that in the usual course of things we may move in after the 25th of October, and shall be ready to migrate by that date. If You wish for any reason to remain longer we can put it off since our tenancy here expires only in December.

Nothing could suit me better than to have you for my landlord. I only hope you won't find me too objectionable. Your wife's suggestion[1] is lovely and excellent whether derived from the Romans or not. Why should I be alarmed? I had in years gone by a certain reputation for courage. Now, no doubt, all this is changed the spirit being brushed out of me by the tyranny of mysterious sensations, yet still a spark, a dim spark exists somewhere—a vestige of the old fire under the tepid ruins. And in any case I could not look upon you as an invading enemy.

I hope that whenever we leave Pent Farm for a time You shall step in as a matter of course; and the time also could be arranged to suit both our tribes.

I shall make my appearance before many days to have a preliminary look around. Should you have coals or such things in store we could take them over from You—perhaps?

What is it about Your eyes? It sounds so very serious. Is it something you have experienced before? I put these questions but I don't want to give you the trouble of writing—really. I shall no doubt turn up next week.

With our kind regards faithfully
yours

Jph. Conrad.

To E. L. Sanderson
Text MS Yale; Unpublished

Stanford-le-Hope
3ᵈ Oct 98

My dearest Ted

Jack[2] has been here and tells me Your wife has been ill, he thinks rather seriously. Do send me news. I understood him to say she was getting better. I want to hear the confirmation of this from you.

I am like a wounded animal—withdrawing from my kind from a sense of my own weakness. How absurd and even wicked it is I know well,

---

[1] That they might sometimes stay with the Conrads.   [2] Galsworthy.

since I've experienced nothing but kindness even from those who may be regarded as strangers. Towards you, of whom I am sure, I am inexcusable, but then don't you see I am so sure that I do not even attempt to excuse myself. I may only tell you this is not a case for anger (not that I think You are angry) but for (horrid word) compassion.

Tell me about you all. It can be done in very few lines. The story of my purgatorial experiences cannot be so shortly told so I don't begin.[1] I would like to know I am not cast out tho'.

Ever Yours

Jph. Conrad.

To ? [an American admirer]
Text MS Rosenbach; Unpublished

4th Oct^{er} 98
[Stanford-le-Hope]

Dear Sir.[2]

Thanks for your appreciation. Besides the two books you mention I have published last year a study of sea and seamen entitled "Children of the Sea" *A tale of the Forecastle* published by Messrs Dodd Mead & C° and early this year a volume of short stories called "Tales of Unrest" published by Messrs: Scribners—I think.

My next book which shall appear serially in the US very soon (I don't know in what periodicals) is a Romance of the shallows called the *Rescue*.

It will come out as book at the end of next year under the imprint of the S. S Maclure* P[ublishin]g C° of New York.

You have here the complete information You seek. Pardon a busy man for not enlarging upon the pleasure of hearing from one of his readers, and believe me very faithfully Yours

Jph. Conrad.

To Ford Madox Ford
Text MS Yale; Unpublished

Thursday 6th Oct 98
[Stanford-le-Hope]

Dear Mr. Hueffer.

Here I am again. May I descend on You tomorrow Friday some time in the afternoon and stay till Sat midday?

---

[1] He had written to Helen Sanderson on 31 August. Since then, he had continued to worry about debts and the halting progress of work that could pay some of them off.

[2] Use of *The Nigger*'s American title affords the only clue to the recipient's identity.

I reckon You will get this about 9 am. If you want to stop me please wire Conrad % Editorship London.[1]

If I get nothing by noon I shall come on without fear.

With infinite apologies to Mrs Hueffer and less so to you I am yours faithfully.

Jph. Conrad.

To Edward Garnett
Text G. 138

Sunday [9 October 1898][2]
[Stanford-le-Hope]

My dear Edward,

I am very anxious to see the horrors of the *Academy*.[3] You are a dear old generaliser. I fancy you've generalised me into a region of such glory that no mortal henceforth will succeed in finding me in my work. However this letter is not written for the purpose of abusing you but strange as it may seem—on business which may concern you.

I went on Friday to Pent Farm. On my way I called on Robert McClure[4] whom I had not seen since the letter and telegram I showed you—as you may remember. He insisted upon feeding me and, while we chewed, the conversation which turned upon famous criminals of history by some strange association of ideas reached your name. Robert must have heard of you from Pawling—or rather *about* you—and wanted to know more. Then by gradations too subtle to record he came out plainly with his desire to make your acquaintance. He means something. I am pretty sure he has some definite idea in his mind. What it is I don't know—but I encouraged it all I could for this reason that anything I may have said not engaging you by any possibility yet gave him the notion that you were open at any rate to listen to any proposal he might make. I wish I may be shot if I don't think he wants to carry you off from Unwin.[5] However that may be he asked me whether I could bring you two together—dinner or something. I told him it could be done almost any Thursday or Friday in the week. I don't suppose you can have any

---

[1] The telegraphic address of McClure's London office.

[2] The mention of visiting the Pent (see letter to Ford, 6 October) confirms Garnett's dating.

[3] See first letter to Garnett, 12 October.

[4] The youngest brother of Samuel S. McClure, whose *Magazine* and syndicate were powerful forces in turn-of-the-century publishing.

[5] Unwin dismissed Garnett at the end of 1899; his next employer was S. S. Pawling at Heinemann's.

objection to meeting McClure—a very decent little chap. You know how well he behaves to me. He is quite in earnest. At parting he told me "I have a matter of business to bring before him" or words to that effect, the word *business* being pronounced. Upon that I said I would arrange the thing. As my train went off he shouted "don't forget" about Garnett?—Now when, how, do you wish it to come off? If you do wish? I think there's no possible harm. Could we manage a lunch on next Friday or Friday after next.[1] I want to officiate and it would be more convenient for me to make it a lunch instead of a dinner because of the wretched trains. Drop me a line and then I shall know what to say to McClure.

—I like Pent. It will do. We're going there for the 26th.—Ford tells me you don't like the place. I hope tho' you like me well enough to come and stay. I fancy I'll get on there all right. I always hope. Oh well.

Ever yours
Conrad

To H. G. Wells

Text MS Illinois; J-A, 1, 249

11th Oct 98[2]
Stanford-le-Hope
Essex.

My dear Mr Wells.

I am writing in a state of jubilation at the thought we are going to be nearer neighbours than I dared to hope a fortnight ago. We are coming to live in Pent farm which is only a mile or so from Sandling Junction.[3] The other day I met Pugh[4] who told me you are much better and in good spirits. We render thanks to Eshmûn the Liberator the same who in the country of the Greeks is called Aesculapius[5] and we pour, after the Ph[o]enician manner, a libation of clear water out of a glass cup for our means do not run to a cup of gold. As to sacrifices of goats, bulls, lambs and pigs these are for kings or rich merchants to be offered on altars of temples with priests and ceremonies—but when we meet (soon—let us hope) we shall offer up a piece of ox-flesh on the altar of domestic gods and partake of the holy viands according to prescribed rites in gratitude for Your return to health and work.

[1] 14 or 21 October.   [2] Jean-Aubry misreads the date as September.
[3] The Pent is about five miles from Sandgate, where Wells was living at 2 Beach Cottages.
[4] Edwin Pugh (1874–1930), novelist of London life.
[5] In Sidon and in Carthage, the god of health was Eshmun. Conrad echoes the beginning of Flaubert's *Salammbô*.

I am still wretched and ashamed of what I am doing and only the hope that you all for whose opinion I care will forgive me for the sake of what went before, gives me the courage to struggle on. We take up our residence at Pent on the 26th of this month and I shall wander out your way soon after that date. Always faithfully yours

Jph. Conrad.

To David Meldrum
Text MS Duke; Blackburn 29

12th Oct. 98.
Stanford le Hope
Essex.

Dear Mr Meldrum.

That was a good and kind letter you wrote and I ought to have answered at once. But I seldom do things I ought; if I did I would be a better man, by a long sight.

Jessie's and my thanks to you and Mrs Meldrum for the invitation which delighted us. The state of affairs however is this.

We leave here on the 26th of this month to go to another farm house but this time in Kent. My new address will be *Pent Farm Postling. Stanford N^r Hythe.*

I got it from a man called Hueffer a grandson of Madox Brown and nephew to D.G. Rossetti. He is an exceedingly decent chap who lets me have the thing awfully cheap. Besides the whole old place is full of rubbishy relics of Browns and Rossettis.[1] There's Brown's first picture, likewise that of Dante Gabriel; Christina Rossetti's writing table which I intend to profane by my own wretched MSS.—and so on. It's a great · solitude about a mile and quarter from Sandling Junction Station on S[outh] E[eastern] R[ailway] and within 3 miles (by road) of Hythe. Chalk soil and a vast view on the valley of the Stour.

What with this and having no one to leave our precious baby with I don't see how we could avail ourselves of Your invitation very soon. But we lay it back carefully in our memory for use at the very earliest opportunity. Now we are unsettled and soon we shall be still more unsettled till we shake into our new place. And then I must write with

[1] Ford grew up in a Pre-Raphaelite clan that included Ford Madox Brown (who painted his grandson as the son of William Tell) and the Rossettis; one of Ford's aunts was married to William Michael Rossetti, brother of Christina and Dante Gabriel. At the start of his tenancy, Ford had returned the Pent 'to its original antique condition of great rafters and huge ingles' (Mizener, p. 36).

fear at my back and ruin before me if I don't make good time. The Rescue begins in first April's issue of the Ill*d* Lond. News to run 3 months.[1]

The people in Edinburgh did their little best to ruin me because the delay of sending proof of *Youth* to McClure made the copyrighting of that story fall through[2] and the Atlantic Monthly which was going to publish it cancelled the arrangement in consequence. However it's past, no use lamenting and for *Jim* I shall have a duplicate copy typewritten to make sure.

I called on you last Friday with the intention to carry You off to lunch with McClure but was told You weren't in town at all. Better luck next time. With very kind regards from us both I am always faithfully yours

Jph. Conrad.

PS As soon as the decks of our new ship are cleared you must come and affront the hardships of our household on a Saturday to Monday expedition. And if the weather is clement and Mrs Meldrum has the courage I trust we shall have the great pleasure of seeing her with you. *Miss Meldrum too.*[3] There is a spare cot, and it's high time Borys was introduced to ladies of his own age. I'll be writing to you soon.

To Edward Garnett
Text MS Colgate; G. 140

Wednesday [12 October 1898][4]
[Stanford-le-Hope]

Dearest Edward.

It is magnificent.[5] I can't conceive how You could find in me the source of such vibrating, tender and illuminating utterance. I can't conceive but I can accept. It is absorbingly interesting to me not as

---

[1] The plan fell through.
[2] Later, Conrad blamed McClure (letter to Blackwood, 31 December 1898). 'Youth' was published in New York in the *Outlook*, 1 October.
[3] Elizabeth A. S. Meldrum, born 1 March 1897.
[4] This letter must come between that of 9 October and the publication of Garnett's 'Mr. Joseph Conrad' in the 18 October *Academy*. The second letter is obviously the promised sequel.
[5] Garnett's unsigned appreciation was the first general survey of Conrad's work in the English press (but see the letter to Blackwood, 13 December). Conrad's 'faculty of seeing man's life in relation to the seen and unseen forces of Nature … is pre-eminently the poet's gift, and is very rarely conjoined with insight into human nature and a power of conceiving character. When the two gifts come together we have the poetic realism of the great Russian novels. Mr. Conrad's art is true realism of that high order.'

appreciation of myself but as disclosure of you. And I appear to myself wrapped in the glamour of Your intention—not of what has been done, but of what should be done, what should be tried for, what should be desired—what cannot be attained.

I send back the proof without more words because I feel I can't arrange them into an artistic expression of gratitude—not for what You say but for what You feel. But I am very proud of what You feel and also a little humiliated. There is likewise a grim delight in the thought that now You have spoken you can't take it back—never—never.

Ever Yours

Conrad.

I wire to McClure and shall write You tonight where and when we meet.

To Edward Garnett

Text MS Colgate; G. 141

Stanford-le-Hope

Wednesday [12 October 1898]

Dearest G.

I propose that little (Hotel d'Italie?)[1] shop at the back of Palace Music Hall where they have tolerable Asti. The time to be 1.15 pm. Say first floor—or still better private room. I know they've got one. You shall be there first no doubt and if so pray use your judgment. If the public room on 1st floor is crowded retain the *cabinet*—if not, retain a table good for three. Or if you think privacy desirable you had better retain the *cabinet* in any case. I shall bring Mac along which probably may detain me a little. If place does not commend itself to you write at once proposing something more suitable. There is however no need to be ceremonious with Mac and the food if I remember rightly is tolerable in that gargotte[2]—We mustn't pamper editors (this is a joke). I've destroyed all I did write last month but my brain feels alive and my heart is not afraid now. Permanent state?—who knows. Always hope.

Ever Yours

Jph Conrad.

Write pc to say you got this all right.

---

[1] 52 Old Compton Street.   [2] *Une gargote*: a cheap eating-house.

To the Hon. A. E. Bontine

Text MS Castle; J-A, 1, 250

16th Oct^{er} 1898.
Stanford-le-Hope
Essex.

Dear Mrs Bontine[1]

I need not tell you with what pleasure I've read your letter so full of that kind of appreciation for which the author's heart yearns and so seldom obtains; and thanks being mostly ineffective I will not enlarge on my sentiments of gratitude. The com[m]endation of your son Charles is very precious to me. He can appreciate the intention and also the *detail* of my work.[2] His praise has an especial significance to me, for, though no two lives could have been more dissimilar, there is between us that subtle and strong bond of the sea—the common experience of aspects of sky and water—of the sensations, emotions and thoughts that are in greater or lesser degree the companions of men who live upon the ocean. Perhaps you would let him know my feelings lamely expressed above. I would have written direct had I not been held back by the thought he is a busy man—and a sailor—and in this double capacity no doubt averse to increasing his correspondence.

My last letter from Robert was from Tangier, the day after he landed. I can well understand your anxiety. Want of water and wild tribes are dangers but the absolute magnitude of such perils depends in a great measure upon the man who affronts them. Robert is courageous and foresighted. He has also experience. With his qualities and knowledge he is not likely to proceed rashly. Firmness and tact—which he possesses—go a long way towards minimizing the danger from wild tribes. The scarcity of water means privation and a call upon endurance, perhaps, but not necessarily serious danger. I have the greatest confidence in his management and in the success of his journey. We shall get news—and good news—soon, I think.[3]

"Higginson's dream" is super-excellent.[4] It is much too good to remind me of any of my work, but I am immensely flattered to learn you discern some points of similitude. Of course I am in complete sympathy

---

[1] The Hon. Mrs Bontine (née Fleeming, 1828–1925) was R. B. Cunninghame Graham's widowed mother. Of Scottish Whig and Spanish parentage, she lived in London, taking a well-informed interest in politics and the arts.

[2] Charles Cunninghame Graham (1853–1917), naval officer and inspector of lifeboats.

[3] On Robert's visit to Morocco the previous year, he had been imprisoned by a local chieftain.

[4] *Saturday Review*, 1 October: a story of colonial squalor in the South Seas.

with the point of view. For the same accomplishment in expression I can never hope—and Robert is too strong an individuality to be influenced by any one's writing. He desired me to correct the proofs but the *Sat. Rev* people did *not* send me the proofs. I am very much annoyed for there is a misprint which makes nonsense of a French phrase. I wrote them reproachfully when sending the MS of "Pulperia"[1] which I did four days ago, and now I clear my character before you as Robert's literary representative.

To your kind inquiries about my wife and boy I am lucky enough to say they are both very well. In fact Jessie is better than she has been for some time. We are leaving Stanford-le-Hope on the 26 Oct*er* for good. Our new residence is also a farm-house in Kent, near Hythe, and thus near the sea though not absolutely in sight of it. I have no ship (but I still have la nostalgie de la mer) though Robert has really done almost the impossible for me. I did take a run to Glasgow for a day and saw Dr McIntyre[2] who was kindness itself. I am afraid nothing will come of it. Il y a trop de tirage, from novel writing to the command of a ship, I fear. Moreover I am tied just now by my engagements to American and English publishers—engagements I failed lamentably to keep through nervous ill-health and I can't think of going away till I've liberated myself from the incubus of that horrid novel I am trying to write now. Early next year, when the torment is over, (and I am hardly able to realise that such a time will ever come) I will without scruple use and abuse everybody's good will, influence, friendship to get back on the blue water. I am by no means happy on shore.

The fact is that in the Academy photograph it is not my clothes that are endimanchés but my face[3]—the artistic! photographer's aim being always to obliterate every trace of individuality in his subject—so as to make a *respectable* picture. "Voilà. La bêtise etant respectable" he did not obliterate that. "Je trouve que j'ai l'air idiot la dedands".[4] But the notice is sympathetic and not commonplace. The man who wrote it is Edward Garnett a great and discriminating admirer not only of Robert's work but of his personality which he—in a measure— understands. This cannot be said of many men (especially literary men) in England.

I do not know whether I outrage "les règles de la bienséance" by

[1] 'La Pulperia', 16 October: both pieces reappeared in *Thirteen Stories* (1900).
[2] Robert's friend, the radiologist.
[3] Conrad with a Sunday-best expression: in the picture accompanying Garnett's article, 18 October.
[4] 'There. Stupidity being respectable ... I think I look absurd in there'.

writing such a long letter. If so you must forgive me in consideration of
my answer to your first letter having been telegraphic. I did not do it for
the sake of conciseness however. I was from home when your letter
arrived and on my return knowing you were about to start on a journey I
wished my answer to find you at home yet. If this excuse is not valid then
by invoking the name of the absent I am sure to be pardonned.* Since I
learned it was you who first put my work before Robert I consider I owe
to you alone one of the most fortunate events of my life—and these are
not numerous. With such a thought and such an obligation a purely
ceremonious attitude is impossible. Thence the "abandon" in the
matter of the lenght* of this letter. I promise however not to sin very
often.

I have grievously sinned towards your nephew. He gave me in the
kindest way an invitation to call on him, which I promised to do and did
not do. It is not so much through my fault as it may look. I beg for your
intercession in getting my "pardon" for what looks like unexcusable
negligence. May I be permitted to keep the invitation for future use—as
soon as possible. I have been worried horribly and I have not been well
at all. I am haunted by the idea I cannot write—I dare say a very correct
idea it is too. The harm is in its haunting me. For the last six months I've
not known a minute's real peace of mind. "Enfin! On se fait a tout." I
got* hardened now—"mais j'ai eu des bien mauvais moments".[1] With
many thanks for remembering me I beg you to believe me, dear Mrs
Bontine, your most faithful and obedient servant

Jph. Conrad.

To W. E. Henley
Text MS Morgan; Baines 217

Stanford-le-Hope Essex.
18 Oct 98

Dear Mr Henley.[2]

I don't know how to thank You for your letter. I don't know how to
begin. I won't begin. I shall accept my good fortune "sans phrases", but
I would have answered yesterday, by return, had I not been in the midst
of concocting a letter to the "Times" about the "Mohegan" affair.

---

[1] 'Well! One gets used to everything ... but I have had some quite bad moments.'
[2] William Ernest Henley (1847–1903), poet, critic, and editor, published the serial
version of *The Nigger* in his *New Review*.

Whether they will print I don't know.[1] I have relieved my feelings by firing off three thousand words. I've never worked so fast with pen and ink before, and I wouldn't stop, feeling that if I did I would never take up the job again. The difficulty to keep swear words out of that communication was very great. There were also other difficulties. That of writing at all is always the greatest with me.

I have meditated your letter. The line of your argument has surprised me. R. L. S.—Dumas—these are big names and I assure You it had never occurred to me they could be pronounced in connection with my plan to work with Hueffer.[2] But You have judged proper to pronounce them and I am bound to look seriously at that aspect of the matter. When talking with Hueffer my first thought was that the man there who couldn't find a publisher had some good stuff to use and that if we worked it up together my name, probably, would get a publisher for it. On the other hand I thought that working with him would keep under the particular devil that spoils my work for me as quick as I turn it out (that's why I work so slow and break my word to publishers), and that the material being of the kind that appeals to my imagination and the man being an honest workman we could turn out something tolerable— perhaps; and if not he would be no worse off than before. It struck me the expression he cared for was in verse;[3] he has the faculty; I have not; I reasoned that partnership in prose would not affect any chances he may have to attain distinction—of the real kind—in verse. It seemed to me that a man capable of the higher form could not care much for the lower. These considerations encouraged me in my idea. It never entered my head I could be dangerous to Hueffer in the way you point out. The affair had a material rather than an artistic aspect for me. It would give—I reflected—more time to Hueffer for tinkering at his verses; for digging hammering, chiselling or whatever process by which that mysterious thing—a poem—is shaped out of that barren thing—inspiration. As for myself I meant to keep the right to descend into my own private little hell—whenever the spirit moved me to do that foolish

---

[1] They did not. On 14 October, the S. S. *Mohegan* had gone off course and smashed against the Manacles reef. The crew's bravery was greater than its skill; since the lifeboats were not readied in time, only a few passengers were saved. Because of his work on *Lord Jim*, Conrad would have been even more aroused than the average sailor by this case of ineptitude and inexperience.

[2] Since 1896, Ford had been at work on 'Seraphina', a tale of Caribbean piracy. Conrad's offer to help him resulted in *Romance* (1903). Henley had had his own experience of collaboration—with Robert Louis Stevenson, one of the two names he had invoked as masters of the adventure story.

[3] Ford had published his first volume of poetry in 1893; a second came out in 1900.

thing—and produce alone from time to time—verbiage no doubt—my own—therefore very dear.

This is the truth—the whole truth. Now of course all this looks otherwise. Were I a Dumas I would eat up Hueffer without compunction. Was it you who called the old man "a natural force"? He was *that*; and a natural force need not be scrupulous. Not being *that* I must navigate cautiously at this juncture lest my battered, ill-ballasted craft should run down a boat with youth at the helm and hope at the prow[1]—pursuing shapes—shapes. I know a man who at the end of a long talk was moved to tell me—"You don't seem to have a conception of what Sin is." Perhaps not! but it seems to me it would be sinful to sink Hueffer's boat which for all I know may be loaded with splendid gems or delicate roses—and all for my private ends. No. I shall not go mad and bite him—at least not without a fair warning. If I do speak at all I shall recite to him faithfully the substance of your letter—that is if he does not kick me out before we get so far. If he does he shall never know he had the high fortune to occupy Your thought for an appreciable space of time. He will miss a fine chance for gratitude. I—thanks to Pawling— haven't missed mine.[2]

And this brings me to what was in my mind all the time when writing this, for months before, not only in my mind—a poor habitation—but in me, from the crown of my head to the tips of my fingers. That I've during the last year composed, walking up and down my room (a quarter-deck habit) several letters to you need not be an alarming intelligence. I've forgotten them—and it is well. Words blow away like mist, and like mist they serve only to obscure, to make vague the real shape of one's feelings. I have let out some of these words before Edwin Pugh at one o'clock in the morning before the steps of the Mansion House[3] and— since nothing is lost in this world—they may be knocking about yet amongst the stones. He said, I remember, "You're with me; the best—the kindest"—well "we will let it go at that" as the Baboo in Kipling's tale of "The finest Story in the World" says.[4] It has been a fine story to me; so fine that I have suddenly regretted the years gone by, regretted not being young when the future seems as vast as all eternity and the story could go on without end; so fine—you are to understand—

---

[1] 'Youth on the prow, and Pleasure at the helm': Thomas Gray, 'The Bard'.
[2] Pawling made the contact between Conrad and Henley.
[3] In the heart of the City of London, official home of the Lord Mayor.
[4] Kipling's story about authorship, the sea, and reincarnation (in *Many Inventions*, 1893) begins with a four-line quotation from Henley's *Echoes*.

that when it comes to setting it down the gods of life say nay and one can only mutter "no doubt—but the door is shut."[1]

And what you say of "Youth" is part, another line, of my "Finest Story in the World." Yes—but the door is shut. Were I to write and talk till Doomsday you would never really know what it all means to me. You would not know because You never had just the same experience. Therein I have the advantage of you and I shall hug this incredible, amazing, fabulous precious advantage with both hands, I shall hug it as long as I can grip anything at all "in this valley."[2] A chance comes once in life to all of us. Not the chance to get on; that only comes to good men. Fate is inexorably just. But Fate also is merciful and even to the poorest there comes sometimes the chance of an intimate, full, complete and pure satisfaction. That chance comes to me when you accepted the *Nigger*. I've got it, I hold it, I keep it, and all the machinations of my private devil cannot rob me of it. No man, either, can do ought* against it. Even you, yourself, have no power. You have given it and it is out of your hands.

This last reflexion is prompted not by impudence but by a less useful and a shade more honourable sentiment. I ask myself sometimes whether you know exactly what you have given, to whom, how much. But I love to think that if You perceive the shade of meaning within these lines you will not—perhaps—regret your gift—whatever happens to morrow or the day after.

Satis. Enough words. The postman will carry away this letter, the mist shall blow away and in the morning I shall discern clearly what to-night I am trying to interpret into writing—which remains. Let it remain, to show with what thundering kick the gods of life shut the door between our feeling and its expression. It is the old tale, the eternal grievance. If it were not for the illusion of the open door—sometimes— we would all be dumb, and it wouldn't matter, for no one would care to listen.

I've run on trying to tell you something and haven't told you how concerned I am at the news of your ill-health.[3] Had I know I would have been still more appalled when Pawling told me he had sent my letter to you. I never dreamt of his doing that. I am very glad, inexpressibly glad though not a little remorseful, now I know the full extent of your generosity. If I could honestly think myself worth your trouble it is to

---

[1] The door between present and previous lives: Conrad quotes the Indian student in the story.
[2] Of the shadow?   [3] Henley suffered from a tubercular leg.

You I would turn for advice, with perfect confidence with certain trust. And for what You have given I am honestly grateful I am faithfully and affectionately grateful.

Jph. Conrad

To Ford Madox Ford

Text MS Yale; *Listy* 148; Original unpublished

Thursday. [20 October 1898]¹
[Stanford-le-Hope]

Honoured and Dear Landlord.

The time approaches for me to step in amongst your relics. That you do feel the impending desecration I do not doubt. Let me exhort you to be a man, and bear up—they are not lost—only left behind. You must be unselfish (it's our *duty* to be so) and in the midst of your sorrow be consoled by the thought that *I* (a fellow creature with a soul and sensibilities) am very happy.

Ethel² and I shall leave London at 11 am on Wednesday. We shall have a heavy breakfast-lunch in London. I mention this for I do not wish Mrs Hueffer to undertake the slightest trouble on our account. We are both most grateful to Her for Her efforts to get us a servant. If there's one of any kind to be got I beg she may be engaged if her wages are anything less than £100 per month. I engage myself never to address her but bareheaded and with the signs of the most profound respect. We cheerfully agree to call her Miss or Your Ladyship—or Your Majesty. We don't stick at trifles. We are puir, servant-ridden fules—Heaven help us!

If there be no girl perhaps Mrs Nash could be bribed to come on Wednesday and also on Thursday when Jess arrives? And could you order the funereal animal with a vehicle attached to meet our train on Wednesday? I don't know the address of the man who keeps him, but if he be difficult to get at from Pent please send me same on scrap of paper and I shall wire to him.

I understand it still holds good You do not leave till some time in the afternoon. Perhaps if the day is fine (when in doubt consult the prophet) you could instruct the carriage man to call at Pent first, and Mr, Mrs & Miss Hueffer could drive out to meet us; in that way as we drive back Your Wife could with less trouble point out to Ethel the places where

---

¹ Conrad's intention of moving in on Wednesday, 26 October, places this letter.

² Jessie Conrad's younger sister.

milk is to be got for that precious baby and eggs for his precious papa
—but enough! I am overcome by the magnitude of the interests of
which I treat!

There are also other interests—not mentioned here. No room. They
are big, big. Fact is I would be glad of a quiet half-hour with you. I've a
word for your ear. Hist! Mystery! Silence! Codlin's your friend—not
Short.[1]

I hope you are better You are well in mind and body—same thing
tho'.

I beg to be remembered to Mrs Hueffer. My wife sends her kind
regards. All our loves to Christina.

> Faithfully Yours,
>
> Jph. Conrad

still in Stanford-le-Hope, Essex
PS I've read Two Magics Henry James's last.[2] The first story is all there.
He extracts an intellectual thrill out of the subject. The second is
unutterable rubbish. Quite a shock to one of the faithful.

To Ford Madox Ford
Text MS Yale; Unpublished

> Friday [21 October 1898][3]
> [Stanford-le-Hope]

My dear Hueffer

Just had your note. We had been all along under the impression it was
the *26th.* I think I said 26th at any rate I was so much under the
impression I had said it that we did act upon that impression.

I am afraid we cant put off our departure from here, the van arrangements being made. So Ethel and I are coming on the 26th.

But suppose you stay on? May I get a room in the village? While Ethel
can be stowed away in Pent. Jess is coming on the 27th. If you write us to
that effect she may stay one day longer in London. The furniture won't
be there till the 29th I suppose.

Let me know how You decide.

> Faithfully Yours
>
> Conrad.

[1] 'Codlin's the friend, not Short': advice from *The Old Curiosity Shop.*
[2] *The Two Magics* (1898) included 'The Turn of the Screw' and 'Covering End'.
[3] Date from the sequence of events.

To John Galsworthy
Text MS Forbes; J-A, 1, 252

Pent Farm. Postling.
Stanford nr Hythe.
28 Oct 98.

My dear Jack.

Thanks for your letter and the cheque for £10 for which let this letter be an acknowledgment.

I turned to You confidently. Your words of cheer are more valuable than all the money in the world—they help one to live—while the money enables one only to exist. And yet one must exist before one can even begin to live.

I feel pretty hopeful—not extravagantly so, which is rather a good sign than otherwise.

I concluded arrangement for collaboration with Hueffer.[1] He was pleased. I think it's all right. Details when we meet.

The first letter in my new home was from You, and you must be the first visitor—the first friend under the new roof

Ever Yours

Jph. Conrad

Jessie's kind regards.

To Cora Crane
Text MS Columbia; Stallman 191

Pent Farm. Postling
Stanford
N^r Hythe.
28th Oct 98.

My dear Mrs Crane.

Just a word in haste to tell you I shall try to do what I can. Don't build any hopes on it. It is a *most* remote chance—but it's the only thing I can think of.[2]

---

[1] On 'Seraphina', the inchoate origin of *Romance*.
[2] During the summer and autumn, Cora Crane was tortured by anxiety. While English publishers plagiarised his work, Stephen was in Cuba, but none of his letters reached her. Instead, she heard a babble of rumours: he was dying, imprisoned, had vanished, had run away to California with a general's wife. Meanwhile, Harold Frederic had died and Kate Lyon Frederic, a Christian Scientist, had been charged with his manslaughter by neglect. Cora took in their children and, despite her own near-destitution, was trying to raise money for Kate Frederic's defence. (See Gilkes, *Cora Crane*, pp. 150–64.)

What kind of trouble is Stephen in? You made me very uneasy. Are you *sure* you can bring him back. I don't doubt your influence mind! but not knowing the circumstances I do not know how far it would be feasible. In Stephen's coming back to England is *salvation* there is no doubt about that.

Will he come? *Can* he come? I am utterly in the dark as to the state of affairs.

We recognise your good heart in your acts. God forbid that we should throw the first—or even the last stone. What the world calls *scandal* does not affect me in the least.[1] My sincere approval and high recognition of the course You've taken is not based on Christian grounds. I do not pretend to that name—not from irreverence but from my exalted idea of that faith's morality. I can't pretend to such morality but I hold that those that *do* pretend and boast of it should *carry it out* at the *cost of personal sacrifice*, and in *every respect*. My admiration of your courageous conduct exists side by side with an utter disapproval of those whom You (in your own extremity) befriend.[2] They invoke the name of a faith and they've dragged its substance pretty well through the mud. It may be only folly—of course—unutterable *folly*. But it looks worse. The only Christian in sight in this whole affair is you, my dear Mrs Crane—exercising that rarest of the Creed's virtues: that of charity.

I would not have said all this but your good friendly letter, I consider, has in a sense authorised me to speak.

I would of course have done what you wish without a moment's delay but the exact truth is I've only £8 in the bank and am in debt to publishers so heavily that I can't go to them for more. Or else I would do it, believe me. I've tried however to do something but *don't reckon on it* and do not relax your efforts in other directions. I am a poor business man and can't give you any hints as to raising money on life insurance. Couldn't Stokes advise you?[3]

Jess shall write to morrow. I will let You know shortly (I hope) whether my plan has been of any good. Affectionately and faithfully Yours

Jph. Conrad.

Having just heard that Stephen had been found in a dingy Havana rooming-house, Cora Crane turned to Conrad. As the following letters show, he intended to ask Blackwood for a loan on her behalf.

[1] Among possible scandals were the alleged affair with General Chaffee's wife and Crane's visit to Washington to see an old lover, Lily Brandon Munroe. It is also possible that Conrad may have learned the truth about Cora and Stephen's liaison.

[2] Several clergymen had taken up the Frederic case.

[3] Either John Scott-Stokes, a wealthy admirer of Crane's work, or Frederic A. Stokes, who later published some of his poems and stories.

To Cora Crane

Text MS Columbia; Stallman 192

1ˢᵗ Nov 98.
[Pent Farm]

Dear Mrs. Crane.

Yours to hand. That's what I am doing; trying to get at B'wood. I took Mʳ Meldrum into our confidence.[1] He is an admirer of Stephen. What you say about your husband is golden truth.

To B'wood I suggested a loan of £50 on three securities. *One* (for which they would care most) *Stephen's work second* Your property *third* my own undertaking to furnish them copy to the amount advanced should unforeseen circumstances prevent you and Stephen from paying him back as soon as he may expect.

We must approach B'wood through Meldrum who is *most* friendly. B'wood himself is a good, kind man but must be handled cautiously. It is better done through me and Meldrum. How it will turn out it is impossible to say. It will also require time. I am writing to M. again this post.

Before you give *bill of sale* on furniture *make sure* the furniture dealer or dealers (from whom You bought) are paid *in full* as in the contrary case you would make Yourself liable to prosecution.

My letter to Stephen was sent through *Reynolds*.[2]

I am sure you are doing and planning for the best. That is the way to rescue poor Stephen. I only wish I had something to pawn or sell; you would not have to wait long for means. As it is I have only my work and that I've offered to B'wood for what it is worth.

Most faithfully Yours

Conrad.

Jessie sends lots of love. She is very much concerned and anxious about your health.

---

[1] Blackburn reproduces Meldrum's letter to Blackwood of 30 November (pp. 31–3). Meldrum warned Blackwood that Crane (who had had £60 on account earlier in the year) was 'far more foolish than you know'. Conrad's proposal to raise £75 or £100 against his next volume of short stories, a bill of sale on the Crane's furniture, and the rights to Crane's next story had not been placed before Blackwood. However, Meldrum had offered to borrow money from his own friends and on his own security: 'chiefly I wished to oblige Conrad whom I admire as a writer and like as a man, and wished to keep attached to the House'.

[2] Paul Revere Reynolds, the literary agent.

To Cora Crane

Text MS Columbia; Stallman 193

Thursday [3? November 1898][1]
[Pent Farm]

Dear Mrs Crane.

I forward you Meldrum's letter. He is a man of good counsel and you can see for yourself that he is anxious to do something. Please read his letter with care. His suggestion is worth consideration. The same ideas occurred to me. If I had the means there would have been no need to mention them, but as you see if we are to do something we must have recourse to strangers.[2] I must mention here that the originals of your letters are destroyed and that the whole matter is treated on a perfectly confidential footing. I had to let M. know the exact state of affairs as far as we all on this side are aware of them.

Would Stephen come back by himself if written to? Would he tell us *how much* is wanted to enable him to leave Havana? Would he recognize the engagements we would enter into here for means to bring him back? His future is here—I firmly believe—but will he see it? Whatever happens the matter must be kept quiet, and his reputation shielded. I know of personal knowledge that B'wood is a little angry.[3] A short letter from Stephen saying he could not send anything would have made all the difference. It is too late now. What do you think of me writing him a strong letter urging his return and saying that we keep £50 ready for that purpose if he gives his word. Please write. Always yours

Conrad.

To Edward Garnett

Text MS Colgate; G. 141

Monday [7 November 1898][4]
[Pent Farm]

Dearest Edward,

Did you think I had died? We are here—over a week now and the place is a success. I reckon Ford told you. I reckon you disapprove. "I rebel! I said I would rebel." (d'you know the quotation)[5] I send you

---

[1] Although other Thursdays are conceivable, the urgency of the exchange suggests this date.

[2] Meldrum's friends, among them the young publisher John Macqueen.

[3] About not hearing from Crane, and about the quality of Crane's recent work. In the end, he was cabled an advance of £50 from Heinemann.

[4] Conrad's reference to living at the Pent for 'over a week now' confirms Garnett's dating.

[5] Turgenev's *Fathers and Sons*, 27: quoted in Garnett's Introduction (1895).

here Henley's letter over the matter.[1] I feel hopeful about my own work. Completely changed. When do you come here. When? Both of you with Bunny. Or you alone to begin with. I feel orphaned. Are You in Constple?[2] Ever Yours

Conrad

Love from us all.

To R. B. Cunninghame Graham
Text MS Dartmouth; J-A, 1, 253; Watts 105

Pent Farm.
Stanford near Hythe.
9[th] Nov 98

Très cher et excellent ami.

I only got your letter on Monday and the tray came this morning. And for both thanks. We shout cries of welcome.[3] Travel[l]ing is victory.

As to returning bredouille[4] well that's better than a crack on the head—if not for yourself perhaps (note how habit of cynicism clings to me) then for your friends. A virtuous man lives for his friends. "Remember this!" as the edicts of the Emperor of China conclude.

I was just thinking of sending a note to the Dev[onshi]re Club to meet you when your letter arrived "announcing presents". Days had slipped disregarded full to the brim with the botheration of moving. Now I am here I like it. I can write a little a very little. A little is better than nothing but it is so little that out of the present worries I look with terror into the future still. Oh the weariness of it, the weariness of it.

They did not send me the proofs of Higg[ins]on's Dream. There is a misprint in French. When sending *Pulperia* I repproached* them.[5] They sent me proofs of that but without the MS, so if there is anything wrong it is not so much of my fault as it may look.

I had a most enjoyable trip to Glasgow. I saw Neil Munro and heaps of shipowners and that's all I can say. The fact is from novel writing to skippering il y a trop de tirage. This confounded literature has ruined me entirely. There is a time in the affairs of men when the tide of folly

---

[1] Of collaboration.
[2] 'A Constantinople project which came to nothing' (Garnett's note).
[3] On his return from North Africa.
[4] 'Empty-headed': political unrest had interfered with Graham's plans.
[5] For these stories, see the letter to Mrs Bontine, 16 October.

taken at the flood sweeps them to destruction. La mer monte cher ami; la mer monte and the phenomenon is not worth a thought.

My letter is disjointed because I can't think to-night. I am touched to think that when wandering through the brass-workers' bazaar (in Fez—was it?) you thought: There's that Conrad. Well yes—there he is—for a little while yet. I have been looking at the thing all day. It has a fascination. I seem to see the face bending over it the hands that touched it. A brown meagre hand, a hooked profile, a skullcap on a shaven head, lean shanks ending in splay slippers, thus I picture the man who hammered the brass according to the design known to his remote forefathers.

> Pressing both your hands   Ever
> Yours
>
> > Conrad.

I didn't know the review was by your Wife.[1] I liked it immensely. I noted it. I hope her health is good. Mes hommages les plus respectueux. I shall levy toll of one copy upon your book—comme de juste.[2]

To Neil Munro
Text MS NLS; Unpublished

> 9th Nov 1898.
> Pent Farm.
> Stanford Near Hythe.
> Kent.

My dear Munro.[3]

I feel like a wretch for not having written to tell you how touched I was by Your friendliness. Yet the feeling is abiding and loses no strenght* by the lapse of time.

My congratulations upon the advertisement of the fourth edition of John Splendid.[4] And splendid indeed it is. I've no gift of critical expression. I feel the beauty strongly but I cannot liberate my artistic emotion in art terms or in any other terms. You must take me on trust. If I had you there, in the room, and the book with us two, then, then perhaps thumping the pages out of your own heart and art with your

---

[1] She wrote for a wide range of periodicals.   [2] A copy of *Mogreb-el-Acksa* – 'of course'.

[3] Neil Munro (1864–1930), poet, novelist, and critic, was a fellow *Blackwood's* author. Conrad had seen him during the visit to Scotland in September.

[4] *A Highland Romance*, published that year and obviously selling well.

own words[1] I could give you a glimmer of my sensations. And some day
I love to think it will be. Remember me when you come south. I look
forward to seeing you and seeing you here. We shan't stir from home for
months ahead. Believe me Always most faithfully Yours

Jph. Conrad.

To Ford Madox Ford
Text MS Yale; Unpublished

Saturday. [12] Nov 98.[2]
[Pent Farm]

My dear Hueffer.

We are very happy here from which you may guess we haven't yet set
fire to the house. The acceptance of our joint work is assured as far as
Pawling is concerned. McClure I guess is all right.[3] We must serialise
next year on both sides of the pond.

I have read the *Shifting of the Fire*.[4] I have read it several times looking
for your "inside" in that book; the first impression being that there is a
considerable "inside" in you. The book is delightfully young. Mind I
say *delightfully* instead of drearily, or morally, or sadly, or frightfully or
any of these things which politeness would have induced me to
paraphrase. The movement, the imagination, the conviction of it *are*
delightful (in the literary sense too). Felicitous phrasing is plentiful and
with that the writing is wonderfully level. There is certainly crudeness in
the presentation of the idea. The facts, the emotions the sensations are
painted somewhat as the scenery for the stage is painted but Youth does
not make for fineness – except in inexpressible ideals, in acted dreams, in
the spoiling or making of a life. Never in writing about it. More could
have been made out of the situations by a more spiritual method. The
analysis however if not crafty is true and every fact is significant. That's
indubitable. Nevertheless it is apparent only on reflection. And that's *the*
fault. Why exactly it is so I am of course unable to say. It is a matter of

---

[1] Even if one puts commas around 'thumping the pages', the details here are blurred; the
general meaning is clear, however: 'face to face, in the heat of the moment, I could tell
you what I mean'. Cf. end of letter to Bennett, p. 390.

[2] Date from postmark.

[3] The 'joint work' is 'Seraphina', but Ford's manuscript was later put aside so that the
collaborators might concentrate on *The Inheritors*. S. S. McClure, who handled
American magazine rights for Stevenson, Doyle, and Rider Haggard, was always eager
for new adventure stories.

[4] Ford's first novel, written in his teens, adopted by Garnett and published in 1892 by
T. Fisher Unwin.

fact to me only so far that it is a matter of feeling. I feel that the effects are partly lost. But I am not like Homocea.[1] I don't touch the spot. No doubt the general cause is (O! happy man) youth—inexperience. How it worked I can't say. These belated remarks are asinine, but not so asinine as the charge of immorality propounded by the D[aily] T[elegraph]. What is mostly obvious is the talent of the writer and that I have the sense to recognise. I need not say I am in accord with the idea—in complete accord.——

Have you written for *Serafina* (or Seraphina?). I get on dreamily with the *Rescue*, dreamily dreaming how fine it could be if the thought did not escape, if the expression did not hide underground, if the idea had a substance and words a magic power, if the invisible could be snared into a shape. And it is sad to think that even if all this came to pass—even then it could never be so fine to anybody as it is fine to me now, lurking in blank pages, in an intensity of existence, without voice, without form—but without blemish.

Faithfully yours

Jph. Conrad

Our kindest regards to Mrs Hueffer and love to Christina.

To Ford Madox Ford
Text MS Yale; Unpublished

17 Nov 89* [1898]
[Pent Farm]

My dear Hueffer.

Herewith some notices which came within the last 3 days.

Had youre* letter. I did hear from G[arnett]. He doesn't think of snakes—not he. He hasn't enough imagination;—as to You, you have too much and that causes you to call yourself zoological names. I hear from Pawling G wrote him a letter commending our partnership on grounds that evidently appeal to P. G is not so bad as he pretends to be.

Come when you like. Next Sunday week (27ᵗʰ) to Mond: I shall have two men for one night here. Except this you may just walk in with or without notice, into the Pent. You will always find me here. I would be very, very pleased to *hear* Seraphina *read*. I would *afterwards* read it myself. Consult your own convenience and (especially) your own—whim. It's the only thing worth deferring to.

Our kindest regards to you both.

Ever yours

Conrad.

[1] 'Homocea touches the spot': advertizing slogan.

To H. G. Wells

Text MS Illinois; J-A, 1, 254

[letterhead: Pent Farm][1]

17 nov. 98

My dear Wells.

I was glad to find you well enough to be out for an airing though of course horribly sorry to miss you. I couldn't wait. A man was coming to see me whom I had to meet at Sandling. I only made a dash to Sandgate to hear how you were getting on. My dear fellow don't you talk of sunsets in connection with your health or your anything else. Nothing more beastly than a sunset—in the abstract. But practically it argues the possibility of sunrise. I ain't clear. I want to say—think of sunrises. This is obscure. Try to understand and believe I am not intoxicated. Too early. It is the first hour of the day and after breakfast I will be more articulate—but the post will be gone. So I write now—7 am. One is still capable of heroism.

I've been bothering Pugh[2] to come and see me. He may turn up next Saturday week in sheer desperation. If he comes, in decent time we might invade you for a couple of hours. Or would you be well enough to come along and sit on us boys. Veni, vidi, vici.[3] You may veni by a train that gets to Sandling about 12.40. I would meet you on wheels if you write in time. There is a return train about 5—another at six.

We would have called together before this but Jess is tied to the house. Our girl's temperament was too artistic. She would wander off and disappear for hours at a time. What she found to dream about on country roads in the mud and after dark I can't imagine. We aren't straitlaced ourselves but—dash my buttons—she was too unconventional. So we parted—suddenly. The noise of that wrench had a melancholy shrillness like the screams of sea gulls. I kept my head throughout but wouldn't like to go t[h]rough it again. She departed; another's coming soon, of a philistinish aspect; meantime we stop at home and look after the baby. It takes a minimum of two wide awake persons to ward off the dangers besetting his reckless infancy. So as I said we sit at home—and watch.

Let me know about your health. I am not very bright myself. I beg to

---

[1] For the varieties of Pent Farm letterhead, see pp. xxxvi-xxxvii. In accordance with Conrad's changing habits, supplied dates go below supplied locations from here on.

[2] Edwin Pugh, the novelist.   [3] 'I came, I saw, I conquered': Julius Caesar.

be remembered to Mrs Wells. The first fine day (baby permitting) I
shall bring my wife along to be introduced to her.

Upon that threat I remain

Ever Yours.

Jph. Conrad.

To the Hon. A. E. Bontine
Text MS Dartmouth; J-A, 1, 255

[letterhead: Pent Farm]
22ᵈ Nov 1898

Dear Mrs Bontine.

Many thanks for Your good letter and the enclosed Max Nordau
autograph.[1] Would Robert[2] let me keep it? I own myself surprised.
There is not the slightest doubt M.N. has understood my intention. He
has absolutely detected the whole idea. This to me is so startling that I
do not know what to think of myself now. However I am pleased. Praise
is sweet no matter whence it comes. What strikes me as strange is that he
writes as though Robert had asked him why he (Robert) liked the book![3]
The expounding attitude is funny—and characteristic too. He *is* a
Doctor and a Teacher—no doubt about it. But for all that he is
wondrous kind.

When I heard of Robert's decision to return my first impulse was to
rush to a telegraph office and wire You my jubilation, exultation,
congratulation. You will not deny he has justified my trust in his
judgment and good sense. He has done so much in his life and knows so
well what he can do that he would not attempt the impossible as an
untried man could be tempted to do. We exchanged two letters. I think
that the trip anyhow has done him good.

My wretched novel begins in April in the *Illᵈ Lond. News* as a serial to
run 3 months. It will appear in book form in Octᵉʳ next.[4] I am afraid that
You and Robert will be disappointed. You will *see* but you will be
disappointed. Everybody else won't see—the idea has the bluish tenuity
of dry wood smoke. It is lost in the words, as the smoke is lost in the air.

---

[1] Max Nordau (born in Hungary as Max Simon Südfeld, 1849–1924), whose best-selling
Degeneration (1895) belaboured the social and artistic decadence of contemporary
Europe.

[2] Cunninghame Graham, Mrs Bontine's son.

[3] Perhaps *The Nigger*, in which Conrad takes a view of reformers and agitators very
different from Graham's. Nordau detested most modern fiction.

[4] *The Rescue*, completed in 1919.

Attempting to tell romantically a love story in which the word love is not to be pronounced, seems to be courting disaster deliberately. Add to this that an inextricable confusion of sensations is of the very essence of the tale and you may judge how much success material or otherwise I may expect. Le lecteur demande une situation nette et des motifs definis.[1] He will not find it in the Rescue.

I can't imagine where we could find a reviewer worthy of Robert and of Roberts book.[2] If I could review myself I would do it, and, under the mask of anonimity* give full play to the baseness of my nature. Robert being my friend, *the* friend, it would be sweet to abuse him with safety and propriety. But seriously speaking I do not see anybody. Wells (H. G.) does that kind of thing, has some intelligence, partly understands Robert—(only partly) and perhaps would like to review. Yet he is scarcely the man. There is Garnett also. But the man is slow and sometimes inarticulate out of the fulness of his heart. There would be no doubt of *his* sympathy and intelligence. Shall I write to him? Perhaps I could work the *Academy*. Ask Garnett first and then set Lucas[3] (one of the Academy gang) to work the oracle within the temple, so as to get the book sent to Garnett? I live like a silly hermit and can be of no good to my friends. Je ne suis pas dans le mouvement.

Of Henry James's last I share your opinion. The second of the *Two magics* is unworthy of his talent.[4] The first evades one but leaves a kind of phosphorescent trail in one's mind. Frederic[5] for me is unreadable. Mr Fitzmaurice Kelly's book[6] I have not seen yet but would like to and shall before long.

Thanks for your kind enquiries. My wife and boy are well. We like our new place. I have been horribly seedy with some kind of gout. It always leaves me demoralised and gloomy. I only got up yesterday. Tears besprinkle my manuscript, but my bad language can be heard across the fields even as far as the sea. Believe me dear Mrs Bontine always Your most faithful and most obedient servant

Jph. Conrad.

---

[1] 'The reader wants an obvious predicament and clear-cut motives.'
[2] *Mogreb-el-Acksa*, about to appear.
[3] E. V. Lucas, Garnett's friend.
[4] 'Covering End'; the first story is 'The Turn of the Screw'.
[5] Probably Crane's friend Harold Frederic (1856–1898). His best known novel is *The Damnation of Theron Ware* (1896, published in England as *Illumination*), the story of a Methodist minister's downfall.
[6] His edition of *Don Quixote*, much admired by Graham.

To H. G. Wells

Text MS Illinois; J-A, 1, 256

Friday. [25] Nov. 98[1]
Pent Farm

My dear Wells.

I did not nourish robust hopes of seeing You on Sat. The weather is infamous. I have been laid up also, with a kind of gout entertainment which lasted 3 days and of course I can only hobble now it is over. As to struggling over darkling hills I thought I made it plain there are wheels—not of chance, but of certitude.[2] Of course our carcases for the sake of their inhabitants require careful handling, but at all events I am telling you that I shall be (on wheels) at Sand. Junc: on Sat at *12:30* to remove Pugh. Thereafter same wheels could take you back at five or six. Bringing P to lunch is another matter. As I tell you one of my propellers is damaged and done up in flannel—an obscene sight—not to speak of the pain and impiety, for swear words issue from my lips at every step I take. I don't think I really could undertake a journey to Sandgate either tomorrow or on Sunday. I go to the station because P is a stranger and may starve or otherwise perish in the fields like any other beast unless he is taken care of. But I shall not leave the fly, and I intend to hoot like a sick Martian[3] outside the station. He is sure to be interested by such a remarkable noise and thus he shall find me.

Re Henley.[4] There is a furnished house in Hythe standing isolated at the Sandgate end of Hythe High Street. A red brick thing, rather large. It would do at a pinch—perhaps.

If you have a copy of the *Invisible man*[5] send it to me. I lent mine to a god-fearing person who stole it. Thus wags the world. I ain't cadging for a gift—it's a loan I want and I will try my best not to steal. ————————

Really why shouldn't you both come? I take all the transport arrangements upon myself on this end. They *won't* fail. At your end you have omnibuses if you are not too hightoned to use them. And you may be home at six—and that's virtuous enough. Well Well. I don't want to be a nuisance. I throw out a suggestion like the angler his hook—the rest is with fate—and the gullibility of the fish. Let me also mention that with Mrs Wells to take care of you You can't come to any harm. On the other hand Mrs Well[s] with Your support can affront for a few hours

---

[1] The circumstances of Pugh's visit give the date.
[2] An allusion to Wells' *The Wheels of Chance* (1896), a novel about a cycling holiday.
[3] In *The War of the Worlds* (1898).   [4] W. E. Henley, who was in constant ill-health.
[5] Wells' *Grotesque Romance* (1897).

our shabby, wretched, rural bohemianism with a fair chance of surviving the adventure. And we will leave it at that.

With kindest and hopeful regards to your wife

Ever Yours

Jph Conrad.

To R. B. Cunninghame Graham
Text MS Dartmouth; J-A, 1, 257; Watts 109

[letterhead: Pent Farm]
1st Dec 1898

Cherissime et excellentissime.

Your photograph came yesterday (It's good!) and the book[1] arrived by this evening's post. I dropped everything—as you may imagine and rushed at it paper knife in hand. It is with great difficulty I interrupt my reading at the 100th page—and I interrupt it only to write to you.

A man staying here has been reading over my shoulder; for we share our best with the stranger within our tent. No thirsty men drank water as we have been drinking in, swallowing, tasting, blessing, enjoying, gurgling, choking over, absorbing, your thought, your phrases, your irony, the spirit of your wisdom and of Your expression. The individuality of the book is amazing even to me who know you or pretend to. It is wealth tossed on the roadside, it is a creative achievement, it is alive with conviction and truth. Men, living men are tossed to these dogs—the readers, pictures are flung out for the blind, wisdom—brilliant wisdom—showered upon fools. You are magnificently generous. You seem to be plunging your hand into an inexhaustible bag of treasure and fling precious things at every paragraph. We have been shouting slapping our legs, leaping up, stamping about. There was such an enthusiasm in this solitude as will meet no other book.

I do not know really how to express the kind of intellectual exultation your book has awakened in me; and I will not stay to try; I am in too great a hurry to get back to the book. My applause, slaps on the back, salaams benedictions, cheers. Take what you like best of these, what you think most expressive. Or take them all. I *can't* be too demonstrative.

Ever Yours with yells

Conrad.

---

[1] *Mogreb-el-Acksa.*

Why did you lug in J.C. into your pages.[1] Oh why? Why take a sinner on your back when crossing a stream.

To the Hon. A. E. Bontine
Text MS Dartmouth; J-A, 1, 258

[letterhead: Pent Farm]
4th Dec. 1898

Dear Mrs. Bontine.

Just a word or two about Robert's book. It is a glorious performance. Much as we expected of him, I, and two men who were staying with me when my copy arrived,[2] have been astounded by the completeness of this achievement. One said—"This is *the* book of travel of the century." And it is true. Nothing approaching it had appeared since Burton's *Mecca*.[3] And, as the other man pointed out, judging the work strictly as a book—as a production of an unique temperament—Burton's *Mecca* is nowhere near it. And it is true. The Journey in Morocco is a work of art. A book of travel written like this is no longer a book of travel—it is a creative work. It is a contribution not towards mere knowledge but towards *truth*—to the *truth* hidden in men—in things—in life—in nature—to the truth only exceptional men can see, and not every exceptional man can present to the ordinary dim eyes of the crowd. He is unappro[a]chable in acuteness of vision—of sympathy; he is alone in his power of expression; and through vision, sympathy and expression runs an informing current of thought as noble, unselfish and human as is only the gift of the best.

The book pulled at my very heart-strings. Et voilà! I've been trying to tell you this—and only this—from the first page to this line. Je ne parle pas de son esprit. Chaque page en est un example, chaque phrase en est une preuve. Le livre est rempli d'un charme étrange et pénétrant. C'est bien là la terre, les hommes, le ciel, la vie! Cette oeuvre brilliante laisse dans l'âme du lecteur comme une traînée de lumière.[4]

I must close this macaronic letter. I could write on for ever and just to

---

[1] On pp. 52–3, he praises 'An Outpost of Progress': 'told without heroics and without spread-eagleism, and true to life; therefore unpopular'.

[2] Conrad had entertained at least three guests in the preceding week: one of them was Pugh, another may have been Ford.

[3] Sir Richard Burton's *Personal Narrative of a Pilgrimage to El-Medinah and Meccah* (1855).

[4] 'I do not speak of its inner being. Every page is an example of it, every phrase is evidence of it. The book is filled with a keen and unfamiliar enchantment. Indeed it's there—the land, the people, the sky, the life! On the reader's soul, this brilliant work leaves [an impression] like a streak of light.'

so little purpose. Believe me, dear Mrs Bontine, Your most faithful and most obedient servant.

Jph. Conrad.

PS Je viens de recevoir une lettre du sérénissime Seigneur. Il se dit triste. Pourquoi![1] He seems also uncertain about the book. Exactly. The poor man is quite incapable of judging impartially or even sensibly, the work of Mr C. Graham. A man who can write like this is a creator—not a critic.

To H. G. Wells
Text MS Illinois; J-A, 1, 259

[letterhead: Pent Farm]
4th Dec 1898

My dear Wells.

Thanks ever so much for the *Invisible Man*. I shall keep him a few days longer.

Frankly—it is uncommonly fine. One can always *see* a lot in your work—there is always a 'beyond' to your books—but into this (with due regard to theme and lenght*) you've managed to put an amazing quantity of effects. If it just misses being tremendous it is because you didn't make it so—and if you didn't there isn't a man in England who could. As to b—y furriners they ain't in it at all.

I suppose you'll have the common decency to believe me when I tell you I am always powerfully impressed by your work. Impressed is *the* word O! Realist of the Fantastic, whether you like it or not. And if you want to know what impresses me it is to see how you contrive to give over humanity into the clutches of the Impossible and yet manage to keep it down (or up) to its humanity, to its flesh, blood, sorrow, folly. *That* is the achievement! In this little book you do it with an appalling completeness. I'll not insist upon the felicity of incident. This must be obvious even to yourself. Three of us have been reading the book (I had two men staying here after Pugh left) and we have been tracking with delight the cunning method of your logic. It is masterly—it is ironic—it is very relentless—and it is very true. We all three (the two others are no fools) place the *I.M.* above the War of the Worlds. Whether we are right—and if so why—I am not sure, and can not tell. I fancy the book

---

[1] 'I have just had a letter from his most serene lordship [Cunninghame Graham]. He calls himself sad. Why!'

is more strictly human and thus your diabolical psychology plants its points right into a man's bowels. To me the W of the W has less of that sinister air of truth that arrests the reader in reflexion at the turn of the page so often in the *I.M.* In reading this last, one is touched by the anguish of it as by something that any day may happen to oneself. It is a great triumph for you.

Ever Yours

Conrad.

My compliments to Mrs Wells. How are you? I am not well. I am eating my heart out over the rottenest book that ever was—or will be.

To Cora Crane
Text MS Columbia; Stallman 197

[letterhead: Pent Farm]
4th Dec 1898.

My dear Mrs Crane.

You made us quite happy with your letter. I had a couple of pretty bad days just before; having heard from Meldrum about that wretched McQueen.[1] You may imagine how sick I felt. I did not write to you at once because I did set to think of some other expedient. I would have gone to London to seek had it not been for my r[h]eumatism which kept me on my back in bed 2 days and even when I got up I could not do more than hobble across the room. I was at my wit's end. Luckily it's over. I dreaded opening your letter, having nothing to propose or suggest. It was an immense relief to hear you had been lucky in some other quarter.[2] Do you think Stephen will be in England before Christmas? His story in B. is magnificent.[3] It is the very best thing he has done since the Red Badge—and it has even something the Red Badge had not—or not so much of. He is maturing. He is expanding. There is more breath[4] and somehow more substance in this war-picture. We (I had two men visiting me last week) are delighted with this bit of work. It is Stephen all himself—and a little more. It is the very truth of art. There is an added ampleness in his method which makes me augur a magnificent future for his coming work. Let him only come—and work!

---

[1] Macqueen had refused to lend any money.   [2] An advance from Heinemann.
[3] 'The Price of the Harness' in the December *Blackwood's*.
[4] 'breadth'? – or inspiration?

Excuse me if I end here. I am in arrears with my correspondence—besides other worries. Ah! but I do feel relieved.

Jess sends congratulations and best love.

> Believe me always most faithfully
>
> Yours
>
> Jph Conrad.

To R. B. Cunninghame Graham
Text MS Dartmouth; J-A, 1, 260; Watts 110

> [letterhead: Pent Farm]
>
> 9th Dec 1898

My dearest amigo.

I wrote to your mother about your book. I found it easier to speak to a third person—at first. I do not know what to tell you. If I tell you that You have surpassed my greatest expectations you may be offended—and this piece of paper is not big enough to explain how great my expectations were. Anyway they are left behind. I am ashamed of my moderation[1] and now I am looking at the performance I ask myself what kind of friend was I not to foresee, not to understand that the book would just be *that*—no less. Well it is there—for our joy, for our thought, for our triumph. I am speaking of those who understand and love you. The preface is a gem—I knew it, I remembered it[2]—and yet it came with a fresh force. To be understood is not everything—one must be understood as one would like to be. This probably you won't have.

Yes—the book is Art. Art without a trace of Art's theories in its incomparably effective execution. It isn't anybody's art—it is C-Graham's art. The individuality of the work imposes itself on the reader—from the first. Then come other things, skill, pathos, humour, wit, indignation. Above all a continuous feeling of delight; the persuasion that there one has got hold of a good thing. This should work for material success. Yet who knows! No doubt it is too good.

You haven't been careful in correcting your proofs. Are you too grand seigneur for that infect labour?[3] Surely I, twenty others, would be only too proud to do it for you. Tenez vous le pour dit.[4] I own I was exasperated by the errors. Twice the wretched printers perverted your meaning. It is twice too often. They should die!

---

[1] 'I stand astonished at my own moderation!': Robert Clive under parliamentary questioning about his alleged extravagance in India, 1773.
[2] See the letter of 26 August.
[3] A common complaint among Graham's friends. 'Infect' means 'noisome'.
[4] 'Take it as said.'

I write because I can't come.[1] Can't is the truth. I am sorry to hear of your depression—but O friend who isn't—(I mean depressed). I am not able to say one cheering word. It seems to me I am desintegrating* slowly. Cold shadows stand around. Never mind.

I thought it was next Tuesday you were coming to town. Stupid of me. Now this letter'll be probably too late to catch you. I am very sorry to hear of Your wife's indisposition. Remember me to her please. I trust she is better.

I daren't ask you to come down. I am too wretched, and its worse than the plague. Au revoir. Ever Yours

Jph. Conrad.

To William Blackwood

Text MS NLS; Blackburn 33

[letterhead: Pent Farm]
13th Dec 1898

Dear Mr Blackwood.

I owe you a great many thanks for the *Maga* which reaches me with a most charming regularity. In truth it is the only monthly I care to read, and each number is very welcome, though each is a sharp jog to my conscience. And yet, God knows, it is wide-awake enough and daily avenges the many wrongs my patient publishers suffer at my hands.

And this is all I can say unless I were to unfold for the nth time the miserable tale of my inefficiency. I trust however that in Jany I'll be able to send you about 30000 words or perhaps a little less,[2] towards the Vol: of short stories.[3] Apart from my interest it is such a pleasure for me to appear in the *Maga* that you may well believe it is not laziness that keeps me back. It is, alas, something—I don't know what—not so easy to overcome. With immense effort a thin trickle of MS is produced—and

---

[1] The last three paragraphs are written on a half-sheet. That in itself is not unusual: since Conrad could not be prodigal with expensive stationery, he often finished a letter with odd pieces of cheaper stock. The tone, however, changes abruptly, and the handwriting is less controlled. Either Conrad's powers of cheerfulness suddenly failed him—an entirely possible event—or these are the fragments of two letters that do not match any other manuscripts at Dartmouth. If the latter case is true, the second fragment could belong anywhere between late 1897 and early 1900, the period during which he kept the type of paper used here. Nevertheless, this fragment (if it is one) could fit between 9 and 21 December, the date of the next known letter to Graham, a letter that echoes the mood and perhaps the circumstances of the paragraphs at issue.

[2] Either 'Jim: A Sketch' or 'Heart of Darkness': see letters of 31 December 1898 and 14 February 1899.

[3] Which became *Youth*.

that, just now, must be kept in one channel only lest no one gets anything and I am completely undone.

The Stephen Crane in the last number[1] has given me great satisfaction. The man will develop. I find this story, broader, gentler, less tricky and just as individual as the best of his work. It is the best bit of work he has done since the *Red Badge*. One or two competent men wrote to me about it and they share my opinion.

I had a treat in the shape of a N° of the *Singapore Free Press* 2½ columns about "Mr Conrad at home and abroad".[2] Extremely laudatory but in fact telling me I don't know anything about it. Well I never did set up as an authority on Malaysia. I looked for a medium in which to express myself. I am inexact and ignorant no doubt (most of us are) but I don't think I sinned so recklessly. Curiously enough all the details about the little characteristic acts and customs which they hold up as proof I have taken out (to be safe) from undoubted sources—dull, wise books. It is rather staggering to find myself so far astray. In *Karain*, for instance, there's not a single action of my man (and good many of his expressions) that can not be backed by a traveller's tale—I mean a serious traveller's. And yet this story "can only be called Malay in Mr Conrad's sense". Sad.

Well. I only wanted you to know I am alive and not utterly lost to sense of my shortcomings. Accept my best wishes for the coming year. It is near enough already to make sinners of my sort think about turning over a new leaf and so on. I hope you will like my new leaves however belated they may be. I am dear Mr Blackwood always Yours faithfully

Jph Conrad.

I am most sincerely glad to see Munro's book[3] in its 4th Edition. Munro *is* an artist—besides being an excellent fellow with a pretty weakness for my work.

---

[1] 'The Price of the Harness'.

[2] The article appeared in the weekly edition, 1 September, as the regular feature by 'The Book-Worm'. Although Conrad did not know it yet, the author was Hugh Clifford, whose *Studies in Brown Humanity* he had reviewed for the *Academy*. In a survey of Conrad's work (perhaps the first one to be published) Clifford applauds *Almayer* and *The Nigger* with special warmth. Yet he finds that even *Almayer*, with all its atmospheric power, is flawed by ignorance: a real Nina would not go back to native ways, a real Babalatchi would never dare to yawn and scratch himself in the royal presence. Turning to the short stories, Clifford argues that their strength – the power of atmosphere again – is also their weakness: 'They should not be four parts description to one part narrative, or they fail in their object, and are apt to exhaust rather than to please.'

[3] *John Splendid*.

To Aniela Zagórska

Text J-A, 1, 261; Najder 226[1]

Pent Farm, Stanford.
18.12.1898.

My dear Aniela,

If I did not believe in the constancy of your sentiments towards me I would not dare write to you after so long a silence. As a matter of fact, my dear, I have been in a sad state of health—miserable rather than bad—and I preferred not to weary or tire you with the sadness of my letters. And also I was ashamed to display before you—who are so brave among the difficulties and sufferings of life—my foolish and not very praiseworthy pessimism.

This is how the days, weeks, and months have gone by; I waited—always thinking of you, with my pen ready to write—I waited for a moment of lucidity, of calmness, of hope. It is hard to attain. And here comes Christmas and the end of the year. One has to ask for pardon, express one's feelings—promise to amend for the hundredth or thousandth time, as all sinners do.

As you will see, we have come to live here; this is also a farmhouse, somewhat smaller but more convenient and, what is most important, it is situated on higher ground. I found that I could not work in our old place. It is better here although I have nothing to boast about. We are only five kilometres from the sea. The railway station is 3 kilometres and Canterbury 1½ kilometres[2] away. Before my window I can see the buildings of the farm, and on leaning out and looking to the right, I see the valley of the Stour, the source of which is so to speak behind the third hedge from the farmyard. Behind the house are the hills (Kentish Downs) which slope in zigzag fashion down to the sea, like the battlements of a big fortress. A road runs along the foot of the hills near the house—a very lonely and straight road, and along which (so it is whispered) old Lord Roxby—he died 80 years ago—rides sometimes at night in a four-in-hand driven by himself. What is rather strange, however, is that he has no head. Why he should leave his head at home while he takes a ride, nobody can explain. But I must tell you that during the two months we have lived here, we have not yet heard the noise of any wheels and although I sometimes walk along this road near midnight, I have never met a four-in-hand. On the other side of the little garden stretches out quiet and waste land intersected by hedges and

[1] For textual source, see n. 5 to letter of 6 February 1898. The texts lack a formal ending.
[2] More like twenty.

here and there stands an oak or a group of young ash trees. Three little villages are hidden among the hillocks and only the steeples of their churches can be seen. The colouring of the country presents brown and pale yellow tints—and in between, in the distance one can see the meadows, as green as emeralds. And not a sound is to be heard but the laboured panting of the engines of the London–Dover express trains.

We live like a family of anchorites. From time to time a pious pilgrim belonging to la grande fraternité des lettres comes to pay a visit to the celebrated Joseph Conrad—and to obtain his blessing. Sometimes he gets it and sometimes he does not, for the hermit is severe and dyspeptic et n'entend pas la plaisanterie en matière d'Art![1] At all events, the pilgrim receives an acceptable dinner, a Spartan bed—and he vanishes. I am just expecting one today, the author of *Jocelyn*,[2] which is dedicated to me! The novel is not remarkable, but the man is very pleasant and kind—and rich, que diable fait-il dans cette galère—where we are navigating whilst using pens by way of oars—on an ocean of ink—pour n'arriver nulle part, hélas!

Jessie is dreaming of a visit to Poland—which to her means a visit to you. And ĩ am dreaming the same. Pourquoi pas? It costs nothing to journey in thought to those we love. It costs nothing—only a little heartache when we find how far the dream is from reality.

Now Christmas is drawing near.

To Edward Garnett
Text MS Sutton; G. 142

[letterhead: Pent Farm]
[18 December 1898][3]

My dearest Garnett.

I was glad to see thy fist. The Crane thing is just[4]—precisely just a ray flashed in and showing all there is.

Jess' and my love to you, and best wishes—and through to all yours please when you write.

Before Mrs Garnett comes back you must come and see me—us.

I've been writing not so badly.

Now I am at a short story for B'wood[5] which I must get out for the sake of the shekels.

---

[1] 'and doesn't listen to jokes on artistic topics'.   [2] Galsworthy.
[3] Garnett's dating, confirmed by the reference to his piece on Crane.
[4] 'Mr Stephen Crane: An Appreciation', *Academy*, 17 December, reprinted in *Friday Nights* (1922).
[5] 'Heart of Darkness'? See the next letter.

Then again at the *R[escue]*.
Come soon. I've read the play.[1] There's something to say about it but viva voce when we meet.

Ever Yours

Jph. Conrad

I don't send you type of R because McCl[ure] is always anxious to get it back at once. And there's nothing to boast of.
Galsworthy is awfully anxious to make your acquaintance.

To David Meldrum
Text MS Duke; Blackburn 35

[letterhead: Pent Farm]
21/12/98

Dear Mr Meldrum
The heartiest wishes to you and yours from us both. I trust next year we shall be able to foregather often.
I don't know whether I've told you that Mrs Crane got the cash[2] and has sent it off to Havana to bring Stephen back. I know you will like to hear that she got over *that* trouble.
I think the *Harness* is first rate.[3] The best bit of work since the Red Badge days. Several men wrote to me about it in almost these very terms.
Excuse hurried scrawl but I've left all my Xmas letters to the last and have a dozen more to write tonight. With kindest regards Always faithfully yours

Jph. Conrad.

I am writing something for *Maga* a tale (short) in the manner of *Youth*, to be ready in a few days.

To R. B. Cunninghame Graham
Text MS Dartmouth; Watts 112

[letterhead: Pent Farm]
21.12.98

Cherissime ami.
With a bad pen by a smoky lamp Hail to you! May all the infernal Gods look upon You with favour; and may all the men who are food for

[1] Garnett's 'A Christmas Play for Children'.   [2] From Heinemann.
[3] 'The Price of the Harness' in *Blackwood's*.

Hell shake their heads at your words and gestures. To be happy we should propitiate the gods of evil and fly in the faces of evil men.

I cannot sufficiently recover from the shock of missing your dear visit to relieve my feelings by strong swears. Not yet. When you come (and you will) I shall explain what infamous thing had me by the neck then. I have eaten shame and my face is black before you.

I toil on. So did the gentleman of the name of Sisiphus. (Did I spell it right?) This is the very marrow of my news.

Mes devoirs les plus respectueux a Madame Votre Femme et mes souhaits de la Nouvelle année. As to you O Friend! Time overtakes us. Time! Voilà l'ennemi. And must I even congratulate you upon a defeat because men lie to each other to conceal their dismay and their fear. Not I! Ever Yours

Conrad.

To E. L. Sanderson
Text MS Yale; Unpublished

[letterhead: Pent Farm]
21st December 1898

My dear Ted.

All hail to your handwriting and your news. Our best wishes go to You both with such strenght* of sincerity that were human wishes of any avail they would secure you earthly happiness beyond the power of all adverse fates.

I am glad you've not given me up. I am going through such a period as would leave any other man without a single friend.[1] But my friends are not like other men's friends and thus I know that when I come out (a better man let us hope) I shall be met by extended hands and by welcoming words.

The "lean and slippered pantaloon"[2] who writes this wishes you to know that the trains for Pent Farm are the trains for Paris—exactly. Also the Vienna express stops to set down and take up my guests. This is not (as You might think) in recognition of my literary achievements but only to suit the ends—the inscrutable ends—of the S[outh] E[astern] R[ailway].

I am torn between the wish to see you get a "pup" (which would

---

[1] In a desperate mood, but working on 'Jim' and 'Heart of Darkness', thinking about the collaboration with Ford, and trying to escape from *The Rescue*.

[2] Jaques on the sixth age of humanity, *As You Like It*, ii.vii.

please You) and the desire to see You here (which [is] the true heart's desire).

I've a *dozen* more letters to write to-night. I left everything to the last. With love from us both to You both

Ever Yours

Conrad.

from Char[in]g X. best train. 11 AM notify the day before Pent being 2 miles from the Station and the fly man mighty touchy.

To Cora Crane
Text MS Columbia; Stallman 198

[letterhead: Pent Farm]
23/12/98

My dear Mrs Crane.

You are indeed good and kind to remember us all so charmingly.

Jess was delighted with this proof of your friendliness and as to the boy he simply went mad over the things. For sometime he looked with suspicion at the big doll but at last he kissed her and they are great friends now. As to the animals he won't part with them. He persists in saying Moo! to the goat. He takes it for a cow—evidently.

I wish you could have given us some news from Stephen. Well, please god you will have your mind and your heart at rest soon.[1] I need not tell you it is the fervent wish of those who live here and however ineffectually, but not the less sincerely take part in your anxieties and hopes. May the Xmas be a season of joy indeed and the new year a year of peace to you. Amen.

Our heartiest and friendliest wishes to the good Auntie Ruedy.[2] We trust to see you all *three* here before the young year has the time to grow old or even middle aged. Let me share in all that befal[l]s you as you have done me the hono[u]r to allow me heretofore.

I am dear Mrs Crane Your faithful
friend and servant

Jph. Conrad

[1] Stephen landed at Gravesend, 11 January. [2] Cora Crane's friend.

To H. G. Wells
Text MS Illinois; J-A, 1, 263

[letterhead: Pent Farm]
23/12/98

My dear Wells.

We called yesterday by an act of inspiration so to speak, and with the neglect of common civilities did so at 2.45 pm. for which we were very properly punished by not finding you at home. We would have waited but we'd left the baby in the gutter (there was a fly[1] under him tho') and the days are too short to allow of camping in a friend's drawing room. So we went despondently. And by the bye. There was an Invisible Man (apparently of a jocose disposition) on your doorstep because when I rang (modestly) an invisible finger kept the button down (or in rather) and the bell jingling continuously to my extreme confusion (and the evident surprise of your girl). I wish you would keep your creations in some kind of order, confined in books or locked up in the cells of your brain to be let out at stated times (frequently, frequently of course!) instead of letting them wander about the premises, startling visitors who mean you no harm—anyhow. My nerves can't stand that kind of thing—and now I shan't come near you till next year. There!

Coming back we found Your Card. We haven't cards. We ain't civilized enough—not yet. But the wishes for the health, happiness and peace of you both I am writing down here in mine and my wife's name are formulated with primitive sincerity, and the only conventional thing about them is the time of their voicing prescribed by the superstitions of men. Thus are we the slaves of a gang of fools unable to read your work aright and unwilling to buy a single entire edition of any of mine. Verily they deserve to have the Heat-Ray[2] turned upon them—but I suppose it would be unseasonable just now. Conventions stand in the way of the most meritorious undertakings.

Has Henley come down here after all? When you favour me with a missive let me know how he is, if You know.

Ever Yours

Jph Conrad.

---

[1] Of the wheeled variety.   [2] As used by the Martians in *The War of the Worlds*.

To Aniela Zagórska

Text J-A, 1, 263; Najder 227[1]

[Pent Farm]
Christmas 1898.

My dear Aniela,

I have just received your letter and I am replying to it at once. The news that you give me distresses me. La vie est dure—très dure, for me also, my dearest.

I shall send you some cuttings (in envelopes, like letters) from the *Saturday Review* and other periodicals which deal with literature—and I shall add occasionally some notes taken by myself.

Grant Allen's *Woman Who Did*,[2] c'est un livre mort. Gr. Allen is a man of inferior intelligence and his work is not art in any sense. The *Woman Who Did* had a kind of success, of curiosity mostly and that only among the philistines—the sort of people who read Marie Corelli and Hall Caine.[3] Neither of these writers belongs to literature. All three are very popular with the public—and they are also puffed in the press. There are no lasting qualities in their work. The thought is commonplace and the style (?) without any distinction. They are popular because they express the common thought, and the common man is delighted to find himself in accord with people he supposes distinguished. This is the secret of many popularities. (You can develop this idea as an explanation of the enthusiasm of the public for books which are of no value). Grant Allen is considered a man of letters among scholars and a scholar among men of letters. He writes popular scientific manuals equally well. En somme—un imbécile. Marie Corelli is *not* noticed critically by the serious reviews. She is simply ignored. Her books sell largely. Hall Caine is a kind of male Marie Corelli. He is the great master of the art of self-advertising. He is always being interviewed by reporters and is simply mad with vanity. He is a megalomaniac, who thinks himself the

---

[1] For textual source, see n. 5 to letter of 6 February 1898.

[2] Grant Allen (1848–99), novelist and speculative writer, published his notorious book in 1895; its story of a 'new woman' who rejects the orthodox sexual arrangements caused a furore; among the rejoinders it provoked was *The Woman Who Didn't*, written by the appropriately named 'Victoria Cross'.

[3] Two of the day's most admired authors. Corelli (really Mary Mackay, 1855–1924) wrote *A Romance of Two Worlds* (1886), *Barabbas* (1893), and *The Mighty Atom* (1896); her house at Stratford-upon-Avon became a major tourist attraction. Once a friend of D. G. Rossetti, and later knighted for services to literature, Thomas Henry Hall Caine (1853–1931) loved to grant interviews at his castle on the Isle of Man, bought with the proceeds of such works as *The Scapegoat* (1891), *The Manxman* (1894), and *The Christian* (1897).

greatest man of the century, quite a prodigy. He maintains that the lower part of his face is like Shakespeare and the upper like Jesus Christ. (This gives you an idea about the man.) Du reste aucune valeur, as you will see reading that book. Besides, one should say that he certainly made more than 60 thousand roubles on this book. His publisher is my publisher too—and I know it from this source. For the American edition he got almost another 60,000 roubles.

Among the writers who deserve attention the first is Rudyard Kipling (his last book *The Day's Work*, a novel). J. M. Barrie—a Scotsman. His last book *Sentimental Tommy* (last year). George Meredith did not bring out anything this year. The last volumes of the charming translation of Turgenev came out a fortnight ago. The translation is by Mrs. Constance Garnett.[1] George Moore has published the novel *Evelyn Innes*—un succès d'estime. He is supposed to belong to the naturalistic school and Zola is his prophet. Tout ça, c'est très vieux jeu. A certain Mr. T. Watts-Dunton published the novel *Aylwin*, a curiosity success, as this Watts-Dunton (who is a barrister) is apparently a friend of different celebrities in the world of Fine Arts (especially in the pre-Raphaelite School).[2] He has crammed them all into his book. H. G. Wells published this year *The War of the Worlds* and *The Invisible Man*. He is a very original writer, romancier du fantastique, with a very individualistic judgment in all things and an astonishing imagination.

But, my dearest, really I read nothing and I *never* look at the papers, so I know nothing of politics and literature. I have barely time to write, for I find work very hard and it is only with difficulty that I can earn a little bread. This is the whole truth.

I shall see Mr. Wells in a few days and I will ask him on your behalf for permission to translate *The Invisible Man* into Polish. If I can arrange this I will send you the book. The language is easy—the story very interesting; it would make a very good serial for a paper. If you undertook this work and if you would send me the sheets as and when you finish them, I shall put notes in the margin which may help you. But you certainly know English as well as I do—and I do not speak of your Polish!

For the moment I am not writing anything. Since the month of January! I have been in such a state that I have been unable to write

---

[1] *The Day's Work* is a collection of stories; *Sentimental Tommy* came out in 1896; Meredith's most recent novel was *The Amazing Marriage* (1895); Constance Garnett finished her series of Turgenev translations in 1899.

[2] Theodore Watts-Dunton (1834–1914) shared his suburban villa with Swinburne, sedately.

anything. It was not until November that I started to work. The novel which was ordered from me is 10 months behind. This is catastrophe! and even now I am not at all well.

I kiss your hands. I embrace my little cousins.

Yours with all my heart,
K. Korzeniowski.

PS. With what I have written you and two books to review, on peut faire un article,—pas une chose profonde, mais du bon journalisme. Try. I shall send you, at the same time as the cuttings, a few notes about the authors—if I know anything about them. This is what the papers need. A chat, an appreciation, something light and interesting. Du journalisme tout pur. If you begin writing, try to do it. It always pays.

To William Blackwood

Text MS NLS; Blackburn 36

[letterhead: Pent Farm]
31/12/98

Dear Mr Blackwood.

Come this moment to hand is your good le[t]ter whose kind wishes, believe me, I reciprocate with all my heart.

Your proposal delights me.[1] As it happens I am (and have been for the last 10 days) working for *Maga*. The thing is far advanced and would have been finished by this only our little boy fell ill, I was disturbed and upset and the work suffered. I expect to be ready in a very few days. It is a narrative after the manner of *youth* told by the same man dealing with his experiences on a river in Central Africa. The *idea* in it is not as obvious as in *youth*—or at least not so obviously presented. I tell you all this, for tho' I have no doubts as to the *workmanship* I do not know whether the *subject* will commend itself to you for that particular number.[2] Of course I should be very glad to appear in it and shall try to hurry up the copy for that express purpose, but I wish you to understand that I am prepared to leave the ultimate decision as to the date of appearance to your decision after perusal.

The title I am thinking of is "*The Heart of Darkness*" but the narrative is not gloomy The criminality of inefficiency and pure selfishness when

---

[1] Blackwood had written from Edinburgh the previous day soliciting a contribution for the February issue of *Blackwood's* – the thousandth number.

[2] 'Heart of Darkness' did begin in that issue.

tackling the civilizing work in Africa is a justifiable idea. The subject is of our time distinc[t]ly—though not topically treated. It is a story as much as my *Outpost of Progress* was but, so to speak 'takes in' more—is a little wider—is less concentrated upon individuals. I destine it for the vol: which is to bear Your imprint. Its lenght* will be under 20.000 words as I see it now.[1] If suitable and you wish to curtail it a couple of pars: could be taken out—from the proof, perhaps.

There is also the question of McClure securing copyright in the States. They bungled the *Youth* affair[2] and I am not in a position to despise the almighty dollar—as yet.

All I can do is to hurry up. Meantime many thanks for thinking of me.

Friendly greetings to Your Nephew.[3] I am delighted to be remembered by him.

I am dear Mr Blackwood, most
sincerely yours

Jph. Conrad

To Minnie Brooke

Text MS Texas; Unpublished

Tuesday. [1898 ?][4]

Dear Mrs. Brooke.

I write at once these few lines to tell you how grieved we both were to hear of your illness.

You had indeed a rough time of it lately!

You do say a lot of nice, kind things about my work. I am very grateful to You for the friendship and the interest you display. It is in the coin of sympathy and good will that my efforts towards literature are recompensed; and indeed it is the most precious kind of reward.

Thanks for kind enquiries about Jess and the boy. They are both well. My wife is going to write to you very soon. I am very unwilling to have their photographs taken. I hate photographs anyhow! But if there are any You shall be remembered first.

Believe me Your grateful and
faithful servant

Jph Conrad.

---

[1] In final form, closer to 40,000.   [2] See letter of 12 October 1898.
[3] George Blackwood, later head of the firm.
[4] Placing arbitrary: there are no dated letters to Mrs Brooke after 1898.

To E. L. Sanderson

Text MS Taylor; Unpublished

Sunday. [1897–1900]¹

Dearest Ted

I hoped to invade you to-day, but got held up in the usual way. I am tired of the persistency and regularity of this odious infirmity.

We were grieved to hear of your elbow. Indeed I noticed at Elstree that it was worrying you, and told Jessie on my return. We saw lately the wonderful good effects of the treatment of which You speak and hope that it will not fail with You. The weather too will be improving before long—or it ought to. I want to see You and *shall* [. . .]² dare not run the risk of being laid up. I've been idle (or rather unproductive) too long already. Our dear love to you

¹ Arbitrary placing: the spring following Conrad's marriage and Sanderson's departure for South Africa early in 1900 provide the limiting dates.
² MS damaged.

1899

To David Meldrum

Text MS Duke; Blackburn 37

[letterhead: Pent Farm]

2 Jan 1899

Dear Mr Meldrum.

I enclose here a letter from Mr Blackwood and a note (at the back of my reply).

This will make it clear to You how matters are. I am very pleased Mr B'wood thought of me; but his letter coming just now makes it difficult for me to do what I intended doing[1]—or at least I fancy so.

I began the story for Maga 10 days ago. It would have been finished Yesterday had it not been our boy fell ill (he is better now) and thus knocked on the head my peace of mind and, say, inspiration. At any rate there is a delay. Now my intention was to ask Mr Blackwood to let me have £40 before the 10th Jan. on the *general* account of my short stories (ser & book). The story would have covered the sum or more; but now the story is not quite ready and my necessity remains all the same. Still I would have asked for the cheque had it not been for this extremely pleasant letter. I don't want M^r B'wood to think I am taking advantage of his ouverture*. In this difficulty real or fancied may I ask you whether you could arrange the matter for me with Mr B'wood. The story shall be in your hands shortly it will be about 20000 words (at the agreed rate for serial it would be about £50). My necessity is not a matter of life or death but of the very greatest inconvenience of which I would fain be relieved by your good offices.[2] If you think I could ask Mr B'wood without gross indecency please mediate. I've just written to him and don't want to fire off another letter. And you can put a better look on the thing.

If you want to refer to the story its title so far is *The Heart of Darkness*. A Central Afr: narrative in the manner of Youth—told by the same man. It would stand dividing into two instalments.

I would like you particularly to read the story and the type shall go to London. As I write this one in pencil my wife *must* type, herself or I would send you the *MS* of what is ready. A mere shadow of love interest

---

[1] The volume of sea stories that Conrad had first discussed with Meldrum in June 1898.
[2] Blackburn (p. 40) gives Meldrum's eloquent and generous plea on Conrad's behalf.

just in the last pages—but I hope it will have the effect I intend. With our kindest regards to Mrs Meldrum and yourself

I am most faithfully yours

Jph. Conrad.

Mrs Crane still without news.[1] I don't know what to think

To Ford Madox Ford

Text MS Yale; Unpublished

[Pent Farm]
Tuesday. [3 January 1899][2]

My dear Hueffer.

Just a word of thanks. The story I told you of holds me. It grows like the genii out of the bottle in the Tale. Won't be done till *Sat*. Till then I am distracted.

With kindest regards to You both from us two.

Ever Yours

Jph. Conrad.

To H. G. Wells

Text MS Illinois; Unpublished

Pent Farm
Tuesday. [3 January 1899][3]

My dear Wells.

Thanks ever so much. The trans: of the T. M. is really *very* first rate.[4]

What an admirably good thing it is, this T. M. How true, clever, ingenious, full of thought and beauty. I read on in the trans: neglecting my work. I haven't looked into the W[heels] of C[hance] yet. I can't till I am done with my infernal tale. It grows like the genii from the bottle in the Arabian Tale. Seventy pages—pencil pencil—since I saw you. Also the boy has been ill. My wife's kind regards to Mrs Wells and you. She wants to know how you got home. Anyway let me know how you are. I fancy I shall turn up at Granville St[?] before long.

Your

Conrad.

[1] Instead of coming directly from New York, Crane returned by way of Havana.
[2] Postmarked Wednesday, 4 January.
[3] An almost identical reference to 'Heart of Darkness' suggests the same date as the letter to Ford.
[4] *The Time Machine* was serialized in *Mercure de France*.

To William Blackwood
Text MS NLS; Blackburn 39

[letterhead: Pent Farm]
6th Jan 1899

Dear Mr Blackwood.

Thanks very much for the cheque for £40 (on account of short stories) which I received to-day.

I am, dear Sir always faithfully
yours

Jph. Conrad.

P.S. I assure you I appreciate your prompt readiness. I am—alas! not so prompt. Still to morrow I shall send off about 12.000 of *H. of D* to Mr Meldrum. I shall also request him to have a copy typewritten on my ac^t to hand to *McClure*.[1]

Lots more of the story is written—not typed, and in a few days shall be despatched. I am afraid it will be too long for one n°

It has grown upon me a bit—and anyhow the value is in the detail.

J. C.

To the Baroness Janina de Brunnow
Text L.fr. 36; Najder 230

Pent Farm.
Stanford. near Hythe.
Kent
6th Jan. 1899[?][2]

Chère Madame,[3]

Rien qu'un mot tout de suite pour vous dire combien je suis désolé d'apprendre l'affreux accident qui vous est arrivé.[4] Mais surtout pour vous dire que je suis bien heureux de savoir que vous daignez me garder une place dans votre mémoire. Rien qu'un mot en toute hâte, car je suis fort occupé au milieu d'un travail qui attend et que l'on attend de moi

---

[1] For the North American market.   [2] The date is questionable: see n. 1, overleaf.
[3] Mme la Baronne de Brunnow (née Taube, 1865–1943), a boyhood friend now married to a general in the Russian army.
[4] According to Jean-Aubry, the loss of a close relation.

avec impatience puisqu'il devait ètre fini en Novembre et qu'il est encore là,[1]—sur ma table.

Mes meilleurs souhaits pour vous et tous les vôtres. Ceci vient du coeur qui n'est guère éloquent. Plus un sentiment est vrai, moins on se trouve en état de l'exprimer.

Donc je finis,—pour cette fois—avec mille remerciements et l'assurance de ma profonde et sincère amitié.

Toujours votre très fidèle
serviteur.
Conrad Korzeniowski.

Je me ferai le plaisir d'écrire bientôt une longue lettre à votre adresse. Mes amitiés et mille souhaits à Monsieur votre mari.

Translation

Dear Madame,

Only a word at once to tell you how saddened I am to learn of the frightful misfortune which has happened to you. But above all to tell you I am indeed happy to know you are good enough to keep me a place in your memory. Only a word in all haste, for I am extremely busy: in the middle of a piece of work waiting and impatiently waited for because it should have been finished in November and is still there—on my table.

My best wishes to you and all yours. This comes, by no means eloquently, from the heart. The more a feeling is true, the less one is in a position to express it.

So I finish—for the time being—with a thousand thanks and the assurance of my deep and genuine friendship.

Always your very faithful servant,
Conrad Korzeniowski

I shall soon give myself the pleasure of directing a long letter to you. My compliments and a thousand good wishes to your husband.

---

[1] 'Heart of Darkness', if Conrad dated (and Jean-Aubry copied) this letter accurately. Far from expecting that work in November, however, Blackwood did not even know of it until the end of December. On 27 December 1899, Conrad again sent his condolences. Although the texts do not fit together smoothly ('un mot tout de suite' in one, 'je n'osais pas prendre la plume' in the other), they may both concern the same event. If so, the present letter would have been written on 6 January 1900, when Conrad was toiling over *Lord Jim*. Alternatively, 27 December may be a Russian date, the equivalent in the Roman calendar of 8 January 1900.

To W. H. Chesson

Text MS Rosenbach; *Listy* 156; Original unpublished

[letterhead: Pent Farm]
7th Jan 1899.

My dear Mr Chesson.

I am a brute. Your letter so unexpected so charming, so appreciative ought to have been answered at once to the neglect of everything— though indeed to let you understand the pleasure it gave me would have been well nigh impossible.

Well You must forgive me and in that Christian spirit accept my belated wishes for the New Year—and my assurance as to the value I attach to every word of Your favourable appreciation.

The above heading is the address of my burial place and if you are not afraid of Ghosts (nothing Ibsenish) you must come and spend a Sunday in the sepulchre. Trains to this mausoleum are good. On Sat: *2.40* to come by and there is a good one on Mond: to return by to the "busy haunts of men".[1]

Drop advice *early* as the visitors to the shrine may have to walk two miles if they neglect that precaution. Cho[o]se a promising day. Sunshine would rob the experience of half its horrors. Bring a firm mind and an ascetic disposition and you shall survive the trial. Most faithfully Yours

Jph Conrad.

How's Garnett. I haven't heard of him for ages.

To David Meldrum

Text MS Duke; Blackburn 40

[letterhead: Pent Farm]
Monday. [9 January 1899][2]

Dear Mr Meldrum.

I send you pp. *1. to 35* typed of *The Heart of Darkness* and from 35 (typed) it goes on to p. 58 of Manuscript.

pp 58 to 90

which is all written up to yesterday. I am awfully sorry to send the pencil *MS* but my wife is not well enough to go on and I want you to have the first half of the story at once. May I ask you to have *the whole* typed out on

---

[1] Felicia Hemans, *Tale of the Secret Tribunal.*
[2] This letter must fit between those of 6 and 13 January.

my acc/t in at least 2 copies. One for Mr McClure and one for *Maga*. The type *from the MS* should be corrected by me before going to printers so You perhaps will let me have that portion for that purpose as soon as ready.

I had a friendly letter and cheque £40 from Mr Blackwood. I am in doubt as to the 1000th N°. There will be no time for US. Copyright. And I can't forego a penny. Are you angry with me for the bother I am giving? I am working under difficulties and that's the truth. Thanks.

Apologies. Cordially Yours
Joseph Conrad.

PS Where MS. illegible let them leave blank spaces I can fill up when correcting.

Stephen left for Europe I hear.

To the Hon. A. E. Bontine

Text J-A, 1, 265

Pent Farm.
12th Jan. 1899.

Dear Mrs. Bontine,

My humble apology for not thanking you before for the volume of verses. I share your opinion of Maupassant.[1] The man is a great artist, who sees the essential in everything. He is not a great poet,—perhaps no poet at all, yet I like his verses. I like them immensely.

To-day, from your kindness, I received the *Chronicle* with Robert's letter.[2] C'est bien ça,—c'est bien lui!

Is he in London now? I have it on my conscience that I did not reply yet to his last letter. I couldn't. A fit of silence. I had too much to say perhaps,—and perhaps nothing. Je deviens bête et sauvage.

Pardon this hurried scrawl. I am finishing in a frightful hurry a story for *B'wood* and it's an immense effort.

With many things I am, dear Mrs. Bontine, always your most faithful and obedient servant.

---

[1] For Conrad's opinion see *Letters*, 1, 184–5 and the appreciation in *Notes on Life and Letters*. Mrs Bontine had sent a copy of *Des Vers* (1880).

[2] 'Pax Britannica', *Daily Chronicle*, 11 January: an attack on colonial double-think and 'the safe massacre of spear-armed men falling like corn before the reaper two miles away from our brave fellows'.

To Stephen Crane
Text MS Columbia; Stallman 205

[letterhead: Pent Farm]
13th Jan 99.

My dear Stephen.

I am more glad than I can say to hear of you being here at last. You haven't lost time in looking up the old *Academy*.[1] I only heard of it to-day. Thanks very much for your second wire. All this would be damnable bosh but for the 50gs which just save me from battering my head against the walls.

I long to hear your news. And let me tell you at once that the *Harness*[2] is the best bit of work you've done (for its size) since the *Red Badge*. There is a mellowness in the vigour of that story that simply delighted me. Several fellows wrote to me about it as soon as it came out. Lucas, Hueffer, Graham and others you don't know. More power to your pen. I feel a new man since this morning's wire. It was good of you to think of me at once. I intended to wire myself to-day inquiring. Well that's all over now. I know where to locate you when I think of you—which is often—very. I've been nearly dead and several times quite mad since you left. This is no joke it is the sober truth. I haven't been able to write and felt like cutting my throat. Not a ghost of a notion in my head, not a sentence under the pen. Well. Never mind. It's a little better now.—What have you got in *Your* head? You must be full of stuff. I suppose the 'Dead Man' story[3] will have to wait till you unload your new experience. I know whatever it is it will be *good*. It will be great! You think I might have given a whole sheet of paper for your welcome, but may I be shot if can find another piece. I am coming to see you directly I finish a rotten thing I am writing for B'wood. It *is* rotten—and I can't help it. All I write is rotten now. I am pretty well decayed myself. I ought to be taken out and flung into a dusthole—along with the dead cats—by heavens! Well. Enough. I don't want to bore you into a faint in your first week in Merry England.

Ever yours

Conrad

---

[1] The 14 January issue of the *Academy* (pp. 66–7) announced the 'crowning' of *Tales of Unrest* as one of the most significant publications in the previous year and associated with the award 'Youth', 'Mr. Conrad's most humanly touching work'. The honour brought with it a prize of fifty guineas. Other crowns went to Sidney Lee's *A Life of William Shakespeare* and Maurice Hewlett's *The Forest Lovers*.
[2] 'The Price of the Harness'.   [3] 'The Upturned Face', not yet written.

To David Meldrum
Text MS Duke; Blackburn 42

[letterhead: Pent Farm]
13 Jan 99.

My dear Mr Meldrum.

Very, very many thanks for your wire. *That* was a real pleasure. As for the thing itself—it is convenient truly and amazing enough. But I am so little conscious of any kind of merit that I ask myself whether the affair is serious. It looks like a piece of luck. Now, luck is all very well.

—I suppose you'll think I am a poor, discontented creature. It isn't that at all. I can take a blessing in no matter what disguise. I can't get rid of a suspicion of injustice. I don't see anything very *solid* in my prose. However I shall keep all this to myself. I couldn't help let[t]ing You see a little of what's inside my thoughts.

I shall come up as soon as *H of D* is finished. I've sent the balance of type to Ed: I am infinitely grateful to you for your patience with me. Believe me most sincerely yours

Jph Conrad.

To Edward Garnett
Text MS Colgate; G. 147

[letterhead: Pent Farm]
13 Jan 99.

My dear Garnett

Have you seen *it*! *It*! The Academy. When I opened the letter I thought it was a mistake. But it was too true, alas. I've lost the last ounce of respect for my art. I am lost—gone—done for—for the consideration of 50 g[uinea]s.

I suppose Lucas[1] worked like a horse to get this awful, awful job through. I suppose you worked too—or no— I won't suppose. Where do you chaps expect to go to when You die?

Ah if I could only write! If I could write, write, write! But I can not. No 50 gs. will help me to that. However I am turning out some rotten stuff for B.wood's 1000ᵗʰ Nº. Been asked to! Honours will never cease. 'House' wrote autograph![2] Ah will you—says I. Thereupon I cram them with rubbish. As soon as I turn out the last line I shall come to town for a

---

[1] E. V. Lucas, critic, journalist, and Garnett's friend.
[2] William Blackwood himself wrote the invitation to appear in the thousandth number.

couple of days. Must see you. Also others. Let me know where You perch. Where You hop too.

Ever Yours

Jph C.

What news of your wife and boy?

To E. L. Sanderson
Text MS Yale; Unpublished

[letterhead: Pent Farm]
Monday [16? January 1899][1]

Dearest Ted

I am delighted and overjoyed, and with all my heart with you both. My wife shares my jubilation and the joyful and excellent news. Keep us informed (by the shortest word) of the state of affairs.

What a relief to your mind! And to your heart too. We here have been speculating dimly but anxiously tho we did not think the event was so near.

I must catch the post. Congratulations in words as affectionate as You can imagine.

Ever Yours

Jph Conrad.

To David Meldrum
Text MS Duke; Blackburn 43

[letterhead: Pent Farm]
Monday [16 January 1899][2]

Dear Mr Meldrum.

Pardon my brutally bad behaviour. Of course I would be delighted and it is very good of you to ask me. As soon as I am done with the *H of D* I shall write you and the day after call on you in Paternoster Row.[3] It will be before end of this month for certain.

The thing has grown on me. I don't think it will be bad.

With very kind regards

Most sincerely Yours

Jph. Conrad.

[1] The type of letterhead places this congratulatory note between November and February. Katherine, the Sandersons' first child, was born 12 January.

[2] 16 and 23 January are the only possible Mondays; in view of the 13 January letter to Meldrum, the earlier date looks more likely.

[3] They met before Conrad had finished.

To Ford Madox Ford

Text MS Yale; Unpublished

[London][1]
Monday [30 January 1899][2]

Dear Hueffer

Saw Meldrum today. He had been in Holland. Your proposal of Cinque Ports book[3] gone to Edinburgh with very warm recommendation. M likes the idea very much. Where's the play?[4]

I am here for two days when[5] I return to work. Excuse my brutal silence. I was simply silly with the hatching of that story.

Always Yours,

Jph Conrad

My kindest regards to your wife.

To R. B. Cunninghame Graham

Text MS Dartmouth; J-A, 1, 266; Watts 114

[letterhead: Pent Farm]
2[d] Febr 99

Cher et excellent ami.

I haven't two ideas in my head and I want to talk to you all the same. Horrid state to be in.

Pawling[6] says your book is going off. The reviews are *good* tho' positively repulsive. Que voulez-vous. They are good selling reviews.

We sang songs of praise before your greatness this morning with G[arnett]. G is preparing your Unwin vol.[7] for the press. May the best of lucks attend it.

A thing of mine began in B'wood's 1000th N[o] to conclude in Feb[y].[8] I am shy of sending it to you—but have no objection to you looking at it if it should come in your way.

Don't, don't ask about the Rescue. It will [be] finished about end March unless it makes an end of me before.

I was in London one day, amongst publishers and other horrors. My heart is heavy but my spirits are a little better.

[1] Letter written on Junior Carlton Club stationery with the embossed letterhead crossed out. Galsworthy belonged to the Junior Carlton from 1896 to 1904 (Marrot, p. 112).
[2] Meldrum's report to Blackwood (2 February: Blackburn, p. 44) fixes the date.
[3] Blackwood published a small edition of this 'Historical and Descriptive Record' of the Kent and Sussex ports in 1900.
[4] It came to nothing.   [5] 'and then'.   [6] Of Heinemann's, the publishers of *Mogreb*.
[7] *The Ipané*.   [8] It came out in the February, March, and April issues.

McIntyre is really "impayable"[1]—and so are you. D'ye think the shipowners of "Glesga" are gone mad. They will never never give a ship to a "chiel"[2] that can write prose—or who is even suspected of such criminal practices.

I am writing an idiotic letter.

If I could tell really what I feel for you for your work and for the spirit that abides in the acts and the thoughts of your passage amongst this jumble of shadows and—well—filth which is called the earth You would think it fulsome adulation. So I won't say anything and shall hug myself with both hands in the assurance of your friendship.

This is stupidly put and a cynic would say it was stupidly felt. *Are* you a cynic?

Quelle bête de vie! Nom de nom quelle bête de vie! Sometimes I lose all sense of reality in a kind of nightmare effect produced by existence. Then I try to think of you—to wake myself. And it does wake me. I don't know how you feel about yourself but to me you appear extremely real—even when I perceive you enveloped in the cloud of Your irremediable illusions.

I had better stop before I say something that would end in bloodshed.

Now I haven't said anything and that's enough. Ever desperately yours

Conrad.

To William Blackwood and Sons
Text MS NLS; Blackburn 45

[Pent Farm]
[7 February 1899][3]

Dear Sirs.

I have marked (on the last page p65) the place where the first instalment might end.

It would be about *half* of the whole story or perhaps a little more.

I shall hurry up the rest as fast as I can. Excuse this scrap of paper and the pencil.

In great haste
Yours faithfully

Jph. Conrad.

---

[1] The radiologist who had looked after Conrad on his visit to Scotland is 'invaluable'.
[2] 'fellow'.
[3] The packet of MS went off by 'Tuesdays morning post': letter to Meldrum of 8 February.

To Aniela Zagórska

Text J-A, 1, 267; Najder 230[1]

Pent Farm,
7.2.'99.

My dear Aniela,

Just a few lines in answer to your letter, for which I thank you. I have seen Mr. Wells, who considers it an honour that his works should be translated into Polish. You must know that the *Mercure de France* has finished the publication of his novel, *The Time-Machine*.

In two days I will send you the book. You can introduce the translation as being authorized by the author. If you plan to publish it in a newspaper, you could suggest a summary to the editor and an appreciation of the author—introduced to the Polish public, as it were—by myself—about 500–1,000 words.[2] But only in the event of this being of any use to place the novel.

I am not sending you any cuttings, as there is nothing of any interest. I will send you soon a note on Miss Kingsley's book on Africa.[3] C'est un voyageur et un écrivain très remarquable. Her opinions on questions dealing with colonies are thought a great deal of.

Here is the photo of Mr. Borys, agé d'un an et deux jours. His mamma, who sends you 'lots of love', is not well. She looks like a very stout old woman—which she is not yet.

Your card written in English is almost without a mistake. Evidently you have a practical knowledge of the language. Cela se voit.

Forgive this hasty letter, but I am awfully busy and surrounded with these wretched editors.

A thousand embraces
Your Konrad Korzeniowski.

---

[1] For textual source, see n. 5 to letter of 6 February 1898.
[2] He did not write such an appreciation.
[3] Mary Henrietta Kingsley (born 1862), explorer and reformer, published an account of her travels in *West African Studies* (1898). The following year she died while nursing Boer prisoners of war.

To Algernon Methuen
Text MS Berg; J-A, 1, 267

[letterhead: Pent Farm][1]
7th Feby 99.

Dear Sir.[2]

Forgive the delay in answering your friendly and flat[t]ering letter; but I was away from home and on my return having a story to finish for 'Maga' I left according to my practice all my letters unopened. Thus the delay is the fault of the system not of the man.

Frankly, I am such an unsatisfactory person that giving promises for books should be the last thing for me to do. I am so unsatisfactory that I am not at all sure of appearing in the Ill: London News. I've inconvenienced Mr Shorter.[3] I know it because he said so to me in writing a few days ago. I made a suitable reply—I mean suitable to my state of mind. And this is the last I know of the affair. However the book is promised; had been so for this year past.

Candidly I dare not make any promises. I write with difficulty, I don't keep my word, I worry my publishers, I try their tempers. I am afraid it would take much better writing than mine to make up for these defects—of character.

I am, dear Sir, faithfully yours
Jph Conrad.

To R. B. Cunninghame Graham
Text MS Yale; J-A, 1, 268; Watts 116

[Pent Farm]
8 Feb^r 99.

Cherissime ami.

I am simply in the seventh heaven to find you like the *H of D* so far. You bless me indeed. Mind you don't curse me by and bye for the very same thing. There are two more instalments in which the idea is so wrapped up in secondary notions that You—even You!—may miss it. And also You must remember that I don't start with an abstract notion.

---

[1] First use of the new letterhead.
[2] Jean-Aubry identified the recipient as Algernon Methuen. Methuen (whose name was originally Stedman, 1856–1924) founded his company in 1889. Besides text-books, which were the source of the firm's prosperity, he published works by Kipling, Stevenson, Maeterlinck and, later, six titles by Conrad.
[3] The editor – by not delivering *The Rescue*.

I start with definite images and as their rendering is true some little effect is produced. So far the note struck chimes in with your convictions—mais après? There is an après. But I think that if you look a little into the episodes you will find in them the right intention though I fear nothing that is practically effective. Somme toute c'est une bête d'histoire qui aurait pu être quelque chose de très bien si j'avais su l'écrire.[1]

The thing in West. Gaz. is excellent, excellent.[2] I am most interested in your plans of work and travel. I don't know in which most. Nous allons causer de tout cela.[3]

As to the peace meeting.[4] If you want me to come I want still more to hear you. But—I am not a peace man, nor a democrat (I don't know what the word means really) and if I come I shall go into the body of the hall. I want to hear you—just as I want always to read you. I can't be an accomplice after or before the fact to any sort of fraternity that includes the westerners whom I so dislike.[5] The platform! I pensez-Vous?[6] Il y aura des Russes. Impossible! I can not admit the idea of fraternity not so much because I believe it impracticable, but because its propaganda (the only thing really tangible about it) tends to weaken the national sentiment the preservation of which is my concern. When I was in Poland 5 years ago[7] and managed to get in contact with the youth of the university in Warsaw I preached at them and abused them for their social democratic tendencies. L'idée democratique est un très beau phantôme, and to run after it may be fine sport, but I confess I do not see what evils it is destined to remedy. It confers distinction on Messieurs Jaurès, Liebknecht & C[o8] and your adhesion confers distinction upon it.

---

[1] 'In short, it's a stupid story that would have been very good, if I had known how to write it.'

[2] 'A Pakeha' (the Maori word for European), *Westminster Gazette*, 31 January, reports a conversation with a neighbour about the old days of territorial plunder in New Zealand (reprinted in *Thirteen Stories*).

[3] 'We are going to chat about all that.'

[4] Organised by the Social Democratic Federation as a counter-movement to the Tsar of Russia's call for an international conference of heads of state, the meeting was held in London on 8 March. Conrad did attend, and heard his friend say that 'The workers themselves would have to settle the problem of international peace for themselves, as they, and they alone, held the key of the whole situation' (Watts, p. 120).

[5] Conrad may mean the Germans ('westerners' from the Polish standpoint), or he may mean Russians with western sympathies (the 'Russes', some of whom were to be on the platform).

[6] One can make sense here either by imagining a dash after 'I' or by transforming 'I' to the French 'y'.

[7] 1893.

[8] Jean Jaurès (1859–1914), Socialist speaker, writer and member of the French Chamber of Deputies: a fervent pacifist, he was assassinated on the eve of the First World War.

International fraternity may be an object to strive for and, in sober truth, since it has Your support I will try to think it serious, but that illusion imposes by its size alone. Franchement what would you think of an attempt to promote fraternity amongst people living in the same street. I don't even mention two neighbouring streets. Two ends of the same street. There is already as much fraternity as there can be—and thats very little and that very little is no good. What does fraternity mean. Abnegation—self-sacrifice means something. Fraternity means nothing unless the Cain–Abel business. Thats your true fraternity. Assez.

L'homme est un animal méchant.[1] Sa méchanceté doit être organisée. Le crime est une condition néréssaire de l'existence organisée. La société est essentielment criminelle—ou elle n'existerait pas.[2] C'est l'égoisme qui sauve tout—absolument tout—tout ce que nous abhorrons tout ce que nous aimons. Et tout se tient. Voilà pourquoi je respecte les êxtremes anarchistes.[3]—"Je souhaite l'extermination generale"— Très bien. C'est juste et ce qui est plus c'est clair. On fait des compromis avec des paroles. Ça n'en finit plus. C'est comme une forêt ou personne ne connait la route. On est perdu pendant que l'on crie—"Je suis sauvé!"

Non. Il faut un principe défini. Si l'idée nationale aporte la souffrance et son service donne la mort ça vaut toujours mieux que de servir les ombres d'une eloquence qui est morte, justement par ce qu'elle n'a pas de corps. Croyez-moi si je Vous dis que ces questions là sont pour moi très sérieuses—beaucoup plus que pour Messieurs Jaurès, Liebknecht et Cie. Vous—vous pouvez tout faire. Vous êtes essentielment un frondeur. Cela Vous est permis. Ce sont les Nobles qui ont fait la Fronde du reste.[4] Moi je regarde l'avenir du fond d'un passé très noir et je

---

Wilhelm Liebknecht (1826–1900), a disciple of Marx but founder of the German Social Democratic party, was a member of the Reichstag and had been imprisoned for his beliefs. Both men spoke at the meeting.

[1] A translation of the whole passage follows the main text.

[2] Watts (p. 121) points out parallels in Anatole France's *Les Opinions de M. Jérôme Coignard* (1893).

[3] Although most self-professed anarchists refused to kill, and others sought to assassinate only those they chose to regard as enemies of humanity, a few interpreted the idea of propaganda by deed as a licence for mass murder. In 1894, when asked why he had exploded a bomb in a crowded and unpretentious Parisian café, Emile Henry replied 'Il n'y a pas d'innocents' (James Joll, *The Anarchists* [1966], p. 137).

[4] There were two Frondes – rebellions against the young Louis XIV – between 1648 and 1653. Conrad may have remembered that the aggrieved noblemen who sponsored them asked help from Spain, even though that country was at war with their own.

trouve que rien ne m'est permis hormis la fidélité a une cause absolument perdue, a une idée sans avénir.

Aussi souvent je n'y pense pas. Tout disparait. Il ne reste que la
verité—une ombre sinistre et fuyante dont il est impossible de fixer
l'image. Je ne regrette rien—je n'espère rien car je m'aperçoit que ni le
regret ni l'espérance ne signifient rien a ma personalité. C'est un
egoisme rational et féroce que j'exerce envers moi même. Je me repose
la-dedans. Puis la pensée revient. La vie recommence, les regrets, les
souvenirs et un desespoir plus sombre que la nuit.

Je ne sais pas pourquoi je Vous dis tout cela aujourd'hui. C'est que je
ne veux pas que Vous me croyez indifferent. Je ne suis pas indifferent a
ce qui Vous interesse. Seulement mon interet est ailleurs, ma pensée suit
une autre route, mon coeur desire autre chose, mon âme souffre d'une
autre espèce d'impuissance. Comprenez Vous? Vous qui devouez Votre
enthousiasme et Vos talents a la cause de l'humanité, vous comprendrez
sans doute pourquoi je dois—j'ai besoin—de garder ma pensée intacte
comme dernier hommage de fidelité a une cause qui est perdue. C'est
tout ce que je peux faire. J'ai jété ma vie a tous les vents du ciel mais j'ai
gardé ma pensée. C'est peu de chose—c'est tout—ce n'est rien—c'est la
vie même. Cette lettre est incoherente comme mon existence mais la
logique suprême y est pourtant—la logique qui mène a la folie. Mais les
soucis de tous les jours nous font oublier la cruelle verité. C'est heureux.

Toujours à Vous de coeur

Jph Conrad.

PS Jessie sends her kind regards and thanks for message about the
story. It delights her. I shall talk with Garnett about your work. He is a
good fellow. Eye and ear? Eh? Not so bad. Only if I *could* write like
you—if I *knew* all you know—if I *believed* all you believe. If, if if!

Translation

Man is a vicious animal. His viciousness must be organised. Crime is
a necessary condition of organised existence. Society is fundamentally
criminal—or it would not exist. Selfishness preserves everything—
absolutely everything—everything we hate and everything we love. And
everything holds together. That is why I respect the extreme anarchists.—'I hope for general extermination'. Very well. It's justifiable
and, moreover, it is plain. One compromises with words. There's no end
to it. It's like a forest where no one knows the way. One is lost even as
one is calling out 'I am saved!'

No. A definite first principle is needed. If the idea of nationhood brings suffering and its service brings death, that is always worth more than service to the ghosts of a dead eloquence—precisely because the eloquence is disembodied. Believe me if I tell you that these questions are very real to me—much more so than to Messrs Jaurès, Liebknecht and Co. You—you can do everything. Essentially, you are a *frondeur* [see n. 4]. You are allowed to be. The Fronde, moreover, was conducted by the aristocracy. For myself, I look at the future from the depths of a very dark past, and I find I am allowed nothing but fidelity to an absolutely lost cause, to an idea without a future.

And so, I often do not think about it. Everything vanishes. Only truth remains—a sinister and fleeting ghost whose image is impossible to fix. I regret nothing, I hope for nothing, for I realise that neither regret nor hope means anything to my own being. Towards myself, I practice a fierce and rational selfishness. Therein I pause. Then thinking returns. Life starts again, regrets, memories, and a hopelessness darker than night.

I don't know why I'm telling you all this today. It's that I don't want you to believe me indifferent. I'm not indifferent to what concerns you. But my concern is elsewhere, my thinking follows another path, my heart wants something else, my soul suffers from another kind of impotence. Do you understand? You who devote your talents and your enthusiasm to the cause of humanity, you will understand no doubt why I must—I need to—keep my thinking inviolate as a final act of fidelity to a lost cause. It's all I can do. I've thrown my life to all the winds of heaven, but I have kept my way of thinking. It's a little thing—it's everything—it's nothing—it's life itself. This letter is incoherent, like my life, but the highest logic is there nevertheless—the logic that leads to madness. But everyday worries make us forget the cruel truth. It's fortunate.

Always yours from the heart...

To William Blackwood

Text MS NLS; Blackburn 45

[letterhead: Pent Farm]

8th Feby 1899

Dear Mr Blackwood.

Thanks very much for your wire. It put my mind at ease for I felt the balance of the story was a little long for one instalment. For the rest I was pretty well to time with it; only 24 hours late and this solely through missing the post by some ten minutes.

I got letters from various people who seem to like the thing, so far.

I was delighted with the number. Gibbon especially fetched me quite.[1] But everything is good. Munro's verses—excellent, and Whibley very interesting—very appreciative very fair.[2] I happen to know Rimbaud's verses.

I must own that I regret the old type. One misses the familiar aspect of the pages when opening the familiar cover. I am "plus royaliste que le roi"[3]—more conservative than Maga.

I am glad to see that the majority (in fact all) of the people for whose opinion I care seem to think I am on the right track in my work for Maga. When talking with Mr Meldrum about the forthcoming volume he seemed to agree with my idea of keeping to that line. I call it idea but probably it is a necessity. When I sit down to write for you I feel as if in a friendly atmosphere, untrammeled—like one is with people that understand, of whom one is perfectly sure. It is a special mood and a most enjoyable one.

Well, I must go on with the wretched novel[4] which seems to have no end and whose beginning I declare I've forgotten. It is a weird sensation; the African nightmare feeling I've tried to put into *H of D* is a mere trifle to it. Believe me, dear Sir, always very faithfully yours

Jph Conrad.

To David Meldrum
Text MS Duke; Blackburn 47

[letterhead: Pent Farm]
Wednesday. [8 February 1899][5]

Dear Mr Meldrum.

I had a wire from Mr B'wood advising me that the story is to go into three numbers.

I've send* the completed MS. to Edinburgh direct, by Tuesdays morning post.

I think it will be 40000 words. The first inst^mt was about 14000 (27 pages) and the two others should run to 12000 each. I had £40 on account and (oppressed by my usual impecuniosity) would like to have

[1] 'From the New Gibbon', Vol. 165, pp. 241–9, an unsigned essay by G. W. Steevens, the don turned war correspondent. Steevens argues that humanitarianism has corrupted modern society.
[2] Neil Munro's 'To Exiles', pp. 179–80; Charles Whibley's piece on Rimbaud, 'A Vagabond Poet', pp. 402–12.
[3] 'Il ne faut pas être plus royaliste que le roi', a maxim from the reign of Louis XVI.
[4] *The Rescue.*   [5] The telegram from Blackwood establishes the date.

the balance at once (£50–60). If you remember our conversation[1] you may perhaps guess why I am so anxious.

Pardon me for invading your home with my business. I won't offend again.

I like the story, tho' it is terribly bad in places and falls short of my intention as a whole. Still I am glad I wrote it.

>With kindest regards
>very faithfully yours
>Jph Conrad.

To David Meldrum
Text MS Duke; Blackburn 49

>[letterhead: Pent Farm]
>Friday. [10 February 1899][2]

My dear Mr Meldrum.

I got your good letter this morning and at the same time the enclosed which please read. This is the third message of the sort since I saw you. Either the man is nervously anxious or he wants to put pressure on me—or he is in a bad way.[3] In any case this kind of thing will drive me crazy. I can't work after I get such letters. I did send him the £50 of the Academy and I owe him 130 yet. I rather owe it to someone else. You know the whole absurd and painful story of the broken friendship— without provocation and even any cause I could remotely guess at. Their business which he started 14 years ago with my money is very good—perfectly sound. And here I am worried with these miserable letters.

This must be stopped. I don't know where to turn. I can't tell you how distressed I am. I am averse to mortgaging my future and yet I must do it in some way because with this idiotic affair bothering me I can not sleep. The man (Hope)[4] he mentions in the letter is utterly ruined and even if I had the heart to squeeze him I would not get any blood out of

---

[1] On 30 January: for the 'conversation', see Blackburn, pp. 47–8.
[2] Meldrum noted on the letter that he answered it on 11 February (a Saturday).
[3] He had known Adolf Krieger since the beginning of the 1880s. Krieger had lent him money and helped him find jobs, including the position at Barr, Moering, where Krieger was a partner and Conrad (with the aid of his uncle's funds) an investor. Although Conrad dedicated *Tales of Unrest* to him, the friendship had already chilled (*Letters*, 1, 416–17).
[4] Another old friend, G. F. W. Hope had lost his (and probably Conrad's) money in South African mining speculations.

that stone. He will come ultimately into some money but meantime he is hopeless.

Could Mr Blackwood besides the amount I have been asking for (*H of D*. balance) (with shame I assure you) send me an advance of £50 on the *volume*. I say distinc[t]ly the vol. because when I send in more copy I shall most likely need the serial money. All this is too wretched for words. I wish Mr Blackwood to know why I apply to him. It is not for my pleasure or even for my health I want the money—tho' my doctor has urged me to go to Nice for a hydropathic cure. It is for my peace of mind. Peace of mind. Would you tell him? Send also the enclosed letter in conf*ce*—if you judge it necessary. If not please burn it. If I can get £*100 in all* I shall pay it to him—and pull another hole in my own belt —by Jove!

You may imagine how well the Rescue is going on with all this. And I don't know how to apologise to you for the constant worry I cause. Yours very faithful[ly] always

J. Conrad

To William Blackwood
Text MS NLS; Blackburn 50

[letterhead: Pent Farm]
12th Febr. 1899.

Dear Mr Blackwood.

The delay in acknowledging your kind letter and enclosure arises from the fact that in Stanford we have no Sunday post and I was not in time for the Sat: night's mail.

Thanks very much for what you send and still more for what you say.[1] The cheque for £*60* now received and the previous one of £*40* on account of the same tale (*H of D*) will probably overpay it as I do not think it will run to 40000 words. I did write that number or even more but I've been revising and compressing the end not a little. The proof of the second instalment I kept only twelve hours—not knowing but it might have been wanted at once. I marked a place—on p. 24—where a break is, at least, practicable. If it does not commend itself to your judgment there may be a better place, somewhere within the last inst*t* of typed MS, I've sent to Edinburgh on Tuesday last. My own MS copy is in such

---

[1] Of 'Heart of Darkness', part two: 'It is very powerful and a wonderful piece of descriptive word painting with the weird African nightmare sensation sustained all through in a marvellous manner' (Blackburn, p. 49).

confusion and moreover so unlike the final 'type' that I could not venture on its authority to indicate any final sentence or paragraph for the ending of part 2^d.

I am delighted to hear you like the story. Very good of You to write me when so painfully indisposed. I trust the attack has not been severe. Mine always are and I am subject to them at least once a year.[1]

I wonder what you will think of the end of the story. I've been writing up to it and it loomed rather effective till I came to it actually. Still I am not altogether dissatisfied with the manner of it; but of course one cannot judge one's own *fresh* work—at any rate.

Re volume of short stories. I wished for some time to ask you whether you would object to my dedicating the Vol: to R. B. Cunninghame Graham. Strictly speaking it is a matter between the dedicator and the other person, but in this case—considering the imprint of the House and your own convictions I would prefer to defer to your wishes.[2] I do not dedicate to C. Graham the aristocrat (he is both—you know) but to one of the few men I *know*—in the full sense of the word—and knowing cannot but appreciate and respect—abstractedly as human beings. I do not share his political convictions or even all his ideas of art, but we have enough ideas in common to base a strong friendship upon.

Should you dislike the notion I'll inscribe the *Rescue* to him instead of the Tales.[3]

Pardon the lenght* of this letter and pray believe me always yours faithfully

Jph. Conrad.

To David Meldrum
Text MS Duke; Blackburn 53

[letterhead: Pent Farm]
Monday—ev^g [13 February
1899][4]

My dear Mr Meldrum.

Ever so many thanks for your kind letter. Yes I ought to be more sensible and not let those things disturb me; but I am still in a wretched nervous state and thus to be sensible is quite out of question with me.

---

[1] Attacks of gout.
[2] Blackwood was as devoted to high Toryism and the cause of Anglo-Scottish union as Graham was to Socialism and Scottish nationalism.
[3] *Typhoon* (Heinemann, 1903) was dedicated to Graham.
[4] Dated by the sequence of events.

I had a most kind letter from Mr Blackwood's private house enclosing me a cheque for £60. I sent on £50 to the man[1] and kept 10 for myself. This morning I had another letter from him. Well, well.

I do not want Mr B'wood to think I am taking an advantage of his readiness to accom[m]odate me. The £*100* he paid me cover the *H of D* and even more as I don't think the story will run up to 40000 words. All this makes me wretched. I don't get on with the *R[escue]* which requires a special mood difficult to attain and still more difficult to preserve. Meantime I am anxious to get on with the Maga stories. I am exasperated at my own stupidity.

You are awfully good and patient with me. I acknowledged M^r B'wood's letter but said nothing about the distressful business leaving it wholly in your hands and not knowing then whether you would consider it opportune.

My wife sends her kind regards. Believe me dear Mr Meldrum very Gratefully Yours

Jph Conrad.

PS I hear the *Spectator* noticed the story.[2] My press agency did not send any cutting. Is it a fact and is the notice good?

To William Blackwood
Text MS NLS; Blackburn 54

[letterhead: Pent Farm]
14 Febr. 1899

Dear Mr Blackwood.

I don't know how to thank you for the very real and friendly service you are doing me by the advance of £*100* on the volume of short tales. The cheque for the above sum came to hand to day.

In reply to points touched upon in Your letter:[3]

I, myself, am very desirous to take advantage of the kind of popularity conferred by the *Ac^{my}* award. I am still more desirous to meet your views as to the date of publication. I have a story *Jim* half-written or one-third written (10.000 words) which is intended for the volume. There are with *Youth* (13.000) and *H of D* (38.000?) say 50 to 52 thousand words ready. *Jim* being 20 or 30 thou: would almost make up matter enough for a

---

[1] Krieger.   [2] 4 February: an approving mention in a survey of the latest magazines.
[3] Blackwood's cordial letter: Blackburn, p. 52.

book. But—are 3 stories only, enough? And supposing even I finished *Jim* in time could it go serially into Maga before the date you contemplate?[1] Besides I thought of two other stories (more in the 'note' of my 'Maga' work) one of them being called *First Command* and the other (a sketch) entitled *A Seaman*.[2] These are not written. They creep about in my head but got to be caught and tortured into some kind of shape. I think—I think they would turn out good as good as (they say) *Youth* is. But the whole thing is complicated by my horrible inability to finish the *Rescue* for which McClure has made arrangements. I must peg away at it.

It seems horribly ungrateful of me to talk about the difficulty of doing what you wish, but I must face the consequences not of my neglect or laziness but of positive ill-health which has caused the shameful delay in writing the *R*. It is small consolation to think I could *not* help it though I did my best. My best has been so very bad after all.

—Yet: if in your opinion *Youth. H of D* and *Jim* would make a volume I shall *try* to get *Jim* finished in April (my heart sinks when I think how days pass and how slow my work is). In that case I would forego the serial pub: of *Jim* not to delay the appearance of the volume. I only can say I shall *try*. I dare say no more after my recent experiences as to being punctual. The Vol of the 3 stories would not be positively bad. Whether you would judge such a publication opportune or not I shall do my best to finish *Jim* in April.

Even in the matter of the title I am unable to answer you decisively. I've not thought of it yet—and it is by no means easy to invent something telling and comprehensive. "Youth and Other Tales" would not do? I wish to convey the notion of something lived through and remembered. *Tales from Memory*(.?) you may think a clumsy title. It is so. I don't seem able to think of anything to-night. Why not: "Three Tales" by Joseph Conrad. Flaubert (mutatis mutandis) published Trois contes.[3] The titles of the three tales could be printed on the cover in smaller capitals thus: Youth; A Narrative. Heart of Dark: Jim: A sketch. That is only if the vol: is to be of the three stories. Pardon the lenght* of this letter, and the unsatisfactory nature of its contents. I *am* an unsatisfactory person, and to no one more than to myself.

I am very sorry to see you have not yet left your room. The

---

[1] Late April or early May. Conrad, of course, did not see 'Jim' as a full-scale novel.
[2] 'First Command': ancestor of *The Shadow-Line*; 'A Seaman': perhaps the sketch of Captain Louttit (letter to Meldrum, 22 August).
[3] *Trois contes* (1877).

acknowledgment of your previous letter I addressed to Edinburgh. By this post I send the letter itself (10th of Febr) to 45 George Street asking for its return after copy taken. Is that right? I am so pleased you approve the break-off of the 2^d inst. I was in doubt. You have removed an immense load from my mind by your kind and sympathetic action. I enclose here a formal acknowledgement of the sum received in advance.

Believe me dear Mr Blackwood
your[s] very faithfully
Jph Conrad

To David Meldrum
Text MS Duke; Blackburn 56

[letterhead: Pent Farm]
14 Febr 99.

Dear Mr Meldrum.

Mr Blackwood has done more than I expected and more than I hoped. I've sent him a formal ackn^{*gment*} for the £*100* stating distinctly they are on acct/ of royalties on book of Tales and the whole sum agreed upon as advance.

Of course I also wrote a letter of thanks.

He wishes me to get the volume ready for May. How can I? I'll *try* to finish *Jim* by that time and am ready to forego its serial appearance for the sake of meeting Mr B'wood's views. But would it be a good vol? Only three stories. Still it would be 70.000 words. I have two more stories in my head which would run the copy to 120000 words, but I can't possibly be ready with them before say—July. (I include Jim too to be finished first.) I must now peg on at the Rescue.

I said that much in my reply to Mr B'wood. If he really desires to send out a vol: by me in Ap: or May it must be a three-story vol. I suggested for titlle*— (in that case) page

Three Tales.
by
Jph Conr.
Youth. A Narrative
Heart of Darkness
Tuan Jim: A sketch.

I can't think of anything else. Can You? Of course I am not anxious to lose the serial value of *Jim*, if that could be helped. But *if I can* finish him in time and Mr B'wood decides on immediate pub^{*on*} I am prepared to let *Jim* go. I've said this to Mr B'wood. In that case the stories: "First

Command"; the one about a Captains wife; "A Seaman" sketch; and "Equitable Division" (a story of a typhoon)[1] would perhaps find hospitality in the Maga and go to make another Vol, later on.

Of this idea I've said nothing in my letter to Mr B'wood, but put it before you, should M. B'wood stick to the may publication *and Jim is ready*, which last upon my conscience I dare not promise.

Many thanks to You for Your friendly offices.

Always yours

Jph. Conrad.

To Edward Garnett
Text MS Sutton; G. 148

[Pent Farm]
Tuesday [21 or 28 February
1899][2]

My dear good Garnett.

I saw Shorter who did't eat me.[3] I can't appear in the Ill[d] Lond News not so much because I am not ready but because McClure told Shorter that the story shall be 60–65000 words long only and Shorter had calculated upon that for the *News*. (14 weekly instalments).

How McClure made that mistake I can't imagine, as the synopsis stated distinc[t]ly minimum of *90.000* words; probably *110.000*.

I set Shorter right on that point. He didn't seem sorry to get a lot of copy for his money but said I must go into the Eng Ill: Magazine. Hopes the *News* will get some other work of mine by and by. Ran out after me to ask whether I had a short story by me to appear in *News* at once. Told him hadn't. Salaams. Then ran out again to ask whether I had a friend who would write something about me in the *Eng. Ill. Mag.* I said I hadn't a friend but had a good enemy Edward Garnett who perhaps could be induced to commit such an atrocity. He hastened to inform me that he knew your Father.[4] I had the baseness to give him Your address and

---

[1] The Captain's wife story may be the origin of *Chance*; 'Equitable Division' became *Typhoon*.

[2] Garnett places this letter in February. Conrad, when he wrote to Methuen on 7 February, had had a letter from Shorter but not seen him. The other Tuesdays in the month were 14, 21, and 28, but Conrad was too preoccupied to have had time for an interview with Shorter between 7 and 14.

[3] Shorter edited both the *Illustrated London News* (for which *The Rescue* had been promised) and the *English Illustrated Magazine*.

[4] Richard Garnett (1835–1906), poet, scholar, then in his last year as Keeper of Printed Books at the British Museum.

escaped without a particle of self respect from that horrid den. So You know what to expect. Are you angry with me? When I know how you feel about this my mind shall be at ease. It's a pity, in a sense, I missed the *News*. On the other hand it's fortunate the thing is arranged. I shall drive ahead all the same, and probably invade you—if You still will have me after what I've done. I fancy Shorter wants to see whether my story can't give a fillip to the circulation of the wretched Magazine. If so he prepares a bitter disappointment for himself.

Thanks for Your visit my dear dear fellow. Water in the desert could not have been more welcome.

Heaps of blessings on your head

Ever ·Yours

Conrad

Since I wrote this I got this letter from Shorter. What a damned barnacle!

To Gabriela Cunninghame Graham[1]
Text L. fr., p. 37

Pent Farm
24th Feb 99

Je viens de lire "Family Portraits".[2] Je suis mauvais critique: il m'est difficile d'exprimer avec des mots justes le plaisir que la lecture de votre charmante esquisse m'a donné; mais quand j'ai levé mes yeux de dessus la page, c'est avec le sentiment très vif d'avoir vu non seulement la longue ligne des portraits mais encore la beauté de l'idée profonde et tendre qui éclairait pour vous tous les visages peints, les yeux tristes des morts avec la flamme d'une pitié très douce et d'une pénétrante sympathie.

Je ne sais pas si je vous ai compris, mais j'ai toujours à vous remercier pour le plaisir de la lecture et encore plus pour le moment de rêverie qui a suivi. J'étais sous le charme de votre pensée et de votre expression. Vous avez fait vivre le passé pendant un court et précieux moment, et je vous en suis infiniment reconnaissant.

---

[1] Robert Cunninghame Graham's wife (née de la Balmondière, 1860?–1906), born in Chile, wrote stories, essays, and poems, studied mysticism, and was active in the Spanish women's movement. Her biography of Saint Teresa of Avila appeared in 1894.

[2] Reprinted in *The Christ of Toro* (1908).

J'espère que vous m'avez pardonné d'avoir retenu Robert. Sa visite m'a semblé bien courte en vérité. Nous avons fait des excès de causerie, mais j'aime à croire qu'il n'a pas été trop fatigué.

Daignez me croire, chère Madame, votre très sincère admirateur et très obéissant serviteur.

Translation

I have just read "Family Portraits". I am a bad critic: it is difficult for me to express with the right words the pleasure that the reading of your charming sketch has given me; but when I raised my eyes from the page, it was with the very vivid feeling of having seen not only the long line of the portraits, but also the beauty of the profound and tender idea which illuminated for you all the faces portrayed, the sad eyes of the dead with the flame of a gentle pity and a penetrating sympathy.

I do not know if I have understood you, but I must always thank you for the pleasure of the reading and still more for the moment of reverie which followed. I was under the spell of your thought and your expression. You have made the past live for a short and precious moment, and I am infinitely grateful to you.

I hope you have forgiven me for detaining Robert. To me, indeed, his visit seemed very short. We had an immoderate amount of talk, but I like to believe he was not too tired.

Deign to believe me, dear Madame, your very sincere admirer and very obedient servant.

To R. B. Cunninghame Graham
Text MS Dartmouth; J-A, 1, 273; Watts 123

[letterhead: Pent Farm]
26th Feb 99.

Très cher et excellent ami.

The portrait came. It is gorgeous. I like its atmosphere. It is a likeness too besides being a picture.

In a little while came the books. Vous me gâtez.[1] I've read Vathek at once.[2] C'est très bien. What an infernal imagination! The style is cold

---

[1] 'You spoil me.'
[2] William Beckford's Arabian tale (1784), originally written in French. The scenes in the Hall of Eblis are quite literally 'infernal'.

and I do not see in the work that immense promise as set forth by the introduction.[1] Chaucer I have dipped into, reading aloud as you advised. I am afraid I am not English enough to appreciate fully the father of English literature.[2] Moreover I am in general insensible to verse.

Thereupon came the "Stealing of the Mare".[3] This I delight in. I've read it at once and right through. It is quite inspiring most curious and altogether fascinating. I've written to your wife a few words in the language of the Franks about Fam: Port: which is a delicious bit. The tenderness of the idea and the feeling for the past have delighted me. C'est tout à fait dans sa note.[4] The quality that made the extraordinary charm of Sta Theresa is in that short article as visible as in the great work. Ever yours with infinite thanks

Conrad.

To Helen Sanderson
Text MS Yale; J-A, 1, 271

[letterhead: Pent Farm]
26th Febr 99

Dear Mrs Sanderson.

I ought to have thanked You for your letter before. We have read it with delight, and we take the full share of friendship in your happiness and joy.

How good of you to write at lenght* of your dear daughter. The names are pretty, very pretty and I have not the slightest doubt she lives and shall live up to her names.[5]

I am glad to hear Ted makes a satisfactory nurse. I was a complete duffer at that business being, as a matter of fact, horribly frightened of the baby. I've now got over my timidity but then the boy is no longer a baby. He only disconcerts me by his unexpected knowledge of the world and of human nature so that I feel I cannot be cautious enough in my dealings with him. As it is he has me always at a disadvantage in every personal discussion. He is also very rowdy and can be naughty in more different ways than I could have imagined. One is amused and at the same time one has a feeling of being confronted by a grave problem.

---

[1] Probably the one by Richard Garnett (1893).
[2] The epigraph to *The Rescue* comes from 'The Franklin's Tale'.
[3] Abu Zaid, *The Celebrated Romance of the Stealing of the Mare* (1892), translated by Lady Anne Blunt and rendered into verse by Wilfrid Scawen Blunt.
[4] 'It's entirely in her idiom.'   [5] Katherine Graham Sanderson.

I do not mind owning I wished for a daughter. I can't help feeling she would have resembled me more and would have been perhaps easier to understand. This is a selfish feeling I admit; but boy or girl they are very interesting and infinitely touching. I can't confess to any reverential feeling for childhood. I've heard people, more or less sentimental, talk about it but I question whether it is not a rather artificial attitude. It is their humanity that is so endearing, their nearness to us, not their nearness to the angels. Perhaps it is only my propensity to make the best not of things in general but to make the best of the worst, which induces me to take this view. It may be bad for me but I am sure it is good for Borys because if my affection for him depended on his angel-like qualities it would be very evanescent. At the age of thirteen months he is an accomplished and fascinating barbarian full of charming wiles and of pitiless selfishness. It is not his innocence but his unconsciousness that makes him pathetic—besides making him just bearable.

I am writing you a twaddling letter. You must forgive—if you can detect—the tinge of cynicism upon my opinions. It is a false light after all. At the bottom of all these cheap reflections there is love for the young souls committed to our blind guardianship which must fit them for the hazard of life.

I would immensely like to meet Mr Lynch[1]—but in any case as soon as I am out of my difficulties I shall come to Elstree. My difficulties may appear to you interminable. It seems to me it is years and years since I first began to afflict and exasperate my friends with these dark allusions to a perfectly clear matter: my inability to work fast enough to get my living. It is ridiculous and sad and wearisome, and that it is true does not make it any less offensive.

Jess sends her love to You and the baby. She has declared to me she "imagines" the baby perfectly. I fancy I also do. We trust we may hear often from You three, but I've become such a wretched correspondent that I hardly dare to hope for forgiveness from my best friends.

Believe me, dear Mrs Sanderson Your very affectionate friend and obedient servant

Jph Conrad.

PS Love to dear Ted and the baby.

---

[1] Unidentified.

To John Galsworthy
Text MS POSK; J-A, 1, 270

[letterhead: Pent Farm]
Sunday evening [12 March? 1899][1]

Dearest Jack

Yes, it is good criticism.[2] Only I think that to say Henry James does not write from the heart is maybe hasty. He is cosmopolitan, civilised, very much "homme du monde" and the acquired ("educated" if you like) side of his temperament that is—restraint the instinctive, the nurtured, fostered, cherished side is always presented to the reader first. To me even the *R. T.*[3] seems to flow from the heart because and only because the work approaching so near perfection yet does not strike cold. Technical perfection unless there is some real glow to illumine and warm it from within must necessarily be cold. I argue that in H. J. there is such a glow and not a dim one either, but to us used, absolutely accustomed, to unartistic expression of fine, headlong, honest (or dishonest) sentiments the art of H. J. does appear heartless. The outlines are so clear the figures so finished, chiselled, carved and brought out that we exclaim—we, used to the Shades of the contemporary fiction, to the more or less malformed shades—we exclaim—Stone! Not at all. I say flesh and blood—very perfectly presented—perhaps with too much perfection *of method*. The volume of short stories entitled I think *"The lesson of the Master"* contains a tale called "The Pupil" if I remember rightly where the underlying feeling of the man—his really wide sympathy—is seen nearer the surface. Of course he does not deal in primitive emotions. I maintain he is the most civilised of modern writers. He is also an idealiser. His heart shows itself in the delicacy of his handling. Things like *The Middle years* and *The altar of the dead* in the vol entitled *Terminations* would illustrate my meaning. Moreover your cousin admits the element of pathos. Mere technique won't give the element of pathos. I admit he is not *forcible*—or, let us say, the only forcible thing in his work is his technique. Now a literary intelligence would be naturally struck by the wonderful technique and that is so wonderful in its way that it dominates the bare expression. The more so

---

[1] Jean-Aubry dates this letter 11 February, but that was not a Sunday. In any case, the closing remarks suggest that more time has passed since finishing 'Heart of Darkness'. If 'next Sunday' were 19 March, the following letter could be read as an apology for putting Galsworthy off.

[2] By Galsworthy's unidentified cousin.

[3] 'The Real Thing' (1893); other works referred to are 'The Pupil' (1892) and the collection *Terminations* (1895).

that the expression is only of delicate shades. He is never in deep gloom or in violent sunshine. But he feels deeply and vividly every delicate shade. We can not ask for more. Not every one is a Turgeniew. Moreover Turg: is not civilised (therein much of his charm for us) in the sense H. J. is civilised. Satis. Please convey my defence of the 'Master' with my compliments. My kindest and grateful regards to Mrs Sauter[1] and love to the boy. I am looking forward to next Sunday. The finishing of *H of D* took a lot out of me. I haven't been able to do much since.

Ever Yours

Conrad.

To John Galsworthy

Text MS Forbes; Unpublished

[letterhead: Pent Farm]
Saturday. [25 March 1899][2]

Dearest Jack.

I'm a brute. But let that pass. The Hueffers with their kid camp here on a house hunt[3] and McClure is coming to morrow to knock spots out of me.

I am in a curious state. I wish I could have You here to myself. Well. Will You come next Sunday? I am trying to work. Not much success—tho'. Still, pages accumulate at my left hand and rage grows within my breast.

I am anxious to see *Your* work. Hueffer fell in love with the *Four Winds*.[4] Without sharing all his enthusiasm (I know your capacities better) I admit (and always did) that the qualities he points out are rare —and are also solid. He is struck most by *Acc^{dg} to his Lights* where I share his opinion that Your temperament and expression are in best accord. Pardon haste. Post due.

Ever Yours

Conrad.

We shall have a crack about Shopp^{er}[5] and Harry James bless him!

---

[1] Galsworthy's sister Lilian, married to the Austrian painter Georg Sauter.
[2] Taken with the following letter to Garnett, the reference to Conrad's visitors fixes the date.
[3] They were about to move into a cottage in Aldington, close by.
[4] Galsworthy's first book, published pseudonymously in 1897; it includes the short story 'According to His Lights'.
[5] Perhaps the cousin who had written on Henry James.

To Edward Garnett
Text MS Sutton; G. 149

[Pent Farm]
in Sorrow and tribulation   Good Friday.
[31 March 1899]

Dearest Garnett.

What do You think of me? Think I love you though I am a dumb dog or no better than a whining dog. There's not a bark left in me. I am overwhelmed and utterly flattened. Hueffers are gone—yesterday. So is McClure[1] who came for the night. A decent little chap I say if I got to die for it!

Is trying to ram the *Rescue* into the Atlantic Monthly but the *R* is *not* finished yet—not Yet—not yet.

"I'll be your banker" says little McClure—this is better than a kick on the shinbone I guess; but the spirit suffers.

Give our love to Your restored household. Restored to You—I mean. H[ueffer] said You reproached him for his fleeting sojourn here. It is not conclusive evidence but if so learn that our friends can not save us from the effects of our own folly.

Are You angry with me?

If so learn that I am so hardened by adversity that your anger glides off me as a dart glances off a turtle's back, and I still continue to radiate affection on You—my affection which is not so offensive as Wells' Martian's Heat-ray[2]—but nearly as warm.

It won't set the Thames on fire tho'. Nothing of mine will. I think of You with gentle melancholy as of one who has put his money on the wrong horse. I am literally lame. Gout. Brought on by—by—by agitation, exasperation, botheration—You know; those things you laugh at and bite your thumbs at—O! Lord! And I write! I write! write! I write! Certainly. Write quick. Not quick enough to make up for the frightful leeway. But I write.

And à propos of writing. Have you seen p III of *H of D*?[3] My dear fellow I daren't send you my *MS*. I feel it would worry you. I feel my existence alone worries you enough. This is not conceit; quite the contrary.

But drop me word of p III.

---

[1] Robert, who represented the British interests of his brother Sam.
[2] From *The War of the Worlds*.
[3] In the April *Blackwood's*.

Fact is I am not worthy to take up your thought. The more I write the less substance do I see in my work. The scales are falling off my eyes. It is tolerably awful. And I face it, I face it but the fright is growing on me. My fortitude is shaken by the view of the monster. It does not move; its eyes are baleful; it is as still as death itself—and it will devour me. Its stare has eaten into my soul already deep, deep. I am alone with it in a chasm with perpendicular sides of black basalt. Never were sides so perpendicular and smooth, and high. Above, your anxious head against a bit of sky peers down—in vain—in vain. There's not rope long enough for that rescue.

Why didn't you come? I expected you and fate has sent Hueffer. Let this be written on my tombstone.

Ever yours

Conrad

To Aniela Zagórska
Text J-A, 1, 274; Najder 231[1]

Pent Farm,

12th April, 1899.

My dear Aniela,

Excuse these few words. I am anxious about Karola.[2] Please be so kind and let me know how she is—and how you all are. Since your last letter I have sent: 1.—the photo of the boy; 2.—3 packets of cuttings; 3.—a number of *Literature*; 4.—Wells's novel *The Invisible Man*. Let me know, my dearest, if you have received all this; especially the photo and the book. If the cuttings have gone astray, it will be necessary to send them in envelopes. If you have received *Literature*[3] I will send it to you regularly. If the book has not reached you, I will send another copy at once.

I have been in bed for a whole week with gout. I do not feel at all well. But that does not matter. My wife and the youngster are both well. God grant that all may go well with you. A few lines will reassure me. I embrace you affectionately and kiss your hand.

Your

K. Korzeniowski

---

[1] For textual source, see n. 5 to letter of 6 February 1898.
[2] Her younger daughter, born 1885.
[3] A weekly review published by *The Times*.

To John Galsworthy

Text MS Forbes; J-A, 1, 276

[letterhead: Pent Farm][1]

17 Ap 99

Dearest Jack.

We were awfully disappointed but perhaps you are right. It would have been like the glimpse of a ship in a fog, tormenting, disturbing, conveying no sense of companionship. I had nothing to show You, so You haven't lost much; but I am anxious about these thousand words You've written.[2] At this juncture *every* word is an object to be considered anxiously with heart searchings and in a spirit of severe resolution. Don't write them (words) hurriedly. I am glad you have written no more than one thousand. If it had been only one hundred I would have said: it is well. Don't smile and think that it is only my own cursed tongue-tied state that gives me that point of view.'There may be something of that of course—but for the most part it is sheer conviction. And I think of your prose just as I think of mine own.

I am sincerely pleased with what you say of Elstree.[3] You know that I am loyal enough; that my memory is good and sane even if my mind is diseased and on the verge of craziness. I am glad they think well of me; it is the only kind of treasure I want to lay up, the only sort of wealth I prize. And I am not ungrateful to those who contribute. I've been more moved by your letter than I intend telling You. I wait as patiently as I can for your return trusting that you will come here with the MS without loss of time. Jess sends kindest regards. Ever Yours,

Conrad.

To R. B. Cunninghame Graham

Text MS Dartmouth; J-A, 1, 275; Watts 124

[letterhead: Pent Farm]

17 Ap. 1899.

Très cher ami

Your letter this morning made me feel better. Is it possible that you like the thing so much?[4] Well, you say so and I believe you but—do you quite believe it yourself soit dit sans vous offenser. The element of friendship comes in. But still I am willing, even eager, to believe in your

---

[1] The first type three letterhead.
[2] Galsworthy was at work on the novel *Villa Rubein* and a group of short stories (Marrot, p. 120).
[3] Home of the Sandersons.   [4] 'Heart of Darkness', presumably.

scrupulous literary honesty. And in any case my blessing on your intention.

I hold "*Ipane*".[1] Hoch! Hurra! Vivat! May you live! And now I know I am virtuous because I read and had no pang of jealousy. There are things in that volume that are like magic and through space through the distance of regretted years convey to one the actual feeling, the sights, the sounds, the thoughts; one steps on the earth, breathes the air, and has the sensations of your past. I knew of course every sketch; what was almost a surprise was the extraordinarily good, convincing effect of the whole. It is not always so with a collection. The style grows on one from page to page. It is as wonderful in a slightly different way as the Morocco book. How do you do it? How? I do not say which I like best. I like best the one I happen to be reading. I think the sequence of the sketches has been arranged very well.

I have read it already three times.

I am cursedly tongue tied. Not only in my own work but when I want to talk of a friend's work too. From a full heart nothing comes. A weariness has laid its hand on my lips—I ask myself at times whether it is for ever. Then I ought to die.

However one is never sure, and thus one hangs on to life. Can there be anything more awful than such an incertitude and more pathetic than such hanging on? Shall I see you before you leave for the Sahara O Fortunate Man? I'll come to town 'a-purpose' you know!

Jess sends her kindest regards   Ever Yours

Conrad.

To Hugh Clifford
Text MS Clifford; J-A, I, 237

[letterhead: Pent Farm]
17 May 1899.[2]

Dear Mr. Clifford[3]

It is very good of you to have forgiven me my review of your *Studies*.[4] I suppose You have seen between the lines the feeling which dictated the

---

[1] Just published by T. Fisher Unwin.

[2] Jean-Aubry misread the date as 1898. The present letter was the first to Clifford: see his account in the *Empire Review* (London), Vol. 47 (1928), pp. 287–94.

[3] Hugh Clifford (1866–1941) began his career as a colonial civil servant in 1883. When he wrote to Conrad, he had just returned from a tour of duty as British Resident in the State of Pahang, Malaya. Later, he was appointed to the governorships of the Gold Coast, Nigeria, Ceylon, and the Straits Settlements. He published many volumes of stories and sketches, collaborated on a Malay dictionary, and produced a Malay translation of the colonial penal code.

[4] Conrad reviewed *Studies in Brown Humanity* for the *Academy*, 23 April 1898.

words. For me to review Your work would have been a mere impertinence and I would have left it to some journalist who lives by that kind
of thing had it not been that I meant it for a tribute not only to the charm
of the book but to the toil of the man; to the years of patient and devoted
work at the back of the pages. This is why when approached by the
Academy, I stipulated for my signature. Reviewing is not in my way; I
had never done any before and none since.[1] I had rather use my
ignorance in other ways—for writing novels, for instance.

I appreciate the more the kind things you say in your letter because I
suspect my assumption of malay colouring for my fiction must be
exasperating to those who *know*.[2] It seems as though you had found in
my prose some reason for forgiving me. Nothing could be more flattering
to a scribbler's vanity or more soothing to the conscience of a man who
even in his fiction, tries to be tolerably[3]

To Hugh Clifford
Text MS Clifford; J-A, 1, 276

[letterhead: Pent Farm]
24 May 99

My Dear Sir.

If we haven't met last Saturday it is the P.O.'s fault.

Thanks very much for your kind letter. I am sure you won't take it ill if
[I] confess my inability to take immediately advantage of your friendly
invitation. The reasons that keep me at home just now are too many to
be set down but you may well believe that if they are not good they are
uncommonly strong or else I would break through them, for my desire to
meet you is not only prompted by a very natural gratitude for Your
appreciation (the most flattering and welcome recognition my work had
brought me) but by a profound regard for your personality, for your
life-work, for Your large and generous sympathies—as far as it is given
to my ignorance to understand these things.

The institution of domestic slavery having broken down in this
country and my wife being far from well just now I simply dare not take
you at Your word, tho' my restraint costs me something I assure You.
You would probably get nothing to eat, and though You have known

---

[1] Except the essay on Daudet (*Outlook*, 9 April 1898) and the unpublished piece on
Kipling.
[2] Conrad did not yet know that Clifford had written an article on him: see letter to
Blackwood, 13 December 1898.
[3] The MS ends here; Jean-Aubry supplies 'true'.

worse hardships think how black my face would be after such a misfortune.

I take it I have your permission to let you know when I come to town next and if then you can spare an hour I will be most happy (this is no conventional phrase) to call on you; and I live even in hopes that before next Nov^{er1} you'll sacrifice a whole day to seek me out in my jungle. Believe me, my dear Sir always very faithfully yours

Jph Conrad.

To E. L. Sanderson
Text MS Yale; Unpublished

[letterhead: Pent Farm]
24 May 99

Dearest Ted.

Your letter came as a blessing for indeed a man is blessed in his friends; and when I think of all the honest affections given me by men much too good for me I feel bitterly ashamed of my pessimism, of my ineradicable tendency to quarrel with fate.

And in the depth of Your friendship You can find words that are sweeter than balsam to the soul of the scribe; after reading your messages I think a little better of myself and thus You confer on me not a small benefit O! Friend long unseen but never forgotten.

I close this with the word—thanks, without my usual jeremiads. You don't say anything of wife and child, but fortunately I had news through Your mother, so I know you are tolerably well. My affectionate regards to Your Wife, love to Miss Katherine (I hear she looks best[?] taking a walk 'in maiden meditation fancy free'^{2} under the Elstree elms) and I am

Ever Yours

Conrad.

To Algernon Methuen
Text J-A, 1, 277

Pent Farm.
25th May, 1899.

My Dear Sir, ·

My letter to you^3 was not a coy manoeuvre with a view to a vast amount of shekels. The facts are these: I am engaged to Mr. Heinemann

---

^{1} When Clifford was to return east.　^{2} *A Midsummer Night's Dream*, II.i.
^{3} 7 February.

here, and to the McClure Co. over there, for the *Rescue*. I am almost a
year behind my date with that extremely long story and I am beyond
measure distressed by the delay. The thing simply *won't* come out as
quick as I fondly hoped. I am also engaged to Mr. Blackwood for a vol.
of three stories which is still 80,000 words short. It is clear to me that my
power of production is as uncertain as the weather of these Isles. If H.
and McC. get tired of my irregularity (to pick out a mild name) I shall
come to you and I don't think you'll find me exceptionally rapacious. I
have no reason, however, to think that such would be the case, and these
two houses have treated me with such consideration, patience and
friendliness, that I don't see myself going elsewhere of my own
movement. Apart from very friendly relations, *Blackwood's* is the only
periodical *always* open to me—and is the only one for which I really care
to work. Such being the true state of the case, to talk about any future
work of mine would be futile and not very sincere. Nevertheless I am
very grateful to you for your generous suggestions. The disposal of my
work cannot be governed purely by questions of payment. That is at
least how I feel about it, tho' nowise bound to these firms except by their
good offices rendered to me at a time when they were needed rather
badly.

Pardon the length of this. It is just because I appreciate the spirit of
your offer that I am anxious to make my position clear to you.

To Cora Crane

Text MS Columbia; *Bookman* (NY) 69,232[1]

[letterhead: Pent Farm]
Monday [29 May 1899][2]

Dear Mrs. Crane.

Just a word. Your expected letter did not come this morning. Ever so
many thanks for allowing Dolly[3] to come. I think if you dont mind we
shall come on Sat^y as we made arrangements with whitewashers and
such like ruffians to come into the house on Monday. I shall bring my
dress clothes along and we shall both try to be a credit to you and
Stephen.[4]

---

[1] In 1929, a group of letters to the Cranes appeared in the *Bookman*. As the texts are very
unreliable, their existence is noted only in the case of letters not republished by Stallman
and Gilkes.

[2] Date established by the next day's letter.   [3] Conrad's sister-in-law.

[4] For details of the two-week visit, see Gilkes, *Cora Crane*, pp. 196–9. The Cranes were now
at Brede Place.

Please say if we may come *early* on Sat? About noon. Unless we hear from you we shall do so.—and write on Thursday the exact time.

In awful haste. Your most afect^t and faithful servant

Jph Conrad.

Jessie's love.

To Cora Crane
Text MS Columbia; *Bookman* (NY) 69,371

[letterhead: Pent Farm]
30 May.
99

My dear Mrs Crane.

I am afraid we are giving you a certain amount of trouble but as the milk is—in a way—already spilt—I trust you will not cry—or at any rate not much. Seriously—if I had the cheek to ask about Dolly it was with the idea of saving you the bother about the little girl and under the impression you would have a clear house. Now Dolly knows, it would simply break her heart if she were stopped; moreover this excitable Borys is more likely to be good with her than with a stranger. Would you believe that since you left he has been quite sleepless getting up in the middle of the night to talk about the 'nice man' and the 'Ann-ann' (which means aunties) and generally behaving like a man in the first stages of lunacy.

My letter of yesterday has no doubt reached you by this. If we may we shall come by the train arriving at Rye *11.14 am*. Would Stephen write to some livery stable at Rye for a landau to meet us at that time? and then we can manage. We invade you so early of course on account of the boy the only practicable train in the afternoon arriving only about six. Jess is sorry your sponge bag has been detained. Mrs Nash[1] put it away carefully so that we did not even know it was here. It goes by this post.

Unless we hear from you we shall carry out our dreadful purposes as set forth in my two letters.

Jess sends her love. She's too busy to write herself—or says so.

In haste to catch post I am dear Mrs Crane your affectionate and obedient servant

Conrad.

[1] Housekeeper at the Pent: the Cranes and Mrs Ruedy had been staying there.

To Edward Garnett
Text G. 151

[June 1899][1]

Dearest Edward.

This is the sort of rot I am writing now.[2] Frankly it is not worth troubling about but still I send you this—the first part of a B'wood story in two parts.

Ever yours

Conrad

Send it back at your leisure. Of course you can see it is not corrected in any way.

To David Meldrum
Text MS Duke; Blackburn 58

[letterhead: Pent Farm]
Thursday.
6th July 99.

My dear Mr Meldrum.

Herewith 3 chap:^{rs} 31 pp. of Lord Jim, or to speak correctly two complete chapters and as much of the third as is ready.

Confiding in Your friendly offices I ask you for a typewritten copy of this batch for myself, together with the return of my own type. The text is pretty correct as it stands now and any small changes I may wish to make shall wait till I get the proof from Maga. This is not enough for one instalment but I will be sending you pages (a few at a time) and work at it steadily till the end. I trust the end of the month will come together with the end of the story. Youre* good letter has cheered me. The story will improve as it goes on. You will arrange the time for publication with McClure; I should not like to lose the American serial of this story if it can be avoided.

The story will be fully 40000 words and I shall ask Mr Blackwood for £*120* which is a little more than the agreed rate but expect to do more work for Maga before the year is out—that is if you want me—and make it right in that way. We must talk this matter over when we meet next as I have had proposals made for a series of short stories (or rather short

---

[1] Garnett's dating, confirmed by the reference to work in progress.
[2] According to Garnett, *Lord Jim*.

serials)[1] and would like to know M^r B'wood's intentions. I may say at once that I would rather work for *Maga* at a less rate than those people offer me; but some revision of terms must take place. However there is plenty of time for that discussion. The important thing now for me is to get rid of my deplorable Jim with honour and satisfaction to all concerned.

My wife's kind regards. She wants to know whether You would risk a visit here—and so do I. We could arrange the time. What do You say?

Very faithfully Yours

Conrad.

To H.-D. Davray
Text MS Yale; *L. fr.* 38

[letterhead: Pent Farm]
10 July 1899.

Cher Monsieur Devray.[2]

J'ai eu un moment de bien vif plaisir en lisant le dernier N° du Mercure,[3] et c'est à Vous que je le dois. Merci. Vous avez dit Votre opinion avec des mots qui vont droit au coeur. La phrase "qui est des notres"[4] m'a touché car en vérité je me sens lié à la France par une profonde sympathie, par des vieilles amitiés (maintenant disparues— hélas!) par le charme durable des souvenirs sans amertume. J'aime a croire que quand Vous enjamberez le Pas-de-Calais[5] la prochaine fois Vous prendrez le chemin de Pent-Farm. Après tout ce ne serait qu'un autre pas a faire.

Croyez moi, cher Monsieur a
Vous bien cordialement
Joseph Conrad.

[1] One of these proposals may have been from Methuen & Co, but see also letter to Meldrum, 22 August, re working for Heinemann.

[2] Properly Davray: Henry-Durand Davray (1873–1944) devoted his life to presenting British literature in France and French literature in Britain. A member of Mallarmé's circle, he wrote for the influential *Mercure de France* and edited its Collection of Foreign Authors. Among those he translated were Meredith, Kipling, Wells, and Conrad himself.

[3] In the July 1899 issue of the *Mercure*, Davray's regular article on new British and Irish works covered, among others, *The Importance of Being Earnest*, *The Wind among the Reeds*, *When the Sleeper Wakes*, and *The Nigger*. Davray praised Conrad for an un-English seriousness about writing: 'ce livre est *écrit* par un écrivain soucieux de la forme, et en même temps capable de belles et profondes émotions'.

[4] Recalling a sea-side conversation (they had met by courtesy of Wells), Davray uses this phrase to indicate Conrad's fealty to the modern French tradition. In a very different context, to be sure, the phrase 'one of us' echoes through *Lord Jim*.

[5] The French département nearest to England – and the journey over.

Translation

Dear Monsieur Davray,

In reading the last number of the Mercure, I had a moment of very lively pleasure, and I owe it to you. Thanks. You have given your opinion in words that go straight to the heart. The phrase 'who is one of ours' touched me, for, truly, I feel bound to France by a deep sympathy, by some old friendships (now vanished, alas), by the lasting charm of memories without bitterness. I like to believe that, the next time you step across the Channel, you will take the road for Pent Farm. This, after all, would only be one step more.

Believe me, dear Sir, very
cordially yours,

Joseph Conrad

To Neil Munro
Text MS NLS; Unpublished

[letterhead: Pent Farm]
10th July 99

My dear Munro.

Blessings on your head for your good letter. I've been thinking of you I may say daily and watching the B'wood adv*ts* with the idea of seeing your name and the title of a new book. When are we to have more of you?

I saw the notice in the G[lasgow] E[vening] H[erald][1] on the occasion of the Ac[adem]y award. No one was more surprised than myself and even yet (when the cash is spent and gone) I feel like an impostor and a thief. I wanted to write to you then; I was immensely touched by what you—for it was you—said "coram publico"[2] about my work. Verily you and two or three others for whose word I care would give me a swelled head if I did not save myself from that disease by suspecting You all of a mysterious insanity. No—my head is not swelled, but behold! My heart is dilated and my ribs ready to burst with gratitude and joy.

I've seen Mr Hamish Hendy's short things in the Sat: Rev.[3] By the

---

[1] Since the piece in the *Herald* (14 January) praises *John Splendid* at Conrad's expense, one presumes Munro was not responsible. His must be the enthusiastic notice – 'the book has stuff in it quite beyond the power – the technical capacity even – of any other English writer' – in the Glasgow *Evening News* of 19 January.

[2] 'In public'.

[3] Hamish Hendry often contributed book reviews and essays to the *Saturday Review*: 6 and 27 August 1898, for example. The nature of Hendry's proposal is unknown.

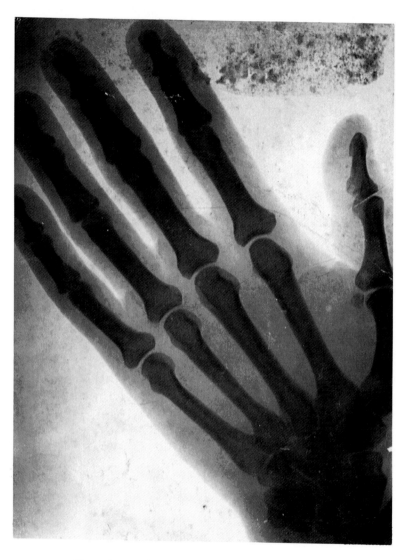

1. X-ray photograph of Conrad's hand: Conrad was intrigued by
contemporary physics

transverse section of deck.

P.   S.

chain   chain   big link   Lanyard. rope. several turns.

Deck   Deck   Ringbolt on the deck

P.S. Re-reading your letter.
That's how a stack would go
perhaps. And this would give
you an idea how to secure
it again {these both lanyards to 5 have them carried
away — say by a roll. the thing is then to
catch the ends of chains hook quick a
spare tackle into the big link and the ring
on deck and set taut. Should chains go
same principle of action might be followed}

Ah! Amigo. I've thought
of Rajah Laut in London and
if not in the W-H then next
thing to it. But I haven't
the heart. I haven't! not yet.
I am now busy about his youth — a gorgeous romance — gorgeous as to feeling I mean. Battles and loves and
so on.

or should only one of each d chains ^pair of go then could secure in a hurry thus with a rope [5 inch line]

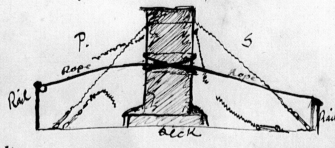

P.   S

Rope   Rope

Rail   Rail

deck

the steam-pipe would check the fall of a funnel and it would go over slowly and land on one of the ship's boats – probably – and smash it no doubt. Or if pitched forward it would damage the bridge – and the man on it too very likely. But the most dramatic circumstance would be the hellish mess of soot blowing about or washing over the deck. Does the plot hinge on the funnel? You must have a _plot_! If you haven't, every fool reviewer will kick you because there can't be literature without plot. I am in a state of a wild excitement about the stack. Let's know quick what happened in the tramp. A Scotch tramp is a very good tramp – The Engineers tell anecdotes, the mates are grim and over all floats the flavour of an accent that gives a special value to every word pronounced on her deck – You must know I've a soft spot for Scotchmen. Be easy on the tramp.

2–3. How to secure a funnel: Conrad to Graham, 7 January 1898

4. Joseph Conrad, *c.* 1900, taken by Wells

5. Jessie and Borys Conrad

6. Stephen Crane shows a smugglers' den at Brede Place

7. Cora Crane, war correspondent

8. Helen and Katherine Sanderson, 1899

9. Ted Sanderson with oboe, *c.* 1896

10. Gabriela Cunninghame Graham at Gartmore, 1900

11. Ivy Walls Farm

12. W. E. Henley, by William Rothenstein

13. John Galsworthy, by R. A. Souter

14. G. F. W. Hope

15. George Gissing, taken by Wells

16.   Wells pedals off: presentation inscription in *Tales of Space and Time*

blind stars that in their courses make us what we are the stuff is *written*! I like it immensely. As to myself I would write for him if I could—if I could! But you all who have undertaken the task to dilate my heart till it crack my ribs should know I am a dumb dog. Who am I—I who accidentally write a sentence a day—to promise books and stand up before publishers. My hands are empty and my tongue is tied from day to day. Now and then for a moment or so the spell is removed from me—to the end that I might the better taste the despair of thought without expression, of the wandering soul without a body. However please tell him with my thanks that I am very much flattered by what his proposal implies. It's better than all the wealth of Grant Richards.[1] And that's all I can say— a poor return for his and your kind thought of me.

There! Enough. But I *was* glad to hear from You. I am now writing for *Maga* a long short story to complete a vol: of three. I am writing with my teeth set very hard, and yet I will bring shame on all your heads, and my heart will shrivel to the size of a pea.

Affectionately Yours

Conrad

To H. G. Wells
Text MS Illinois; Unpublished

[letterhead: Pent Farm]

Tuesday [July 1899?][2]

My dear Wells.

I am confoundedly lame and want wife to stop here and look after me. It may be better to-morrow but I don't reckon on it. It's no use me writing to You to groan and swear.

I feel pretty wretched; Jess on her side has scalded her hand during cooking operations today. We are physically and mentally cripples, and not fit to be let lo[o]se. As soon as I can I shall sail up to Sandgate.

I haven't had much sailing. O! gosh! Life is full of deceptions. Our kindest regards, and humble apologies for unreadiness, to your wife and yourself.

Faithfully Yours

Conrad

Thanks! I've got the N° of *Mercure*. Nice. I.O.U. twenty five pounds.

Jph. Conrad

---

[1] The London publisher: he started business in 1897.
[2] The type three letterhead implies a date in 1899; the issue of *Mercure de France* most likely to interest Conrad was that of July 1899, with its article by Davray.

To Helen Sanderson
Text MS Yale; Unpublished

[letterhead: Pent Farm]
22 July 99.

Dear Mrs Sanderson.

I ought to have thanked you weeks before for the photograph of your charming and very young daughter. We have been delighted with it and we had a good look every day. It is the dearest little face! Of you however there is not much to see.

I am glad You're going to Scotland. There is such a thing as native air—and native atmosphere; and even such a hopeless vagabond as myself understands the need of it—the longing for it—that comes upon one in the midst of cares, in the midst of happiness as well.

The unrest of human thought is like the unrest of the sea, disturbing and futile. There is always something stirring under the surface of accepted beliefs. Nothing new however; nothing enduring. It seems to me I am looking at the rush and recoil of the waves at the foot of a cliff;[1] but a Church should be like a rock in the midst of an ocean—unmoved. The mad individualism of Niet[z]sche[2] the exaggerated altruism of the next man tainted with selfishness and pride come with their noise and froth, pass away and are forgotten. Faith remains; but a faith that seeks a compromise with every outbreak of human levity ceases to be a faith, becomes an expedient, a system a social institution—and perishes. Truth is immovable—it is eternal, it is one; and a church as the repository of the highest truth cannot listen, cannot absorb what is unstable, complex and doomed to die.

These are my vague thoughts. They could be made the ground of a defensible position. I would not advocate a blind intolerance. The church should be indulgent like a mother to the capricious vagaries of her child; but to surrender to such vagaries or even make the smallest concession to them would be fatal, would be destructive.

Pardon these platitudes and many thanks for your delightful letter. Your affte and obe[t] servant

Jph Conrad.

Love to Ted and to Katherine.

[1] And recalling Arnold's 'Dover Beach'?
[2] Much later, in 'The Crime of Partition', Conrad associated Nietzsche with the morality of 'Germanic Tribes': *Notes on Life and Letters*, pp. 124–5. Conrad had seen Garnett's article on Nietzsche in the *Outlook* of 8 July (see letters to Garnett, 26 October and 9 November; the latter witnesses to Helen Sanderson's interest as well).

To Hugh Clifford
Text MS Clifford; Hunter

[letterhead: Pent Farm]
23 July 99

My dear Sir.

I trust you and Mrs Clifford will find it in your hearts to give us a day of your time.

I think you mentionned* the first half of Aug^st. I want only two days in that fortnight one for a visit to Henry James (who is almost my neighbour in Rye)[1] and another for W. E. Henley who has sent me a reproachful message the other day. I've not fixed the dates for these visits and shall not do so till I hear from you.

If Your fortitude does not flinch at the awful prospect we can put You up for the night—and this would be the better way. Only in any case I trust you will come early. There is a decent train about 11 am from Char X which I venture to recommend.

I've been very busy and not a little seedy or I would have written before.

Believe me dear Mr Clifford very
faithfully yours

Jph. Conrad.

To Hugh Clifford
Text MS Clifford; Hunter

[letterhead: Pent Farm]
28 July 99

My dear Sir.

In a tremendous hurry to catch this post. Many thanks for the book[2] which I've only just seen on my return from a couple of days cruising.

There's much to say—also about B'wood contributions.[3] Very excellent.

Faithfully yours

Jph. Conrad

---

[1] About eighteen miles away.
[2] Dr Allan Hunter identifies this as *Since the Beginning* (1898), Clifford's first novel.
[3] The most recent was 'In Chains' in the August issue: Clifford was a regular contributor.

To David Meldrum

Text MS Duke; Blackburn 59

[letterhead: Pent Farm]
31st July 99

My dear Mr Meldrum.

Thanks for your letter. I have been seedy and interrupted in various ways; this explains the delay and the small quantity of copy I am sending you now.

Here's the end of Chap III. Chap IV whole and the beginning of Chap V. pp of my type *32 to 50* which I should like to be doubly copied—one set for me and the other for E'burgh.

I shall be sending you MS almost daily if only a few pages at a time keeping it up till the end which, I pray, may be soon but is not in sight yet—not by a long way.

I had proof from E'burgh which I return there by the same post that takes this letter to you.

I would like to get £50 on acct of *Jim* at once.

These three tales will make a thick vol or I am much mistaken. Jim may turn out longer than *H of D* even. Whether as good?—that's a question. Let us hope.

I make note of the new agreement[1] entered into with Mr B'wood. *£5 per 1000 words serial rights (in England) and 20% book. No advance.* And once more thanks very much for arranging the matter.

I am my dear Mr Meldrum very
faithfully Yours

Jph. Conrad.

To David Meldrum

Text MS Duke; Blackburn 26

[letterhead: Pent Farm]
Friday 10h August 98
[10/11 August 1899][2]

My dear Mr Meldrum.

Very many thanks for the cheque for *£20* which You have so kindly sent me. It shall be paid back as soon as I get my advance from Mr Bwood.

---

[1] For another volume of short stories after the one intended to include 'Jim' and 'Heart of Darkness': see letter of 19 May 1900.

[2] The manuscript does read '98', and Blackburn places it in that year. The circumstances of its writing, however, must place it in August 1899, between the letters of 31 July and 22

As to Jim: I think that September *is* safe *quite*. Strictly speaking you have enough for two instalments now in hand. If you divide in that way the story may run into 4 No^s. But even if you distribute the whole into three I am confident of coming to time.[1] This work isn't like the *Rescue* where I aim at purely [a]esthetic (if I dare say so) effects. I am now in tolerable health. There's really nothing to stand in the way of a happy termination of Jim's troubles; and its as likely as not the story will be finished a long time before the second instalment comes out.

If America is in the way of the dates I shall not write any slower for it. I *never mean* to be slow. The stuff comes out at its own rate. I am always ready to put it down; nothing would induce me to lay down my pen if I *feel* a sentence—or even a word ready to my hand. The trouble is that too often—alas!—I've to wait for the sentence—for the word.

What wonder then that during the long blank hours the doubt creeps into the mind and I ask myself whether I am fitted for that work. The worst is that while I am thus powerless to produce my imagination is extremely active: whole paragraphs, whole pages, whole chapters pass through my mind. Everything is there: descriptions, dialogue, reflexion—everything—everything but the belief, the conviction, the only thing needed to make me put pen to paper. I've thought out a volume in a day till I felt sick in mind and heart and gone to bed, completely done up, without having written a line. The effort I put out should give birth to masterpieces as big as mountains—and it brings forth a ridiculous mouse now and then.

Therefore I must sell my mice as dear as I can since I must live; that's why I beg you very earnestly to arrange matters so as not to give McClure any excuse for losing my Am: Ser: rights of *Jim*.[2] It looks as if I were very mercenary but, God knows, it is not so. I am impatient of material anxieties and they frighten me too because I feel how mysteriously independent of myself is my power of expression. It is there—I believe—and some thought, and a little insight. All this is there; but I am not as the workmen who can take up and lay down their tools. I am, so to speak, only the agent of an unreliable master.

Once more—many thanks for all and every one of the good offices I

August (see also the letters from Meldrum and Blackwood, Blackburn pp. 60–1). Presumably the letter was written on Thursday, 10 August, Friday 11 August, or both those days. It was not unusual for Conrad to muddle his dates.

[1] *Lord Jim* ran for fourteen monthly issues of *Blackwood's*, starting in October; Conrad finished the manuscript in July 1900.

[2] In the United States, *Lord Jim* appeared as a book (Doubleday, McClure), but not as a serial.

receive at your hands. We haven't given up the hope of seeing you here before the 'rainy season' sets in. With kindest regards from us both.

Always yours

Jph. Conrad

I've received 2^d batch of *Jim* last night. There will be a good many corrections to make in proof for Maga. Upon the whole I don't think the story very bad. I am cheered.

To David Meldrum

Text MS Duke; Blackburn 62

[letterhead: Pent Farm]
22 Augst 99

Dear Mr Meldrum.

I've dispatched today 12 pp. more of Jim—addressed to the office. More would have been sent but my wife not being very well could not type yesterday. They shall be coming in very soon: I am going straight ahead with Jim and am rather pleased with him so far.

I haven't heard yet from Mr B'wood, neither in reference to the advance I asked for *Jim* nor to the arrangement for future work. Did I read Your letter aright that that last is 'fixed' on conditions proposed by me? As to the first, to have to go a-begging is bad enough—and nothing but dire necessity would drive me to it; therefore the delay in the effect of it is most tormenting. All these are miserable cares.

Speaking of future work it is I suppose understood that I have a free hand in placing my stories elsewhere too than in *Maga*. Or do you think Mr B'wood wishes to have *everything* till the next vol (after the Three Tales) is completed? I ask for two reasons. One that—don't you think?—there may be too much Conrad in *Maga* by and by. The other is this: That having made a beastly hash of my *Rescue* engagements (the book itself is right enough) I feel I would like to let Heinemann have something of mine in the meantime. Now there is a law of Medes and Persians[1] that anything appearing in *Maga* must be published in book form by the Firm—isn't there? This being so the stuff destined for H. must appear serially somewhere else. I have enough matter laid up in my head for two more vols in the style—or, let us say as they do of men-of-war cruisers—in the class "Youth" and if possible I would like

---

[1] 'Which altereth not': Daniel 6.8.

to share it between B'wood and H'nn—unless I get on (in the next few months) much quicker with the *Rescue* than I expect.

This for your consideration. Moreover after Jim is finished I would like to give Mr B'wood the sketch of old Captain Loutit[1] and another story—at new rates—together about 30 to 35000 words (or more). Will he want them so soon after Jim—will he want them at all? I wouldn't want to hurry the publication. I would be only anxious to sell them.

Of course my dear Sir I never for a moment supposed you would want to criticize my method (or no-method) of work. If I wrote touching my difficulties it is because sometimes it is very hard to keep one's trouble to oneself, and writing to you I was sure of 'comprehension'. You have been so friendly to me that you must bear the penalty of my occasional confidences.

If you could jog their memories in E'gh without breaking any sacred usages or compromising my good standing—you would be doing a good action. My wife's kind regards.

Always yours faithfully
Jph. Conrad.

I dare say McClure is right in everything. So I've written him. By this time you have 20000 words of Jim in hand, and I want £50. You may reckon on 40-42000 as the whole.

To William Blackwood

Text MS NLS; Blackburn 63

[letterhead: Pent Farm]
22 Augst 99.

Dear Mr Blackwood.

I've this afternoon received your letter enclosing a cheque for £50 on acc^t/ of *Jim*. Many thanks for your unwearied readiness to answer my unceremonious—to say the least—demands.

I am glad you like Jim so far. Your good opinion gives one confidence. From the nature of things treated the story can not be as dramatic (in a certain sense) as the *H of D*. It is certainly more like *Youth*. It is however longer and more varied. The structure of it is a little loose—this however

---

[1] When Conrad sailed aboard the *Duke of Sutherland* in 1878, Thomas Louttit (born in Wick, Scotland, 1821) had just completed his last voyage as master; he had commanded the ship since it was built in 1865. Registered in Wick, the *Duke of Sutherland* was owned by Daniel Louttit. (PRO: BT 100/21 and 115/116.) In the MS of 'The End of the Tether', Captain Whalley was originally called Loutit.

need not detract from its interest—from the "general reader" point of view. The question of *art* is so endless, so involved and so obscure that one is tempted to turn one's face resolutely away from it. I've certainly an idea—apart from the idea and the subject of the story—which guides me in my writing, but I would be hard put to it if requested to give it out in the shape of a fixed formula. After all in this as in every other human endeavour one is answerable only to one's conscience.

I have this day sent off another 3000 words to your London office. 2000 more are actually written or rather scrawled and awaiting the domestic typewriter. I devote myself exclusively to *Jim*. I find I can't live with more than one story at a time. It's a kind of literary monogamism. You know how desperately slow I work. Scores of notions present themselves—expressions suggest themselves by the dozen, but the inward voice that decides:—this is well—this is right—is not heard sometimes for days together. And meantime one must live!

Very good of you to delay *Jim's* app'ce out of regard for my american business. It's obvious the matter is of prime importance to me. My unsatisfactory manner of production is at fault here. If the thing can't be managed, well, then it must go. Let no horrid Yank stand in the way of Maga's convenience.

Hugh Clifford with his wife paid me a flying visit. Actually came down all the way to make my acquaintance. I was quite touched. We sang Maga's praises. His last thing (Augst N^o) was rather good—I mean as a piece of writing. His knowledge is unique. If I only knew one hundre[d]th part of what he knows I would move a mountain or two. This is an endless letter. I've had news of your health from Meldrum. I trust you are quite well now. I've suffered from excruciating headaches all the summer. Believe me dear Mr Blackwood always very faithfully yours

Joseph Conrad.

To J. B. Pinker

Text MS Berg; J-A, I, 278

[letterhead: Pent Farm]
23^d Augst 99

Dear Sir[1].

Thanks very much for your letter.

The Am: Publisher need not be ashamed, tho' the fact is that all my

---

[1] James Brand Pinker (1863–1922), a Scotsman, was one of the first literary agents in London. At various times he represented Ford, James, Crane, Bennett, and D. H. Lawrence. Although the present letter turns Pinker down, in September 1900 Conrad began a working relationship with Pinker and, later, his son that lasted until Conrad's death. This letter is the first of over 1200.

prose has been published in the states. Publishers are not supposed to be able to read. I can write a little but God forbid that I should break upon the blessed ignorance of a stranger far from his native land.

My method of writing is so unbusiness-like that I don't think you could have any use for such an unsatisfactory person. I generally sell a work before it is begun, get paid when it is half done and don't do the other half till the spirit moves me. I must add that I have no control whatever over the spirit—neither has the man who has paid the money.

The above may appear fanciful to you but it is the sober truth. I live in hopes of reformation and whenever that takes place you and you alone shall have the working of the New Conrad. Meantime I must be content to pander to my absurd weaknesses, and hobble along the line of the least resistance.

> I am my dear Sir faithfully yours
> Jph. Conrad.

To Cora Crane
Text 101 MS Columbia; Stallman 225

> [letterhead: Pent Farm]
> 27 Aug 99

Dear Mrs. Crane.

I am so sorry Stephen worried about the payment. Thanks ever so much for cheque. I've sent Hope[1] yesterday *£15* in Stephen's name.

A series of visits from Jessie's people has begun. There are now four in the house and this state of things shall last for a fortnight at least. We have put them off till now having lived in hopes of Your visit early this month.

Could you come in September—second half? We are extremely sorry to suggest the delay of an event we have been looking forward to with eagerness and delight. Jessie's tearful. She sends her love and would write herself only she is bad with neuralgia. This is the second day of it.

I am at work and doing very little as usual.

> With affectionate regards from us
> both Yours most faithfully
> Jph Conrad

---

[1] Conrad's friend, who was in serious financial trouble.

To David Meldrum

Text MS Duke; Blackburn 65

[letterhead: Pent Farm]

27 Augst 99

My dear Mr Meldrum.

My wife's and mine heartiest congratulations on the safe arrival of a boy.[1] I trust that in a few days You will find time to drop us a word as to his and his mother's welfare.

The matter I mentioned is not at all pressing. I just wanted to hear Your opinion of it. It is more than kind of you to write at such a lenght.* If my thoughts ran that way it is only out of regard for Heinemann. I am not anxious to fling myself on sixpenny or even shilling magazines. I am quite content to work for 102Maga and I always meant to have one vol for M^r B'wood and only now and then divert a story for an eventual vol for H.

Why not bring Mr B'wood's manager here? Coming to lunch you may be back in London for dinner.

I return the advance You have been so kind as to accom[m]odate me with.[2] Many thanks.

Always yours

Jph. Conrad.

To William Blackwood and Sons

Text MS Duke; Blackburn 65

1st Sept 99
Pent Farm
Stanford.
N^r Hythe.

Dear Sirs.

I beg to acknowledge receipt of 'type' of *Jim*. Allow me to point out that I've this time got only *one* copy of type and that my original text has not been returned to me. Would You kindly send me the duplicate and also the original.

Very faithfully Yours

Jph. Conrad.

---

[1] Jan, born 25 August.   [2] Pending the arrival of Blackwood's £50.

To John Galsworthy
Text MS Forbes; J-A, 1, 278

Pent Farm
2ᵈ Sept. 99

Dearest Jack

Horrors. I think I am too late in writing. The days dropped by so fast, so fast!

Dear of you to drop me a line to think of me and my work. You have no idea how your interest in me *keeps me up*. I am unutterably weary of thinking, of writing, of seeing of feeling of living.

Jim will be finished end this month. I plod on without much faith. Its money. Thats all.

I think of your work. Hueffer has been here inquiring about You and your prose. We are all interested. You've made the conquest of C. Graham whom I treat worse than a dog not having answered two of his letters.

Jessie's kindest regards. Borys talks about "nice man Jack." Forgive this familiarity.

Yours ever

Conrad.

To Stephen Crane
Text MS Columbia; Stallman 230

Sunday [10 September? 1899]¹
Pent Farm.
Stanford
Nr Hythe.

Dear old Pard.

Right. Bully for you. You are the greatest of the boys—and you are as good as I want you so you needn't trouble to apologise.

Could you come? You would make me happy. And will you pardon me for not coming to you. Dear Stephen I am like a damned paralyzed mud turtle. I can't move. I can't write. I can't do anything. But I can be wretched and, by God! I am! Jess sends her love to the whole house. Give my affectionate regards and compliments. Let me know *the day before* when you are coming. You are a dear old chap.

Ever Yours

Conrad.

Station: Sandling Junction. From Charg X good train a[t] *11 am* and *4.25 pm* (S.E.R)

¹ Dating by Stallman and Gilkes: they offer no evidence.

To Edward Garnett
Text MS Indiana; G. 152

[letterhead: Pent Farm]
16th Sept 99.

Dearest Edward.

To drop me a line was a generous action. I had not the courage to write; I feel to you like a son who has gone wrong and what with shame and recklessness remains silent—and yet nourishes the hope of rehabilitation and keeps his eye fixed steadily on some distant day of pardon and embraces.

It will come, it will come, and whether the prodigal comes to you or you come to the prodigal some poor innocent calf is sure to suffer.

I had nothing to write—or else too much—so much that no piece of paper seemed long enough no ink-well of adequate depth! And yet when some day we sit together at last over the remains of the obese heifer of forgiveness half a dozen words or a judicious wink of the eye shall make everything clear—everything clear!

I wouldn't trust C Graham's literary judgment—wouldn't—not much. I am writing—it is true—but this is only piling crime upon crime: every line is odious like a bad action. I mean odious to me—because I still have some pretences to the possession of a conscience though my morality is gone to the dogs. I am like a man who has lost his gods. My efforts seem unrelated to anything in heaven and everything under heaven is impalpable to the touch like shapes of mist. Do you see how easy writing must be under such conditions? Do you see? Even writing to a friend—to a person one has heard, touched, drank* with, quar[r]elled with—does not give me a sense of reality. All is illusion—the words written, the mind at which they are aimed, the truth they are intended to express, the hands that will hold the paper, the eyes that will glance at the lines. Every image floats vaguely in a sea of doubt—and the doubt itself is lost in an unexpected universe of incertitudes.

I've written. Are you any the wiser? Are you disposed to forgive?

I end here because I must to catch the post.

Ever Yours

Conrad.

Jessie's love. We are well enough—considering.

To David Meldrum

Text MS Duke; Blackburn 66

[letterhead: Pent Farm]
Monday. 17 Sep^t 99

My dear Mr Meldrum.

Many thanks for your letter. Will you convey my cordial invitation to Mr Morton.[1] If You go to Rye in the morning why not come on here for dinner and the night. You could be back in London next day at 10.30 am were it necessary. Any day *after Tuesday* will do.

I trust Mrs Meldrum and the boy are going on well.

Always yours

Jph. Conrad.

Please wire or write in time. Wire best as letters do go astray. I will be sending more Jim in a day or two.

To David Meldrum

Text MS Duke; Blackburn 66

[Pent Farm]
2^d Oct 99.

My dear Mr Meldrum

Just time for a word of thanks before the post goes.[2]

If I had a year to write before me I wouldn't know what adequate I could say.

Always yours

Jph Conrad.

To Hugh Clifford

Text MS Clifford; J-A, 1, 279

[letterhead: Pent Farm]
Monday.
9th Oct 99

My Dear Mr. Clifford.

I received the book three hours ago and—it is only too short![3] I've read it twice. I've also read the inscription the wording of which I prize

---

[1] George A. Morton, Blackwood's manager.

[2] Occasion unknown: the letter Blackburn assigned to 29 September belongs to spring or early summer 1900.

[3] *In a Corner of Asia*, just published by T. Fisher Unwin in the Overseas Library. Conrad discusses 'In the Central Gaol', 'The Vigil of Pa' Tûa, the Thief', and 'The Death March of Kûlop-Sumbing'.

immensely, though I vow and protest that I never looked upon your critical notice[1] in the light of an act requiring expiation. I am only too conscious of my ignorance my audacity—and of all my other failings, which at your hands have received such a generous treatment.

Many thanks. I've lived for a few hours in your pages. Of the sketches I've not previously seen, *The Central Gaol* and *The Vigil of Pa' Tûa* are the two I like the best. Of the others, *The Death March* has been always my favourite; but indeed all are absorbing—to me at least. I would like to talk about them long—interminably; of the matter and of the manner too.

Of course the matter is admirable—the knowledge, the feeling, the sympathy; it is sure to win perfect and full recognition. It is all sterling metal; a thing of absolute value. There can be no question of it not only for those who know but even for those who approach the book with blank minds on the subject of the race you have, in more than one sense, made your own. And as to the manner—well! I know you are not a seeker after mere expression and I beg leave to offer only one remark.

You do not leave enough to the imagination.[2] I do not mean as to facts—the facts can not be too explicitly stated; I am alluding simply to the phrasing. True a man who knows so much (without taking into account the manner in which his knowledge was acquired) may well spare himself the trouble of meditating over the words, only that words, groups of words, words standing alone, are symbols of life, have the power in their sound or their aspect to present the very thing you wish to hold up before the mental vision of your readers. The things "as they are" exist in words; therefore words should be handled with care lest the picture, the image of truth abiding in facts should become distorted—or blurred.

These are the considerations for a mere craftsman—you may say; and you may also conceivably say that I have nothing else to trouble my head about. However the *whole* of the truth lies in the presentation; therefore the expression should be studied in the interest of veracity. This is the only morality of *art* apart from *subject*.

I have travelled a good way from my original remark. Not enough left to the imagination in the phrasing. I beg leave to illustrate my meaning

---

[1] See letter to Blackwood, 13 December 1898.
[2] Conrad gives another dimension to some remarks in the Preface: 'since I have striven throughout to convey a picture of realities, not merely to write fiction, it is possible that I may occasionally have sacrificed dramatic effects in the cause of truth. The descriptions of native character, of customs, manners, superstitions and social practices owe nothing at all to my imagination' (pp. v-vi).

from extracts on p. *261*—not that I pose for an accomplished craftsman or fondly think I am free from that very fault and others much worse. No; it is only to explain what I mean.

—When the whole horror of his position forced itself with an agony of realization upon his frightened mind, Pa' Tûa for a space lost his reason.—

In this sentence the reader is borne down by the full expression. The words *with an agony of realisation* completely destroy the effect—therefore interfere with the truth of the statement. The word *frightened* is fatal. It seems as if it had been written withought* any thought at all. It takes away all sense of reality—for if you read the sentence *in its place on the page* You will see that the word *frightened* (or indeed any word of the sort) is inadequate to express the true state of that man's mind. No word is adequate. The imagination of the reader should be left free to arouse his feeling.

—When the whole horror of his position forced itself upon his mind, Pa' Tûa for a space lost his reason.—

This is truth; this is* which thus stated carries conviction because it is a *picture* of a mental state. And look how finely it goes on with a perfectly legitimate effect

—He screamed aloud, and the hollow of the rocks took up his cries
It is magnificent! It is suggestive. It is truth effectively stated. But
and hurled them back to him mockingly
is nothing at all. It is a phrase anybody can write to fit any sort of situation; it is the sort of thing that writes itself; it is the sort of thing I write twenty times a day and (with the fear of overtaking fate behind me) spend half my nights in taking out of my work—upon which depends the daily bread of the house: (literally—from day to day); not to mention (I dare hardly think of it) the future of my child, of those nearest and dearest to me, between whom and the bleakest want there is only my pen—as long as life lasts. And I can sell all I write—as much as I can write!

This is said to make it manifest that I practise the faith which I take the liberty to preach—if You will allow me to say so—in a brotherly spirit. To return.

Please observe how strikingly the effect is carried on.

—When the whole horror of his position forced itself upon his mind, Pa' Tûa for a space lost his reason. He screamed aloud, and the hollow of the rocks took up his cries; the bats awoke in thousands and joined the band that rustled and squeaked above the man etc. etc.

In the last two lines the words hurrying—motiveless—already—defenceless—are not essential and therefore not true to the fact. The impression of *hurrying motiveless* has been given already in lines 2. 3. 4. at the top of the page. If they *joined* it is because the others were *already* flying. *Already* is repetition. *Defenceless* is inadequate for a man held in the merciless grip of a rock.

And pray believe me that if I have selected this passage it is because I am alive to its qualities and not because I have looked consciously for its defects.

For the same reason I do not apologise for my remarks. They are not an impertinence, they are a tribute to the work, that appeals so strongly to me by its subject, partly—but most by its humanity, its comprehension, by its spirit and by its expression too—which I have made a subject of critical analysis. If I have everlastingly bored you, you must forgive me. I trust you will find no other cause of offence.

Our meeting—Your visit here[1]—mark an epoch in my life. I wish my work would allow me to run up to town and see you before you return to the East; but I have been unwell, mentally powerless and physically unfit, my work has suffered a disastrous delay. I am a slave of mean preoccupations, alas!

"Friend"—says the inscription—and I feel distinctly the richer for your friendship. Your and Mrs Clifford's short apparition amongst us has left an abiding and valued memory. Jessie joins me in kindest regards to your wife and yourself.

Pardon this corrected and interlined letter. It's past midnight and I had a rough time with MS all day.

Always Yours faithfully
Joseph Conrad.

To John Galsworthy
Text MS Forbes; Unpublished

[letterhead: Pent Farm]
Tuesday. [10? October 1899][2]

Dear Jack

How goes the chapter?[3] When are you coming? Hueffer has been here inquiring with quite an anxiety. Meldrum spent a day and is gone

---

[1] In August.

[2] The £20 arrived on 12 October. Prompt as well as generous, Galsworthy had probably replied by return of post. He was always ready to lend Conrad money – without much hope of seeing it again. Jean-Aubry suppressed all references to Galsworthy's generosity, perhaps at his own request.

[3] Of *Villa Rubein*.

yesterday to Harrowgate where old B'wood is nursing himself.[1] There will be no difficulty about a cheque but the old chap is so leisurely that if you can meantime send me twenty?

I am a horrible skunk.

Jim takes his time to come out but it never stops for long. I've done nothing on Sund and Mond. Today I write with a little rush. Oh I *am* weary.

Maupassant? Eh? Bring him soon.

Ever yours

Conrad.

To John Galsworthy
Text MS Forbes; Unpublished

[letterhead: Pent Farm]
12 Oct. 99

Dearest Jack

Just time for a word of thanks for cheque £20 received this morning.

Drop me a line soon to say when you are coming. I am all impatience to see that Chapter. You are the best of fellows!

Ever yours

Jph Conrad.

I am sincerely and seriously glad Your Sister likes the book. It is a good sign. I surmise she has seen the last chap.?

To E. L. Sanderson
Text MS Yale; J-A, 1, 281

[letterhead: Pent Farm]
12 Oct 99

My dear Ted.

Were you to come with a horsewhip you would be still welcome. It's the only kind of visit I can imagine myself as deserving from You. Only the other day Jessie asked me whether I had written to you and overwhelmed me with reproaches. Why wait another day? But I am incorrigible; I will always look to another day to bring something something good, something one would like to share with a friend— something—if only a fortunate thought. But the days bring nothing at

---

[1] Having returned from Harrogate the day before, Blackwood sent an advance of £50 on 26 October (Blackburn, p. 68).

all—and thus they go by empty-handed—till the last day of all. I am always looking forward to some date to some event: when I finish this; before I begin that other thing—and there never seems to be any breathing time, not because I do much but because the toil is great. I try at times to persuade myself that it is my honesty that makes the burden so heavy, but, alas! the suspicion will force itself upon one that maybe it is only lack of strenght,* of power—of an uplifting belief in oneself. Whatever the cause the struggle is hard, and this may be no more than justice.

I haven't been in town since last March. If I haven't been to see you I have not gone to visit other people. My dear Ted you have much to forgive me; but try to imagine yourself trying your hardest to save the School[1] (God forefend) from downfall, annihilation and disaster; and the thing going on and on endlessly. That's exactly how I am situated; and the worst is that the menace (in my case) does not seem to come from outside but from within; that the menace and danger or weakness are in me—in myself alone. I fear I have not the capacity and the power to go on—to satisfy the just expectations of those who are dependent on my exertion. I fear! I fear! And sometimes I hope. But it is the fear that abides. But even were I wrong in my fear the very fact that such a fear exists would argue that everything is not right—would in itself be a danger and a menace. So I turn in this vicious circle and the work itself becomes like the work in a treadmill—a thing without joy—a punishing task.

You can see now why I am so often remiss in my correspondence. There is nothing one would gladly write under that shadow. This is the sort of thing that one writes and the more one loves his friends, the more belief one has in their affection, the less one is disposed to cast upon them the gloom of one's intimate thoughts. My silence is seldom selfish and never forgetful. It is often a kind of reserve, "pudor", something in the nature of instinctive decency. One expects to fall every instant and one would like to fall with a covered face, with a decorous arrangement of draperies with no more words than greater men have used. One would! And when one sits down it is to write eight pages without coming to the end of one's groans.

I am ashamed, bitterly ashamed to make the same eternal answer, the same eternal wail of incertitude to your hospitable voice. I am now trying to finish a story which began in the Oct N° of *Blackwood*. I am at it day after day and I want all day, every minute of a day to produce a

1 Elstree, the Sanderson family's preparatory school.

beggarly tale of words or perhaps to produce nothing at all. And when that is finished (I thought it would be so on the first of this month—but no fear!) I must go on, even go on at once and drag out of myself another 20000 words if the boy is to have his milk and I my beer (this is a figure of speech—I don't drink beer. I drink weak tea and yearn after dry champagne) and if the world is not absolutely to come to an end. And after I have written and have been paid I shall have the satisfaction of knowing I can't allow myself the relaxation of being ill, more than three days, under the penalty of starvation; nor the luxury of going off the books altogether without playing the part of a thief regarding various confiding persons whose desire to serve me was greater than their wisdom. Do you take me, sir? Verb: sap: that is, circomlocution* is clear to the wise.

And yet—one hopes, as I had the honour to remark above.

A book of mine—(Joseph Conrad's last)[1] is to come out in March. Three stories in one volume. If only five thousand copies of that *could* be sold! If only! But why dream of the wealth of the Indies? I am not the man for whom Pactolus flows and the mines of Golconda distil priceless jewels[2] (What an absurd style. Don't *you* think I am deteriorating?) Style or no style—I am *not* the man. And oh! dear Ted—it *is* a fool's business to write fiction for a living. It is indeed.

It is strange. The unreality of it seems to enter one's real life, penetrate into the bones, make the very heart beats pulsate illusions through the arteries. One's will becomes the slave of hallucinations, responds only to shadowy impulses, waits on imagination alone. A strange state, a trying experience, a kind of fiery trial of untruthfulness. And one goes through it with an exaltation as false as all the rest of it. One goes through it—and there's nothing to show at the end. Nothing! Nothing Nothing!

Let me remark with due solemnity that it is to morrow morning already. For an apparently domesticated man to be 'abroad' (in the 17th century sense) with friends at 1.30 AM is (to say the least) reprehensible. Suffer me to leave you here at this turning that heads nowhere. That very turning is my way, my only way. You are going straight and, perchance, you know where—and, perchance, you are right! You are right! Upon the whole I shall suffer most from that separation. But I shall soon come out of my land of mist peopled by shadows, and we shall

[1] In the sense of 'latest'?
[2] The golden sands of Pactolus and the diamond mines of Golconda were fabulous sources of wealth.

meet again for another midnight communion—as though we too also had been ghosts, shadows. I question however whether the most desolate Shade that ever haunted this earth of ours carried in its misty form a heart as heavy as mine is—sometimes.

I wanted to write you a sober sensible letter; to explain, to make clear, to apologise—and before all to thank you for that fidelity which is for me one of the few real things in this world. Perhaps with the intuition of a heart not rebuked by appearances you will divine what I've not been able to set down—for want of space—yes; let us say, for want of space. Jessie sends her kind regards. She is writing to your wife.

Affectionately your[s] ever

Jph Conrad

PS You don't speak of Kitty[1]—therefore it is a kind of negative evidence she is well. My little chap begins to talk. It is very amusing, charming, even touching. One gets to love the voice and sometimes it makes a cold shiver run down my back it rings so unconscious of life!

PS My affectionate regards to Your wife. The first time I come to town I shall push on to Elstree; that will be as soon as *Jim* is finished. You must be patient with me and bear with me and not cast me off in anger. Never!

To R. B. Cunninghame Graham

Text MS Dartmouth; J-A, 1, 284; Watts 126

[letterhead: Pent Farm]

14 Oct 99

Très chèr ami.

I was just wondering where you were when your dear letter arrived. I mean, dear—precious. Well! Vous me mettez du coeur au ventre;[2] and that's no small service for I live in a perpetual state of intellectual funk. I only wish I knew how to thank you.

Shall I see you on your return from Madrid? The book that's gone to Heinemann is the "History of the Jesuits" I suppose[3]—and I should think for next year. Now with this idiotic war[4] there will be a bad time coming for print. All that's art, thought, idea will have to step back and hide its head before the intolerable war inanities. Grand bien leur en

---

[1] The Sandersons' baby daughter.   [2] 'You buck me up.'

[3] The history of the Jesuit missions in Paraguay, *A Vanished Arcadia*, published in 1901.

[4] The Boer War, which Graham regarded as a struggle between two burglars. On 26 October Conrad wrote to Sanderson, who took a very different view of the conflict.

fasse.[1] The whole business is inexpressibly stupid—even on general principles; for evidently a war should be a conclusive proceeding while this noble enterprise (no matter what it's* first result) must be the beginning of an endless contest. It is always unwise to begin a war which to be effective must be a war of extermination; it is positively imbecile to start it without a clear notion of what it means and to force on questions for immediate solution which are eminently fit to be left to time. From time only one solution could be expected—and that one favourable to this country. The war brings in an element of incertitude which will be not eliminated by military success. There is an appalling fatuity in this business. If I am to believe Kipling this is a war undertaken for the cause of democracy. C'est a crever de rire.[2] However, now the fun has commenced, I trust British successes will be crushing from the first—on the same principle that if there's murder being done in the next room and you can't stop it you wish the head of the victim to be bashed in forthwith and the whole thing over for the sake of your own feelings. Assez de ces bêtises. Borys wears the heart[3] every day and says Gram-ma has given it to him. Jessie's kind regards. We must be in town in Nov'' for your Wife's play.[4] Rappelez moi a son bienveillant souvenir.[5]

Drop me a line to say when you return.

Ever Yours

Conrad

To David Meldrum
Text MS Duke; Blackburn 67

[letterhead: Pent Farm]
18th Oct'' 99

My dear Meldrum.

Thanks for all you've done and for all you say. As ill-luck would have it Jessie got rh[e]umatism in the right wrist. The worst of the pain is over but it is still quite powerless. She couldn't travel alone with the child in that state; as to me I protest I dare not stray far away from my table. Jim

---

[1] 'Much good may it do them.'
[2] 'It's enough to make you die laughing.' The campaign to enfranchise the Uitlanders (white Britons) in the mineral-rich Transvaal was one of the issues in the war.
[3] A gift from Graham: a gold heart set with a turquoise.
[4] Gabriela Cunninghame Graham had translated Zorrilla's *Don Juan Tenorio*; the production opened in February.
[5] 'Remember me kindly to her.'

is approaching his climax. I have a good few pages more but I must attend to my own typewriting just now. I had a fair copy and am dispatching it to E'burgh tomorrow along with some proofs.

I haven't heard from Mr B'wood yet; but after your letter my mind is at ease—for a bit anyhow.

Pardon hurried scrawl. Pray convey our heartfelt blessing to Your Wife and also our regret. We trust Betty is getting on. You say nothing of the Man.[1]

With kindest regard from us both to Mrs. Meldrum and yourself I am always your[s] faithfully

Jph. Conrad.

To David Meldrum
Text MS Duke; Blackburn 67

[letterhead: Pent Farm]
Tuesday. [24 October 1899][2]

My dear Mr Meldrum—

Here's some more Jim. The Jany inst is well advanced if not wholly finished. I've dispatched the proofs and additional type for the Dec^er Number yesterday, proposing that the inst^t should include Chap VIII if possible. I hope they will see their way. In that case Jan and Febr instalments without being unduly long will contain the end of the story.

I've *not* heard from Mr Blackwood, as yet. I may get a letter this morning but I must post this at once.

I hope Betty is getting on and both your wife and yourself are well. Our kindest regards

Always yours

Jph Conrad.

To Edward Garnett
Text MS Sutton; G. 153

[letterhead: Pent Farm]
26 Otc^er* 99

Dearest Edward.

Thanks for your letter. If I don't send proofs or type it is because there is, alas, so little to send and what there is, is not worthy. I *feel* it bad; and,

---

[1] Their son Jan and daughter Elizabeth.
[2] On the MS, Meldrum noted replying on 26 October.

unless I am hopelessly morbid, I can not be altogether wrong. So much I am conceited; I fancy that I know a good thing when I see it.

I am weary of the difficulty of it. The game is not worth the candle; of course there is no question of throwing up the hand. It must be played out to the end but it is the other men who hold the trumps and the prospect is not inspiriting.

I don't know what to say to Your projected dedication.[1] Not that I feel averse to take the utmost from your affection. Generous as you are you can never give me enough; for of the proofs—such proofs—of such friendship one is insatiable as of the most real form of happiness. You've made me happy, and sad, and frightened; you've startled my secret dream as the report of the first gun may interrupt a dream of battle. *Vous avez remué le plus profond de mon âme.*[2] Never have I felt less worthy as now when my name is to be borne on the stream of time with Your wife's achievement and your criticism. Is it possible that I should deserve to stand so close to the great creator, to his great interpreter and to the man who, in this country, alone had penetrated the Master. But You have said it and I can only bow my head before this fabulous good fortune.

When you send me that volume ask your dear wife to write her name in it for me. I almost think I understand better than any one all the perfection of her finished task. That is why I said Interpreter and not translator. She is in that work what a great musician is to a great composer—with something more, something greater. It is as if the Interpreter had looked into the very mind of the Master and had a share in his inspiration. I had letters about your Nietzsche from all sorts of people. You have stirred some brains! I don't think there's anything wrong with *your* wits. Galsworthy brought the *Outlook* the other day and began to read aloud from your Ibsen. He read a couple of pars: and asked—Now who's this? I said Garnett or the devil. At that time I had no idea You wrote for that paper with a horrid caste-mark on its forepage.[3] I am taking it in now. You never even *tell* me what *You* are doing. As to Jim. I entreat you: wait till the 2ᵈ inst: comes out (in a few days) and I shall send you the two together. The first is too bad to stand alone. The fifth (and last inst) is not written yet—and what it will be God only knows.

[1] Constance Garnett dedicated her translation of Turgenev's *A Desperate Character* to Conrad.
[2] 'You have stirred the deepest part of my soul.'
[3] The front page of the *Outlook* carried a red seal showing a classical design; for Conrad's involvement in this weekly's early days, see letter to Sanderson, 3 February 1898. The article on Nietzsche appeared 8 July and the article on Ibsen 23 September 1899.

When! Oh when! Shall we speak face to face?

The news about the Patron is grave.[1] Is it grave? Surely you—You! are wanted in too many places to bother much about the placing of youre* wits. I keep mum but let me know the finality of this thusness.

Ever Yours

Conrad.

Jessie sends her love. We are in fair health.

To E. L. Sanderson
Text MS Yale; J-A, 1, 285

[letterhead: Pent Farm]
26th Oct 99

My dearest Ted

I had no idea my wail had been so loud and so lamentable and though I am sorry I have intruded with my miseries on your serious preoccupations, I congratulate myself on my lack of restraint since it had drawn from you such a priceless, such a fraternal answer. I never doubted the nature of your sentiments but this inward certitude does not make their expression the less welcome. I am indeed a fortunate man. When the heart is full it is not full of words whatever the proverb may say; and if you had come and shot a sack of diamonds at my feet I could not have felt richer than when reading your letter; but as to understanding it as it should be answered it is vain for me to try. You must put the finishing touch to your friendship by giving me the credit of such feelings as to make me worthy of it.

I've been especially thinking of you since I read the Proclamation.[2] A sacrifice of that kind a man is always ready for though in your case it must be, to say the least of it, a grave inconvenience.[3] As to the war itself much might be said. I am a little out of touch with facts (though not totally ignorant of them) but one can apply general principles. Now it seems to me that—from the point of view of statecraft—no war is justifiable which does not solve a question. A war should be a final act—while this war is an initial act. This is the weak point. It will create

---

[1] Garnett's note reads: 'Mr. Fisher Unwin dispensed with my services as his literary adviser at the end of 1899.'

[2] Kruger's ultimatum to the British government had expired on 10 October. From that date Great Britain and the Boer republics were at war. As an officer in a territorial battalion, Sanderson was liable for service.

[3] For a married man in his thirties with a young child, delicate health, and an established career.

a situation of which, unless I am much mistaken, the country will get weary. The victory—unless it is to be thrown away—shall have to be followed by ruthless repression. The situation will become repugnant to the nation. The *"reasonable English ideals"* (I am quoting Sir F. Milner's words)[1] are not attained in that way. Their instruments are time and the deepseated convictions of the race—the expansive force of its enterprise and its morality. We all know, we know instinctively that the danger to the Empire is elsewhere—that the conspiracy (to oust the Briton) of which we hear is ready to be hatched in other regions. It has peeped out at the time of the last Eastern crisis and is ever-lastingly skulking in the Far East.[2] A war there or anywhere but in S Africa would have been conclusive—would have cleared the air—would have been worth the sacrifices. We have heard much of the sorrows of the Outlanders (which did not prevent them from growing fat) but now real sorrows have come in the last few days.[3] May they be mitigated by a speedy and complete triumph since the work is begun and the price is being daily paid.

I can't say that I shared in the hysterical transports of some public organs for the simple reason that I expected to see displayed all the valour, perseverance, devotion which in fact have been displayed. Confound these papers. From the tone of some of them one would have thought they expected the artillery to clear out at a gallop across hills and ravines and every regiment to bolt throwing away arms and accoutrements. Those infernal scribblers are rank outsiders. No matter. It was very, very fine.[4] Much finer than the generalship I can't help fancying. To have an intelligent idea of these matters one must have a good map and I do not possess anything that's worth a cent in that way. But it seems to me that if his "internal" lines were too short, the ground unfavourable or his force not sufficiently mobile to strike east or west with his whole strenght,* Sir G. White would have been better in Ladysmith;[5] for the presence of his force in an intrenched camp would have anyhow checked an invasion of Natal, while an assault on a chosen

---

[1] Sir Alfred Milner, High Commissioner for South Africa 1897–1905, had been vehement in his demands for the Uitlander vote.
[2] Where Russia and Germany were competing for influence.
[3] The Boers had invaded Natal, the first battles had been fought, and refugees were pouring south.
[4] G. W. Steevens, the *Daily Mail*'s correspondent described the final charge at Eland-slaagte, 21 October, in a characteristically jaunty way: 'The merry bugles rang out like cockcrow on a fine morning. The pipes shrieked of blood and the lust of glorious death. Fix bayonets!': *From Capetown to Ladysmith* (1900), p. 54.
[5] General Sir George White, who left Ladysmith in order to observe the Battle of Elandslaagte.

position decisively repulsed would have had all the consequences of a defeat upon the Boer army. Am I too imbecile for anything? The chamber criticism of strategy *is* generally imbecile. As far as I can see he clawed with one arm here and with the other there—scratched pretty well too—but in the end stopped nothing. However we shall see. To a really great general these converging movements in his front would perhaps have given an opportunity. I revel in my imbecility.

I wonder *how* Buller will do it.[1] I am glad he goes there and the papers shall have another general to talk about. I had Kitchener on the nerves.[2] There was a correspondent who wrote of that extremely clever organiser in terms that would not have been unbecoming if applied to the Archangel of War himself. The men in India had done real military work without all that bell ringing and horn-blowing. I dare say Buller is no Archangel either but I pin my faith on him.

Tell your dear wife with our best love—that Jess had some wretched trouble in her right wrist and it is still almost powerless. She can typewrite with her left hand but she "didn't like" to write in type. Shy, I suppose. I ought to have written. I ought to! My fault, my great fault.[3] I plead forgiveness but if you stand my friend I doubt not I shall be forgiven.

It was good and sweet of Her to ask us. Your Mother too has been most kind. I simply dare not leave my table; I must go on and wait for more fortunate days.

You will drop me a line to tell me where you are stationed. Have you got your company?[4] My dearest Ted your letter did me good. It is *great* to hear you talk like this of my work. I wish I could be sure the partiality of your affection does not mislead you. Ah my dear fellow. If You knew how ambitious I am, how my ambition checks my pen at every turn. Doubts assail me from every side. The doubt of form—the doubt of tendency—a mistrust of my own conceptions—and scruples of the moral order. Ridiculous—isn't it? As if my soul mattered to the universe! But even as the ant bringing its grain of sand to the common edifice may justly think itself important, so I would like to think that I am doing my appointed work. With love

Ever yours

Conrad

[1] General Sir Redvers Buller, in charge of the Army Corps.
[2] Kitchener was in Egypt. There was heated public and private debate about the merits and ideas of rival generals.
[3] 'Mea culpa, mea culpa, mea maxima culpa': the words of contrition from the Roman Mass.
[4] For Sanderson's military career, see the letter of 19 February 1900.

To William Blackwood

Text MS NLS; Blackburn 68

[letterhead: Pent Farm]
27 Oct 99

Dear Mr Blackwood.

Many thanks for the cheque for £50—second payment on acc' of Jim—which I received an hour ago. I could have dispatched the Dec^{er} inst' ten days sooner only I wished to take full advantage of the time. There is always a correction to make on every day—no matter how long I keep proof or type by me; but at last I felt I must part with that batch and devote myself to the next.

The greater part of the Ja^{ny} inst. is written and practically ready; some of it in London for a fair copy and seventeen pages on the table before me to be pecked at, slashed, turned over, for two days more, and depart for Paternoster Row[1] on Monday. I *am* glad you like it—for tho' the thing were not absolutely bad it might not have been exactly to your mind. The beginning wobbles a good deal; I did cut up shamefully the proofs without being able to put it firmly on its feet; however my little band of faithfuls professes itself (in various letters) to be immensely pleased. You express yourself hopefully about the book. You may be sure that none of your kind words are wasted. The man here wants them, wants everything he can get of such genuine encouragement.

I think Zack may be congratulated on the novel.[2] It is an advance on the short stories—a *promising* advance. I've just finished reading it having waited for the last inst: Of course I could argue vehemently (with the *Writer* not with the *Lady*) about this and that par: this and that page; but the distinction is undeniable the vision at times most remarkably artistic. The French article in the last number I dislike frankly as to *tone*.[3] It is not Maga's tone either; it does not give an impression of intelligence behind the words—it is not quite candid. Why this superficial acrimony while much more severe things—much more!—could have been said? The navy article awful[l]y interesting and the Fashion in fiction simply delightful—the perfection of mannor!* with its tactful banter and a serious intention behind. The *London* is remarkable though this kind of thing does not appeal to me. It is a very literary thing and, I

---

[1] Meldrum's office in London.

[2] 'Zack' was the pseudonym of Gwendoline Keats. Her novel *On Trial* finished in October, the month that *Lord Jim* began.

[3] 'France To-day' (Vol. 166, pp. 543–55): an attack on the conduct of the Dreyfus case. The other articles selected from the October number are 'The Naval Manoeuvres of 1899', 'Fashions in Fiction', and 'London'.

apprehend, a little beyond me. I do not know where to place it in the scale of my liking. And the number as a whole is excellent—but what number isn't?

I shall of course read Buchan at once and write you *all* I think.[1] I've heard of him but have not read anything of his. I read very little—too little, I sometimes think. I look forward to the Nov: issue. Maga is the bulk of my reading.

And now dear Mr Blackwood I shall just slip these sheets under an envelope ready for to-morrow's post and go back to my grind till midnight or so. Pages of Jim are under my elbow to the right and left and in front of me and if I can screw up one page more (that when written doesn't look particularly valuable) it will be so much done towards duty and peace of mind. I suppose Meldrum told you that I intend to waylay you this year with 20 000 words more (after Jim); the beginning of a new vol: If I can get my weapon ready I shall; for, joke as I may about it, it is a question of life and death.

Pardon all this twaddle and the untidy aspect of the sheets. They've been filling my inkstand for me—with the best intentions, no doubt.

Believe me my dear Sir always
very faithfully yours
Jph. Conrad.

Isn't it a funny coincidence me following Zack on essentially the same subject?[2] I hope nobody will suspect Maga of having started a 'literary' competition for the best story on the State of Funk and that Zack and I rivalise for the possession of a nickel-plated chronometer or a lath-and-plaster palace, or whatever other 'literary' rewards are going now in the great world of democracy.

To David Meldrum

Text MS Duke; Blackburn 71

[letterhead: Pent Farm][3]
Monday. 9. AM. [30 October
1899]

My dear Mr Meldrum

I am sending by this post (to the office) another 16 pp of *Jim*; I've got a good few more written—and I have no fear as to the rest. I was very

---

[1] John Buchan (1875–1940) near the start of his literary career. For Conrad's reaction to 'The Far Islands' see letter of 8 November.

[2] Dishonourable conduct.

[3] The 'friendly letter' from Blackwood fixes the date as the first Monday after 27 October. Meldrum replied 1 November (note on MS).

glad of your letter and the good news about yourself and your 'House' as an Arab would say.

The post before I had a very friendly letter from Mr B'wood with enclosure (£50) on account of Jim. I wrote immediately a long letter in reply. So far all's well. He seems to like the story.

As you said I might put it off I do not immediately discharge my debt to you—putting it off till the story is finished. It is very convenient to me and I need not tell you—indeed I could not express it adequately—how sensible I am of your good offices, of your patience with me, of your kindness.

I've returned all the proofs and forwarded more copy to Edinburgh. My mind is eased by what you say about Jim's lenght.* It would be to my interest to cut it short as possible, but I would just as soon think of cutting off my head. With kind regards from us both

Always yours

Jph. Conrad.

PS Last inst^t of fair copy received; it goes north in a day or two.

To William Blackwood

Text MS NLS; Blackburn 71

[letterhead: Pent Farm]
8th Nov 99

Dear Mr Blackwood.

Criticism is poor work, and to expose the weaknesses of humanity as exhibited in literary (?) work is a thankless and futile task. I've always thought that Macaulay's smashing of R. Montgomery's poems(!)[1] was a pathetic example of mighty truth powerless before the falsehood of pretences, like the great sea before a very small rock. To point out to the crowd beauties not manifest to the common eye, to flash the light of one's sympathetic perception upon great, if not obvious, qualities, and even upon generous failings that hold the promise of better things this is indeed a toil worthy of a man's pen, a task that would repay for the time given up, for the strenght* expended for that sadness that comes of thinking over the sincere endeavour of a soul—for ever debarred from attaining perfection. But the blind distribution of praise or blame, done with a light heart and an empty mind, which is of the very essence of

[1] Thomas Babington Macaulay savaged Robert Montgomery's *Omnipresence of the Deity* in the *Edinburgh Review*, 1830.

'periodical' criticism seems to me to be a work less useful than skirt-dancing and not quite as honourable as pocket-picking.

There is too a sort of curse upon the critical exercise of human thought. Should one attempt honestly an analysis of another man's production it is ten to one that one will get the credit for all sorts of motives except for that of sincere conviction; thier* is the taint of the literary life; and though writing to you I would not expose myself to the risk of being misunderstood I prefer to say nothing critical about John Buchan's story.[1] I am willing to admit it is grammatically written—(I know nothing of grammar myself as he who runs may see)—if anybody desires to make that assertion. I do happen however to know one or two things that might conceivably be found to have a bearing upon the story and on these I shall hold my peace.

There is one thing (though hardly pertaining to criticism proper) which ought to be said of that—production. It is this: it's* idea, its feeling, its suggestion and even *the most subtly significant incidents* have been wrenched alive out of Kipling's tale "*The finest story in the world*".[2] What became of the idea, of the feeling, of the suggestion and of the incidents, in the process of that wrenching I leave it for the pronouncement not of posterity but of any contemporary mind that would be brought (for less than ten minutes) to the consideration of Mr Buchan's story. The thing is patent—it is the only impression that remains after reading the last words—it argues naïveness of an appalling kind or else a most serene impudence. I write strongly—because I feel strongly.

One does not expect style, construction, or even common intelligence in the fabrication of story; but one has the right to demand some sort of sincerity and to expect common honesty. When that fails—what remains?

If my remarks are unwelcome I can only express my regret without in the least apologising for my opinion. No amount of money would have extracted it from me—I have hardly time enough to think of and combat my own shortcomings—but at your request I've found leisure to set it down here and it must be accepted for what it is worth. Some men who *can* write (and even one or two who *sell*) do me the honour to say that it is worth something—at least to them.

---

[1] 'The Far Islands' in the November issue of *Blackwood's*.

[2] For an earlier mention of this story (from *Many Inventions*, 1893), consult the letter to Henley, 18 October 1898. In both stories a dream-life is more vivid than the everyday, and in both stories sea-faring has a part, but the resemblances seem more a case of 1890s *Zeitgeist* than of plagiarism.

I shall *without fail* dispatch tomorrow the corr^d proofs of the Dec^{er} instalment—and also some more typed matter. The last number of Jim is practically ready and Febr is on the way to completion. The March issue will see the end of the story—and of the Vol:

I don't think that these 20000 words I've been threatening you with for this year have the slightest chance of coming to light. Just now it is all for Jim! And no amount of sacrifice seems too much for him.

I trust you are well—as well as the truly awful weather permits. I am holding my own tolerably well against the winds and rains that beat upon the Pent. Always faithfully yours.

Jph. Conrad.

To David Meldrum

Text MS Duke; Blackburn 74

[letterhead: Pent Farm]
9th Nov 99

Dear Mr Meldrum.

Many many thanks for the copy of the stories. It *does* look a nice book[1] and I am glad to have it by me to work upon at odd times.

I took the liberty to send you a lady a Mrs Blake who has some jolly good stories[2] which she wishes to place in *Maga* if possible. I've written her a letter of introduction (to you) which I am forwarding today. (She will probably call on Monday in Paternoster Row.)

There is a lot of Jim in MS and you shall have it soon.

Always yours
Jph. Conrad.

To David Meldrum

Text MS Duke; Blackburn 74

[letterhead: Pent Farm]
9th Nov 99.

My dear Mr Meldrum.

This is to introduce Mrs Blake of 24 Montague Street wc. She has one or two stories which she wishes to submit to Mr Blackwood for *Maga*, and she would like them to be considered as quickly as possible.

---

[1] A mock-up of the proposed collection of stories, consisting of 'Youth' and 'Heart of Darkness' but not, of course, *Lord Jim*.

[2] Of life in Rhodesia: she may have been the C. T. Blake who published *Chris Wharton: A Tale of Life in South Africa* in 1904. Conrad originally wrote 'Mrs Ritchie'.

I have the less hesitation in asking You to do all you can in the matters because Edward Garnett thinks very highly indeed of Mrs Blake's work and has in fact advised her to come to you.

I am yours very faithfully

Jph. Conrad.

To Edward Garnett
Text MS Rosenbach; G. 155

[letterhead: Pent Farm]
9th Nov 99

Dear Edward.

I've written the required letter but it can't go till to morrow morning's post. I've also written privately to *Mel^d*. preparing him for Mrs Blake's visit—probably on Monday; and in a note to the lady herself I advise her to call on Monday.

My dear fellow I don't know how to thank You for all you say in your critical letter anent Lord Jim. Of the faults You point out I've been aware all along, but that the thing had any good at all in it I vow and declare I was ignorant. The faults are mine and the good (since you say there is some good in it) comes from devil knows whence. Well! As long as it *is* there.

Turg^v: in the Academy is rather so so.[1] Who wrote it? And who are your wife's *associates*?!! She had not any ... The people who wrote me about your Nietzsche were Sauter (a German painter)[2] and Mrs Helen Sanderson a scotch girl of great intelligence. She was immensely struck. Wells also said something appreciative at the time. The pub^s *are* fools. B^{wood} is fussing now over a fraud called John Buchan. Asked me to give him my opinion of that unspeakable impostor's story in the last *Maga*. And I did give it to him too. I said it was too contemptible to be thought about and moreover that it was stolen from Kipling as to matter and imitated from Munro as to style. I *couldn't* keep my temper.

Ever yours

Conrad

---

[1] 'Ivan Turgenev: An Enquiry' by 'E. A. B.': 4 November.
[2] Galsworthy's brother-in-law.

To Ford Madox Ford
Text MS Yale; Unpublished

[letterhead: Pent Farm]
[12] Nov. 99 Sunday.[1]

My dear Ford.

Your letter distressed me a little by the signs of nervous irritation and its exasperated tone. I can quite enter into your feelings. I am sorry your wife seems to think I've induced you to waste your time.[2] I had no idea you had any profitable work to do—for otherwise effort after expression is not wasted even if it is not paid for. What you have written now is infinitely nearer to actuality, to life to reality than anything (in prose) you've written before. It is nearer 'creation' than the *Shifting of the Fire*.[3] That much for the substance. I do not want to repeat here how highly I think of the purely literary side of your work. You know my opinion.

But beautiful lines do not make a drawing nor splashes of beautiful colour a picture. Out of discussion there may come conception however. For discussion I am ready, willing and even anxious. If I had influence enough with the publishers I would make them publish the book in your name alone—because the *work* is all yours[4]—I've shared only a little of your worry. Well—you worry very much—and so do I—over my own stuff. I sweat and worry, and I have no illusions about it. I stick to it with death for the brightest prospect—for there may be even a more sordid end to my endeavours—some abject ruin material or physical for me—and almost inevitably some ghastly form of poverty for those I love. Voilà. Am I on a bed of roses?

Whether I am worth anything to you or not it is for you to determine. The proposal certainly came from me under a false impression of my power for work. I am much weaker than I thought I was but this does not affect you fundamentally. Heinemann (and McClure too I fancy) are waiting for our joint book and I am not going to draw back if You will only consent to sweat long enough. I am not going to make any sort of difficulty about it—I shall take the money if you make a point of that. I am not going to stick at that trifle.

Do come when you like. Bring only one (or at most two) chapters at a time and we shall have it out over each separately. Don't you good

---

[1] Postmarked the following day.
[2] Having put 'Seraphina' aside, they were now collaborating on *The Inheritors*.
[3] Ford's first novel (1892).
[4] For Conrad's attitude to the collaboration, see the letter to Garnett of 26 March 1900. The conception and most of the writing were Ford's.

people think hardly of me. I've been—I am!—animated by the best intentions. I shall always be!

We expected you both to day. Come as soon as You feel you want to. Kindest regards.

Yours

Jph Conrad

To Edward Garnett
Text MS Virginia; G. 157

[Pent Farm]
13 Nov 99.

Dearest Edward.

I am delighted to hear of the critical book[1]—and more interested than I can say. At last! I am sure it will attract attention if not extract shekels. Only you must not have me there. An article in a weekly that's dead as soon as it's born does not matter—but in a book you must not give anybody an opening to impugn your judgment. —No! Not even to serve me who am your spoiled child. I've no place in literature though I may have one in your affection. Be original—be *awakening* as much as you like, but be also guarded as to what material you use to develop upon your theory and practice of criticism. Deal only with people that are *unquestionable* in this your first book of criticism. Reject dubious personalities (like me)—even if in your conscience they are deserving. Afterwards! Well! You'll do what you like and may even cram *me* down their narrow gullets. But now think only of E.G. and of E G alone—of what E G stands for to us who have heard him, who know him—and of what he may stand for even for the wise man in the street, who is instructed, shocked and amused by innumerable swarms of geniuses.

I shall send Bridges this week;[2] also the title of all your books now staying with me. Your question about the Rescue sent a shiver down my back. Jim's dragging his slow lenght* along[3]—après—nous verrons. Annihilation perhaps. I repeat: Nous verrons! Love from us to you both.

Ever yours

Conrad.

---

[1] *Friday Nights*, Garnett's collection of the critical pieces he had been writing since the late 1890s, did not appear until 1922. On 1 September 1900, Conrad wrote to Meldrum about Garnett's plans.

[2] Garnett had sent Conrad a copy of *The Shorter Poems of Robert Bridges* (1890): *Letters*, 1, p. 413.

[3] Like the Alexandrine in Pope's *An Essay on Criticism* 'That . . . drags its slow length along.'

To Edward Garnett
Text MS Free; G. 158

[letterhead: Pent Farm]
Sunday. [19 November 1899][1]

Dearest Edward.

I send you the vol of Bridges. It is not yours. I find I can't lay my hands on it so I got a paper copy meanwhile.

I shall send you titles of others in a day or so.

I also send you 2d inst of *Jim*—which is too wretched for words. It would have been less shocking if it had included another chapter.

Meldrum wrote saying he shall report on Mrs Blake's work to old B'wood forthwith. I hope it will come off.

Ever Yours

Conrad.

To Edward Garnett
Text MS Sutton; G. 158

[letterhead: Pent Farm]
Friday evening [24 November 1899][2]

Dearest Edward.

The letter to McClure goes by to morrow morning's post. I play the honest broker to the best of my ability. I've said all you wished me to say; and as I remember perfectly that you did rather 'choke off' poor little Robert[3] at the time I suggest that at a hint from me *you* would approach him on the matter. (At the same time I send him your address).

Robert is perfectly harmless; knows nothing of literature; is proud of the success of the firm but is not *low minded.* Simply ignorant. Of Doubleday the world had heard in connection with Kipling's pneumonia.[4] That's enough!

S.S. McClure is a sort of Holy Terror—I hear but *why* he is terrible

---

[1] The only Sunday between 13 and 25 November: by the latter date, Blackwood had turned down Mrs Blake.

[2] Garnett's dating, confirmed by the correspondence with McClure (see note to following letter).

[3] Robert McClure, brother and London representative of Samuel S.

[4] Frank N. Doubleday, and S. S. McClure were partners from 1897 to 1899. When Kipling fell dangerously ill on a visit to New York, Doubleday looked after him.

I'm damned if I know. Sort of Silas Lapham I understand.[1] I dare say he is no more beastly than any other animal of that sort—nor more intelligent; nor more stupid. He has *made* the business. Personally I've found Robert very nice extremely decent—not more so than Pawling—and rather deferential. And this is all I know of them.

You are a dear good old critic—you are! You've a way of saying things that would make an old sign-post take to writing. You put soul and spunk into me—You, so to speak, bamboozle me into going on—and going on and going on. You can detect the shape of a mangled idea and the shadow of an intention in the worst of one's work—and you make the best of it. You would almost persuade me that I exist. Almost!

Love to you all from us all

Ever Yours

Jph Conrad.

To Ford Madox Ford

Text MS Yale; Unpublished

[Pent Farm]
[24? November 1899][2]

Dear Ford—

Let this cheer you up in your arduous labour. I wrote McClure that the thing is making good progress.

Yours

C.

---

[1] *The Rise of Silas Lapham* (1885), by William Dean Howells: McClure (1857–1949), now an influential editor and publisher with radical sympathies, came from a poor farming family in the north of Ireland.

[2] This note is scribbled on the typescript of a letter from Robert McClure dated 23 November. McClure wrote:

> I was glad to get your long letter and to learn of your plans for more stories. Yes, I think we can say that the stories will be out by March. I will see Meldrum on the matter.
>
> Will you let me see the "Extravagant" novel [*The Inheritors*] when it is finished? We are certain to want the book for United States, and I particularly want to serialise it too, if it will cut up reasonably well.
>
> On receipt of yours I telephoned Pawling to send you £20, and later in the day I sent him my cheque for the amount. Please let me know if you got it all right.

To David Meldrum

Text MS Duke; Blackburn 75

[letterhead: Pent Farm]
25 Nov 99.

My dear Mr Meldrum.

I was very glad to hear from you and your invitation is most delightful enticing and irresistible. We shall certainly come if Mrs Meldrum—to whom pray convey our thanks—can put up with us for two days.

Yes. Every day making the children older, delay in this can may* make things easier for your wife. You must choose a time quite convenient to you and give us notice.

I am still at Jim. I've sent 6 more pages yesterday. I shall send 7 more today to end Chap XIII. The Story will be finished of course this year. I trust they will give me as much space as possible in the Jan. Febr. & Mch numbers. I shall want all I can get.

I've sent last proofs to E'gh the other day and can't have more till they get further copy. I am sorry Mrs Blake won't do for Maga. She is no friend of mine in any real sense. I thought her work (what I had seen of it) had something real—very real, in it.

I trust Mr B'wood has not been offended by a critical letter I wrote about that story by Buchan in the last N° of Maga. I did hit hard but then Mr Blackwood asked me to say what I thought of it. I considered it an outrageous performance and speaking confidentially—in a way—made no secret of my opinion.[1] In fact I shouted it out. Being a person of no consequence the noise I make when I am hurt (and bad work *hurts* when you set yourself to think over it seriously) need not disturb any one very much. And I am not forward with my opinions either.

With kindest regards from us both to Mrs Meldrum and yourself I am always faithfully Yours

Jph. Conrad.

---

[1] On 20 November, Meldrum told Blackwood about his invitation to the Conrads: 'He, I am sure, would like a little change from Pent Farm. We'll see. I had hoped to get hold of Buchan and bring him and Conrad together—but not now!' (Blackburn, p. 75).

To Edward Garnett

Text MS Sutton; G. 160

[letterhead: Pent Farm]
2^d Dec 99.

My dear Edward.

I was on the point of sitting down to write to you yesterday when a despairing note from poor Hope informed me that his eldest boy Jack was drowned. Jess and I started at once to see them. We spent two hours in Stanford and returned home feeling horribly wretched and tired. There's no doubt the poor boy had been murdered on the marshes not far from the place where you and I looked upon the river. They found him in the creek.[1]

I am too upset to be able to write you a connected letter. I wanted to thank you for the volume you've sent me. The preface is *jolly good* let me tell you.[2] It is wonderfully good—and true. Thanks to you both. I want to catch the post.

Ever Yours

Jph. Conrad.

To David Meldrum

Text MS Duke; Blackburn 76

[letterhead: Pent Farm]
3^d Dec 99

My dear Mr Meldrum.

A terrible misfortune happening to my oldest English friends has completely upset all our plans and jumbled my thoughts. Their eldest son has been killed last Tuesday night on the Essex marshes. He was a promising boy seventeen and his death is made more bitter to them by the appalling circumstances of his end. The spot where he was found is not quite a mile from the Farm where we used to live.

On receipt of news we rushed off to see them and returned home the same day. The poor people have not realised yet their loss and I fear a breakdown by and by for them both. I have urged them to come here and stay with us for some time.

I am sure Mrs Meldrum and yourself will understand why it is

---

[1] The bruised and naked body of Fountaine Hope, a clerk at an engineering works, was found in a ditch. The coroner's inquest returned an open verdict (*Southend-on-Sea Observer*, 7 and 21 December).

[2] Garnett's Preface to Turgenev's *A Desperate Character*, translated by Constance Garnett.

impossible for us to keep our engagement. But if you would have us in Jan*y* for a day we shall be more than delighted to come.

I am awfully cut up. It has checked my work for two days but now the grind goes on. Many thanks for your letter. In the matter of space—if Maga gives room in Jan*y* N*o* to all *nearly all* of the copy I am sending to-morrow the end of the story may be divided between the Febr*y* and March numbers. Forgive my stupid letter. I can write my stuff but feel quite incapable to concentrate my thought upon any other sort of writing.

Kindest regards from us both to Your wife and Yourself. I am

Always yours

J. Conrad.

To John Galsworthy
Text MS Forbes; Unpublished

[letterhead: Pent Farm]
Tuesday. [12 or 19 December
1899]¹

My dearest Jack.

Ever so many apologies. I've read the Seven Seas[2] and Jessie has used the scent (after heroic struggles with Kipling's diction and the glass stopper) and we are full of gratitude. Both things are excellent—the scent in its way better than the poems. But this we can discuss.

We had the poor Hopes here for three days. They left yesterday a little the better for their visit. It is a peculiarly abominable affair.

Come by all means. I've mislaid your letter but if I remember rightly you intend to arrive by the 12.30 train. Just drop me a word that this is so.

I've done very little work but have worried a great deal. Jessie's kindest regards.

Ever Yours

Jph. Conrad

---

[1] On Tuesday 5 December, the Hopes had not yet come to the Pent. Although 19 December seems too close to the next letter, to Galsworthy, a letter from Meldrum to Blackwood (Blackburn, p. 78) suggests that the Hopes may have visited near that date.

[2] A volume of Kipling's poems published 1896.

To Hugh Clifford
Text MS SO; Hunter

[letterhead: Pent Farm]
13th Dec 99

My Dear Excellency.

I was delighted with the gazetting of Your name and still more delighted to see You are pleased with the prospect before you.[1] I hope that at first You will have no war on your hands; not at any rate till you get good hold. Who is Mat Saleh?[2] I've seen the name in the papers some time ago. Should think he is none of the Brunei Royal gang. Is he? One would think the name of a villager. It has a plebeian sound.

Your letter warmed my heart. May good fortune attend you and your people; and thinking of your 'House' I wonder whether Sandakan is as healthy as Pahang?[3]

You will have the Sulu people for next door neighbours.[4] When the expanding Yanks begin to gallop their imperial gunboats up and down the Archipelago you may have some queer refugees in your Kingdom. I once knew a gentleman of that sort—but he was from Basilan.[5] He traded in coconuts and—I regret to say—in women. Incidentally he endeavoured to split my skull with a horrid wood chopper. This kind intention was unfortunately frustrated by some people who really had nothing to see in the matter, and now my head is ready to burst with worries of sorts. And this brings me naturally to *Jim*. Perfectly right! Your criticism is just and wise but the whole story is made up of such side shows just because the main show is not particularly interesting— or engaging I should rather say. I want to put into that sketch a good many people I've met—or at least seen for a moment—and several things overheard about the world. It is going to be a hash of episodes,

[1] Clifford's appointment as Governor of Labuan and North Borneo (the territories administered by the British North Borneo Company) had just been announced.

[2] Mat or Mohamed Salleh, originally a petty chieftain from the east coast, after raiding along the coasts and rivers of the west, had now retreated to a fortress in the deep interior; he was killed there by a punitive expedition in 1900. His raids in areas subject to Brunei started a dispute over jurisdiction between the Sultan and the Company. By ancestry, Salleh belonged to the Sulu and the Bajau, two sea-faring peoples.

[3] Prompted not by his health but by his distaste for Company ways, Clifford resigned after only six months in Sandakan, the capital. He then returned to Pahang, where he took up his old post as British Resident.

[4] The Sulu Archipelago lies between North Borneo and the Philippines; it had just come under United States control and was to be the scene of a vigorous campaign against slavery.

[5] At the other end of the archipelago: Conrad probably had his dangerous encounter with him while mate of the *Vidar*, 1887–8.

little thumbnail sketches of fellows one has rubbed shoulders with and so on. I crave your indulgence; and I think that read in the lump it will be less of a patchwork than it seems now.

As to *Your* sketch (for it is that) in last B'wood,[1] it has pleased me immensely. The simplicity of treatment is effective. Of course you are favoured by the subject while I have always to struggle with a moral horror of some sort. It looks like my choice but it may be only my fate. Our kindest regards and best wishes for a prosperous voyage and the prosperity of the new life. We prize the memory of Your visit and we beg You both to give us a small place in your memory. I am always my dear Clifford yours most sincerely

Joseph Conrad.

I shall await the new B'wood with impatience.[2] May I hope to hear sometimes from You?

To David Meldrum
Text MS NLS; Blackburn 77

[letterhead: Pent Farm]
Sunday. [17 December 1899][3]

My dear Mr Meldrum.

I send here a MS lot of Jim which would be most of the Febr^y instalment. My poor wife is too taken up just now with domestic worries to be able to type for me and I do not want to stop the trickle of copy.

The lot published and in proof together at present in Edinburgh amounts to 40000 words already. I trust I am not making myself objectionable by unduly lenghtening* my contribution. As things go now there will be no hurry to publish the book early next year? Or am I mistaken? I have been so upset by the turn of this war[4] as to be hindered in my work.

If my calculation of 40000 words (now set up) is correct (and I cannot be very far wrong) then I've written up to the value of £100 advanced me by Mr B'wood. I would be glad—if at all feasible—to have £20 further on acct/. I am ashamed to everlastingly proclaim my destitution—and

---

[1] 'Father Rouellot' in the December *Blackwood's*: the story of a selfless French missionary in Malaya.

[2] Clifford's 'Bush-whacking', an account of a war in Malaya, was to appear in the January and February numbers. On the evidence of this letter's opening paragraph, Dr Allan Hunter suggests that Clifford may have discussed the topic with Conrad.

[3] Meldrum sent an answer next day.   [4] In South Africa.

weary of the thing itself. The balance I would get on delivery of the conclusion. I still think I shall finish the story this year. With kindest regards from us both to Mrs Meldrum and yourself

I am always yours

Jph Conrad.

To R. B. Cunninghame Graham
Text MS Dartmouth; J-A, 1, 287; Watts 127

[letterhead: Pent Farm]
19th Dec 99

Cher et excellent ami.

I was so glad to hear from you. Borys got his card the day after. You are emphatically a *nice man*.

This country does not want any writers; it wants a general or two that aren't valorous frauds. I am so utterly and radically sick of this African business that if I could take a sleeping draught on the chance of not waking till it is all over I would let *Jim* go and take the consequences.

As it is—in the way of writing I am not much more good than if I were sleeping. It is silly of me to take a thing so much to heart but as things go there's not a ray of comfort for a man of my complex way of thinking, or rather feeling.

It would do me good to hear you talk. I don't know why I feel so damnably lonely. My health is tolerable but my brain is as though somebody had stirred it all with a stick.

Allah *is* careless. The loss of your MS is a pretty bad instance; but look—here's His very own chosen people (of assorted denominations) getting banged about and not a sign from the sky but a snowfall and a fiendish frost. Perhaps Kipling's Recessional (if He understood it—which I doubt) had offended Him?[1]

I should think Lord Salisbury's dying nation[2] must be enjoying the fun.

I can't write sense and I disdain to write Xmas platitudes so here I end. My wife and I send you unconventional greetings and as to Borys

---

[1] Kipling's hymn was written for the Queen's Diamond Jubilee in 1897 and reprinted in *Recessional and Other Poems* (1899): its closing line implores 'Thy mercy on Thy People, Lord!'

[2] The Boers, whose military campaigns were going well: in a speech in London on 4 May 1898, the Prime Minister had predicted that 'From the necessities of politics or under the pretence of philanthropy—the living nations will gradually encroach on the territory of the dying' (*The Times*, 5 May).

he *has* said you are a *nice man*—what more can you want to be made
happy for a whole year? When do you return? Shall I see you here before
you go north? I am vexed about the preface.[1] Your prefaces are so good!
It is quite an art by itself.

Well. This time I am really done.

Ever Yours

Jph Conrad

To John Galsworthy

Text MS POSK; Danilewicz 6

[letterhead: Pent Farm]
21 Dec^{er} 99.

Dearest Jacko.

You could not have had a greater pleasure in giving me the books
than I had in receiving them. I express it so because I know You; you
take a delight in spoiling me in the tenderest way imaginable; and I'll
not conceal from you that it is good, it feels very good to be thus spoiled.

Another year gone; and one beholds in fear and trembling another
year approaching. The newcomer does not wear a very cheerful face, but
there may not be much in its scowl for real misfortunes come stealthily.

I do not know why I should pursue you with my lugubrious
meditations. I had better stay my pen. I feel tonight as though a load of
untold years had descended upon my spirit. So, Silence.

May all possible good attend your steps.

Ever Yours

Conrad.

To Aniela Zagórska

Text J-A, 1, 288; Najder 232[2]

Pent Farm,
25.12.1899

My dearest Aniela,

Your letters, dearest, are very interesting; they give me courage and
are very precious to me; my ingratitude is all the blacker—but it is only
in appearance that I am ungrateful. In reality I am not—I am only a
man with a weak will—and full of good intentions, with which—as they

---

[1] Presumably the missing MS. Watts (p. 129) suggests a Preface to *Thirteen Stories* or *A Vanished Arcadia*.

[2] For textual source, see n. 5 to letter of 6 February 1898. The ending has not survived.

say— hell is paved. What would you have, my dear? The Malays say: 'The tiger cannot change his stripes'—and I—my ultra-Slav nature.

Much might be said about the war. My feelings are very complex—as you may guess. That they are struggling in good faith for their independence cannot be doubted;[1] but it is also a fact that they have no idea of liberty, which can only be found under the English flag all over the world. C'est un peuple essentiellement despotique, like by the way all the Dutch. This war is not so much a war against the Transvaal as a struggle against the doings of German influence.[2] It is the Germans who have forced the issue. There can be no doubt about it.

You are mistaken in saying that it is the Government who sends soldiers. The English Government has no right to make a single Englishman move, if he does not consent to it.[3] Le pour et le contre of this issue have been weighed not only in the conscience of the people but of the whole race. Canada and Australia are taking part in this, which could not influence their material interests. Why? Europe rejoices and is moved because Europe is jealous and here in England there is more real sympathy and regard for the Boers than on the whole Continent, which proclaims its compassion at the top of its voice. Quelle bourde![4]

To William Blackwood
Text MS NLS; Blackburn 79

[letterhead: Pent Farm]
26th Dec 99

Dear Mr. Blackwood.

Many thanks for your friendly letter with enclosure (£20) which came to hand this morning.[5] I wished to time my letter to you for the New Year's day and to send together with the most sincere wishes of happiness for prosperity some good report of the tale.

The tale progresses and in five more days' time it will be still nearer the end which seems well in view now.[6] I say seems, because I do suffer at times from optical delusions (and others) where my work is concerned.

---

[1] A telling argument, of course, in Poland.
[2] Germany, France, and Russia all threatened to intervene on the Boers' behalf; German power was already established in South-West Africa (present-day Namibia).
[3] The continental armies relied heavily on conscription.
[4] 'What a lie!' Feelings did indeed run high in the rest of Europe, while Britain stood in what Joseph Chamberlain called 'splendid isolation'.
[5] Blackburn (p. 79) gives Blackwood's letter.   [6] He finished in mid-July.

I mentioned the number of words in my letter to Meldrum in a casual way and not in the least because I thought it any justification for my request or any argument for you granting the same. I turned to you with perfect confidence remembering how generously ready you were last year—when all the words were counted and there were no more to come.

What made me allude to words too was my preoccupation as to the forthcoming volume. It'll be a fat book—and not, perhaps, well balanced to the eye. Still we are in for it now I fancy. *Lord Jim* would have hardly the lenght* and certainly has not the sub[s]tance to stand alone; and the three tales, each being inspired by a similar moral idea (or is it only one of my optical delusions?) will make (in that sense) a homogeneous book.[1] Of the matter I am not ashamed and the mere size won't, I hope, militate against such commercial success as is within my reach.

And so this year which began with work for you ends also with copy for *Maga* on my table. Nothing can please me better; and it is also a fact that of my year's writing all that's worth anything is gone to you. You have helped me through these twelve months in more than one sense, for the conditions of our intercourse made work easier to me. There are of course other pages scribbled over[2]—pages not destined for the 'House' but I can't pretend to look upon them with satisfaction. Their existence does not cheer me—it frightens me rather—for everything is dangerous that has even ever so little doubt in it, that dims the guiding light of one's confidence.

The war disturbed me not a little. I do not share the slightly frantic state of the press. They write as if they had expected the soldiers to run and the Empire to collapse and can't possess their souls for joy that these things did not happen. To me, seeing the initial nonsuccess the development of the national will on the lines of unflinching resolution seemed from the first as inevitable as the preordained motion of the stars. It may be that I do not know enough of England and that the journalists have very good reasons for that jubilation which strikes me as unseemly. At any rate it is expressed so stupidly that it is exasperating to a man whose faith is as deep as the sea and more stable.

And on this I shall close this interminable letter and turn to the MS to grind out another page or two. I am spending Xmas not forgotten certainly, but very solitary. It's all the better for my work. Festivities jumble my crazy thoughts and visitors leave me as a rule in a state

---

[1] Containing besides 'Lord Jim', 'Youth' and 'Heart of Darkness'.
[2] *The Rescue* and perhaps some work on *The Inheritors*.

bordering upon idiocy. Believe me dear Mr Blackwood very faithfully
yours

Jph. Conrad.

To the Baroness Janina de Brunnow
Text L.fr. 39; Najder 233

Pent Farm
27 Dec. 1899. [?][1]

Chère Madame,

En vérité j'avais reçu la lettre de faire-part il y a quelques jours et je
n'osais pas prendre la plume: mais depuis l'arrivée de la douloureuse
nouvelle, vous et Monsieur votre Mari, vous avez été constamment
présent à mon esprit.

Que peut-on dire, chère Madame! C'est en présence d'une douleur
comme la vôtre que l'on s'aperçoit que les mots sont vides de sens. Il y a
toujours l'espoir d'une vie meilleure et la certitude consolatrice que
l'amertume de l'existence ici-bas a été épargnée au cher mort dont la
perte nous déchire le coeur.

Vous devez puiser la consolation dans les coeurs qui vous entourent:
et moi, éloigné et solitaire, j'envoie vers mon amie d'enfance à qui le sort
a réservé une si dure épreuve l'assurance de ma profonde et affectueuse
sympathie.

Mille et mille fois merci pour votre lettre dont la franche amitié m'a
ému profondément. Mes salutations cordiales à Monsieur votre Mari.
Une autre lettre suivra bientôt si vous permettez.

Croyez moi, chère Madame, avec vous de coeur et toujours votre très
dévoué serviteur.

Conrad N. Korzeniowski.

Translation

Dear Madame,

Indeed I did receive the obituary letter some days ago, but I dared not
pick up my pen; nevertheless, since the arrival of the painful news, you
and your husband have been constantly in my mind.

What can one say, dear Madame! In the presence of a pain like yours,
one finds that words are meaningless. There is always the hope of a
better life and the consoling certainty that the dear departed, whose loss
rends our hearts, has been spared the bitterness of life below.

[1] See n. 1, p. 148.

You must draw consolation from the affections that surround you, while I, far away and solitary, send my childhood friend for whom fate has reserved such a difficult ordeal the assurance of my deep and affectionate sympathy.

A thousand, thousand thanks for your letter whose open friendship has moved me profoundly. My cordial greetings to your husband. If you permit, another letter will follow soon.

Believe me, dear Madame, to be with you in heart and always your very devoted servant,

Conrad N. Korzeniowski.

To E. L. Sanderson
Text MS Yale; J-A, 1, 289

Pent Farm
28 Dec 99.

Dearest Ted.

Thanks for your dear note. I didn't write not knowing where You were—and we only sent a card to your wife addressed to Elstree. I had a notion she would be away, either with You or in Scotland.

All possible and imaginable good to you my dear fellow. There's not a day I do not think of you. I was in hopes you would turn up in Shorncliffe[1] which would have been all the same to you (once away from home and school) but would have made a great difference to me.

I am upset by this war more than enough. From every point of view it is an unsatisfactory business. I say from every point because the disclosure of our military weakness is not compensated by the manifestation of colonial loyalty. That was a thing one would have taken for granted. We who know how loosely the colonies were hanging to mother's skirts are impressed and cheered[2]—but on the continent they never understood the conditions and they take it as a matter of course. But the disclosure is a pleasant surprise to them, with nothing to counteract their satisfaction.

I hope you won't have to go; but I am very glad Roberts is going—or gone. To Kitchener by himself I would not have liked to pin my faith.[3] And may it all end speedily—and well.

[1] The army camp five miles from the Pent.

[2] During the course of the war, Canada, New Zealand, and Australia sent about 30,000 troops to South Africa. Australia became a political entity by the federation of six colonies in 1900.

[3] By his spectacular success in the Sudan, Kitchener had won a reputation for military dash. Roberts had had similar success in Afghanistan but, during his time in India, had also proved himself a thoughtful organiser and a soldiers' general.

I am at work but my mental state is very bad—and is made worse by a constant gnawing anxiety. One incites the other and vice versa. It is a vicious circle in which the creature struggles.

Wife sends her best wishes and kind regards.

With love my dear Ted

Ever Yours

Jph. Conrad.

To Ford Madox Ford
Text MS Yale; Unpublished

[1899?]¹

My dear Ford

The MS came back in fair copy. I read it and am quite struck. There are excellencies there. I don't send you the 2d copy because I don't want you to be disturbed at your last chap.

It will want correcting here and there and in places "il y a des longueurs." The effect is remarkably weird as a whole.

We must read together and talk a little.

Ever yours

Conrad.

---

¹ The 'remarkably weird' nature of the work suggests *The Inheritors*. Ford delivered the first few chapters on 6 October (Mizener, p. 51); any date from then until early 1900 is possible. As Conrad often takes 'last' to mean 'latest' rather than 'final', his delicacy about 'your last chap' does not solve the problem.

1900

To David Meldrum

Text MS Duke; Blackburn 81

[letterhead: Pent Farm]

3^d Jan 1900

My dear Mr Meldrum.

I hope you have all begun the year in good health and with easy minds. May luck and happiness attend you as long as the years keep rolling.

I am sending by this post a batch of MS. Lord Jim to end Ch XVII.[1] Of course the chap^s. are short.

The next batch should be the last, unless I were to forward an instalment before the 15th inst^t.

L. J. is a rather bad business for me on account of its length that is to say. Otherwise I am pleased with it and, I think, with some shadow of a reason.

But the artistic pleasure is neither here nor there. Bread is the thing.

When the end is delivered I hope Mr Blackwood will be kind enough to send me at least £80 (100 if possible). I have innumerable bills flapping about my ears! Thereupon I shall proceed to write 20000 words (either *A seaman* or *First Command* or a *Skittish Cargo*[2] or any two of them to make up the number) for publication serially when he thinks fit and convenient (if you only knew how sick I am of this contriving and of being always behind!) when we shall see how we stand for words v. sovereigns. By that time the book shall be out too, perhaps and fallen into the bottomless hole as likely as not. Well never mind. Some day, something will come up out of the pit.

Drop me a line as to yourself and family. Borys is not at all well with a cold and a cough. The grown-ups are so-so.

With my duty to Mrs Meldrum I
am always yours

Jph Conrad.

---

[1] In its final form, *Lord Jim* has 45 chapters. The original notes for the story (written on blank pages of a family poetry album now at Harvard) do anticipate Jim's exile to Patusan. Nevertheless, in January 1900, Conrad still apparently envisioned a novel half its ultimate length.

[2] 'A Skittish Cargo' became 'Typhoon' and 'First Command' *The Shadow-Line*; 'A Seaman' may have been the genesis of 'The End of the Tether'. See letters of 14 February and 22 August 1899.

To John Galsworthy

Text MS POSK; Danilewicz 7

[letterhead: Pent Farm]
4 Jan 1900

Dearest Jack.

And I thought you were on "the shoot"! It is somehow more odious to think of you laid away in bed than of any other man I know. We all—including Borys—are very much concerned. He's very anxious to know whether you have a dog to lie on your bed till you get well. I can't imagine whence that form of anxiety. But it's well meant.

I *am* writing whether or no. But what a grind! I must stick to my hole and to my post to fight the awful shadows. It is an endless job. Thereupon 'so long' for the present as the Australians say. Let me know how you progress. It is hard to be kept from running up to you.

With all our affectionate
regards
Ever Your

Conrad.

To R. B. Cunninghame Graham

Text MS Dartmouth; Watts 129

[letterhead: Pent Farm]
4th Jan 1900

Cher ami

I just write a word to thank you for putting a little heart into me. I was glad to know You are back. And what of the affair?[1] I am pretty miserable—nothing new that! But difficulties are as it were closing round me; an irresistible march of black beetles I figure it to myself. What a fate to be so ingloriously devoured.

I think the historian is quite right.[2] It's a pity my style is not more popular and a thousand pities I don't write less slow. Of such that do is the Kingdom of the Earth. I don't care a damn for the best heaven ever invented by Jew or Gentile. And that's a fact.

And if the Kg^{om} of Earth were mine I would forthwith proceed to

---

[1] Graham had been in Madrid, seeking trading concessions from the Spanish government.

[2] Perhaps Graham's friend Martin Hume, a prolific popular historian and a stern critic.

London to waylay you for a talk. As it is it shall not be—alas! Borys is
not well. Heavy cold. He sends his How do you do. Ipsissima verba.[1]

> Jessie's kind regards.
> Weather beastly.
> Ever yours
>   Jph. Conrad.

To H. G. Wells

Text MS Illinois; Unpublished

                                                    [letterhead: Pent Farm]
                                                    6th Jan 1900

My dear H G.

I send you my affectionate thanks for the book[2] and for the terms of
the inscription on the fly-leaf; for the more I know of you—in our inconclusive talks—the more I feel that such should be the terms of our
intercourse.

I've of course read the book more than once.

You get hold of one by your immense power of presentation, by your
capacity to give shape, colour, *aspect* to the invisible; and the same power
of presentation brings out the *depth* of things common and visible.
Therefore to a man like me you are doubly fascinating. I think of the
Plattner Story on one part and of *A Catastrophe* and *The lost inheritance* on the
other. I can't and won't write platitudes about the power of your fancy.
The strenght*—the creative strenght*—of your imagination is the most
obvious of Your gifts. I prefer to contemplate your qualities: the lucidity
of expression which is admirable and often poetic, the wonderful
'easiness' of your work, your fidelity to that ideal *intention* which stands
before the artist's eyes like a veiled figure at the end of a long gallery;
distant and, perhaps forever, mysterious.

I feel very small before the concrete power of your phrases, and before
your rectitude of purpose I feel like a fraud. This does not prevent me
from taking your achievements to my heart and in that sense making
them my own. I flatter myself that I have a capacity for that at least!

I don't go in for a detailed (and futile) review of the stories. The '*Cone*'
is weak. That and one or two others (two) seem to have dropped off

---

[1] 'His very own words.'

[2] A belated copy, now at Yale, of *The Plattner Story and Others* (1897), which includes the
stories discussed in paragraphs three and five. Wells inscribed his book 'To Joseph
Conrad with affection'.

before they were ripe. The *stuff is* in them indubitably. You've never—as far as I know—written anything *hollow*.

And with this last tribute to your manifold worth and affectionate regards from us both to you both I am my dear Wells Ever Yours

Conrad.

The poor little chap has been seedy with coughs and colds and shut up for days. I am sorry for him. His disposition is fiendish.

To William Blackwood and Sons

Text MS Duke; Blackburn 82

[letterhead: Pent Farm]
7 Jan 1900

Messrs. Wm Blackwood & Sons London.
Dear Sirs.

Herewith further inst[t] of Lord Jim p 376–394. *Chap.xviii.*

I trust You've received all eight previous inst[ts] p. 342–375 sent by registered packet.

When returning MS and type kindly register or keep back MS till type is received as in case of loss we would have no other copy available.

I am dear Sirs very faithfully yours
Joseph Conrad.

To David Meldrum

Text MS Duke; Blackburn 82

[letterhead: Pent Farm]
Tuesday. [9 January 1900][1]

My dear Mr Meldrum.

I fully intended to let you know in my last letter that Mr B'wood had written to me and sent £20 which I received on Xmas day I believe.

My wife and I are very much distressed at her apparent neglect in answering Mrs Meldrum's letter; but the fact is that we had not the letter. Whether I—after extracting your note—have dropped the envelope with Mrs Meldrum's message into the waste paper basket, I can't say. It would be just like me—my wife says. Unless we didn't get your last letter at all—which is just barely possible. Most likely it isn't the P.O. but I who am the culprit. Pray present my apologies to Mrs Meldrum and Jessie's expressions of regret. I really ought to have a

---

[1] The only Tuesday between 3 January (Conrad's previous letter) and 15 January (Meldrum's answer to this one).

nurse—since my wife must look also after the other child, to say nothing of the everlasting cooking.

I've sent off last Friday another ins*t* of *Jim* Ch XVIII, rather longer than either of the three previous ones. I am driving on with the story and you may expect another Chap: shortly. And then the end! I do wish for the end. After the end a visit to you—if convenient. Even if Jess couldn't come I would take a run up to town. But the pressing necessity to write more hangs over me. I don't know when and how I will ever fight my way back to the *Rescue*. I try not to think of it.

With our kind regards to you[r] wife and yourself I am always yours

Jph. Conrad.

To David Meldrum

Text MS Duke; Blackburn 83

[Pent Farm]
15 Jan 1900

My Dear Mr Meldrum.

Just a line to tell you I've found Mrs Meldrum's and your own letter amongst the pages of returned *MS*! I had never looked for anything from you thinking the envelope was dispatched from the office.

You must have thought me wretchedly ungrateful—while the truth is I am immensely touched by the warm tone of Your New Year's message. I do not know how to tell you how much I appreciate every proof of your friendly feeling—and you have given me not a little of them. I reciprocate with all my heart every wish of yours.

Post waits.

Ever yours most sincerely
Conrad.

Jessie is going to write

To Edward Garnett

Text MS Colgate; G. 163

[letterhead: Pent Farm]
15 Jan 1900

Dearest Edward.

Thanks for the vol. of Turg:[1] I haven't yet looked in.

I shall send You the B'woods only I am trying to collect all the stray

---

[1] *The Jew*, a collection of Turgenev's stories translated by Constance Garnett and just published by Heinemann. Garnett records his inscription in the presentation copy: '"An

proofs so as to send you a lot of copy, since you won't wait till it is
finished.

    Our love to you three

Ever yours

Jph. Conrad.

—Tell me what are your plans? Ford has been talking about some
weekly paper. Is there anything in it.

Times are deucedly hard here. But it's no use talking. This imbecile
war has just about done for me.

To R. B. Cunninghame Graham
Text MS Dartmouth; Watts 130

Pent Farm.
19 Jan. 1900.

Très cher ami.

    It's worse than brutal of me not to have answered your letter sooner.
To say the truth I haven't the heart to write either MS or letters; but
now since I received the Sat Review I've something to write about. The
German Tramp is not only excellent et bien tapé but it is something
more.[1] Of your short pieces I don't know but this is the one I like best.
The execution has a vigour—the right touch—and an ease that delight
me. It is wonderful how you perceive and how you succeed in making
your perception obey and bend to your thought. The *gold fish* the escaped
Indians sketch[2] and this one stand in a group by themselves waiting for
more with just that easy probing touch which no one but you can give.
There is nothing in these that the most cantankerous caviller could
pronounce out of focus. They are much more of course than mere
Crane-like impressionism but even as impressionism these three
sketches are well nigh perfect.[3]

    Well, I want to know—you know, so you should write to me. I would
write to you too if it were not for shame of having nothing to write. Out of

Unhappy Girl" is the most remarkable in psychology. "Enough" is very like the
philosophy of your novels. Send me the Dec. & Jan. Blackwood, please. I return you the
Nov. Number.'

[1] 'In a German Tramp', *Saturday Review*, 13 January; 'bien tapé': 'well and boldly painted'.

[2] Both *Saturday Review* stories: 'The Gold Fish', 18 February and 'A Hegira', 8 April 1899.
All three pieces, set respectively off the West African coast, in Morocco, and in Mexico,
reappeared in *Thirteen Stories* (1900).

[3] For Crane's 'impressionism', see *Letters*, 1, p. 416 and *A Personal Record*, p. 103. Graham
called himself an impressionist: Watts and Davies, p. 173.

that a good letter could be concocted but my mind is not enough at ease for such exercises. And I don't think you would care to get a mere exercise in vacuo from me.

The leaden hours pass in pain but the days go in a flash; weeks disappear into the bottomless pit before I can stretch out my hand and with all this there is an abiding sense of heavy endless drag upon the time. I am one of those who are condemned to run in a circle.[1] Now and then only I have an illusion of progress but I disbelieve even illusions by this time. And where indeed could I progress!

Of course there is a material basis for every state of mind, and so for mine. Fame is a fraud—and, scurvy thing as it is at best, it is beyond my reach. Profit I do not get—since you did ask whether that was the matter. There may be the illusion of being a writer—but I had the honour to remark that I no longer believe in illusions. This particular one I leave to my friends—it's something to have even this to give.

The fact of the matter is things go badly with me, and nobody can help—not even you unless you could invent something to make me write quicker. Palliatives won't do. And yet in the fourteen months I've been at the Pent I've written upwards of 100 000 words—that's a fact too—including of course some unutterable bosh for the unfinished *Rescue*. But I have lost all sense of reality; I look at the fields or sit before the blank sheet of paper as if I were in a dream. Want of mental vigour I suppose—or perhaps it is all the fault of the body? I am discouraged and weary and

Satis! Send me everything you publish. When is Heinemann going to 'produce' your book?[2]

Presentez mes devoirs a Madame Votre Femme. Jessie sends you her kind regards and Borys wishes to know whether you are coming to-morrow. And I wish you were here. Ever Yours

J Conrad.

To Edward Garnett

Text J-A, 1, 289; G. 163[3]

Pent Farm,
20 Jan. 1900.

Dearest Edward,

You make my head whirl when you write like this. What a letter for a poor devil to get! You've knocked my evening's work on the head; I

---

[1] Dante, *Inferno* III and XVIII, *Purgatorio* XVIII?

[2] *Thirteen Stories* (1900).

[3] Text from Garnett, with correction of obvious errors such as 'Sobariska' for 'Sobańska'. Last paragraph from facsimile, American Art Association sale, 24 April 1928.

found it impossible to write any copy. You frighten me; because were I to let you take me up on these heights by your appreciation the fall before my own conscience's smile would be so heavy as to break every bone in my body. And yet what, oh! what would become of me if it were not for your brave words that warm like fire and feed like bread and make me drunk like wine!

No. I didn't know anything about *Jim*; and all I know now is that it pleases you; and I declare as true as there are blind, deaf-mute gods sitting above us (who are so clear-eyed; eloquent and sharp of hearing) I declare it is enough for me; for if you think that because I've not been sending you my MS., your opinion has ceased to be a living factor in my individual and artistic existence, you are lamentably mistaken. I was simply afraid. And I am afraid still. You see the work fragmentarily; and the blessed thing is so defective that even that far within it you can not possibly (with all your penetration and sympathy) you cannot possibly know where I tend and how I shall conclude this most inconclusive attempt. You don't; and the truth is that it is not my depth but my shallowness which makes me so inscrutable (?). Thus, (I go cold to think) the surprise reserved for you will be in the nature of a chair withdrawn from under one; something like a bad joke—it will strike you no doubt. Bad and vile. Now had you taken the whole thing the fall would not have been so heavy, I imagine.

There has been a *John Kochanowski* a 15th century poet who wrote a threnody amongst other things and really our literature dates from him.[1] Of course his name is no more like mine than Brown is like Robinson. His name is derived from the word which in Polish means *love* while mine derives from the word *root*.[2]

Then in the thirties of the 19th century (or forties) there was a novelist of about say—Trollope's rank (but not so good in his way) named *Joseph Korzeniowski*.[3] That is also my name but the family is different, my full name being Joseph Theodor Konrad *Nałęcz* Korzeniowski, the underlined word being the appelation of our trade mark as thus [SEAL HERE]=Nałęcz without which none are genuine. As a matter of fact I and Alfred Borys Konrad Korzeniowski are the only two of that particular brand of Korzeniowski in existence. There are other families

---

[1] Jan Kochanowski (1530–84), the first great Polish poet, and the first to write a tragedy in the vernacular. He wrote a series of laments on the death of his daughter.

[2] *kochanie*: love; *korzeń*: root.

[3] Józef Korzeniowski (1797–1863), novelist and playwright; on 14 February 1901, Conrad wrote to the scholar who also bore that name.

whose arms are like mine but whose names are altogether different.[1] This is a distinct *bond*—though not a relationship in any sense. It may indicate a common origin lost in the midst of ages? It was always recognised as a title to good offices from a powerful family towards a humbler one—and so on.

My paternal grandfather Theodor N. Korzeniowski served in the cavalry. Decorated with the cross of 'Virtuti Militari' (a plain white enamel with a green wreath of laurel and these words in the centre) something in the nature of V.C. Attained the rank of captain in 1830 when the Russo-Polish war occurred after which the so-called Polish Army ceased to exist. Two wounds.[2] Retired to a little hereditary estate adjoining the extensive possessions of the family of *Sobański* (they are in the Almanach de Gotha) great friends and I fancy distant relations. Administered the territorial fortune of Madame Melanie Sobańska.[3] Wrote a tragedy in 5 Acts, Verse, privately printed, and so extremely dull that no one was ever known to have read it through. I know I couldn't notwithstanding my family pride and the general piety of my disposition.

My other grandfather *Joseph Bobrowski*[4] landowner, man of wit, owner of a famous stud of Steppe horses, lived and died on his estate of Oratów; popular, greatly lamented. Never wrote but letters (and very few of these) and a large number of promissory notes dedicated to various Jews. Left a large family of sons and one daughter *Eva*—my mother.[5] There was an extraordinary Sister-Cult in that family from which I profited when left an orphan at the age of ten. And my mother certainly was no ordinary woman. Her correspondence with my father and with her brothers which in the year 1890 I have read and afterwards destroyed[6] was a revelation to me; I shall never forget my delight, admiration and unutterable regret at my loss, (before I could appreciate her) which only then I fully understood. One of her brothers Thaddeus

---

[1] The Nałęcz arms, which Conrad bore on his signet-ring, display a knotted handkerchief, said to commemorate the field-dressed wounds of a patriotic ancestor. A grant of arms signified membership of the *szlachta*, the Polish gentry.

[2] During the Napoleonic campaigns, Teodor Korzeniowski fought for the Duchy of Warsaw against the Austrians; he fought against the Russians in the uprising of 1830–1 and was on his way to fight them again when he died in 1863. According to Stefan Buszczyński, he won the Military Cross twice.

[3] It was Conrad's father who, from 1852 onwards, managed a Sobański estate; his grandfather managed Korytna.

[4] Józef, 1790–1850.

[5] Ewa Bobrowska (1833–65) had a younger sister, Teofila, who died in 1851.

[6] Her letters to her husband have, however, survived: consult Najder, *Conrad under Familial Eyes*.

to whom I stand more in the relation of a son than of a nephew was a man of powerful intelligence and great force of character and possessed an enormous influence in the Three Provinces (Ukraïne, Volhynia and Podolia). A most distinguished man.[1] Another *Stephen* was in 1862 chief of the Polish Revolutionary Committee in Warsaw, and died assassinated soon after the Polish outbreak of 1863.[2]

None of the members of the many families to which these two are related was a literary man; all made sacrifices of fortune, liberty and life for the cause in which they believed; and very few had any illusions as to its success.

My father Apollonius N. Korzeniowski. Educated in the University of St. Petersburg. Department of Oriental Studies and Philology. No degree.[3] Debts. Social successes and any amount of "bonnes fortunes". Poet. Married in 1855. Came to Warsaw in 1860. Arrested in 1862 and after 10 months detention in the Citadel condemned to deportation into Russia. First in Archangel,[4] then in Tshernigow. My mother died in exile. My father liberated in '67 on the representation of Prince Gallitzin that he was no longer dangerous.[5] He was dying. Comedy in 5 acts in verse of modern life (date about 1854).[6] Trans: V. Hugo, *Legende du Siècles. Travailleurs de la Mer. Hernani.* Alf. de Vigny Chatterton.[7] Drama. (Verse) Shakespeare. *Much Ado About Nothing. As you Like it. Two Gentlemen of Verona. Comedy of Errors. Othello.*[8] (These I remember seeing in proofs when sent for his correction.[9] There may have been others. Some of these I've read when I could be no more than eight or nine years old.) After his liberation, in Cracow (Austrian Poland), one of the Editorial Committee of a Newspaper (Kraj) then founded if I remember

---

[1] Conrad's uncle Tadeusz (1829–94), his guardian and benefactor, a powerful influence on his life and mind.

[2] Stefan Bobrowski (1840–63), a member of the clandestine National Government, his brother Kazimierz, and his sister Ewa did not accept Tadeusz's policy of enduring rather than resisting foreign hegemony. Stefan was killed in a duel contrived by right-wing enemies.

[3] Apollo (1820–69) also studied law; it is not known whether he graduated (Najder, *Chronicle*, p. 5).

[4] Actually Vologda, much farther south but cursed with an abominable climate.

[5] Prince Golitsyn was Governor of Chernikhov.   [6] *Komedia*, his satirical first play.

[7] Korzeniowski planned a complete translation of Hugo's plays (Najder, *Chronicle*, p. 26) but did not live to complete the project; parts of a version of *La Légende des siècles* appeared posthumously; the translation of *Les Travailleurs de la mer* was not published; the translation of de Vigny's *Chatterton* came out in 1857.

[8] He published only *The Comedy of Errors* (1866) and an essay on Shakespeare (1867).

[9] See *A Personal Record*, pp. 71–3.

rightly by Prince Leo Sapieha (?)[1] but too ill to continue actively in the direction.

A man of great sensibilities; of exalted and dreamy temperament; with a terrible gift of irony and of gloomy disposition; withal of strong religious feeling degenerating after the loss of his wife into mysticism touched with despair. His aspect was distinguished; his conversation very fascinating; his face in repose sombre, lighted all over when he smiled. I remember him well. For the last two years of his life I lived alone with him—but why go on?

There were piles of MS. Dramas, verse, prose, burnt after his death according to his last will. A friend of his a Polish critic of distinction wrote a pamphlet entitled "A little known Poet" after his death.[2] And so finis.

Have I written enough? I certainly did not mean to write so much, when I began. I always intended to write something of the kind for Borys, so as to save all this from the abyss a few years longer. And probably he wouldn't care. What's Hecuba to him or he to Hecuba.[3] Tempi Passati brother! Tempi passati. Let them go.

Ever yours

Jph. Conrad.

To David Meldrum
Text MS Duke; Blackburn 83

[Pent Farm]
Thursday. [8 February 1900][4]

My dear Mr Meldrum.

Since the 25 of Jan I've been ill. Ten days in bed and it is only today that I managed to leave my bedroom.

Bad! Thank God tho' there is enough copy ahead to keep Maga going. They've been sending me proofs of the book but I haven't had the strength to look at them yet. I shall do so to-day perhaps.

I can't write any longer. Believe me always

Yours

Jph Conrad.

---

[1] Prince Adam Sapieha (1828–1903), a left-wing nationalist. Ironically, it was in *Kraj* (23 April 1899) that Eliza Orzeszkowa attacked Conrad for working abroad.
[2] Stefan Buszczyński's memoir, published in Cracow, 1870.   [3] *Hamlet*, II.ii.
[4] Meldrum replied 11 February.

To William Blackwood

Text MS NLS; Blackburn 84

[letterhead: Pent Farm]
12 Febr 1900

My dear Mr Blackwood.

I've had an exceedingly rough time of it since the 25th of last month when beginning with a severe fit of malaria I continued with bronchities* and an attack of gout, giving my wife a variety entertainment. The poor woman can hardly stand, and as to myself I managed yesterday to totter downstairs for the first time.

This sorry news will explain my delay in returning proofs of Maga: and book,[1] and the stoppage of further copy.

To-day (monday) I send off proofs of chap. xvi and xvii and also proofs of book, up to page *208*. I have yet ch xviii in proof, which I shall forward very soon together with two more chap^{rs} of copy. After these another two chapters will see the end of Jim.[2]

You have no idea what an anxious time I had. The illness looked much more serious than it has turned out to be and the thought of 'copy' nearly distracted me. All's well that ends well.

Believe me dear Mr Blackwood
always very faithfully yours
Jph. Conrad.

To R. B. Cunninghame Graham

Text MS Dartmouth; J-A, 1, 292; Watts 132

[letterhead: Pent Farm]
13 Febr 1900.

Cher ami.

Je me suis collété avec la mort ou peu s'en faut.[3] However not this time yet it seems. I've been ill since the 26th of Jany. and have only tottered downstairs yesterday.

Malaria, bronchitis and gout. In reality a breakdown. I am better but I've no sense of *rebound* don't you know; I remain under the shadow.

Ma pauvre femme est extenuée.[4] Nursing me, looking after the child,

---

[1] *Lord Jim* was still being set in type for the projected *Three Tales of Land and Sea* as well as for *Blackwood's.*

[2] For Blackwood's reply, offering a further sum on account and proposing to finish *Jim* in the May number, see Blackburn, p. 85.

[3] 'I have come to grips with death—or something very close.'

[4] 'My poor wife is worn out.'

doing the housework. She could not find a moment to drop you a line of thanks for Borys' purse.[1] He was delighted with it, and she wanted badly to write and tell you so. I suppose it isn't so much want of time but weariness that prevented her. I am afraid she'll break down next and that would [be] the end of the world. I wish I could give her a little change but—quelle misère.

I think that to-morrow I'll be able to begin writing again. What sort of stuff it'll be devil only knows. Moi aussi je suis extenué. Il faut se raidir.[2] Pardon this jeremiad. Ever yours

Jph Conrad.

To David Meldrum
Text MS Duke; Blackburn 85

[letterhead: Pent Farm]
Tuesday.
14 Febr 1900

My dear Mr Meldrum

Ever so many thanks for your letter. I am able to write you that I am somewhat better but still cast down a bit. In an hour we shall leave here to go to H. G. Wells for two days. It'll do me good I think and perhaps when I get back I shall be able to grapple with pen ink and paper. I haven't done anything yet tho' my head is full (too full) of Jim's end but when it comes to putting it down black on white the brain wanders. When I start 10 days will be enough to finish the thing.

I've sent 208 pp. of proofs corrected for book and also proofs for Maga of Ch: XVI XVII. I've been able to do that much anyhow. I've also written a few lines to Mr Blackwood.

If I could get £20 it would be a great convenience for my balance is very near zero; this worries one—you know.

With kindest regards from us both to Mrs Meldrum and yourself believe me

Always Yours

Jph. Conrad.

---

[1] He was two years old on 15 January.   [2] 'I must be steadfast.'

To Ford Madox Ford

Text MS Yale; Unpublished

The Pent Stanford Kent
Sat. 17th Febr. 1900

My dear Hueffer

Thanks for your letter which I received in Sandgate where we went on Tuesday to stay with H.G. Wells for two days.

I have nothing to boast of as regards my physical or mental condition; I am low and fanciful. On Tuesday I got so worried about your Christina that I made my wife wire to Ethel for news[1] my forebodings being of so gloomy a character that I could not bear the idea of asking you directly. This will illustrate my morbid condition at the time.

To-day I am less of an ass but my distaste to every form of literary exertion persists. What will be the end of this I can't imagine or rather I imagine only too well. I don't wonder You are not disposed to write. You had some anxiety and bother—hadn't you? Would it do you good to come and talk over the last chap: again?[2] I am ready for that now. The MS is in Heinemann's hands.

I trust You are all well. Our love to you all

Ever Yours

Jph. Conrad.

To E. L. Sanderson

Text MS Yale; Unpublished

[letterhead: Pent Farm]
19 Febr. 1900

Dearest Ted.

I had put off replying to your letter till I felt better. I had ten days in bed and so on with gout, bronchitis and malaria; a debauch of disease. It flattened me like a pancake, emptied my head and gave me a horror of every exertion. I am rather better now.

Jack[3] who came charitably to see me last Sunday told me You are ordered to the front.[4] As I understood him there's nothing between you and South Africa but a medical examination.

This news has interfered with my peace of mind not a little. However ready you may be for every sacrifice I deplore the necessity which

---

[1] To add to the worries of Christina's illness, Elsie Hueffer was seven months pregnant.

[2] The precise nature of the collaboration is debatable, but Conrad probably had much more to do with revising *The Inheritors* than with drafting it.

[3] Galsworthy.   [4] As a captain in the Princess of Wales's Own Yorkshire Regiment.

removes you from the sphere of your real usefulness. Knowing as I do your moral worth, your intelligence and your sense of duty I cannot help feeling that your life-work would serve your country more than all the military virtues of courage and endurance you may be called upon to display. War is a wasteful business at best.

For Grey[1] I have nothing but congratulations and every wish of good luck and for the opportunities of distinction. He is young; it is his career after all.

It is sad for me, though a perfectly useless person with shattered nerves and a depressed mind, to sit here in my shell and think of you who are going and of those who remain. Let me know *when* you start and will it be from London or from South[ampt]on? I don't ask for a long letter; just a word. With our love.

Ever yours

Conrad.

To Helen Sanderson
Text MS Yale; Unpublished

[letterhead: Pent Farm]
19 Febr 1900

My dear Mrs Sanderson.

Your letter reached me just as I was entering upon the period of convalescence after a rather sharp illness. Before I was mentally fit to answer You as I wished to answer, Jack Galsworthy brought me the news of Ted being ordered to South Africa.

I've just written to him trying to express some part of my thoughts; but to you I find it much more difficult to write. I know you are both ready for every sacrifice and ones heart goes out to you. That's all one can say. Since we heard the news you have not been out of our thoughts for a moment.

It is fortunate that—as I firmly believe—the campaign has taken a decisive turn. Thus your separation need not be very long after all. I think events shall move quickly now and I wouldn't be surprised if the heaviest of the fighting were actually over before Ted lands at Cape-town.[2] There is some comfort in that thought. If Ted must go, then (even apart from the feelings of those who love him) the sooner he is

---

[1] A twenty-year-old brother, second lieutenant in the same regiment.

[2] A pessimist could point to the Battle of Spion Kop (24–5 January), in which the British losses were five times heavier than the Boer; an optimist to General French's dramatic advance on Kimberley. The war dragged on until the end of May 1902.

back the better it will be. He can do more for his country in Elstree[1] than in the field though wherever he is I know he will give of his best. May I ask you for a line or two about yourselves. I am very anxious and the truth is I am not fit to travel yet or you would see me in Elstree. Pardon this disconnected letter. I am so absurdly weak that I can't think clearly. Jessie sends her love and assurances of her heartfelt sympathy. She is completely knocked up with the nursing and anxiety. Believe me, dear Mrs Sanderson always your affectionate and faithful servant

Conrad.

To William Blackwood

Text MS NLS; Blackburn 86

[letterhead: Pent Farm]
20th Febr 1900.

Dear Mr Blackwood.

Many thanks for your letter. When it arrived here I was away in Sandgate (only seven miles from here) staying with H.G. Wells for a much needed change.

It has done me some good so that yesterday I got hold of Jim again. When I get into the stride a fortnight will see the end of the story, though I shall not hurry myself since the end of a story is a very important and difficult part; the *most* difficult for me, to execute—that is. It is always *thought out* before the story is begun.

The last proof and some more *copy* shall be sent in a couple of days.

As to your very kind offer of some money the truth is I had already written to Mr Meldrum asking whether it was feasible. I cannot tell you how much I appreciate your kindness which seems proof against all my wearisome imperfections.

Believe me, dear Sir always very
faithfully yours
Joseph Conrad.

---

[1] At the school.

To William Blackwood

Text MS NLS; Blackburn 87

The Pent.
Stanford
N^r Hythe.
26th Febr 1900.

Dear Mr Blackwood.

Many thanks for the cheque for £40 in further payment on acc^t of *Lord Jim* which I received this morning.

I am at work at last. Proofs leave here to-morrow morning together with 2 new chap:

I trust I shall be a credit to Maga with Lord Jim—even to the very end. I mean to try hard.

Believe me, dear Mr Blackwood, always very faithfully yours[1]

To Ford Madox Ford

Text MS Yale; Unpublished

[Pent Farm]
27 Febr 1900

My dear Ford.

Many thanks for cheque for six guineas. The man has been here with his horse. I think we can do a trade tho' I am not enamoured of the animal.

Heinemann writes will do his damnedest to serialise our story here.[2]

Come next week not this, because Jess is going to London for two days and there will be precious little to eat.

Ever Yours

Jph Conrad.

My love to Your House.

To David Meldrum

Text MS Duke; Blackburn 88

The Pent.
Stanford. N^r Hythe.
3 Mch 1900

My dear Mr Meldrum.

If I didn't write to you I did write a little—as much as I could. Now I send You 14 pp. of pretty rough MS to be typed in two copies and I shall

[1] Signature excised.   [2] *The Inheritors* on this side of the Atlantic.

keep up that kind of dribble if you don't mind so as to write and revise at the same time for greater speed in getting the copy ready for the press. I've 'got hold' again, thank God. It seemed at first as though I had written my last line.

I have, inexcusably, neglected to let you know of Mr. B'wood's cheque (£40), which reached me a few days ago, and was made very welcome. Though, speaking frankly, I don't doubt I am giving Mr B'wood the equivalent of his money I am very touched by his patient acceptance of my unpunctuality and by his readiness to respond to my demands. I hope he does not doubt it.

I do long for a pause—but I am afraid my illness has done away with my holiday. I must drive on. One decent success with a book would give me a chance to breathe freely. But will it ever come? I fear that from this vol: I must not expect relief. There's the war!

I trust Mrs Meldrum yourself and the children are all well. My wife sends her kind regards Believe me always yours

Jph Conrad.

To R. B. Cunninghame Graham
Text MS Dartmouth; J-A, 1, 293; Watts 133

The Pent.
3 March [1900]¹

Très cher ami.

Just a word to thank you for your letter. Vous me mettez du coeur au ventre² though I can't possibly agree to your praises of Jim. But as to *Buta*³ it is altogether and fundamentally *good*; good in matter—that's of course—but good wonderfully good in form and especially in expression.

I am sad we don't meet but I couldn't come to town for the play⁴ as I very much wished to do. No doubt managers are as stupid as the majority of publishers. I don't see the papers only the Standard. It had a rigmarole but not even an attempt at any sort of appreciation so I don't know how Don Juan went.⁵ Is it going to be printed?

---

¹ References to work by Conrad and the Grahams fix the year.
² 'You put new heart in me.'
³ Graham's story-within-a-story, *Saturday Review*, 3 March.
⁴ Gabriela Cunninghame Graham's translation of *Don Juan Tenorio*, the play about Don Juan's redemption, by José de Zorrilla y Moral. It ran from 27 February to 31 March.
⁵ According to the unanimous opinion of the press, the company, and the Grahams, very badly.

I am trying to go on with my work. It is hard but damn it all if it is only *half* as good as you say then why groan? Have you seen the last *vol* of Mrs Garnett's Turgeniev?[1] There's a story there *Three Portraits* really fine. Also *Enough*, worth reading.

Mes devoirs très respectueux à Madame Votre Femme. Jessie sends her kindest regards. Borys is very fat and unruly but wears the heart you've given him round his neck and thinks no end of it. Poor little devil; if he had a decent father he would come to something perhaps.

Ever Yours

Jph Conrad.

To Helen Sanderson

Text MS Yale; J-A, 1, 294[2]

The Pent
Stanford
N^r Hythe
17 Mch 1900

My dear Mrs Sanderson.

My wife thought I had written while I was under the impression she had done so days ago. The mutual recriminations of the "You're another" sort which ensued were the most violent that ever troubled the peace of this bucolic spot. You being of a charitable and forgiving disposition will be glad to hear we've made it up; and it is in consequence of a friendly agreement that I write to offer excuses for us both, and to thank You for the good and friendly thought of sending us your and Bab's photograph. Baby[3] is very delightful; it is indeed over the contemplation of her and her mother's portrait that the light was thrown upon the horrible situation and the scenes of recrimination took place. And it is a pleasure to have you too; for in truth we have Miss Helen Watson but of Mrs Sanderson who is so often in our thoughts (and now more than ever) we had no portrait. You have changed, a little, I think. It is difficult to say how much for on the photograph you are sacrificed to the child. She is a dear, cheerful, intelligent little woman and we are very much in love with her.

I doubly congratulate you on the recent victories.[4] The sooner the war comes to its unavoidable conclusion the better for those we love; and the

---

[1] *The Jew.* [2] Jean-Aubry omits most of paragraph one.
[3] The Sandersons' year-old child, Katherine.
[4] Notably the relief of Ladysmith, 28 February.

better for the national conscience which in my view is as much part of the Empire as the extent of the earth it holds; and of as great importance to its future and to its power. Nations, like men, often act first and reflect afterwards; the responsability* is with the leaders and the verdict with history, when the generations are gone and the truth of their sins and virtues alone remains.

But I don't know why I should inflict upon you my valueless meditations; and besides it is late. I had better refrain. You will share with me the first news of our dear Ted? Will you not? I am not anxious in any way but every day he is in my thoughts—he has his part in the silent life within, which goes on deep and steady under the noise, the exertions, the clashing thoughts of our daily existence.

Believe me, dear Mrs Sanderson, always your most affectionate friend and servant

Joseph Conrad.

Jessie sends her love and her thanks; she would also send the boy's photograph only we have nothing recent.

To Ford Madox Ford
Text Telegram, Yale; Unpublished

[26 March 1900][1]

Hueffer Aldington

Splendid reports of novel original popular great hopes society hit McClure takes serialising in both countries[2] as he has good connection wirepullers suggested by Edward[3] as more catching and first chapter a little thin but the last three completely convincing my heartiest congratulation love from us all

Conrad

To Edward Garnett
Text MS Colgate; G. 168

The Pent.
26 Mch 1900

Dearest Edward.

All my bits of luck come through you! You must be—indeed—as Jess says—the best of men. I consider the accept^{ce} of the *Inh:*^{ors} a distinct bit of luck.[4] Jove! What a lark!

---

[1] Post office date-stamp.   [2] *The Inheritors*, never serialized, appeared in 1901.
[3] Garnett.
[4] Acceptance by Heinemann, Garnett's current employer.

I set myself to look upon the thing as a sort of skit upon the political (?!) novel, fools of the Morley Roberts[1] sort do write. This in my heart of hearts. And poor *H* was dead in earnest! Oh Lord. How he worked! There is not a chapter I haven't made him write twice—most of them three times over.

This is collaboration if you like! Joking apart the expenditure of nervous fluid was immense. There were moments when I cursed the day I was born and dared not look up at the light of day I had to live through with this thing on my mind. H has been as patient as no angel had ever been. I've been fiendish. I've been rude to him; if I've not called him names I've *implied* in my remarks and in the course of our discussions the most opprobrious epithets. He wouldn't recognize them. 'Pon my word it was touching. And there's no doubt that in the course of that agony I have been ready to weep more than once. Yet not for him. Not for him.

You'll have to burn this letter[2]—but I shall say no more. Some day we shall meet and then—!

I am still at *Jim*. I've been beastly ill in Febr^y. Jessie is hunting all over the house for the *Febr^y* N^{o3} to send you. I am old and sick and in debt—but lately I've found I can still write—*it* comes! *it* comes!—and I am young and healthy and rich.

The question is *will* I ever <u>*write*</u> anything?

I've been cutting and slashing whole pars out of Jim. How bad Oh! how bad! Why is it that a weary heaven has not pulverised me with a wee little teeny weeny thunderbolt?

Love from us to you three. I shall write again when I get time to gasp once or twice.

Ever yours

Jph Conrad.

I suppose you've scornfully detected whole slabs of my own precious writing in that precious novel?[4]

---

[1] E.g. *The Colossus: A Story of To-Day* (1899). Roberts (1857–1942), friend of Hudson and Gissing, was widely travelled and prolific: between 1895 and 1899, he published fourteen titles.

[2] Garnett's publication of this letter in 1928 upset Ford very much: Mizener, pp. 54–5.

[3] Of *Blackwood's*.

[4] Ford identified the Conrad passages in 1924 (*Conrad*, pp. 134–42). Conrad's remarks in presentation copies now at Dartmouth and Yale confirm the smallness of his contribution.

To Ford Madox Ford
Text MS Yale; Unpublished

[Pent Farm]
[late March 1900][1]

My dear Ford.

I am sending you P[awling]'s letter about Inh^{ors} and Cheque £15 together with receipt for £30 which we sign jointly. The report of Stephen Gwynn[2] to McClure was also *very* hopeful. I am driving hard. It's awful Shall write soon. Send receipt on to Heinemann.

Our love

Ever Yours

J Conrad.

To Ford Madox Ford
Text MS Yale; Unpublished

Pent Farm
Saturday 31 Mch [1900][3]

My dear Ford.

My aunt[4] is coming on Monday to stay a week. I would be awfully glad if your wife and yourself could come on Wednesday to lunch. Jessie thinks that if you started early to arrive here about 10 so as to give your wife some time to rest on a couch before lunch and also a couple of hours after the meal before You start for home, there would be no imprudence in the proceeding. I am of course anxious very anxious to introduce my 'collaborateur' to the good woman who represents to me so much of my family—she had known so many of them on whom no eye of man'll rest again. And the pleasure would be more than doubled if Auntie Elsie could come too. I would have given You longer notice but for the fact that I didn't know till this morning the exact day of my visitor's arrival.

I think Jess is writing too, but she has been unwell (Borys too) and is awfully busy.

McClure's letter[5] is most satisfactory. Stephen Gwynn (connaissez-Vous ça?) read the MS for him and is distracted with admiration. Is consumed with the desire to make our acquaintance. McC. also wishes to

---

[1] The news of *The Inheritors* suggests a date between the telegram of 26 and the letter of 31 March.
[2] The Irish novelist and poet (1864–1950) was supporting himself as a publisher's scout; later, he became a Nationalist MP.
[3] Gwynn's report supplies the year.
[4] Marguerite Poradowska: see the letter to her of 16 April.
[5] About possible serial rights in the United States.

see us. They propose to come down here and beg me to let you know what day I fix for the visit. I fancy you would not mind Friday next. Would you? At any rate I want to see McC on my own affairs[1] and if anything prevented you we shall later on extort a lunch from our Yankee editor. It's so much to the good. S. Gwynn says in his report "It is a work no publisher anxious to produce literature should think of refusing." The literary quality (and most other things) is all *your own* in that book. I've written these ipsissima verba to McClure.

With love Ever yours

J. Conrad.

To T. Fisher Unwin

Text MS Rosenbach; Unpublished

Pent Farm.
Stanford
N^r Hythe.
2 Ap. 1900

Dear Sir.

My letter must have miscarried. I wrote you about the 25th ult. about contributing to Mr J. E. Nash's vol of short stories.[2] I also wrote him by the same post. From his letter enclosing Yours I see that neither of You received my note.

Will you consent to Mr Nash using one of the stories in the *Unrest* vol for his patriotic charitable publication. I've given my consent.

I am dear sir Yours faithfully

Jph Conrad.

To David Meldrum

Text MS Duke; Blackburn 89

[letterhead: Pent Farm]
3 Ap. 1900

My dear Mr Meldrum.

I am sending a fresh inst. of *Jim* and now I start to write the last chap.

I don't know how my answer was taken in Edinburgh and what they meant by this inquiry. As a matter of fact they have already—(considering the length of each inst^t). enough matter for *two* numbers.

---

[1] *The Rescue* would have been an unavoidable topic.

[2] James Eveleigh Nash, *The Ladysmith Treasury* (1900), published by Sands & Co without any *Tales of Unrest*.

I've been horribly disappointed by the shortness of the inst^t in the Ap. N^{o1} the more so that the break just there destroyed an effect. If one only could do without serial publication! Don't think me an ungrateful beast. Jim is very near my heart. I don't apologise now for springing on Mr Blackwood such a long affair and for the unfortunate dragging manner of its production. Apologies butter no parsnips—to adapt the popular saying. It won't happen again.

My story in collaboration with H[ueffer] seems to have produced a very good impression on Heine:'s and McClure's readers. There's something in it no doubt. *What*, exactly, I can't say myself.

I am always thinking of a *long* book for Mr Blackwood and, if the collaboration stuff goes well, the thing shall be managed sooner than I hoped for. The *R[escue]* shall be finished before long—and then we shall see what can be done for the *House*.

Meantime what I want Mr Blackwood to do is to advance me on completed delivery of *Jim* something like £150. Of course that will over pay *Jim* a lot, but I shall at once write something that will reduce if not extinguish the surplus. Only I have pressing liabilities to discharge just now.

Please pardon this constant screwing. Fact is I can't help it.

Jim shall be finished by the 12th inst and I shall want the cash then.

Well this is the end for the present of the old tune. I shall certainly run up to see you directly Jim is finished.

Believe me

Always yours

Jph Conrad.

To David Meldrum

Text MS Duke; Blackburn 66

[letterhead: Pent Farm]
[spring or early summer 1900]^2

My dear Mr Meldrum.

I wrote you this morning but since a horrid bill came in. I am awfully sorry to bother you but if You could lend me another ten pounds till *Jim* is finished you would render me a service.

Pardon this In haste

Yours

Conrad.

---

^{1} Chapters 14 and 15.
^{2} Type five letterhead, first used for the preceding letter. Conrad also wrote to Meldrum on 19 and 22 May and 7 June, all possible dates for this note.

To William Blackwood
Text MS NLS; Blackburn 90

[letterhead: Pent Farm]
12 Ap. 1900

Dear Mr Blackwood.

Yesterday I sent off to Edinburgh proofs of Maga and book, together with an instalment of type-written matter, and to London a batch of further MS. I feel the need of telling you that I've done something anyway and to assure you that *Lord Jim has* an end, which last I am afraid you may be beginning to doubt. It has though—and I am now trying to write it out. A dog's life! this writing out, this endlessness of effort and this endless discontent; with remorse, thrown in, for the massacre of so many good intentions.

This by the way. The real object of this letter is to tell you that should you find Jim unconscionably long (for Maga—I mean) I am ready to shorten (what remains) by excision. I am however in such a state of mind about the story—so inextricably mixed up with it in my daily life—that I feel unequal to doing the cutting myself; so, addressing you in your character of Editor of *Maga*, I declare my readiness to make conscientious joints, if the parts that can be taken out are marked for me and the MS with such indications is returned. I would not keep it for more than a day or two—and, as (I trust) you will have the story complete in a week or so, there would be time to look through it before the copy is required for setting up.

Perhaps you've heard that Hueffer and I have finished a novel in collaboration. I did not show it to Mr Meldrum for two and even three reasons. First of all I did not wish to offer you a work in its nature necessarily tentative—an initial experiment, in fact. The second reason was my running actually singlehanded in Maga and of course my partner and myself are very anxious for serial publication. The third reason for you not having had the refusal of these first-fruits is that you have (virtually) a book of mine while poor Heineman[n] (who had been awfully decent to me)[1] has nothing to show for his decency but a few receipts for moneys paid out and half a novel which is hung up, to ripen—I trust. He seemed very anxious to see it. I am not enthusiastic about it myself but it seems to have hit Heinemann's readers in a soft spot, and Mr Stephen Gwynn (on behalf of McClure) has delivered a

---

[1] In publishing *The Nigger* and in paying an advance on *The Rescue*, the ripening 'half-a-novel'.

favourable judgment. Well—as our good friends the Russians[1] say—"God give them health and the rank of generals." If this goes down well with the public we shall try our hand at an adventure story[2] of which the skeleton is set up—with some modelling here and there already worked up.

I hope your health does not suffer from this cold and blustering spring. I've had something in the nature of a slight relapse in March, but am very fit now. Believe me dear Mr Blackwood always very faithfully yours.

                                                                            Jph. Conrad.

To Marguerite Poradowska
Text MS Yale; Rapin 171; G. & S. 101

                                                            [letterhead: Pent Farm]
                                                            16th Ap. 1900.
Très chère et bonne.[3]

Ce matin j'ai reçu Votre lettre contenant celle de la Dame "Odonie" et en ce moment je viens de finir la lettre que je lui adresse au Couvent de Lille.[4] Après avoir médité quelque temps sur le mot *entretien* j'ai pris le parti d'ecrire a Dame Odonie franchement qui si le mot etait equivalent au *board* (en Anglais) et l'instruction seule devait être gratuite les moyens de ma belle-mère ne lui permettaient pas d'accepter l'offre généreuse des Dames Bernardines. Il est évident que dans un pension-nat comme Slough cela signifierait trente livres ou plus pour chacune des petites par an: Une dépense hors de question pour une personne qui n'a absolument rien. Quand à moi Vous savez ou j'en suis. Il y aura bien assez de tirage pour le trousseau si modeste qu'il soit. Dautre part si *entretien* veux dire les petites dépenses courantes on pourrait s'arranger.

J'ai pensé qu'il valait mieux declarer la situation nettement afin d'épargner a la bonne Dame Odonie le temps et la peine d'une plus longue correspondence. Du reste il serait trop triste pour les enfants

---

[1] Blackwood shared Conrad's opinions on the subject.

[2] 'Seraphina', which became *Romance*.

[3] Mme Poradowska (1848–1937) was the widow of Conrad's cousin Aleksander; more significant, at least in the early stages of an intimate friendship, was her success as a novelist in French. The letters to her between 9/10 June 1895 and this one are missing: see *Letters*, 1, pp. 228, 428.

[4] Conrad's mother-in-law, Mrs George, was a widow; this letter was written in the interest of her two youngest daughters. The Dames Bernardines, a teaching order originating in Belgium, had recently opened a boarding-school at St Bernard's Convent in Slough, Buckinghamshire. The two girls did go there, and, as Conrad's application to the Royal Literary Fund (File 2629: 17 June 1902) reveals, he undertook the costs of their education.

d'aller à Slough rien que pour subir une deception qu'elles ressenti-
raient vivement. Ai-je bien fait?

Ma chère Marguerite Vous avez été on ne peut plus bonne pour ces
enfants et pour nous tous. Il est impossible de Vous dire combien Vous
nous manquez! Borys m'a demandé ce soir si Vous reveniez demain? Il
semble attendre Votre retour chaque jour. Nous n'avons pas cette
consolation.

Il est fort tard. J'ai envoyé Jessie se coucher et je suis resté a travailler.
Quel métier de chien. On en est assommé, Je n'ai même pas la force de
Vous dire combien je Vous aime, combien je Vous sais gré de Votre
solide amitié pour nous—de Votre tendresse! Jess m'a chargé de Vous
transmettre une quantité des baisers. Les deux petites sont remplies de
gratitude et d'affection pour Vous.

Je vous embrasse bien fort.

Toujours Vôtre

Conrad.

Translation

Very kind and dear,

This morning I had your letter enclosing the one from Dame Odonie,
and I have just now finished the one I am sending to her at the convent
in Lille. Having thought about the word *entretien* for some time, I decided
to write frankly to Dame Odonie that if the word was the equivalent of
the English *board*, and only the tuition was to be free, my mother-in-
law's means would not permit her to accept the Dames Bernardines'
generous offer. In a boarding-school like Slough, it stands to reason that
that could mean thirty or more pounds a year for each child: an
unthinkable outlay for someone who has absolutely nothing. As for me,
you know my situation. There will be quite enough difficulty with the
outfit, however simple it may be. On the other hand, if *entretien* means
minor current expenses, one could make do.

I thought it better to state the situation clearly in order to save Dame
Odonie the time and trouble of a longer correspondence. Besides, it
would be too painful for the children to go to Slough only to suffer a
disappointment they would feel acutely. Have I done the right thing?

My dear Marguerite, you could not have been kinder to these
children and to us all. It's impossible to tell you how much we miss you!
Borys asked me this evening if you were coming back tomorrow. Every
day he seems to wait for your return. We don't have that consolation.

It is very late. I have sent Jessie to bed and I have stayed behind to work. What a dog's life. One's exhausted by it. I don't even have the strength to tell you how much I love you, how much I am thankful for your firm friendship for us—for your fondness. Jess has told me to send you an abundance of kisses. The two little girls are full of gratitude and affection for you.

To Elsie Hueffer and Ford Madox Ford
Text Telegram, Yale; Unpublished

[17 April 1900][1]

Hueffer   Marine House   Slade St   Hythe
Felicitations affectueuses et notre cienvienne[2] a la jeune personne[3]
Conrad

To William Blackwood
Text MS NLS; Blackburn 92

[letterhead: Pent Farm]
26th Ap. 1900

Dear Mr Blackwood.

I hurry up to catch this post. Fact is I only opened the envelope from Edinburgh this moment thinking it contained only the proofs. Somehow it did not occur to me it might have contained a letter from you[4]—still less the enclosure.

Many thanks for the cheque for £25. You need not for a moment apprehend I would extend the story, but I am immensely pleased with what you say about there being no necessity for cutting down what remains.

Both my partner and myself would be delighted if our adventure story seemed to you worthy of Maga.

My wrist (left one thank God) is swollen to the size of an ordinary ankle. You may imagine how I enjoyed the process of swelling. This has

[1] Date-stamp.   [2] A clerk's misreading of 'bienvenue'?
[3] Katharine, born the previous evening.
[4] Blackburn (p. 91) prints the letter. Concerning *Lord Jim*, Blackwood wrote: 'I do not think the story loses anything by the method of telling. I would not recommend any cutting down in these three chapters merely for the sake of bringing the serial issue to an earlier close. The end must now justify the length of the story, & to hurry it up for any reason but the right one be assured would be a mistake. I therefore as heretofore leave you a free hand with regard to it. But do not from anything I have said expand it to a greater length than you have already sketched out.' Blackwood also set Conrad's mind at rest about Heinemann's publishing *The Inheritors* and told Conrad that he would be glad to consider 'Seraphina'.

been a bad year for me. However as usual in such attacks my head is clear and having the use of my right hand I can manage to write, with a heavy paper-weight to hold the sheet. I've only lost one day.

Thanks for your kind inquiries. Believe me, dear Sir,

Very faithfully yours

Jph. Conrad.

To Ford Madox Ford

Text MS Yale; Unpublished

[Pent Farm]
Wednesday. [Spring 1900?][1]

Dear Hueffer.

Why won't you believe that in any house in which I may live you are too much appreciated by the permanent and the floating population to be a nuisance to anybody—or even to suggest the thought of a nuisance. This is absurd and wounding. I went off with Hope on that Monday because I didn't think You would come. I am quite aware that many people I know can not be interesting to You. But frankly I would have gone even if [I] had expected you, for this reason that the poor man (whom I had known for over 20 years now)[2] was in a fearful state of depression. He must have been very unhappy to volunteer to come for four days—as it is very difficult for him to leave his work. There are states of mind when even one's wife is less of a help than a friend. I rushed him out on that rainy day because I didn't know what to do to prevent him giving away to something very like suicidal melancholia. If my manner displeased you in any way that evening this is the explanation. Si Vous avez cru que je m'amusai Vous Vous trompez étrangement.[3] You must have noticed I tried to make him talk of his mining days.[4] I have heard these stories years ago and ever since, and did not think they would entertain you either. I couldn't attend to you because I was worried. Vous comprenez? That's all there is to it.

Yours

Conrad.

Love to you all. Shall be home Thursday of course.

[1] The only other letter on this stationery (18×11 cm, watermark WILLOW BROOK EXTRA FINE) is also to Ford, 31 March 1900. The contents account for the formality of the greeting.

[2] Conrad met G. F. W. Hope in 1880, between service on the *Europa* and the *Lock Etive*. With the violent death of his son and the collapse of his business interests, Hope had much to be sad about.

[3] 'If you thought I enjoyed myself, you are strangely mistaken.'   [4] In South Africa.

To John Galsworthy

Text MS Forbes; Unpublished

[letterhead: Pent Farm]
5th May [1900][1]

Dear Jack

Just a word to say I am going to morrow to stay a week with Stephen
Crane.[2] Things aren't very bright. Still! ... And you?

I am anxious to see you *and* the book.[3] Shall drop you a line as soon as
I am back here

Ever yours

Conrad

To Marguerite Poradowska

Text MS Yale; Rapin 172; G. & S. 102

[letterhead: Pent Farm]
May 10th, 1900.[4]

Très chère.

J'ajoute quelques mots surtout pour Vous parler du Volume.[5] J'ai lu
le roman pour la troisième fois religieusement—d'un bout a l'autre.
C'est très bien. C'est très bien! Les charactères sont definis avec une
précision que je Vous envie. La scène finale est on ne peut plus
touchante, jusqu'a a la dernière ligne. J'aime le livre. Il y a un charme
très doux dans le stile et aussi il y a de la force. Tout se tient. Il n'y a pas
des trous. Vous savez ce que je veux dire. Mes felicitations. Quand au

---

[1] The Crane reference gives the year.

[2] Crane was dying of tuberculosis; the visit was abandoned.

[3] Galsworthy's *Villa Rubein*.

[4] Jessie Conrad dated the letter and began it:

My dear Auntie.

Conrad's hand is better but he is dreadfully busy. I can never thank you enough for all
you have done for the girls. I had a letter from Dollie last week and she said how very
happy they both were in Slough. I enjoy your visit to us by simply looking back to it, and
Borys often talks of his dear Auntie. When you write will you tell us what you can of
Bruges. I am so looking forward to going there but even more to seeing you in Paris
before the year is out. Mrs. Hueffer has another daughter nearly a month old. I am afraid
they are both awfully disappointed it is not a son. Borys grows much quicker than I like
and is quite a boy. Sometimes I heartily wish he were again a tiny baby; one feels more
sure of children when they are very young, I think. When dear Conrad has finished his
book we mean to take a little holiday. I will write again very soon

With love from all three of us
Believe me dear Marguerite
Yours very lovingly

Jessie

[5] Mme Poradowska's *Pour Noémi*, just published.

succès de librairie—nous verrons bien. Pour moi cependant il me semble hors de doute; mais le public est un animal capricieux qui broute ou il veut et préfere se nourrir de chardons. Vous m'enverrez un mot pour me dire comment va la vente—n'est-ce pas? Hueffer est surtout frappé par la delicatess de Votre procédé artistique. Il a raison, là. Du reste, nous avons joliment épluché le cher bouquin—ce qui pour nous qui refusons de discuter, ou même de regarder les romans est un acte d'hommage a Votre beau talent. Il vient d'emporter Yaga[1] et me prie de Vous presenter ses respectueux hommages. Je vous embrasse bien fort.
Toujours à Vous

Conrad.

PS Les deux petites sont au septième ciel.[2] On est si bon pour elles. Ces enfants Vous doivent une fière chandelle. Du reste il faut dire elles Vous sont reconnaissantes et Dolly surtout a pour Vous une espèce d'adoration. Jessie aussi. Vous ètes venue comme une bonne et charmante fée et Vous avez laissé votre image dans les coeurs.

Translation

Very dear,

I add a few words, above all to talk to you about the book. I've read the novel for the third time, faithfully—from one end to the other. It's very good. It's very good! The characters are defined with a precision which I envy in you. The final scene could not be more touching, right up to the last line. I love the book. There is a very gentle charm and also power in the style. Everything holds together. There are no gaps. You know what I mean. My congratulations. As for success in the book-shops—we shall see. For me, however, it seems beyond doubt, but the public is a wayward beast that browses where it will and prefers to feed on thistles. You'll send me a word to tell me how the wind blows—won't you? Hueffer is particularly struck by the delicacy of your artistic method. He's right, there. Moreover, we have well and truly picked over the precious volume—for us, who refuse to discuss or even look at novels, that's an act of homage to your fine talent. He has just carried off *Yaga* and asked me to pay you his respectful compliments. I embrace you warmly.

Always yours

Conrad

[1] *Yaga*, a novel of Ruthenian life, published as a book in 1888.
[2] At the convent in Slough. Dolly, the elder, had helped look after her baby nephew, Borys.

PS The two girls are in seventh heaven. It is so fortunate for them. These children should be most grateful to you. I must say they are grateful, moreover, and Dolly, especially, feels a kind of worship for you. Jessie too. You've come as a kind and enchanting fairy and you have left your image in their hearts.

To Cora Crane

Text MS Columbia; Stallman 281

[letterhead: Pent Farm]
10th May 1900.

My dear Mrs Crane.

Your letter distresses me beyond measure and confirms my fears as to your material situation.[1] It has been the object of my anxiety and of many sad thoughts. You may imagine that had it been in my power to render you any sort of service I would not have waited for any sort of appeal. I've kept quiet because I feel myself powerless. I am a man without connections, without influence and without means. The daily subsistence is a matter of anxious thought for me. What *can* I do? I am already in debt to my two publishers, in arrears with my work, and know no one who could be of the slightest use. It is not even in my power to jeopardise my own future to serve you. If it had been, such is my affection for Stephen and my admiration of his genius, that I would do so without hesitation, to save him.[2] But my future, such as it is, is already pawned. You can't imagine how much I suffer in writing thus to you. I have been almost distracted since I had your letter. Won't Stephen's relations come forward?

Pardon me for not saying more. I feel too unhappy.

Always yours

Jph. Conrad

PS I am writing to the boatman.[3]

[1] Stephen Crane's doctors held out as a last hope a costly stay in the Black Forest. Cora Crane was trying to raise money for the journey; her long-range prospects were equally distressing: see Gilkes, *Cora Crane*, Chapters 6 and 7.

[2] A mutual affection: in the last letter he ever wrote, Crane told Sanford Bennett: 'I have Conrad on my mind very much just now. Garnett does not think it likely that his writing will ever be popular outside the ring of men who write. He is poor and a gentleman and proud. His wife is not strong and they have a kid. If Garnett should ask you to help pull wires for a place on the Civil List for Conrad please do me the last favor' (14 May: Stallman, pp. 283–4).

[3] About *La Reine*: Conrad and Crane had wanted to be joint owners of this boat (Jessie Conrad, *Joseph Conrad and His Circle*, p. 74).

To Cora Crane
Text MS Columbia; Stallman 282

[letterhead: Pent Farm]
Sunday. [13 May? 1900][1]

Dear Mrs Crane.

What awful news you are giving me! And yet people given up by the doctors have been known to live for years.

Of course I will take the boat over. I didn't offer to come near your place knowing myself powerless to help you, not wishing to bring my barren sympathy and my helpless sorrow only to hinder You who are fighting the battle.

Believe, our hearts are with You. May Heaven give You strenght* and the supreme consolation of faith. I can't give you an idea how unhappy I am since I have received your letter.

Always yours

Jph. Conrad.

To Marguerite Poradowska
Text MS Yale; Rapin 174; G. & S. 103

[letterhead: Pent Farm]
16 May [1900][2]

Très Chère

Ce que je suis heureux et fier! Oui! envoyez la traduction.[3] Je brule du desir de la voir.

Moi—mieux. Jessie pas tres bien. Borys fort bien mais pas sage. Merci de details.[4] Nous irons a Bruges ou a Neuport. On verra. Facteur attend.

Toujours a Vous

Conrad

Embrassades de tout le monde.

---

[1] Stallman assigns this letter to Sunday, 13 May, just before Crane was moved from Brede Place to Dover. However, the one time that any of his doctors pronounced his case hopeless was 'around April 30' (Gilkes, *Cora Crane*, p. 250); thus the right date may be Sunday, 29 April.

[2] Year added in another hand.

[3] Of 'An Outpost of Progress', never published: for Conrad's judgment, see letter to Davray, 2 April 1902.

[4] Jessie Conrad had asked for information about Bruges in her letter of 10 May.

Translation

Very dear,
How happy and proud I am! Yes! send the translation. I'm burning to see it.
Me—better. Jessie not very well. Borys very well but naughty.
Thanks for the particulars. We shall go to Bruges or to Nieuport. We shall see.
Postman waiting.

Ever yours
Conrad

Hugs from everyone.

To John Galsworthy
Text MS Forbes; J-A, 1, 294

[letterhead: Pent Farm]
Thursday. [17 or 24 May 1900][1]

Dearest Jack
Impossible on Monday, but shall let you know soon the day of my liberation.[2]
Went to see Crane yesterday at Dover. Been with him 20 minutes. Supported move from Brede pretty well. I was awfully shocked of course and had to put on jolly manners. He may yet escape.
The Frewens[3] (owners of Brede) pay *all* his transit to the Black forest—rather more than £100. A doctor friend goes with them. It is a long goodbye to England and Stephen seems to feel it very much. And it may be for ever! He is not *too* hopeful about himself. One lung quite intact at any rate.
Do tell me about the McClure interview

Yours Ever
Conrad.

---

[1] The J-A date, 7 May, must be wrong. On his way to Germany, Crane stayed at the Lord Warden Hotel in Dover from 14 to 24 May, gathering his strength and waiting for the sea to calm. As visits were discouraged in the last few days (Stallman, p. 284), the earlier date seems likely, but in 1919 Conrad remembered seeing his friend on the last day in England (*Notes on Life and Letters*, pp. 51–2).
[2] From *Lord Jim*.   [3] Crane dedicated *Wounds in the Rain* (1900) to Moreton Frewen.

To David Meldrum
Text Blackburn 94[1]

> Pent Farm
> Stanford
> Hythe.
> 19th May 1900.

My dear Mr Meldrum.

I enclose here the letter I received from Ed'gh last night.[2] I daresay you know all about it anyhow. I wired in reply *"Think arrangement suggested judicious. Conclusion in a few days"*—both statements being true enough. I think it judicious but can't profess myself pleased. I've felt that something of the kind would have to be done, though, and I am not unreasonably upset. Now the proposal has come from Mr Blackwood the thing seems unavoidable. Perhaps the story will please. Perhaps! I would like to know what you think. I am too fond of it myself to be very hopeful. It has not been planned to stand alone. *H of D* was meant in my mind as a foil, and *Youth* was supposed to give the note. All this is foolishness—no doubt. The public does not care—can not possibly care—for foils and notes. But it cares for stories and *Jim* is as near a story as I will ever get. The title will have to be altered to *Lord Jim. A tale*—instead of *A sketch*. And yet it is a sketch! I would like to put it as *A simple tale A plain tale*—something of the sort—if possible. No matter.

I think that the conditions of production should be altered a little. I wouldn't think about it, much less say anything, if it was not a matter of self-preservation almost. I must be enabled to draw breath or I will choke. I've been gasping for months now and doing my best all the time too. The question is what Mr Blackwood will do for me? What I suggest would be this:—

Lord Jim should be considered separately of course. It will be (it seems incredible) of, apparently, 100000 words[3] or very little short of that. In fact it shall take the place really of that *second book* to follow 3 tales which

---

[1] Blackburn lists this letter and its sequel as held at Duke; the originals are not there, nor are they in NLS or the firm's archives.

[2] Blackburn prints the letter (pp. 93–4). Although not written by him, it states William Blackwood's position: with the arrival of Chapters 28–30 and part of 31, *Lord Jim* had overrun its estimated length. The novel would need another ten or so pages to complete (Conrad actually wrote another fourteen chapters); rather than appear with 'Youth' and 'Heart of Darkness', a work this size had better stand alone. Doubleday's agent also preferred separate publication. The independent *Lord Jim* should come out on 15 September, after all or most of the serial version. In order to replace *Jim*, Conrad could make up the volume of stories with one or two new ones.

[3] Finally about 130,000.

we have talked over and which was to be paid at the rate of £5 p. 1000 (serial) with a shilling royalty but *no* advance on book form.[1] However the circumstances are not the same if only for the reason it is going to appear first—and besides *Lord Jim* was not meant when we settled the terms. On the other hand it is a long story—a novel—and this, I am told, is an advantage from the publisher's point of view. What I would propose then would be that Mr Blackwood should pay me at the rate of £5 p 1000 but that of the whole sum £200† should be put as on account of a shilling royalty. This would make the serial payment (assuming 100,000 words) to be at the rate of £3 p. 1000—10/- higher than the serial rate of the short stories volume that was to be. I engage myself to furnish between 30 and 40 thousand words to complete the vol: of stories at the old rate of *£2.10* per thousand if Mr Blackwood should wish to use these serially. But as Maga has been pretty full of Conrad of late I would try to serialise them elsewhere reserving them for Mr Blackwood's vol without any further payment—naturally—since *that* volume has been already paid for.

I ask for these terms with the less hesitation because I know that Mr X . . . (pardon this discretion) would give me £200 on acc[t] of royalties for a long book.[2] Hang Mr X. The fact is I don't hesitate because if I hesitate I am lost—like many a better man; and if I AM worth anything I had rather be helped over the stile by Mr Blackwood than by any publisher in the three kingdoms. The long and the short of it is I want £300 to pay my debts (which are not great but very awful) and to go abroad for a couple of months. I fear I must go, and that soon, or I shall become a complete idiot. My nerves are like fiddle strings. I think of going to Bruges directly I deliver the last of Jim. Hueffer is going too and we shall bring two-thirds of a novel from there or the devil's in it! Should the length of *Lord Jim* not cover my demands Mr Blackwood would always have that collaboration novel[3] to fall back upon. (He said he would like to see it). But the crux is that I must have (from somewhere) the 300 in question. For *L. J.* I had already £165 I think—maybe more; (my wife is out for the day and has locked her drawer so I am not certain). I had £65 this year and fancy a 100 (or 130?) last year.[4]

Of course I am aware that Mr Blackwood may with perfect fairness return to the original plan. In that case I say—very well. Let the whole thing appear in Septb[er] or never appear. I am so utterly weary of myself

[1] Letter of 31 July 1899.
[2] The total advance on *The Rescue* from Heinemann and McClure.
[3] 'Seraphina.'   [4] For the serial rights, £65 in 1900, £120 in 1899.

(not of my work) that I verily believe I don't care. I ought to have been writing MS instead of this. There's a tidy pile ready and it seems good stuff too. Lord Jim brings me letters. From Spain to day! They take in Maga in Madrid. Where is it they don't take Maga! Believe me Always yours

Joseph Conrad.

PS I would be rather anxious to know the result of this.

———

† *The Nigger* which seems to be selling yet has brought me (at 17½%) nearly that amount.

To David Meldrum

Text Blackburn 96

[letterhead: Pent Farm]
22 May 1900

My dear Mr Meldrum.

I can easily imagine how awfully you must be bored with all these affairs; and yet my very good sir I even must have another go at you. You will perceive that I have no option and indeed I trust you are not angry with me for worrying you.

It is of course my earnest desire that you would communicate with Mr Blackwood in respect of the arrangements I propose.[1] Herewith I enclose a statement of the position as I see it; and the matter is pressing. I stated my view on a separate piece of paper so that you may forward it to Ed'gh if you judge it expedient.

And now I must go back to the *MS*. I write no letters to anybody. People think I am dead. Now the thing comes out alone I must modify the end a little bit.

Yes. Your remarks are just. The book would have been ill-balanced and I think I've good matter ("First Command"[2] especially) for the volume of *Tales*. It will turn out to be a record of personal experience purely. Just as well—maybe!

Always most gratefully yours
Jph. Conrad.

[1] In replying to the previous letter, Meldrum had taken issue with the confusing reference to a rate of £5 per 1,000 words of *Jim*. (In the present letter, Conrad clarifies his request for a rate of £3 – ten shillings more than the original agreement – and an advance of £200 on the book). Meldrum also pointed out that, because he had had no say in the expansion of *Jim* from story to novel, Blackwood might not accept the new terms. Blackwood accepted them nevertheless (Blackburn, pp. 98–100).

[2] Ancestor of *The Shadow-Line*.

Draft of arrangements and payments for Lord Jim and Volume of Tales follows.

A *Three Tales*. Conditions: £2.10 p *1000* words for serial pub and £100 ad^{vce} for a volume (of about 70000 words.)

Youth—paid for ⎫ serial appearance. (about 50000 words).
H of D—paid for ⎭

(Lord Jim was included in this arrangement.) *partly paid for* as serial. The *book form* has also been PAID FOR already.[1]

B Then we planned another book of short tales 70,000 words for which the terms were: £5 per thousand words serially. Royalty 1/- per copy.[2] *No* advance on publication.

Instead of which *Lord Jim* (of about 100000 words) is to appear as a long novel. Therefore let us leave the work A to be finished on the old conditions at a future time by one or two tales, to complete the number of words agreed upon, to make a 6/- volume. A is PAID FOR unless Mr Blackwood desires the balance of it to appear serially in *Maga* when he shall pay £2.10 per thousand of further copy.

A then remains unfinished for the time and *Lord Jim* takes the place of *B* with the following modifications of terms:—

£300 for appearance *serially* and £200 for the *book form* on acc^t of 1/- per copy royalty. Mr Blackwood on delivery of completed MS (for which I've received already payments on acc^t to the amount of nearly (or quite) £200) shall pay me £300 as balance of serial rights *and advance on book-form*. He shall publish the book at such date as he thinks best for his interests.

PS I engage myself to furnish balance of copy for Volume A within a year from Lord Jim's appearance in book form.

PS You see from the statement that in consideration of Jim being an unexpected development, I, *by no means*, ask for it to be paid at the rate of £5 per 1000 *serially*. The most I ask for is an increase of 10/- on the serial rate agreed for A. If you think that this is too much you may perhaps suggest a modification. The sum (£500) is the same (assuming 100000 words) which is important to me but £200 of it go to the royalties which is not so good for me as £500 for *serial only* even if I had to wait a year for my royalty.

As to Jim's expansion—well, I am sorry. Mr Blackwood must now forgive me and we won't let it happen again. But the story *is* good for all that.

---

[1] In February 1899.   [2] Assuming sales at five shillings a copy: letter of 31 July 1899.

To Marguerite Poradowska
Text MS Yale; Rapin 175; G. & S. 104

> [letterhead: Pent Farm]
> 1 Juin
> 1900

Très chère

Oui. J'ai reçu le manuscrit.[1] Permettez moi de le garder pendant quelques jours car en ce moment je suis fort occupé avec mon roman et je veux avoir l'esprit tout a fait libre.

Vout êtes bonne comme tout.

En toute hâte

> Toujours a Vous
>
> Conrad.

Translation

Very dear,

Yes, I have had the manuscript. Let me keep it for a few days, because at present I am very busy with my novel, and I want to be entirely free of distractions.

You are kind as ever.

In all haste

> Always yours
>
> Conrad.

To William Blackwood
Text MS NLS; Blackburn 100

> [letterhead: Pent Farm]
> 4[5] June 1900[2]

Dear Mr Blackwood.

I enclose here with many thanks a formal receipt for £100[3] received on acct of *Lord Jim*.

Poor Stephen Crane died this morning. I am too upset by the news to touch to-day upon one or two matters I wished to communicate with you about. One is as to a MS (not mine)[4] which I shall send off to M^r

---

[1] The translation of 'An Outpost of Progress'?

[2] Conrad is replying to a letter posted in Scotland on 4 June; Crane died in Germany early in the morning of 5 June.

[3] The final instalment of the £300. Meldrum had pressed Blackwood to act quickly.

[4] Galsworthy's 'A Man of Devon', which Blackwood published in a collection of stories with the same title (1901).

Meldrum on Thursday for a preliminary examination. But that will keep.

> Believe me always very faithfully
> yours
> > Jph. Conrad.

To David Meldrum
Text MS Duke; Blackburn 100

> [letterhead: Pent Farm]
> Thursday [7 June 1900][1]

Dear Mr Meldrum

I venture to send my friend's MS; Last post I had your good note and the typed matter. I hope You will enjoy Your holiday.

I've wired you of M^r B's remittance reaching me two days ago. Thanks for everything you have done for me.

The news of Stephen's death had been a shock for I did not expect it so soon—at any rate.

Our kindest regards to Mrs Meldrum and yourself

> Always yours
> > Jph Conrad.

To John Galsworthy
Text MS Forbes; Unpublished

> Pent Farm.
> 19 June 1900.

My dear Jack.

I did not want to bother you with correspondence and that is why I invaded Mrs Sauter's[2] leisure. In these influenza affairs one fears a relapse. I am inexpressibly glad to know you are out of the wood. I got nervous not being myself very well. Stupid of me.

Of course come; we wait with joy. I must tell you poor Montague is lame and an invalid in the stable for a month. An awful sell to have a lame horse. I am sorry for poor Jess. She isn't very bright either. What bothers me is how to get you from the station. Write in good time day and train so that I may try to make 'bundobast'[3] for Your transport to

---

[1] Date fixed by preceding letter.
[2] Galsworthy's sister, Blanche Lilian, married to the painter Georg Sauter. *Villa Rubein* is a fictional portrait of their marriage.
[3] Anglo-Indian: 'arrangements'.

Pent. The outlook is gloomy because poor Divers (the fly owner) is in articulo mortis and the organisation of the business gone to pieces.

So on this comparatively cheerful note I end. Were I to write anything of myself I would depress You too much. I trust in you to put some little spring into me. Heavens! Who would like to have friends like me!

Ever yours

Conrad.

Brow ague I had myself every afternoon for a month when in the Archipelago.[1] It was rather fiendish. I do hope You will get rid of it soon. I had to take to whisky—medicinally!

To William Blackwood

Text MS NLS; Blackburn 102

[letterhead: Pent Farm]
29 June 1900.

Dear Mr Blackwood.

I return agreements duly signed.[2] I would have much to say to you but the last words of Jim are waiting to be written and shall be before midnight if so God wills ...

Re Canadian proposals.[3] I should say—"*Gage*" unless Messrs: Copp Clark & C° are much better—as I know Mr Fairholm Gage's agent here and hear that he is very (?) anxious to secure the book for them.

However I am perfectly content to leave all matters in your friendly hands.

Believe me always faithfully Yours
Jph. Conrad.

---

[1] At the time of his service on the *Vidar*, plying between Singapore and Borneo? Brow ague is 'supra-orbital neuralgia of malarious origin' (*Shorter OED*).

[2] On 26 June, Blackwood sent the new contracts for *Lord Jim* and the 'Youth'/'Heart of Darkness' volume (Blackburn, p. 101).

[3] W. J. Gage & Co. and G. N. Morang & Co. had made offers for Canadian rights; Blackwood also wanted to sound out Copp, Clark & Co. Gage brought out the Canadian edition in 1900 – the first Conrad book published outside Great Britain or the United States.

To H. G. Wells

Text MS Illinois; Unpublished

[letterhead: Pent Farm]
Monday [June? 1900][1]

My dear Wells

Thanks for the vol. Chaffery is immense. The thing as a whole remarkable in its effects. The ease and the charm of execution have given moments of unalloyed pleasure. It gives a sense of the shallowness of life which yet may be made a deep hole for any of us. The light touch with which the story is fashioned is very clever. There is tact in it.

Upon the whole hurrah! These are things I want to talk over when we meet.

Affectionately Yours

J. Conrad

This is silly but is meant to express intelligent appreciation. I am stupid today.

To William Blackwood & Sons

Text MS Duke; Blackburn 102

[letterhead: Pent Farm]
9 July 1900.

Dear Sirs

Pray have the enclosed copy typed as fast as can be done; as the book is finished (I intend to bring the last pages on Thursday),[2] and I shall want urgently the whole of the end for revision. Be kind enough to let me know *where* is the last inst^l of my org^l MS? And allow me to point out that you've sent the last inst^t of typed copy to Edngh instead of forwarding it to me. The typed copy unless corrected by me is not fit to go to the printers.

I am dear Sirs
faithfully yours

Jph Conrad

Messrs: *Wm Blackwood & Sons*

---

[1] Mention of Chaffery identifies the book as *Love and Mr. Lewisham*, published in June.
[2] 9 July was a Monday. They were not finished until Saturday morning.

To Ford Madox Ford

Text MS BL Ashley 2923; Unpublished

[letterhead: Pent Farm]
Monday. [9 July 1900][1]

Dearest Ford.

I really hope to be done on Thursday and we shall arrive on Monday. I am in a state of excitement. You'll be either struck with what I am doing now or else find it beneath contempt. I don't know anything myself except that it is either hit or miss with it. Devil only knows.

I shall bring you £20 in cash francs and cheque for the balance. I shall write to Mrs Dear[2] on Thursday if I've done the trick by that day. If she can't manage I shall ask her to tell you this. Then on Fr: and Sat: you could look out for something for us—provisional if not able to achieve the permanent. If not we may catch on to a Hotel for a day or two.

As to arrangements for meals (at Mrs Dear should that come off) and so on: I fancy we had better not fetter each other (in our collective capacities). You have a help for the children and Jessie has not and is averse to having one. Let us preserve our "liberté d'allures."[3] Moreover by the time we've arrived You shall have settled down to a certain system. My (or our) constant scolding and drilling of the boy at table will "a la longue" be a horrid bore to you both. I feel it; I know it; I can't help it. We couldn't talk—nor could our wives. Let us be together in the intervals of vile (but indispensable) sensual gorging of dead matter, when we can feast on reason and drink of the flowing soul.[4] Love to You both [...] chicks.[5] Ever Yours

Jph Conrad

Pray for me these days.

---

[1] The circumstances match those of the letter to Blackwood.
[2] Proprietor of the English Pension in Bruges.
[3] 'Freedom of action.'
[4] 'The feast of reason and the flow of soul': Pope, 'To Mr. Fortescue', *Epistles and Satires of Horace Imitated.*
[5] The page is torn.

To H.-D. Davray

Text MS Yale; *L. fr.* 40

[letterhead: Pent Farm]
10 Juin [Juillet] 1900[1]

Mon cher Davray.

Le diable s'en mêle pour sûr. Je suis en train de finir un gros bouquin que j'espère (et que je dois) terminer, terminer dans deux jours d'ici. Ensuite nous partons rendre quelques visites que nous devons depuis des siècles, et puis des amis sont a nous attendre a Bruges ou je compte me reposer un mois; car a force de gâcher du papier je deviens idiot. Tout ceci, livre, visites, repos, e[s]t tellement en retard que je n'ose ni ne peux me permettre de toucher a nos plans; malgré le plus vif désir que j'ai de lâcher le sale encrier et Vous tomber sur le dos pour une bonne et longue causerie.

Quand Vous arriverez chez Wells je ne serai plus là. Je serai a m'embêter chez de braves gens en Essex[2] ou en Surrey. Mais vous manquer comme ceci c'est vraiment le comble de la guigne!

Souvent j'ai pensé a Vous travaillant dans Votre fourmillère—la-bàs; tandis que moi ici, solitaire comme une taupe, je suis a creuser, a creuser sans fin ni trève, sans jamais arriver a y voir clair.

Il faudra cependant nous re[n]contrer. Ne manquez pas de me prevenir de votre prochaine visite en Angleterre et gardez nous un jour *au moins* pour le Pent. De mon côté si je viens, comme je l'espère a Paris cette année je vous enverrai un mot d'avance.

A vous très sincèrement.

Joseph Conrad.

My dear Davray,

The devil's in it for sure. I am in the middle of ending a fat volume which I hope to (and I must) finish, finish by two days from now. Afterwards we go off to pay some visits that we've owed for ages, and then some friends are to wait for us in Bruges, where I intend to take a month's rest, because by dint of wasting paper I've turned into an idiot. All this, book, visits, rest, is so far in arrears that I neither dare nor can change our plans—in spite of my very strong desire to abandon the wretched ink-pot and descend on you for a good, long chat.

---

[1] The circumstances of this letter – a commitment to finish *Lord Jim* within two days, the imminent departure for Bruges – suggest that, not for the first time, Conrad has put the wrong month.

[2] The Hopes lived in Essex.

Again I won't be there when you come to Wells's place. I shall be boring myself at the house of some good people in Essex or in Surrey. But to miss you like this is really the height of bad luck.

I have often thought of you over there toiling away in your ant-heap; while over here, lonely as a mole, I must dig, dig without end or pause, without ever seeing the light.

We must meet, however. Don't fail to tell me in advance about your next visit to England, and save us at least a day at the Pent. For my part, if I come to Paris this year, as I hope to, I shall warn you in advance.

Yours very sincerely
Joseph Conrad

To William Blackwood
Text MS NLS; Blackburn 103

[letterhead: Pent Farm]
[14 July 1900][1]

Dear Mr Blackwood.

The last word of Lord Jim is written but before I retire to rest I must with the same impulse, the same dip of the pen as it were say a word to you.

Whatever satisfaction I have now or shall have out of the book I owe very much to you—not only in the way of material help but in the conditions which you have created for me to work in by your friendly and unwearied indulgence.

I feel I owe you also an apology—many apologies for this long work about which the only thing I am sure of is the good faith I brought to its writing. I can't say much more. I would like to express something that would not be mere banality. But I can't. I've been now for 23 hours at work and feel unable to collect my thoughts.

We should like to leave for Bruges on Wednesday next.[2] The type of the last part of MS will be sent to me here. I must live with the end for a bit. There are many places which a bit* judicious cutting would improve and so on. As there is enough copy set up to go on with I suppose I may take a little time. But it will be only a matter of few days

---

[1] This is 'the letter penned after sunrise on the fourteenth' (to Blackwood, 18 July). Meldrum wrote to Blackwood on Saturday 14 July, 'Fortunately, I was in the office this morning when Conrad called with the conclusion of *Jim*, which went off to the type-writer *instanter*. He was, of course, in great spirits' (Blackburn, p. 104).

[2] They left on Friday, 20 July.

at most. In a few hours I start for London with the last pages. I am too tired to feel either glad or sorry just now. But it is a relief of some sort.

Believe me dear Mr Blackwood

very faithfully Yours

Jph. Conrad.

To William Blackwood

Text MS NLS; Blackburn 105

[letterhead: Pent Farm]

18th July 1900.

My dear Mr Blackwood.

I hope you'll find this less incoherent than the letter penned after sunrise on the fourteenth. Thanks very much for the wire which I found on my return home yesterday. At once I posted the corrected proofs of Ch: 28 to 30 (revise) and 31 to 35 (first proof) rather badly cut about—which is not altogether my fault as the type of that part had been sent off straight to Scotland without passing through my hands.

From end of 30 to end of 35 will make (unless I am mistaken) another instalment, and the next (Chap 36 en seq.) will conclude the story in the October issue.[1]

It seems to me that *Lord Jim* as title for the book is meagre—perhaps misleading? Could not a sub-title be invented? I am hammering the sorry remnant of my brain without being able to get sound or sense out of it. Perhaps even thus *Lord Jim: A romance* in one line would be better. I feel it's a poor suggestion.[2]

Another matter, if it is not too late already, has occurred to me. Would it not be better seeing the form of the novel (personal narrative from a third party as it were) to dispense with the word *Chapter* throughout the book, leaving only the Roman numerals. After all, these divisions (some of them very short) are not chapters in the usual sense each carrying the action a step further or embodying a complete episode. I meant them only as pauses—rests for the reader's attention while he is following the development of *one* situation, only *one* really from beginning to end. I fear however that it may be now too late to make the alteration.[3]

Mr Meldrum has told me that a story by my friend Galsworthy ('John

[1] Eventually, Chapters 31–5 in September, 36–40 in October, 41–5 in November.
[2] The Blackwood edition calls it *A Tale*; the Doubleday, McClure, *A Romance*.
[3] It was.

Sinjohn)'[1] is in your hands; my friendship has of course nothing to do with my opinion of the work; I didn't think it unworthy (on literary grounds) of being submitted to you.

Believe me, dear Mr Blackwood,

always yours faithfully

Jph Conrad.[2]

To William Blackwood

Text MS NLS; Blackburn 106

[letterhead: Pent Farm]

19th July 1900

Dear Mr Blackwood.

I am in receipt of your very kind letter enclosing a cheque for *£100* on acct of *Lord Jim*.[3]

I think that you shall have the typed copy (corrected) by the end of this month. I am sending my address in Bruges to Mr Meldrum and if there is no delay in typing [t]here shall be no delay in correcting.

I am exceedingly unwilling to cut about a proof. I prefer correcting the type where I can interline, erase and slash out without the feeling of causing extra work to be done.

Indeed my dear Sir I couldn't adequately express my appreciation of your unvarying and much tried kindness.

The end of Lord Jim in accordance with a meditated resolve is presented in a bare almost bald relation of matters of fact. The situation—the problem if you will—of that sensitive nature has been already commented upon, illustrated and contrasted. It is my opinion that in the working out of the catastrophe psychologic disquisition should have no place. The reader ought to know enough by that time. I enlarge a little upon the new character which is introduced (that of Brown the desperate adventurer) so as to preserve the sense of verisimi-

---

[1] *Villa Rubein* and *A Man of Devon* (in which the story appeared) were the last to be written under this pseudonym.

[2] A pencilled note by Blackwood follows: he sees that the serial must run beyond October and asks advice about the title.

[3] Meldrum told Blackwood that Conrad could not leave for Belgium until he had a cheque. With a very friendly letter, Blackwood sent £100 'leaving a balance of £115 still to be paid you on account when the completion of the story [the corrected typescript] reaches me. I shall then have paid you . . . £300 for the serial rights and £200 in advance of the royalties on the book' (Blackburn, pp. 104–5). Neither Conrad nor Blackwood chose to point out that the serial payment was for a work of 100,000 words; Conrad wrote 130,000 and should have received another £90.

litude and for the sake of final contrast; but all the rest is nothing but a relation of events—strictly, a narrative.

Pardon this egotism. My head is full of this thing yet.

> Believe me, dear Mr Blackwood,
> very faithfully yours
> Joseph Conrad.

To John Galsworthy

Text MS Forbes; J-A, 1, 295

> [letterhead: Pent Farm]
> Friday. [20 July 1900][1]

Dearest Jack

We are off in an hour—at last, and shall be back on the 16 or 17 Aug. to give their holidays to various children.

I've written to Blackwood mainly for the purpose of insinuating amongst other matters that a quick decision as to your story would be welcome. He has your address; but hurry of any sort is not in the traditions of the 'House'.

Meldrum professes great admiration for the *M[an] of D[evon]*. It is evident to me he has been struck plumb-center,* and I am glad to find him discriminative. This does not settle the question of publication, but his opinion has a certain weight with M^r B'wood.

The end of *L.J.* has been pulled off with a steady drag of 21 hours. I sent wife and child out of the house (to London) and sat down at 9 am, with a desperate resolve to be done with it. Now and then I took a walk round the house out at one door in at the other. Ten-minute meals. A great hush. Cigarette ends growing into a mound similar to a cairn over a dead hero. Moon rose over the barn looked in at the window and climbed out of sight. Dawn broke, brightened. I put the lamp out and went on, with the morning breeze blowing the sheets of MS all over the room. Sun rose. I wrote the last word and went into the dining room. Six o'clock. I shared a piece of cold chicken with Escamillo[2] (who was very miserable and in want of sympathy having missed the child dreadfully all day). Felt very well only sleepy; had a bath at seven and at 8.30 was on my way to London.

Same day we journeyed to Slough and saw the children.[3] They are

---

[1] The only Friday between the end of *Jim* and the arrival in Belgium.
[2] Borys's dog, named after the toreador in *Carmen*, a present from Stephen Crane.
[3] The George sisters at the convent.

improved, very much liked, very happy. That's a success. From there we rushed straight on to the poor Hopes where we slept two nights. Yesterday morning cheque from B'wood arrived and today we are off to join the disconsolate and much enduring Hueffer. Address: *4: Rue Anglaise Bruges.*

I am still well. Jessie too, notwithstanding the heat. Borys in great form but exceedingly naughty except when actually travelling when he is simply angelic.

This is all that will go on this piece of paper. Our love.

Ever Yours

Conrad.

To William Blackwood

Text MS NLS; Blackburn 107

Hotel de la Plage
Knocke-sur-Mer
Belgium
23^d July 1900

Dear Mr Blackwood

The enclosed letter[1] written on the eve of our departure from the Pent got itself carried off here in my writing case.

I don't know what you must have thought of me?

Besides your letter that to Mr Meldrum (giving my address) has been also found here by my horrified wife. No wonder I haven't got yet the type of *L. J.* It is a stupid accident. First thing to-morrow morning I shall wire my address to 37 Paternoster Row[2] and I've no doubt that by the end of this month the corrected copy shall reach your hands.

Pray accept my apologies for this delay in acknowledging your good letter and the cheque.

Always very faithfully Yours

Joseph Conrad.

PS We've found Bruges too hot so came on to this little seaside place

---

[1] i.e. that of 19 July; the letter to Meldrum has not survived.
[2] Blackwood's London office.

To R. B. Cunninghame Graham
Text MS Dartmouth; Watts 135

[letterhead:
Grand Hôtel de la Plage
DIGUE
KNOCKE-SUR-MER]
In a hurry to catch post
Belgium.
28 July 1900

Très cher ami

Yesterday I dispatched a letter to Morrocco,* with apologies and news and a lot of loose chat which is no loss to you.[1]

Jim finished on the 16th inst.[2] At last. It is going to appear in book form (by itself) in October.

I started upon a small holiday at once even before the last inst' of Jim had been typed and corrected. I shall do that here.

Youth, Heart of darkness and some story of the same kind which I shall write before long are to form a vol of Tales which (unless forbidden) it is my intention to dedicate to You.[3]

My brain reduced to the size of a pea seems to rattle about in my head. I can't rope in a complete thought; I am exhausted mentally and very depressed.

Pity I miss you. It would have done my heart good to see and hear you—you the most alive man of the century.

I am awfully sickened by "public affairs". They made me positively ill in Febr^y last. Ten days in bed and six weeks of suspended animation.

Drop me a line here. We return to the Pent on the 15th of August. I *must* see you when you come to London again. Jessie's kindest regards. Borys (who's grown very ugly) remembers you perfectly and still wears the heart. Ever Yours

Conrad.

---

[1] And is lost to us.   [2] Really 14 July.

[3] See letter to Blackwood, 12 February 1899; in the end, *Typhoon* (a Heinemann title) was dedicated to Graham and *Youth* to Jessie Conrad. Writing to Meldrum about Garnett (1 September 1900), Conrad again tried to bridge the political chasm between Blackwood and a radical friend.

To John Galsworthy

Text MS Forbes; J-A, 1, 296

[letterhead:
Grand Hôtel de la Plage]
11 Aug 1900

Dearest Jack.

Pardon me not answering your letter. The boy has been very ill indeed—dysentery; and the danger of a fatal termination has not been over till yesterday. Jess showed lots of pluck. The poor little chap is a miserable object to behold. As soon as he has picked up a little strenght* we are coming back. I had enough of this holiday.[1]

Fortunately I had done with Jim before the boy fell ill. The corrected type went off five days ago and the very next day I had to devote all my energies to nursing, along with Jess, who, all the same, had to bear the brunt of it as You may imagine.

The whole Hotel was in a commotion; Dutch Belgians and French prowled about the corridor on the lookout for news. Women with babies of their own offered to sit up, and a painter of religious subjects Paulus by name[2] rose up and declared himself ready to do likewise. Elsie Hueffer helped a bit but poor H. did not get much collaboration out of me this tide.[3]

Well, it's over. We shall try to be home by the 20th. I've done nothing except as I said getting the end of Jim fit for print. There was a good deal to do to it as a matter of fact.

The plan of your story is excellent. I can't enlarge just now, only this is certain that such a story shall want an immense amount of execution. You must make the personal note very strong. Delighted to hear M^{te} *Carlo* finished.[4] I can't get any news from B'wood as to the *M of D*. The delay is a good sign. They refused something of Hueffer's in four days. They were 3 weeks accepting *Karain*.[5]

Always yours

Conrad.

---

[1] 'It was a nightmarish time, that terrible August we spent in Knocke': Jessie Conrad, *Joseph Conrad and His Circle*, p. 71. They returned on 18 August (Jessie Conrad to Cora Crane, 25 August, MS Columbia).

[2] Francis Petrus Paulus, born in Detroit, 1862, but long settled in Bruges – he specialised in picturesque views of ancient towns.

[3] Nor could he do much work of his own. Ford describes the ordeal in *Joseph Conrad*, pp. 219–29.

[4] Renamed 'A Knight', it appeared in the collection *A Man of Devon* (1901).

[5] Closer to nine: *Letters*, 1, pp. 356, 364.

To David Meldrum
Text MS Duke; Blackburn 108

Pent Farm.
1 Sep^t 1900.

My dear Mr Meldrum.

Thanks for your note; I was very sorry I couldn't see you, but I came up rather unexpectedly and there was no time to warn You.

I've dispatched to Edinburgh the last Maga proofs of *Jim*; a good bit cut about but undoubtedly bettered. I am glad *that* at least is off my mind as I am blessed with enough worries to prevent me from going to sleep.

The day I came up I ran accross* McArthur[1] whom I did not know before. He seemed to be animated by most friendly sentiments towards Your servant. I was at lunch with Edward Garnett when he turned up—and this brings me to one of the objects of this letter.

E. Garnett thinks of publishing (in due time) a vol: of criticism. It will be something fresh and intelligent too—and it is about time intelligence had its say in those matters. What he would like to do would be to publish very soon, what is intended for a sort of introduction to such a volume, as a paper in some magazine. This would be a general view, a sort of philosophy of criticism as he conceives it illustrated by examples (from Lyolf Tolstoi[2] to Joseph Conrad I believe) giving his idea of the relation between literature and life in their modern conditions. A large order for 6000 words. Still the man is quite capable of it; and I am sure there will be no platitudes in it whatever amount of sound truth there may be. Do you think he would have any chance of being given room in Maga?

For myself I don't see why not. Whatever his political and social opinions may be[3] (and he is not one to obtrude them in questions of art) his attitude towards literature is, one may say, aristocratic. This obviously is not the same thing as conservative—still. And, at any rate, it would be a fresh utterance. If the idea commended itself to you and you were to drop him a friendly line he would call on you and explain exactly what it is he wishes to say—and thus you could judge better whether he would be acceptable to Mr Blackwood.[4]

I haven't heard from Mr Blackwood lately. Do you have any idea whether the "Man of Devon" is accepted or rejected? Jack Galsworthy

---

[1] London agent of Doubleday, McClure.   [2] Leo Nikolayevich?
[3] Anarchist and pro-Boer.
[4] See letters to Blackwood, 3 and 26 August 1901.

has been down to see me since my return and I rather think the poor fellow is worrying a bit about it. He finished another thing called *The Cosmopolitan* quite as good as the *Man of Devon* but a little shorter.[1] There's stuff in the chap.

Now as to myself. I must make a fresh start without further delay. I think of writing something that would be suitable for the vol: of Tales. I would like to know whether Mr Blackwood would wish to serialise that too (First Command would be the title probably).[2] The fact is I could I think place it elsewhere (especially after *L. Jim* comes out) at an advantageous rate and I think I shall be ready in about six weeks. Of course were Mr Blackwood to take it I wouldn't expect immediate publication, but I would expect (can't help myself) immediate payment. I would also—supposing the story completed the vol:—beg that the book should not be published in the Spring. My collaboration story[3] shall appear in March and the two would clash.

If Jim has any selling success (which I doubt) I would have a clear road to run after the end of the *Rescue*. Otherwise I can see I shall have a difficult existence before me. Sometimes I feel utterly crushed at the prospect; and yet I can not but feel that I've been exceptionally fortunate in the appreciation my work has met with, and in the friendliness and generosity of my publishers. Surely if I go under I shan't have the divine consolation of railing bitterly at the unkindness of mankind. This, as you perceive, is a serious disadvantage.

Anyhow I shall try to swim as long as I am able. My wife joins me in kind regards to Mrs Meldrum and yourself. Believe me yours always.

Jph. Conrad.

PS Will you forgive me if I put off wiping out my indebt[ed]ness to you till I get my Canadian rights advance?
PPS Does Tauchnitz take up the books published by the Messrs. Blackwood. I should like to place my Jim in Germany with Tauchnitz.[4] Unwin always managed that for me (so he said at least), or is it Tauchnitz himself who approaches the author or the publishers?

---

[1] Another name for 'A Knight': Conrad had not yet seen the finished story.
[2] There are no more references in the Meldrum or Blackwood correspondence to this prototype of *The Shadow-Line*. As the story of a personal crisis, it would have kept good company with 'Youth' and 'Heart of Darkness'.
[3] *The Inheritors*.
[4] Tauchnitz did not bring out *Lord Jim* until 1927. For Conrad's dealings with this immensely successful English-language publisher, see *Letters*, 1, p. 298.

To Mabel Reynolds

Text J-A, 1, 297

Pent Farm,
5th Sept. 1900

Dear Mrs. Reynolds,[1]

The MS. heralded by your letter arrived this morning. I've had the time to read it.[2] It is wonderfully well done: technically and in the clearness of the idea it is superior to the *Villa*.[3] Jack is making giant strides; there is in his latest work,—notwithstanding the first person form,—a truly artistic aloofness even more pronounced than in the *Villa*. He is coming on! It is for me a wonderful example of what a determined singleness of purpose can achieve when there is a solid basis of a remarkable talent that I verily believe will go very far,—practically as far as he chooses to push it.

That I have detected the existence of that talent, when in the nature of things it could not be very obvious, I shall always remember with pride, but in all conscience I must disclaim the credit you give me of being of help to him.[4] One needs to be a very exceptional person to be of real use to his fellow men. I've certainly talked, but had I never existed someone else would have found the same things to say,—though perhaps not with the same loving care for his promise. That much I may admit without self-deception.

Recognition shall come. Strictly speaking, what people think does not matter,—and yet everything is in that. I am afraid he can never look forward to other than limited appreciation.[5] That he shall have it I feel certain,—and even the other kind is possible too. I say this deliberately, having my reasons for such a hope both of the artistic and also "human" order. But they are too many to be set down at length here.

With kindest regards to your husband[6] and yourself, believe me, dear Mrs. Reynolds, your most obedient and faithful servant.

---

[1] The younger of Galsworthy's sisters, born 1871. In 1936, she published *Memories of John Galsworthy*. One of Ted Sanderson's sisters recalled Lilian and Mabel Galsworthy as 'well educated and very "Arty" . . . They scarcely spoke above a whisper, and were very serious. They were good linguists, and never used slang': Catherine Dupré, *John Galsworthy* (New York, 1976), p. 30.

[2] 'The Cosmopolitan': see preceding and following letters.   [3] *Villa Rubein*, a novel.

[4] Although the early correspondence is lost, their friendship went back to the voyage on the *Torrens* in 1893. Conrad read his work and helped him find publishers: see, e.g., *Letters*, 1, p. 341.

[5] In view of his Nobel Prize and copious sales, one could say that Galsworthy had more success than Conrad with the contemporary public – but less with critical posterity.

[6] Tom Reynolds, a musician.

To John Galsworthy

Text MS Forbes; Unpublished

[Pent Farm]
Sunday. [9 September 1900][1]

Dearest Jack.

I did not notice that your first letter did say 2 o'clock. However if it does not shock you very much let it be one or soon after instead so that we can have a little longer time. I shall come with Garnett.

The Cosmopolitan is now in Hueffer's hands. My dear fellow the sketch is very fine—in tone, in expression, in conception; and fine too in innumerable touches that are born of artistic insight. I am delighted with it; I am—I am grateful to you for it.

Now go and do even better.

The *Villa* is in the hands of Garnett. He shall no doubt talk to you about it. H[ueffer] has not written to me yet. He seemed touched by your appreciation of his verse.[2]

I've pointedly asked Meldrum to find out B'w's intentions as to *M of D*.

Au revoir. Ever Yours

Conrad

To Helen Sanderson

Text MS Yale; Unpublished

The Pent.
Stanford N^r Hythe
9th Sept 1900.

My dear Mrs Sanderson.

I've only just learned that you are returning to Elstree and that Ted is returning home.[3] I won't offer any lame excuses for my long silence; even my quiet life I find almost too distracting so that I am not always quite responsible for my actions—which are mostly misdeeds wearing often an ugly look but not so black as they seem. I would have written no doubt (for my memory is not paralysed if my hand often is) had I not been in receipt of indirect news of you and the babies. You were

---

[1] Conrad asked Meldrum about 'A Man of Devon' on 1 September and received the MS of 'The Cosmopolitan' on 5 September: these circumstances suggest the following Sunday.

[2] Hueffer published *Poems for Pictures* in 1900.

[3] Only temporarily: because of Ted's health, the Sandersons spent several years in the Transvaal and then moved to Kenya.

well—and that was all that could be expected while Ted was away from his fireside.

And now we both allow ourselves to think with delight of your happiness in re-union; and may its first priceless flush last, enduring valiantly the assaults of comparatively petty but wearing—oh! so wearing—troubles. Anyway now they'll be easier to bear when you can meet them shoulder to shoulder—all the four of you.[1] Quite a little army. Let it be named the Ever-victorious in the face of life's cares which are a pertinacious legion—alas!—as we all well know.

I won't pretend to ignorance as to the state of affairs. I've been biting my thumbs at my uselessness to my friends. That's all I could bite. I haven't barked because my bark is no better than my bite, and I made no sound because I didn't think that my well-meant howling would have cheered you much.

When do you expect Ted? Perhaps soon? This week? I do not ask; I speculate with as much excitement as the return of any living man may awaken in my breast. I don't deserve that you should answer this letter. I do not ask and do not even hope. I've no more taste for coals on fire upon my head than the next man. I just speculate joyfully and when he *has* returned I shall know through my intelligence department. Then in time—in time—I may even hear from either of you. Meantime I shall be at rest and as much with you at heart as the best correspondent of them all.

When we heard of the boy I had a great mind to cable congratulations to Ted. Finally I decided upon a letter and I am glad now because I should have, as likely as not, cabled to East London.[2] Why? I don't know—unless that I've been during the writing of my lame book mad for all practical purposes. The letter has gone there I fear—it dawns upon me—or perhaps to Durban. There is just a chance that I did sanely put Port Eli[izabe]th on the envelope. But I don't know. Nobody knows. Jessie had not looked over the letters that morning; the old lady who runs our post office can't remember by this time; rather thinks there was no letter for S. Africa at all.

These are humiliating confessions. Sometimes I fancy I am breaking up mentally. I've been much worried this year. First illness; afterwards the death of poor Stephen Crane upset me horribly delaying my work, and all the time Maga's next number hanging over my head. Yet I've written 120000 words in ten months; (such as the words are). I finished in July and felt limp done up, dazed, like a man waking up from a

---

[1] Mrs Sanderson had recently given birth to a son, Ian.   [2] In South Africa.

nightmare. We went abroad and then Borys fell ill. We've nearly lost him. Since our return Jess has been on the rack with neuralgia; the after result of anxiety I suppose. She rejoices with all her heart at the lifting up of *your* anxiety. My heart is lighter than it has been for many a month now.

My love to husband, wife and children. I know that you and Ted never doubt that I am always yours affectionately.

Jph. Conrad.

PS My affec^te regards to Mrs Sanderson[1] and to such members of the family as have not cast me out and you can get at.

To Ford Madox Ford
Text MS Yale; Unpublished

[letterhead: Pent Farm]
[mid-September ? 1900][2]

Dear Ford.

Here's the chap. I am at work and beastly seedy with cold, cough, piles and a derangement of the bowels. No doubt paralysis isn't far off.

Arranged with Pawling to pub^sh *Inheritors early* spring. Very early. I reckon Febr. They want to give B'wood's publications a sort of start. Bless you all

J.C.

To John Galsworthy
Text MS POSK; Danilewicz 10

[letterhead: Pent Farm]
Thursday. [13 September 1900][3]

Dearest Jack.

We talked of you with Garnett and he was struck with the *M of D.* much more than it is in his nature to show to the author himself.

In Zachary there is just the lack of some one illustrative detail. Plenty of *telling* ones, but there is somewhere one—perhaps not so telling, but as

---

[1] Ted's mother.

[2] Type six letterhead, whose first dated use is 19 September; up to 9 September, Conrad wrote on blank sheets. He mentioned a March publication of *The Inheritors* to Meldrum on 1 September and would not have kept Ford in the dark for long.

[3] On 9 September, Conrad promised a luncheon with Garnett. This letter reports what was said after Galsworthy left.

it were, bringing him within reach of the hand that is missing and is, as a matter of fact, missed.

This I took to be the essence of G's criticism developed in his talk with me. I am glad you like G.

Won't you come down on Sat: or Sund: Jess thinks you will. I don't want to worry you but it seems ages since You've been. I want to see what You've done. I've been seedy and low. I've worked too; trying for a new manner. I would say more but no space.

Ever Yours

J Conrad.

To J. B. Pinker
Text MS Berg; Unpublished

[letterhead: Pent Farm][1]

19 Sept 1900

Dear Mr Pinker

Your letter found here my collaborator Mr Ford M. Hueffer and this circumstance allows me to answer your proposal with the suggestion that you should take in hand a joint work of ours which is nearing completion.[2] Whether this is what Constables want I don't know but our meaning is that you should handle that stuff with a free hand: that is *serialise it* and arrange for book form.

We could let you have 14 chap^{rs} out of twenty the work contains, for a specimen. The rest shall be out of hand in Dec^{er} for certain.[3] It is a story of adventure relating to the first 20 years of 19th century.

As to my own singlehanded work I can't say anything nor hold out any hopes. I wish that in Am: you would give McClure the first chance. The title of the book is *Seraphina*; action in West Indies, Havana and England. It concerns itself with the last of the pirates in those parts. The hero is English.

Would you let me know how it strikes you. Yours faithfully

Jph. Conrad.

PS The serialising is *the important* part.

---

[1] First dated use of letterhead type six.

[2] The saw him on 3 October (telegram Berg). Conrad rejected an earlier overture from Pinker on 23 August 1899.

[3] *Romance* was finished 10 March 1902, but then, for the sake of Pinker's luckless endeavours to place it as a serial, Conrad and Ford had to set about heavy cutting. The final version has 34 chapters.

To John Galsworthy

Text MS Forbes; Unpublished

[letterhead: Pent Farm]
19th Sept 1900

Dearest Jack.

This is well. Hoch! for Morrah.[1]

Why I am so late is because Jess forgot to post my original letter. This is written in its place. On consideration: Yes. Try B.'wood if you mean to try him for book form publishing. As to *M of D*. it occurs to me it would do for the Bampton Mag. (formerly Chapman's) O. Crawfurd is the editor[2]—or was. Hueffer however thinks it no good.

I am drooping still. Working at Seraphina. Bosh! Horrors!

Ever Yours

Conrad.

To J. B. Pinker

Text MS Berg; Unpublished

[letterhead: Pent Farm]
8th Oct 1900.

Dear Mr Pinker.

This word is to inform You that you shall have *two* stories from me to place serially, of which one shall probably be ready by the 15th inst. It is not the story I spoke* you about; it is nothing so horrible and deals with a lot of Chinamen coolies and a few seamen on board a steamer in a gale of wind in the China Seas.[3] Its title is *Typhoon* and length as far as I can see 12000 words. Why however I mention it now is because it struck me casually that it is quite the thing that finds room in Xmas numbers. I may be too late with the stuff by this time, for that purpose, but here's the suggestion.

The other story shorter and much more horrible[4] shall be finished early in Nov^{er}. I fancy I can do it in about 5000 words.[5] I'll forward it to you in due course.

And now I go back to my MS.

Believe me faithfully yours

Jph. Conrad.

[1] Unidentified.

[2] In 1897, Oswald Crawfurd had thought of accepting 'The Return' for *Chapman's Magazine of Fiction* (*Letters*, 1, p. 394).

[3] First proposed in a letter to Meldrum, 14 February 1899, finished January 1901.

[4] 'Falk', a confession of cannibalism.

[5] The stories came to about 25,000 words each.

To R. B. Cunninghame Graham

Text MS Dartmouth; Watts 137

[letterhead: Pent Farm]
10th Oct 1900.

Très cher ami.

I know I am a beast. I've read Cruz Alta four days ago. C'est tout simplement *magnifique*. I knew most of the sketches, in fact nearly all, except Cruz Alta itself.[1]

I shall write you about them in a few days. I am oppressed by the sense of my scoundrelism. This is only to let you know that I am writing by this post to P[awling] telling him to send me 20 pounds which I shall forward to you at once as soon as I get the cheque.

I've been in bed ill and hopeless. Now I am tottering about and trying to write.

Don't cast me out utterly—but anyhow ever yours

J Conrad

To S. S. Pawling

Text MS Heinemann; Unpublished

[letterhead: Pent Farm]
10th Oct^{er} 1900

My dear Pawling.

I just got a letter from a man you know. I can't and mustn't say more. I am awfully sorry to strike you again but I am forced (really) to ask you for a cheque for *£20* either on acc/t of *Inheritors* or a short story vol. whichever you like to make it. (NB. *Inheritors we* had *£30* on acct. of £100. £15 each. This 20 would be out of my share of the balance of *70* when the time comes).

I wouldn't say anything if the matter was not distressing.[2]

I am a precious acquaintance am I not?

Always Yours

Jph Conrad.

---

[1] A long reminiscence of frustration in a remote Brazilian town, it appeared for the first time in *Thirteen Stories* (1900). For its possible influence on *Nostromo*, see Watts, p. 38.

[2] Its nature is unknown. Graham had just had to sell off his ancestral home – he left it for good on 6 October – and was under great mental stress.

To David Meldrum

Text MS Duke; Blackburn 111

[letterhead: Pent Farm]
Thursday. [11 October 1900][1]

My dear Mr Meldrum.

I've been beastly seedy again. The fact is I ought to have a winter out of England. So the doc. says.

Still I've been working. Would you send me back the specimen of the story I've left with you. I want to look at it and perhaps expunge a par. or two.

Upon the whole I hardly think it would be worthy of Maga. But the end is not yet (though it is not far) and it's impossible to say till the thing is done.

Our kindest regards

Ever Yours

Jph. Conrad.

To David Meldrum

Text MS Duke; Blackburn 112

[letterhead: Pent Farm]
17 Oct 1900

My dear Mr Meldrum.

Pardon the delay in answering. I've been in bed.

I would like to come, if able, which I hope.

Would you let me know the day?

May I ask for 4 more copies of *Jim* which I wish to send abroad. One is for my German translator[2] and the others for relations.

When coming must I bring sable garments?[3] I know Mrs Meldrum would let me off the conventional disguise but it is better to be sure.

My wife's kind regards.

Always Yours

Jph Conrad

PS. The MS Typhoon to hand. Thanks.

---

[1] The nearest Thursday to 17 October, when Conrad acknowledged the return of 'Typhoon'.
[2] A translation appeared in 1927.   [3] Evening clothes.

To David Meldrum

Text MS Duke; Blackburn 110

[letterhead: Pent Farm]
31 Oct. 1900[1]

My dear Mr Meldrum.

Very many thanks for the cuttings. I had a letter from E'gh with details as to the start of the book in the way of subscription. It isn't exactly like Marie Corelli's[2] but let us hope it will improve.

Could you tell me whether my advance from Canada (£30) is to come through Mr Blackwood? I want it pretty badly since I've not yet finished the *Typhoon* which is to prolong my wretched existence. That infernal story does not seem to come off somehow. Meantime the Canadian dollars would be welcome. I can't let the pony starve. I can't explain to him that it is because of my high principles in story writing. And could you perhaps give me an idea how long one has to wait.

The M[anchester] G[uardian]'s notice is good.[3] The D[aily] Chr[onicle] notice is good too[4]—should say best for selling. I do want to write something that would be *really* good.

I ought to have written to you before but on my return[5] I was distracted with Hueffer. When he went away I was half dead and crawled into bed for two days.

Always Yours

Js Conrad.

---

[1] Blackburn misreads the date as 3 October, an impossibility given the reviews cited below.
[2] The sensational novelist's.
[3] 29 October, reprinted in *Critical Heritage*, pp. 111–13. The nameless reviewer likes Conrad's artistic energy and originality; the book makes 'a whole greatly conceived and finely executed'.
[4] This reviewer (29 October) has less to say about the novel's artistic merits: 'The story itself takes you far away from the triviality of literary coteries, and the mean little streets of cities.' It is 'a strong, sincere and reticent piece of work, a human document if ever there was one'.
[5] From London. On Wednesday, 24 October, Meldrum gave a dinner-party at the Garrick Club; among the guests were Conrad, George Blackwood, and Stephen Gwynn. 'I would have asked Buchan', Meldrum reported, 'but remembered Conrad's violent antipathy to his work' (Blackburn, p. 113).

To Edward Garnett
Text MS Colgate; G. 170

[letterhead: Pent Farm]
Friday. [2 November 1900][1]

Dearest E.

What Meldrum says is this:

He is most anxious to see (what he calls) your essay in criticism but lately he was greatly annoyed by having one or two things he sent to E'gh refused. He thinks it deplorable to ask a man for stuff, then have it fired back after 3 weeks, or more.

Consequently were You to send anything he would be delighted and do all he can with alacrity but says he—I am unwilling to ask E. G. in so many words and then hear that his work has been refused.

As to George B'wood[2] from few words I've exchanged with him I fancy the idea has a fearful fascination for him. They step delicately round you as though you were a box of dynamite, they would like to pick up but daren't. It's most impressive. If I talk much more about you with that lot I'll get frightened myself. It seems to me you do not realise this extraordinary prestige you possess—the prestige of a quiescent bomb about whose deadly quality there is no doubt whatever. All these priests of imbecile idols seem to think that you may go off—if given a chance—and shatter their commodious temple to pieces.

May you do so! To me you are not a bomb—you are a righteous club which I imagine forever suspended over my head. And I don't think you realise either how much this conception of E. G. influences the course of my existence.

If you've written to me about *L J* keep back your letter for a week. I am in a state bordering on distraction. Most unhappy about it and yet idiotically exalted. I want to settle down before I hear what you have to say—for to me it is your voice that really matters.

Ever Yours

Jph. Conrad.

---

[1] Here Conrad asks Garnett to delay his comments on *Lord Jim* by a week; by 12 November he had seen them. 9 November is too close to that date, and on 26 October, two days after the talk with George Blackwood, Conrad had Ford to contend with (see preceding letter).

[2] William's nephew, a member of the firm.

To John Galsworthy
Text MS Forbes; Unpublished

[letterhead: Pent Farm]
Friday. [2 November 1900][1]

Dearest Jack

Thanks for your letter. We expect You on Sunday.

Hueffer has been here and we talked of you. H said some intelligent things about *Villa Rubein*.[2]

I am informed that *A Knight* is gone to Edinburgh on the initiative of young George B'wood who came to London the other day and read the story, himself. Meldrum was very much upset when *M of D* was sent back to You. M considers *M of D* as superior to the *Knight*—as it were in *theme*—an opinion in which I share.

Bring MS when You come.

Ever Yours

Jph. Conrad

To William Blackwood
Text MS NLS; Blackburn 113

[letterhead: Pent Farm]
7th Nov. 1900.

My dear M[r] Blackwood.

Many thanks for the Cinque Ports[3] which came to-day as a most agreeable surprise.

In the matter of outward characteristics the book has substance, appearance an air of sober finish which to me is very pleasing. As to the inside—Hyde's art is undeniable[4] and is done justice to, in a remarkably successful manner. Of the letter-press I had always a good opinion. Hueffer's talent has been from the first sympathetic to me. Throughout, his feeling is true and its expression genuine with ease and moderation. He does not stand on his head for the purpose of getting a new and striking view of his subject. Such a method of procedure may be in favour nowadays but I prefer the old way, with the feet on the ground.

---

[1] George Blackwood was in London on 24 October, 'the other day'. Conrad would not have encouraged a visit on 28 October, when he was either sick or still playing host to Ford; 'Sunday' must be 4 November.

[2] For his comments, see *Letters of Ford Madox Ford*, ed. Richard M. Ludwig (Princeton U.P., 1965), pp. 10–14.

[3] Ford's book on the old Kent and Sussex towns (one of the ports was Hythe, near the Pent); just published by Blackwood in an edition of 525 three-guinea copies.

[4] William Hyde, the illustrator.

Neither does he tear his hair with enthusiasm and paint his Ports red; but there is—it seems to me—a good deal of force in his quiet phrasing. His facts I believe to be right and his theories have some authority to back them and at any rate are no worse—I believe—than many theories of all sorts that born yesterday jostle us to-day, and shall fall to pieces to-morrow.

Upon the whole the criticism in the excellent last N° of Maga[1] is fair and in the main judicious.

I had the pleasure of dining with Mr George Blackwood a few days ago, and was very happy to hear that your health was good. I trust we shall have a merciful winter. Even now, after dire experience, it seems to me impossible that a little cold or a little more or less wet should affect one's efficiency and even happiness. I can't forget the days when 'climate' did not exist for me as long as there was enough air to breathe and not too much wind to keep my feet.

Believe me, dear Mr Blackwood,
very faithfully yours
Jph. Conrad.

To John Galsworthy
Text MS Forbes; J-A, 1, 297

[letterhead: Pent Farm]
7 Nov 1900.

Dearest Jack.

I was so touched by your letter! Believe me I was, though I did not answer it at once. Indeed it is very difficult to answer such a message from the very force of the emotions it awakens. I thought I was very fortunate to get such a response for my work. You've done so much for me and in so many ways that I have felt myself silenced a long time ago—but never have you done so much for me as when you wrote that letter.

I wanted to write to you about Your book;[2] that is really one of the reasons why [I] had not acknowledged your letter—which I could do if I couldn't answer it with adequate expression. But my dear Jack I've been in such a state of wretchedness and worry that I could not find three words that would hang together. You know how paralyzed one is sometimes—and then we had talked—I had tried to talk—of the book so many times that it seemed to have become part of me—that part of belief

---

[1] A long review of Ford's book in the November issue. [2] *Villa Rubein.*

and thought so intimate that it cannot be put into speech as if it could not live apart from one's conscious self.[1]

The preliminary note in the *Academy*[1] was at least decent. 'Sense of style and eye for character'. That's something—and not a little thing to have come home to a casual reviewer. Now what we want is to get the *A* to get out a review which would have at least that amount of intelligence and discrimination. Lucas wrote to me that he no longer reviews for the *A* unless books of verse. I am afraid they are awfully crowded there is such a rush of fiction which had been held back by the Krüger–Chamberlain combination.[2]

How are You? When are you coming? My flesh is weary and my spirit sinks. But I shan't treat you to any of that. Ever Yours.

Conrad.

To Edward Garnett
Text MS Free; J-A, 1, 298; G. 172

[letterhead: Pent Farm]
12 Nov 1900

Dearest E.

You are great and good.

Yes! you've put your finger on the plague spot. The division of the book into two parts which is the basis of your criticism demonstrates to me once more your amazing insight; and your analysis of the *effect* of the book puts into words precisely and suggestively the dumb thoughts of every reader—and my own.

Such is indeed the effect of the book; the effect which *you* can name and others can only feel. I admit I strove for a great triumph and I have only succeeded in giving myself utterly away. Nobody'll see it, but you have detected me falling back with my lump of clay I had been lugging up from the very bottom of the pit, with the idea of breathing big life into it. And all I have done was to let it fall with a silly crash.

For what is fundamentally wrong with the book—the cause of the effect—is want of power. I do not mean the 'power' of reviewer's jargon. I mean the want of *illuminating* imagination. I wanted to obtain a sort of lurid light out* the very events. You know what I have done—alas! I haven't been strong enough to breathe the right sort of life into my clay—the *revealing* life.

I've been satanically ambitious, but there's nothing of a devil in me,

---

[1] Fiction supplement, 3 November, p. 420.   [2] The Boer War.

worse luck. The *Outcast* is a heap of sand, the *Nigger* a splash of water, *Jim* a lump of clay. A stone, I suppose will be my next gift to the impatient mankind—before I get drowned in mud to which even my supreme struggles won't give a simulacrum of life. Poor mankind! Drop a tear for it—but look how infinitely more pathetic *I* am! This Pathos *is* a kind of triumph no criticism can touch. Like the philosopher who crowed at the Universe[1] I shall know when I am utterly squashed. This time I am only very bruised, very sore, very humiliated.

This is the effect of the book upon me; the intimate and personal effect. Humiliation. Not extinction. Not yet. All of you stand by me so nobly that I must still exist. There is *You*, always and never dismayed. I had an amazing note from Lucas. Amazing! This morning a letter came from Henry James.[2] Ah! You rub in the balm till every sore smarts—therefore I exist. The time will come when you shall get tired of tending this true and most well-intentioned sham—and then the end'll come too.

But keep up! keep up! Let me exhort you earnestly to keep up! as long as you can.

I send you the H.J. letter. A draught from the Fountain of Eternal Youth. Wouldn't you think a boy had written it? Such enthusiasm! Wonderful old man, with his record of wonderful work! It is, I believe seriously intended (the letter) as confidential. And to you alone I show it—keep *his* secret for us both. No more now. I've read *Petersburg tales*[3] Phew! That *is* something! That is many things—and the only thing—it is written! It is. That work is genuine, undeniable, constructed and inhabited. It hath foundation and life. I hope the writer will deign to recognise my most fraternal welcome!

Yours ever

J.C.

PS Pray send the James autograph back—registered. Our great love to You three. We *must* meet soon.

---

[1] Democritus? See Juvenal, *Satire* x ll. 28 ff.

[2] Like nearly all Conrad's incoming correspondence, the letters from E. V. Lucas and James have vanished.

[3] By Garnett's sister Olive: just published. She was close to Stepniak and other revolutionary exiles.

To J. B. Pinker

Text MS Berg; Unpublished

[Pent Farm]
Monday. [November ? 1900][1]

My dear Sir.

Seraphina is finished and shall be ready for you in a fortnight.

I send you 33 pp of my *Typhoon*, all but two thirds of the whole. (7.000 words or 7500)

I sent it unfinished because you may judge it necessary to have it re-typed, though my corrections if numerous are perfectly clear.

I had rather not but if you think it should be done they may type the meantime so as to avoid delay at the end.

This is my first attempt at treating a subject jocularly so to speak. You shall have the end shortly.

Yours

Jph. Conrad.

To H.-D. Davray

Text MS Yale; *L.fr.* 41

[letterhead: Pent Farm]
20. Nov. 1900

Mon cher Davrey.*

Votre bonne et amicale lettre m'a attristé. Avez-vous donc été sérieusement malade? Moi aussi du reste j'ai besoin (a ce que l'on me dit) de passer un hiver dans un climat plus doux. Mais voilà! Le public, le grand et gros public ne veut pas. Donc je ne pourrai pas Vous rejoindre a Naples, a Capri. C'est dommage. On aurait pu causer sous un ciel moins gris. Il me pèse; il pèse sur la pensée; sur la plume aussi.

Je vous expédie le bouquin que vous êtes assez bon et assez charitable de me demander. Edition américaine. Je la prefère a l'anglaise. C'est moins lourd, et le papier est blanc au lieu d'être jaune sale. Blackwood a produit quelque chose qui ressemble a une bible verte. On pourrait assomer un homme avec. Ces gens-là sont idiots!

Comme oeuvre d'art cette machine n'existe pas. Peut-être y verrez vous quelque intention. Pour ma part je regarde ce monstre avec un ébahissment d'avoir fait cela. C'est lourd, lourd comme une pierre. Mais peut-être les pierres ont-elles une âme, une toute petite âme cachée dans le grès.

---

[1] Conrad described 'Typhoon' on 8 October and sent the next batch of MS on 25 November; the first possible Monday is 15 October and the last 19 November. Given the optimism about 'Seraphina', one of the later dates would be more likely.

Voilà notre rencontre, dont je me faisais fête a l'avance, bien eloignée. Enfin! Le diable dispose des choses a son gré—et n'est pas Enchanteur qui veut!

Je vous serre la main bien cordialement. Je vous souhaite une douce convalescence, bien abritée, bien ensoleillée. Du reste, patience et courage, mon cher—car tout change à la fin a celui qui sait attendre.

Donnez-moi de vos nouvelles, un petit mot de temps en temps, et croyez moi

toujours à vous

Jph. Conrad.

Translation

My dear Davray,

Your kind and friendly letter saddened me. Have you indeed been seriously ill? I, too (so they tell me), need to spend a winter in a milder climate. But there it is! The public, the great and considerable public, does not wish it. Thus I shall not be able to join you in Naples [or] on Capri. It's a shame! We could have chatted under a less grey sky. It weighs me down; it weighs on my thought, my pen as well.

I have sent off the book that you are good and generous enough to request from me. American edition. I prefer it to the English. It is less heavy, and the paper is white rather than dirty yellow. Blackwood has produced something that looks like a green bible. One could knock a man down with it. These people are idiots!

As a work of art, this contrivance does not exist. Perhaps you will see some intention there. For my part, I look on this monster with astonishment at having made it. It is heavy, heavy as a stone. But perhaps stones themselves have a soul, a very little soul hidden in the sandstone.

There's our meeting—I was really looking forward to it—well and truly postponed. So! The devil arranges matters to his liking—not everyone who wants to be a magician can be!

I shake your hand very cordially. I wish you a gentle convalescence, very sheltered, very sunny. Patience and courage as well—because for him who knows how to wait, everything changes in the end.

Give me your news, just a word from time to time, and believe me

Always yours,

Joseph Conrad.

To J. B. Pinker

Text MS Berg; Unpublished

> Pent Farm. Stanford. N^r Hythe.
> Kent.
> 25 Nov 1900

Dear Sir.

I send you pages 34 to 53 (inclve) of *Typhoon*. The end shall follow shortly.

A bad wrist and other worries prevented me from writing.

> Faithfully Yours
> Jph. Conrad.

PS Kindly acknowledge safe receipt, by a post-card.

To David Meldrum

Text MS Duke; Blackburn 115

> [letterhead: Pent Farm]
> Tuesday morning. [27 November
> 1900][1]

My dear Mr Meldrum.

Many thanks for the *Spectator*, I received yesterday morning. Be assured that all the little and all the great proofs of your friendly feeling are appreciated by your recipient—if he does often neglect to acknowledge them as promptly and as adequately as is proper and seemly and as, indeed, is his desire to do.

The review is good is it not. The *Speaker* too reviewed me the same week—Whig and Tory.[2] That was also a good review. Upon the whole the 'Press' is good. The provincial papers seem to catch on to Jim. They sent me some cuttings from Ed'gh. The Bradford Obs^{er} was most appreciative.

Last Sat: I had a cheque from my Canadian pub^{rs} through Mr Blackwood. It has come none too soon, for I must tell you that taking advantage of feeling pretty fit just now I've made an endeavour to get my life insured. I trust the matter will go through. I've undergone

---

[1] Dated by the reference to payment of Canadian rights, forwarded from Edinburgh 22 November (Blackburn, p. 114).

[2] The Tory *Spectator* (24 November) congratulated 'him on an achievement at once superlatively artistic in treatment and entirely original in its subject'; the Liberal *Speaker* (same date) observed that the book's construction 'seems to have solved one of the great difficulties of the philosophical romance'. Both reviews appear in *Critical Heritage*, pp. 119–22.

yesterday the Med^l exam^{on}. Nothing's radically wrong; but there is my wretched gout in the way.

I work more or less ineffectually. The Typhoon is still blowing. I find it extremely difficult to express the simplest idea clearly. It is a sort of temporary fog on the brain; and it has kept me back.

Henry James wrote me an absolutely enthusiastic letter about the book. That was a great pleasure.

My wife sends her kindest regards. We trust you are all well. Post waits

Ever Yours

Jph Conrad.

PS Do the B'woods think of the Tauchnitz business for *L. J.*? and is there any chance?

To David Meldrum
Text MS Duke; Blackburn 117

Pent Farm.
Stanford N^r Hythe.
Kent.
6 Dec. 1900.

My dear Mr Meldrum.

Pardon these scraps of paper. I can't find anything else, and the matter is pressing. I wish to consult you.

Briefly the affair is this: I've been accepted by the Standard Life Ins^{ce} C^o for the sum of £*1000*. I've got my bankers (Wm. Watson & Co 7. Waterloo Place) to pay the premium for the first quarter so that so far the matter has been carried through; but in order to get my affairs into some short* of shape I must raise £*150* which would enable me to discharge my liabilities (to you[1] amongst others). I can get this from the Ins. C^o at 5%.[2] And in fact this transaction must be carried out to make my Ins^{ce} arrangement permanent.

To carry it out (as suggested by my bankers) I must find two *good* sureties which would guarantee the premium and interest on loan. I thought Heinemann would undertake to be one and I wish to ask you whether Mr Blackwood would be the other? Of course I would write direct to Mr B'wood if you thought such a step possible and effective.

[1] Apparently a private debt rather than the advances from Blackwood.
[2] Conrad had been fascinated by the financial possibilities of life insurance for many years; he broached the subject with Kliszczewski in 1885 (*Letters*, 1, p. 14).

Were Heinemann unwilling Jack Galsworthy (he has plenty of money and a great affection for me) would join the Firm of B'wood as second surety, or he would join the *two* firms as *third* surety thus making the individual responsibility of each, less.

I am not likely to go utterly wrong on the payments and very soon each of these firms shall have two books from me. I am in a tight corner and this would give me a chance to breathe for a while. The liability would not be very imminent for with a guarantee at the back my bankers would always make up any deficiency on the premium should this be temporarily required. They are in fact doing it *now* without any such security. I shall go on working as long as I live and my debt would end their liability leaving always £850 clear to my creditors. The repayment of the sum borrowed would remove also their liability and such repayment (by instalments) shall be one of my endeavours. And I could not pledge my policy any further without the knowledge and consent of my guarantors. This is the matter. Pardon me for this endless bothering you with my affairs. I await your opinion.

Ever yours

Jph Conrad.

The premium for £1000 is £*35–1–8* yearly. (First quarter paid) The interest on loan would be £*7–10–*: Together £*42–11–8* which would be the sum guaranteed.

The Typhoon is all but finished and pleases me now so that I am sorry it isn't for *Maga*.

P.P.S. As there is now some *estate*[1] (at least for the next 3 months) I send you an IOU in case I should kick the bucket before the matter treated in this letter comes to pass.

To John Galsworthy
Text MS Forbes; Unpublished

[letterhead: Pent Farm]
Saturday [8 December 1900?][2]

Dearest Jack.

Unless you hear again from me before Tuesday You may take this for an eager acceptance.

---

[1] I.e. literary estate.
[2] A conjecture: Conrad wrote a letter of thanks the following Friday. The letterhead is type six.

I shall drop you a line as to train. Could I meet you at the club[1] in the evening? Or perhaps go straight to Kettner?[2]

You're right. I have to see Watson, Pawling, Meldrum, Pinker, McClure and desire greatly to see Garnett.

Your invitation converts a frightful grind into a pleasure. You are a man of lovely inspirations.

Foot painful to day but I hope it is only a threat and no more.

Love from us all

J. Conrad.

If you could put me up it would be lovely.

To William Blackwood

Text MS NLS; Blackburn 119

[letterhead: Pent Farm]
14 Dec 1900.

Dear Mr Blackwood.

I trust you will read what follows in a forgiving spirit—and as the matter is pressing I proceed to state it without further preamble.

I have, lately, insured my life for £1000 with the Standard Life Ins^ce C^o. and now I desire to raise two hundred pounds on the same. This loan is, I scarcely need to tell you, not for the purpose of indulging any sort of whim, and not even for the purpose of spending the winter abroad (which my doctor has recommended)—but to clear up generally my financial situation and to discharge a certain obligation which weighs on me the more, because it cannot be legally enforced.[3] I may mention incidentally that my bankers Messrs: Wm. Watson & Co of 7 Waterloo Place SW. think this step advisable since I can get the money from the Ins^ce C^o at 5% for a term of five years.

For this the Company requires two sureties to join me in a bond guaranteeing the principal, interest and premium. It is not easy for me to find two sureties which would be considered *good* by the C^oy. Discussing this matter with M^r Wm. Watson yesterday he said that *if* Mr Blackwood would consent to become one of the sureties he, himself, would be the other.

I venture therefore to put this request before you. You would be

---

[1] Galsworthy's club, the Junior Carlton.   [2] Kettner's Restaurant, 37 Greek St.
[3] Presumably the debt to Adolf Krieger, who was in financial trouble himself and must have sent the 'distressing communication' mentioned in the PPS.

rendering me a very great service. No doubt the thing could have been managed in some other way but really my dear M[r] Blackwood I am so worried with the thoughts of my work and the pain of my gouty foot that I have not the courage or the energy to go 'flying around' as a Yank would say. And there is also the fact that I find it easier to put myself under obligation to you than to any other man—a fact not particularly fortunate for you perhaps—but illustrative of my feelings.

The only thing I am anxious about is that you should not take it ill.

I took my gouty foot to London yesterday to see Watson; and I also called on Meldrum whom I acquainted with my intention of writing to you on that matter.

> Believe me, dear M[r] Blackwood,
> always very faithfully yours
> Jph. Conrad.

PS. The annual premium is £35–8– and the interest on £200 would be £10 yearly. The loan is for five years to be paid off by instalments. The policy is made out to my estate.

PPS Before I could send off this letter I received a distressing communication which in my at present helpless state (I am in bed) forces me to ask you whether you would not—whatever your decision on the main matter—lend me now £50 to be repaid as soon as my loan from the Insurance C[o] is negotiated. Negociated* in one way or another it must be and it would be anticipating one of the purposes for which it is intended. It is not a fresh liability. Only *time* in this case is of the greatest importance. You may imagine how pressing the case must be to prod me into such an appeal.

> JC.

To John Galsworthy
Text MS Forbes; Unpublished

> [letterhead: Pent Farm]
> Friday. [14 December 1900][1]

Dearest Jack

I got back without damage. You will never know how much your friendship and your warm affection are to me—what a help in life your personality is to my shadow.

We talked of You with M. after you left. He told me that M[r] B'wood is

---

[1] The day after the interview with Meldrum (preceding letter and Blackburn, p. 118).

anxious to have from You something that would fit into Maga. It is *purely* a question of size and space.

Then he *asked* me to mention to you that B'woods would be glad of the book. These are the ipsissima verba. They would like to publish you. They never go to a man who has a publisher but in some indirect way and no doubt (certain in fact) Meld: has been instructed. He began by asking me whether You were in any way *bound* to Duckworth.[1] I said no.

I havent a word against Duckworth only I think it would be to your advantage to be published by B. Afterwards when Your position is assured you may give D a book. He has not ruined himself for you after all and would have no right to complain.

Besides the B'woods would pay you something. Then You would get better advertised.

I cant help thinking you ought to give yourself a chance with a publisher having a certain prestige and a name for not publishing rubbish.

Think it over and write to *M* or write to me if you like better and I shall write *M* who then would write to you. See? A beginning publisher and a beginning author are not a good combination.[2] Then You get at the scotch public directly.

I am still a bit seedy and in more pain than I like. When I came home I gasped like a fish. With our love

Ever Yours

Conrad.

Pray you to "presenter mes devoirs" to your father and mother and thanks for their most kind hospitality.

To David Meldrum
Text MS Duke; Blackburn 120

[letterhead: Pent Farm]
18 Dec 1900

My dear Mr Meldrum.

I have mentioned to Jack Galsworthy that Messrs: Blackwoods were disposed to publish the vol: containing The *Man of Devon, Knight* and *Swithin.*

He is immensely pleased at the idea. Says he: "*If Blackwoods take to me I*

---

[1] Gerald Duckworth had published *Jocelyn* at his own risk.
[2] Duckworth began business in 1898.

want no better luck." I earnestly hope, now I started the matter, the thing will come to pass.

The *Knight* (or the Cosmopolitan) is to appear in Febr. Mch. Ap: numbers of the Argosy. The *M of D* is now held by Lippincotts Mag: but what their answer may be is not known yet. The third story I do not think he intends to try to serialise.

Jack is gone abroad but shall be back for the New Year and remain in London a few days. If he could hear anything by that time it would make him glad, and me too.

I've written to M^r B'wood about my affair. I haven't had an answer yet. However I don't worry for if this fails the Firm of H[einemann] will lend me the amount without any difficulty.

I shall let you know as soon as I hear. Believe me always yours

Conrad.

Have you seen the notice in *Literature*? I am glad somebody arose to slate me properly.[1] That means that I *exist* anyhow.

To John Galsworthy

Text MS Forbes; Unpublished

[letterhead: Pent Farm]
18 Dec 1900

Dearest Jack

I am so glad you placed the *Knight.*

I wrote to M. at once—saying you would be in London about NY's day and would like to hear something definite by then.

Are you anxious to come out in the spring? As matters are now it is possible; but what about Lipp[inco]tt's? Will they print at once if they accept? Or would you abandon Ltt's? I want to know. May I hint at terms and accept the same provisionally of course?

We can't ask for much on acct because of previous sales. Could you give me a note of Your Duckworth Agreement? Just the bare terms.

Love from us all and affec^te best wishes.

Ever Yours

Conrad.

---

[1] 15 December, p. 489: 'while we find in it infinite power of phrase, infinite observation, infinite volubility, we consider the narrative ... terribly involved, bewilderingly crowded, frequently turgid, painfully phantasmagoric, in no way a thing of beauty or fashioned for our delight'.

To William Blackwood
Text MS NLS; Blackburn 122

[letterhead: Pent Farm]
19th Dec. 1900

Dear Mr Blackwood.

Many thanks for your letter and the enclosure.[1] You should have heard before from me but last night the postman did not turn up and the weather was so infamous that I hadn't the heart to send the sort of errand boy we have, a mile across the fields to the post office.

I can't tell how sensible I am to all you say and are doing for me.

I am communicating your answer to Watson.

'Literature' went for me heavily—otherwise I am the spoiled child of the critics.

Jack Galsworthy came down to see me. He is very pleased with the kind letter you wrote him—though the *Knight* is declined.[2] He would like to be published by you in book form;[3] and I have written to M[r] Meldrum on the subject. I trust you will see your way to take up Galsworthy. He is genuine and has the making of a stylist in him, with a well-balanced temperament and a poetical vision. There's not a grain of humbug in the man.

> Believe me, dear M[r] Blackwood
> your most obliged and faithful
> Jph Conrad

To William Blackwood
Text MS NLS; Blackburn 123

[letterhead: Pent Farm]
30 Dec 1900.

Dear Mr Blackwood.

My best wishes for the New Year and for the New Century

You have made the last year of the Old Century very memorable to me, by your kindness. I am alluding to the production of Lord Jim—an Old Book by this time.

I can't think of that work without thinking of you. As it went on I appreciated more and more your helpful words your helpful silence and your helpful acts; and this feeling shall never grow old, or cold or faint.

> Very faithfully yours
> Jph. Conrad.

---

[1] For his sympathetic letter of the day before, see Blackburn, p. 121. Blackwood agreed to guarantee the insurance premiums and sent a cheque for the extra £50 Conrad had requested on 14 December.

[2] By Blackwood's.   [3] As *A Man of Devon* would be in 1901.

To H. G. Wells

Text MS Illinois; Unpublished

[Pent Farm]
Tuesday. [1900 or 1901?][1]

Dearest H G

I didn't thank you for the books always thinking I would be able to call to express gratitude and admiration (mingled with proper quantity of abuse) in person. And such is my intention still only I must put off the invasion on account of wretched state of my own work—if work it may be called. Seriously I much rather talk with you than write, as in the last case one tries to be brief and thus runs the risk of being misunderstood. Our love to you three.

Ever yours

Conrad.

---

[1] The Wells family had three members from July 1900 to October 1903. During that period, Wells gave Conrad at least seven books, as evidenced by the correspondence, the presentation copies at Yale, and Hans van Marle's note in *The Conradian*, 9 (1983), 44. The titles that cannot be matched with a surviving thank-you letter are *Tales of Space and Time* (1900), *The First Men in the Moon* (presented 20 November 1900), and *Anticipations* (a 1902 imprint published in December 1901).

1901

To William Blackwood

Text MS NLS; Blackburn 123

[letterhead: Pent Farm]

3 Jan 1901.

Dear Mr Blackwood.

I am advised by Watson & Co that they are sending you my Loan application Form (on which they figure as second sureties) for the needful filling up. I wish to explain that instead of One policy for a £1000 I have taken two for 500 each and on one of these the loan is raised.

They acquaint me also that they have made the loan £250 instead of two hundred as originally contemplated. They seem to think it advisable and they are certainly good judges of my financial situation.

I could only write to them that I have asked you to be joint surety with them for £200 only. Obviously it is to my interest to borrow enough. The bungling as to the amount was probably my fault. Now the matter rests with you.

> Believe me, dear Sir, always very
> faithfully Yours
>
> Jph. Conrad.

To John Galsworthy

Text MS Forbes; Unpublished

[letterhead: Pent Farm]

Sunday evening. [6 January 1901?][1]

My dearest Jack.

Before I wrote my letter to Watson I studied the tables of the Company and have elected to take out my insurance under the, so-called, half premium system.

In this way I can be insured for *£1000* at a premium of *£22* p year for the first five years and after that I must pay for all the subsequent years *£44.* per year.

The participation in the profits in that case does not *begin* till the sixth year (included). The division of profits taking place every five years (according to the date of the policy) I wouldn't actually *touch* anything in the way of profits till the 10th year of my policy. From that time forward

---

[1] The plan to split the insurance policies suggests a date close to that of the 3 January letter; 30 December is also possible. Letterhead is type six

the aforesaid profits could be applied towards the reduction of the premium.

This seems to me the best under the circumstances. Otherwise I would have to pay *£37.4.0* from the first; having my profit at the end of five years. But the difference in premiums is material to begin with. In five years I shall be either dead or able to pay £44 per year.

The increase on a policy of £1000 by accumulated profit is *£425* in 30 years. By my scheme I lose 5 years profit and the extra 7 per year after the first five years; on the other hand I gain £15 p.y. (reduced premium) on the first five years. Calculating by the company table I arrive at this result; that if I lived 30 years I should be £123 worse off than the man who would have paid £37.4 from the start to the end. But if I lived only 15 years I would be only £10 worse off—that is as regards profits. So I decided for the Table II scheme and write accordingly to Watson. Do you think I am right? Ever Yours

Conrad.

To J. B. Pinker
Text MS Berg; Unpublished

[letterhead: Pent Farm]
14 Jan 1901.

Dear Mr Pinker.

On reckoning up with the situation I see that I must take advantage of your proposal.

Would you, therefore, advance me as much as the prospect of placing the story[1] would justify—leaving you on the safe side.

I feel I am not fair to you with all my reservations of book-rights to certain publishers and so on. However, later on, when I've cleared up my position vis-a-vis Heinemann—principally[2]—we may be able to put our connection on a sounder basis, as far as *you* are concerned.

The 'knot' in the situation is in the finishing of the *Rescue*. That would clear the air—but on the other side I must for the present write stuff that'll bring immediate bread and butter. The position looks without issue but really what is wanted is time, and nothing else.

I would like to have back *my own* typed copy of story when your typist has done with it.

Very faithfully yours.

Jph. Conrad.

[1] 'Typhoon', finished midnight 10 (MS), hand delivered 11 January (telegram Berg).
[2] Conrad owed Heinemann (and McClure) *The Rescue* and a collection of stories, but he also owed Blackwood a new collection and a final story for *Youth*.

PS I wish, whatever publisher you capture, could be induced to make a certain amount of fuss about the story "Mr. J Conrad's new tale Typhoon begins in ... etc etc" That kind of thing. The public's so used to the guidance of Advertis[e]ment! Why! even I myself feel the spell of such emphasis.

To J. B. Pinker
Text MS Berg; Unpublished

[letterhead: Pent Farm]
15 Jan 1901.

Dear Mr Pinker.

Many thanks for Your letter and enclosure.

I never doubted that our connection would be of advantage to *me*. I only feel that as long as I am entangled by old obligations You must be handicapped in a measure which of course is disadvantageous to You as well as to myself.

Will there be a chance of American serial for Typhoon? I am afraid in this case too McClure's claims to *the book* must be recognised.

I haven't a stamp in the house but the formal ack^{*gmt*} of the amount rec^{*d*} is on the other page.

Very faithfully Yours

Jph. Conrad.

15 Jan. 1901

Received from James B. Pinker Esq^{*re*} the sum of one hundred pounds (*£100*) on acct of ser: rights of 'Typhoon'.

Joseph Conrad.

To Edmund Gosse
Text J-A, 1, 300

Pent Farm,
18 Jan. 1901.

Dear Mr. Gosse,[1]

Very many thanks for the names, which are lovely; and for all the additional information.[2]

---

[1] Gosse (1849–1928), poet, literary historian, and biographer, had very wide connections in publishing and academia. His autobiographical *Father and Son* appeared in 1907; his critical enthusiasms included Ibsen and Donne. In 1894 he read the MS of *Almayer's Folly*, and in 1902 he procured Conrad's grant from the Royal Literary Fund.

[2] According to Jean-Aubry's note, material for 'Falk'.

It is indeed very kind of you to write in such terms—and thus I am exceedingly rewarded for my cheek in setting Pawling on you.[1]

Nevertheless I am very much ashamed. If I were to make an inroad upon your time I wish it had been on some more promising occasion. This story promises to turn out a deplorable pot-boiler; unless, before it is too late, the gods wake up and are good to me. I don't see why they should. However the way of the gods (as those of Chinamen, *pace* Bret Harte),[2] are dark, and there may be salvation, somewhere, before the last line is written.

To J. B. Pinker
Text MS Berg; Unpublished

[letterhead: Pent Farm]
18 Jan 1901

Dear Mr Pinker.

Many thanks for my copy of T[yphoon] received to day.

You who have a connection with the US. could perhaps tell me whether there would be a chance *there* of disposing of a collection of autographs—a big lot—some 300 letters including Burne Jones with sketches and caricatures; Holman Hunt ditto; Wm Morris, Rossetti Millais, Leighton, and all the preraphaelites. Carlyle—2 long letters; Swinburne—and so on. I could furnish a list; especially if you found it possible or worth Your while to act in the matter—perhaps?

I submit this to you as a matter of business, acting for a friend who does not want to dispose of that lot *here*.[3] He wishes them to go over the water.

Yours very sincerely

Jph. Conrad.

To J. B. Pinker
Text MS Berg; Unpublished

[letterhead: Pent Farm]
23 Jan 1901.

Dear Mr Pinker.

I've wired my friend to send you a selection of his autographs. My friend is, as you may have guessed, F. M. Hueffer. In this matter pray keep the secret of ownership.

[1] Both Pawling and Gosse were associated with Heinemann's.
[2] The opinion of the outsmarted card-sharper in 'Plain Language from Truthful James': 'for ways that are dark / And for tricks that are vain, / The heathen Chinee is peculiar'.
[3] Where Ford (the friend) would be embarrassed to sell off the correspondence of his Pre-Raphaelite grandfather, Ford Madox Brown.

I think—since you ask me—that £75 is a disappointing price.[1] But for all practical purposes I have no opinion in this business. I wired you that I could get a 100 from B for the story. However I don't want to go to B for the present for many reasons—one of them being that I wish to reach another public than *Maga's*.

No doubt You'll find me difficult to handle very profitably. At any rate at first, I am afraid you shall.

The 2ᵈ story progresses having taken a start since last Monday.[2]

> With kind regards faithfully yours
> Jph. Conrad.

To John Galsworthy
Text MS POSK; Danilewicz 8

> [Pent Farm]
> Friday night [January? 1901][3]

Dearest Jack

I am awaiting the news, the story YOURSELF, with the greatest impatience.

Do let me know what You arrange with B[lackwood] at once. For the rest—we shall talk. Only do come as soon as You can.

Borys wanted to know whether You are a relation of Jack the Giant Killer? Otherwise he is well. I had another touch of gout and Jess had a week of most awful torture with neuralgia. However we are all on the active list again. Typhoon finished. It is too silly for words.

I am trying not to think but the prospect of going on living on the present terms frightens me when I do think.

> With love from us all
> Ever Yours
> Jph. Conrad.

---

[1] Offered by George R. Halkett, editor of the *Pall Mall Magazine*, who told Pinker (21 January, MS Berg) that 'Typhoon' was too long and too expensive.

[2] 'Falk', 14 or 21 January.

[3] The date falls between the ending of 'Typhoon' and the letter of 23 February; 11, 18, and 25 are possible January days.

To Józef Korzeniowski

Text MS Warsaw; *Listy* (facsimile) 184; Najder 233

[letterhead: Pent Farm]
14th February 1901.

Dear Sir,[1]

I hasten to acknowledge the receipt of the Memoirs,[2] which reached me yesterday morning, and at the same time to thank you for your kindness in sending them.

Your so friendly letter, Sir, has given me the greatest pleasure. As we are bearers of the same name and have the same family crest there must surely be between us if not actual kinship at least an affinity,[3]—this is a great honour to me and its mention by you, dear Sir, has been most gratifying.

Incidentally, I heard from Mrs. Poradowska as well as from Mrs. A. Zagórska—a relation of mine from Lublin—that the Memoirs had met with a most unpleasant response.[4] It has upset me greatly, for that uproar (if it was such an uproar as they say) concerns the memory of a man for whom mind and heart I have always cherished the greatest admiration, to say nothing of my deep attachment to him as my Uncle, guardian, and benefactor!

It must only be due to the indulgent eyes of good Mrs. Poradowska, who has always been well disposed towards me, that she sees me as eminent in English literature. Apart from the fact that it is not easy for anyone to achieve a position of eminence, it is still a question whether my (and other peoples') mawkish romances can justifiably count at all as works of literature? However, I am not ashamed of my undertaking, as the path I have chosen is by no means an easy one—on the contrary, it is difficult and precarious—striving for recognition not by inventing plots, but by writing in a style which serves the truth as I see and feel it.

And please let me add, dear Sir (for you may still be hearing this and that said of me), that I have in no way disavowed either my nationality or the name we share for the sake of success.[5] It is widely known that I am a Pole and that Józef Konrad are my two Christian names, the latter being used by me as a surname so that foreign mouths should not distort

---

[1] Korzeniowski (1863–1921), a historian and librarian, lived in Cracow.
[2] Of Conrad's uncle, Tadeusz Bobrowski (1829–94): an anecdotal and reflective survey of nineteenth-century Polish life published in two volumes, Lwów, 1900.
[3] For names and affinities, see the letter to Garnett, 20 January 1900.
[4] Provoked by Bobrowski's caustic tone and his contempt for Polish chauvinism.
[5] As certain Polish writers (notably Eliza Orzeszkowa) had accused him of doing. See *Letters*, 1, p. 360 and Najder, *Conrad under Familial Eyes*, pp. 178–92.

my real surname—a distortion which I cannot stand. It does not seem to me that I have been unfaithful to my country by having proved to the English that a gentleman from the Ukraine can be as good a sailor as they, and has something to tell them in their own language. I consider such recognition as I have won from this particular point of view, and offer it in silent homage where it is due.

With renewed thanks, I beg you, dear Sir, to accept my friendly expression of profound respect.

Konrad Korzeniowski.

To John Galsworthy
Text MS Forbes; Unpublished

[letterhead: Pent Farm]
23 Febr 1901

Dearest Jack

I don't know about Mrs Bontine.[1] I fancy she might. She is interested in the artistic movements of all sorts. A wonderful old woman.

I am glad you are settled. I am not very happy finding a great difficulty in writing. I am either getting stale or becoming an idiot.

MacIlwaine[2] was here and at one's own fireside he gains on acquaintance. He is harmless and quiet. Borys took a great fancy to him. He isn't amusing—at least not very. That's certain.

Jessie has been on the go since 7 o'clock this morning. Poor Nash is dying. Inflam[m]ation of the veins and clot of blood in the circulation. I dont think he has a ghost of a chance. Those people are curiously helpless. Anyway Jess went off this morning to Folkestone to fetch the daughters. They weep, Mrs Nash[3] weeps, and poor Nash, gasping for breath, weeps too.

This is all the news. I shall come down on You as soon as I can.

Ever Yours

Conrad

To John Galsworthy
Text MS Forbes; Unpublished

[letterhead: Pent Farm]
6 March 1901

Dearest Jack

The whole mystery is that on returning from my visit to McClure I found the letter I had written you, last Tuesday week, on my table. In it I explained why I could not come to stay with You on Thursday.

[1] Cunninghame Graham's mother.   [2] Unidentified.   [3] Housekeeper at the Pent.

It's too absurd. However I never supposed you would be angry but I was relieved on hearing from you this morning. I did not write an explanatory letter sooner for the reason that ever since I returned (Friday night)[1] I've been violently seedy with a thorough chill which involved my liver, my face, my back (which got respectively swollen congested and stiff) but principally my intellect which became withered. I really thought I was in for a big thing. It's all over now though. I crawled downstairs this morning and am feeling shaky but otherwise unharmed.

I've read *The Silence*[2] once but shall keep it till tomorrow. Certain remarks I keep for a note which I shall send You together with the MS. Here I can only say that I feel strongly my good fortune in being able to sympathise more and more with your work, with its spirit, feeling and fundamental conception. I don't mention especially the felicities of your style because in that matter we all who've read you critically are agreed in our admiration.

I don't know when I shall be really well, clear of my work and able to come to you. Everything, every achievement seems so hopelessly, hopelessly far away—as it were beyond one's own region of time, the tiny minute ring within which one is trying to bustle about.

Ever Yours

Conrad.

To John Galsworthy
Text MS Forbes; Unpublished

[letterhead: Pent Farm]
Sunday. [10 March? 1901][3]

Dearest Jack

I am afraid I won't be fit to come of* Thursday. I'm as weak as a cat and haven't been out since last Friday week being forbidden by

---

[1] 1 March. [2] The last story in *A Man of Devon*.

[3] The references to Mrs George's illness and the fate of Galsworthy's stories point to a date in February or March. This cannot be the forgotten letter mentioned on 6 March: (a) that one was written on a Tuesday; (b) this one pleads illness – a reason for not coming to town at all, rather than an excuse for seeing McClure but not Galsworthy. An earlier date might fit, but 24 February or 3 March would not go with the letter of 23 February, and 17 March comes too close to the news of Mrs George's recovery. 10 March matches the circumstances best: 'last Friday week' would be 1 March, when Conrad returned from London; Galsworthy must have suggested another Thursday meeting to make up for the previous one.

Hackney.[1] I am writing a little but otherwise seem incapable of any sort of effort. To complete the situation Mrs George[2] came here and fell ill, seriously rather. She's been a bad seven days, and devil only knows when she'll be able to get up. In any case it must be a long business. Jess keeps up wonderfully well. Only I can't ask you to come here just yet.

I tried to see Meldrum in the matter of your stories but failed. Have you heard anything? I shall send back your MS tomorrow (Monday) morning.

Best love from us all. Ever Yours.

Conrad.

To John Galsworthy

Text MS Forbes; Unpublished

[letterhead: Pent Farm]
Mch 24 1901

My excellent Jack.

I've been having an uncommonly rough time of it what with toothache and gout and other things.

I only crawled downstairs two days ago after being in bed since last monday.

Time lost. Spirits low. Weather too horrible. Also one tooth gone (forcibly removed) which seems to me like the beginning of the end. Irritability, weakness, pain, with their natural train of consequences. That's the budget.

If You want to lay up some exceptional merit against the Day of Last Judgment You had better come swiftly and visit this sick. I had a good mind to call upon You before—but refrained. Ever Yours,

Jph. Conrad.

Mrs George left here discharged cured a few days ago.

To Cora Crane

Text MS Columbia; *Bookman* (NY) 69, 374

[letterhead: Pent Farm]
24 Mch 1901.

Dear Mrs Crane.

Jessie must have written you about my gout which absolutely prevents me not only writing but even thinking. I had an extremely bad

[1] John Hackney, a doctor from Hythe.   [2] Jessie Conrad's mother.

bout of it, and let this be my excuse for not replying sooner to your kind letter.

I am *so* really and truly glad your work finds space *and* recognition.[1] No news could have been more welcome. As to what You propose, pray believe me when I say that any change, as to the disposal of my work, in that direction is impossible.[2] I am bound in too many ways, though of that I do not complain. I've found much kindness and even generosity in my difficult way.

You *must* come to us for rest as soon as the weather is a little improved.

Believe me always most faithfully Yours

Jph Conrad.

To Cora Crane

Text MS Columbia; *Bookman* (NY) 69, 374

[letterhead: Pent Farm]
9 Ap 1901.

Dear Mrs Crane.

I've been bad again with gout and could not interview the farmer who had stipulated when we first came here that we should not have any dogs. There is upwards of a thousand sheep in the fields around the house and this is the reason he objects to the tenants having dogs. We had a lot of trouble in getting him to admit Escamillo[3]—and a lot of unpleasantness afterwards about sheep and chickens which the dog did chase till we broke him of it. He had a narrow escape from being shot, once or twice.

Moreover our position here is very uncertain. And the truth is dear Mrs Crane it is growing worse. I can't say what we may have to do, where we may have to go! It is the holy truth. And I am afraid we could not take proper care of the dog.[4] Of course if You positively cannot make a satisfactory arrangement anywhere we will try to do our best. But don't you think You will miss the dog awfully yourself? And I fear the dog won't be happy either, away from you.[5]

You must pardon the long delay in reply. Jess has been blind with

---

[1] She had placed some of her own stories and was finishing some of Stephen's.
[2] She thought of becoming a literary agent herself and also offered her services to Curtis Brown, who wanted to represent British authors in the USA (Gilkes, *Cora Crane*, pp. 299–300).
[3] Stephen's gift to Borys.   [4] Tolstoi by name.
[5] Cora Crane was leaving for the USA at the end of the month.

neuralgia for the last week. It was a wretched time. Believe me always faithfully Yours

Jph Conrad.

Jessie's best Love.
PS The Farmer won't hear of another dog. As I think he wants this house for himself if I insist he will I fear give notice to Hueffer who will have to give me notice. Still—consider us as a last resource.

To Ford Madox Ford
Text MS Yale; *Listy* 182; Original unpublished

[letterhead: Pent Farm]
28 Ap. 1901

Dearest Ford.

I think I shall run down in two–three days to you, make arrangements and then fetch wife and boy for 3 weeks.[1] Something must be done.

I am finishing the Falk story but with me such a statement may mean anything.

You two are excellent, worthy people deserving of testimonials in jewelled caskets and your own portraits in gold frames.

Meantime accept my thanks.

With love to you all
Yours J Conrad

I shall wire the day before.

To William Blackwood
Text MS NLS; Blackburn 125

[letterhead: Pent Farm]
24 May 1901.

My Dear Mr Blackwood.

Many thanks for your letter. The enclosure was most interesting.[2] It reveals an original personality and, to me, attractive. It is at the same time a most flattering recognition of my qualities and shortcomings. I shall write to Mr Constable in a day or two.

---

[1] To stay in Winchelsea, Sussex, where Ford had just moved. He and Conrad planned to work on 'Seraphina'.
[2] A letter from Frank Challice Constable, formerly of the Indian civil service, and one of Blackwood's novelists; he lived near Bristol.

I own, with shame, that too long I've not written to you;[1] I have been writing hard however, trying to get over the work which lies between me and Maga. It loomed as big as a mountain, but now it is more than half scaled at last. Another 20000 words separate me from the summit. And then I shall begin another climb forthwith on behalf of the vol: of *Youth*. The simile of hill climbing is not used to hint at the loftiness of my work, but simply as conveying a notion of its arduousness.

Do you think that another *20000* added to *Youth* and *H of D* would make a satisfactory volume. I ask the question in view of treating the subject I reserve for that vol:—and am I right in thinking that it shall be favoured by Maga's hospitality? It may in that way extinguish my debt to you (of £50) which I have incurred with every appearance of false pretences. I have been bitterly ashamed ever since. But there is in me yet some of the unreasonable Jack ashore spirit, and not a little of that truly Polish hopefulness which nothing either nationally or individually has ever justified. In extenuation I may only say that my ambarrasments,* worrying and humiliating, did not arise from any personal extrava-gance. I've taken up certain obligations which are heavier than I expected. It is a poor excuse enough but it will serve like a straw to a drowning man; and that hopefulness of which I've spoken shall always prevent me from sinking as long as I can move hand or foot.

I have been in Winchelsea (returned yesterday) for a fortnight; finishing a story for Heinemann,[2] drinking bottled Carlsbad water and working with Ford Hueffer on our romance of Seraphina. That will be ready in a few days. It is something. How much of a thing it is hard to say. It has a certain originality—of *exposition*, I may say. Would you care to look at it? I would in that case direct Pinker to submit it to you. Pinker is doing some business for me and shall be entrusted with Seraphina; but for reasons which I trust you will understand without explanation, I have barred our relations from his influence. As to my *own* work especially—and as to our joint productions at least by implication.

I put all these questions because I intend to run up especially to see Mr Meldrum—probably in some 10 days' time—and if you were to let him know your wishes we could talk matters over.

> Believe me my dear M^r
> Blackwood, always faithfully
> yours
>
> Jph. Conrad

---

[1] Blackwood had politely inquired about the work Conrad owed him (Blackburn, p. 125).
[2] 'Falk'.

To J. B. Pinker

Text MS Berg; Unpublished

[Pent Farm]

[25 May? 1901][1]

My dear Mr Pinker

This is the first part of the story.

I haven't received up to now (Saturday evening) the typed pages of the end.

I trust you will find it possible to dispose of this story without difficulty. I am anxious for my name to appear now and then. A short story of 7–9 thousand shall be sent to you before many days.

Yours faithfully

Jph. Conrad.

Hadn't you better send me one copy of the *whole* type to look over.

To William Blackwood

Text MS NLS; Blackburn 127

[letterhead: Pent Farm]

3 June 1901.

Dear Mr Blackwood.

Thanks for your encouraging letter.[2]

In reference to the *Youth* volume I have two subjects which will do—I hope. I am cheered to think I shall again see daylight through the Maga window. Pinker has got a couple of my stories—good too—but no one seems anxious to print them. They make more than half of the vol destined for Heinemann. I regret they are not for you.

I would like to see Mr Constable—and I've not yet written to him. But I must—soon. As to getting as far as Bristol I can't think of it just yet. I run on with leaden feet and do not seem to advance an inch. I see no one read nothing but Maga which is a solace a treat, an event!

I like Linesman immensely. The last one of Zack was admirably done. Lawson's sketches are beyond praise—the more so that in such a subject it takes a first rate man not to break through the thin ice of sentimentalism. My best wishes go with Doom Castle for the sake of the author and

---

[1] The most likely Saturday in the sequence of revising 'Falk' and projecting 'Amy Foster'.

[2] Asking to read 'Seraphina' and estimating that the *Youth* volume would need another one or two stories, about 40,000 words (Blackburn, p. 127).

the publisher.[1] The value of the work is undeniable without any wishing.

> Believe me yours faithfully.
>
> Jph Conrad.

To J. B. Pinker
Text MS Berg; Unpublished

> [letterhead: Pent Farm]
> 3 June 1901

Dear Pinker

Thanks for Seraphina MS received all right. We wanted to look up certain things and modify a few lines. You shall have the work complete before long.

I had a letter from B'wood, in which he says he would like to see *Seraphina*. This may be of use. At any rate the thing is in your hands but I hope you will submit it to B'wood. It would be good to appear in Maga unless you have something much better in view. As things stand now S would not be in the way of my own work.

I am anxiously waiting for *Falk*. I greatly desire to appear somewhere soon.

The short story (entitled—either *A Husband* or *A Castaway*)[2] will be ready in a week.

> Yours
>
> Conrad.

To Richard Garnett
Text MS NYPL; Unpublished

> [letterhead: Pent Farm]
> 6 June 1901

My dear Garnett.[3]

Pardon my brutality—or rather brutishness in delaying so long to thank you for your letter.

---

[1] Of short stories by 'Linesman' (Captain M. H. Grant), 'Zack' (Gwendoline Keats), and Henry Lawson, and an episode of Neil Munro's *Doom Castle*: all contributions to the latest *Blackwood's*, Vol. 169, pp. 616–778.

[2] 'Amy Foster'.

[3] Richard Garnett (1835–1906), Edward's father, wrote *The Twilight of the Gods* (1888) and many literary biographies. He had recently retired as keeper of Printed Books at the British Museum; his unequalled knowledge of the collection made him the ideal person to consult about any bookish problem.

I am fixed now as to the rights of the business. My man shall be born in Italy six months before the ceremony takes place, so that 'decency' shall be completely outraged.[1] Other details I must think out.

I am delighted by the quotation from Brackstone.[2] If the rest of his immortal work is written in that style I want to read it all. It would be a liberal education.

I am physically incapable of expressing just now my gratitude in an adequate manner; it is 2 am; I've written since 10 pm four harrowing pages. My head buzzes. I am buried in cigarette-ends and feel as if I could give all I have (my Kingdom in short) to anybody who would drag me out and carry me up to bed.

Kindest regards. Yours faithfully
Jph. Conrad

To J. B. Pinker

Text MS Berg; Unpublished

[Pent Farm]
7 June 1901

My dear Pinker.

I return both copies of T.M.S. *Falk* corrected for press.[3] I would want to see the proofs of course.

I shall send next (perhaps on Monday) the short story. Really short this time, and worth the more money. You will have to adv^{ce} something on that too if you don't want me to roll over on my side and give up writing altogether.[4] It's awful. awful.

Seraphina is now complete in MS.[5] But we must type and correct about 20000 words of it before we can send you the work. This shall be my next task.

Kindest regards
Yours Jph Conrad

---

[1] An unused idea for 'Seraphina'?
[2] Conrad wrote 'Brackstone' but must have meant Sir William Blackstone, author of the magisterial *Commentaries on the Laws of England* (1765–9).
[3] A TS for setting the story as it would appear in *Typhoon* (1903).
[4] Conrad stayed in debt to Pinker until the commercial success of *Chance* in 1913.
[5] A fragmentary draft.

To Ford Madox Ford
Text MS Yale; Unpublished

[Pent Farm]
Thursday. [13 June 1901]¹

Dearest Ford.

Don't think evil of me. I am doing my damnedest. I've been interrupted; I've been upset too; and generally I am not allowed to forget how
impossible my position is daily becoming. Anyhow I've worked as hard
as I know how. I think I'll finish my castaway² to morrow; and at any rate
I intend if at all possible and you will have me to come up to you for a
couple of days on Monday and work there at Seraphina. Then Jess would
come up for a night and take me home again. I think this the best scheme
for getting forward. Only pray beg Elsie not to make preparations and
not to treat me as a guest—if I am permitted to come. Or are you going to
London just then? *Do not let me interfere with your plans.* I can work here too;
and *shall* work—never fear. Ah! for three days' peace of mind. If I had
that I would move mountains. Three days only!

Write me frankly what you think of my intentions.

As to *married*.³ I say: go on by all means. I shall bring the pages with
me (if I can come) and then offer certain minor remarks. The value of
creative work of any kind is in the *whole* of it. Till that is seen no
judgment is possible. Questions of phrasing and such like—*technique*—
may be discussed upon a fragmentary examination; but phrasing,
expression—*technique* in short has importance only when the Conception
of the whole has a significance of its own apart from the details that go to
make it up—if it (the Conception) is imaginative, distinct and has an
independent life of its own—as apart from the 'life' of the style.

My love to you all

Yours ever

Jph. Conrad

To J. B. Pinker
Text MS Berg; Unpublished

[letterhead: Pent Farm]
Sunday late. [16 June 1901]⁴

My dear Pinker.

It is accomplished! I am off (after a good sleep) to Winchelsea by a
midday train and my wife shall type and send you the end of the story to

---

¹ The closest Thursday to the completion of 'Amy Foster'.   ² 'Amy Foster'.
³ Should John Kemp and Seraphina be married?
⁴ Completion of 'Amy Foster' and the visit to Winchelsea fix the date.

morrow (Monday) evening. I am afraid it is just over 9.000. But the subject is big too. Anyhow if an editor accepts it I may try to take a thousand out should it be necessary. Now however I am a bit sick of it.

It should fetch £5 p thou: At all events I must ask you for forty and if you be so kind, to send the cheque straight to *Wm Watson & C° of Waterloo Place. SW.* for the reason that I shall be working at S. with H on Tuesday but on Wednesday I shall be out all day in a Rye fishing boat if I can arrange it. I am thinking of a fisher-story.[1] On Thursday I hope S shall be ready to go to you.

If I am asking too much for the story pray take into account *S.* shall be in your hands this week. All this is beastly. But imagine my dear fellow the state of mind in which I am writing these stories! I wonder I don't go off my chump. Always, always, in a damned hole! But never mind. Some day I too shall put out my 'Diana of the Crossways'[2]—be it said without instituting comparisons. I intend to turn up in person with the MS of *S.* Kindest regards

Ever Yours

Jph Conrad.

To J. B. Pinker

Text MS Berg; Unpublished

Winchelsea
19 [June] 1901.[3]

My dear Pinker

I suposse* You've understood what was in the note (intended for you which my wife received) was this:

I was asking You to send me for 24[4] the clean double copy of *The Castaway* for certain corrections which I didn't make on my own type because I was too worried to do it well. By the time your typist is ready my brain shall be too. These would be mere corrections of phrasing.

I am staying here till Monday—on which day I shall reach the Pent. If the copy is sent off to me there on Saturday—(let us say) You'll have it back corrected on Tuesday or at the latest on Wednesday next. And if you put a few blank pages in my wife would type clean in duplicate any page I would have too much messed. This would involve no delay. I am working now at S

Kindest regards

Yours Jph Conrad

---

[1] Without result.

[2] George Meredith's novel, 1885, consolidated his reputation as the leading English writer of the day.

[3] Conrad stayed in Winchelsea from 17 to 24 June.   [4] June.

To John Galsworthy

Text MS Forbes; J-A, I, 300

[letterhead: The Bungalow,
Winchelsea, Nr. Rye,
Sussex.]¹
20ᵗʰ June 1901

My dear Jack

Jess sent me on your letter. Yes next Sunday week will do excellently well. I've been longing to see you and like Anteus² in touching the earth draw some strenght* from the contact of your friendship.

I've finished Falk, and I've written another story since. Now I am here working at seraphina. There are 10000 words which I am going to write in, manu prop[r]ia.³ I reckon to be done Sunday sometime. On Mond: we go to the Pent. And on Wednesday perhaps I may run up to London with the MS of S to see Pinker, Meldrum and Watson my banker. It is a weary life. But I am cheered to hear from you. I am *most* anxious to see the play—also the verses. The story in the Outlook Ford sent me some time ago.⁴ We enjoyed it!

Ever Yours

Conrad.

PS Jess is coming here tomorrow Friday to stay till Monday.

To Ford Madox Ford

Text MS Yale; Unpublished

[Pent Farm]
[late June? 1901]⁵

My dear Ford.

You can not really suppose that there is anything between us except our mutual regard and our partnership—in crime. "Voyons, señorita, quelle folie!"⁶ Upon my word I am quite confounded by your letter which my speaking a coeur ouvert to Auntie Elsie did not deserve. I was afraid of taking a course that would seem heartless or offensive to you—especially in your low state of health; and I mistrusted my own

¹ An eighteenth-century cottage owned by Elsie Hueffer's father.
² Antaeus, the great wrestler killed by Hercules.
³ 'In my own hand.'   ⁴ From the 18 May issue, 'A Reversion to Type'.
⁵ The newly written scene reported in the PS belongs to *Romance* III, 4; Conrad worked on Part Three in late June and July, so this letter should come from the first few days after his return from Winchelsea on 24 June.
⁶ A near quotation from *Romance*, II, 3.

nerves which, as you may have perceived, are and were devilishly attuned to the concert pitch of gloom and absurd irritation. But of irritation or of any thought about you but of the most affectionate nature I have been utterly unconscious then or now.

It is a fact I work better in your house in touch with your sympathy. Still I can do something here too. I am very grateful to you for the days I've passed in W'sea. I could write much more in the strain of thanks but Hoyle is here[1] (The mare dead lame); and the postman's due in 10 minutes or so. Ever Yours with love to you all

Jph Conrad.

Report: O'Brien just out of Kemp's rooms.—another 2 hours work'll push the story along.

To Ford Madox Ford
Text MS Yale; Unpublished

[letterhead: Pent Farm]
Friday. [28 June? 1901][2]

Dearest H.

So sorry to hear Elsie is unwell, and the crew left the ship.

On the other hand Your valliant* tone delights me. The time of our conjunction approaches and from shock heavenly fire struck would base metals into gold transmute! (in other words: from Bsh Public's pocket extract shekels.)

I am hard at it with *S.* night and day. More anon

Love

Your Conrad

To J. B. Pinker
Text MS Berg; Unpublished

[letterhead: Pent Farm]
3d July 1901.

My dear Pinker.

I do not know whether I've made it clear that the disposal of Seraphina in the states, serial and bookform, is in your hands com-

---

[1] John George Hoile, the veterinary surgeon from Lympne.
[2] *The Inheritors* appeared on 26 June: this letter must be close in time to that mystical but unprofitable conjunction. 28 is the only Friday in May or June not ruled out by visits to Winchelsea, absence of the 'Seraphina' MS, or frenzied work on 'Amy Foster'.

pletely. Blackwoods generally (I fancy) try to secure Am: business for Dodd Mead.

I am just writing to Ed'gh sending them an epitome of part III. I am at work at it but really I have no force for a break neck performance. I shall take a fortnight and intend to send you chapters as they are ready.

From what I see Hein: is going to make a certain amount of fuss over the Inheritors. Garnett will write something about me. There will be some paragraphing too. This may help to place one or two of the stories You have in hand as well here as in America where McClure says they are going to do their best for the book in the way of publicity.

Now I am really very sorry but I must ask you whether you could not pay in another £40 to my acct at Watson & Cº. To secure this further advance you shall have Seraphina till I am ready with another short story.[1] I delay the writing of the short story only to get Seraphina off my mind, and off my partner's mind too. All the same I am ashamed to be everlastingly after your cash. But the devil drives—you know the proverb.

I have been considering my position vis a vis McClure and would like your opinion upon what follows:—I reckon that I owe them about £180—more or less. This money had been advanced on account of *The Rescue* in various sums since 98.

The agreement under which I attained these payments gives to McClure the serial rights both *here* and in America and the American book rights for the sum of £250. (I can't find my copy of agreement but I think it specifies also 10% royalty) *NB* at that time McClure and Doubleday were one firm.

Since then I delivered to them *Lord Jim*. However Doubleday got that but I understand that when the final division takes place the book is to go to McClure Phillips. (For *Lord Jim* I had £20 from Doubleday alone so far on a 10% royalty.)

You will note that I delivered one long novel (Jim) and as far as I knew when I was writing it I was writing it for McClure.

Now the thing is to finish the *Rescue*. Much of it is written and much remains to be done. I don't see how I can set out about it (living as I do from hand to mouth) unless I can get something for it; I mean something more. It is an evident necessity. As to why I went writing Jim and the short stories while it was my evident duty to go on writing the *R* I simply can't explain. It has caused me worry and pain enough, goodness knows.

The next was 'To-morrow', finished in January 1902.

However while I owed them the Rescue every line of the other work was also for them. Thus (besides Jim) all the matter of the two vols: of short stories is destined for McClure, without formal agreement but on a general understanding of 10% royalty in America.

Looking at the position from all sides I think that it would be better for me to surrender to McClure *completely* the copyright of the two vols of stories (and even of *Jim* as far as their interest in that book goes) on condition that they would write off the debt and cancel the agreement as to *The Rescue*.

In other words I propose to sell them outright for America the book rights of the two vols of stories (The *Youth* vol (B'wood) and The Typhoon vol (Hein)) and such interest as they may have in *Jim* for say £180 and the release from the agreement as to *Rescue*. I seek to be thus released really for the purpose of being enabled to finish that story in some peace of mind. I am animated by the most friendly sentiments towards McClure and admit I have failed in my part of the agreement lamentably. But if I am ever to work to some purpose at that book I must have my liberty to go into the market with it and thus insure the means to finish it.

Do you think my idea feasible from a business point of view.

Pray tell me your opinion for indeed I would only wish to be released from the McC agreement on the assurance that you would handle the book (when free) unreservedly in the states and with the reserve of Heinemann's book rights on this side. From that last I can't get free.

If the thing strikes you as, after all, advantageous I would ask You to undertake the negociation.* It would be always a step towards freedom.

Pardon this lenght.* I wanted You to understand the position clearly.

> Kindest regards
>> Yours Conrad.

To Edward Garnett
Text MS Colgate; G. 177

> [letterhead: Pent Farm]
> 3ᵈ July 1901

Dearest Edward.

Am I to understand that, like the hero of the Inheritors, you have fallen amongst the Dimensionists and are about to become an interviewer? Then I must be the Great Callan—who, Pawling says, must be meant for Crockett.[1] And so be it.

But to see you, and to see you here, I am ready to turn myself into a Callan. I believe Fox paid Granger's expenses, so Pawling can't do less than buy you a return ticket for Sandling.[2] But come under any pretence and at whatever cost and help me to inherit the Earth before I die. There is no time to lose.

I feel as if I were asking you to come and see the last of me. A sort of invincible oppression bears me down and whether it is the mind or the body that is suffering it is literally—all one. It is a bad sign—and a great sadness.

Ever Yours,

Jph Conrad.

Our love to you three.—

P.S. I came up to London on Monday calculating I would see you at the oar in your galley.

To William Blackwood

Text MS NLS; Blackburn 129

[letterhead: Pent Farm]

4 July 1901

Dear Mr Blackwood.

I have asked Pinker to send you parts I. II and IV of our joint novel *Seraphina*. Part III I keep by me yet. It is as a matter of fact completely written. We had done with it. The whole secret of its being held back lies in this that since the prospect of its appearing in Maga I have given rein to my unholy passion for revising, reconsidering, re-writting.* I don't mean to say that there is anything, in that part, unsuitable for the pages of Maga. It is a part of adventure (and a good many of them) my concern being not the matter—which is all right—but the expression which on my final reading (all by myself) seems to me not—what shall I say?—consciencious* enough. Pray don't smile! Some passages struck me as lacking vigour—others as wrong in tone—too much *written* in fact; and therefore I want to write them once more, after my own fashion.

[1] S. R. Crockett (1860–1914), a former minister of the Free Church of Scotland, and a prolific member of the Kailyard school of sentimental fiction. See, however, n. 2, p. 345.

[2] In *The Inheritors*, Fox, a newspaper proprietor, sends Etchingham Granger to interview Callan, a pompous writer. Garnett appears as Lea, a sympathetic publisher's reader. His interview with Conrad is untraced.

This is what I am engaged in doing now and shall take a fortnight and perhaps a day or two more over it.

Meantime I enclose here an epitome of the part stating the events with which it deals. From parts I. II & IV you will be able to judge of the literary qualities and defects of our tale. This tale—which we call a romance—has been grubbed out of the British Museum by Hueffer.[1] All the details of the political feeling in Jamaica (about 1821) are authentic. There was really a perfectly innocent young Englishman who was tried for piracy and escaped the gallows by the merest hair's-breadth. There did exist a nest of pirates about that time on the coast of Cuba. They were a sorry lot—I admit. O'Brien is our own invention, and he is possible enough—I mean historically possible. Good many Irishmen took refuge in Spain, made careers, and founded families. For the rest you'll see we do not go in for analysis of character seeking rather to present a succession of picturesque scenes and personalities. We try to produce a variation from the usual type of romance our point of view being that the feeling of the romantic in life lies principally in the glamour memory throws over the past and arises from contact with a different race and a different temperament; so that the Spanish girl seems romantic to Kemp while that ordinary good young man seems romantic and even heroic not only to Seraphina but to Sanchez and Don Riego too.

Pardon this long letter; and pray believe me always very faithfully yours

Jph. Conrad.

To Ford Madox Ford

Text MS Yale; Unpublished

[letterhead: Pent Farm]
11/7/1901

My dear Ford

Thanks. Ten days or a fortnight will be plenty of time. There's no precise date by which I *must* have the money. It is intended to pay off the first instal^t of the loan (from the ins^{ce} Co)=£25 and the premium for the next 6 months £22.10. Its due on the 28th inst. but Watson would settle.

---

[1] Ford came across the story while working on his biography of Ford Madox Brown (1896): 'Cuban Pirates: A True Narrative', *All the Year Round*, N.S. Vol. 3 (1870), pp. 172–8.

The extra pounds I intended to send to my grocer. So you see 60 is not a precise sum. Anything between 50 & 60 will do.

My dear fellow you are very good. I must pay you some interest for my own sake and I mentioned 5% because it's easy to calculate—not because I suspected You of being first cousin to Shadrach and godson to Isaac Gordon.[1]

If you hold anything which you dont want to sell now, perhaps you could transfer to my name and I would lodge them with Watson and get credited that way?

Note the Scotsman's review. Obscurity![2]

Do you see what's the matter? It is the typographical trick of broken phrases: ... that upsets the critic. Obviously. He says the characters have a *difficulty of expressing themselves*; and he says it *only* on that account.

We must be careful as to that with our next.

I've got clean copy of Sera:. Just arrived.

Sorry for your bother with the hired Nymph. What's the matter! Anyway come soon. Little Nell and Dolly will help look after all the Children. Love

Yours ever

Conrad.

To J. B. Pinker
Text MS Berg; Unpublished

[Pent Farm]

Sunday [14 July 1901][3]

My dear Pinker.

I send you here the letter I received last night, thinking this may be of some use.

Let us leave the M'Clure business till we can talk it over.

And in connection with the stories you have I think that it would be no bad policy to let them out as soon as possible even if they don't fetch as much as you would like to get. As long as you can recoop* yourself (or very nearly) by the Am & English rights. It would, in my opinion, be

---

[1] The much-libelled Scottish Jew.

[2] *Scotsman* (Edinburgh), 4 July: despite the collaboration, the book 'has all the characteristic features' of Conrad's work, 'notably a certain curious obscurity. His characters never seem quite to understand what they want to say or have a singular difficulty in expressing themselves.'

[3] The only Sunday between the dates of the *Guardian* and *Daily Mail* pieces.

important to me to have a book out in November—one of my own. Its publication also would be so much towards my liberation vis-à-vis Heine^{nn}. I shall be ready with a final story may be by the end of Aug.

The *Inheritors* if they do no other good will bring my name forward. There's a Daily Mail man coming to see me on Tuesday. An excellent review came out in the Mch^{er} Guard: of the 10th.[1] The review in the Chronicle gives a basis for my talk with the D. M. man.[2] We may expect there one or two pars. Kindest regards

Yours

J. Conrad.

Many thanks for £40 paid in to Watson.

To John Galsworthy

Text MS Forbes; Unpublished

[letterhead: Pent Farm]
Sunday. [14 July 1901][3]

Dearest Jack.

Do come!

All you say of the book is all right. Let it go.

But I've been thinking of Your play.[4] I have indeed. That's too promising to let go. And I believe there is a solution.

Let the child have died—don't you see.

To my mind this makes everything possible and the position is scarcely touched except in so far that the *old people* should be presented as having greatly loved that grandson and therefore as in sympathy with the daughter-in-law who—they of course know—is not happy with their son. *The Son* remains as you meant him (subject to the remarks I made as to his character). And as a matter of fact the 2^d act may remain as

---

[1] 'It is a ghost story of a new kind, with the vulgar thrills eliminated for a strange quality of mental disturbance. Its great merit lies in the extraordinary delicacy of its literary presentment.'

[2] The *Daily Chronicle* reviewer (11 July) was not impressed: 'We felt that we had been bamboozled ... The style is spasmodic, the dialogue gaspy; the interlocutors would seem to suffer from shortness of breath, as well as from confusion of ideas.' The *Daily Mail* reporter (19 July) was more respectful: 'his plots have ... a sense of reality unequalled in modern literature'. Conrad told this interviewer that the idea for *The Inheritors* came 'from a striking sentence' by H. G. Wells. 'The Master Mariner Turned Novelist' put his early longing for the sea down to reading Marryat in Polish, and his choice of English over French to the former's 'infinite variety' and 'boundless possibility'.

[3] Contents match the preceding letter.

[4] *The Civilised*, a play about the Forsytes; it was never finished (Marrot, pp. 133–51).

written with modifications of phrasing. Then in the 3^d the story would develop as You contemplated. The old people no longer loving their daughter-in-law want to stick to her for purposes of respectability. There can be inserted there a tremendous development of the family idea—but of that viva voce.

Pray my dear fellow don't be angry for this my meddling with Your art and Your work. I dare say my suggestion may be imbecile. However this is not written in any excitement. I have considered the notion since Friday last. Give it as much consideration as it deserves and we shall have a talk ready when you come. Don't come on Tuesday (unless in the evening) for a Daily mail man is coming in the middle of the day for a parag[ra]ph or two.

To Ford Madox Ford

Text MS Yale; Unpublished

[letterhead: Pent Farm]
19 July 1901

My dear Ford.

It's all right. I didn't bother You and after all Robert[1] is doing his duty.

I daresay he has written You of my new proposal.[2] So I shan't worry you who have a good "homme d'affaires" with details here. Briefly, for the policy, I ask you to advance me £100 in actual cash. You are safe and I am pleased.

Let us talk of other things. Very pleased to hear of ex^{llt} review in the rotten Telegraph.[3] This indeed is fame. Gals^{thy}, here for a day (yesterday), has sung the praise of your art, as shown in the Inh^{tors}. He is really and truly struck. So is Mme Poradowska from whom I just had a letter this afternoon. Her general disquisition on You is remarkable by the force and justness of outside observation—so clever as to amount almost to the reading of character. I have had a greatly enhanced opinion of the excellent woman since she—French!—has been so fascinated by Your verse and impressed by Your personality. In comparison with her insight—(shallow if you like)—James's "Un jeune homme modeste"

[1] Edward Garnett's brother, Ford's solicitor.
[2] Another loan on the insurance policy: for details of Conrad and Ford's manoeuvrings, see Mizener, pp. 64–5, 536–7.
[3] 'Not food for everyone, but . . . a work to be read and well weighed by the thoughtful, and of no small interest to the psychological student of the times' (*Daily Telegraph*, 14 July).

has an effect of farcical blindness.[1] After all give me the French for that sort of intelligence that picturesque intelligence that does not want to go digging holes into people's stomachs to look for moral significance before it could form an opinion.

Satis! for the present. Our love to You all

Yours

Conrad.

I send you the page relating to the book and premise she had read three chapters only so far. I also admit that the book being by us two to sign the gift with my own name would have looked invidious. So I wrote '*A Mme Poradowska avec les hommages des Auteurs.*'

To Ford Madox Ford

Text MS BL Ashley 2923; J-A, 1, 312

Private and Conf*al*

[letterhead: Pent Farm]
Tuesday. [23 July 1901][2]

My dear Ford.

This is what I've done:

I've sent parts I. II & IV of Seraphina to Pinker with instructions to send on to Edinburgh as soon as clean typed.[3] The second copy goes to the States. Our copy of Pts II & IV to come here. Pt I does not want any tinkering any more.

Part II I've worked at a little—reducing and bringing into line in matters of detail which we have overlooked here and there. Then to give the story a fair chance I have given up the idea of presenting the *Rescue* to B'wood. This was McClure's wish and intention. However without my consent he can't do that. I had reserved B. to myself.

Meldrum seems to think the acceptance of Seraphina a fairly certain thing. *M* goes north next week and will help M*r* B'wood to read the parts I. II. & IV. I write an epitome of p III and shall send it to Scotland in a day or two.

I've studied p III as a whole very earnestly. It is most important and it wants doing over. It must be given hard *reality*. The treatment as it

[1] Nevertheless, Ford was still repeating the judgment in 1921: *Thus to Revisit*, p. 115.
[2] The first Tuesday after the 'preliminary whisper' in the 20 July *Academy* (the next letter to Ford refers to the same piece). Misdated in Jean-Aubry and the BL catalogue.
[3] Meldrum sent the TS north on 5 August (Blackburn, p. 131).

stands is too much in the air—in places. I don't want to bother you now by going into the argument. I shall do the thing myself but of course I would want to speak to you about it. Don't let this interrupt your work on the dear old Harry.[1] I hear You've been gathering the pollen and the sweetness off the B'sh Museum and assume you are fabricating now the specimen combs.

I've made no combs. I've been (like Soane) ill—very ill—but if my arrangements come off I won't "stop the confounded presses and spoof old Hueffer."[2]

On the other hand pray don't curse me in your heart. I am surprised I've preserved my sanity all these days—but never mind.

There's no doubt that Heinemann means to work up the Inheritors. In Pawling's opinion there is nothing against the book's success but the general slump in the trade. Of the slump alas, there can be no doubt. I had heard of it from Meldrum who has no conceivable reason to mislead me.

Otherwise P would be *certain* of success. I've never before heard such talk of anything with my name to it. So hopeful, I mean. There shall be a campai[g]n. Different plans are under consideration. One of them is to start a general discussion on methods of collaboration. Have you noticed in the last *Aca*[y] a sort of preliminary whisper?[3] That's it. The other hare it seems is to be a philosophical hare. That's what Niet[z]sche's phil[phy] leads to—here's your overman—I said.[4] I kept my gravity in the big armchair and with extreme sobriety made suggestions: the authors by the introduction of the *4*[th] *D* tried to remove their work from the sphere of mere personalities. They attack not individuals but the spirit of the age—the immoral tendencies arising from a purely materialistic view of life which even reach the lower classes (Slingsby,[5] I suppose).

I had hard work to keep my countenance with the photo of the Great Callan, on the mantelpiece, looking at me. Pawling wanted to know who Fox was. I smiled enigmatically. P *has* read the book. He talked glibly of

---

[1] Henry VIII; preliminary work on *The Fifth Queen* (1906).

[2] 'Deuced good idea', says Soane in *The Inheritors*, 'to stop the confounded presses and spoof old Fox' (p. 187).

[3] A note in the 'Literary Week' column of the *Academy*, 20 July. 'A Correspondent' 'suggests that a very good subject, *The Collaborators*, remains to be handled by some clever writer'. He also hints that *The Inheritors* was drafted by the younger and revised by the older author.

[4] The *Daily Chronicle* review (11 July) had already seen a connection between Fourth Dimensionists and *Übermensch*.

[5] A modest investor taken in by de Mersch's swindle.

the D de Mers[c]h, of your aunt (she's no aunt of mine) in Paris, of Churchill of Gurnard (he called him Chamberlain half the time) of Polehampton[1] (he winked and I winked), of Callan

—"That's Crockett". My lower jaw fell.

(I swear that this is exactly and verbatim what happened) He looked me hard in the eye.

"Of course it's Crockett. There's no man who had worked that kind of business more."[2]

I asked him not to let it out; and he said "oh no. Of course not."

By the immortal Jove it was like a chapter out of the very book itself.

Anyway that's what's in the wind. When you good people come along I shall tell you more. Burn this letter for fear Your German Girl should sell it to a Belgian newspaper[3] and we should stand revealed as 4th Dim[ists] ourselves.

I am much better for the rush to town. Otherwise all goes badly with me. But never fear. S[eraphina] shall get herself written before very long.

Let us know when You good people are coming. Love from us all

Yours

C.

I am sending you 4 copies of the Eng. Edition, your share of the eight which arrived today.

---

[1] If the book be understood as a *roman à clef*, Fox comes from Alfred Harmsworth (soon to be Lord Northcliffe), de Mersch from King Leopold II of the Belgians, Churchill from A. J. Balfour, Gurnard from Joseph Chamberlain, and Polehampton from T. Fisher Unwin; beyond being well-connected in France, the narrator's aunt bears little resemblance to Mme Poradowska.

[2] Arguably there was. The novelist most given to vapid public pronouncements against materialism was not Crocket but Hall Caine. (Conrad said what he thought of him in the letter to Aniela Zagórska of Christmas 1898.) It was Caine who provided the gold (if not the literary jewels) for the crown of Heinemann's success and, as the first author Heinemann had ever published, no doubt it was Caine whose photograph adorned the office mantelpiece.

[3] Which might spot the resemblance between the Congo Free State and the fictional Système Groenlandais. 'Your German Girl': one of Ford's cousins?

To Ford Madox Ford
Text MS Yale; Unpublished

[letterhead: Pent Farm]
Thursday. [25 July 1901][1]

Dearest Ford.

I have to day received the cheque from Robert—and many thanks to You for staving off the impending annihilation.

Poor Jessie is very bad with gastric neuralgia and I've had a hell of a time. Mrs. George arrived tonight so I hope I shall be able to get on with my—Our—work to morrow.

Sometimes I feel as if my brain were on the point of boiling over the top of my miserable skull.

Yes. D[aily] T[elegraph] is all right. And so in a measure is the D[aily] N[ews][2] and I feel more and more like a thief of Your cleverness. Upon the whole (apart from cash) this thing must do us good—at any rate as far as our next book is concerned. The note in the Academy originates from 21 Bedford S[t3] as you may've guessed.

I'm weary, weary, weary—but I trust and hope you good people are well and happy. With love Yours

Jph. Conrad

PS Jess is better and in a couple of days shall've picked up her strength again.

To the *New York Times* 'Saturday Review'
Text New York Times, 24 August 1901, p. 603

Pent Farm, Kent
Aug. 2, 1901.

Referring to *The New York Times Saturday Review* of July 13, it is impossible not to recognize in the review of one "extravagant story" the high impartiality exercised in estimating a work which, I fear, remains not wholly sympathetic to the critic.[4]

A feeling of regret mingles with gratitude on that account. It is a great good fortune for a writer to be understood; and greater still to feel that he

---

[1] Although the following Thursday is possible, the earlier date better suits the pace of the dealings with Robert Garnett.

[2] Which called their book a 'very interesting study of the loveless race for power and wealth' (24 July).

[3] Heinemann's office.

[4] 'The book lacks the emotional power of "Lord Jim," but it is clean, vigorous, and not machine made' ('Saturday Review', p. 499).

has made his aim perfectly clear. It might have been wished, too, that the fact of collaboration had been made more evident on the face of the notice. The book is emphatically an experiment in collaboration; but only the first paragraph of the review mentions "the authors" in the plural—afterward it seems as if Mr. Conrad alone were credited with the qualities of style and conception detected by the friendly glance of the critic.

The elder of the authors is well aware how much of these generously estimated qualities the book owes to the younger collaborator. Without disclaiming his own share of the praise or evading the blame, the older man is conscious that his scruples in the matter of treatment, however sincere in themselves, may have stood in the way of a very individual talent deferring to him more out of friendship, perhaps, than from conviction; that they may have robbed the book of much freshness and of many flashes of that "private vision" (as our critic calls them) which would have made the story more actual and more convincing.[1]

It is this feeling that gives him the courage to speak about the book—already written, printed, delivered, and cast to the four winds of publicity. Doubtless a novel that wants explaining is a bad novel: but this is only an extravagant story—and it is an experiment. An experiment may bear a certain amount of explanation without confessing itself a failure.

Therefore it may perhaps be permissible to point out that the story is not directed against "some of the most cherished traditions and achievements of Englishmen."[2] It is rather directed at the self-seeking, at the falsehood that had been (to quote the book) "hiding under the words that for ages had spurred men to noble deeds, to self-sacrifice, and to heroism."[3] And apart from this view, to direct one's little satire at the tradition and the achievements of a race would have been an imbecile futility—something like making a face at the great pyramid. Judge them as we may, the spirit of tradition and the body of achievement are the very spirit and the very body not only of any single race, but of the entire mankind, which, without the vast breadth and colossal form of the past would be resolved into a handful of the dying, struggling feebly in the

---

[1] 'If he sometimes flashes before us what we have fondly hoped was a private view, he does it without malice or coarseness.'

[2] According to the reviewer, the reader's verdict will depend on being able to appreciate satire against these 'cherished traditions', yet the book as a whole 'is more than a clever study of contemporary manners, morals and ideals. Mr. Conrad sees the significant facts of life and character.'

[3] The first British edition reads: 'to noble deeds, to self-sacrifice, to heroism' (p. 282).

darkness under an overwhelming multitude of the dead. Thus our Etchingham Granger, when in the solitude that falls upon his soul, he sees the form of the approaching Nemesis, is made to understand that no man is permitted "to throw away with impunity the treasure of his past—the past of his kind—whence springs the promise of his future."[1]

This is the note struck—we hoped with sufficient emphasis—among the other emotions of the hero. And, besides, we may appeal to the general tone of the book. It is not directed against tradition; still less does it attack personalities. The extravagance of its form is meant to point out forcibly the materialistic exaggeration of individualism, whose unscrupulous efficiency it is the temper of the time to worship.

It points it out simply—and no more, because the business of a work striving to be art is not to teach or to prophesy (as we have been charged, on this side, with attempting,) nor yet to pronounce a definite conclusion.

This, the teaching, the conclusions, even to the prophesying, may be safely left to science, which, whatever authority it may claim, is not concerned with truth at all, but with the exact order of such phenomena as fall under the perception of the senses. Its conclusions are quite true enough if they can be made useful to the furtherance of our little schemes to make our earth a little more habitable. The laws it discovers remain certain and immovable for the time of several generations. But in the sphere of an art dealing with a subject matter whose origin and end are alike unknown there is no possible conclusion. The only indisputable truth of life is our ignorance. Besides this there is nothing evident, nothing absolute, nothing uncontradicted; there is no principle, no instinct, no impulse that can stand alone at the beginning of things and look confidently to the end. Egoism, which is the moving force of the world, and altruism, which is its morality, these two contradictory instincts of which one is so plain and the other so mysterious, cannot serve us unless in the incomprehensible alliance of their irreconcilable antagonism. Each alone would be fatal to our ambition. For, in the hour of undivided triumph, one would make our inheritance too arid to be worth having and the other too sorrowful to own.

Fiction, at the point of development at which it has arrived, demands from the writer a spirit of scrupulous abnegation. The only legitimate basis of creative work lies in the courageous recognition of all the irreconcilable antagonisms that make our life so enigmatic, so burden-

---

[1] 'It is permitted to no man to break with his past, with the past of his kind, and to throw away the treasure of his future' (p. 305).

some, so fascinating, so dangerous—so full of hope. They exist! And this is the only fundamental truth of fiction. Its recognition must be critical in its nature, inasmuch that in its character it may be joyous, it may be sad; it may be angry with revolt, or submissive in resignation. The mood does not matter. It is only the writer's self-forgetful fidelity to his sensations that matters. But, whatever light he flashes on it, the fundamental truth remains, and it is only in its name that the barren struggle of contradictions assumes the dignity of moral strife going on ceaselessly to a mysterious end- -with our consciousness powerless but concerned sitting enthroned like a melancholy parody of eternal wisdom above the dust of the contest.

Joseph Conrad

To William Blackwood
Text MS NLS; Blackburn 130

[letterhead: Pent Farm]
3^d Aug 1901.

My Dear Mr Blackwood.

Some time ago Edward Garnett telling me he was about to terminate his connection with Mr Heinemann spoke of his intention of doing some work in the sphere of criticism. A fundamental study of critical work as a whole, under the title of: "The Contemporary Critic" was to begin a series of appreciations including the work of modern poets and novelists with a philosopher or two thrown in.

I have been always anxious to see him do something off his own bat instead of judging in obscurity the more or less deplorable play of countless others. His unaffected desire to appeal to that part of the public which the Editors of "Maga" had known how to group around their magazine—the *only* magazine—my great belief in his talent and abilities, our general agreement upon the subject in hand—have induced me to promise that I would forward his Introductory study to you, with an earnest request to give it your consideration, basing myself on such rights as my status of contributor gives me of access to my chief—but more still on my experience of your open mind and of your kindness.

Therefore I forward here P I of the Cont^{ry} Critic. Part II (of about the same number of pages) shall be ready very soon. The matter of it is interesting and true. The expression studiously moderate. I need not say that Mr Lang[1] is by no means attacked there. On the contrary his utterances are used as the text of the argument because his position in the first rank is recognized as indisputable. Believe me, dear Mr Blackwood most faithfully yrs

Jph. Conrad.

To Edward Garnett
Text G. 178

The Pent
4th August 1901

My dear Edward,

We have been very much shocked at the awful catastrophe of which I've read without ever dreaming it touched your wife so close.[2] Pray assure her of our most affectionate sympathy. I would like exceedingly to see you both and may try to come over but things are damnably bad with me anyhow—Your stuff is absolutely right, interesting, first rate, written judiciously and excellently well in tone with Maga in her unpolitical mood. I of course am completely convinced by this preliminary exposé and have the greatest confidence in what is to come. And without flattery I am interested and eager to see more of it. The thing goes on most felicitously as to phrasing, is developed with a pleasing assurance. Here, you feel, is a man who knows what he is writing. A sort of air of meditation broods over it all and is positively seductive. What Blackwood may think I don't know and am not enough of a devil to guess at. I've sent off tonight the MS of the first instalment with a pressing letter of mine advocating not so much the man (you) as the expounder of opinions views and feelings very near my own heart, but which I could never hope to express with anything like such certitude and effect. (This because B. had hinted *I* would be acceptable in critical wandering which is all I am capable of). I've also warned Meldrum who I am sure will do what's right by your copy. I mentioned that you are leaving H[einemann] for good in a short time.

I've been unable to think but the writing had not been the easier for

---

[1] Andrew Lang (1844–1912), the Scottish poet, editor, translator, historian, and student of folklore and mythology. Rejected by Blackwood, the article was taken by the *Monthly Review* (and reprinted in *Friday Nights*). It did indeed attack Lang – for his hostility to modern literature.

[2] Her brother, Robert Black, a surgeon from Brighton, was killed on the Matterhorn during a 'hopelessly underguided' climb (letter from another member of the party, *The Times*, 30 July).

that. Tell good old Ford that he is not utterly undone as yet by the Fatal Partnership, but there is gathering a pretty lot of material for a sombre drama of the literary-domestic order—which he may have an opportunity to write and make his fortune thereby.

My love to all the houseful

Always yours

Conrad

To Edward Garnett

Text MS Berg; G. 179

[Pent Farm]

Monday evening. [5 August

1901][1]

Dearest Edward.

Last night I posted you a letter care of Hueffer who will no doubt forward. We did not know Dr Black was your wife's brother till Hueffer wrote. We were greatly shocked but as at the same time Ford said you were coming directly to Winchelsea I did not write to the Cearne. One never has anything to say unless one is completely and stonily indifferent. Assure your wife of our profound sympathy—and we are concerned about her health. It must have been a cruel shock. Drop us a line because Jess imagines that you delay the visit to W. on account of your wife's unsatisfactory state. I trust not.——The MS. went off to E'gh on Sat evening, backed by a letter to B pressing for immediate consideration not so much on account of my interest in Your work as in the views expressed with which I am in complete accord and could never hope to put forward in a manner so effective and fundamental. I wrote in that strain just because B has been asking me to contribute some critical views—and so this pins him down so to speak. I've also warned Meldrum who is friendly and is sure to put his shoulder to the coach if B sticks in the mud of hesitation with it. My impressions I have put down in the other letter to you and here only say emphatically First rate! Get on with the IId instalment. It is the right thought, the right tone, the right words. Ever Yours

J.C.

PS Of course it is impossible to guess how it'll strike B. I build my hopes on the judicial tone. Anyway speak with authority! I mean—force

---

[1] See previous letter.

the note of it. *That* is your line. You do it so well. And after all you have the right to be magistral. You <u>*know*</u>!

To Edward Garnett
Text G. 180

[Pent Farm]
Wednesday [7 ? August 1901][1]

My dearest Edward.

I've written to B—saying that the end of the paper shall be ready next week and'll reach him through my hands.

The fact is my dear fellow that if the machine runs stiffly (as *you* say—because no creaking is audible in part I) it is because of dis-use, of non-use. The raw thought is with you—valuable, weighty, informed by sensitive feeling and justice, flowing from instinct and therefore the more valuable. The distilling apparatus may be clogged as to pipes, but it has only to be kept at work to clear itself. Meantime no one would guess or suspect that there is anything the matter.

I repeat: the authoritative attitude is the attitude for you. Every truth requires some pretence to make it live. Let this be your pretence, your pose. Speak magistrally no matter how you may feel.

I am with you, in thought, during every spare minute, but with all my hopefulness I don't find anything really convincing to say. So vale.

Ever yours

Conrad

To Ford Madox Ford
Text MS Yale; Unpublished

[Pent Farm]
Wednesday. [21 August 1901][2]

My dear Ford.

All my faculties being concentrated on my inadequate collaboration had Rossetti[3] required the very roof I would have only grunted.

---

[1] Garnett dates this letter 7 August, and it does echo the language of two days before. Yet the reference to the essay's being ready 'next week' recalls a similar statement in the 26 August letter to Blackwood. Conrad, however, had not yet seen either version of the ending, a fact suggesting the earlier date.

[2] Blackwood's letter rejecting 'Seraphina' would have reached Conrad on Friday, 16 August. It seems improbable that he would dawdle over passing the news to Ford.

[3] Work on Ford's study of Dante Gabriel (1902).

Jessie has been again seedy but not so bad this time. Did you see the Reviews? Even *Literature* was benign.[1]

Do you feel up to running over here for a day (and night). I should like to have a talk and a sort of consultation as to disposal of Seraphina which B with many circumlocutions declines.[2] Pity. But on the other hand it may be of advantage by leaving P[inker] quite free. Love to you all.

Yours always

Jph. Conrad.

To Edward Garnett
Text G. 181

[Pent Farm]
[23? August 1901][3]

Dearest Edward,

... I think that it would be impolitic to spring upon B'wood the 2d version. The fact is that the first version gave me a very favourable impression—and at any rate since you leave the decision to me I simply dare not interfere now. The paper as a whole is very good. I consider the first version of part II simply too short but in no other way defective. I regretted a certain lack of development. You should have spread your elbows more—taken room, spoken louder. Now the 2d version of part II is even shorter than the first version. On that ground alone (the thing being left to me) I would refrain from putting it before B'wood. We want weight, volume, a more opulent roll of your particular thunder—that's how I feel.

I write as I think. Of course if you instruct me definitely to forward the 2d version I shall do so at once and write to B'wood in the sense suggested in your letter. Only I repeat: we had better not.

I trust they won't keep us in suspense very long but the method of their madness is leisurely.

Love to you all

Ever yours

Joseph Conrad

---

[1] Finding *The Inheritors* 'more unsatisfactory than absurd' but 'extremely original' (17 August).

[2] With a consoling request for 'a light paper now and then' on literary topics (Blackburn, p. 132).

[3] Garnett misdates the letter of 20 September as 23 August. He may have done this by assigning an envelope postmarked on the latter date to the wrong MS. The present MS, in any case, must come after that of 7[?] August.

To William Blackwood

Text MS NLS; Blackburn 133

[letterhead: Pent Farm]
26 Aug. 1901.

Dear Mr Blackwood.

I am very delighted to hear you are well and "going strong" as Admiral Kennedy says. I've never had the pleasure of meeting him; but I've read and admired his book.[1] Now a book of that sort *is* the man—the man disclosed absolutely; and the contact of such a genuine personality is like an invigorating bath for one's mind jaded by infinite effort after literary expression, wearied by all the unrealities of a writing life, discouraged by a sunless, starless sort of mental solitude, having lost its reckoning in a grey sea of words, words, words; an unruly choppy sea running crosswise in all the endless shifts of thought. Oh! for a cutter and the Fatshan Creek, or for that wonderful beat-up from Mozambique Channel to Zanzibar![2] A wrestle with wind and weather has a moral value like the primitive acts of faith on which may be built a doctrine of salvation and a rule of life. At any rate men engaged in such contests have been my spiritual fathers too long for me to change my convictions—if I have pulled off my sea-boots, hung the sou-wester on a peg and made a tasteful trophy of my pet marline spikes. I re-read Admiral Kennedy's book with gratitude and have a great affection for the man; for, with due regard to all the differences, even a cat may nourish a tender sentiment for a king.

I hear from Garnett that the 2^d part of the critical essay shall be ready early next week. I've dropped him a note recommending the greatest possible diligence. I own that I am very anxious he should find a way to your convictions; for this man too is very genuine, capable under encouragement of achieving even brilliance and at any rate solidity of not an obscure sort. I think I forgot to say in my last letter that in the matter of writing over his signature he is indifferent. If it comes to publication it shall be as you prefer.

Thanks for your kind inquiries. My health is better than my industry which seems to depend on something mysterious and even more capricious than the weather. Still something is written every day.[3]

> Believe me dear Mr Blackwood
> always most faithfully yours
> Jph. Conrad.

[1] Blackwood published Admiral Sir William Robert Kennedy's *Hurrah for the Life of a Sailor: Fifty Years in the Navy* in 1901.

[2] Pp. 84–93 and 127–31 of Kennedy's book.

[3] On seeing this, Meldrum asked 'Is this the only letter you have had from Conrad? And did he not say anything about *Seraphina*?' (Blackburn, p. 134).

To Ford Madox Ford
Text MS Yale; Unpublished

[letterhead: Pent Farm]
Friday [6 September or 6 December 1901][1]

Dear Ford

To our everlasting confusion the man Mungeam (or Munn)[2] (may his father's grave be a browsing place for goats!) declares in writing he will bespeak the truck and put the furniture on board *packed in straw* for 12/- (twelve shgs sterling).

I am deafened by Jessie's crowing over that job. Obviously the man is courting ruin but if he *will* do it I wash my hands of this iniquity. You had better send on the address and the key of the bureau.

The disastrous transaction is to take place on Wednesday the 11th inst.

Our love

Yours

J. Conrad

To Edward Garnett
Text MS Colgate; G. 182

[Pent Farm]
Friday. [20 September 1901][3]

Dearest Edward.

I am bitterly disappointed at B'wood refusing your paper. The act seems to me unqualifiable; neither does he qualify it getting off the track with vague civilities.[4] One can only say "damn!"—

I haven't the heart to say anything else, besides mentioning that the addition of the matter you sent me last would not, as far as I can see, have influenced the issue of this attempt.

I shall send you the MS by the next post. You may work at it a little; but I despair of the current intelligence which nothing seems capable of

---

[1] Within the duration of the letterhead (type seven), only two months have a Wednesday the eleventh.

[2] Both common names around Hythe, but P. Munn of 134 High St was carter 'by appointment' to the S.E. Railway.

[3] Garnett's date, 23 August, must be wrong; Conrad would have heard of the rejection on Wednesday, 18 September.

[4] In a letter to Conrad: 'I have little sympathy with articles of this kind, which to my mind are somewhat futile as nobody reads them' (17 September, Blackburn, p. 134).

stirring. It is like a viscous pool. Things at most can fall into it and be lost, and give no ripple. Is it worth throwing things into it?

Love to you all

Ever yours

Conrad

To William Blackwood

Text MS NLS; Blackburn 134

[letterhead: Pent Farm]
7th Nov 1901

Dear Mr Blackwood.

My conduct is certainly outrageous but I am getting such a hardened sinner that even a plausible apology does not run easily from my pen. It seems to me that I have already used all the forms of them, and I daren't or care not to produce the old excuses—so truthful after all, and so threadbare.

Of course I was sorry (without in the least questioning your judgment) that you did not see your way to accept Garnett's article; and I will admit the rejection of *Seraphina* had shaken the confidence with which I looked upon that work. So, as one can not turn back till the furrow is ploughed to the end, I took it in hand: and whether I've finally spoiled a big lot of paper or made some sort of tale I can't say. In any case I suppose the seasons shall follow each other in their secular course, and I would not have mentioned the matter at all, only that I wish you to know I've not been exactly lying on the floor and groaning. Such was the practice of a certain shipmaster I've known in my very young days and I remember well my astonishment at such an irrelevant conduct. Truth to say looking back now I am not so astonished. We live and learn; only I haven't got a man at *£8.10* p month, to write my confounded stuff for me and save the ship.

I hope by the 15th of Jan[y] next to place in your hands about 30000 words for the *Youth Vol*—perhaps a little more. Characteristic matter suitable for binding together with what is already written—and essentially autobiographical. That is, more in the note of *Youth* than in that of the *H of D*.

Of the three stories which are the sum of my remarkable work for the year ending last July one is accepted by the *P.M.M* and another by the Ill: Lond: News.[1] The third, 'Falk' (the name of the principal man) no

---

[1] 'Amy Foster' by the *Illustrated London News*, 'Typhoon' by the *Pall Mall Magazine*.

one seems anxious to gather in. Probably on account of his size, because his behaviour, if cannibalistic, is extremely nice throughout—or at any rate perfectly straightforward. I think so well of the story that if it handn't* been for very shame after the avalanche of *Jim* I would have sent it North to try its luck with you. But it was impossible, and moreover it must go for Mr Heinemann's volume.

The last *Linesman* was of a really superior excellence. I've ordered the book.[1] As to *Charlotte*[2] the genuine[ne]ss of its conception the honesty of its feeling make that work as welcome as a breath of fresh air to a breast oppressed by all the fumes and cheap perfumes of fiction that is thrown on the altar of publicity in the hopes of propitiating the god of big sales. It is refreshing indeed. And of course, I won't say the display, but the *outlay* of skill, very quiet, very sure skill, is of no mean order. Altogether a delightful piece of work.

Street's critical article is (apart from undeniable literary quality) first rate and gets home most convincingly.[3]

I shall be writing soon to Mr Meldrum and as I get a handful of pages ready shall be sending them to him for transmission in Edinburgh.

Believe me, dear Mr Blackwood always very faithfully yours

Jph. Conrad.

To J. B. Pinker
Text MS Berg; Unpublished

[letterhead: Pent Farm]
7 Nov. 1901.

My dear Pinker.

I am of course glad that Amy Foster is placed at last at the price you mention; but don't for a moment suppose I have felt at any time that anything whatever was 'unsatisfactory'.

I've at last finished <u>S</u>. I've put remarkable guts into that story. It goes now to Hueffer to make a few alterations necessary to square Part II and IV with part III which is practically my work. I have no doubt the thing is greatly improved, made more interesting and exciting. It is, you understand, a story of adventure but written not exactly according to the usual formula for work of that kind. We have tried to convey a

---

[1] Captain M. H. Grant ('Linesman'), *Blackwood's*, Vol. 170, pp. 579–90, and *Words of an Eyewitness: The Struggle in Natal* (Blackwood, 1901).
[2] *The Conquest of Charlotte* by David Meldrum, running as a serial.
[3] G. S. Street, 'Three Novels', pp. 271–6.

certain impression of picturesqueness—something new in its effect as a whole.

I wish, if practicable, that you should keep the account of *Seraphina* separately—quite distinct from my own work. I think you have advanced me something (I fancy £30 or else 40) on *that tale*. Is that so? Would you tell me?

Half of proceeds would belong to Hueffer of course. But now the book is completed and beyond the ordinary hazards of uncertain life I would be glad if you could advance me a little more. Let's put it that the story serial & book, Eng. & Am: shall bring, say £240. That's a very low estimate of which £120 would come to me. If I had 40 already could you let me have another *40* on that expectation? Then, as soon as I send you the short story we spoke about (6–7 thous)[1] you'll give something for that too. Hang it all I must keep my head above water if only some day to make a splash—a big one. For indeed even *that* is possible. Many thanks for your friendly labours.

Your[s] faithfully

J Conrad.

Will you tell me if I am correct in the statement below. I've lost or mislaid the little book where I enter my miseries.
I had from you this year:

---

for—'Typhoon'—£100)
,, —'Falk'—£60   )   200
,, —'Amy Foster'—40)
        and
for '*Seraphina*' on acct of my share £40. (?).

To John Galsworthy
Text MS POSK; J-A, 1, 301

[Pent Farm]
11th Nov. 1901.

Dearest Jack.

I didn't write about the book[2] before, first because Jess had it—and she reads slowly—and then I had at last some proofs of mine a whole batch which it took me several days to correct. Nevertheless I've read

---

[1] 'To-morrow'? For the circumstances of its creation, see the letters of early January 1902.
[2] *A Man of Devon*, a newly published collection of stories.

the book twice—watching the effect of it impersonally during the second reading—trying to ponder upon its reception by the public and discover the grounds of *general* success—or the reverse.

There is a certain caution of touch which will militate against popularity. After all to please the public (if one isn't a sugary imbecile or an inflated fraud) one must handle one's subject intimately. Mere intimacy with the subject won't do. And conviction is found (for others—not for the author) only in certain contradictions and irrelevancies to the general conception of character (or characters) and of the subject. Say what you like man lives in his eccentricities (so called) alone. They give a vigour to his personality which mere consistency can never do. One must explore deep and believe the incredible to find the few particles of truth floating in an ocean of insignificance. And before all one must divest oneself of every particle of respect for one's characters. You are really most profound and attain the greatest art in handling the people you do not respect. For instance the minor characters in V[illa] R[ubein]. And in this volume I am bound to recognise that Forsythe[1] is the best. I recognise this with a certain reluctance because indubitably there is more beauty (and more felicity of style too) in the M of D. The story of the mine[2] shows best your strenght* and your weakness. There is hardly a word I would have changed; there are things in it that I would give a pound of my flesh to have written. Honestly—there are. And your mine-manager remains unconvincing because he is too confoundedly perfect in his very imperfections. The fact is you want more scepticism at the very foundation of your work. Scepticism the tonic of minds, the tonic of life, the agent of truth—the way of art and salvation. In a book you should love the idea and be scrupulously faithful to your conception of life. There lies the honour of the writer, not in the fidelity to his personages. You must never allow them to decoy you out of yourself. As against your people you must preserve an attitude of perfect indifference—the part of creative power. A creator must be indifferent; because directly the 'Fiat!' had issued from his lips there are the creatures made in his image that'll try to drag him down from his eminence—and belittle him by their worship. Your attitude to them should be purely intellectual, more independant,* freer, less rigorous than it is. You seem for their sake to hug your conceptions of right or wrong too closely. There is exquisite atmosphere in your tales. What they want now is more air.

---

[1] 'The Salvation of Swithin Forsyte', Galsworthy's first story of that family.
[2] 'The Silence'.

You may wonder why I write you these generalities. But first of all in the matter of technique, where your advance has been phenomenal and which has almost (if not quite) reached the point of crystallisation, we have talked so much and so variously that I could tell you now nothing that you have not heard already. And secondly these considerations are not so general as they look. They are even particular in as much that they have been inspired by the examination of your work as a whole. I have looked into all the volumes; and this—put briefly, imperfectly and obscurely—is what they suggested to me.

That the man who has written once the *Four Winds*[1] has written now the M of D volume is a source of infinite gratification to me. It vindicates my insight, my opinion, my judgment—and it satisfies my affection for you—in whom I believed and am believing. Because that *is* the point: I *am* believing. You've gone now beyond the point where I could be of any rse to you otherwise than just by my belief. It is if anything firmer than ever before, whether my remarks above find their way to your conviction or not. You may disagree with what I said here but in our main convictions we are at one.

Ever Yours

Conrad

To R. B. Cunninghame Graham
Text MS Dartmouth; Watts 138

[letterhead: The Bungalow,
Winchelsea]
New Year's Eve 1901

Très cher ami.

We have been here since the 24[th] and your letter did not reach me till yesterday, sent on by my wife who has gone home. I remain here to work up the last of our coll[aborati]on stuff.

I was under the impression that neither your wife nor yourself were in London—or even in England. So we only sent a card. For the same reason I did not write of the *Vanished Arcadia*.[2]

I am altogether under the charm of that book, in accord with its spirit and full of admiration for its expression. My very highest appreciation of your work (your written work—your lived word) can not be news to you. To word it efficiently I can not. The more one likes a book the less there

---

[1] *From the Four Winds* (1897).
[2] A history of the Jesuit missions in Paraguay, published in September.

seems to be in our power to say it. I haven't the vol here. Hueffer lent his copy. I should like to write to you with the book at my elbow. There are supreme places—but the *evenness* of inspiration feeling and effort is amazing

Ever Yours

Conrad.

My best wishes to you both for the coming year.

You are very good to commend typhoon so much. It causes me the greatest pleasure. If you can see N^{os} of Ill^d Lond: News for the *14th 21st 28th* Dec^{er} there is a story of mine—Amy Foster. J'ai des doutes là dessus. Dites moi ce que Vous en pensez.

1902

To J. B. Pinker

Text MS Berg; Unpublished

[letterhead: The Bungalow,
Winchelsea]
6 Jany 1902

My dear Pinker.

I've been here since Xmas, very hard at work. There is always some sort of a devil interfering with Seraphina. Hueffer had a beastly accident with a chicken bone in his throat a few days before Xmas. It shook his nerves all to pieces as you may imagine—and indeed the affair looked dangerous enough. The cursed bone was got rid of on Box[ing] day but the man was as limp as a rag afterwards and totally unable to work. Then he developed a swollen face, a mild abscess in the cheek. That's better too.——Of course I had *all* the work to do and I have worked like a nigger abandoning 2 short stories begun and waiting for me at home. One fairly advanced and which I hoped to send you before new years' day.

I tried to keep my word with you—but don't you see the whole thing is not my fault though it looks as if it were. *H* is quite incapable just now to undertake the revision and filling in of parts which he should have commenced doing on the 10th of Dec. Consequently when I discovered the state of affairs I had to buckle to at once. I came here for two days and have been slaving ever since. To night I finished rearranging and fixing finally P[art] I—work which I never expected to do.

Meantime I am nearly going mad with worry. You may imagine I am hard pushed if I come to you again without a scrap of *MS*. But you must do the best you can for me—and if you can not or are disinclined to make a further advance pray tell me so at once (by return of post *to the Pent*) and I'll see what I can do with B'wood. This life will drive me mad. My ½ years premium on my policies together with int^t and paying off instalment of loan is what lies on my mind. I thought the two stories would have done it. Really all these anxieties do drive me to the verge of madness—but death would be the best thing. It would pay off all my debts and there would be no question of *MS*. Really if one hadn't wife & child I don't know——There are also some pressing bills. Damn. And with all this my bodily health is excellent it is the brain only that is fagged.—

Returning: I intend to stick now to *S[eraphina]*. Devil only knows when H. will catch on again but I can do it single handed. To make sure lets say end Jany for the *whole*. Meantime we shall send you in a few days

Parts I. II. III—this last will be short of the last few pages which I must keep to join with part IV which part is written and finished to the *end of the book*. Only Chap: 1 & 2 in it want recasting in consequence of the changes that have been made in the preceding part III.

I hope I am clear in this report of the state of the work. I am going home now (today) and intend to stick on blindly to the work till it is done with. It has been a worry—but I do firmly believe that here at least we hold something with a promise of popular success. There's easy style, plenty of action, a romantic atmosphere and a happy ending after no end of real hair's breadth escapes. I am sure the story can be placed on *its merits*. If you can only get some confounded good old Editor to read it success in that way is assured. With the first batch of *MS* we shall send you a note relating to the book. We shall be prepared if length (about 120000) is too great to reduce the whole affair considerably for purposes of serialising going to the point of taking out the whole of last part and replacing it with one chapter ending the adventure of hero and heroine there and then in a manner perfectly effective and satisfactory. But we desire that the book shall be submitted in full the alternative and shortening being a matter for the editor to decide. You may describe and introduce the book (if You do such things in that way) as a Straight romantic narrative of adventure where the hero is a Kent youth of good birth, the heroine a Spanish girl, the scene in England, Jamaica, Cuba, and on the sea—the personages involved besides Hero and Heroine smugglers, planters, sailors and authentic pirates—the last of the West Indian pirates; the whole story being founded on a fact carefully looked up in contemporary press and report of trial in Eng.—but by us brought about Romantically—the Romantic feeling being the basis of the book which is *not* a boy's story. You may take my word for it that it is a piece of literature of which we are neither of us at all ashamed.

It is rather the old thing (if you like) done in a way that is new only through the artistic care of the execution. The aim being to present the scenes and events and people *strictly realistically* in a glamour of *Romance*. The hero goes (accidentally so to speak) to seek Romance and finds it—a thing rather hard and difficult to live through. The time about 1823 is just far enough to bear the glamour of the past and near enough to enable us to dispense with elaborate explanations. In fact it is a serious attempt at *interesting, animated Romance*, with no more psychology than comes naturally into the action.

The two stories that I have by to finish are *one* the story of a retired skipper who lives in a cottage and expects his long lost son to return every day. He even plans a marriage for him with the daughter of their neighbour—who is the girl of the story. At last a young man arrives. He is the son but his behaviour is so extremely unlike what the capt expected (in fact he runs off with the spoons) that the father comforts himself with the idea that the fellow is an impostor. But a shipmate comes upon the scene and the capt is convinced at last. The girl is his consolation. 6000 words.[1]

The *other* is the story of a barge collision on the Thames and trial in court arising therefrom.[2] A rather funny affair which happened lately. Say 5 to 6000. Pray do what you can to tide me over. Faithfully yours

Conrad.

To David Meldrum

Text MS Duke; Blackburn 136

[letterhead: Pent Farm]
7 Jan 1902

My dear M[r] Meldrum

I know I behave most abominably to you, giving no sign of life till I got* to ask for something. But do not suspect me of ingratitude or forgetfulness. The fact is I seem unable to write a letter most of the time. Many a time have I sat down with you in my mind—and then laid the paper aside thinking that later on something more satisfactory could be written. But things do not improve.

Seraphina seems to hang about me like a curse. There is always something wrong turning up about that story. After M[r] B'wood's refusal of the same I first dropped it in disgust; then took it up again and have been working very hard at it. It is now a satisfactory piece of work but not quite rearranged and adjusted all through to the changes in action and in the reading of characters which I have introduced. Hueffer was to do all that—instead of which he goes and tries to swallow a chicken bone, gets nearly choked, awfully shaken up, unable to work and so on. I could have wept. Still there was no remedy so I buckled-to again and am still at it driving hard. I had just one days respite—Xmas—that's all—but the book is a new book and really not bad at all this time.

A few days'll see all the loose ends gathered up the tangle unravelled and the last knot tied. I long for the day! The last has been a disastrous year for me. I have wasted[3]—not idled—it away, tinkering here,

---

[1] The final version of 'To-morrow', 9,000 words long, has no spoons and no shipmate.
[2] He did not pursue the topic.   [3] Originally 'idled'.

tinkering there—a little on *Rescue*, more on that fatal *Seraphina* with only three stories (5000w) finished and *two* others begun lying in a drawer with no profit or pleasure to anybody.

On the other hand my health has been remarkably even and very tolerable—while when writing *Lord Jim* in ten months or less I had been feeling always on the brink of the grave. Explain it who may. And perhaps true literature (when you "get it") is something like a disease which one feels in one's bones, sinews and joints.

However I feel that if I can only tide over all the beastly bothers (that very naturally beset a man who has not worked enough to keep body and soul together) I shall get my feet on the firm ground or my head above water—whatever is the proper metaphor for this kind of situation. The delay in placing the three stories I had achieved dispirited me for a time in a most ridiculous and lamentable manner—for after all I *do* know fairly well what I am doing and the unwillingness of editors to publish the stuff does not affect its value.

I wish M^r B'wood could be induced to—so to speak—*hire* me permanently take all my stuff as it comes—lock it up—in a desk if he likes—publish when he likes, never publish! Anything! That would be an ideal state of affairs for me.

However thats a sort of dream that's not likely to come true.

Upon the whole Pinker I believe has tried and upon the whole has done his best for me. To appear in P[all] M[all] M[agazine] and the Ill: Lond: News is advantageous no doubt—but I only care for *Maga*, my first and only Love!

I am, as soon as ever I can, going to work for *Maga* at last. My idea is to do some autobiographical matter about Ships, skippers, and an adventure or two. How will that do? Pray tell me. *Youth* style upon the whole only not with the note of Youth in it but of the *wonderfulness* of things, events, people,—when looked back upon.[1] Do I make the idea clear? Of course it shall be 'fiction' in the same sense that *Youth* is fiction. Some critics, at the time, called it a short story! Q did, for instance.[2] And, by the bye his *fiction* in Maga is *x* well I won't say.[3] On the other hand the *C of C* is in many respects admirably done; with a sincerity of feeling and a skill! I am simply *fond* of that piece of work. Hueffer maintains, and has always maintained that it is *you*.[4] I wrote to Mr B'wood some time ago of the story putting the question. I've had no

[1] *The Mirror of the Sea* (1906)?   [2] *Speaker* (17 September 1898), p. 343.
[3] Quiller-Couch's *The Westcotes* ran from October to January.
[4] Meldrum's *The Conquest of Charlotte*, then in mid-serial.

answer to that letter. If it is you pray accept my congratulations in which there is nothing affected; they are as sincere as the story—though not of the same value.

Do you think M^r B'wood is in any way offended or annoyed. He need not be. One does what one can; and I've not wasted time or substance in riotous living tho' things are in a rather bad way with me just now. But that is nothing new.

And in this connection do you think M^r B'wood would advance me £50 after I send in say 5000 words. The whole contribution either in one or two *stories* (of the kind I mentioned) I intend to be of about 30000 words. Could you manage to convey him a hint to that effect. I don't ask how much he will pay me per 1000 but £4 would not be unreasonable. It is (in confidence) what Pinker advances me on my stuff on delivery. But he had a better price for my Ill. Lond News story. PMM paid me a little more. Why I so pointedly ask you the question is because the affirmative would set my mind a little at ease—and I expect to have the 5000 words done shortly. Of course I would be sending on more to you as fast as possible.

I am inutterably* weary of all this.

Thanks for your kindness, for your good wishes. I intended to write to you for the NY's day but being in Winchelsea, with Hueffer very unwell, and the wretched work on my hands I absolutely had no knowledge of the day incredible as it may appear. And after missing *the* day I waited with my wishes and congratulations till I had got away from the place. I arrived home only a couple of hours ago with the piles of MS of our Romance and in a worry that almost drives me out of my mind.

Believe me dear Mr Meldrum
always yours most faithfully,
Jph. Conrad.

PS I have also by me a paper comparing the spirit of Elisabethan* times with ours as expressed in the respective literatures.[1] Nothing heavy. I would polish it up if you think there is any chance of acceptance for Maga. Unsigned of course.

---

[1] Vanished.

To J. B. Pinker

Text MS Berg; Unpublished

[Pent Farm]
8 Jan: 1902.

My dear Pinker.

I fail to apprehend what inspired the extraordinary contents of your letter which I received this morning. All you had to do was to say yes or no. Mine was written fully not to get the easier at your pocket but from another motive—not worth explaining now. But it was never intended to give you an opening for a lecture. It will take more than the delay in delivering *S* to make *me* a failure; neither do I believe it will put you into the B'cy Court. And I am not just now in the right frame of mind for the proper appreciation of a lecture. I am working twelve hours in the twenty four with the full knowledge of my ideal and of my risk. What do you imagine? What is my purpose do you think?

What of my letter of the 7th of Nov? On that date I did say that my particular part which (you might have understood) only our scrupulous sense of what is due to our work induced us to reconsider, was finished and the book as a whole actually existed; but at the same time or shortly after (in fact as soon as I was informed of it) I wrote to you saying that the putting together and altering made necessary by the modified scheme would be delayed by my excellent collaborator's engagement to write a short book of art criticism at the demand of a publisher.[1] He could not be expected to sit idle waiting for the moment I was ready for him to come in with his revision. When his work was done he went to London with it. There, unfortunately, he had an accident of a dangerous nature,[2] and though still greatly suffering from the shock is doing his best now; but of course a delay was bound to ensue. What prevented us sending the stuff to [you] as it stood? It was intrinsically as good as any fifty MS you sell in the year. Pray do not write to me as I were a fool blundering in the dark. There are other virtues than punctuality. Have you the slightest idea of what I am trying for? Of what is my guiding principle which I follow in anxiety, and poverty, and daily and unremitting toil of my very heart. Come, my dear fellow, I am not one of your 25-year-old geniuses you have in your pocket, or one of your saleable people who drive three serials abreast.[3] I am another kind of person. If you don't want the bother of my stuff saddled with my other imperfections tell me

---

[1] *Rossetti* (1902).
[2] Nearly choking himself to death at his birthday party.
[3] Like Pinker's client Arnold Bennett, capable of writing an entire novel in a month.

to go to the devil. That won't offend me and I'll go as soon as ever you had your money back. But don't address me as if I were a man lost in sloth, ignorance or folly. Were you as rich as Croesus and as omnipotent as all the editors rolled into one I would not let such a tone pass without resenting it in the most outspoken manner. And don't write to me of failure, confound it! because you and I have very different notions of failure. It is an impertinence if You want to know my name for it. And I am willing to let the future judge whether the name does apply.

I had asked you for £40 I believe. To this demand in the given circumstances there was the reply of no—in business—or in friendly—terms. I was prepared for it. But what does the last par: of your letter mean? Who are the people I am to send to you? My tradesmen? Or my banker who has known me for some few years and does not talk to me of failure because my acct/ is overdrawn. This is the sort of thing one writes to a grub street dipsomaniac to stop him bothering one—not to a man of my value. Am I a confounded boy? I have had to look death in the eye once or twice. It was nothing. I had not then a wife and child. It was nothing to what I have to go through now pen in hand before what to *me* spells failure. I am no sort of airy R. L. Stevenson who considered his art a prostitute and the artist as no better than one.[1] I dare say he was punctual—but I don't envy him. What could you say to the "people"? "Oh Conrad. I know him. I had two stories of his for some eight months and another for nearly six. I did advance him money and may do so again if he takes my advice and writes 'straight on'". —Frankly I don't see much in that offer and if my letter displeases pray consider that sincerity for sincerity we are quits.

Sincerely yours

Joseph Conrad.

---

[1] Stevenson's attitude to literature was moral (or even moralistic) rather than meretricious; given the difficult birth of *Romance*, his real offence in Conrad's eyes must have been his facility in making up adventure stories.

To Ford Madox Ford

Text MS Yale; Unpublished

[Pent Farm]
Friday morning [10 January
1902][1]

Dearest Ford.

The crisis has come. To day Watson has kicked.[2] You may imagine how it soothed me for work. I haven't had a morsel of food to day. Don't worry about me. I only tell you this to explain why the Romance got hung up for to-day. For the Lord's sake drive on with your fixing. I feel *most confident* that you got the hang of it (from what you told me as to beginni[n]g of P II.) P I *is* all right. Chapter my bally rot[3] and look it over without killing yourself however. A great wheel has been buzzing in my head but half of the Son[4] is written and even typed. *All your* suggestion and *absolutely my* conception. Its most interesting and funny to see. It seems to me I could go on for ever but look how good I am. It is one AM. and I am going to bed instanter. As to sleep—nous verrons.

Love to you all

Yours Conrad.

I shall send you commencement of Spanish prison[5] with an indicatory note of the situations to be worked out. I intended to do it all myself—but—vous comprenez. Now is your time to back me up.

To J. B. Pinker

Text MS Berg; Unpublished

[Pent Farm]
Sunday Ev^g [12 January 1902][6]

My dear Pinker.

Cheque to hand all right. I shall send you by to morrow (Monday) evening's post the short story; that is if my wife can finish typing early enough to give me time for corrections.

Your refusal before was quite justified; Your compliance now is the more kind; for I don't suppose you had heard from Wells when you

---

[1] The circumstances point to a date in early January 1902: Ford is revising Part Two of *Romance*; Conrad is expanding Part Five and also writing 'To-morrow', which he sent to Pinker on 16 January. On Friday 3 January, however, Conrad was still at Ford's house.
[2] Demanding payment of his life-insurance obligations?   [3] Break it into chapters?
[4] 'To-morrow', the story of a son returning.   [5] *Romance*, v, 2.
[6] References to finishing 'To-morrow' and enlisting Wells's help with *Seraphina* place this letter between those of 6 and 16 January.

dispatched the money. The offer came from Wells (I assume you have *now* his letter). What I had asked him to come to me for was to show him the MS of Seraphina.[1] I recognised so much your point of view, that I wanted him to give you his fair judgment as to the sort of thing that was being produced.

In haste for post
Yours sincerely

Jph Conrad

To J. B. Pinker

Text MS Berg; Unpublished

The Pent.
Thursday. 16th Jan. 1902

My dear Pinker.

Herewith the story—title proposed "To-morrow" but he who buys it may call it as he jolly well likes. About 8000 words but I think rather less than more. The MS is in a devil of a state but my wife has been down with one of her headaches and I haven't had the heart to ask her to retype the blotted pages.

Generally: it is 'Conrad' adapted down to the needs of a magazine. By no means a potboiler; on the contrary. It has given me no end of trouble; but I hate restraint in size and tone; and I've had to cut out 2000 words and smooth down a few passages. Consequently I resent the thing's existence.

I need not say that during the writing (since Friday last) Seraphina had been suspended. Yesterday had a wire from H. saying Part II is done. There is therefore ready: Pts I. II. III. To part IV a few pages are wanting at the end. To part V. a few need re-writing at the beginning. We divide into five pts to equalize the length. Say 22000 each. We shall be sending you whats definitively ready so that they may begin the copies.

Saw Wells yesterday. I need not assure you that the proposal came from him—I mean as to guaranteeing the fresh *S.* advance. For the story here enclosed pray advance me as much as you safely may straight to *Watson* & Co 7. Waterloo Place. SW. and kindly drop me a line to say how much.

I am in a devil of a fix and very sick of it all. Directly you get all *S* I shall have to turn-to and do some 30000 for B'wood. That'll end the vol.

---

[1] Wells, one of Pinker's most profitable clients, had offered to guarantee another advance.

for him. The story enclosed here ends the vol: for Heinemann.[1] So far, good. I long for the day when *you* shall have *all* my stuff with no conditions, restrictions and arrears to make up. Remains on my overburdened neck the *Rescue*. A good thing in itself but eaten up with debt. If McClure will give me back my right of serialising 'Rescue' *in England* I offer him the 2 vols of stories (The B'wood and the H'mann vols) in exchange—I mean I am ready to give them up to him in absolute property. Not that I consider it a good bargain for me but simply because I require the Engsh serial rights to live on. Of course he would keep the *Am. Serial rights and book* against the advances he had made me. If you don't care to open that negociation* I shall do so myself. But at any rate give me your opinion of it. Something of the sort must be done—I fear—if I am ever to clear myself.

Yours very faithfully

J. Conrad

To J. B. Pinker
Text MS Berg; Unpublished

[Pent Farm]
24 Jan 1902

My dear Pinker.

I am afraid we must *not* accept Putnam's book offer for *Typhoon*. You might hold out possibilities of further work and so on. If you could place it serially with the *NY Critic*[2] it would relieve my mind because you've advanced me on that story more than the Engsh serial rights will cover. I hope you will be successful.

My dear fellow can you tell me how about serializing *Falk*? and that last story? Are there any prospects. Heinemann is waiting for the book. The few pounds I would get from him for it would be very welcome. And besides I don't want to make them too sick of me. Mind this is no grumble of any sort. I must tell You. Is there any chance—the remotest chance of coming out with the Typhoon Volume this spring.

I have had a touch of the liver. Ford is here; to-morrow night we shall post you 3/4 of Seraphina and the rest before end Jan^y.

Yours faithfully

Jph Conrad.

---

[1] *Youth* for Blackwood, *Typhoon* for Heinemann.
[2] It appeared there in February and March.

Yes; as to *McClure*. I would abandon to them propriety* in two vols of short stories *The Typhoon* (now complete) and *Youth* vol (to be ready next) in exchange for release serial rights of Rescue as far as *England and Col^{ies}* is concerned. Or better terms if you can get them.

To George Blackwood
Text MS NLS; Blackburn 140

> Pent Farm
> Stanford N^r Hythe
> Kent
> 28th Jany 1902

Dear Mr Blackwood.[1]

I am ready now, thank God! to take in hand the completion of the *Youth* volume of stories. I say: thank God, because it is an unspeakable relief to write for *Maga* instead of for "the market"—confound *it* and all its snippetty works. To open one of their Magazines is like opening your tailor's book of patterns for trouserings—only the book of patterns would be the more genuine production of the two.

But first of all I wish to ask you whether you could see your way to take up for *serial* pub^{on} a story which I have on hand. What lies at the bottom of this cool request is this: I want Mr Heinemann's volume of short stories (now ready) *out of the way* (together with the Coronation)[2] for the sake of the *Youth* book. Otherwise I would not seek to add to the obligations under which I am to the House already.

You would really be rendering me a great service. The story is good; its size alone (24000 w) is against the speedy placing of it, and placed serially it must be because I had an advance on it from Pinker. It's* title is *Falk: A Reminiscence* and it would go into two numbers, each inst*lmt* being a little shorter than the one inst^{mt} of *Karain: A Memory* which, as you may remember was published in Maga under similar conditions. In its way it is superior to *Karain*. On the other hand it is not a thing intimately felt, like Youth or H of D. not to be used in the same volume. I plan other sort of stuff for its completion. Besides the tale is specifically intended for Mr H's book; designed to go with the other of that group. Would you permit Pinker to send you the MS, and make him an offer for it?

[1] George Blackwood (1876–1942), nephew of William, and the next in line as head of the house; 'primarily a fine printer and businessman', George was less indulgent to authors than his uncle (Blackburn, p.xxxii).
[2] Of Edward VII, planned for 26 June.

I've commenced working for the Youth vol: and by the 15th of Febr^y shall be sending in copy—either to Meldrum as before, or to Ed'gh, according as you shall direct me. I have 30 000 words laid up in my cranium; remains only the writing of them; no trifle I'll admit. It shall be maritime stuff in the manner of *Youth* and *H of D*. Very personal.[1]

The advance on royalties on book-form I've had already some time ago. As to the serial appearance of this portion of the vol: I would suggest £4 per thousand (30 000 words). Also I would ask you to make me an advance on that of a fifty, about the middle of next month, providing that there is ten thousand words at least in the copy sent in by that time.

If we had negotiated through an agent I would not have had to bother you with this last request; only, this time I preferred to approach you personally—as indeed I would at any time. Since the subject of liter: Ag^t has cropped up, should he in the future ever approach you with my work pray don't believe that he has any "squeezing" mission. As Pinker is attending to my affairs, it is only fair that, after I had cleared up my arrears, he should be allowed to attend to them all. I told him that in the future you are to be given the first refusal of all my work—for indeed I had much rather work for *Maga* and the House than for the "market": were the "market" stuffed with solid gold throughout.

May I beg your answer on all these points, and also on the point whether 30 000 words are enough to make up the volume. I reckon *Youth* at 15000. *H of D* at 32 000. I ask the question because I understand that these two stories are already in plates.

Pray remember me to your uncle. I was sorry to hear he had been so unlucky in the matter of the weather; but at this time Sicily ought to be all right. With kind regards, very faithfully yours

Jph. Conrad

To J. B. Pinker
Text MS Berg; Unpublished

[Pent Farm]
28 Jan 1902

My dear Pinker

On consideration of a thought which occurred to me after I left you I shall approach B'wood myself. I've written to Mr George B'wood re *Falk*.

[1] Although not as severely as Captain Whalley in 'The End of the Tether', Conrad had trouble with his eyes (draft of letter from Pawling to Gosse [June 1902], MS Yale).

I have seen the books at H. and McClure coming in I have arranged the affair of serial rights of Rescue.

I have got them back in America as well as in England. He has given me these back on the only condition that from the proceeds I should repay the sum he had advanced me on *acct*. That is *£180*. The book-rights in America he keeps of course—and the book right[s] in this country remain with Heinemann who has also advanced me £180 on 17½% royalty. After that we shall be free! and You shall run the show.

Yours faithfully

J. Conrad

From what I heard reported I fancy Halkett of the P[all] M[all] M[agazine] would be likely to consider the Rescue. He has already seen some of the MS.

To Ford Madox Ford
Text MS Yale; Unpublished

[Pent Farm]
Tuesday [28 January 1902][1]

My dear Ford

All well I delivered the MS yesterday with severe recommendations.

I am at work with end of Part IV.

Your burial stuff came in quite lovely at the end of Part III. Quite! With love

Ever Yours

Conrad.

To J. B. Pinker
Text MS Berg; Unpublished

[Pent Farm]
[late January or February 1902?][2]

My dear Pinker

I send you second part corrected proof. The first lot I returned to the P.M.M. not knowing they passed through your hands.

---

[1] Date from postmark, confirmed by the previous day's visit to Pinker.
[2] This note seems to be about 'Typhoon', which ran in serial from January to March; in late January, Pinker had also placed it with the New York *Critic*.

You'll note the typewritten MS for AM.[1] would require correction by
the proof. P. M. M. text shall be taken to set the book form of the story.

Always yours

Jph Conrad.

To Ford Madox Ford

Text MS Yale; Unpublished

[Pent Farm]
Monday evening [3 February
1902][2]

My dear Ford,

I have been greatly moved by your letter and I am still under the
painful impression, after a day in London, a day of worries during which
the idea of your wife and yourself had not left me for a moment. You
must have had a most awful time.[3]

I hope she stood this cruel shock with the firmness I imagine to be the
foundation of her character. I can't say much to her. Indeed unless one
is perfectly heartless death is no time for words. The touch of it gives a
vision of the world in which words have no place; it unlocks feelings, it
sets free thoughts unsuspected in form and substance; and nothing
outside matters much: but pray, not obtruding my sympathy, tell her
that as one who had known death and its work upon the living I take my
part in her affliction in virtue of my great regard for her, no small
admiration and that very sincere sentiment of friendship in which it had
been my privilege to include you both.

The effect of your letter quite staggered me; to think of you hung up in
that hotel, waiting under the burden of that God-forsaken errand was
too awful. I am glad you found it in your heart to write to me. I had not
much taste for my journey to London but had to go having arranged
interviews—and so on.[4] I left Jessie greatly affected. I hope you did not
think our wire misplaced. She begged me to ask whether she could be
useful in that or any other way; and I had just five minutes in Sandling.
We thought you could not very well take the children to London and
faute de mieux it may have eased her mind to know them with a woman
who is fairly sensible with children anyhow and very certainly likes them

---

[1] America?

[2] Letter postmarked 4 February.

[3] Elsie's father, Dr Martindale, had been found dead on 2 February. He may have killed
himself (Mizener, p. 76).

[4] See the letter to George Blackwood, 5 February.

very much—not to mention myself. Command us in that way at any rate. If you would prefer we could come to W[inchelsea] for the days you are going to be away, and staying in the hotel she could keep on them an unobtrusive eye. I mention this because when I asked Elsie to come here with you she said she did not like leaving the girls with the servants for any time. No more. With our love always Your

J. Conrad.

To David Meldrum
Text MS Duke; Blackburn 143

[Pent Farm]
Tuesday. [4 February 1902][1]

Dear Mr Meldrum.

I send you the letter from G[eorge] B[lackwood] and the précis of my answer which goes north by the same post with this.

As you see he mentions the £50.[2] This may give an opening for approaching the subject of a further advance, the two to be consolidated and secured on copyright of *Lord Jim* and *Youth* as you have suggested. As I am going to get so much less than I expected for my serial rights of the forthcoming 80000 words[3] that matter is more important than ever. Could you then make the preliminary soundings as You have in Your kindness proposed to do.

The question is: Can it be done at all—first. And if it can be done can I ask for a *100* or more—or if not for a 100 then for how much?

I do not like to part with the copyright altogether but I must offer them something. Could I surrender it for a certain number of years for instance? Or up to a certain amount of copies sold?

I want of course to get as much as possible, and give them something not altogether illusory in exchange. If they believe in a future not so much for myself as *for my work* the thing can be done and I don't mind a sacrifice; since I cannot wait and the firm of B'wood & Sons can afford to bide the time.

Many thanks for your really unwearied kindness.

Always faithfully yours
Jph. Conrad.

---

[1] George Blackwood wrote on 3 February (text Blackburn, pp. 141–2) and Conrad replied on 5 February.

[2] See Conrad to William Blackwood, 14 and 19 December 1900.

[3] Conrad had asked for £4 per 1,000 words, but as 'Mr George' reminded him, he had previously (19 May 1900) agreed to £2.10.

Answered. The agreement (made at the time Lord Jim was published) for the completion of Youth vol: must of course stand at the rate of £2.10 per 1000 serially. Say £75 for 30000 words. Whatever more may be judged necessary for the *vol* would be forthcoming at same rate; but hope that 30000 would do.[1]

(It would make about 85000 in all which is a fair size for a vol).

In reference to the £50. lent by Mr B'wood said: that am not in a position *at present* to work it off or otherwise discharge my indebt[ed]ness.

Explained: Am not responsible for the terms Pinker may ask for *Falk* as he has a lien on the story.

To George Blackwood

Text MS NLS; Blackburn 144

[letterhead: Pent Farm]
5th Febr 1902

Dear Mr Blackwood.

I regret that you should have to remind me of the agreement as to the rate of serial payment for the balance of the serial form of Youth and other stories. Of course the thing is perfectly clear since it was mentioned when the arrangements for a separate publication of Lord Jim were being made—that novel itself being paid for (as a serial) at a higher rate.[2] And in this connection (since the lapse of time, as you suggest, is responsible for my error) let me assure you that nothing but hard necessity had kept me from completing the volume. Every one of the 80000 words I've written (solus—because there's another 80000 or so in collaboration) since the end of Lord Jim, has been written with the regret that they were not destined for *Maga*. My ambition had never been to see myself drawn, quartered and illustrated in a Magazine run for the Million by a Millionaire.[3]

I had not forgotten the advance of £50 made me by your uncle at the time you mention. I said nothing about it for the reason that I am not in a position *at present* to propose working it off or otherwise discharging that particular debt. I am still in a very thick wood of arrears but I begin to see daylight.

---

[1] He had been told that a 30,000 word story could complete *Youth*, 'but if you have another and strong story there is no reason why we should not include it and make the volume a full one'.
[2] £3 per 1,000.   [3] His fate in the *Illustrated London News*.

Thanks for your promptitude in looking at Falk. In this connection I must observe that I would not be responsible for the terms Pinker may ask. He has a lien on the story.

Whatever shall be necessary for the completion of the volume shall be forthcoming at the agreed rate—say £75 for 30 000 words; and if you would when 10000 w. are to hand send me £30 it would be very convenient.

I was in London on Monday and had the pleasure of making your brother's acquaintance.[1] We lunched with Meldrum. Though I had my arm in a sling and most horrid twinges of gout in my wrist I enjoyed myself greatly. I fear however your brother carried away the impression of a loquacious lunatic, from that smoking-room.

Should you accept *Falk* I would beg for the MS to look over. I haven't seen the thing for six months and have no copy at home. It would probably save much cutting up of proof; and this is my reason for asking. But pray do not imagine that I take acceptance for granted in the least.

Believe me very faithfully yours

Jph. Conrad

To J. B. Pinker
Text MS Berg; Unpublished

[letterhead: Pent Farm]
5th Febr 1902

My dear Pinker

I feel I owe You an apology for the way I changed my mind;[2] I trust You never supposed that it had anything to do with *you* personally. It would have been too absurd. It had to do of course with the consideration of *my* personal position vis-a-vis B'woods—a matter I don't set out a[t] length here because no talk could remedy the evil of such a situation.

I would have written this sooner only I had a gouty wrist and have not been able to write at all for the last few days. It's all right now and I feel very well as usual after an attack of gout. Sorry I had been forced to hold up that miserable chapter. I am at it again and you shan't have more than a couple of days to wait.

Could you send me back my own copy of *To-Morrow*? It's of no

---

[1] James Hugh Blackwood (1878–1951).
[2] Deciding to approach the Blackwoods directly rather than leaving that to Pinker.

importance but I like to have my corrected type for reference and so on. The pen and ink MS is only a rough draft.

George B'wood says he has Falk and promises to decide quickly. Hope we shall have some luck with him. Pray push in To-Morrow somewhere as soon as you can, so that I may be delivered from 21 Bedford Str.[1] Yours

Conrad.

To J. B. Pinker
Text MS Berg; Unpublished

Pent Farm.
25 Febr 1902

My dear Pinker.

I send you the whole of Chap VIII of part IV of Romance. I did find it necessary to write a short Chap. IX. concerned with facts making a transition to the part V and last of the story. I could forward you more than half of that last chap: (IX) too, but I refrain till it is ready quite. It is my desire to make that Chap: IX *short* which delays me. Moreover I have been too worried to work with ease. You can have no idea how really and truly I am anxious to complete these few pages; but they must be up to the mark of the rest. Another 1500 to 2000 words have to be written. That's all. Meantime you may have Ch: VIII typed and see the escape from the cavern, and the end of Manuel.[2]

So much for *Romance*. Have you read it? And if so what is your opinion of its being to the taste of the public? Your impression would be valuable to me. Thanks for original MS safely to hand.

Now I want to expose to you a difficulty not strictly connected with my writing.

Rather more than a year ago I've insured my life with the Standard life in two policies one *A* for £600 and the other *B* for £500.[3] Together £1100. (*The policy A is held by my bankers as security for occ^l overdrafts and has nothing to do with the matter of this letter.*)

I have managed to pay the premiums which amount for the policy *B* to £9.13 *half yearly*. On that *B* policy however I borrowed from the Ins^{ce} Comp^y itself the sum of £250 at 5% p. a. with the proviso that the capital is to be repaid in instalments of £25 every half year. My banker *Watson* of

---

[1] Heinemann's office.   [2] For the division of chapters, see letter of 12 March.
[3] See Conrad to Blackwood, 14 December 1900.

7 Waterloo Place was *one* of the sureties on that agreement. And as the Comp^y required *two* sureties M^r Wm. Blackwood is now the other.

(I need not say that the loan was spent not in riotous living but *mostly* for the purpose of paying off other liabilities that could not wait)

My difficulty, the incubus, is the obligation of paying off the borrowed capital—that half yearly £25. This is always the difficulty; and I have a positive dread of the Insur: Comp: coming down on my sureties. If once B'wood is involved in that paying off business it means unending slavery for me. I say this without reflecting on his character at all. He has been very friendly and helpful—but you know how it is between author and publisher.

I've paid off one £25 last June. The one which came due in Jany this year I can not manage. Altogether instal^t: of capital, interest and ½ yearly premium it comes to £40. I have induced the company to wait till now.

I owe them now altogether £225 the half year's interest and the premium in all *£240.5.6* of which the *40.5.6* must be paid off this time. Of course my sureties Watson and B'wood are liable and will have to pay this time (though I am trying to avoid this). But it is the ever recurring anxiety that distracts me. I don't want B'wood to have to pay—just *because* he is a most likely publisher for me.

I could not and I would not ask you to help me with this payment. It would be of no use, because next June the same difficulty would occur. But if you could see your way to do something in appearance much more considerable and in reality much more business-like, I would propose this:

That you should *pay off* the Insurance C^o completely (£240.5.6 as near as I can reckon to a shilling or two) and I would *assign to you* my policy *B* (for £500) which your action would totally liberate. My work passing through your hands (I do not mind a formal engagement that with exception of 30000 words owing to B'wood every line shall go to you) would always cover the yearly premium to the Comp^y of roughly £19 per year and the interest to you at say 6% on £240.5.6—again, roughly, about £15 per year—or a few shillings less. Together £36 or so per year. Of course I hope to write more than that—but when making me advances on short stories or on a long novel you would keep in mind that charge. Your capital would be secured by the policy and as my position improved we would reduce my indebtedness to you, the policy remaining assigned to you *absolutely* till the last pound has been paid off.

What encourages me to make this proposal to you is this, that, dealing with a needy man like me, it makes your position safer really, by all the margin between £240 and the £500 which at my death would be available to cover any advances that there might be outstanding between us. The means of paying the premium and interest would be in your hands all the time and I can produce 100,000 words a year on an average. With the delivery of the *Rescue* to you for placing serially I shall be clear of every entanglement and you shall have an absolutely free hand for dealing with my stuff all over the world.

Moreover this is the very thing that some time ago the firm of H[einemann] professed themselves ready to do for me; so I do know that the transaction is not of an impossible kind. The only consideration is for You.—of expediency. Is it worth your while—am I worth your making that outlay (perfectly secured as it is)? I need not say that whatever your decision it shall not affect our relations. I shall write on and I hope you'll place the stuff for me to the best advantage.

---

p.t.o.

There are in addition a few considerations which I wish to present to you:

That I have no weakness or vice which would prevent me pursuing a litterary* calling or likely to affect my mental capacity. And at my age a man is not so likely to go wrong suddenly.

That hereditarily I am not likely to develop a lingering disabling disease—which of course is the only chance of risk for you.

My life is not very good, certainly. That, however, in the given case, does not matter—as you perceive. On the other hand I may hang on. Gouty people do. They also go out suddenly. That's so much the better. I am not worrying about the last scene except in novels. But what is a worry is this struggle with wretched embarras[s]ments, this scheming and planning for which my previous existence has utterly unfitted me. And if you can do this big bit towards giving me peace pray do so. Of course I don't want you to conclude offhand. But if you can *at all* consent to take the matter into consideration I beg you will drop me a line to that effect. It'll not engage your ultimate decision—only I would stay my hand in dealing with Edinburgh.

Very sincerely yours

Jph Conrad.

PS The policy is a perfectly safe one proof of age having been furnished and *accepted* by the C°.

To J. B. Pinker
Text MS Berg; Unpublished

Pent Farm
28 *Febr*ʸ [1902][1]

My dear Pinker.

Thanks for the friendly spirit of your answer. Do not suppose that it engages you *in the least* in my eyes.

I wrote you *all* that I had thought on the matter and this accounts for the length of the letter. Here I only repeat that if there is a way of giving you a legal lien on the proceeds of my *future* work (including 'Romance' but *excepting Typhoon and B'wood volumes*) and also in three of my past publications, namely: *Outcast of the Islands, Tales of Unrest, Nigger of the Narcissus*—I am perfectly ready and willing to do what's necessary. The *Rescue* book form is unfortunately arranged for; but there's nothing to prevent you looking after all these books and, as my agent, receiving all the moneys they may bring in the future. On Rescue I am to get 17½% royalty and I've had already £180 on acct from H[einemann]. From MᶜClure I had as much but only on acct/ of serial rights in both countries. These we have back from him on condition of paying off that advance—but only when the work has been placed serially. Without any mental reservations and in perfect sincerity I do feel (and she does so too) that in case of my early death my wife would be perfectly safe in your hands.

So much for the past. For the future I only may express my honest conviction that I haven't done my best work yet; and at any rate I've plenty of material to try my hand on.

———————

I am no end pleased "Romance" is to your liking. Your remark that it does not *read* long is a most complimentary thing to hear—because that is the very effect I aimed for. As to shortening: in my opinion Part II (at the beginning) is the one to go for. I feel with you there. If it had not been for the considerable delay already incurred I would have tried to do it before I sent you the MS at all.

Upon my word McClure's suggestion is impossible. Hueffer has done as much and more to the book than I did. I would not *dare* to suggest anything of the sort to him even if I could bring my own conscience to accept such a swindle. With Hueffer it is not a matter of money at all. As a literary man he considers it (rightly or wrongly) an honour to

[1] Content gives the year.

collaborate with me. The book must be accepted on its merits by the public—as a romantic story not as Conrad's work specifically.

Very truly yours

Jph. Conrad.

To H. G. Wells

Text MS Illinois; J-A, 1, 323; Ray

Monday. [February 1902?]]¹

Dear H. G.

The lecture is splendid. It is striking in its *expression* and as nearly perfect as things of today can be in its tone and temper; and in its eloquence too, which is undeniable and of a sort most attractive to me. I call it scientific eloquence—that is eloquence appealing not to the passions like the eloquence of the orator but to the reason. That in this case it is calculated for the smaller capacity of the general public makes it no less scientific; for it is calculated perfectly for the understandings you have had to address and *there* is the test of a successful achievement whether in art in letters or in politics.

Its sheer *pronouncement* is difficult to criticise because of its extremely skilful moderation. Indeed that skill is extremely striking. You make a case. All the criticisms I've seen (now, after reading the lecture) strike me as extremely unfair—I would say uncandid did I not know how honest a total misapprehension of the plainest meaning can be.

When I try to analyse to myself the merits of its *substance* I find the difficulty of weighing the imponderable. Do not suspect that I have in my mind the uselessness of such an inquiry. I am I flatter myself too intelligent to take such a stand. But with my rooted idea of the whole value of the future (whatever we wish to make it or find it) consisting in what we do, endure and shape *today* I can't help wishing you had emphasized that view—which surely is not foreign to your conviction? Is it? The future is of our own making—and (for me) the most striking characteristic of the century is just that development, that maturing of our consciousness which should open our eyes to that truth—or that illusion. Anything that would help our intelligences towards a clearer

---

¹ Jean-Aubry placed this letter in 1903, but Martin Ray offers persuasive arguments for assigning it to 1902. He sees it as a response to Wells's *The Discovery of the Future*, published as a 96 page book in February 1902. It is a lecture, originally given at the Royal Institution on 24 January.

view of the consequences of our social action is of the very greatest value—and as such a guide I salute you.

I shall try to descend on you for a talk very soon.

Always yours

J. Conrad.

To David Meldrum
Text MS Duke; Blackburn 146

[letterhead: Pent Farm]
8 Mch 1902

My dear Mr Meldrum.

I am so sorry I worried you. Calling on Friday at paternoster Row I heard you were seedy.

Many thanks. I'll wait till M^r B'wood is in London.

It's wonderful how well sustained is the excellence of Charlotte. I've just read the last instalment;[1] for finishing our Romance, I had no time to read anything for the last fortnight. The ease of the narrative is fascinating by itself. I may well believe it cost you much labour—unless you are luckier than most of us who write.

I trust I'll soon hear of Your complete recovery. Many thanks.

Very faithfully yours,

Jph. Conrad.

To Ford Madox Ford
Text MS Yale; Unpublished

[letterhead: Pent Farm]
Sunday. [9 March 1902][2]

My dear Ford.

I took the last of *Romance*[3] to London on Friday. I had to engineer an affair with Pinker besides—and I wanted (besides) to hear him talk.

I am confirmed in my judgment as to the great excellence of *R's* last part—for though I appreciate it on other grounds than P, the fact is that he is greatly impressed by it. Now if *he* isn't an average reader I want to know who is? My cleverness however lies in the fact that I did perceive the side that would impress a mind (?) of that sort.

---

[1] I.e. 'latest': *The Conquest of Charlotte* ended in the July issue.
[2] Conrad went to London on 7 March (telegram Berg).
[3] Conrad had sometimes called *Seraphina* 'the romance'; now it becomes *Romance*.

You mustn't think of suppressing that part for serial pub:. No editor would wish us to do that either, I firmly believe. But that a demand for shortening the thing may be made is very probable; because (don't faint!) the book as it stands contains *166,000* words.

I confess this piece of information did not take me so much aback as you may suppose.

Says Pinker: "but it *reads* short."[1] (So it does and that emphatically since his dull senses received that impression) This being so, I observed, is it worth while operating on it? By the severest pruning we could not hope to eliminate more than 6000 words. Not one tenth, not one twentieth of it—I said.

He of course does not complain of the size. On the contrary he says, there could not be too much of such admirable stuff for the book-form. Only he did not want to be a year placing it serially. Thereupon he confessed that the MS was already in Fisher Unwin's (!!!!) hands with a proposal to make it a serial for the New Eng*sh* Mag*ne* which is going to be enlarged and generally worked up. The point is that F.U. would begin publication at once. The N.E.M. is not choked up with contracts. As to the money Pinker's opinion is that F.U. can find money when he likes.

I made no objection. After all the man must be allowed to do the business, or there could be no point of employing him at all.

For America McClure has the MS to look over but unless he accepts the terms stated he shall not have it. He would syndicate the story of course. Otherwise P who is off to the states in a week or so shall take it with him—to Putnam perhaps. Voilà. Upon the whole I have good hopes.

I feel slightly fagged out—and I must begin at once something for B'wood! I haven't a single notion in my head. The 'wonderfulness' You have suggested is nowhere for the moment. 'Blankness' is the impression of life past and future; and tho' it is no doubt true and correct one can hardly fabricate Maga-stuff out of it. 'Tis too subtle. 'Taint raw enough. By the bye B'wood (George) has refused *Falk*.

What's wrong with that dam' thing? They seem to treat it as though it had the pest.

How are you good people getting on. We were glad to hear that Xina[2] is getting better.

Elsie may say that "l'air tranquille de ce bonhomme est odieux"

---

[1] Cf. the letter of 28 February.   [2] Christina.

(Flaubert Ed. Sent:)[1] but generally I may say that children are seldom constitutionally touched. They grow out of early predispositions. I had inflam[m]ation of the lungs twice (at five and seven) but whatever else's wrong there's nothing the matter with my lungs now. Had she been 15 I would share Elsie's apprehensions—which now have my heartfelt sympathy. After all Xina is a much better *animal* (not to speak of her vivacious mind) than Borys who nearly went down before half a dozen grapes.[2] But life is full of these terrors and on that general ground I take part in Your feelings.

We have been smothered in fogs. Jessie has an awful cough and it makes me wretched no end. I have nothing to read and nothing to think about. The bleating of sheep is the only sound. There is a pause in the drama.

Our love to you all

Ever yours

Jph Conrad.

To Arnold Bennett

Text MS UCL; J-A, 1, 302

[letterhead: Pent Farm]
10 Mch 1902

My dear Sir.[3]

The reading of the Man from the North[4] has inspired me with the greatest respect for your artistic conscience. I am profoundly impressed with the achievement of style. The root of the matter—which is expression—is there, and the sacred fire too. I hope you will give me the credit for understanding what you have tried for there. My dear Sir I do envy you the power of coming so near to your desire.

The thing as written is undeniable. To read it was to me quite a new experience of the language; and the delight was great enough to make me completely disregard the subject.

This at first; but as you may suppose I've read the book more than once. Unfortunately, I don't know how to criticise; to discuss however I

---

[1] Words describing the doctor who visits Mme Arnoux's dying son (*L'Education senti-mentale*, II, 6).

[2] In Bruges.

[3] Enoch Arnold Bennett (1867–1931) had recently given up the editorship of *Woman* in order to become a full-time novelist. His publications in 1902 were *Anna of the Five Towns* and *The Grand Babylon Hotel*.

[4] *A Man from the North* (1898).

am ready. Now the book (as a novel not as a piece of writing) *is* discutable.[1]

Generally, however, I may say that the die has not been struck hard enough. Here's a piece of pure metal scrupulously shaped, with a true—and more—a beautiful ring: but the die has not been struck hard enough. I admit that the outlines of the design are sharp enough. What it wants is a more emphatic modelling; more relief. And one could even quarrel with the design itself.

Nothing would give me greater pleasure than to have it out with you, the book there on the table, to be thumped and caressed. I would quarrel not with the truth of your conception but with the realism thereof. You just stop short of being absolutely real because you are faithful to your dogmas of realism.[2] Now realism in art will never approach reality. And your art, your gift should be put to the service of a larger and freer faith.

Believe me yours faithfully

Jph Conrad.

PS Of course I may have misunderstood your standpoint utterly. I want to hear what you have to say if you think it worth while to say anything to me. Only let it be viva voce. Come when you can spare a day. I won't be likely to have forgotten the book. We shall be back at home after next Monday. We can put you up and next day I could deliver you safe at H. G's palatial residence.[3]

To John Galsworthy
Text MS Forbes; Unpublished

[letterhead: Pent Farm]
10th March 1902

Dearest Jack

We send you the monkey[4] at the age of four. He's gone to bed but has left instructions it should be done to-night without fail.

"Que devenez-vous?" How goes the work? How soon will you be able to spare me a day?

---

[1] James wrote in 'The Art of Fiction': 'only a short time ago it might have been supposed that the English novel was not what the French call *discutable*. It had no air of having a theory, a conviction, a consciousness of itself behind it' (Leon Edel, ed., *The Future of the Novel* (New York, 1956), p. 3).
[2] Bennett much admired the French Naturalists.
[3] Spade House, designed for the Wells family by C. F. A. Voysey.
[4] Borys.

Next Sunday we shall be in Winch*ˢᵉᵃ* leaving here on Friday returning on Mond.

Seraphina is finished and gone out the house she has haunted for this year past. I do really hope it will hit the taste of the street—unless the devil's in it.

I am afraid we shall have to leave the Pent before long. No end of worry in that thought.[1]

Otherwise there's a pause in the drama. I feel idle. I am idle. I can't remain idle. Blackwood's at the door.

It seems at times as though I could give my head to be quit of this scribbling life. But you know all that.

I engaged myself to let Pinker handle all my stuff—and on consideration of that agreement he has paid off my loan to the Ins*ᶜᵉ* company (on the £500 policy). Of course I have assigned the policy to him. The advantage to me is that I need not bother as to paying off any of the capital, and he will look to the premiums out of the proceeds of my work. I need have no uneasiness on that score; therefore my dearest Jack pray let me release you from Your voluntary engagement to pay half my yearly premiums. Do not believe I am in a hurry to discard your help; only really now there is not that necessity which would justify me in increasing my obligations to you ad infinitum as it were.

Do come and shake me up if it is at all possible. Love. Yours ever

Jph Conrad

To Jane Wells
Text MS Illinois; Unpublished

[letterhead: Pent Farm]
11ᵗʰ Mch 1902.

Dear Mrs Wells[2]

You do write immensely nice notes; if I were many times a better man I could never compose anything that would give a greater pleasure to the readers.

So You and H. G. think the thing comes off?[3] It is very delightful to hear this; though for my own part I can't help thinking that I have tried

---

[1] Cf. the letter to Ford, 24 March.

[2] Born Amy Catherine Robbins (1872–1927), she had been Wells's student and, changing her first as well as her family name, became his second wife. He collected some of her work in *The Book of Catherine Wells* (1928).

[3] 'Amy Foster'?

to make too much of a simple anecdote. I am just now in one of my very sober moods.

We send you the monkey at the age of four and by the same token put in our claim for the first time Gyp[1] is taken in a more or less erect attitude. And let it be soon and often. We want a series of Gyp and he shall have an album all to himself as he has an exclusive place in our hearts.

Believe me dear Mrs Wells,
always most faithfully yours
Joseph Conrad.

PS Jessie's love. I've at last achieved a letter to Bennett.

To J. B. Pinker
Text MS Yale; Unpublished

[letterhead: Pent Farm]
12th Mch 1902

My dear Pinker.

Cheque safely to hand. Many thanks.

You are right no doubt as to the *numbering* of the chapters.[2] The 8 and 9 of my MS must be the 10 and 11 of the clean copy. But there is nothing missing between the 10 and 11. They follow strictly and clearly tho' to a cursory glance they may not appear so. At the end of *10*th Kemp and Seraphina are found in the ravine and rescued by two peons; and the 11th opens with their arrival at the door of the hacienda; but the very first paragraph describes concisely their journey at night over the plain and the forest to the gate. It is only a few lines but all that is necessary since the journey is uneventful. However if You think it necessary a line or two more may state the fact in so many words. But for anybody reading consecutively (which you had no opportunity of doing) the inference is clear. In Chap *10*th there are constant allusions to the hacienda as the goal they wish to reach. In Ch: 11th they are there and afterwards make a fresh start for Havana carrying out strictly Sebright's plan as laid down for them earlier in the part. Nevertheless if you doubt my contention pray send me the two chapters and I promise to write in a bare statement of no more than 20 words.

Yours faithfully
J Conrad.

---

[1] George Philip Wells, nearly eight months old.   [2] In Part Four of *Romance*.

To Elsie Hueffer

Text MS Yale; Unpublished

[letterhead: Pent Farm]
[17] March 1902 Monday.[1]

Dear Auntie Elsie.[2]

I write instead of Jess not to miss this post as she was too lazy yesterday and is too busy this morning.

We had a windy drive but on the whole pleasant.

We feel greatly refreshed by our little holiday with you. I am in an hour or so going to begin writing my B'wood stuff "The End of the Song"[3]—as Ford has suggested and advised.

Many thanks for your charming hospitality; and our love to you all

Yours very faithfully

Jph Conrad.

PS. Pray has Ford come upon, lying about on his table, three green pieces of paper—receipts of the Ins^{ce} Comp^y. If so I should like to have them.

To J. B. Pinker

Text MS Berg; Unpublished

[letterhead: Pent Farm]
17 Mch 1902

My dear Pinker.

I am finishing here my yesterday's letter interrupted at post-time. Thanks for the good news you give me as to To-morrow.[4] I suppose they won't delay the story too long. Could you ask (if opportunity offers) the Editor to send the proof early for the thing wants some looking through. It had very little of that before it went to you.

I am glad the Yanks did not carry their point by bullying. It was my imbecile joke of course. What Pawling has told you is alas! very true. It all rests with him. No need to enlarge upon that fact.

I have to ask you for two things. First: would you talk to McClure about sending me whatever money is due as royalty on the *Inheritors*.

---

[1] The letter to Galsworthy of 10 March mentions a visit to Winchelsea the following weekend.
[2] Elsie Martindale had married Ford in 1894, when she was seventeen. Later in 1902 she began to translate Maupassant.
[3] 'The End of the Tether'.
[4] Accepted by the *Pall Mall Magazine*: published in August.

There is something as Robert[1] told me himself. Second: could you let me know whether Mr William Blackwood has arrived in London from abroad. I don't want to ask the office myself, and Meldrum I am afraid is ill at home yet and not to be bothered with my affairs.

I am glad you got forty from PMM. Frankly the story is worth it. Now if we only could be relieved of *Falk* I would feel easy as to the volume.

How the devil are Putnams to publish Typhoon by itself? As a booklet at 75 cents—or what?[2] It's too short. However devil take them.

I am at work and till that job is over there's no use talking of the Rescue: A Romance of Shallow waters. But of course You will keep in mind that that is coming next and that a good half of it is written already.

Always yours faithfully.

Jph Conrad

To Harriet Mary Capes

Text MS Yale; J-A, 1, 303

[letterhead: Pent Farm]

22^d Mch 1902

Dear Miss Capes.[3]

Your fancy is most kind but I fear it is a far cry from Prospero's Island to Patusan.

I have been greatly moved by your letter, by the kindness of your thought, by the generosity of your appreciation; and my wife, a person of simple feelings guided by the intelligence of the heart has begged me for it to put into her own copy of the book. As it is only just that she should have her share of whatever's best in the hazard of our indifferent fortunes I have presented it to her for that purpose.

It is very late, it is very still; I have pushed my work aside to take up this sheet: and I only wish I had some part of your gift of convincing expression in which to clothe adequately the truth of my gratitude.

I have just re-read Your gracious message. I can not believe that I deserve so high a commendation. That you should give it to me is not my merit but yours alone—for the reader collaborates with the author. What I am most grateful for is the *artistic* sympathy and the delicate intelligence of your praise. But how to thank you I do not know, with my

---

[1] McClure.   [2] As a 205 page book illustrated by Maurice Greiffenhagen.
[3] Miss Capes, who lived in Winchester, wrote inspirational stories for children. She became a lifelong admirer of Conrad's works, and he dedicated *A Set of Six* to her.

weary hand ministering to my jaded thought. I find my mind lame and outdistanced and all I can say is that if you have found me worthy of your praise you have made me feel that your praise is eminently worth having: for to confer upon my unworthiness the greatest favour an author may receive You have found the just word and the penetrating phrase.

As soon as my next volume comes out I promise to myself the happiness of sending You a copy. Meantime pray let me assure You that your letter is not a small part of my reward for these anxious and perplexed hours which fall to the lot of us who write.

I am, dear Miss Capes, with a very sincere gratitude Your most obedient servant

Jph. Conrad.

To J. B. Pinker
Text MS Berg; Unpublished

[letterhead: Pent Farm]
22 Mch 1902

My dear Pinker

I am quite prepared to do what's required to Romance. At the same time a story of that sort can't be all fat as it were. What I feel is that the matter at the beginning necessary to create the situation may be put perhaps in a more interesting way. Once the story is placed I would have more heart to handle the opening again. Also I take it that from the moment Kemp is kidnapped the thing is satisfactory. It's what goes before that must be retouched for the serial? Is that so?

I haven't received yet the policy. I am writing to the Standard C° to hurry up. When are you leaving for the States? You'll leave instructions with your man in charge as to that affair no doubt, and I shall communicate with your office should you be gone when the document reaches me. But I suppose I'll hear from you once more before you launch yourself upon the stormy ocean.

Yours

Conrad.

To J. B. Pinker
Text MS Berg; Unpublished

[letterhead: Pent Farm]
Sunday
23 Mch 1902

My dear Pinker.

I wrote to you yesterday to your office and later on heard from Wells that you were not likely to appear there before leaving for the states. This is the reason I write to your private address.

I would not have bothered you at all but for Wells saying you would not take it amiss. I generally tell HG all my troubles and I happened to mention how awkward M^r B'wood's absence for another fortnight was for me.

The fact is that I wish to sell to them my copyright of Lord Jim and also of the tales now being completed.[1] The wisdom of that step I do not defend. It is a matter of necessity about which I am extremely anxious. As you may imagine I am almost broken hearted about it too, believing in the future as I must confess I do. No matter. I don't think there will be any difficulty in the matter and I shall try to get as much as I can. I have opened no negotiations as yet with the young man preferring to wait for the return of the uncle. This return announced more than a fortnight ago is, I judge from your letter, again delayed. Meantime there's urgency in the case.

If you let me have £50 now I shall repay you as soon as the transaction is completed. The copyrights are sure to fetch more than that as Lord Jim's sales have nearly covered the advance if not altogether. I have no reason to think that M^r Wm B'wood would refuse to entertain my proposal.

I am so muddled in everything but my work that I imagined the dinner to you was for the 28th. I seem to live in a sort of dream till something of that sort wakes me up to the sense of my absurdity. I never answered Pett Ridge's letter either.[2] I must apologise now to him. I don't apologise to you; your knowledge of my distressed personality will enable you to look at my vagaries with an indulgent eye. I am not fit to live in the world. If I don't hear from You by Tuesday I shall conclude my letter has missed you, but anyway on the chance good voyage and good luck to you as we sailors say.

Very faithfully yours
Jph Conrad.

---

[1] The *Youth* volume.
[2] William Pett Ridge, a prolific novelist. In *Who's Who* he listed his recreation as 'roaming east of Aldgate'.

Pray tell me whether you have left instructions as to my policy. I shall forward it to the office as soon as I get it. I did not hurry up the Standard life thinking I had all ten days before your departure. I've written them yesterday.

To Ford Madox Ford
Text MS Yale; Unpublished

[letterhead: Pent Farm]
Monday. [24th March 1902][1]

Dearest Ford

Just a word to catch this post. I am afraid we can't afford to move from here.[2] Simply can not. Il ne faut pas y penser.

Our love to you all. Pardon this brevity.

Ever Yours,

Jph Conrad.

I've put on a screw upon McClure:[3]

To John Galsworthy
Text MS POSK; Danilewicz 9

[letterhead: Pent Farm]
Tuesday. [March–November 1902][4]

Dearest Jack

Of course come next Sunday. We are sorry for the doggie and sent wishes for speedy recovery. Ourselves had a spill and are stiff. No bones broken though; only the poor mare has cut herself about a good deal.[5]

Love. Ever Yours

Conrad.

---

[1] Date from envelope.
[2] Ford had sub-let the Pent to Conrad. See also the letter of 15 April.
[3] To squeeze out royalties on *The Inheritors*.
[4] Letterhead type eight, first used on 17 March 1902.
[5] The accident described by Jessie Conrad in *Joseph Conrad As I Knew Him*, pp. 111–12?

To J. B. Pinker

Text MS Berg; Unpublished

[letterhead: Pent Farm]
[March–November 1902][1]

Dear Pinker

I return the docts signed as requested.

Yours in haste

J Conrad

To H.-D. Davray

Text MS Williams; *L.fr.* 42

[letterhead: Pent Farm]
2 Avril. 1902

Cher Ami.

Votre proposition me fait le plus grand plaisir imaginable.

Heinemann a acquis tous les droits du volume qui contiendra *Typhoon* et trois autres nouvelles: *Amy Foster* (parue dans le Ill^d *London News*, 3 numeros en Decembre 1901), *Falk: A narrative*, et *To-morrow* (qui paraitra dans le Pall Mall Mag: en Août 1902).

Heinemann me mande dans sa lettre que j'ai reçue ce matin qu'il vous a écrit directement en acceptant Vos conditions. Ceci vous comprenez bien est son affaire. Mon interét dans la traduction est tout autre et bien plus près de mon coeur.

Donc, s'il vous convient de commencer par là, vous pouvez aller de l'avant (go ahead) avec *Typhoon*. Je puis Vous assurer d'ailleurs que les quatre machines ci-dessus feront un bon volume. Ci-jointe une petite note des sujets.

Quand au *Tales of Unrest*: l'Editeur est Fisher Unwin avec qui mes relations sont tant soit peu tendues. Mais cela ne fait rien. Il y a autre chose. Voici:

Ma parente et bonne amie Mme Marguerite Poradowska (née Gachet) a traduit, il y a un an déjà, la nouvelle *Outpost of Progress* dans le volume en question. J'ai le manuscrit ici chez moi. C'est assez bien mais il faudrait corser le style un peu. Je crois que son intention etait de placer la chose dans la Revue des deux mondes. Vous voyez la position, car a vrai dire sans ma faute la nouvelle aurait parue depuis longtemps. Peut-être vous pourriez Vous arranger avec elle et vous servir de son travail? Je ne voudrais pas l'offenser pour rien au monde.

---

[1] Type eight letterhead. Pinker was away throughout April.

Envoyez-moi un petit mot à ce sujet; mais comme mon desir le plus vif est d'être traduit par Vous ou du moins sous votre direction et inspiration[1] je trouverais toujours le moyen de m'entendre avec elle.

Wells m'a donné des vos nouvelles de temps en temps. Mille remerciments, mon cher pour votre note sympathique sur moi dans le Mercure.[2]

Toujours votre devoué.

Jph. Conrad.

Typhoon. Vous connaissez. 28000 mots. (Pall Mall Mag.)

Amy Foster.—Histoire d'un montagnard autrichien-polonais[3] émigrant en Amerique, qui est naufragé sur la côte Anglaise. Il vagabonde par le pays. On ne le comprend pas. Il est traqué comme une bête sauvage. Un fermier[4] le recueille. Il se marie avec une bonne bête de fille, une villageoise. Mais il s'entête a parler sa langue a lui a leur enfant. Cela ennuie sa femme. Elle commence a en avoir peur. Il tombe malade. Elle le garde. Il a soif et demande a boire—mais dans sa langue a lui, sans se rendre compte de cela du reste. Elle ne comprend pas. Lui non plus ne comprend pas pourquoi elle ne bouge pas. Il se fâche, il se lève—l'effroi de ses sons étranges la gagne et elle se sauve en emportant l'enfant. Il meurt sans jamais comprendre. 11000 mots. Idée: difference essentielle des races. Histoire lugubre quoique le Illust*ed* Lond: News a eu le courage de la publier. (3 nos en decembre 1901).

NB.—Je vais essayer de les obtenir pour Vous les envoyer.

Falk: A Narrative Traite d'un norvégien, capitaine de remorqueur, et de la niece d'un allemand, capitaine de la barque 'Diana' de Bremen. Il y a aussi le proprietaire d'un hotel qui fait des potins, et le narrateur Capitaine Anglais, qui se trouve mêlé a toutes ces histoires d'une façon ridicule. La-dessous un petit gout de cannibalisme—autrefois—bien loin—dans les Mers du Sud. Le tout se passe a Bankok capitale de Siam. J'ose dire c'est bien fait. Idée: Contraste du sentimentalisme commun avec le point de vue net d'un homme a peu près primitif (Falk lui-même) qui considère la preservation de la vie comme la loi suprême et morale. Pas encore placée. 26000 mots.

To-morrow. Très difficile a traduire a moins que *C'est pour demain* ne fasse l'affaire. Mais vous verrez. Il s'agit d'un vieux maître au cabotage

---

[1] It is not known how many of the stories Davray translated, but the only translation to be published was 'Karain' (*Mercure de France*, 1906).

[2] The most recent mention came in the July 1901 issue: Vol. 39, p. 253.

[3] The story itself does not specify his origins.

[4] 'Fermier' usually means 'tenant-farmer', but Swaffer is a substantial land-owner.

en retraite. Son idéal est le chez soi, la vie du foyer. Sa femme est morte et il a eu le malheur d'avoir chassé son fils unique dans un moment de colère. Depuis il est devenu fou avec l'idée fixe que ce fils reviendra. Mais comme on se moque de lui en peu, il n'en parle plus a personne; mais sa folie augmente; il espère ce retour pour demain. Une jeune fille, sa voisine, esclave resignée d'un père aveugle et tyran prends en pitié ce vieux solitaire. Il en fait sa confidente. Il fait des plans, il achète des meubles pour etablir son fils quand il reviendra. Il faudra que le jeune homme se marie. Ce sera avec elle. Il lui promet monts et merveilles; elle l'ecoute par pitié. Il causent par-dessus la haie du jardin[1] et à la fin cette folie du vieux communique a la fille un vague espoir. En effet un beau soir pluvieux le fils revient. Il arrive en flanant le long de la haie. Le vieux en train de bêcher dans jardin ne veut pas le reconnaître. Son fils reviendra demain. L'autre insiste. Le fou lui jette sa pioche[2] par la tête et court s'enfermer dans sa maison. Au bruit la jeune fille sort de chez elle. Le fils naturellement se tourne vers elle pour une explication. Dans le dialogue de ces deux personnes le conte est devellopé. Lui est un marin avec les gouts, l'indépendance l'âme même d'un vrai aventurier. Tout doucement elle s'enhardit a lui confier les projets de son père. L'autre se révolte. C'est trop fort. Autrefois son père voulait faire de lui une espèce de monsieur, un clerc d'huissier, et voilà qu'a présent il veut le faire vivre comme un lapin dans une cage. Ça, jamais. Il rit, éxaspéré. Et peut-être, dit-il, vous connaissez la femme qu'il me destine? Il a élévé sa voix; le fou dans sa maison l'entend. Il ouvre la fenêtre et crie: ne l'écoute pas ma fille. C'est un vagabond. Mon fils revient demain. C'est le mari qu'il vous faut. Vous serez sa femme, et s'il ose refuser je le desherite—moi. Il ferme la fenêtre. Alors le jeune homme dit: "C'est donc vous—la femme." Elle baisse la tête. Une pause. Tout a coup il l'etreint a plein bras lui jette une grêle de baisers a travers la figure, puis s'en va. A travers le bruit de la mer, sur la grève elle l'entend s'eloigner d'un pas flaneur. Son père, l'aveugle qui a faim, gueule dans la cuisine: Arrive donc Bessie. Le fou ouvre la fenêtre et crie: il est parti donc ce vagabond. C'est ça ma fille. Mon fils fera un excellent mari. Tu n'en a pas pour longtemps à l'attendre. C'est pour demain. Elle rentre.

Vous voyez l'idée. 9000 mots. Paraîtra dans *Pall Mall* N° d'Août prochain.

---

[1] In the story a fence rather than a hedge.
[2] 'Pickaxe': in the story, Captain Hagberd has a shovel, which he takes with him into the house.

Translation

Dear Friend,

Your proposal has given me the greatest imaginable pleasure. Heine-mann has acquired all the rights for the volume that is to include *Typhoon* and three other stories: *Amy Foster* (appeared in the *Illustrated London News*, three issues, December 1901), *Falk: A Narrative*, and *To-morrow* (which will come out in the *Pall Mall Magazine* in August 1902).

In his letter, which I received this morning, Heinemann tells me he has written to you directly, accepting your terms. This, you understand, is his affair. My interest in the translation is quite different and much closer to my heart.

So, if it suits you to start there, you can 'go ahead' with *Typhoon*. I can assure you, moreover, that the four contrivances above will make a good volume. Attached, a little note about the subjects.

As for *Tales of Unrest*, the publisher is Fisher Unwin, with whom my relations are just a little strained. But that doesn't matter. There is something else. Here it is.

A year ago, my relative and good friend Mme Marguerite Pora-dowska (born Gachet) translated the story *Outpost of Progress*, which is in the volume in question. I have the manuscript with me. It's quite good, but the style needs a little fortification. I believe she intended to place the piece in the *Revue des Deux Mondes*. You see the situation for, to be honest, without my negligence the story would have appeared a long time ago. Perhaps you will be able to come to an arrangement with her and avail yourself of her work? I wouldn't want to offend her for anything in the world.

Send me a word or two on this topic; but as my liveliest wish is to be translated by you or at least under your direction and inspiration, I should still find the means of staying on good terms with her.

Wells has given me news of you from time to time. A thousand thanks, my dear fellow, for your sympathetic notice of me in the *Mercure*.

Always yours truly,

Jph. Conrad

Typhoon. You know. 28,000 words. (*Pall Mall Magazine*) *Amy Foster.*— Story of an Austro-Polish highlander emigrating to America who is shipwrecked on the English coast. He roams around the countryside. No one understands him. He is tracked down like a wild beast. A farmer takes him in. He marries a good fool of a girl, a villager. But he persists in speaking his language to her and their child. That annoys his wife. She begins to fear him. He falls ill. She watches over him. He is thirsty and asks for a drink—but in his own language rather than hers. She doesn't understand. He can no longer understand why she doesn't stir. He becomes angry, he gets up—his alien noises frighten her and she runs away, carrying the child. He dies without ever understanding. 11,000 words. Idea: the essential difference of the races. A dismal story, although the *Illustrated London News* has had the courage to publish it. (Three numbers in December 1901).

NB—I shall try to obtain them in order to send them on to you.

Falk: A Narrative deals with a Norwegian, captain of a tug-boat, and the niece of a German, captain of the barque *Diana*, of Bremen. There are also a gossipy hotel proprietor and the narrator, an English skipper, who in a ridiculous way finds himself mixed up in all these affairs. The undertone a little taste of cannibalism—in the past—a long way off—in the South Seas. Everything happens in Bangkok, capital of Siam. I venture to say it's well done. The idea: contrast of commonplace sentimentality with the uncorrupted point-of-view of an almost primitive man (Falk himself) who regards the preservation of life as the supreme and moral law. Not placed yet. 26,000 words.

To-morrow: a very hard title to translate, unless 'One day more' does the job. But you will see. It's about a former master retired from the coasting trade. His ideal is his own home, life around the hearth. His wife is dead and he suffered the misfortune of banishing his only son in a fit of rage. Since then he has been obsessed with the idea that this son will come back. But because people make fun of him he soon stops talking about it. But his madness grows; he expects the return tomorrow. A young girl, his neighbour, the submissive slave of a blind and tyrannical father, takes pity on the old recluse. He confides in her. He makes plans; he buys some furniture in order to establish his son when he returns. The young man must get married. It will be to her. He promises her the earth; she listens out of pity. They talk over the garden fence, and eventually this old man's obsession imparts to the girl a faint hope. Indeed, one fine, rainy evening the son returns, strolling past the front-railings. The old man, in the middle of digging in the garden, doesn't want to acknowledge him. His son will return tomorrow. The other insists. The madman throws his spade at him and runs to shut himself in his house. At the noise, the young girl comes out of her house. Of course the son turns to her for an explanation. The story unfolds in a conversation between these two characters. He is a sailor with the tastes, the independence, the very soul of a true adventurer. Very slowly, she nerves herself to confide his father's schemes to him. He is indignant. It is too much. Formerly, his father had wanted to turn him into a sort of gentleman, a lawyer's clerk, and now here he is wanting to make his son live like a rabbit in a cage. That, never. He laughs in exasperation. 'And perhaps', he says, 'you know the woman he's looked out for me?' He has raised his voice; the madman hears him from the house. He opens the window and shouts 'Don't listen to him, my girl. He's a tramp. My son is coming tomorrow, the sailor who's the very man for you. You'll be his wife, and if he dares to refuse, I'll disinherit him—I shall.' He shuts the window. Then the young man says 'So it's you—the woman.' She bows her head. A pause. Suddenly he clasps her in his arms and showers kisses on her face; then he goes off. Through the noise of the sea, she hears him on the beach, wandering away at a leisurely pace. Her father, the blind man, who is hungry, makes a row in the kitchen—so back comes Bessie. The maniac opens the window and shouts 'The tramp has gone, then. That's that, my girl. My son will make an excellent husband. You won't have to wait long for him. One day more.' She goes in.

   You see the idea. 9,000 words. It will appear in the *Pall Mall* next August.

To T. Fisher Unwin

Text MS Colgate; Unpublished

[letterhead: Pent Farm]
4 April. 1902

Dear Sir.

   Mr. Henry Davray of the *Mercure de France* well known for his translations of English works proposes to translate mine. He wishes to begin with the Tales of Unrest.

   As this is a serious offer I hasten to communicate with you at once. He would of course place some at least of the tales serially and ultimately publish the volume.

   For my part I have cordially agreed to his proposal, and I do not suppose you are likely to object either to the idea or to the person. Davray's translations of my friend H. G. Wells' tales have been very successful. The terms he proposes are 20% of profits.

   This is all I know of the financial aspect of the matter. According to our agreements (except for Almayer's Folly in which I have no interest) we share alike in such proceeds. What I would suggest is that Davray should be referred to you for that part of the business. I'll do mine by revising his proofs, as he proposes. The payments for all the books published with your imprint to be made to you for future settlement between ourselves.

Perhaps, if You think the affair worth while (I think it is) You would communicate with Davray (c/o "Mercure de France") and arrange the matter on the lines suggested above.

I am, dear Sir

faithfully yours

Jph. Conrad

T. Fisher Unwin Esqre

To Hugh Clifford
Text MS Clifford; Hunter

[letterhead: Pent Farm]
5th April 1902

My dear Clifford.

I have been too worried and too wretched generally to write anything worth reading or even to write at all. But that's nothing new for me.

We have been truly concerned at the unsatisfactory state of your health. A few days before your letter I had heard something of it in B'wood's London office. Till then I did not even know you were in England at all.

In the labour and pain of its sons shall this great Empire live—and not otherwise. And its daughters shall have their heavy share of one and the other. This is the law.

Pray allay my anxiety by a word. You may well believe it genuine though I am late in voicing it. Fact is I expected to hear some news of you from Meldrum but he has been laid up with unromantic influenza.

As to Bushwhacking you know I prize it beyond anything that may be written in acknowledgment of a presentation volume.[1] You don't mean to say I did not acknowledge it? It would be too horrible. My notion is that I did—all too briefly I confess and after a delay.—If I did not then indeed I am not fit to cumber this world which but for You and two or three more does not seem to want me particularly.

The book I consider as the best expression of Your talent. All is seen and all is felt, with that gift of expression peculiar to you which suggests action itself under the record of vision and emotion. You are lucky to have lived, and lived consciously to such excellent purpose.

[1] *Bushwhacking and Other Sketches*, published August 1901.

No more at present. We must meet and talk. But I seem rooted in the carpet here. I am ashamed of my inertia. However let me remind you that Mahomed (on whom be the mercy of God) had condescended once to go to a mountain.[1] I have no pretensions to any sort of loftiness but I assure you I feel as invincibly and desolately passive as any soulless heap of earth on this globe.

My wife joins me in kindest regards to Mrs Clifford and Yourself. Pray believe me always ever faithfully yours

Jph. Conrad.

To John Galsworthy

Text MS Forbes; Unpublished

[letterhead: Pent Farm]
Wednesday. 9th Ap [1902][2]

Dearest Jack

Do come along, and bring all the MS. I am very impatient to see Your work.

Could you find out for me whether Meldrum is up and doing. When I last heard he was at home with influenza. It is rather important for me to know and I do not want to write to the office direct.

Write to us day and train. I have done very little alas.

Yours ever

Jph. Conrad.

To H.-D. Davray

Text L.fr. 47

Pent Farm
10 Avril 1902.

Mon cher Davray,

J'ai reçu votre lettre et la carte postale. Tant mieux! Je me promets le plus grand plaisir de votre entreprise. Je suis persuadé que vous donnerez à mon oeuvre (qui me semble, quand je la regarde, rien que cendre et poussière) non seulement un corps nouveau, mais aussi le souffle qui la rendra vivante.

J'ai écrit à madame Poradowska. Elle est en ce moment en Belgique,

---

[1] Proverbial, of course, but the story passed into English by way of Francis Bacon's essay on 'Boldness'.
[2] The only year at the Pent in which 9 April fell on a Wednesday.

mais on fera suivre ma lettre. Aussitôt son adresse reçue je vous la ferai parvenir.

De même j'ai fait part à Fisher Unwin (Éditeur de *Tales of Unrest*) de votre offre. L'animal (cette épithète est en confidence) consentira sans aucun doute et vous aurez à régler les questions d'argent avec lui.

Le volume de Blackwood contiendra: 1° *Youth: a narrative* (J'ai fait erreur en vous donnant le titre de *Falk*, vol: Heinemann, comme *Falk: a narrative*. C'est FALK: A REMINISCENCE) 2° *Heart of Darkness*, et 3° Une histoire que je suis en train de fabriquer en ce moment-ci et dont le titre est *The End of the Tether* comme qui dirait: A bout de ressources. C'est ça l'idée—mais le titre a l'air bête. Le tout à peu près 75.000 mots. 1 et 2 ont déjà paru dans B'wood's Magazine. 3 paraitra prochainement. 1 et 2 à la première personne racontés par Marlow—le sieur qui raconte Lord Jim si vous vous rappelez. 1 Histoire d'un navire qui brûle en mer. 2 se passe au Congo Belge. Histoire farouche d'un journaliste qui devient chef de station à l'intérieur et se fait adorer par une tribu de sauvages. Ainsi décrit le sujet a l'air rigolo, mais il ne l'est pas. 3, écrit à la troisième personne, est plutôt sentimental. Il s'agit d'un vieux Capitaine. Pour le moment ça n'a ni queue ni tête. Enfin.

Là-dessus je vous serre la main bien cordialement et vais me coucher.

Tout a vous.

Translation

My dear Davray,

I have had your letter and the post-card. So much the better! I promise myself the greatest of pleasure in your undertaking. I am convinced that you will give my work (which, when I look at it, seems nothing but dust and ashes) not only a new body, but also the breath that will bring it to life.

I have written to Mme Poradowska. At the moment she is in Belgium, but my letter will be forwarded. As soon as I have her address, I shall send it on to you.

Likewise I have communicated your offer to Fisher Unwin (publisher of *Tales of Unrest*). Without a doubt, the animal (this epithet in confidence) will agree, and you will have to settle financial matters with him).

The Blackwood volume will contain: first, *Youth: a narrative* (In giving you the title of *Falk* in the Heinemann volume as *Falk: a narrative*, I was wrong. It's *Falk: A Reminiscence*.); second, *Heart of Darkness*; and third, a story I am now in the middle of composing, whose title is *The End of the*

Tether, at the end of one's resources, in other words. That's the idea, but the title looks stupid. Nearly 75,000 words in all. One and two have already appeared in *Blackwood's Magazine*. Three will appear shortly. One and two are told in the first person by Marlow—the gentleman who, if you recall, narrates *Lord Jim*. One, the story of a ship on fire at sea. Two happens in the Belgian Congo. A wild story of a journalist who becomes manager of a station in the interior and makes himself worshipped by a tribe of savages. Thus described, the subject seems comic, but it isn't. Three, written in the third person, is rather sentimental. It is about an old captain. At present it has neither head nor tail. That's it.

With that I give you a very cordial handshake and go to bed.

Yours truly.

To T. Fisher Unwin
Text MS Colgate; Unpublished

[letterhead: Pent Farm]
11th April 1902

Dear Sir.

You are no doubt right in the view you take; and there can be no harm in putting it before Davray, as long as it is *not* made a condition sine qua non. He has come to an arrangement with Mr Heinemann for a forthcoming vol: of stories. As to the terms for the Tales I have referred him to You and he is now awaiting Your consent.

His address is: H. D. Davray. Marlotte Seine & Marne.

Yours faithfully

Jph. Conrad

T. Fisher Unwin Esqre

To H.-D. Davray
Text MS Yale; *L.fr.* 48

[letterhead: Pent Farm]
12 Ap. 1902

Cher Ami.

L'addresse de Mme Poradowska est pour le moment a Bruxelles: R. Caroly. 10.

Comme je lui ai dit que Vous avez une communication a lui faire veuillez lui écrire un mot au sujet de l'*Outpost* car il me tarde de Vous envoyer sa traduction.

La chère femme est fort bien disposée. Elle même fait des romans plus au moins Polonais que Buloz acceptait autrefois et Brunetière[1] accepte a présent.

Unwin vous a-t-il écrit encore?

Tout à vous
J. Conrad

Translation

Dear Friend,

For the present, Mme Poradowska's address is in Brussels: Rue Caroly 10.

As I have told her you have something to say, please write her a word about the *Outpost*, for I am anxious to send you her translation.

The dear woman is very well disposed. She herself produces more or less Polish novels that Buloz used to take, and Brunetière takes now.

Has Unwin written to you yet?

Yours sincerely,
J. Conrad

To Ford Madox Ford
Text MS Yale; Unpublished

[Pent Farm]
15 Ap 1902

Dearest Ford,

What becomes of You two and your work?[2] And what of your young women?

These interrupted relations must be taken up again. The cause of my silence is as usual the worry about stuff that won't get itself written. Vous connaissez cela.

I miss collaboration in a most ridiculous manner. I hope you don't intend dropping me altogether. I see You have not given notice to old Hog:[3] Mon cher I appreciate Your regard for my wretched affairs.

In haste to catch post I ask: are you thinking of coming this way and of staying here? I am fairly wretched but still could take in a little. I don't know how it is but with the end of Seraphina everything in the world

---

[1] The literary critic Ferdinand Brunetière, who edited the *Revue des Deux Mondes*.
[2] Elsie Hueffer was working on a novel, Ford on a novel and some poems.
[3] Richard Hogben, owner of the Pent.

seemed to come to an end. Pinker gone to states and McClure too. I wrote a stiff letter to Robert McClure, about Inheritor Royalties. How rotten everything is!

Our love to You all.

Ever yours

Conrad.

To Ford Madox Ford

Text MS Yale; Unpublished

[Pent Farm]
Wednesday. [23 April 1902][1]

Dearest Ford

I wired asking you to come on Monday, meaning also any day after Monday which may be convenient to you. We do not want to be disturbed and Jack's[2] presence announced for Saturday would be distinctly disturbing. And we want time too. A day is not enough. The matter, to us two at least is serious and these considerations seem to me weighty enough to repress my impatience to see you and to see, hear, taste, absorb your George.[3] I felt so strongly that to have a third person hanging about would be unbearable that I had no hesitation in putting you off, since it was not very feasible to wriggle out of a freshly extended invitation.

Your letters have been touching in their suggestion of your mental state. I am truly impatient and anxious. I say anxious, frankly, because not distrusting you in the least, I have from personal experience a rooted mistrust towards our work—yours and mine—which is under the patronage of a Devil. For indeed unless beguiled by a malicious fiend what man would undertake it? What creature would be mad enough to take upon itself the task of a creator? It is a thing unlawful. Une chose néfaste, carrying with it its own punishment of toil, unceasing doubt and deception.

Therefore I am anxious. And I am quite excited for there is an excitement in braving heaven itself as it were, in giving form to an idea, in clothing the breath of our life with day. How fine and how insane! And so the gods encompass our destruction—prius dementat![4]

From the above remarks you may guess I am not on a bed of roses. But that is of no consequence. The great thing is that you are about to

---

[1] Postmarked 24 April.   [2] Galsworthy's.   [3] Ford was at work on *The Benefactor*.
[4] 'Quem Juppiter vult perdere dementat prius' ('Whom God would destroy He first makes mad'): James Duport (1606–79).

step down from your gridiron; the great point what during torture you have snatched from the fire—what form of baked clay. I have no doubt of the breathing of life but the fact remains that without baked clay there is no art, no success, no honesty as you and I understand these terms. Your paper in the Academy mutilated as it is by the mystic mind illustrates my meaning.[1]

In any case, even if its entrails *are* torn out as you say it is all right. One does not write for the Academy for the glory of the whole truth and the paper as it stands is just as much as I and the other fools that read this preposterous weekly can embrace. For the rest we shall talk of that amongst other things. I'll remark however that I am surprised that you with your sane, disillusioned outlook can regret being made to appear superficial. Are you like the rest of us and know not what is good for you? Fear God!—as a Mohamedan would exclaim.

Love to you both and your small woman. Get power of attorney from Elsie to arrange movements, déplacements and interviews on the lines shadowed forth in her good letter.

Ever yours

Conrad

To J. B. Pinker

Text MS Berg; Unpublished

[Pent Farm]
1st May 1902

My dear Pinker.

I am glad you are back home and I presume well in health. I observed the weather in view of your passage and fear that, if the easterly winds we had here extended far into the Atlantic, you must have had it pretty rough towards the end.

It is very friendly of you to write in reference to my letter. I assure you I was very loth to bother you at the moment of departure; and as you see I have managed to exist during your absence though in the usual state of worry. My work for B'wood has not progressed as far as I hoped it would have done by this time. Fact is I fancy that my efforts to throw off Romance must have been really greater than I supposed. My health has been good; I simply could not write anything that would go down with myself. But I am recovering my tone and there is 10000 words ready

---

[1] 'The Making of Modern Verse', *Academy*, 19 and 26 April, pp. 412–14, 438–9.

towards the first instalment for *Maga*.[1] I can't however sent* them on yet. I want 2000 more which will be half the story. The next half is bound to come easier and then—the 'Rescue' or the ex-Rescue since the title must be changed now.[2]

M^r B has *not* turned up yet; so the abominable sacrifice is not consummated. I try not to think of it tho' the necessity is unavoidable and pressing. In this connection I must tell you I had the account of Lord Jim's sales for last year—the second of the book's existence. Six hundred copies have been disposed off,* not counting the 137 of Colonial Ed: This is not brilliant but still it shows a certain vitality in the book. At any rate 4000 copies *did* go off—all but a hundred or so.

You would of course oblige me greatly if you could pay in to Watson now the 50 I had asked you for in my last letter. I would repay you as soon as I get a cheque in advance on the first instalment of my story (serial) or as soon as I had concluded the affair with M^r B—whichever first happens. When I come up to see him (he is expected daily) I shall call on you.

I trust You will find the policy in order when You have time to look into that matter. The assignment should be effected without delay.

> Kindest regards. Yours faithfully
> Jph. Conrad.

To J. B. Pinker
Text MS Berg; Unpublished

> Pent Farm.
> 7 May 1902

My dear Pinker

Many thanks. You shall be kept informed of the course of the affair and paid back as soon as it is concluded. I am a worry to you but am worrying myself much more.

I enclose here this communication from Unwin. I've signed it at all events; but I think you should decide. The books in question are *Outcast* and *Tales of Unrest*. I was afraid you should catch it on the passage. M^r B is coming next week[3] and I shall then see you for sure. Meantime thanks once more

> Yours faithfully
> Jph Conrad.

[1] Of 'The End of the Tether'.
[2] Because of the tangled negotiations over serial rights? See letters of 16, 24, and 28 January.
[3] He returned from Italy at the end of May.

To J. B. Pinker

Text MS Berg; Unpublished

[Pent Farm]
[May 1902?][1]

My dear Pinker.

I return the Document duly signed. As to the Unwin affair it was he himself who arranged the Tauchnitz publication of all my books which he has published: *Alm. Folly. Outcast & Tales*. What this new move of his means I cannot tell. Kindest regards

Yours

J. Conrad

To Ford Madox Ford

Text MS BL Ashley 2923; Unpublished

[Pent Farm]
1902
Thursday. [15?] May[2]

Dearest Ford.

I had to dash to London and found time to look in upon the Pinker of Literary Agents. I reckon he had been very sea-sick and the yanks must have been bullying him brutally between the two spells.

He placed *Romance* for Serial rights and book form with McClure. The Royalty arrang^{nt} is fairly good 12½% for the first thou: and 15% after. Serial £100. (for the McC Syndicate of Newspapers). Advance on pub: £30. Together in America £130. He says we could have had elsewhere £100 for book (adv^{ce}) but no guarantee of serial in that case. He elected to close with McC. The "trade" in an awful state he says. I've generally approved his bargain so far. It gives us £65 each to begin with anyhow. The condition that the beginning should be shortened for serial pub^{on} will give you some light occupation. He intends to forward you the MS. When you come here we may have a look at it together if you are too sick of the thing to tackle it alone.

In England he has tried only three people so far. Unwin is one; the second I do not know. The third refusal came from the Times. He means to interview Longman now.

Postman turned up. Love to you all. Yours

Conrad.

---

[1] A sequel to the letter of 7 May?

[2] The contents suggest a date fairly soon after Pinker's return. On 7 May Conrad had not yet seen him but intended to do so 'for sure' the following week.

To George Blackwood
Text MS NLS; Blackburn 147

[letterhead: Pent Farm]
20th May. 1902

Dear Mr Blackwood.

You may well say: at last—but if you knew how hard on me too are my delays you would feel relieved out of pure human compassion.

This is 14 000 words.[1] There are more written and you need not apprehend anything in the nature of Lord Jim's development. That sort of thing does not happen twice.[2]

There will be about *30000* words. If you make one instalment of this the other two may be shorter—say 8 000 each. However this first batch may be cut anywhere. I am read for my quality and cannot regard anything else. My quality is my truth. The rest may go.

I have now blocked out in MS about 6 000 words besides what you receive.[3] Probably before I get the proofs of this I shall be ready to send you another batch.

Pray send me £30 pounds. I would not ask if I did not need the money urgently; and you cannot be more disgusted with me than I am with myself.

In haste. Kind regards

faithfully yours

Jph Conrad.

To William Blackwood
Text MS NLS; Blackburn 148

[letterhead: Pent Farm]
27th May 1902.

Dear Mr Blackwood.

During your absence I've been in communication with Mr George Blackwood regarding the completion of the Youth volume. Six days ago I forwarded Part the First of *The End of the Tether* containing rather more than 14 000 words. Part the II^d now being finished off, shall be ready by the 20th of next month.[4] The whole will not fall short of the 30 000 words

---

[1] Chapters One to Five, four of which appeared in the July issue.   [2] But it did.

[3] In the final version, Chapters Six to Eight amount to about 6,800 words.

[4] On 20 May, Conrad suggested dividing the remainder of the story into two instalments, but 'Part' does not necessarily mean *instalment*. Paragraph four of the letter of 5 June shows that he hoped to finish the entire story by the end of the month.

which were needed to make up the volume. From his last letter I am glad to learn he thinks the story suitable for *Maga*.[1]

In my correspondence with him (which through a blunder of mine had to touch upon my money-indebt[ed]ness to the 'House') I have said nothing as to the loan from the Insurance Office being paid off; this now is done and the Indenture with the cancelled signatures of my sureties is now in my possession.

My gratitude for your assistance at that time does not come to an end with the transaction; neither is it (as the epigrammatist defines it) "a lively sense of the favours to come":[2] though I proceed now to ask you for the favour of an interview during your stay in London. Half an hour of your time (on as early a day as you may find convenient) would set my mind at rest as to the proposal I wish to make. It is of great importance to me; and I think—as far as it concerns you—it is fairly "presentable"—or of course I would not entertain the notion of presenting it. I don't put it down on paper because—apart from the very real pleasure of seeing you—I would rather face the matter out than try to write about it plausibly.

Believe me, dear Mr Blackwood, always faithfully yours

Joseph Conrad.

To Ford Madox Ford

Text MS Yale; Unpublished

[Pent Farm]
[30 May 1902][3]

My dear Ford

Our letters always cross.

I suggest that you should write Pinker saying that as co-author of *R* you object to its being disposed of to McClure till a statement and remittance of Inheritors is sent us.[4] I am off to see B'wood about the fatal act and if he entertains the proposal I'll be able to chime in with a small cheque. I am afraid all this will take time. In your letter to P say that you can not enter into Conrad's position vis-a-vis of McClure and

---

[1] But see the letter to Blackwood, p. 418, n.2.

[2] 'Sir Robert Walpole's definition of the gratitude of place-expectants, "That it is a lively sense of *future* favours"': Hazlitt, *Lectures on the English Comic Writers*. Sir Robert, in his turn, was paraphrasing La Rochefoucauld.

[3] The day when Blackwood's offer of an interview would have arrived, and the day of the note to Pinker.

[4] Ford wanted to sue the McClures; they were behind with the statement of account but not, according to standard trade terms, with the royalty payments (Mizener, p. 78).

that you insist on payment of *your* half of such proceeds as there are before anything is done to R^{ce}. I am dropping a note to P saying: Hueffer's angry and my position most unpleasant.

This is all I can do just now. I am nearly out of my mind with anxiety as to B's action as if he should refuse to acquire the books I am indeed at the end of my tether. With love—

Always yours

Conrad.

To J. B. Pinker
Text MS Berg; Unpublished

[Pent Farm]
30th May 1902

My dear Pinker.

Hueffer is exasperated at McClure's action and in effect says that the idea of selling them *Rce* is distasteful to him. It is really a shame that the acct/ of the Inheritors is not sent yet. Why? Pray let them know they must pay Hueffer *his* half of the proceeds. Let them keep mine— whatever it is. Upon my word it looks as if I had pawned his part of the work too. I warned R.[1] that our joint work must not be involved (as far as his half goes) in my indebt[ed]ness to the firm.

Can you do anything?

Yours faithfully

J. Conrad.

To William Blackwood
Text MS NLS; Blackburn 152

[letterhead: Pent Farm]
31 May 1902

Dear Mr Blackwood.

Directly on my return I sit down to thank you for your very kind and patient hearing.[2] That the occasion was painful to me (it is always painful to be 'asking') makes your friendly attitude the more valuable: and to say this is the primary object of my letter. But there is something more.

I admit that after leaving you I remained for some time under the impression of my 'worthlessness'; but I beg to assure you that I've never

[1] Robert McClure – whom Conrad owed at least £180 (letter to Pinker, 28 January).
[2] They had talked that morning at a London hotel.

fostered any illusions as to my value. You may believe me implicitly when I say that I never work in a self satisfied elation, which to my mind is no better than a state of inebriety unworthy of a man who means to achieve something. That—labouring against an anxious tomorrow, under the stress of an uncertain future, I have been at times consoled, re-assured and uplifted by a finished page—I'll not deny. This however is not intoxication: it is the Grace of God that will not pass by even an unsuccessful novelist. For the rest I am conscious of having pursued with pain and labour a calm conception of a definite ideal in a perfect soberness of spirit.

That strong sense of sober endeavour and of calm conception has helped me to shake off the painful impression I had, notwithstanding your kindness, carried away from our interview. I don't—in the remotest degree—mean to imply that you wished to crush me. Nothing's further from my thought; but you are aware, I hope, that your words carry a considerable weight with me; and now I have no longer the buoyancy of youth to bear me up through the deep hours of depression. I have nothing but a faith—a little against the world—in my reasoned conviction.

I've rejected the idea of worthlessness and I'll tell you, dear Mr Blackwood, on what ground mainly. It is this:—that, given my talent (which appeals to such widely different personalities as W. H.* Henley and Bernard Shaw—H. G. Wells and professor Yrgö Hirn of the Finland University—to Maurice Greiffenhagen a painter and to the skipper of a Persian Gulf steamer who wrote to the papers of my 'Typhoon'—to the Ed. of PMM to a charming old lady in Winchester)[1] given my talent, the fundamental and permanent failure could be only the outcome of an inherent worthlessness of character. Now my character is formed: it has been tried by experience. I have looked upon the worst life can do—and I . m sure of myself, even against the demoralising effect of straitenec circumstances.

I know exactly what I am doing. Mr George Blackwood's incidental remark in his last letter that the story is not fairly begun yet[2] is in a

[1] W. E. Henley published *The Nigger* in the *New Review*. Shaw, whom Conrad despised, was a recent visitor (letter to Garnett, 28 August ? 1902). Wells praised *Almayer* and *An Outcast* in the *Saturday Review*. Yrjö Hirn was a professor at Helsingfors: his wife, Karin, translated some of the *Tales of Unrest* into Swedish (*Fredlösa historier*, Stockholm, 1903), and he wrote the introduction. Greiffenhagen illustrated many of Conrad's works, including 'Typhoon' for the *Pall Mall Magazine*, whose editor was George Roland Halkett. Harriet Capes was the 'charming old lady'.

[2] He had written: 'this story should suit Maga, though as far as it goes at present one can hardly say one has got into the story yet' (letter of 23 May, Blackburn, p. 148).

measure correct but, on a large view, beside the point. For, the writing is as good as I can make it (first duty), and in the light of the final incident, the whole story in all its descriptive detail shall fall into its place—acquire its value and its significance. This is my method based on deliberate conviction. I've never departed from it. I call your own kind self to witness and I beg to instance Karain—Lord Jim (where the method is fully developed)—the last pages of Heart of Darkness where the interview of the man and the girl locks in—as it were—the whole 30000 words of narrative description into one suggestive view of a whole phase of life and makes of that story something quite on another plane than an anecdote of a man who went mad in the Centre of Africa. And *Youth* itself (which I delight to know you like so well) exists only in virtue of my fidelity to the idea and the method. The favourable critics of that story, Q amongst others remarked with a sort of surprise "This after all is a story for boys yet – – – – –"[1]

Exactly. Out of the material of a boys' story I've made *Youth* by the force of the idea expressed in accordance with a strict conception of my method. And however unfavourably it may affect the business in hand I must confess that I shall not depart from my method. I am at need prepared to explain on what grounds I think it a true method. All my endeavours shall be directed to understand it better, to develop its great possibilities, to acquire greater skill in the handling—to mastery in short. You may wonder why I am telling you all this.

First because I am sure of your sympathy. I hope that this letter will find its place in that memoir which one or two of my young faithfuls have promised to offer to my 'manes'.[2] It would be good for people to know that in the 20th century in the age of Besants, Authors' Clubs and Literary agents[3] there existed a Publisher to whom not an altogether contemptible author could write safely in that strain. Next because I want to make good my contention that I am not writing "in the air". It is not the haphazard business of a mere temperament. There is in it as much intelligent action guided by a deliberate view of the effect to be attained as in any business enterprise. Therefore I am emboldened to say that ultimate and irretrievable failure is *not* to be my lot. I know that it is not necessary to say to You but I may just as well point out that I

---

[1] 'Youth', according to Quiller-Couch (*Speaker*, 17 September 1898, p. 343), 'might be one of the ordinary stories told by ordinary writers for ordinary boys at Christmas. But the framework goes for little; for the story contains an idea.'

[2] To propitiate his spirit.

[3] Who, like Pinker, came between writer and publisher. Sir Walter Besant was a philanthropist, popular novelist, and founding member of the Society of Authors.

must not by any means be taken for a gifted loafer intent on living upon credulous publishers. Pardon this remark—but in a time when Sherlock Holmes looms so big[1] I may be excused my little bit of self-assertion.

I am long in my development. What of that? Is not Thackeray's penny worth of mediocre fact drowned in an ocean of twaddle? And yet he lives. And Sir Walter, himself, was not the writer of concise anecdotes I fancy. And G. Elliot*—is she as swift as the present public (incapable of fixing its attention for five consecutive minutes) requires us to be at the cost of all honesty, of all truth, and even the most elementary conception of art? But these are great names.[2] I don't compare myself with them. I am *modern*, and I would rather recall Wagner the musician and Rodin the Sculptor who both had to starve a little in their day—and Whistler the painter who made Ruskin the critic foam at the mouth with scorn and indignation. They too have arrived. They had to suffer for being 'new'.[3] And I too hope to find my place in the rear of my betters. But still—my place. My work shall not be an utter failure because it has the solid basis of a definite intention—first: and next because it is not an endless analysis of affected sentiments but in its essence it is action (strange as this affirmation may sound at the present time) nothing but action—action observed, felt and interpreted with an absolute truth to my sensations (which are the basis of art in literature)—action of human beings that will bleed to a prick,[4] and are moving in a visible world.

This is my creed. Time will show. And this you may say is my overweening conceit. Well, no. I know well enough that I know nothing. I should like to think that some of my casual critics are in the possession of that piece of information about themselves. Starting from that knowledge one may learn to look on with some attention—at least. But enough of that.

Believe me, dear Mr Blackwood in all trust and confidence yours

Jph Conrad.

---

[1] *The Hound of the Baskervilles* came out in 1902.
[2] Intentionally or not, three hits: John Blackwood, William's father, befriended Thackeray and published every Eliot novel but *Romola*; in Edinburgh, the name of Sir Walter Scott was great above all others.
[3] And, in two cases out of three, on suspicion of not working hard enough. Rodin was falsely accused of casting rather than sculpting his models. Whistler was denounced for lack of 'finish' in his paintings. Whether or not Blackwood had accused him openly, Conrad is answering a charge of laziness.
[4] 'If you prick us, do we not bleed?' *Merchant of Venice*, iii.i.

To David Meldrum
Text MS Duke; Blackburn 150

[Pent Farm]
[31 May 1902]¹

My dear Mr Meldrum.

The affair looks shaky. Still M^r B said finally that he would consider and "consult Mr Meldrum, Mr Morton"²—and so on. I send him a letter today and a *memo* of what I propose, of which the copy I enclose here for your judgment. He was very kind but told me plainly that I was a loss to the Firm. Thats hard enough to hear at any time. I do think that he resented a bit my going to Pinker; but I think I've explained away that bad impression—and towards the end the *tone* of the conversation was changed in a subtle way.

If you think this agreement at all fair I know you will back me up. Mr B seems half-anxious to feel he will get a look in with my future work. I gave assurances—but pledge it I will not. If it comes to pledging my work a year ahead I can with a *guaranteed* policy get 300 somewhere else. And would have to do it too. All this horrible and the time passes the story is hung up.

Pray directly you see how the wind veers, good or bad, let me know, if you can without breaking confidence of course. The anxiety is great.

Kindest regards
Always Yours

Conrad.

The cheque has not come yet.³ M^r B only told me he would send it at once. It's the most humiliating thing in the world.

Copy.

Pray believe that I am assuming nothing as to your action. But as you said most kindly that you "would consider" I set down here a memorandum of what I wished to propose.

The copyright in Eng^d & the Col^ies and USA of *Jim* (on which £200. has been paid on ad^vce of royalties) and of *Youth* (on which £150 has been paid in ad^ce of roy^es) becomes your absolute property in consideration of a further pay^t of £50 *and* a loan of £300 bearing interest at 5%. No date shall be specified for the repayment of the principal. I shall assign to you a life policy for £400 (or if margin seems inadequate then £450) and Mr

¹ The same day as the letter to Blackwood.
² George A. Morton, Blackwood's manager.
³ An advance on 'The End of the Tether' in serial form.

John Galsworthy shall *guarantee* the payments of half-yearly premiums necessary to keep the policy in force—say for ten years. *At my death you repay yourself the principal and such interest as may be due to date and hand the balance over to my wife.* I am at liberty to extinguish the debt by partial payments in the manner most convenient to me, paying interest on the residue till the final settlement. On the day the sale of these works should have reached 15000 copies[1] at 6/- (or a larger number of cheaper copies equivalent to 15000 at 6/-) half the debt (150) shall be considered as extinguished interest reduced and the balance of insce money handed to my wife proportionately increased—unless I pay off the remaining half then and there when the policy reverts to me. But should my death occur before the number of copies is reached Messrs: Blackwood repay themselves in full as stated in the underlined passage. Only if at any time between my death and the expiration of copyright that number of copies sold is reached Messrs: Blackwood would pay my heirs the sum of £100. In introducing this condition I waive any right its acceptance would give me of seeking information or inspecting the books of the Firm either by myself or my agents the books being absolutely and without reserve the property of Messrs: Blackwood and my confidence in them complete.

The weak point of the scheme is of course that it provides no guarantee for the regular pay^t of interest. I don't see how to meet this. But *without specifically pledging* my future work to you I would suggest that as Mr Pinker has definite instructions to submit my productions to you in the first instance any terms agreed upon the same may include a stipulation as to arrears of interest if any. Otherwise my works shall come before you in no way affected and without any lien on them in consequence of this arrangement: it being clearly understood that the privilige* of priority in acquiring my work is a matter voluntary on my part quite distinct from the existence of this arrangement and in which I am solely moved by my great personal regard for the Head of the House.

To John Galsworthy

Text MS Forbes; Najder (1970)

[Pent Farm]
1 June 1902

Dearest Jack.

I am indeed sorry that I wired too late to catch you at home; the more so that I have been led into taking an atrocious liberty—or what would have been one if you had not been what you are to me.

---

[1] So far about 4,000 copies of *Lord Jim* had been sold.

I was coming to see B'wood by appt^t. You know on what errand. I was going to try and sell him outright the copyright both of Jim and Youth—just to get a fresh start again out of the slough of perpetual despond. He was kind but atrocious. Demonstrated to me that I've been a loss to the firm and at first would not—apparently—even look at the idea. Methinks George is none of my friends; and also I fancy the old boy was huffed at my connexion with Pinker. At last he seemed to be half inclined to condescend to be bribed by the offer of these two books to *lend* me some money. Comprenez-Vous? No matter. I shall explain the transaction (which is only under consideration at that) when we meet. In short, discussing the terms which would involve my taking out a fresh policy of £*450* he said: "Yes; but there is also the question of premiums." Then I my dear Jack remembering your offer some time ago (forgive me) said that very likely you would guarantee that at least for some time. If the thing comes off I shall square up everybody, pay the first half-year premium and have about £70 in hand to begin the Rescue again on. Therefore in six months you would find yourself liable for about £*8.10* and thereafter as God shall will it; but I dare say I would be more or less able to meet the premiums—(in greater part at any rate). You would render me the greatest service by giving this guarantee if B'wood finally decides to do what I want. If he does not . . . but I can't be bothered looking at this. It would be a dead wall and I haven't the pluck to face it in imagination.

He seemed impressed by my words—as to my confidence in you I mean. And apart from that he suddenly expressed such an evidently, unquestionably, genuine appreciation of your person and your work (intelligent too) that I found it in my heart to love him. I should not wonder if that impulsive bringing in of your personality (I spoke under the impulse of desperation) were to carry through this for me infinitely important matter. But you must understand that I did in no way engage you. I said in effect that I could venture to ask you—and no more. I also added—what I believed then—that I thought you were out of town— perhaps abroad. So my dear Jack if there is impossibility you have only to say nothing. You understand clearly what is required—do you not! You are *not* asked to guarantee the principal of the loan, or the interest on the same. You would be asked to guarantee the punctual payment of half-yearly premiums which I would do my best to meet myself, of course. In the worst case you would undertake a liability of £20 a year *on the outside*. No trifle to ask for I am well aware; only I really believe that having got rid by that means of all tormenting debts I could always raise the necessary cash for that 'service'. Thus my dear Jack *if there is possibility* a letter from you to B saying that you had heard from me and that you consent to give the guarantee if required would be of the best possible effect on my fortunes now hanging in the balance. The old boy is staying for the next few days at Neumeister's Hotel 30 Bryanston Street Portman Sq. W.——At any rate write your forgiveness to me or best bring it here. The terms roughly are: *Jim* (£200 paid) and *Youth* (£150 paid) become B's absolute property. *Consideration*: £50 in further payment *and* loan of £300. at 5%. but this last secured by a £450 life policy with *guarantee of premiums* to keep it in force. No term fixed for repayment of principal—to be carried out in my time and at my convenience. There are other conditions where I try to reserve for myself something in case of sudden popularity coming on—a dream! Too complicated to set down here.

With love ever Your

Jph. Conrad.

PS I shall also in a day or two ask you to swap cheques with me. That is I shall send you B's cheque for £30 and you shall give me yours—(if no objection) which I shall use to pay off Meldrum. I don't want to pass the cheque through my bank and he wishes to cover up the tracks. But this is another story.

To John Galsworthy

Text MS Forbes; Unpublished

[letterhead: Pent Farm]

Wednesday. [4 June 1902?]¹

My dearest Jack

Thanks. I trust Your letter'll act like magic—but are you not tired of assissting* (in the French and English sense) at my sordid man[o]euvrings?

You do not say anything of Your Father's health. This spring is more horrible and treacherous as it seems to improve.

It is quite on the cards I may have to come to town and I shall certainly let you know in time. Post waiting.

Ever yours

Conrad:

Love from us all.

¹ The type eight letterhead implies a date in 1902. Galsworthy's magical letter could be the one requested on 1 June, although June seems late for talk of spring.

To William Blackwood
Text MS NLS; Blackburn 157

[letterhead: Pent Farm]
5 June 1902

Dear Mr Blackwood.

Many thanks for the cheque for £30 on acct of *The End of the Tether* received to-day.

That story will contain 30 000 words. I understand that this will be sufficient to complete the volume in a satisfactory manner.

I would consider it a kindness if the proofs of the 1st inst:^{nt} were sent to me at your earliest convenience. The corrections however, I may safely promise, shall not be extravagant in extent; only I want time to look *into* the text a little.

This is the really important matter. For the rest pray be assured that I appreciate the tone of your reply.[1] Your decision I regret of course and mainly because it will not allow me to dismiss the subject from my mind which would be exclusively busy with the Troubles of Captain Whalley: —these having to come to their appointed end in the last week of June.[2] How the days fly! From July to Oct: I shall be busy with the last third of my Rescue. Then, at once, I shall begin on a story of about 80000 words for which I shall allow myself a year: thus I have good hopes of being ready in 18 months with another work to try my further luck. It'll be a novel of intrigue with the Mediterranean coast and sea, for the scene.[3]

Believe me, dear Mr Blackwood, with the greatest regard

faithfully yours

Jph. Conrad.

To Ford Madox Ford
Text MS Yale; Unpublished

[Pent Farm]
10 June 1902

Dear Ford.

I am most distressed about poor Xna[4] and the failure of all our plans. Jess is writing to Elsie at length; for on my side I am in the throes of

---

[1] Declining the copyrights and warning that the scheme could harm him (Blackburn, p. 156).
[2] The due date was 20 June.
[3] He turned instead to the Latin American intrigue of *Nostromo*.
[4] Christina was sick.

dissolution; distracted with the backward state of the story and with no idea where to turn.

We can not leave here. There is no possibility. I am still negotiating for dear life with Heine[nn] this time B'wood having declined to have anything more to do with me. I tell you it's no joke. Enough. Love

Yours

Conrad

Thanks for the *Rossetti*.[1] My opinion of it you know: but I am reading it carefully. It is *good*.

To Edward Garnett
Text MS Colgate; G. 183

[Pent Farm]
10 June 1902

Dearest Edward.

In so far as writing goes I hardly dare look you in the face. Why do you introduce the name of Pinker into your letter? It is almost indelicate on your part. The times indeed are changed—and all my art has become artfulness in exploiting agents and publishers.

I am simply afraid to show You my work; and as to writing about it—this I can't do. I have now lost utterly all faith in myself, all sense of style, all belief in my power of telling the simplest fact in a simple way. For no other way do I care now. It is an unattainable way. My expression has become utterly worthless: it is time for the money to come rolling in. The Blackwood vol: shall be coming out in two three months: *Youth, Heart of Dark*[ss] and a thing I am trying to write now called *The End of the Tether*—an inept title to heartbreaking bosh. Pawling's vol shall follow at a decent interval; four stories of which Typhoon is first and best. I am ashamed of them all; I don't believe either in their popularity or in their merit. Strangely enough it is yet my share of '*Romance*' (collab[m] stuff with Ford) that fills me with the least dismay. My mind is becoming base, my hand heavy, my tongue thick—as though I had drunk some subtle poison, some slow poison that will make me die, die as it were without an echo. You understand?

I am always coming to you, and some day I shall appear. I don't suppose you are angry with me: for in truth where would be the sense of expending your fine stock of indignation upon such a base wretch.

[1] Ford's newly published monograph.

The other day I ran into Duck*th*[1] to try and see you. No luck.

Remember me affectionately to your wife whose trans*on* of Karenina is splendid.[2] Of the thing itself I think but little, so that her merit shines with the greater lustre. Jessie joins me in our love to You all. We talk of your boy very often. Oh! My dear dear fellow I am so very disgusted with my mental impotence so afraid of my hollowness—so weary—deadly weary of writing!

Ever Yours

Jph. Conrad

To John Galsworthy

Text MS Forbes; Unpublished

[letterhead: Pent Farm]
11 June 1902

My dearest Jack

I have exchanged some letters with Pawling who is really desirous to do something for me. Indeed I have no delusions as to the true nature of the feeling. This affair—apart from the necessity of paying away a sum of money is all to their advantage; and Heinemann himself does not intend to make any sort of sacrifice or take any risk for my sake.

I felt from the first that the want of a definite provision for paying off the principal would be fatal to the proposal. I did not want to pledge my future to them since Pinker has been impressing upon me the necessity of being free to go "upon the market". With that proviso he (P) is hopeful about my work. But the crux is that I have nothing in the world but my work to point to. Therefore I devised a sort of scheme which I put into my proposal for the gradual extinguishment of the debt.

It is to the effect that on publication of every new work of mine £25 should be paid to H*nn* *no matter who is the publisher*. But as my work would come before them in the usual way should *they* be the publishers then a clause would be inserted in the agreement (as to each such work) providing for part of the usual advance on pub*on* to be set aside for paying off the debt: and upon a sort of sliding scale. That is that: if the agreed ad*ce* on pub*on* is under £200 then £25 should [be] deducted; and if over £250 up 350 then that the amount deducted should be *£50* and so on.

This is the only scheme that I can devise consistent with my keeping

[1] Garnett was now at Duckworth's. Conrad came to town 6 June (telegram Berg).

[2] Published in 1901: she was currently at work on *The Death of Ivan Ilyitch*.

my freedom as to the disposal of my stuff unimpaired. I am quite willing to submit my production to them *in the first place*. This arrangement however will prevent them offering me too low a price; for obviously if some other publisher proposed me substantially better terms it would be to my advantage to go to him—and yet not quite to their disadvantage since the better terms would enable me to pay off a larger portion of my debt. I write confusedly but I dare say you catch on to what is in the back of my head:

Heinemann demurs apparently to that part of my proposal; on what ground precisely Pawling does not say. His hurried note says only that he has asked you for an interview in order to discuss my case. He has written yesterday (Monday) I presume to your club. I've let you in for a pretty bother; but now you *are* in it I want you to know what scheme I proposed. Perhaps You could hammer out some modification of it which would satisfy them. The other thing is this:

The policy being for *500* and the loan of *300* this lets you in for a liability of about £36 a year in case of my utter inability to meet my obligations. (£18 premium guarantee and another £18 or less interest guarantee)

The policy must be assigned to the firm of Heinemann in the first place but pray stipulate for yourself to have a *second charge* on it. To this they cannot object and I want you eventually to get some at least of your money back. In five years' time I'll be either dead or would have done something. Under the two other policies Jessie, in the worst case, is sure to get 700 to 750; and I have been putting my hand in your pocket in a manner that causes me sometimes to break out in a cold sweat in the still watches of the night.

I trust you will get this before the interview with P. Love from us all. Yours

J Conrad.

We are ready for you whenever you like to come for a few days on the plan of country walks. Jess is planning sandwiches of sorts for you to take on these tramps. I am very anxious you should come. I'll work better under the stimulus of your company. Don't fail.

To Ford Madox Ford
Text MS Yale; Unpublished

19 June 1902
The Pent

Dearest Ford.

We have been greatly concerned about the poor child, about Elsie and about yourself. These are the troubles Jessie can understand and feel for. My concern is perhaps wider and it is not diminished by your wife's letter. She is in the mood of self reproach the hardest, the most difficult to overcome—and the most useless of moods. And moreover always and essentially the mood of injustice in which one is misjudging oneself and others fatally. Let her mistrust it and think of picking up the threads— even the thread of her writing. Nobody has been wronged. Let me assure her that in this world—as I have known it—we are made to suffer without the shadow of a reason, of a cause or of guilt. To us who cannot see beyond—I won't say the day but—the instant, it should be a comforting reflexion that ignorance not only makes for bliss but is the f[o]undation of innocence.

It is good of her and of You to think of my troubles. I have scrambled through once more leaving a few more shreds of my self respect amongst the thorms.* I did not know I had so much left to lose. Be it as it may I stand on the other side, to draw a breath or two, raw from head to foot with the body of my thought in tatters and surveying my dishonourable scars. No more just now. My best love to you both and the dear chicks.

Ever Yours

Conrad.

Story for Mag all behind. I am tired! I am tired of sitting on the knees of the unpropitious gods.

To John Galsworthy
Text MS Forbes; Unpublished

[letterhead: Pent Farm]
19th June 1902
Thursday.

Dearest Jack

I have your letter—and this is all I can find to say. Since you left I have worked. I've been able to work; but nothing seems good in the slightest degree. And yet I feel that I must do well to justify before my own eyes and even before yours what your affection has prompted you to do for me.

Tell me in what form the acknowledgment of my debt should be. I don't know. Is there a form? Is a simple IOU the proper and valid thing? Our love.

Always Yours

Jph. Conrad.

To Ford Madox Ford

Text Telegram Yale; Unpublished

[24 June 1902][1]

Reply paid Hueffer Winchelsea
How is Elsie today letter received writing this post.

Conrad

To Ford Madox Ford

Text MS Yale; *Listy* 199; Original unpublished

[letterhead: Pent Farm]
24 June 1902

My dear Ford.

I can't express how sorry we are for the horrors accumulating upon your devoted head. Your note reached us this morning. The thing for you all to do is to come over here for rest and recovery after the infectious part of the convalescence is over. I have a great need to get in touch with you again.

Last night the lamp exploded here and before I could run back into the room the whole round table was in a blaze, books, cigarettes, MS—alas. The whole 2d part of End of Tether, ready to go to E'gh. The whole![2] The fire ran in streams and Jess and I threw blankets and danced around on them; the blaze in the window was remarked in Postling then all was over but the horrid stink. No books of yours have been burnt. The roundtable is charred in one place. The brown carpet damaged by fire and oil. This morning looking at the pile of charred paper—MS and typed copy—my head swam; it seemed to me the earth was turning backwards. I must buckle to. The MS was due today in

---

[1] Date-stamp.

[2] Conrad may have meant the second of three instalments (in the way he describes a reconstituted text in the following letter), but he is more likely to have meant the entire second half (cf n. 4, p. 413).

E'gh. I have wired to B'woods. It's a disaster, but the text is fairly fresh in my mind yet. The thing simply *has* to be done.

A more sensible letter than this, for you, was burnt too in its gummed envelope. I said a lot of things.

Are you quite alone? Jessie's impulse was to rush over—but, que voulez vous! Any illness in my household now would mean the End of the World for me. Now since this catastrophe more than ever. And after all you and I shall yet work and hope together so it's better that I should keep out of the way of infection. When can Xna be moved? Would you trust her with us? Love.

Conrad.

To William Blackwood

Text MS NLS; Blackburn 158

[letterhead: Pent Farm]
24 June 1902

My Dear Mr Blackwood.

The Story was completed (three days late) and lying on my study table, when, while we were,* at dinner the lamp (just carried in) exploded. When I ran back my whole table was in a blaze and unapproachable. All the blankets being upstairs by the time we had smothered and stamped out the flames both the MS and the type of Part II were one mass of charred remnants.

This is what Gen: Buller would call "rank bad luck".[1] I wired you first thing this morning and shall be on tenter-hooks till I get your reply. If the first inst^t contains only the Chap^{rs} I to IV all is well[2]—comparatively well; for I am confident of getting 4–5 thous: words ready again by next Sunday. That would be the 2 first Chap^s:[3] of Part II? Then Chap^s 3 to 6 would make another instalment (the final one) of say 8–9 thou: words.[4]

But if *all* Part Ist has gone into the July N^o the position is more

---

[1] General Sir Redvers Buller, VC, thus described the military chaos at Colenso, 15 December 1899. Blamed for the mistakes of his subordinates, he was demoted and, in 1901, dismissed the service.

[2] Because Blackwood already had Chapter Five (letter of 20 May).

[3] I.e. the first two chapters of the recreated version. As published, they ran to nearly 4,000 words; with Chapter Five they made up the August instalment.

[4] Conrad estimates a work in three instalments, eleven chapters and, at most, 28,000 words (the 12 to 14,000 offered here plus the 14,000 already in Edinburgh). The version in *Maga* numbered 50,000 words, had fourteen chapters, and appeared in six instalments.

difficult. I am buckling-to as if that was the case; and I believe that I shall be ready by the 15th prox: with the last page of the story. Meantime I would send you the copy from day to day. The text is fresh in my mind.

I am more sorry for the bother I cause you than words can express. As far as common prudence goes I've nothing to reproach myself with. Yours faithfully

Jph Conrad.

To Ford Madox Ford
Text MS Yale; Unpublished

[letterhead: Pent Farm]
24 June 1902

Dearest Ford.

Thanks for Your wire. We are greatly relieved. What an awful strain it must have been on you. I feel my head swim when I think of it.

The only damage done is: round table charred slightly on one side and brown carpet badly burnt in several places. This last may be the subject of a claim on the ins^{ce}.

The MS is gone. However the situation may be saved as far as maga is concerned if I furnish 4000 by the 2^d July. That I fancy I can do. Of course the thing puts me back; always back; everlastingly back.

The Pent has been done thoroughly outside; floors mended inside also the defects of inner walls.

The banging and hammering was awful; I wrote on through it: then the lamp blew up: all's up!

However I must have another dying effort. O but the heart break!

At last McClure sends the cheque and his outrageous acct. Pray credit me with my half of it and soon I shall send you another fiver.

In haste. With love

Yours

Conrad.

What about Xna? Seriously. Jessie would come to fetch her. We both would come. Would it not give Elsie a better chance to recover? We both love the child; and she would not be worried or interfered with—only looked after and kept dry faithfully. Consider.

Sign receipt and forward to SS McClure C^o Effingham House Arundel St Strand. WC.

To John Galsworthy

Text MS POSK; J-A, 1, 304

[letterhead: Pent Farm]

25 June 1902

Dearest Jack.

Imagine that with the End of Tether lying on the table ready (or all but)[1] the lamp exploded and the whole thing is consumed. That was on Monday evening. On Tuesday by noon I had a comforting message from B'woods about it. If I can rewrite 4000 words by the 2ᵈ next or so the situation is saved as far as Maga's concerned. But what a set back! Enfin!

Heaven's unkind to Kings[2] and to authors this year.

Ever Yours

Conrad.

My dear fellow you did put new heart into me with your letter about the *Tether*. But Edward is not very far wrong.[3]

To David Meldrum

Text MS Duke; Blackburn 159

The Pent.

25 June 1902

My dear Mr Meldrum.

To begin with—a word of congratulation on *The Conquest of Charlotte* coming to its most harmonious ending.[4] My high opinion of this achievement, as a whole, you know. I have no critical vocabulary to express the very complex impression left upon my mind by the story; which, apart from its many other qualities, possesses the all-important one of being *interesting*. From a craftsman's point of view the ease and the compactness of effect are very striking—especially to a man who knows how much hard toil must be put into *Ease* and how much hard thought is necessary to attain the effect of *compactness* in a work so long and so many-sided. I don't go into detail but I dare say I've missed no point. As to picking holes—which is my instinctive propensity to do with every work of fiction—I confess that in this case I have been unable to lay hold

---

[1] Although this qualification may mean that the story had not been finished after all, it may simply mean that some of the MS had not yet been typed.

[2] The new king had nearly died of appendicitis.

[3] A cancelled PS reads: 'I think thats the correct form of IOU. No date I believe.'

[4] In the July *Blackwood's*.

of any loose ends. Truth to say I would just as soon try to find fault with a blade of grass or the outline of a hill. You will understand that the above remarks are the best tribute I can offer to the humanity and the sincerity of the story. The accomplished simplicity of your method I simply envy you with the real black envy of a man who is thousands of miles away from his heart's desire. And finally, charm—undeniable charm—is the last word I will say to characterize the whole of my feelings in regard to the story. All this is very lame, but it must serve, being insufficient but as far as it goes perfectly genuine.

I hope you have not resented my unceremonious manner of sending you the cheque. I was upset and done up with running about that day, and Jack[1] was just writing to you. And you are always so sympathetic to me that it seemed as if you would understand my state of mind without a word. Then I put off writing to you till the story for Maga was finished. Well, it was finished on Monday evening and it is almost worse as if it had not been written at all because being written it is burnt. The lamp in my room exploded while we were at dinner and I ran back just in time to see all the table in a blaze. We beat out the flames without damage to ourselves but there are only four pages saved entire and the broken fragments of a dozen more out of both MS and typed copy. It is a heavy blow. I wired at once to E'gh whence I had a comforting reply. 4000 words are all that is needed for the next instalment and *that* I can rewrite by 2^d of July I think. For the rest I shall have all the time I need.

Pardon this scrawl all round the paper. I am in fairly good health but of course feel the set back acutely. Kindest regards in which my wife joins.

Always yours

J. Conrad

To William Blackwood

Text MS NLS; Blackburn 161

[letterhead: Pent Farm]
26 June 1902

Dear Mr Blackwood.

Thanks for your welcome letter which I received the day after my little private disaster.[2] I can manage 4 000 words—or perhaps a little more—in good time for the printing of the Augst number; and I promise faithfully to return proofs within 24 hours.

---

[1] Galsworthy: see PS to the letter of 1 June.   [2] Text in Blackburn, p. 158.

The sum (£25) with which you have credited me (against the £30 advanced) covers the 10 000 words instalment according to our agreement.

The pleasure of reading your favo[u]rable opinion was very great. I assure you that for all the unconscionable delay the *Youth* vol: has not been out of my mind for two days together. I am also gratified to see that you consider the subject suitable for the book form with the other two stories. It has been in my mind for this eighteen months past.

I felt the loss of my work acutely. It is completely gone all but 3 pages that escaped mysteriously and the fragments of about eleven more not amounting, all told, to one thousand legible words. The calamitous interruption of what was to be a great national manifestation[1] affected me too—as you may imagine.

However I may confide to you that I have already rebuilt a chapter of 2 000 words. My wife types it to-day, and I take a rest helping my boy to drill holes in his wooden bricks—which is the latest craze. I have also written to Meldrum a few words of felicitation on the excellent end of *Charlotte*. This evening I shall start again and hope in the next three days to complete another chapter. It is a curious experience, like trying desperately to remember a lesson learned years ago. Believe me always faithfully yours.

J. Conrad.

To Arthur Llewelyn Roberts
Text MS RLF; Unpublished

[letterhead: Pent Farm]
11th July 1902

Dear Sir.[2]

In returning the filled in receipt form for £300 I beg You to transmit my thanks to the General Committee of the Royal Literary Fund. I am proud to see stated black on white the grounds on which the grant was made—and this sentiment enters into my natural feeling of gratitude.[3]

Besides the material assistance there is in such recognition an amount

---

[1] Because of the king's illness the coronation, scheduled for 26 June, had been deferred.

[2] Roberts (born 1855) was Secretary of the Royal Literary Fund from 1884 to his death in 1919. The Fund helps needy writers.

[3] Gosse organized the award. Against 'Cause of Distress' on the application form he wrote 'Slowness of composition and want of public appreciation'. He procured letters of support from Mrs Craigie ('John Oliver Hobbes') and Henry James (Royal Literary Fund archives, file 2629).

of moral support which to a worker toiling in anxiety and doubt is altogether priceless.

> I am, dear Sir
> Yours very faithfully
>> Jph. Conrad.

To George Blackwood
Text MS NLS; Blackburn 162

> [Pent Farm]
> July 15/02

Dear Mr George.

Here's the stuff. I am too wretched and ashamed to apologize for the failure to keep decent time.[1]

Anyway the stuff is all right; and the proof-reading of Maga is so near perfection that I am quite willing to forego all correcting of this batch if it is at all inconvenient to let me have the slips. The copy is not typed for my wife is not well. I fancy she had a scare tho' she worked like a professional fireman at the time. My handwriting is not very difficult to read I like to believe. Kind regards

> Yours Conrad.

To John Galsworthy
Text MS Forbes; Unpublished

> [letterhead: Pent Farm]
> 16th July 1902

Dearest Jack.

I get on most damnably badly. However I managed to save the 2^d instalment from utter collapse. It went off last night or rather this morning. I finished a[t] 2am. today. Remains another 8000 words at least[2] to be ready in a fortnight and I feel as if could not write one in a century.

Don't think me a brute for not writing you sooner. I have been greatly struck by a phrase in your letter before the last. I expected You would come but dared not really clamour for You.

I am inexpressibly glad to hear good news of your Father. Where is Leith Hill? When do you come back?—and *when* oh *when* are you coming to see me with MS of course and a pair of wide open ears for a wonderful

---

[1] Chapters Six and Seven had been promised for 2 July.
[2] He still adhered to the estimate of length sent to Blackwood 24 June.

(to me) piece of news which I keep for the living voice. Meantime pray let me know what the pre^m: on my 400 policy amounts to. Love from us all.

Yours ever

Conrad.

To Ford Madox Ford

Text MS Yale; *Listy* 198; Original unpublished

[Pent Farm]
Saturday. [19 July? 1902][1]

My dear Ford.

I send you here £10. Pray credit me with it as against interest and rent; and have no scruples. Something has turned up which enables me to do that easily. I keep the story for the living voice.

The Maupassant idea is good.[2] Pardon me not being able to send the titles just yet. I've a wretched memory and I am most desperately unhappy and harrowed by the awful task of trying to get the *mood* of my End of Tether. Ford—it is terrible! There are also other things but I am like Turgueniev's Governor General who in the midst of "making arrangements" found time to say "enchanté" to Mme Olga.[3] I say "enchanté" to Mme Elsie. She shall tackle *M*. I consider her by temperament eminently fit for the task and her appreciation of the author guarantees success. The fact is "the young ooman can do it on her 'ead" as they would say in a mean street.[4] And I am always at her disposition with pleasure and pride—if I am allowed to take upon myself the office of an intelligent dictionary. We must get into a closer heap together when she is ready to commence—if not sooner! I want you and have wanted you for some time.

Let her bear in mind that there are three requisites for a good translation of M. Imprimis she must be idiomatic, secundo she must be idiomatic, and lastly she must be idiomatic. For in the idiom is the *clearness* of a language and the language's force and its picturesqueness— by which last I mean the picture-producing power of arranged words. It

---

[1] Internal evidence gives the month and external the likely date. As in the preceding letter to Galsworthy, the news 'for the living voice' must be the Royal Literary Fund grant. In the Lamb collection there was an envelope, now lost, post-marked (Sunday) 20 July 1902. No other letter matches that date so well.

[2] Elsie Hueffer wanted to translate Maupassant. She published her selection in 1903.

[3] See *Fathers and Sons*, 14: the Governor does make 'arrangements', but it is Kolyazin who compliments Mme Eudoxia Kukshin.

[4] Talking Cockney, as in Arthur Morrison's *Tales of Mean Streets* (1894).

will be a splendid thing for her and not a bad thing for us—for it's clear that while such a work is going on we shall all *think* Maupassant. C'est forcé.[1]

Thereupon *Vale* for a while with much love from us both to you all. We tried to hunt up more lodgings. Everything is taken. C'est a s'arracher les cheveux![2] Ever Yours

Jph Conrad.

To David Meldrum
Text MS Duke; Blackburn 162

[letterhead: Pent Farm]
22 July 1902

My dear Mr Meldrum.

I delayed acknowledging the volume[3] till I had read the story through to get a connected effect. It is, of course, incomparably greater than in the serial form. The story grips one more and I am very glad that you were not well enough off to suppress the book form as You said You wished to do. Indeed it would have been an illegitimate use of wealth for all your discontent. The artist's destiny is not to be pleased with himself. We must leave that to Mr Carnegie[4] though God knows what flaws *he* too in his dazzling career he may be groaning over in the secret of his heart.

I understand, tho' I do not agree with your discontent. We read over our work in a very wide awake frame of mind; whereas, when actually at work, the Homer nods[5] at times in all of us. The shortcomings come to us with an extraordinary force; the flaws of the mood appear as great as the chasms of an earthquake and as fatal: but what is good we accept as a matter of course as if nothing less in achievement were our due.

I have closed the book with an increased feeling of its absolute value. There is skill and conviction and a wonderfully sustained mood—and not a moment of unworthy artifice. I most sincerely congratulate You on its complex unity so varied and so artistically preserved to the very last scene. To discuss the detail I am not fit; just now less than ever. I am utterly cast down and overwhelmed by the necessity of rewriting a finished thing and the impossibility to find again the mood.

---

[1] 'It's inevitable.'   [2] 'It's enough to make you tear your hair out!'
[3] *The Conquest of Charlotte: A Romance.*
[4] Andrew Carnegie (1835–1919), maker of steel, donor of libraries, and author of *The Gospel of Wealth, and Other Timely Essays* (1901).
[5] Pope's phrase (*Essay on Criticism*, 180), Horace's idea (*Ars Poetica*, 359).

No more for the present but my heartfelt thanks for the book and my wishes for its prosperity in the world.

Ever Yours

Conrad.

To William Blackwood

Text MS NLS; Blackburn 163

Winchelsea,
3^d Aug 1902

Dear Mr Blackwood.

I've just received your letter and cheque for £22.10 for which thanks. I've not yet seen the last Maga which has not been sent after me here. We return home on the fourth whence I shall write in a day or two.

I am glad you like the story and Mr Michie's praise is very pleasant.[1] Proof and more copy shall be posted at the end of this week. Believe me always very faithfully yours

Jph Conrad.

To Elsie Hueffer

Text MS Yale; Unpublished

Pent Farm [letterhead]
5 Aug^{st.} 1902

Dear Auntie Elsie.

Following your admirable directions we had an easy drive home and on the road snatched a consultation from old Hoile.[2] In that village of evil-eyed 'chenapans' and dirty "morveux" children—I mean Court-a[t]-Street[3]—we saw him prowling meditatively round the hairy heels of a tall and philosophical horse. He asked about our health, sympathised with Borys (who had a toothache) and prescribed for Nancy. You'll be glad to hear the animal is now out of danger.

As to ourselves we feel the benefit of the change. I wanted to make a long story but the postman has turned up this moment. Jack sends a cordial message to you in the note I found here. Wells likewise desires to be remembered.

---

[1] Formerly *The Times* correspondent in Tientsin, Alexander Michie (1833–1902) wrote books about China and Siberia.
[2] The local veterinary surgeon.
[3] 'Rogues and ... snotty children', denizens of a hamlet near Aldington.

The rest of the exciting news Jessie shall give. She is making arrangements ever since we arrived.

Our love—in haste. Your devoted servant

Jph Conrad.

To Hallam Murray
Text MS Murray; Stape

[letterhead: Pent Farm]
14 Augst 1902

Dear Sir.[1]

Would you mind giving me half an hour or so—on Sat or even Sunday next to talk about a MS.—that is if you are coming down to Sandling this week end.

The MS is not by myself. The author is an Oxford man and an intimate friend of mine.[2] I believe the thing deserves your attention; but if the idea of being invaded in the country with these matters is distasteful to you I am ready to take back my request.

I trust that if it is you will not think I've presumed too much on our slight acquaintance.

I am, dear Sir very faithfully Yours

Jph. Conrad

To Hallam Murray
Text MS Murray; Stape

[letterhead: Pent Farm]
[18? August 1902][3]

Dear Sir.

This is the MS.

From my friend's letters I gather that:

The title is provisional, in the sense that he has not set his heart on it.—

(Personally I think the title excellent but there would be the public to consider.) The first 40 pages he wishes to remodel.—(My idea is that this impulse is right.) My advice to him shall be to bring the *idea* of the

---

[1] Alexander Henry Hallam Murray (1854–1934) was a partner in the family firm of John Murray, and a writer and illustrator of travel books. He owned a farm near the Pent.

[2] Galsworthy. The MS in question was 'The Flying Goddess', a revision of 'The Pagan'; revised again, it was published by Heinemann as *The Island Pharisees* (1904).

[3] Conrad left the MS on Monday, 18 August: see letter of (Friday) 22 August.

girl forward more distinc[t]ly—make it, as it were, more haunting the man's thoughts—through hints at the purely personal feelings.

The end he expects to reach in 20–30 thousand words more.

As the book is so distinctly episodical (almost a sort of latter-day picaresque form) any episodes you should judge unsuitable for ser: pub:[1] could be taken out and he would be prepared to make suitable joints.

I need not of course point out to you the vigorous realization of incidents and personalities which suggest the passages of analysis. The man has an eye: the visible world exists for him; and as to analysis it is simple in expression but subtle enough in its penetration—just subtle enough. Shelton is saved from fancifulness by the directness of his idealism.

Pardon this feeble twaddle.

Very truly yrs,

Jph. Conrad.

To John Galsworthy

Text MS Forbes; Unpublished

[letterhead: Pent Farm]
22d Aug 1902

Dearest Jack

Last Monday I left the MS with Hallam Murray. It was impossible to manage it earlier. He seemed impressed with what I had to say. It is made clear that serial pub: is what You want. You must give him a little time. We shall talk it over when you appear.

Do not miss us if you can possibly manage it. I would like to meet you in Folkestone. What time do you arrive? At any rate drop me a line to say if there is no obstacle.

I've been and am seedy. Quite broken backed and very low spirited. Love from us all

yours

Conrad.

---

[1] In the *Monthly Review*, edited by Henry Newbolt and published by John Murray.

To Edward Garnett

Text MS Yale; G. 184

[Pent Farm]
Thursday [28 August? 1902][1]

Dearest Edward.

I was glad to see your handwriting and am excitedly interested in the venture. But what *great of the world* do you imagine I have under my roof.—Great buzzing flies, fine large wasps—these are my visitors which make a noise in the world. I see no one from month to month. Four or five months ago G.B.S. towed by Wells came to see me reluctantly and I nearly bit him.[2] Since then—barring Ford there has been no one.

I am trying to rewrite the story *End of Tether* which (perhaps you've heard) has been burnt when completed. The weariness and disgust of that awful toil nearly kill me every day; just leaving breath enough in me every evening to feel the utter misery, the complete foolishness of the undertaking.

How can one believe in one's story when it has to be written for the second time—and if one does not believe how is one to write? Imagine trying to clothe in flesh a naked skeleton, without the faith to help you in the impossible task! Enough.

Our love to you all

Ever yours

Conrad.

PS Galsworthy is coming today. I had not seen *him* for 3 months.

To David Meldrum

Text MS Duke; Blackburn 169

[Pent Farm]
Friday. [August or September?
1902][3]

My dear Mr Meldrum.

I snatch a piece of MS paper to thank your* for your good letter received today. Mine to you went on Thursday morning.

---

[1] Garnett's date is simply [August]. We learn from the letter of 22 August that Galsworthy intended to visit Folkestone, a few miles from the Pent. The following Thursday fell just within the month, and two-and-a-half months from his visit in mid-June.

[2] See Garnett, p. xxx, for further hostile remarks.

[3] The letter refers to the Eliott episode from the August instalment of 'Tether'; the discussion of length at the end suggests a date before the story expanded beyond its original size.

Yes. Hermann and his wife are the people I wanted to *do*: the story of Falk being more or less of a foil to the main purpose.[1] However I thought that I did bring his personality out towards the end distinctly enough. If I did not—as I fear—it is simply want of skill in finding the essential trait in an image clear enough to my own eye. I wanted to make him stand for so much that I neglected, in a manner, to set him on his feet. This is one of my weaknesses—one of these things that make me swear at a finished work so often.

I am heartened greatly by what you say of the wretched "Tether". The old man does not wobble it seems to me. The Elliot* episode has a fundamental significance in so far that it exhibits the first weakening of old Whalley's character before the assault of poverty. As you notice he says nothing of his position but goes off and takes advantage of the information. At the same time it gives me the opportunity to introduce Massy from way back without the formal narrative paragraphs.

But the episode is mainly the first sign of that fate we carry within us. A character like Whalley's cannot cease to be frank with impunity. He is not frank with his old friend—such as the old friend is. For, if Elliot had been a genuine sort of man Whalley's secrecy would have been that of an intolerable fool. The pathos for me is in this that the concealment of his extremity is as it were forced upon him. Nevertheless it is weakness—it is deterioration. Next he conveys a sort of false impression to Massy—on justifiable grounds. I indicate the progress of the shaking the character receives and make it possible thus to by and by present the man as concealing the oncoming of blindness—and so on; till at least* he conceals the criminal wrecking of his ship by com[m]itting suicide. And always there is just that shadow, that ghost of justification which should secure the sympathy of the reader.

Pardon this long discourse. I want to give you an idea how the figure works. Upon the episodes, after all, the effect of reality depends and as to me I depend upon the reader *looking back* upon my story as a whole. This is why I prefer the form which needs for its development 30000 words or so. When it runs into 120 thou:—like *Jim* it reaches failure. But let that pass.

Kindest regards. Always Yours
J. Conrad

---

[1] 'Falk' was not published until September 1903; Meldrum must have seen galleys or a fair-copy.

To William Blackwood
Text MS NLS; Blackburn 164

[letterhead: Pent Farm]
1ˢᵗ Sept 1902

Dear Mʳ Blackwood.

The arrangement of our posts has prevented me acknowledging sooner the receipt of the cheque.

Thanks for kind words and acts. As to the last instalment: I think 13 words in all may do it.[1] I am now straining every fibre to throw it off.

In any case the October N° shall see the end.

Pardon this disjointed letter. Always yours faithfully

Jph. Conrad.

To William Blackwood
Text MS NLS; Blackburn 165

[letterhead: Pent Farm]
[late September 1902][2]

Dear Mʳ Blackwood ·

Our little boy got suddenly ill and my typist[3] had* turn nurse; this is why the last few pages are sent in MS. Another a slightly longer instᵗ shall see the end.

To morrow I shall return to you the corrections of the previous parts for book form.

Is it really possible for the book to be issued in October?

I shall try to send my copy early; this month if possible for I am anxious to see a vol of mine appear at last.

Pardon my disconnected scrawl. I am extremely tired physically and mentally. Always very faithfully yours

Jph. Conrad

---

[1] 13,000: he did it in 26,000.
[2] Blackwood acknowledged receipt of the corrected pages 29 September (Blackburn, p. 165).
[3] Jessie Conrad.

To Elsie Hueffer

Text Sutton; Unpublished

[Pent Farm]
[late September 1902][1]

Dear Elsie

I'm sorry I kept the MS so long.[2] I had my own awful task.

However I've read it more than once; the difficulty was to write something useful.

My opinion you know or you ought to know. Had you the riches of the Indies and a charm greater than Cleopatra's you could not have made me read your work as I've read it. Therefore Your work and your work alone has done it by the force of its promise as well as by the actuality of the performance.

I did not want to deface the pages tho' I have meditated them.

The passages I have written on the loose sheets embody my criticism which is concerned solely with the technique. You will see from them what in my opinion should be done to the whole book. These are examples and I have chosen the two first and three last pages of this part to give you in that way an idea of what I mean. P. 220 I've taken the liberty to correct. I have touched nothing material in the way of your thought and conception.

I congratulate you. If my own stuff were not so damnably bad I could express better my appreciation of yours; but I have just finished with desperate efforts the penultimate inst[t] for Maga and feel greatly depressed.

Borys has been ill with some feverish attack (liver they say) for three days.

He has got up to day. Jessie had no sleep and I have been sitting up with my story—which is the sickliest performance possible.

I trust you are all flourishing. Our love to you all. I shall write to Ford to night for tomorrow's post.

Always Your

J. Conrad

---

[1] Sold at an American Art Association auction in 1928 with an envelope dated 28 October 1901, but Conrad was not writing a serial for *Maga* then. The circumstances match those of the preceding letter to Blackwood.

[2] The MS of her novel *Margaret Hever*: as Elizabeth Martindale, she published it with Duckworth in 1909.

PS Of course my suggestions in the last scene *are* nothing but suggestions. It seems to me that a little of that sort of mending will do no harm. Pray don't imagine I presume to dictate. I throw myself confidently on Your artistic intelligence there. The words of my text may be wrong but its spirit is not. I am thinking of effect.

to p. 219 par. 3
Margaret laid the pen down and sighed Her elbows rested on the black sides of the deep easy chair; she put her finger tips together in front of her face, and the loose sleeves of her grey dressing gown slipped down softly exposing her white arms. A little clock on the table marked 11.30; the house was very still. Mr and Mrs Hever slept on the floor below, with Nell next door to them. The servants were above—there was an empty bedroom by the side of hers.

This is the sort of thing that has got to be done—though of course that particular instance may not seem convincing to you. But of course you'll see from it what I mean. Screwing up here and there is the main thing. Many *little* words should come out. Sometimes a sentence is *too* precisely finished. For grammar your "man" is the authority; but indubitably a less precise expression makes for a greater precision of effect in nine cases out of ten.

to p. 283
"Is that what you think" he said, concealing with a great effort of will the sudden premonition of the infinite agony this woman might give him. She answered: "Thats what I think." He said with a sort of furious and bitter anxiety "And you imagine yourself speaking the truth!" She seemed to defy him monstrously. "I know that I am speaking the truth". "Mad not to believe! ... Mad to think!" he burst out, raving, "Mr Cheyne! O, no—it's ... Ha! Ha! Mr Cheyne! He laughed uproariously and suddenly took his head between his hands "Whats to become of me" he stammered out "You think that I, that I" ... He faltered before her immobility and she summoned to her aid all there was in her of derisive cynicism.

"You" she exclaimed etc etc
(That part must stand)
"His arms fell. She saw his passion working in every nerve of his face, in each line of his forehead; in his eyes that looked at her feverishly; in his lips that quivered for a long time before he managed to say, very

low: "You don't want me! Is it possible ..." She felt as though she had come to the end of her struggle.

"Is it possible?" he repeated in an appalled mutter.

Her lips stirred; she could not utter a word. An unexpected hesitation had come over her feelings. For a moment she thought that she must fail.

He came closer. Her silence gave him a shade of hope. He raised his voice almost menacingly—"Don't you want me?"

She succeeded in breaking out of the numbness of defeat. "No" she cried, "No! Not you! Not you!" He swung away from her as if stabbed. Twice he paced blindly the whole length of the room swearing aloud before he went out slamming the door behind him.

She has permitted herself, motionless, to ... etc etc. (This par may be improved. It's worth improving. At any rate the words *small, remaining* are *not* the words—unless you wish to minimize the preceding scene. *Fearful*, something of the sort, (even *flattering* pleasure)—anything in short would be better than *small remaining*. This is my feeling.)

To John Galsworthy
Text MS Forbes; J-A, 1, 305

[letterhead: Pent Farm]
5 Oct 1902

Dearest Jack.

They are beasts. I've just received a note from H[allam] M[urray] declining with many complimentary expressions.[1]

I am sending you the MS by this same post registered.

After all we must expect this sort of thing. No work is judged on its artistic merits; and there's no doubt that the book must rub many susceptibilities the wrong way. If you remember what tempest of anger Mme Bovary had raised by the sheer sincerity of its method alone you will understand perhaps that your sincerity—extending further than to mere method—must prepare itself for a struggle. Upon my word the book is worth the sweat and dust of it.

The temper of the present time is against it a little. You must not forget that when I (without a tithe of the value you display here) have

---

[1] Stape prints the note rejecting 'Mr. Colesworthy's' MS in *Conradiana*, 14 (1983), 232.

got myself accepted with the Folly it was during a boon* in fiction such as this century is not likely to see for a few years yet. I do not mean to say that you should wait. Of course not. I only point out another difficulty in addition to the book's excellence which stands in its way.

I don't know what you'll resolve on doing at once. I should suggest a certain expenditure of work on it on the lines we have discussed. After all it *is* a short work. It will stand expanding.

Next thing I would suggest is a certain compromise—a concession to the needs of popularity. Something must be done to the end. I will expound my meaning when you come down; and you must come down on the book's business on the first convenient day after the 15th inst. Why after the 15th and not before I'll explain when we meet. That I shall by then be free of the Tether is not the only reason.

Jessie and boy send their love. Let me know what you feel and think and undergo.

Ever Yours

Conrad

PS For god's sake *don't don't* get disgusted.

To John Galsworthy

Text MS Forbes; Unpublished

[letterhead: Pent Farm]

Saturday [11 October? 1902][1]

Dearest Jack.

The temptation is great. Ought we—do you think—really succumb? I suppose we must; You make it all so easy—so very easy.

I am empty headed. I have been trying to read and I haven't been able—nor yet to write. This will never do. Is it laziness? Whatever it is I am humiliated by the defeat of my best intentions. And it spells ruin too!

What have You been doing. How is *the* book. If you would kindly forget my miserable performances and talk to me a little of the "Goddess" I would be obliged to you.

Is there a prospect of seeing the final version as a whole, or are you going to fire it out amongst the pub^{ers} at once. Expliquez Vous la dessus.[2] Ever yours

J Conrad

---

[1] Mention of the reworked 'Flying Goddess' places this letter after the rejection by Hallam Murray. The 'temptation' may be an invitation to stay with Galsworthy, as the Conrads did in late October. On the 18th May they were in Winchelsea; the 11th is therefore the likeliest date.

[2] 'Give an account of yourself.'

To Edward Garnett

Text MS Sutton; G. 185

Winchelsea.

17 Oct. 1902.

Dearest Edward

When the book arrived I had been up two nights trying to finish my Bl'wood story to time. It was a matter of life and death as it were for otherwise I would have missed an instalment. I had neither the time nor even the right to look at the book in this hurry and mental stress. I had 3 hours' sleep for two nights and for the third no sleep at all going to bed at 7 am in a state, I may describe it, as frenetic idiocy.[1]

To-day I am recovering. This evening I shall read the study.

I had urged Wells to order the book[2] before I had your letter. I did not know it was to appear so soon however. Besides my dear fellow with that miserable* I was not conscious of the days passing and did not know whether the sun shone. We are staying till Monday or Tuesday next.

With love to you all

ever yours

Conrad.

To John Galsworthy

Text MS Forbes; J-A, 1, 308

Thursday. [23 October 1902?][3]

Pent Farm.

Dearest Jack.

I shall turn up at Holl^d P.A.[4] sometime between 11 and 12. I can't be more precise because the trains are not trustworthy.

Jessie starting by a later train will arrive at Char: + a few minutes after 12 and shall proceed to Lan^{ce} Mans:[5] at once—unless this would be inconvenient; in which case pray wire to-morrow. But in any case pray don't send the carriage. She will have a big trunk with her and intends to wire from Sandling for a small omnibus.

Up to last Monday I had slight sciatica and a slightly game foot; these slight infirmities (which had no charm of novelty) have departed now

---

[1] Ford gives an operatic account of the final night in *Joseph Conrad* (pp. 243–4), complete with a mounted courier and last pages snatched from the febrile writer's hand.

[2] Garnett records it as E. G. Duckworth's *The Art of Winnifred Matthews* (1902).

[3] The circumstances match those of the week-long visit to London which had ended by Tuesday, 4 November.

[4] 1 Holland Park Avenue, home of Galsworthy's sister Lilian Sauter; her husband was going to paint Conrad's portrait.

[5] From Charing Cross station to Galsworthy's flat, 4 Lawrence Mansions, Chelsea Embankment.

without medicamentation*—on the cheap—and no harm done. Only, with my head full of a story, I have not been able to write a single word—except the title which shall be I think: NOSTROMO; the story belonging to the 'Karain' class of tales ('K' class for short—as you classify the cruisers.)

Will you leave whatever MS is ready in the flat for me? Going back there from H.P.A. about 3 or 4 I shall have time to begin reading it at once. I couldn't wait. I really could not! Don't forget this request of mine my dear Jack.

We have been wondering anxiously how this severe weather may have affected your Father's health.[1] You say nothing. Does this mean the proverbial good news? We hope so.

Your "program" is simply lovely and accepted with enthusiasm. Our love. Always yours

Jph Conrad.

To William Blackwood
Text MS NLS; Blackburn 166

[letterhead: Pent Farm]
25 Oct 1902

Dear Mr Blackwood.

I did not write when sending the last of the copy; I was far from well, and the experience of rewriting a story already dismissed from the mind and with the mood of its production vanished was absolutely nightmarish. Like a man awakening from a bad dream I was glad to lie passively on my back for a while enjoying the feelings of relief.

I am awaiting now the proofs of the book. In that form there'll be another page (of print) to add at the end.[2] I anticipate no other corrections, and forty-eight hours shall suffice to do all that's necessary.

The vol: won't be so bad upon the whole, though not so good as is due to your patience and kindness. *That* could be only recognized adequately by the production of a masterpiece of which I am incapable. So I must even remain in your debt to the end of time.

With the proofs I shall send the epigraph—two lines of Keats—for the title page, and the dedication—*not* to Mʳ Henley,[3] this time. With all

---

[1] The elder John Galsworthy died in 1904.

[2] In Ford's retelling of the final night, he had yelled at Conrad 'In the name of God, don't you know you can write those paragraphs into the proofs when you get them back?'

[3] The volume bears a dedication to Jessie Conrad and an epigraph from the Brothers Grimm.

deference to your better judgment I would suggest that the vol: should be made uniform with *Lord Jim*. Believe me dear Mr Blackwood always yours faithfully

Jph Conrad.

To John Galsworthy

Text MS Forbes; Marrot 118 (in part)

[letterhead: Pent Farm]
4 Nov. 1902

Dearest Jack.

I've never realised so well how fast we travel nowadays. We were home by three and the change was great.

I've come back improved and warmed—thoroughly warmed by your affection and the kindness extended to us for your sake. You've been playing the part of Providence in small things and great and I don't know which—the small or the great—have the greater value. But there are no small things; and I am so fortunate in my relation to you that the very load of indebt[ed]ness is a pleasure in itself—seems in its magnitude a proof of the unchangeable feeling.

We all feel this. Borys absolutely proprio motu[1] has asked to have his hand 'guided' to write to Mr Jack, and I like him the better for this petition and Jessie is delighted. I leave them the next page for their artless effusion.[2] With love. Ever Yours

Jph Conrad.

---

[1] 'Of his own accord.'

[2] They wrote:

Dear Mr Jack,

I want to tell you how much I did like to stay in your flat. Thank you ever so much. I am writing this letter all myself.

Borys

Dear Mr Galsworthy,

This joint letter that Borys insisted on taking a part in could not express one part of the pleasure and gratitude we feel for all your kindness. This week in London will live always in our mind. It has done Conrad so much good not so much the complete change as your kindness and affection all the time.

Believe me, Always Yours
Jessie Conrad.

To Elsie Hueffer
Text MS Colgate; Unpublished

Pent
4 Nov. 1902

My dear Elsie.

I snatch the first piece of paper to hand.

We've been to London and had a week of what to rustics of our sort was a Whirl—(with a capital W). I am trying to collect my scattered senses. B'wood is wiring for proofs and I have done nothing to the end of the story yet. Nothing. I've lazed—tho' I must say I did look through all the stories.[1] It was the first look and I have done no actual inter-lining.

I shall set about it directly—Honour Bright—my dear Confrère. To morrow! (I am not mad, so it is really tomorrow.) Today however and far into the night I shall sit up with the End of the Tether in my hand. The book is to appear on the 15th inst—ruat coelum![2] A great and desperate determination has made the souls of all the B'woods as stiff as pokers.

Our love to you all.

Yours

Conrad.

Jack and his little world excited at the prospect of the Maup: translation of which I've made no secret "dans les salons" to which I've had access. (it's *ten copies off the stalls for sure*)

To William Blackwood
Text MS NLS; Blackburn 168

[letterhead: Pent Farm]
5 Nov. 1902

My Dear Mr Blackwood.

The proofs went last night to the station for the last train as the stupid post leaves here at 4 pm and I wanted to send the additional matter typed and properly corrected.

Now the story is properly finished as originally contemplated and thus it is meant for the book form. It would be a great pleasure to me if

---

[1] Elsie Hueffer's Maupassant translation, first mentioned 19 July and published in 1903.
[2] 'Even if Heaven falls!'

the last instalment in Maga[1] could be extended so as to make the serial form and the book form identical.

I doubt not that your judgment will approve the full ending which is in no sense an amplification of anything. It is almost word for word as it stood in the destroyed MS.

As to the suggestions for the title page I leave it to your experience whether they are to be carried out wholly or partly as it commends itself to you: or not at all if you prefer to let the page stand. To the epigraph I suppose there can be no objection; the dedication is purely a private transaction. With that sort of dedication the public can have no concern. It would not have been the case if I had dedicated to Mr Henley as I had half a mind to do. Later on perhaps I may offer that tribute to the man who befriended my early work and has remained friendly ever since. The time is not yet I think.

I should very much like to see my correction in the list of works adopted, especially in what touches Lord Jim. The other is of lesser importance.

Many thanks for the cheque which I found on my return home from a bout of dissipation in London. We overstayed the leave we have given ourselves and this accounts for the delay in returning the proofs.

I saw Mr James[2] twice and have had with him some discourse whose business part must have been communicated to you by this time. I was very sorry to understand that your health has not been quite weather proof of late. I had also the pleasure of lunching with my good friend Meldrum and with Jack Galsworthy who wishes to be remembered to you. With kind regards I remain, dear Mr Blackwood

Always yours

J. Conrad

---

[1] Blackwood had split the final batch of work into two instalments 'at I think a most interesting part' (Blackburn, p. 167).
[2] James Blackwood, William's nephew.

To David Meldrum

Text MS Duke; Blackburn 165

[Pent Farm]

[autumn 1902][1]

My dear Mr Meldrum.

This is all that Jessie has been able to find. The Q[uiller] C[ouch] thing on Youth[2] however is there and it may be of some use. Another cutting relates to *H of D*

Kindest regards from us both

Always yours

Jph. Conrad

To Arnold Bennett

Text MS UCL; J-A, 1, 305

[letterhead: Pent Farm]

6th Nov 1902

My dear Bennett.

I wonder what you think of me? Well I have deserved some hard thoughts, but only in a certain measure. Obviously I might have sent a civil line to acknowledge the book;[3] but obviously too one does not like to sent* a civil line in acknowledgment of E A Bennett's book. The gift is on another footing of welcome.

Of one thing you may be sure, that my silence my unconscionable delay had not for cause indifference. The word looks monstrous as I write. Neither was I made lazy by an excess of happiness, or busy with riotous living. The reason was worry, the terrible worry of having to re-write a story (completed and then burnt by a fatal accident) with the next instalment of 'Maga' and the impossibility of concocting a reasonable sentence confronting me at every turn. It was like a night mare.

But if I could not write to you I had found time to read your book. I read it once, twice, and then kept it upstairs for dipping into when I came up to bed, jaded with my unavailing efforts to express myself in the absence of any sort of mood; and your firm grip, the firm grip of style and the mastery of the subject have more than once refreshed my weariness.

I doubt if hitherto my mind had been fresh enough to appreciate your work—intellectually as it deserves to be. It's* appeal had been to me emotional, a matter of art purely as apart from underlying thought. Of

---

[1] This note must concern publicity for *Youth*, published mid-November.

[2] See letter to Blackwood, 31 May, p. 417, n.1.

[3] *Anna of the Five Towns*, published in September.

course you understand that my emotion is awakened by the *skill* of your work first—and I may almost say: first and last—this word in my mind embracing everything; from the first co ordination of your inspiration, through the effective processes of your thought down to the last small touches of expression, delightful to trace along the pages and which resume to me the whole extent of the remarkable gifts which you display in the justness and the cadence of your sentences.

It is indeed a thing *done*: good to see and friendly to live with for a space. This is the final impression—the whole feeling freed from that quarrelsomeness of one craftsman appreciating another—if you do me the honour to take me for a fellow craftsman. That I could drag up points for discussion you may be pretty sure; I have no other way of showing my love of the *work* when I meet the *man* face to face; but to criticise in detail (even if to laud) that I can not do on paper: and if you, by chance, should care to receive my argumentative tribute to your excellence you must choose any day after the 16th inst: for a rush into Kent. We can put you up, You know, in a sort of haphazard way and when you get tired of my inanities you may fly to Wells for refuge. It's only seven miles. I would be most truly delighted to receive a warning note from you.

That the advance upon the *Man from the N[orth]* is great is undeniable. Just in what that advance consists it's not so easy to say without losing one's way amongst mere superficialities—for there too the advance is very marked. The other, the deeper change, the essential progress, is felt right through but not so easy to hold up. The excellence (in its place) of the first par of Chap XII is easy to point out, or the mastery—the obvious mastery—of pp 164. 165. My dear fellow it is fine, very fine; I am thankful to see it written. But there are other pars: other pages and the whole spirit of the book informed by a less apparent excellence.

There is too the whole conception of the story whence of course flows the characterisation. On this one could say much. I am afraid of falling into twaddle without the stimulous* of your presence and your voice. I will only then say that the conception seems to me too logical. It's a cryptic saying and does not make my criticism clear in the least—not even to myself.

But on that I end with a congratulatory and hearty handshake. It *is* good my dear Bennett: and You *know* it is good; and I know that you shall do even better.

Kindest regards.
Believe me yours most sincerely
Jph Conrad.

PS I perceive I haven't after all thanked you for sending me the book. The letter however is written with that object as you may have guessed. I shall send a vol of my rot when it appears—or have a copy for you when you come.

To John Galsworthy
Text MS Forbes; Unpublished

1902
[letterhead: Pent Farm]
6th Nov*er*

Dearest Jack.

As to the concert in Chislehurst.[1] We are coming—or going—but my intellect rising to the height of an idea discovered that there is a certain Bull's Head Hotel there, wherein a distinguished party from London may be asked to dine.

The question is the number of the party. You can tell us who is coming—or going—besides Mrs Galsworthy.[2] I assume that you intend to be present, all being well, or at least no worse than at present; I suppose the Reynolds are going and perhaps the Sauters.[3]

You can find out and let us know by Monday and, as I have let the time run on (from the difficulty of collecting information about the country) you can *at once* deliver our invitations with apologies for the informal proceedings—because I am afraid that ere I am in a position to write some other arrangements may be made by the enterprising travallers.* You may explain to Mrs Galsworthy that the natives are friendly—at least the advert*mt* of the Bull Head is couched in a friendly language and with some rude art of eloquence. Its chief belongs to the tribe of Smithe some of whom have been known as cannibals; others again as saints (Mormon). On the whole an interesting people.

Anyway we shall sleep in his wigwam (electric light—bowling green—good stabling) and shall be in time to meet the arrival of the 5 pm train from Char[in]g cross. It arrives at 5.32—the next arrives at 6.15 and I guess between these two the choice of the Expedition must lie. There is also a later one arriving at 6.38 which may do should the concert not begin till sometime after eight. At any rate we must not dine later than 7 I think.

With love from us all

Ever yours

Jph Conrad.

---

[1] In Kent, about ten miles from central London.   [2] His mother.
[3] His sisters and their families.

To John Watson

Text MS Berg; Unpublished

[letterhead: Pent Farm]
26 Nov. 1902

The Editor
Northern Newspaper Syndicate
Dear Sir.[1]

I've nothing to show you at present and for the next four months I shall be engaged in finishing a long novel,[2] begun sometime ago, of which one third is yet to be written.

Mr. James B. Pinker Effingham House Arundel S[t] W.C. is my literary agent, to whom I've forwarded your communication of the 25th inst.

I beg him at the same time to keep your request in view. No doubt something of the sort you desire will be finished in good time next year, since this is the form I like best (30–40000 words) and have a subject or two in reserve for treatment in that shape.[3] Then with the work before you, you could judge of the suitableness for your public.

But I could not bind myself for delivery at any specified time or discuss in any way the nature of my story.

I am, dear sir faithfully yours,

Jph. Conrad.

To J. B. Pinker

Text MS Berg; Unpublished

[Pent Farm]
26[th] Nov 1902

My dear Pinker.

I send you the 2 letters I had from Mc Arthur.[4] I am personally acquainted with him. In answering his first letter I stated distinc[t]ly that You are my agent and that the copy shall come through you.

Generally, I said that: to occasionally furnish a story for Harpers would not be a breach of my tacit understanding with McClure, "and in time—I said—a volume of short (3 or 4) stories could be made up for

---

[1] Editor in chief of a press syndicate based in Kendal, in the Lake District.

[2] *The Rescue* again.

[3] Among them the idea for *Nostromo*? Cf. letters to Galsworthy, 23 October, and Blackwood, 4 December.

[4] Formerly with Doubleday, McClure, now with Harper & Brothers. Conrad first met him in August 1900 (letter to Meldrum, 1 September 1900).

publication by that firm." *I engaged myself to nothing whatever*; neither do I desire to engage me to anything for the future. All I said definitely was this: "That to begin with I could do for them a 6 to 8 thou: story at once *perhaps*."

I am inclined however to do this—this year. M^cA. says they pay well; and I *want* to be well paid. You who know these things can tell me no doubt what it means precisely.

Could you place that story (I've commenced it)[1] in England too? I would want to make by it £70 *at least* (in both countries) serially.

Pray answer these two question[s] in a few words.

———————

Are you pleased with the reduction of *Romance*? You ought to be. Pretty nearly half of the book is gone; but you must not think we broke it up stupidly. On the contrary it cost us some scheming and a lot of work: four days and one whole night. All that's likely to be most popular is preserved and embodied in a rational conception.

The *Youth* vol: has come out on the 17th ult:[2] The subscription before pub^on was roughly 1400 copies. I haven't had a single review yet but I know that this week's Academy will have a column by E. Garnett.[3] I have been working at *Rescue* not very hard however. Still I may say that even at that rate it will be completed by March next.

Kind regards

Yours

J. Conrad.

Have you sent my Copy of 3 stories: *Falk. Amy Foster. To-morrow* to McClure? *Pray do*. There's a row about the delay.

To Edward Garnett
Text G. 186

Pent Farm
Stanford, Near Hythe
27 Nov. [1902][4]

Dearest Edward.

I am glad you review me in the *Academy*, and I am sorry you had the bother. Somehow it never occurred to me that mine would go to you. I am in luck if you are not.

---

[1] If he did indeed write a story of 6 to 8,000 words, it was put aside.
[2] He means inst[ant]. Publication day was really 13 November.
[3] See the letter to him of 22 December.   [4] The *Academy* review supplies the year.

I sent you two the copy as soon as I got it. They were late in sending them to me; then I, myself, lost a day.

Horrible! Horrible! I am like Philip IV—I am overwhelmed: he however was overwhelmed by the death of Velasquez[1] while I am overcome [. . .][2] three-head monster in the green cover. I hate the sight of the thing.[3]

How's David? His books are on the way to me to be inscribed.

Our love to you

To David Meldrum

Text MS Duke; Blackburn 170

[letterhead: Pent Farm]
27 Nov 1902

Private

My dear M[r] Meldrum.

I had rather not; moreover I haven't got a photograph, not a single copy; and I won't sit on purpose as two years ago I've refused to do so for D[r] Robertson Nicoll[4] who wanted to put me into the Bookman.

A criticism of the book is all right, but my face has nothing to do with my writing.

If I were a pretty actress or a first rate athlete I wouldn't deprive an aching democracy of a legitimate satisfaction.

In '96 a photograph of me appeared in the *Sketch* I think. I let myself be persuaded. Two columns of colossally stupid letter press accompanied it.[5] No more.

Believe me always yours

J. Conrad

---

[1] Who was his court painter.
[2] The MS may have been damaged.
[3] He had hated the look of *Lord Jim* too (20 November 1900).
[4] Editor of the *Bookman* since 1891.
[5] *Sketch*, 6 May 1896, p. 62. The anonymous journalist wrote of him: 'he is but a star in the making. His light is all his own, and is unquestionably brilliant, but it is nebulously diffused.'

To J. B. Pinker
Text MS Berg; Unpublished

[letterhead: Pent Farm]
Saturday
28th [29] November 1902[1]

My dear Pinker.

Thanks for your letter and the note received this morning.

Of course it is your mission to put things on a business basis. If I exchanged letters with McA: it was mainly for old acquaintance's sake. It is good, I think, to have in publisher's offices men that believe in one. And I repeat that I only said I was going to do a story which could *perhaps* suit them.

In the same way I answered the Syndicate with the main purpose of informing them that you were the man they must go to if they want any of my work. I had one communication from them three or four months ago which I neglected because it was vague. Their now more definite proposal I put into your hands absolutely, only asking you not to bind me *tight* to anything—at any rate till the *Rescue* is finished.

Regards.
Yours

J Conrad.

To R. B. Cunninghame Graham
Text MS Dartmouth; Watts 140

Pent Farm.
29 Nov. 1902

Très cher ami.

Many thanks for your good and friendly letter. You have lost no time in cheering me up. I however have been thinking of many enthusiastic things to say of *Success*[2] and written none of them. Indeed when trying to talk of your work I am afraid to show myself unintelligent in expression and that's the secret of my taciturnity. But *Success* is a success—there's no doubt of it. The thing is "telling" all along, from the first sentence of your preface. Your prefaces are wonderful.

I feel so dull and muddle-headed that I daren't even attempt to give you now an idea of the effect the little volume had produced on me. One can only feel grateful to you; and, after all I am so much in accord with

---

[1] Saturday was 29 November.
[2] Graham's latest collection of stories, essays, and sketches.

your sentiment (ne pas confondre avec "sentimentalisme") that I can't say anything illuminating as to my feelings. As to any critical remarks, that, from me to you, is impossible; I accept you without reservations; you express yourself too consummately for anything else to matter even if I were stupid enough not to *feel* your logic.

There may be a fallacy somewhere in your view of the world. There may—it's of no consequence. For myself I see with you; your talent has for me the fascination of deeper truth while with others I fall under the spell of your brilliance which is as genuine, I believe, as anything in letters since the invention of printing. Mille amitiés Tout à vous

J. Conrad

To Hugh Clifford
Text MS Clifford; Hunter

[letterhead: Pent Farm]
2 December 1902

My dear Clifford

This is indeed a most gorgeous appreciation.[1] I am delighted with all you say and am made really happy by your sympathy. I got the cutting this morning, on the last day of my forty-fourth year, and thus it becomes a noble birthday offering which I am inexpressibly proud to receive.

I would fain persuade myself that I deserve all you say but I can't succeed in that. I am only happy to think that there is *something* in my work which could have appealed to You to that extent.

What however I know I deserve (tho' you glide gently even tenderly over the point) are your remarks as to the style.[2] I am glad you absolve me from affectation.

[1] His review in the *Spectator*, 29 November, pp. 827–8. Clifford praises Conrad as a writer led by literary conscience rather than literary cynicism. Of the stories, Clifford particularly admires 'Heart of Darkness': 'never, beyond all question, has any writer till now succeeded in bringing the reason and the ghastly unreason of it all home to sheltered folk as does Mr. Conrad in this wonderful, this magnificent, this terrible study'.

[2] After noting that *Youth* demands an intelligent reader who will give the closest attention to its details, Clifford continues 'to be quite honest, the admission must be made that Mr. Conrad's style is occasionally difficult. It does not run in any well-worn groove, for its owner is no apostle of the obvious; to the casual reader it may at times appear to be laboured, even self-conscious. A closer study of it, however, should lead to the conviction that this style is individual, instinctive, moulded on no ready-made model; that it is the one and only mode of expression adapted to the purposes of its author, or indeed possible to him; that it is no sense an affectation; and, moreover, that it is exactly suited to the subjects of which he treats.'

Style is a matter of great concern to me as you know; and perhaps my very anxiety as to the proper use of a language of which I feel myself painfully ignorant produces the effect of laboured construction: whereas as a matter of striving my aim is simplicity and ease. I begin to be afraid I'll never achieve it; that I shall lose myself in a wilderness of endeavour unilluminated by knowledge.

What I am afraid of is: verbiage. Not so much the superfl[u]ous sentence as the superfluous word is my bugbear. You may smile perhaps at this pretence of conciseness; yet (as the French jurymen) "upon my honour and my conscience" that's what I am trying for. The treatment of the subject may be long; there may be too many phrases:—but the phrases should be without excrescences, almost bare.

The trouble is that I have no skill in tracking out of my principle.

However I must stop these confidences. Thanks! from the bottom of my heart. With kindest regards from us both for Mrs Clifford and yourself. Gratefully always yours

Jph Conrad.

To Elsie Hueffer
Text MS Neville; Unpublished

[letterhead: Pent Farm]
3 Dec 1902

My dear Señora

I ought to have answered your letter before this; but I have been plunged in a torpor so profound that even your attack on my pet Heart of Darkness could do no more than make me roll my eyes ferociously. Then for another day I remained prone revolving thoughts of scathing reply. At last—I arose and . . .

Seriously—I don't know that you are wrong. I admit that your strictures are intelligible to me; and every criticism that is intelligible (a quality by no means common) must have some truth in it, if not the whole truth. I mean intelligible to the author of course. As I began by saying—yours is to me; therefore I, in a manner, bear witness to its truth, with (I confess) the greatest reluctance. And, of course, I don't admit the whole of your case. What I distinctly admit is the fault of having made Kurtz too symbolic or rather symbolic at all. But the story being mainly a vehicle for conveying a batch of personal impressions I gave the rein to my mental laziness and took the line of the least resistance. This is then the whole Apologia pro Vita Kurtzii—or rather for the tardiness of his vitality.

My indignation having been (at first) fulgurant my gratitude for all
the charming things you say so well in commendation of your servant
burns with a steady and unalterable glow. Indeed, pray believe me,
your letter has given me a very great pleasure; and I thank you for
writing it; for to write to an author who sends his book is—generally—
an odious task.

I may say then "Au revoir a bientôt." I shall bring the cuttings with
me. Most of them are unintelligible to me and consequently contain no
truth. Jessie sends her love. Believe me always faithfully yours,

Jph Conrad.

To William Blackwood
Text MS NLS; Blackburn 171

[letterhead: Pent Farm]
4th Dec 1902

Dear Mr Blackwood.

Your letter has been a great pleasure in matter and in tone for you
know how much I prize the friendliness of your feeling and your
appreciation of my work.

The reviews are coming in. I've written to thank Clifford for his
Spectator article; and I hear that the Academy has allotted two columns
to Garnett to discourse upon Conrad. This generosity is striking, the
more so that the man pitched upon is not likely to make capital of the
crowning of *Youth*.

Next work to my hand will be to finish a story begun some seven years
ago of which a good third is to be written. I am getting up steam for it,
slowly, very slowly. Nevertheless I hope to be done with it in March.

To follow that I've a subject which may be treated in 30–40 thou:
words: the form I like best but which I believe is in no favour with the
public. The subject is difficult however and it may take up a great part of
the next year in the working out.

I would avail myself eagerly and on every possible occasion of the
hospitality you offer me, so kindly, in the pages of Maga; but the fact is
that I doubt profoundly the value of my ideas upon things in general and
on any single thing in particular; and this not morbidly, I trust, but with
judgment and in view of a definite ideal in the substance of thought as
well as in expression. But of course one doesn't know till one tries.

Excellent, the last number of Maga, especially In the Track of the

War and the N. Munro's instalment.[1] First rate, his new story; most promising.

I trust, dear Mr Blackwood, that this horrid weather has not tried you too much. It has been bad enough here to stop my writing with its gloom and the uproar of wind around the house. My health keeps good however; all I need is a little sunshine now and again.

Believe me, my dear Sir, always faithfully yours

Jph. Conrad.

PS Kind regards to Mr George Blackwood. I forgot to acknowledge in the body of the letter the safe receipt of the cheque for £25 for which my thanks.

To Ernest Dawson
Text MS Yale; J-A, 1, 307

Pent Farm.
12 Dec. Thursday. 1902

My dear Dawson.[2]

I snatch the first piece of MS paper to hand for I have delayed too long my answer to you.

With many thanks for your hospitable scheme I am afraid that it cannot be carried out this month. However, next year is near enough and your plan is too seductive not to be seriously considered. Don't forget however that (with all my qualities(?)) I am reduced to write for dear life, literally; and that when I put forward the claim of my work it is no conventional sense but iron necessity that speaks.

Ceci posé, you may trust my very sincere desire to see you again and to make your brother's acquaintance; but as to a definite answer at this moment I must beg your indulgence. It all depends how I get on with the story begun some six years ago and which *must* be finished in March. "Faudra voir" as our neighbours say. I shall drop you a line early in January. This case apart I think that's a magnificent occasion for me to go wrong, to fling my pen—so to say—par dessus les moulins[3]

---

[1] 'In the Tracks of War' and the second part of *Children of the Tempest*, in the December issue.

[2] H. G. Wells introduced Dawson to Conrad in 1901 or 02. Major Dawson contributed reminiscences of his life in Burma to *Blackwood's*. In 1928 he published 'Some Recollections of Joseph Conrad' in the *Fortnightly Review* (1 August, pp. 204–8). His brother A. J., a novelist and traveller, also became Conrad's friend. They bore no connection to Warrington Dawson, a later correspondent.

[3] 'Uninhibitedly'.

and cease to be a respectable (and bored) workman for two or three days.

I had the Spectator from Clifford a day or two before your letter. Many thanks. As to Clifford I think his reservations (and they are too few in all conscience) are perfectly just and proper as far as they go. As to his commendation I am not so sure; the personal element enters into that; we are on very friendly terms and he is very human.

In regard of what you say of greatness I doubt if greatness can be attained now in imaginative prose work. When it comes it will be in a new form; in a form for which we are not ripe as yet. Till the hour strikes and the man appears we must plod in the beaten track we must eternally "rabâcher"[1] the old formulas of expression. There is no help and no hope; there is only the duty to try, to try everlastingly with no regard for success.

Kindest regards Yours very sincerely,

Jph Conrad.

To Edward Clodd

Text MS Rosenbach; Unpublished

[letterhead: Pent Farm]
21st Dec. 1902

My dear Sir.[2]

I hasten to return Gissing's letter[3] with no end of thanks for communicating to me the whole document and for enclosing it in a message from Yourself, a message so unexpectedly friendly so welcome and so encouraging.

Of course it's a great event to happen to one—a great success! One could be more proud of it if it were possible to weigh in scrupulous scales the part of merit and the part of chance. So much of one's achievement (such as it is) comes from outside—from some unknown and inaccessible region! I tell this to myself very insistently and I don't know why I should trouble you with the expression of that feeling unless because I know that you will understand that this is for me a great occasion—a great success. As to the other sort of success, which you wish me so kindly, not expecting much I shall not be disappointed. Obviously one wishes to be widely accepted; but for that piece of luck (I

---

[1] 'Repeat'.
[2] Edward Clodd (1840–1930) was a banker and a writer on science and folklore.
[3] Full of praise: see also the following letter to Gissing.

believe it is luck mostly) I would not bargain away your appreciative words setting off Gissing's unguardedly generous expression.

Believe me, my dear Sir, yours very sincerely

Jph. Conrad.

To George Gissing

Text MS Mursia; Coustillas

[letterhead: Pent Farm]
21 Dec 1902

My dear Gissing[1]

Like a good Mohamedan at a rash saying or before a rash action I am tempted to exclaim at You: "Remember God!"

I've read your letter to Clodd;[2] and lest that cabinet noir sort of proceeding should shock you, I hasten to explain that the man had sent it to me; for which indiscretion let him be everlastingly blessed in this world and the next.

As to you, my dear Gissing, who have the Lamp and the Treasure,[3] You can afford royally to fling away a priceless jewel of a word. But still—Remember God!

And also remember man—the man—this man. I—who had always had a very human affection for You—am no longer young enough to accept with proper self confidence all that you may think right to give. After forty it is easier to spurn away blame than to embrace the fair form of praise. There is a talking spectre, a ghostly voice whispering incessantly in one's ear of the narrow circle circumscribing all effort, of the shortness of one's vision and of the poverty of one's thought.[4]

But whatever is before me I feel rich enough now standing here with such a Christmas gift in my hands as no lavishness of Dickens' imagination could have contrived for the felicity of a poor devil in a Christmas Tale.

And I am my dear Gissing, as I've been always (but one now

---

[1] George Robert Gissing (1857–1903), the distinguished but unfortunate writer of essays, novels, and short stories. His novels include *New Grub Street* (1891), *The Odd Women* (1893), and *In the Year of Jubilee* (1894). He and Conrad were among the improbable group of collaborators on 'The Ghost', the Christmas play at Brede Place, 1899. Gissing's reply to the present letter is in *Twenty Letters to Joseph Conrad*, ed. G. Jean-Aubry, 1926.

[2] Clodd published the letter in *Memories* (1916), pp. 184–6.

[3] Like Aladdin in the *Thousand and One Nights*.

[4] For the sake of his diseased lungs, Gissing himself had moved to the south of France, where he died the following year.

encouraged to set down the very words) admiringly and affectionately
yours

Jph Conrad.

To William Blackwood
Text MS NLS; Blackburn 173

[letterhead: Pent Farm]
22 Dec. 1902

My Dear Mr Blackwood

I don't know how it is in Scotland but here after the late severe
weather a thaw set in which has melted even the frigidity of the
Athenaeum. They gave me a line in the Contents all to myself and a
column and a half inside.[1] I must say I am pleased.

Edwd Clodd (I've never met him) wrote me an appreciative letter
enclosing one from Gissing to him. What Gissing says of Youth is not
meet for me to repeat, even to you; but he ends by entreating Clodd to
talk about the book to every man and woman he knows.[2] This is
showing a practical interest.

And since finishing the E of the T I have not written anything that I
can bring myself to let stand: that is, practically, I've done just nothing.
It's awful—awful.

This, is all my news.

I trust that some time in 1903 I'll have something to knock at Maga's
door with. But perhaps you won't have me? But let me tell you that I am
no longer obscure. A publication called the "Smart Set"[3]—heavens!
What a name—has asked me, this very day, for a short story of 3–4
thou: words. An airy trifle of a thing—don't you know.

After I had recovered from the fit ... No. I won't go into details.
Suffice it to say that when I reached the stage of cool reflexion and
realized that there were men, good, decent clever men, not only able but
willing to sit down and write the demanded story—I asked myself
seriously whether it would have been my loss or my gain if I too had
been able and willing to sit down and write a story, simply because
somebody was ready to pay for it?

[1] 20 December, p. 824; reprinted, *Critical Heritage*, pp. 137–9. A. J. Dawson wrote, but
did not sign, the review.

[2] And Gissing wrote in similar terms to other correspondents: 'Read Conrad's new book.
He is the strongest writer—in every sense of the word—at present publishing in
England. Marvellous writing!' (24 December 1902 to Miss Collet: quoted in *Critical
Heritage*, p. 140).

[3] *A Magazine of Cleverness*, which began its stylish career in 1900.

I am going to ask the London office for three more copies. I want one for Paris ("Mercure de France"),[1] one for Dr Yrjo Hirn a professor in the university of Helsingfors who, with his wife, has translated some of the Tales of Unrest into Swedish, and had a critical article on my work in a Stockholm paper some time ago.[2] The third I want to send to Poland for the very young lions of an extremely modern literary review in Warsaw, the *Chimera*.[3] Let them chew it up and snarl over the flavour of the fossil. The Putnams published lately a story of mine (Typhoon) in a small vol.[4] They had not the elementary humanity to send me a proof nor the civility to send me a copy. However I obtained one. It has been set up from an uncorrected MS; the consequence is that I am made to provide ventilators for a hole—a contrivance worthy of American genius for invention.

Pardon this long document—which does not require an answer however; and with my best wishes for yourself and your nephews for the coming year, I am, dear Mr Blackwood always faithfully yours.

Jph. Conrad.

To John Galsworthy
Text MS Forbes; Unpublished

[letterhead: Pent Farm]
22 Dec 1902

Dearest Jack

I've been bitterly disappointed.

We are leaving in half an hour for W'sea to spend there a week or so.[5] I don't know whether that sort of thing does me any good nor not, but as I can't work at home it doesn't matter where I am.

I shall expect to see you and your work as early as possible in Jan^y.

I feel seedy and gloomy and discontented with myself. I've been lazy—or paralysed: but the result is the same. Nothing done. Bad! Our love, our thanks and our best wishes to you and for all that are dear to You.

Ever yours

J. Conrad.

---

[1] For Davray.
[2] Collected in *Yrjö Hirns Verksamhet svenska Litteraturällskapet* (Helsingfors, 1953). See also letter to Blackwood, 31 May, p.416, n.1.
[3] A monthly begun in 1901.   [4] Without other stories.   [5] With the Hueffers.

To David Garnett

Text G. 189

[letterhead: Pent Farm]
22 Dec. [1902][1]

My dear boy,[2]

We have sent off three volumes of the "Leather-Stocking Tales"—one from each of us—with our love to you.

You have promised me to read these stories and I would recommend you to begin with the *Last of the Mohicans*—then go on with the *Deerslayer* and end with the *Prairie*. I read them at your age in that order; and I trust that you, of a much later generation, shall find in these pages some at least of the charm which delighted me then and has not evaporated even to this day.[3]

Thirty four years ago is a long long time to look back upon. And then already these stories were not of the day before; now the arrangement of their words has grown old—they say—very old.

It may be. Time spares no one. Even you shall grow old some day. But I have a great confidence in you; and I believe that you shall respond— as I did in my time—to the genuine feeling of the descriptions and the heroic temper of the narrative.

Your affectionate friend

Joseph Conrad

To Edward Garnett

Text MS Yale; G. 187

1902
[letterhead: Pent Farm]
22^{d} Dec

Dearest Edward

I've just finished a long letter to David introducing my old friend Cooper. I am quite excited at the result of the experiment. Will they hit it off together? That's the question.

With my usual brutality I've neglected to express my feelings very much awakened by your review of Youth.[4]

How nice they are I renounce to tell. My dearest fellow you quite overcome me. And your brave attempt to grapple with the foggishness of

---

[1] See the next letter.   [2] The future novelist (1892–1981).

[3] Conrad wrote on Fenimore Cooper's maritime novels in 'Tales of the Sea' (1898), *Notes on Life and Letters*, pp. 53–7.

[4] *Academy and Literature*, 6 December, p. 606, unsigned, *Critical Heritage*, pp. 131–3.

H of D, to explain what I myself have tried to shape blindfold, as it were, has touched me profoundly.[1] You are the Seer of the Figures in the Carpet.[2] The Figure in the Carpet of the E of the T you have seen so perfectly and described in a line and a half with so much precision that even to me it has been a sort of revelation.[3]

Thanks and thanks again.

The ruck takes its tone from you. You know how to serve a friend! I notice the reviews as they come in since your article. Youth is an epic: that's settled. And the H of D is this and that and the other thing—they aren't so positive because in this case they aren't intelligent enough to catch on to your indications. But anyway it's a high water mark.[4] If it hadn't been for you it would have been,* dreary bosh—an incoherent bogie tale. Yes. That note too was sounded only you came just in time. As to the E of T you have seen the Figure—but the miserable threadbare warp and woof of the thing had fascinated them already. They didn't want you there. Touching, tender noble, moving . . .

Let us spit!

However the *Manch^er Guardian* was fairly intelligent[5]—and, I suppose, you have seen the thawing of great snows on the hoary summits of the Athenaeum?

I am still shaking at the august phenomenon.

J[ames] Bl'wood sent me word that the thing sells decently and that if the Christmas does not kill it—if . . .

It's strange how I always, from the age of fourteen, disliked the Christian religion, its doctrines, ceremonies and festivals. Presentiment that some day it will work my undoing, I suppose. Now it's quite on the cards that the Bethleem* legend will kill the epic, and the bogie tale, and the touching tender, noble captain Newcome—Colonel Whalley thing.[6] Hard. Isn't it. And the most galling feature is that nobody—not a single

---

[1] 'For the art of "Heart of Darkness" . . . lies in the relation of the things of the spirit to the things of the flesh, of the invisible life to the visible, of the sub-conscious life within us, our obscure motives and instincts, to our conscious actions, feelings and outlook . . . the art of "Heart of Darkness" implies the catching of infinite shades of the white man's uneasy, disconcerted, and fantastic relations with the exploited barbarism of Africa.'

[2] Echoing Henry James's 'The Figure in the Carpet'?

[3] It is 'a study of an old sea captain who . . . finding himself dispossessed by the perfected routine of the British empire overseas he has helped to build, falls on evil times, and faces ruin calmly, fighting to the last'.

[4] Garnett calls it 'the high-water mark of the author's talent'.

[5] 10 December 1902; *Critical Heritage*, pp. 134–5.

[6] By insisting on Captain Whalley's poignancy (as in the *TLS*, 12 December, p. 372), some reviewers made him fit company for Colonel Newcome, whose death (in Thackeray's *The Newcomes*) is the acme of Victorian pathos.

Bishop of them—believes in it. The business in the stable isn't convincing; whereas my atmosphere (vide reviews) can be positively breathed. Our festive greetings, love and best wishes. Ever yours

Conrad.

To H. G. Wells
Text MS Illinois; Unpublished

1902
[letterhead: Pent Farm]
22 Dec

Dear H. G.

You shall get the official card in due course but here I record our best wishes of the year's end and the year's beginning for you both.

A special message of love and good wishes is set down here for the young Man.[1] I don't write to him personally because I know how busy he must be at this time of the year; but we are sending him by this post, in a card board box, a remarkable example of Evolution; a dog belonging to a species which has developed (in consequence of transference to the new habitat of Nurseries) a small metal wheel under each paw.

In our search for the specimen we have been greatly assisted by the energetic efforts and the sage advice of our son Borys. He sends to G. P a manly greeting together with a peremptory message to "make haste and grow big".

Ever since the Dawson meeting I've been sneezing coughing and groaning. Still we managed to run up to London for a couple of days and I've given three long sittings to G. Sauter[2] for my portrait. It promises well.

And I have done no work! I hear with delight (and some envy) that you have finished a book.[3] I rejoice at your relief and am impatient to know what you have done. I shall descend on You shortly after the new year for a careful inquiry. Now we are off to W'sea for a week at least. Affectionate regards in which Jessie joins. Always yours

Jph Conrad

---

[1] George Philip Wells. [2] Galsworthy's brother-in-law.
[3] Perhaps *Mankind in the Making*, which appeared in serial from September 1902 to September 1903.

To Ford Madox Ford
Text Telegram, Yale; Unpublished

[23 December 1902][1]

Hueffer Winchelsea
Bismillah the sheik of Caravan hopes reach oasis of El Rhayah at 4.30
Salutations[2]

---

[1] Date-stamp.   [2] 'Bismillah': 'God willing'. The oasis is Rye, near Winchelsea.

The letter to Sanderson dated by Conrad 15 July 1905 (J-A, 2, 21) almost certainly belongs to 1901. The text, however, will appear in Volume Three.

CORRECTIONS TO THE TEXT

The following slips of the pen have been silently corrected.

Missing full stop supplied

7 Jan. 1898 (to Garnett): after 'peg out naturally'; 9 Jan. 1898: after 'for a place'; 30 March 1898: after 'not to be found'; [4 June 1898]: before 'I am averse'; 18 Oct. 1898: before 'A chance comes once'; 28 Oct. 1898 (to Galsworthy): after 'when we meet'; 13 Jan. 1899 (to Garnett): before 'Been asked to'; [30 Jan. 1899]: after 'hatching of that story'; 2 Feb. 1899: after 'in your way'; 23 July 1899: after 'first half of August'; 10/11 Aug. 1899: before 'But even if you'; 22 Aug. 1899 (to Meldrum): before 'Will he want them'; 9 Oct. 1899: after 'to arouse his feeling', after 'to your wife and yourself'; 13 Nov. 1899: after 'nous verrons'; 19 Dec. 1899: after 'hear from you'; [8 Feb. 1900]: after 'look at them yet'; 12 Feb. 1900: after '*208*'; [17 or 24 May 1900]: after 'friend goes with them'; [9 July 1900 (to Ford)]: after 'for the balance', before 'Moreover by the time'; 23 Jan. 1901: after '*Maga's*'; 24 May 1901: after 'qualities and shortcomings'; 3 June 1901 (to Pinker): before 'It would be good'; 3 July 1901 (to Pinker): before 'I am at work', after 'so far on a 10% royalty'; 11 July 1901: after 'with our next'; [14 July 1901 (to Pinker)]: before 'I shall be ready'; [23 July 1901]: before 'I write an epitome', after '"That's Crockett"', before '"Of course not"', after 'I shall tell you more', before 'Love from us all'; 31 Dec. 1901: after '*Vanished Arcadia*'; 6 Jan. 1902: after 'a glamour of *Romance*'; 16 Jan. 1902: before 'That'll end the vol.'; 28 Jan. 1902 (to Pinker): before 'The book-rights in America'; [28 Jan 1902 (to Ford)]: before 'Your burial stuff'; 25 February 1902: after 'our relations'; 19 June 1902: after 'I have worked'; 24 June 1902 (first letter to Ford): after 'reached us this morning'; [late September 1902 (to Blackwood)]: after 'disconnected scrawl'.

Dittography

[28 May? 1898]: a second 'we' before 'will be glad'; 29 Sept. 1898 (to Garnett): a second 'matter' after 'composed of the same'; 2 Feb. 1899: a second 'says' after 'Pawling says'; 3 Dec. 1899: an 'all' before 'all *nearly all*'; 22 May 1900: a second 'as' in 'to appear as a long novel'; 13 June 1901: a second 'is' after 'seen no judgment'; 3 Aug. 1901: a second 'a' before 'fundamental study'; 'Friday' [Aug. or Sept.? 1902 (to Meldrum)]: an 'I' before 'If I did not'; 6 Nov. 1902 (to Bennett): a

second 'with' before 'my unavailing efforts'; 2 Dec. 1902: a second 'am'
before 'glad you absolve me'.

Other

Quotation marks supplied: 31 Jan. 1898: after 'Romance of Shallow
Waters'; 14 April 1898: after 'very good!'; 11 June 1898 (to Blackwood):
after 'bis dat qui'; 19 July 1898: before 'would let me know'; 16 Oct.
1898: after 'règles de la bienséance'; 18 Oct. 1898: 'sans phrases'; 8 Nov.
1899: after *'finest story in the world'*; 19 July 1901: at end of PS; 2 April
1902: before 'Elle baisse la tête'.

Quotation marks deleted: 14 Feb. 1899 (to Blackwood): before 'and Other
Tales'.

Question mark supplied: 2 Oct. 1898 (to Ford): after 'about your eyes'.

Semi-colon supplied: 29 Sept. 1898 (to Garnett): after 'Glasgow'.

Bracket deleted: 19 [June] 1901: after 'intended for you'.

Bracket supplied: 3 July 1901 (to Pinker): after '(Hein)'.

Comma supplied: 28 April 1901: before 'make arrangements'.

CORRIGENDA, Volume One

Page ix: 'Berdyczów'; xi: 'Palestine'; xviii, letters to Garnett: 'Indiana-polis: Bobbs-Merrill, 1928'; xxii, l. 3: '12 October 1878'; xlviii, l. 13: 'revolutionary silver'; lxii: 'Paul Briquel (1877–1922), Emilie (c. 1875–1961)', 'de Brunnow (1865–1943)'; lxiii: 'Chesson (1870–1952)'; add: 'William Leonard Courtney (1850–1928), a prolific author, editor of the *Fortnightly Review*, and reviewer for the *Daily Telegraph*'; 'Olivia Garnett (1843–1903)'; lxiv: 'Krieger (c. 1850–1918)'; lxv: 'Meldrum (1864–1940)'; 'Poradowska (1848–1937)'; lxvi: 'Ted Sanderson (1867–1939)'; 'Katherine Sanderson died in 1921'; lxvii: 'John E. Weston (born c. 1848) succeeded his father John Thomas Weston'.

25, n. 3; 'in May'; 28, to Thys, l. 9: 'la peine'; 40, l. 19: 'passe vite'; 42, l. 5: 'embarquées par'; n. 1: 'Luke 23.34'; 43, l. 27: after 'abyss' add: 'Now this soul is liberated; it has known its error; it needs your indulgence'; 46: 'estate of Kazimierówka'; 52, l. 31: comma after 'handwriting'; 54, l. 7: 'beaucoup'; 56, l. 12: delete 'free'; 63, l. 16: after 'I would' add: 'on every voyage'; 87, lls. 1 and 3: delete code after full stop; 96, l. 16: 'rien à dire'.

101, l. 14: 'peut se faire'; 108, published J-A, 1, 149, n. 3; 112, l. 13: add 'plans' after 'tout Vos'; 119, l. 8: add 'de' after 'le desert'; 131, to Poradowska, l. 2: comma before 'pour service'; 137, last line: 'puis-qu'ils'; 171, l. 24: 'health is coming back'; 173, to Poradowska, l. 6: 'moi-même'; 175, l. 5: 'chaque foi'; 177, l. 10: 'Apresant'; 183, l. 21: 'Du reste'; 184, translation, l. 7: 'you should not bother'; 198: letter to Chesson published Mursia 6, 'You' and 'Your' throughout; 199, l. 3: 'about its being'.

203: letter to Unwin published Keating 8; 207, l. 7: 'desespoir'; 223, translation: 'to come up with a selection'; 232, l. 2: 'la tâche'; 238–42: emendations from MS Taylor; 240, l. 13: after 'arguments' add: 'pres[en]t'; l. 18 'travelled in Pullman'; 241, l. 12: 'Jullien et Epstein'; 242, l. 2: 'syndicate for'; l. 12: delete 'me' after 'give'; l. 24: 'common (or garden)'; 271, address: 'Couadou'; last line: 'news from you'; 272, l. 22: 'really exist?'; 277, to C. Garnett, l. 8: 'unfortunate'; 280, l. 1: 'tell me how'; 282, l. 19: 'books lay hold'.

310, l. 26 should read '"I am sitting on my bare ass in the lee scuppers" (Burn this letter: it's indecent!)'; 314, n. 2: '*Tales of Unrest*'; 333, l. 19: comma before 'I feel'; 338, n. 6 and 364, n. 3: 'about 15,600 words'; 340, to Sanderson, l. 17: 'Can't [. . .] I ask' (MS torn); 362, l. 18: 'lest some evil should'; 363, to Krieger, l. 1: 'Ortmans' sweet'; 370, l. 2: 'sees round the corner'; 371, l. 18: 'understood perfectly'; 389, PS, l. 2: 'rappelle'; 396, to Sanderson, l. 5: 'I can do so ignorantly'; 398, to Sanderson, lls. 26–9 should read: 'This conviction makes me cautious not because I care for my dignity, or even because I would be thought wise through the prestige of silence, but because I care for truth—as far as I know it'.

403, to O. Garnett: published *Conradiana*, 8 (1976), 78; 414, translation, l. 5: after 'listen with' add: 'the intensity of'; 420: letter is to W. L. Courtney, who reviewed *The Nigger* in the *Daily Telegraph*, 8 December; published *Nineteenth Century Fiction*, 23 (1968), 201–16; Index of recipients: 'Courtney, W. L., 420'; 'Sanderson, E. L. . . . 366, 368 . . . 400, 433'; 'Zagórska, Aniela, 287, 427'; 'Zagórski, Karol and Aniela, 324'.

INDEX I

In Index I, which identifies recipients, only the first page of each letter is cited.

In Index II, an index of names, run-on pagination may cover more than one letter. References to ships and boats are consolidated under 'Ships'; references to newspapers and magazines under 'Periodicals'. References to works by Conrad appear under his name. A full critical index will appear in the final volume.

Recipients

Bennett, Arnold, 389, 452
Blackwood, George, 375, 380, 413, 434
Blackwood, Messrs William and Sons, 155, 196, 240, 278
Blackwood, William, 67, 129, 139, 147, 161, 164, 166, 193, 213, 215, 230, 248, 252, 253, 261, 264, 275, 277, 281, 282, 283, 285, 300, 309, 313 (2), 317, 327, 329, 338, 349, 354, 356, 413, 415, 423, 429, 432, 437, 442 (2), 448, 450, 461, 465
Bontine, the Hon. A. E., 104, 121, 125, 150
Brooke, Minnie, 3, 20, 27, 140
Brunnow, Baroness Janina de, 147, 232

Capes, Harriet Mary, 394
Chesson, W. H., 19, 32, 149
Clifford, Hugh, 179, 180, 189 (2), 199, 226, 404, 459
Clodd, Edward, 463
Crane, Cora, 28, 45, 46, 48, 58, 72, 112, 114, 115, 127, 135, 182, 183, 195, 268, 269, 325, 326
Crane, Stephen, 13, 21, 38, 42, 151, 197

Davray, H.-D., 185, 280, 304, 398, 405, 407
Dawson, Ernest, 462
Ford, Ford Madox, 93, 96, 98, 110, 111, 118, 119, 146, 154, 219, 222, 234, 250, 253, 256, 258 (2), 264, 265, 279, 293, 327, 332, 334, 335, 339, 342, 343, 346, 352, 355, 372, 377, 378, 387, 397, 408, 409, 412, 414, 423, 427, 428 (2), 430, 435, 470

Galsworthy, John, 11, 21, 26, 112, 174, 175, 178, 197, 202, 203, 225, 229, 238, 266, 270, 276, 284, 287, 291, 293, 295, 300, 301, 308, 310, 312, 317, 321, 323 (2), 324, 325, 334, 341, 358, 390, 397, 405, 420, 422, 425, 427, 431, 434, 439, 445, 446, 447, 449, 454, 466
Garnett, David, 467
Garnett, Edward, 6, 12, 18, 26, 32, 38, 45, 46, 49, 61, 62, 66, 74, 76, 83, 85, 94, 99, 102, 103, 115, 132, 152, 169, 176, 184, 198, 208, 218, 220, 221 (2), 224, 241, 243, 256, 299, 302, 337, 350, 351, 352, 353, 355, 424, 440, 447, 456, 467
Garnett, Richard, 330
Gissing, George, 464
Gosse, Edmund, 319
Graham, Gabriela Cunninghame, 170
Graham, R. B. Cunninghame, 4, 15, 24, 29, 35, 39, 43, 52, 56, 59, 61, 68, 69, 75, 79, 80, 82, 83, 87, 89, 116, 124, 128, 133, 154, 157, 171, 178, 206, 228, 238, 242, 248, 254, 286, 296, 360, 458

Henley, W. E., 106
Hind, C. L., 57, 59
Hueffer, Elsie, 264, 393, 437, 443, 450, 460

Kliszczewski, Spiridion, 40, 41, 54, 77
Korzeniowski, Józef, 322

Meldrum, David, 64, 65, 71, 72, 101,
    133, 145, 149, 152, 153, 162, 163,
    165, 168, 184, 190 (2), 192, 196,
    199 (2), 207, 208, 214, 217 (2), 223,
    224, 227, 237, 240, 241, 247, 249,
    253, 259, 260, 271, 273, 276, 288,
    297 (2), 298, 306, 307, 311, 367,
    379, 387, 419, 431, 436, 440, 452,
    457
Methuen, Algernon, 157, 181
Munro, Neil, 117, 186
Murray, Hallam, 438 (2)

New York Times, 346
Nicholson, William, 65

Pawling, S. S., 42, 296
Pinker, J. B., 194, 294, 295, 304, 306,
    318, 319, 320 (2), 329, 330, 331,
    332, 333, 335, 340, 357, 365, 370,
    372, 373, 374, 376, 377, 381, 382,
    385, 392, 393, 395, 396, 398, 410,
    411, 412, 415, 455, 458
Poradowska, Marguerite, 262, 266, 269,
    275

Quiller-Couch, A. T., 78

Reynolds, Mabel, 290
Roberts, Arthur Llewelyn, 433

Sanderson, E. L., 34, 47, 51, 53, 70, 97,
    134, 141, 153, 181, 203, 210, 233,
    250
Sanderson, Helen, 63, 90, 172, 188, 251,
    255, 291; *see also* Watson
Shorter, C. K., 86 (2)
Spiridion, Joseph, *see* Kliszczewski

Unidentified, 98
Unwin, Jane Cobden, 40
Unwin, T. Fisher, 9, 14, 39, 48, 84, 96,
    259, 403, 407

Watson, Helen, 51; *see also* Sanderson
Watson, John, 455
Wells, H. G., 91, 100, 120, 123, 126,
    136, 146, 187, 239, 278, 314, 386,
    469
Wells, Jane, 391

Zagórska, Aniela, 23, 36, 55, 131, 137,
    156, 177, 229

INDEX II

Names of people, places, ships, organizations and publications

Abel, 159
Aesculapius, 100
Africa, 139–40, 145, 417
Allen, Grant, 137
Antaeus, 334
Arnold, Matthew, 188
Australia, 230, 238

Bacheller Syndicate, 39
Balfour, A. J., 345
Bangkok, 93
Barrie, J. M., 35, 138
Basilan, 226
Beckford, William, 171–2
Belgium, 345
Bennett, Arnold, 392
Besant, Sir Walter, 417
Bethlehem, 468–9
Bible, 5, 24–5, 60, 89, 159, 192
Black, Robert, 350
Blackstone, Sir William, 331
Blackwood, George, 299–301, 376, 379,
    382, 388, 413, 416, 421, 462
Blackwood, James Hugh, 381, 451, 468
Blackwood, William, 7, 12, 43, 46, 48,
    50, 62, 65–6, 71, 73, 78, 102, 114,
    132, 145, 151–2, 162, 166, 168–9,
    182, 190, 192–3, 196, 208, 215, 218,
    221, 223, 227, 240, 249, 271–4, 276,
    285, 288–9, 291, 295, 298–9, 304,
    306, 310–12, 321, 330, 336, 343,
    350–3, 355, 365, 367–9, 373, 376,
    379–81, 383–4, 387–8, 394, 395,
    406, 410–11, 414–15, 419–22, 424,
    429, 450
Blake, Mrs (C. T.?), 217–18, 221, 223
Blunt, Lady Anne, 172
Blunt, Wilfrid Scawen, 81, 172
Bobrowska, Ewa, 245
Bobrowski family, 245–6
Bobrowski, Józef, 245
Bobrowski, Stefan, 246
Bobrowski, Tadeusz, 37, 245–6, 322
Boer War, 207, 210–12, 228, 230–1, 233,
    250–2, 255–6, 286, 302, 357

Bontine, the Hon. A. E., 128, 323
Borneo, 277
Botticelli, Sandro, 50
Brede Place, 73, 182, 270
Bridges, Robert, 220–1
Bristol, 329
British Empire, 211, 231, 233, 256, 404
Brittany, 43
Brown, Ford Madox, 101
Bruges, 269, 272, 279–81, 283, 285
Brunetière, Ferdinand, 408
Buloz et Cie, 408
Brunei, 226
Buchan, John, 214, 216, 223
Buller, General Sir Redvers, 212, 429
Burne Jones, Sir Edward, 320
Burton, Sir Richard, 125
Buszczyński, Stefan, 247
Bussow, Herr, 84

Cain, 159
Caine, Hall, 137, 345
Canada, 230, 277, 298
Canterbury, 131
Capes, Harriet, 416
Capri, 304
Caribbean, the, 294, 339, 366
Carlists, 53
Carlyle, Thomas, 320
Carnegie, Andrew, 436
Castle Line, 83
Catullus, 51
Cearne, The, 42–3, 351
Cervantes, Miguel de, 65, 81, 122
Chamberlain, Joseph, 302, 345
Chaucer, Geoffrey, 172
Chesson, W. H., 18
China, 116
China Sea, 295
Chislehurst, 454
Christianity, 468–9
Cleopatra, 443
Clifford family, 227
Clifford, Hugh, 57, 130, 194, 461, 463
Clive, Robert, 128

Clodd, Edward, 464–5
Congo, 139–40, 145, 406
Conrad, Borys, 17–19, 20, 23, 34, 38,
    48, 50, 55, 74, 76, 83, 90–1, 102,
    105, 111, 228–9, 238, 244, 247, 390,
    392, 437, 469
Conrad family, 27–9, 31, 45, 71, 80,
    101, 122, 135, 140, 156, 177, 183,
    197, 205–6, 207, 210, 243, 248–9,
    255–6, 269, 279, 284–7, 293, 321,
    323, 327, 365, 389, 433, 443–4, 446,
    449
Conrad, Jessie, 3, 14, 20, 24, 33, 37, 41,
    43, 52, 54–6, 58–9, 62, 73–4, 83–4,
    91, 105, 110–11, 113–14, 120–1,
    132, 149, 160, 173, 180, 185, 187,
    195, 203, 212, 225, 227, 240–1,
    252–3, 258, 263, 276, 295, 325,
    332–3, 346, 351, 355, 358, 360, 373,
    378, 393, 423, 426, 430, 438, 447
Conrad, Joseph: Works:
    Almayer's Folly, 6, 403, 412, 446
    'Alphonse Daudet', 32, 34
    'Amy Foster', 330–4, 356–8, 361, 368,
        391–2, 399
    Chance, 62, 169
    'Dynamite': *see Chance*
    'The End of the Tether', 193, 376,
        406, 410–11, 413, 423–4, 427–35,
        440–3, 446–8, 450–1, 465
    'Equitable Division': *see* 'Typhoon'
    'Falk', 295, 319–21, 327–31, 334, 356,
        358, 368, 374–6, 380–2, 388, 399,
        441
    'First Command': *see The Shadow-Line*
    'Heart of Darkness', 129, 132–3,
        139–40, 145–7, 149, 152–5, 157–8,
        161–8, 175–6, 178, 193, 271, 375–6,
        406, 417, 460
    The Inheritors, 231, 234, 256–9, 289,
        293, 296, 335–8, 340–9, 353, 393,
        409, 415
    'Jim: A Sketch': *see Lord Jim*
    'Karain', 57, 130, 287, 375, 417, 448
    Lord Jim, 62, 65, 67, 72, 102, 129, 169,
        184–5, 190–4, 196–7, 198–9, 203–5,
        207–9, 213–15, 217–18, 220–1, 223,
        226–8, 230–1, 237, 240–1, 243–4,
        247, 248–9, 252–4, 257, 259–61,
        270–5, 277–8, 281–9, 292–3, 297–9,
        302–3, 306–7, 312–13, 336–7, 357,
        368, 379–80, 394, 396, 406, 411,
        413, 417, 419–22, 441, 449, 451

The Mirror of the Sea, 368
The Nigger of the 'Narcissus', 3–4, 6–8,
    10–11, 13–14, 16, 18–20, 23, 28,
    31–2, 41, 44, 51, 62, 86, 95, 98, 109,
    273, 303, 385
Nostromo, 448, 455, 461
'An Observer in Malaya', 179–80
An Outcast of the Islands, 6, 84, 92, 303,
    385, 411–12
'An Outpost of Progress', 16, 140,
    398, 407
The Rescue, 6–9, 15, 26–7, 31–2, 42,
    46–7, 49, 54, 59, 62, 66, 71, 73–4,
    76, 78, 83, 85–90, 96, 98, 102, 105,
    119, 121–2, 133, 139, 154, 162,
    164–7, 176, 182, 191–2, 229, 231,
    241, 243, 260, 289, 318, 336–7, 368,
    374, 377, 384–5, 394, 411, 421, 423,
    455–6, 458, 461
'The Return', 7, 9–11, 39
Romance, 107–8, 112, 118–19, 262,
    294, 304, 328, 330–6, 338–40,
    343–6, 353, 356, 357–8, 365–74,
    377, 382, 385–8, 391–2, 395, 408,
    410, 412, 414–15, 424, 456
'A Seaman', 62, 167, 169, 193, 237
'Seraphina': *see Romance*
The Shadow-Line, 167, 169, 237, 273,
    289
'Tales of the Sea', 71, 467
Tales of Unrest, 3, 7, 9–10, 15, 16, 26,
    28, 44–5, 48–9, 98, 259, 385, 398,
    403, 406, 411, 466
'To-morrow', 366–7, 372–3, 381–2,
    393, 399–400
'Typhoon', 169, 237, 295, 297–8, 304,
    306–8, 319–21, 356, 358, 361, 368,
    377, 399, 416, 466
Typhoon, 337, 340–1, 374–5, 385, 394,
    398, 456, 466
'Youth', 59, 63–5, 67, 71, 91–2, 102,
    109, 133, 140, 145, 166, 192–3, 271,
    368, 375–6, 406, 417
Youth, 72, 129, 140, 145, 147, 164–8,
    192–3, 205, 237, 271–4, 286, 328–9,
    337, 356, 374–6, 379–80, 385, 413,
    419–22, 424, 433, 442, 448–9,
    451–2, 456–7, 459, 461, 465, 467–8
Constable & Co., 294
Constable, Frank Challice, 327, 329
Constantinople, 116
Cooper, James Fenimore, 467
Corelli, Marie, 137, 298

Corot, J. B. C., 95
Court-at-Street, 437
Crane, Cora, 32, 36, 43–4, 133, 146
Crane, Stephen, 4, 18, 28–9, 32, 34, 36,
    44–6, 48, 72, 113–15, 130, 132, 133,
    135, 150, 182–3, 195, 242, 266,
    268–70, 292
Crawfurd, Oswald, 295
Crockett, S. R., 338, 345
Currie, Sir Donald, 75, 83

Dames Bernardines, 262–3
Dante Alighieri, 243
D'Annunzio, Gabriele, 31, 33
Daudet, Alphonse, 32
Davray, H.-D., 403–4, 407
Dawson, A. J., 462, 465
Dawson, Ernest, 469
Dear, Mrs, 279
Dickens, Charles, 111, 464
Divers, Mr, 277
Dodd, Mead & Co., 336
Doubleday, Frank N., 221, 336
Dover, 270
Doyle, Arthur Conan, 418
Dreyfus case, 213
Duckworth, Gerald, 311, 425
Dumas, Alexandre, 107–8
Duport, James, 409
Durban, 292

East London, 292
Edinburgh, 162, 193, 215
Edward VII, 375, 431
Eliot, George, 418
Elstree, 51, 63, 70, 90–1, 141, 173, 181,
    233, 291
England, 54, 55, 127, 151, 230, 270,
    294, 296
English language, 20, 138, 156, 460
Escamillo (dog), 284, 326
Eshmûn, 100
Essex, 280
Europe, 230
Evans, Sir Francis, 75, 79

Far East, 211
Fez, 117
Finland, 416
Flaubert, Gustave, 80, 100, 388–9, 445
Folkestone, 439
Ford, Ford Madox, 41, 64, 95, 107–8,
    112, 151, 175–7, 197, 242, 260–1,
    267, 272, 287, 291, 294–5, 298, 300,

320, 327–8, 334, 339, 347, 351,
    357–8, 365–8, 368–70, 374, 385,
    393, 415, 424
Fowey, 78
France, 185, 342–3, 460
Frederic, Harold, 41, 44, 58, 122
French language, 172
Fronde, the, 159

Gage, W. J. & Co., 277, 306
Galsworthy family, 454
Galsworthy, John, 18, 97, 132, 250–1,
    275–6, 282–3, 308, 311–13, 342,
    409, 420, 437–40, 450–1
Galsworthy, John (Senior), 422, 434,
    448
Garnett, Constance, 27, 33, 63, 132,
    138, 209, 255, 350, 425
Garnett, David, 457
Garnett, Edward, 42–3, 61, 68, 73, 89,
    91, 105, 119, 122, 149, 154, 160,
    218, 256, 291, 293–4, 309, 349–50,
    354, 356, 431, 456, 461
Garnett family, 45, 47, 96, 116, 176
Garnett, Olive, 303
Garnett, Richard, 50, 169, 172
Garnett, Robert, 342
Gartmore, 16, 82–4
George, Dolly, 14, 29, 46, 48, 58, 74,
    182
George, Ethel, 110–11
George family, 195, 262–3, 267, 325,
    340
Germany, 81, 84, 158, 230, 289
Gissing, George, 463–4, 465
Glasgow, 93, 94, 116, 155
Globe Venture Syndicate, 36, 53
Golconda, 205
Golitsyn, Prince, 246
Graham, Charles Cunninghame, 4, 31,
    104
Graham, Gabriela Cunninghame,
    16–17, 29–31, 35, 85, 117, 129, 172,
    207
Graham, R. B. Cunninghame, 12–13,
    18, 32, 49–50, 61, 63, 66, 68–70, 85,
    104–6, 121–2, 125–6, 150, 165, 171,
    197–8, 296
Grant, Captain M. H., 329, 357
Grant, Stephen, 275–6
Gray, Thomas, 108
Great Britain, 67
Greiffenhagen, Maurice, 416

Hackney, John, 325
Halkett, George R., 377, 393
Harmsworth, Alfred, 345
Harper & Brothers, 455–6
Harris, Frank, 12, 15, 18, 29, 32
Harrogate, 203
Harte, Bret, 320
Haschem, Sidi, 36
Havana, 115, 133, 294
Hazlitt, William, 414
Heinemann, William, 3, 15–16, 21, 38,
    44, 48, 181–2, 192–3, 196, 206, 219,
    243, 250, 253, 258, 260–1, 308, 312,
    318, 328–9, 336, 341, 344, 346,
    349–50, 357, 374, 377, 384, 398,
    407, 424–6
Helsingfors (Helsinki), 466
Hemans, Felicia, 149
Hendry, Hamish, 186
Henley, W. E., 80, 116, 123, 136, 189,
    416, 448, 451
Henry VIII, 344
Hirn, Yrjö, 416, 466
Hobson, Lieutenant, 73
Hogben, Richard, 93, 326–7, 408
Hoile, John George, 335, 437–40
Homer, 34, 436
Homocea, 119
Hope family, 224–5, 280, 285
Hope, G. F. W., 163–4, 195, 265
Horace, 36
Howells, William Dean, 222
Hueffer, Christina, 429
Hueffer, Elsie, 97, 99, 258, 287, 332,
    334–5, 378–9, 427
Hueffer family, 94, 110–11, 175–6, 250,
    279, 327, 388–9, 408, 410, 423, 430
Hueffer, Ford Madox, *see* Ford, Ford
    Madox
Hueffer, Katharine, 264
Hugo, Victor, 246
Hunt, Holman, 320
Hurd, Percy, 34
Hythe, 123

Ibsen, Henrik, 149, 209
Iceland, 16
Indian Ocean, 41
Ireland, 58, 339
Irving, Sir Henry, 65
Italy, 331
Ivy Walls Farm, 69, 77, 105, 111,
    224

James, Henry, 111, 122, 174, 189, 303,
    307, 342, 468
Jaurès, Jean, 158

Keats, Gwendoline ('Zack'), 213–14,
    329, 357
Keats, John, 448
Kelly, James Fitzmaurice, 79–81, 122
Kennedy, Admiral Sir William Robert,
    354
Kingsley, Mary, 156
Kipling, Rudyard, 31–4, 108–9, 138,
    207, 216, 218, 221, 225, 228
Kitchener, Lord, 212, 233
Kliszczewski family, 41, 54, 77
Knocke-sur-Mer, 285
Kochanowski, Jan, 244
Korzeniowski, Apollo, 246–7
Korzeniowski family, 244–7
Korzeniowski, Józef (author), 244
Korzeniowski, Teodor, 245
Krieger, Adolf P., 163, 166
Krüger, Paul, 302

Labuan, 226
Lang, Andrew, 350
Lavery, John, 56
Lawson, Henry, 329
Leighton, Sir Frederick, 320
Leith Hill, 434
Leopold II, King of the Belgians, 345
Liebknecht, Wilhelm, 158–9
Lingard, Tom, 6
London: I, General: 20, 21, 28, 61, 72,
    75, 76, 110, 127, 154, 204, 282, 284,
    286, 310, 334, 378, 381, 404, 414,
    450–1, 469
  II, Localities etc: British Museum,
    339, 344; Charing Cross, 135, 189,
    447, 454; Chester Square, 56;
    Devonshire Club, 36, 116;
    Fenchurch Street, 45, 66; Garrick
    Club, 48; Holland Park Avenue,
    447–8; Hotel d'Italie, 103; India
    Docks, 92–3; Junior Carlton Club,
    18, 23, 309; Kettner's Restaurant,
    309; Mansion House, 108;
    Neumeister's Hotel, 422;
    Paternoster Row, 153, 387; Savage
    Club, 45; Southwark, 23
Longman & Co., 412
Louttit, Captain, 62, 193
Lowestoft, 35

Lucas, E. V., 91, 122, 151–2, 303
Lynch, Mr, 173

Macaulay, Thomas Babington, 215
MacIlwaine (unidentified), 323
Macqueen, John, 127
Madrid, 206
Mahomed, 405
Malaysia, 130, 180, 200, 230, 277
Manila, 73
Martindale, Dr, 378
Maupassant, Guy de, 150, 203, 435–6, 450
McArthur (publisher's agent), 288, 455–6, 458
McClure, Robert, 62, 86–7, 90, 99–100, 102–3, 133, 147, 150, 169, 175–6, 193–4, 221, 270, 309, 323, 343, 397, 409, 415, 430
McClure, S. S., 42, 44, 49, 62, 78, 88, 98, 140, 182, 184, 191, 219, 221, 256, 294, 319, 340, 374–5, 377, 385, 412, 414–15, 455–6
McIntyre, Dr John, 94, 105, 155
Meldrum, David, 7, 45, 66, 73, 114–15, 127, 147, 154, 162, 194, 214, 218, 221, 231, 261, 276, 282–5, 291, 299–300, 309, 313, 325, 328, 334, 343, 350–1, 357, 376, 381, 394, 404–5, 422, 433, 451
Meldrum family, 101, 196, 208, 223–5, 240–1, 297
Meredith, George, 138, 333
Michie, Alexander, 437
Milan, 50
Millais, Sir John Everett, 320
Milner, Sir F., 211
Mitchell, S. Weir, 11
Montague (horse), 276
Montgomery, Robert, 215
Morang, G. N. & Co., 277
Morocco, 36, 44, 76, 81, 125, 286
Morrah (unidentified), 295
Morris, William, 320
Morton, George A., 196, 199, 419
Munn, P., 355
Munro, Neil, 95, 116, 130, 162, 218, 329–30, 462
Murray, Hallam, 439, 445

Nałecz family, 245
Nancy (horse), 437
Naples, 304

Napoleon III, 60
Nash family, 323
Nash, James Eveleigh, 259
Nash, Mrs, 110, 183
Netherlands, 154
New York, 38, 44, 81
Newcastle-upon-Tyne, 35
Nice, 164
Nicoll, W. Robertson, 457
Nietzsche, Friedrich, 188, 209, 218, 344
Nieuport, 269
Nordau, Max, 121
North Borneo, 226
Northern Newspaper Syndicate, 458

Odonie, Dame, 262–3
Over-Seas Library, 61
Oxted, 28, 36, 38, 40, 43

Pactolus, 205
Paderewski, Ignace Jan, 95
Pahang, 226
Paris, 280
Patagonia, 16
Patusan, 394
Paulus, Francis Petrus, 287
Pawling, S. S., 7–8, 12, 33, 35, 38, 44, 99, 108, 118, 154, 222, 258, 293, 296, 309, 320, 338, 344–5, 393, 424–6
Payn, James, 86
Pent Farm, 93–102, 105, 110–12, 115, 118, 122, 124, 131, 134–5, 149, 181, 185, 217, 243, 265, 280, 286, 333–4, 389–91, 397, 437, 453
Periodicals:
    Academy, 8, 41, 57–9, 99, 102, 105, 122, 151, 152, 163, 166, 180, 218, 302, 344, 346, 410, 456, 461
    Athenaeum, 465, 468
    Atlantic Monthly, 102, 176
    Badminton Magazine, 69
    Bampton Magazine, 295
    Blackwood's, 57, 81, 91, 127, 129–30, 133, 139, 145, 150–2, 154, 157, 162, 167, 182, 184–5, 186–7, 189, 192, 194, 196, 204, 213–14, 217–18, 223, 225, 227, 231, 241, 247, 253, 259, 264, 272, 292, 297, 301, 308, 321, 328, 338, 349, 368–9, 375–6, 380, 406, 411, 414, 431, 434, 437, 447, 452, 461–2, 465
    Bookman, 457

—▾

Periodicals *cont.*
Bradford Observer, 306
Chapman's Magazine, 295
Chimera, 466
Daily Chronicle, 150, 298, 341
Daily Mail, 14, 341
Daily Telegraph, 119
English Illustrated Magazine, 169
Glasgow Evening Herald, 186
Illustrated London News, 86–8, 90, 102,
    121, 157, 169–70, 356, 368–9
Kraj, 246
Labour Leader, 68
Lippincott's Magazine, 312
Literature, 10, 51, 177
Manchester Guardian, 298, 341
Mercure de France, 156, 185, 187, 399,
    403–4
Monthly Review, 439
New English Magazine, 388
New York Critic, 374
New York Times, 346–9
Outlook, 32, 34, 71, 334
Pall Mall Magazine, 9, 10, 356, 368,
    377–8, 393–4, 400
Pearson's Magazine, 43
Revue des Deux Mondes, 398
Saturday Review, 12, 31, 44, 59, 92,
    105, 116, 137, 186, 242, 254
Scotsman, 340
Scribner's Magazine, 12, 33, 35, 38
Singapore Free Press, 130
Sketch, 457
Smart Set, 465
Social-Democrat, 68–9
Speaker, 306, 417
Spectator, 166, 306, 459, 461, 463
Standard, 8, 254
The Times, 106, 412
Westminster Gazette, 158
Philip IV, King of Spain, 457
Philippines, 81
Pinker, J. B., 309, 328, 334, 353, 375,
    380–1, 387–8, 409, 412, 414,
    419–21, 424–5, 455
Poland, 17, 23–4, 34, 44, 51, 132, 158,
    244–7, 322, 328
Polish language, 24, 138, 156
Pompadour, Mme de, 90
Pope, Alexander, 220, 279, 436
Poradowska, Marguerite, 258, 322,
    342–3, 398, 405–8
Port Elizabeth, 292

Postling, 428
Pre-Raphaelites, 101, 138, 320
Pugh, Edwin, 100, 108, 123, 126
Putnam, G. P. Co., 374, 388, 394, 466

Queenstown (Cobh), 58
Quiller-Couch, A. T., 9, 10, 13, 368,
    417, 452

Reynolds family, 454
Reynolds, Mabel, 203
Reynolds, Paul Revere, 114
Richards, Grant, 187
Ridge, William Pett, 396
Rimbaud, Arthur, 89
Roberts, Morley, 257
Rodin, Auguste, 418
Röntgen machine, 95
Rossetti, Christina, 101
Rossetti, Dante Gabriel, 101, 320, 352
Rostand, Edmond, 79, 89
Roxby, Lord, 131
Royal Literary Fund, 433–5
Ruedy, Mrs, 48, 58, 73–4, 135
Runciman, J. F., 35
Ruskin, John, 418
Russia, 54, 158, 246, 262
Rye, 183, 189, 199, 333, 470

Salisbury, Marquess of, 55, 228
Salleh, Mohamed, 226
Sandakan, 226
Sanderson, E. L., 63–4, 91, 251, 256,
    291–3
Sanderson family, 63, 153, 172, 178,
    181, 206, 212, 293
Sanderson, Grey, 251
Sanderson, Helen Mary, 97, 233
Sanderson, Katherine, 188, 255
Sandgate, 120, 123, 187, 250, 252
Sandling, 120, 123, 134–5, 197, 378, 447
Sapieha, Prince Adam, 247
Sassoon, C. E., 275
Sauter family, 454
Sauter, Georg, 218, 469
Sauter, Lilian, 175, 203, 276
Scotland, 188
Scott, Sir Walter, 418
Shakespeare, William, 41, 134, 181,
    246–7, 394, 418
Shaw, George Bernard, 416, 440
Ships:
    Duke of Sutherland, 75

Highland Forest, 75
Mohegan, 106
Palestine, 92
Skimmer of the Sea, 35
Tourmaline, 36
Shorncliffe, 233
Shorter, C. K., 88, 157, 169–70
Sisyphus, 134
Slavs, 230
Slingsby, 3
Slough, 262–3
Smith (editor or publisher), 14
Smithers, Leonard, 80
Sobański family, 245
Social Democratic Federation, 158
Soheil (Canopus), 88
South Africa, 211, 265, 292
Spade House, 390
Spain, 60, 81, 273
Spanish–American War, 73, 81, 127
Spilsbury, Major A. G., 36, 52
Spiridion, *see* Kliszczewski
Standard Life Insurance Co., 307–10,
    317–18, 339, 382–4, 393, 395, 397,
    414
Stanford, 164
Steevens, G. W., 162
Stevenson, Robert Louis, 107, 371
Street, G. S., 357
Sulu Archipelago, 226
Surrey, 280
Swedish language, 466
Swinburne, Algernon, 320
Symons, Arthur, 31, 33

Tangier, 104
Tarver, J. E., 80
Tauchnitz, Baron, 48, 289, 307, 412
Tennessee, 74
Teresa of Avila, Saint, 30, 68, 172
Thackeray, W. M., 418, 468
Thousand and One Nights, The, 78, 146,
    464
Tolstoy, Leo Nikolayevitch, 288, 425
Traill, H. D., 80

Trollope, Anthony, 244
Turgenev, Ivan, 63, 115, 138, 175, 209,
    218, 224, 241, 255, 435

Ukraine, 246, 323
Union Line, 79
United States, 7, 14, 38–9, 44, 54, 60,
    62, 66, 71, 78, 81, 98, 140, 150, 191,
    304, 319, 335–6, 374, 393, 395, 408,
    412, 466
Unwin, T. Fisher, 3, 11, 21–3, 26, 41,
    81, 89, 99, 154, 210, 289, 345, 388,
    398, 406, 408, 411–12

Velázquez, Diego, 457
Vigny, Alfred de, 246

Wagner, Richard, 418
Wales, 28
Walpole, Sir Robert, 414
Warsaw, 158
Watson, Helen, 47, 53
Watson, William & Co., 307, 309, 313,
    317, 333–4, 336, 340, 372–3, 382–3,
    411
Watts, Henry E., 80
Watts-Dunton, Theodore, 138
Wells family, 314
Wells, George Philip, 392, 469
Wells, H. G., 30, 122, 138, 156, 177,
    218, 249–50, 252, 280, 372–3,
    390–1, 396, 399, 403, 416, 437, 440,
    447, 453
Wells, Jane, 121, 123
Whibley, Charles, 162
Whistler, J. M., 95, 418
Winchelsea, 327–8, 332–5, 351, 360,
    369, 379, 391, 393, 437, 466, 469

Zagórska, Aniela, 322
Zagórski family, 24, 37, 177
Zagórski, Karol, 36–7
Zaleski, Stanisław, 24
Zangwill, Israel, 41
Zola, Emile, 81, 138